RECONSIDERING THE CHAVÍN PHENOMENON
IN THE TWENTY-FIRST CENTURY

DUMBARTON OAKS PRE-COLUMBIAN SYMPOSIA AND COLLOQUIA

Series Editor
Frauke Sachse

RECONSIDERING THE CHAVÍN PHENOMENON IN THE TWENTY-FIRST CENTURY

RICHARD L. BURGER AND JASON NESBITT

Editors

DUMBARTON OAKS, TRUSTEES FOR HARVARD UNIVERSITY

WASHINGTON, D.C.

LIBRARY OF CONGRESS CATALOGING-IN-PUBLICATION DATA

NAMES: Pre-Columbian Studies Symposium "Reconsidering the Chavín Phenomenon in the Twenty-First Century"
(2018 : Washington, D.C.) | Burger, Richard L., editor. | Nesbitt, Jason, editor.

TITLE: Reconsidering the Chavín Phenomenon in the twenty-first century / Richard L. Burger and Jason Nesbitt, editors.

OTHER TITLES: Dumbarton Oaks Pre-Columbian symposia and colloquia.

DESCRIPTION: Washington, D.C.: Dumbarton Oaks, Trustees for Harvard University, [2023] | Series: Dumbarton Oaks
Pre-Columbian symposia and colloquia | "Volume based on papers presented at the Pre-Columbian Studies sympo-
sium 'Reconsidering the Chavín Phenomenon in the Twenty-First Century,' held at Dumbarton Oaks, Washington,
D.C., on October 5–6, 2018" | Title page verso. | Includes bibliographical references and index. | Summary: "The
UNESCO World Heritage Site of Chavín de Huántar holds an iconic place in the archaeology of Pre-Columbian
Peru; it is crucial to understanding the emergence of Andean civilization during the early first millennium BC. Best
known for its elaborate religious architecture and distinctive stone sculpture, Chavín de Huántar was the center of
a much wider Andean world, and the synchronicity of widespread socioeconomic changes, coupled with intrusive Chavín material culture and iconography at distant centers, suggests that it influenced a vast region through
the expansion of religious ideology and the intensification of long-distance interaction. *Reconsidering the Chavín
Phenomenon in the Twenty-First Century* builds upon a surge of archaeological research over the last twenty years,
bringing together the work of scholars researching Chavín de Huántar and its neighbors from the coast, highlands,
and *ceja de selva*. The volume offers a cohesive vision of the Chavín Phenomenon at both the local and interregional
level, one which recognizes the high degree of socioeconomic and cultural diversity that existed and the active role
of centers outside the Chavín heartland in shaping the radical transformations that occurred within the Chavín
Interaction Sphere between 1000 and 400 BC."—Provided by publisher.

IDENTIFIERS: LCCN 2022056216 | ISBN 9780884024996 (hardcover)

SUBJECTS: LCSH: Chavín culture—Congresses. | Chavín de Huantar—(Peru)—Congresses.

CLASSIFICATION: LCC F3429.1.C48 P74 2023 | DDC 985/.2101—dc23/eng/20230419

LC record available at https://lccn.loc.gov/2022056216

GENERAL EDITOR: Frauke Sachse
ART DIRECTOR: Kathleen Sparkes
DESIGN AND COMPOSITION: Melissa Tandysh
MANAGING EDITOR: Sara Taylor

Volume based on papers presented at the Pre-Columbian Studies symposium "Reconsidering the Chavín Phenomenon
in the Twenty-First Century," held at Dumbarton Oaks, Washington, D.C., on October 5–6, 2018.

JACKET PHOTOGRAPH: Polychrome frieze AM–52 at Huaca Partida, depicting a raptorial bird. Photograph by
Koichiro Shibata.

www.doaks.org/publications

CONTENTS

This volume is dedicated to the memory of our friend and colleague
Colin McEwan,
director of Pre-Columbian Studies at Dumbarton Oaks from 2012 to 2019.

Participants in the "Reconsidering the Chavín Phenomenon in the Twenty-First Century" symposium, October 2018. From top clockwise: Yuichi Matsumoto, Michelle Young, Lucy C. Salazar, Lisa DeLeonardis, Yuji Seki, Hugo Ikehara-Tsukayama, Ryan Clasby, Rosa Mendoza, Jason Nesbitt, Richard L. Burger, Colin McEwan, John W. Rick, David Chicoine, Christopher A. Pool, Matthew P. Sayre, Jalh Dulanto, and Rebecca E. Bria.

PREFACE

The things we most eagerly seek to understand are those that seem least tangible. The origin of complex societies in the Americas has been an intriguing and challenging research question. Accordingly, the first two Pre-Columbian conferences held at Dumbarton Oaks were dedicated to the Olmec in Mesoamerica (1967) and Chavín in the Andes (1968).

Organized by Elizabeth P. Benson and chaired by Junius Bird, the "Dumbarton Oaks Conference on Chavín" was instrumental in synthesizing the information on the Formative period in the Andes. The resulting volume, published in 1971, became a standard source that summarized the state of knowledge of the time. The site of Chavín de Huántar, with its monumental architecture and distinctive art style, was seen as the center of a religious system and the origin of a civilization that had expanded to other early sites across the Andes.

In 1982, Dumbarton Oaks revisited the topic of Chavín with a conference on "Early Ceremonial Architecture in the Andes" organized by Christopher B. Donnan. The conference drew together evidence from antecedent sites that suggested that Chavín de Huántar may have been the end of a cultural development rather than the origin. The 1985 publication was characterized by Richard L. Burger, who contributed the final discussion chapter, as a "watershed in the history of Peruvian archaeology" because it introduced a new framework that

departed from the precedent of connecting all early complex societies to Chavín.

With the present volume, Dumbarton Oaks hopes to contribute once more to shaping the scholarly debate about Chavín. Richard L. Burger and Jason Nesbitt have brought together leading and rising scholars to share their research and insights on a phenomenon that remains elusive. The symposium was held at Dumbarton Oaks on October 5–6, 2018, under the stewardship of my esteemed predecessor, the late Colin McEwan (1951–2020). The contributions present new archaeological research results that point to a system of complex long-distance interactions of independent and culturally diverse regions. The editors have succeeded in bringing together a range of different voices that contribute to building a new consensus on what Chavín really was and how it may have been formative for Andean cultural development.

Many need to be thanked for creating this fine volume. First and foremost, I thank the editors and contributors, who conceptualized the symposium and engaged in a conversation that generated a marvelous collection of essays. We are indebted to two anonymous reviewers for their valuable comments and suggestions. The production of this beautiful volume is once more the result of the tireless work of a wonderful publications team. I would like to thank managing editor Sara Taylor for her focus and care with this volume and for all the hours she has put into working with the editors and authors. Moreover, I owe thanks to the director of publications, Kathy Sparkes, for her incredible patience in steering this project and keeping us all on track.

We hope that this volume will serve as a reference point for current research, stimulate further debate, and lead to new ways of understanding the Formative period in the Andes.

Frauke Sachse
Director of Pre-Columbian Studies

Introduction

Reconsidering the Chavín Phenomenon in the Twenty-First Century

RICHARD L. BURGER AND JASON NESBITT

For more than a century, Chavín culture has been considered fundamental to understanding the emergence of Andean civilization in the late second and early first millennia BC (Burger 1992; Tello 1943, 1960). The archaeological site at Chavín de Huántar is an iconic symbol of Peru's cultural patrimony and national identity, and in 1985 it was made a UNESCO World Heritage Site. Widely known as an early ceremonial center with ornate stone sculpture, platforms, and sunken plazas, the site features a large masonry temple with a maze of subterranean passageways and rooms and monstrous carved tenoned heads projecting from its outer walls (Rick, this volume). While the core of the Chavín de Huántar complex is characterized by stone-faced platforms and plazas, most of the site consists of the remains of residences and workshops (Burger 1984; Sayre and Rosenfeld, this volume). Scholars have long understood that the ascendancy of Chavín de Huántar was not an isolated phenomenon and investigators have documented that the inhabitants of the late Initial Period/Early Horizon settlement had access to exotic resources that came from distant sources, indicating that the center was enmeshed in far-flung exchange networks spanning much of the Central Andes (Figure 1.1).

During the early first millennium BC, when the center was prospering and growing, much of the Central Andean coast, highlands, and adjacent tropical forest witnessed fundamental socioeconomic and religious changes. The synchronicity of these changes, coupled with the appearance of intrusive elements of Chavín material culture and iconography at distant centers and villages, suggests that Chavín de Huántar influenced a large territory through the expansion of religious ideology, social relations, and intensified long-distance exchange of exotic goods. This intensification of pan-regional interaction associated with the rise of Chavín de Huántar was unprecedented in the Central Andes, and how it should be understood has fascinated archaeologists for the past century.

Reconsidering the Chavín Phenomenon in the Twenty-First Century is the product of a Dumbarton

figure 1.1

Map of key Initial Period and Early Horizon archaeological sites mentioned in this chapter. Map by Bebel Ibarra Asencios.

Legend

■   Modern City

▲   Archaeological Site

0   480

KM

Oaks symposium in Pre-Columbian Studies that was held in October 2018 to revisit and reevaluate the many unresolved issues that continue to bedevil Chavín studies. The timing and location of the event was auspicious because it marked the fiftieth anniversary of "The Dumbarton Oaks Conference on Chavín," organized by Elizabeth P. Benson in 1968 (Benson 1971). The conference volume from this earlier symposium disseminated pioneering research at Chavín de Huántar, Kotosh, and Ancón as well as at sites in the *ceja de selva* and Upper Amazon (Izumi 1971; Lathrap 1971; Lumbreras 1971; Patterson 1971) and it has come to be considered a classic.

However, at the time of its publication, archaeological research on the Initial Period (1800–800 BC) and Early Horizon (800–100 BC) was still in a nascent stage. Chronologies at Chavín de Huántar, both relative and absolute, were poorly established and few coeval sites had been investigated in detail. Despite its acknowledged significance, the conference volume failed to offer a cohesive and consistent vision of the Chavín problem based on empirical data.

Fortunately, since that time a surge in archaeological research at Initial Period and Early Horizon centers (e.g., Burger, Salazar, and Seki 2019; Conklin and Quilter 2008; Fux 2013; Kaulicke and Onuki

2010a, 2010b) has generated a wealth of new data, creating opportunities for a critical reassessment of culture change and interregional interaction during the period encompassing the second and first millennia BC. A Dumbarton Oaks symposium held in 1982 entitled "Early Ceremonial Architecture in the Andes" (Donnan 1985) focused on the third and second millennia BC and highlighted many of the antecedents for Chavín civilization (Burger 1985). In order to sharpen the focus of the 2018 Dumbarton Oaks conference and of this volume, the Late Preceramic and Initial Period antecedents for the Chavín Phenomenon were not the primary focus (but see Bria, this volume). Instead, the emphasis centers on developments from the late second millennium BC until approximately 400 BC; this corresponds to the final centuries of the Initial Period (1100–800 BC) and the first portion of the Early Horizon (800–400 BC), which some scholars refer to as the Middle and Late Formative (Figure 1.2). It was during this time that there is clear evidence for the emergence and eventual florescence of the long-distance connections that were a hallmark of Chavín civilization.

Our goal in this volume is to provide an updated perspective on Chavín de Huántar and its relationships with its contemporaries on the coast, highlands, and tropical forest of Peru based on recent and ongoing research. These studies make it possible to better appreciate the degree of socioeconomic and cultural diversity that existed and the factors involved in the pan-regional spread of cultural elements traditionally associated with the Chavín Phenomenon. To achieve this, the organizers invited a group of archaeologists to the 2018 Dumbarton Oaks symposium whose work focused on the first millennium BC and covered a wide range of sites and regions in what today is central and northern Peru.

In this introductory chapter, we contextualize the volume within historical and ongoing debates regarding Chavín. We begin by considering a group of terms that have been used in these discussions and that are sometimes poorly defined and confusing. These include Chavín culture, Chavín civilization, the Chavín horizon, the Chavín Interaction Sphere, and the Chavín Phenomenon. This is followed by a review of two alternative chronological

terminologies that still appear in the professional literature and the differing theoretical assumptions that underlie them. After this, we offer a review of the organization of the book and some of the salient patterns that emerge from the individual contributions.

Terminological Tools for Discussing Chavín Civilization

Julio C. Tello deserves credit for recognizing both the antiquity and importance of Chavín civilization in Andean culture history, and no discussion of this subject can ignore his pioneering contributions. But one of his legacies was the abstruseness of the term "Chavín." He applied it loosely to a culture, an art style, a mode of architecture, and a kind of pottery, and while he initially defined it based on his first-hand observations of the stylistic and technological attributes at Chavín de Huántar, he gradually broadened his definition by adding new elements that appeared at other coastal and highland sites that he thought reflected Chavín culture because they shared one or more traits with that site. As a result of this approach, Tello came to view Chavín culture or Chavín influence as spanning most of the coast, highlands, and cloud forest of Peru (Tello 1943).

This position was reflected in the work of Tello's protégé, Rebeca Carrión Cachot, who in 1948, the year after his death, described a hypothetical Chavín empire characterized by a multitude of centers throughout Ecuador, Peru, and the Titicaca Basin; its influence was said to extend as far as San Agustín in the highlands of Colombia and Marajó Island at the mouth of the Amazon River in Brazil (Carrión Cachot 1948:169–170, lam. XXVI). Carrión Cachot clarified that the Chavín empire was religious and not political, claiming that "this old civilization was homogeneous in arts, rituals, religion, race, and probably in language" (Carrión Cachot 1948:172, our translation).

Tello's broadly conceived concept of Chavín was criticized by the prominent U.S. anthropologist Alfred Kroeber, who wrote incisively that "it

figure 1.2
Comparative chronologies of sites and regions discussed in this volume.
Illustration by Richard L. Burger and Jason Nesbitt.

Years	GENERAL CHRONOLOGIES		Chavín de Huántar — Temple	Residential	Chavín	Callejón de Huaylas — Huaricoto	Hualcayán	North Highlands — Pacopampa	Huacaloma	Kuntur Wasi	Ceja de Selva — Huayurco	Ingatambo
AD 1 / BC – 200	Early Horizon	Final Formative					Cayán Phase 1		Layzón	Sotera	Las Juntas	
200 – 400		Late Formative	Post-Monumental		Huarás	Huarás		Pacopampa III	EL	Copa		
400 – 600			Support	Janabarriu		Late Capilla					Tabalozo	
600 – 800			Black and White Stage	Chakinani	Late Chavín	Early Capilla	Perolcoto Phase 4	Pacopampa II	Late Huacaloma	Kuntur Wasi	Ambato	Ingatambo
800 – 1000	Initial Period	Middle Formative	Consolidation Stage	Urabarriu	Early Chavín	Huaricoto				Ídolo		
1000 – 1200			Expansion Stage / Separate Mound Stage				Perolcoto Phase 3	Pacopampa I				Pomahuaca
1200 – 1400		Early Formative				Toril	Perolcoto Phase 2		Early Huacaloma			
1400 – 1600								Pandanche				
1600 – 1800												
1800 – 2000						Chaukayan						Huancabamba
2000 – 2200							Perolcoto Phase 1					
2200 – 2400												

REGIONAL CHRONOLOGIES

North Coast				Central Coast	South Coast / Paracas	Upper Huallaga	South Central Highlands		Southern Highlands		Olmec Veracruz
Middle Jequetepeque	Caballo Muerto/ Moche Valley	Nepeña	Cupisnique	Lurín	Palpa/Paracas	Kotosh	Atalla	Campanayuq Rumi	Cusco	Titicaca	
										Pucara	Late Formative
Sotera				Tablada de Lurín	Initial Nasca	Sajarapatac			Chanapata		
		Samanco	Salinar		Late Paracas					Late Chiripa	
Copa				Pampa Chica	Middle Paracas	Kotosh Chavín	Atalla II	Campanayuq II			
Lechuzas	Curaca	Nepeña	Late Cupisnique		Early Paracas				Marcavalle	Middle Chiripa	Middle Formative
						Kotosh Kotosh	Atalla I	Campanayuq I		Late Qaluyu	
Tembladera	San Lorenzo	Cerro Blanco	Middle Cupisnique	Manchay Bajo	Erizo		Early Atalla	Pre-Platform			
				Cardal						Early Qaluyu	Early Formative
Hamacas	Cortijo	Huambocayan	Early Cupisnique			Kotosh Wairajirca					
				Mina Perdida							Initial Formative

Introduction 5

has not been altogether clear just what characterized the Chavín style or culture; and as Tello found its irradiations . . . manifesting themselves in most varied form, the concept has proved difficult to use, even though there appears to have been no one who doubted that the concept contained an essential kernel of validity." Kroeber went on to suggest that it is "desirable first to define the characteristics of Chavín culture as it occurs at Chavín, and second to examine Chavinoid cultures elsewhere for the degree and nature of Chavín [elements] which they contain" (Kroeber 1944:82).

Horizon styles were a basic archaeological concept in New World culture history, and Kroeber thought that Chavín might be a good candidate for Peru's earliest horizon style. A horizon style was intended to serve as a tool to help synthesize complex local historic trajectories into a single coherent framework (Kroeber 1944; Willey 1948; Willey and Phillips 1958). Every horizon was expected to be characterized by a distinctive and homogeneous style that was widespread geographically but restricted chronologically. To be a valid horizon style, it had to have spread rapidly at a pan-regional scale. In his review of the "Chavín problem," Gordon Willey intentionally shifted attention away from the question of Tello's poorly defined Chavín culture or civilization in order to focus on the possible existence of a Chavín horizon style. On the basis of the style of the abundant stone sculpture at Chavín de Huántar, he sought to identify those archaeological remains that could be considered part of a Chavín horizon and those that should be excluded (Willey 1951). Out of the numerous "Chavín" sites mentioned by Tello, Willey accepted seventeen sites or areas with "indisputable Chavín stylistic affiliation" (Willey 1951:125). Following Carrión Cachot, Willey argued that the functional basis of this Chavín horizon style was "the peaceful spread of religious concepts" (Willey 1948:10). Nonetheless, the primary purpose of Willey's hypothetical Chavín horizon was as a chronological tool, since, at a time when radiocarbon dating did not exist, it allowed investigators to assume that the sites in the identified horizon were contemporary with each other, despite the distances that separated them.

The notion of a Chavín horizon or a Chavín horizon style remained popular in the Peruvianist literature for several decades, but it proved difficult to operationalize because outside of Chavín de Huántar, few centers had stone sculpture. Those that did, such as Kuntur Wasi, often featured carvings dissimilar in theme and style to the Chavín de Huántar temple (Burger 1988:102). In many of Willey's seventeen cases, Chavín-related iconography appeared only on one or two objects, and these could have been obtained through exchange. Finally, as more radiocarbon measurements became available in the 1980s and 1990s, it became clear that the distinctive Chavín art style had lasted for at least five centuries at Chavín de Huántar, and the Chavín stylistic elements observed at other sites likewise spanned many centuries, thus making the assumptions underlying the notion of a Chavín horizon style problematic. Moreover, the increasing accuracy and availability of radiocarbon dates made debates over the Chavín horizon concept moot. In a recent review, Richard L. Burger concluded: "With the introduction of increasingly more reliable radiocarbon measurements and the likelihood of developing even more precise chronometric techniques, such as archaeomagnetism, perhaps it is time to acknowledge that the term Chavín horizon has outlived its usefulness and that the confusion it causes is no longer justified by its value as a chronological marker. Yet abandoning the term should not be equated with relinquishing the pan-regional analytical perspective that remains crucial for understanding the complex socioeconomic and cultural dynamics of the first half of the first millennium BC" (Burger 2019a:199).

It is, however, worth returning to Kroeber's suggestion that we begin by defining Chavín culture using the information available from the abundant excavations at Chavín de Huántar. Chavín's iconographic style is distinctive as well as beautiful; it has been described as following a specific set of conventions including metaphorical substitutions (or kennings), double profiles, anatropic organization, and modular width (Burger 1992; Rowe 1962a; Tello 1960). Similarly, there is a consensus that Chavín religious art emphasized elements drawn from Amazonian fauna, including anacondas, jaguars, caimans, and harpy eagles (Lathrap 1971, 1973; Roe 2008). It also features elaborately dressed religious specialists in procession or in the process of transforming from human to feline or avian form (Burger 1992, Lumbreras 1977; Rowe 1962a; Tello 1960). When describing Chavín culture, the central role of hallucinogenic snuffs from the tropical forest and other psychotropic plants such as San Pedro cactus in Chavín ritual should be mentioned, since it can be linked not only to iconography but also to numerous bone-snuffing spoons and tablets, small mortars for hallucinogenic snuff, and even a bimetallic gold and silver spoon for inhaling snuff (Burger 1992, 2011; Cordy-Collins 1977; Torres 2008). Other distinctive aspects of Chavín culture at Chavín de Huántar are the use of carved stone tenon heads emplaced high above the ground surface and the unlit internal passageways and rooms linked to sophisticated systems of stone-lined canals and air ducts. The use of carefully shaped and dressed stone blocks in the temple architecture is also noteworthy, as is the transport of large white granite and black limestone blocks from a distance of many kilometers (Turner, Knight, and Rick 1999).

Moreover, the culture of Chavín de Huántar was not fixed; on the contrary, it was continually changing during the centuries in question. For example, a dependence on wild game from hunting was replaced by a reliance on the meat of domesticated llamas, and the raw materials for stone tools shifted from semi-local raw materials such as quartzite and chert to obsidian, an exotic material brought from the south-central highlands (Burger 1984; Burger et al. 2006; Miller and Burger 1995; Rosenfeld and Sayre 2016).

The larger point, however, is that Chavín culture can now be recognized as being unique to Chavín de Huántar. Contrary to the assumptions of Tello and Carrión Cachot, the culture does not appear at other sites, such as Pacopampa, Kuntur Wasi, or Ancón. In fact, each of the contemporary sites that has been studied in detail has proven to be fundamentally different from Chavín de Huántar in most respects. As seen in many of the chapters of this volume,

similarities, where they occur, are piecemeal, and these sites also show the deep imprint of local cultural traditions, many of which predated intensive contact with Chavín de Huántar.

The widely used term "Chavín civilization" is basically a synonym of "Chavín culture," but by substituting the term "civilization" for "culture," it expresses a subjective judgment that the quality of the art, technology, and lifestyle at Chavín de Huántar had achieved a degree of sophistication or excellence that is comparable to other better known world civilizations, such as the Shang, Indus Valley, Sumerian, or Egyptian. Since Chavín culture or Chavín civilization appears to have existed in a small section of the Mosna Valley, neither Chavín culture nor Chavín civilization is particularly helpful as a tool in analyzing the pan-regional patterns that have attracted the attention of so many scholars. When Chavín civilization is applied to the entire network of centers interacting with Chavín de Huántar, it results in highlighting Chavín emulations and distorting the nature of individual sites.

Toward this end, the term "Chavín Interaction Sphere" is perhaps a more useful tool. It takes its inspiration from a concept originally introduced by Joseph Caldwell (1964). He recognized that the different sites in eastern North America referred to as Hopewell were not part of a single culture but were, despite similarities in their mortuary and religious practices, independent societies within and across areas that interacted within different institutional frameworks. The Hopewell Phenomenon has parallels to that of Chavín, and some Andean scholars have adopted Caldwell's concept by referring to a Chavín Interaction Sphere (or Chavín Sphere of Interaction) (e.g., Burger 2008; Matsumoto et al. 2018; Nesbitt, Matsumoto, and Cavero Palomino 2019). This term has the advantage of making no assumptions about the nature of the interaction in question. Although discussions of archaeological treatment of interaction spheres often emphasize the movement of exotic raw materials or crafts, the concept itself does not imply that the driving force behind the interaction sphere was economic. It could also be religious, social, or political—or some combination of these. Moreover, an interaction sphere could differ in character and intensity between areas within the interaction sphere and could change in character over time.

For the first time, a new term "Chavín Phenomenon" features prominently in this volume. Unlike Chavín Interaction Sphere, the term does not necessarily emphasize the relations between different sites or groups as the primary focus, but rather it refers to the way in which specific communities reacted and changed as they encountered or were incorporated into the Chavín Interaction Sphere. This bottom-up perspective is as interested in the diversity and heterogeneity of late Initial Period/Early Horizon societies and cultures as it is with their similarities to Chavín de Huántar. Given the assumption of agency by the inhabitants of each center or area, it would be expected that the Chavín Phenomenon would be different in each case, depending on the local history, culture, and resources.

Time and Space at Chavín de Huántar

Never forgotten by local inhabitants and known by the Spaniards since colonial times, Chavín was not the focus of scientific research until the early twentieth-century investigations of Julio C. Tello (1934, 1943, 1960). Although foreshadowed by the German traveler Ernst Middendorf ([1893–1895] 1974), Tello was the first archaeologist to hypothesize that Chavín was of great antiquity and was foundational to developments of sociopolitical and religious complexity in the ancient Andes. Perhaps most importantly, Tello supported this hypothesis with stratigraphic excavations demonstrating the early chronological position of Chavín culture and its association with the site's sculptures and monumental architecture. These conclusions were confirmed and reinforced in the subsequent archaeological investigation by Wendell Bennett (1944).

Since that time, numerous projects have been undertaken at Chavín de Huántar by archaeologists including Manuel Chávez Ballón, Jorge Muelle, Marino Gonzales, John Rowe, Luis Lumbreras, Hernán Amat, Rosa Fung, Richard Burger, Federico Kauffmann Doig, and, most recently, by the Stanford University Project led by John Rick (see Rick, this volume; Sayre and Rosenfeld, this volume). Much of the research has focused on the nature of monumental architecture and sculpture at the site, as well as on the clarification of both its relative and absolute chronologies (Burger 1981, 2019b; Kembel and Haas 2015; Rick et al. 2010).

While radiocarbon dating was unavailable at the time, Tello hypothesized that the civilization documented at Chavín de Huántar had temporal precedence over stylistically related sites found on the coast. Tello argued that crucial agricultural and cultural developments in the Amazonian lowlands led to the crystallization of civilization on the eastern slopes of the Andes. For Tello, Chavín de Huántar was the center of Peru's first civilization and Chavín culture spread to other parts of the highlands and coast from Chavín de Huántar, thus providing the matrix from which later Andean civilizations originated.

While this diffusionary hypothesis is now considered to be incorrect in light of new data and more recent archaeological theorizing, Tello's ideas were revolutionary in that they placed highland and Amazonian peoples, typically marginalized groups, at the forefront of Peruvian culture history (Burger 1989, 1993). Moreover, Tello and his students also recognized that Chavín de Huántar exerted influence over a large swath of the ancient Andes due to a rapid widespread system of shared beliefs (Carrión Cachot 1948; Tello 1930, 1943). This idea of the religious character of Chavín influence and its links to pan-regional pilgrimage has been further advanced by later scholars (Burger 1988, 1993, 2013; Cordy-Collins 1977; Patterson 1971; Willey 1948).

Chronology and Terminology

The study of the Chavín Phenomenon has been hindered by a lack of agreement regarding chronological terminology and absolute dating. To start, there is disparity regarding the proper nomenclature to use when referring to the regional developments that characterize the second and first millennia BC (cf. Burger 1993; Carmichael 2019; Kaulicke 2010; T. Pozorski and S. Pozorski 1987; Sayre 2018). Some scholars, including many from Peru and Japan, utilize an evolutionary-based terminology first proposed by Luis Lumbreras (1974). The details of this framework have shifted as new archaeological discoveries have been made. Using this framework as currently conceived, the second and first millennia are divided into Early Formative (1800–1200 BC), Middle Formative (1200–800 BC), and Late Formative (800–400 BC). It should be noted that the time period that Lumbreras (1974) referred to as Middle Formative is now Late Formative, and that some have advocated for the addition of a Final Formative period (400–200 BC) (e.g., Kaulicke 2010).

This system contrasts with the chronological terms proposed by John Rowe (1962b) in a framework that is still favored by many U. S.–based investigators because of the greater precision of their definition (Carmichael 2019; Moseley 2001; Quilter 2022). Based on the "master sequence" from the Ica Valley, blocks of time were designated and subdivided into epochs; these explicitly lacked evolutionary implications. The Initial Period was defined as beginning with the introduction of ceramics in the Ica Valley. The subsequent Early Horizon began with the appearance of Chavín influence in Ica and ended with the introduction of polychrome prefire slip painting on decorated pottery in that same valley. Although the term "Early Horizon" was inspired by Kroeber's observation that Chavín appeared to be the earliest of Peru's three prehispanic horizons (i.e., Chavín, Huari-Tiahuanaco, Inca), in Rowe's system, the Chavín Phenomenon would have begun in the final epochs of the Initial Period and ended in the middle of the Early Horizon. In Ica, the second half of the Early Horizon, referred to as Middle and Late Paracas (or Ocucaje 6–10), would have been characterized by ceramic styles that postdate direct Chavín influence (Unkel et al. 2012). In defense of this system, Rowe (1962b:51) wrote: "The negative advantage of using periods rather than stages to organize archaeological data is that the investigator runs much less danger of assuming what he ought to be trying to prove. Because of the close association of stages with the theory of cultural evolution, virtually every archaeologist who uses stages to organize his data thereby builds into them certain assumptions about cultural development without being aware

that he is doing so." Unfortunately, more than a few scholars have ignored the technical definition of the Early Horizon as proposed by Rowe and assumed that the term is a synonym of the Chavín horizon, thereby increasing confusion rather than providing the chronological clarity that Rowe aspired to with his framework.

Although there is no agreement regarding the application of these two different terminologies, there does seem to be an emerging consensus regarding absolute chronology that is evident in this conference volume. This is an outgrowth of the introduction and spread of AMS dating, with its greater precision and ability to date smaller organic samples. As a result, many of the chapters in this volume are reliant on local or site-based chronologies using local terminologies anchored by suites of radiocarbon dates. Using the AMS dates, these local chronologies can then be placed within the broader pan-regional chronologies in which key processes can be compared (discussed below). As editors, we have let individual scholars use the chronological frameworks that they are most comfortable with. With that in mind, Figure 1.2 presents the different regional chronologies in comparative perspective along with their estimated date-ranges. Critically, the establishment of detailed absolute chronologies permits a much greater appreciation of local diachronic change than was possible even fifteen years ago. As can be seen in Figure 1.2, there are chronological synchronicities that suggest key historical moments that appear to occur at a pan-regional scale.

One of the time periods of special interest is the late second millennium BC (ca. 1100–950 BC). During this time, many major highland centers were founded, including Pacopampa, Kuntur Wasi (Seki, this volume), Chavín de Huántar (Burger 2019b; Kembel and Haas 2015; Rick et al. 2010), Atalla (Young, this volume), and Campanayuq Rumi (Matsumoto and Cavero Palomino, this volume) to name a few. On the coast, this was the time that the classic Cupisnique style appears (Chicoine, Ikehara-Tsukayama, and Shibata, this volume; Nesbitt 2012; Nesbitt, Gutiérrez, and Vásquez 2010; Prieto et al. 2022; Shibata 2010), although Cupisnique centers such as Caballo Muerto in the Moche Valley and Purulén in the Zaña Valley were established many centuries earlier (Alva 1988; Nesbitt 2019; Nesbitt, Gutiérrez, and Vásquez 2010; Pozorski 1983; Watanabe 1976).

A second key process occurs around ca. 900–800 BC, when there is good evidence for the abandonment or decline of many of the monumental coastal cultural centers (Burger and Salazar, this volume; Nesbitt 2012; S. Pozorski and T. Pozorski 1987; Sandweiss et al. 2001). In contrast, highland centers such as Kuntur Wasi and Pacopampa enter a period of fluorescence (Burger 1992; Seki, this volume). The latter period is linked by rapidly expanding trade networks, as well as burial data and other evidence that suggests the emergence of striking social inequalities. A final moment of pan-regional synchronicity occurs around 450 BC with the "collapse" of the Chavín de Huántar center and the long-distance interaction sphere associated with it. We return to these issues later in this chapter, but it is relevant here to note that, with a few exceptions, there is consensus regarding the absolute dates provided here, regardless of the chronological terminology employed in the chapters.

Organization of the Volume: Chavín from the Inside-Out

The chapters in this volume examine long-standing themes central to understanding the Chavín Phenomenon at both the local and interregional level. As noted earlier, progress has been made on many of the unresolved problems as a result of recent investigations. We, therefore, begin this volume with chapters dealing with archaeological investigations of Chavín de Huántar and its immediate heartland, then move to an examination of the highland, coastal, and tropical forest contemporaries that became entangled in the long-distance interaction sphere in which Chavín de Huántar played such an important part.

Chavín de Huántar: Center and Heartland

Chavín de Huántar

In "New Galleries at Chavín de Huántar: An Exploration of Chavín Underground Architecture and Organization," John W. Rick discusses the results of a long-term international research program

figure 1.3
The temple architecture of Chavín de Huántar. Photograph by Richard L. Burger and Jason Nesbitt.

undertaken at Chavín de Huántar by the Stanford University Project (e.g., Kembel 2008; Mesía 2007; Rick 2005, 2008, 2013, 2017; Rick et al. 1998, 2010). Chavín de Huántar is located at an elevation of 3150 masl and is positioned at the junction of the Huachecsa and Mosna Rivers. As already noted, it stands out from its highland and coastal contemporaries by the sophistication and complexity of its public architecture and stone sculpture (e.g., Bennett 1944; Burger 1992; González-Ramírez 2014; Kembel 2001, 2008; Kembel and Rick 2004; Lagarde 2022; Lumbreras 1977, 2007; Rick 2008, 2013, 2017, this volume; Rowe 1962a; Tello 1943, 1960; Weismantel 2015a, 2015b) (Figures 1.3–1.5). Collectively, the art and complex architecture of Chavín de Huántar served to create a ceremonial environment that was radically different from its contemporaries, and this, along with its reputation for oracular pronouncements and efficacious religious ceremonies, probably helped to stimulate pilgrimage to the site from distant regions as evinced by the presence of exotic pottery and other goods in the Ofrendas and Caracolas Galleries (Burger 1992; Burger and Salazar, this volume; Lumbreras 1993, 2007; Rick 2005, 2008, this volume).

figure 1.4
The main deity at Chavín de Huántar; the sculpted figure is holding a strombus shell in its right hand and a spondylus shell in its left hand. Photograph by Richard L. Burger and Jason Nesbitt.

figure 1.5
Tenon heads from Chavín de Huántar. Photographs by Richard L. Burger and Jason Nesbitt.

Recent archaeological investigation at the site has documented the way in which the monumental core was constructed over many centuries in a complex building sequence that expanded both horizontally and vertically beginning, according to the Stanford University Project, in the late second millennium BC and continuing until the mid-first millennium BC (cf. Kembel 2001, 2008; Kembel and Haas 2015; T. Pozorski and S. Pozorski 1987; Rick 2008; Rick et al. 2010). There remains a lack of consensus regarding the dating of the earliest monumental constructions at the site, with Burger favoring 1000–950 BC and Rick and his colleagues advocating an earlier founding in 1200 BC or even earlier (cf. Burger 2019b, 2021; Kembel and Haas 2015; Rick et al. 2010). There is also disagreement regarding the timing of construction in the temple core, with the Stanford University team arguing that its fluorescence occurred prior to 800 BC and Burger arguing that public construction continued unabated for an additional three centuries during most of the Chakinani and Janabarriu phases (Burger 1992, 2019b, 2021; Kembel 2008). Despite these differences in opinion, there is greater agreement about Chavín de Huántar's absolute chronology now as a result of new suites of radiocarbon measurements and the utilization of comparable calibration curves in the presentation of these dates.

Rick's chapter on Chavín de Huántar focuses on the extensive subterranean gallery architecture for which the temple is famous. He presents a detailed description of these features, including newly discovered galleries near the Circular Plaza, which he argues were integral to the extensive planning that characterizes the monumental architecture. He believes that these architectural features had ceremonial functions linked to issues surrounding the evolution of religious and political authority at the site (see also Rick 2005).

Yet Chavín de Huántar was not just a ceremonial center (Rowe 1963:10); instead, it had a large residential population living in a settlement that covered an area of about thirty hectares (Burger 1984, 2019b; Gamboa 2016; Sayre 2010). The first systematic study of the residential complex was undertaken by Burger, who documented the extensive domestic occupation on the west banks of the Mosna River. One of the outcomes of this research was the creation of a detailed ceramic sequence that made it possible to track the growth of this population (Burger 1981, 1984). Based on current radiocarbon data (Burger 2019b), the settlement was founded at the beginning of the Urabarriu phase (950–800 BC); during this time, occupation was apparently limited to a few hectares adjacent to the temple and near a megalithic wall crossing the valley floor at the north end of the modern town. The residential area began to grow around the temple core during the Chakinani phase (800–700 BC), but it was during the Janabarriu phase (700–400 BC) that the residential area grew exponentially to cover an area that includes zones that now lie beneath the modern town of Chavín de Huántar. Burger (1984) hypothesized that the residential population approached three thousand people at this time, and the subsequent discoveries at La Banda by Gamboa (2016) and Sayre (Sayre and Rosenfeld, this volume) on the eastern side of the Mosna River strengthen the plausibility of this estimate. If this estimate is correct, then Chavín de Huántar would have been orders of magnitude larger in demographic terms than any of its contemporaries in the Central Andes.

Different studies of refuse from the residential sector at Chavín de Huántar indicate that the inhabitants were agropastoralists and consumed a variety of locally available cultigens, as well as camelids from the adjacent *puna* grasslands (Burger and Van der Merwe 1990; Miller and Burger 1995; Rosenfeld and Sayre 2016; Sayre 2010). Moreover, numerous studies have noted that the inhabitants of Chavín de Huántar also had access to a variety of exotic goods that came from the coast and highlands (Burger 1984; Burger et al. 2006; Rosenfeld and Sayre 2016; Sayre, Miller, and Rosenfeld 2016).

Matthew P. Sayre and Silvana A. Rosenfeld's chapter, "A River Runs through It: Ritual and Inequality in the La Banda Sector of Chavín de Huántar," provides a valuable contribution to the settlement history of Chavín de Huántar based on their research at La Banda, a residential sector positioned on the banks of the Mosna River opposite the temple core. Radiocarbon dating and ceramic evidence suggest that it was during the Janabarriu phase that this sector was most intensively occupied (see also Gamboa 2016; Sayre 2018). Drawing on a detailed analysis of the artifact and faunal assemblages, Sayre and Rosenfeld tackle the issues of inequality and the relationship of the La Banda inhabitants to the ritual activities undertaken in the ceremonial core of Chavín de Huántar. The authors demonstrate that the residents of La Banda were engaged in craft production activities that supplied temple elites/ leaders with ceremonial paraphernalia made from raw materials imported from distant locales, including sea mammals from the Pacific littoral. This research is significant because it links the temple with the population living at Chavín de Huántar. It also offers new evidence for socioeconomic inequality and craft specialization in the Chavín de Huántar settlement, confirming earlier arguments made for the population living closer to the ceremonial core (Burger 1984; Miller and Burger 1995).

Collectively, the work at Chavín de Huántar suggests that the site clearly stands apart from its neighbors. To our knowledge, no highland site of this period exhibits the size, architectural complexity, dense residential population, and quantity of exotic items that is seen at Chavín de Huántar. In addition, studies of landscape modification (Contreras 2015, 2017; Contreras and Keefer 2009) suggest large labor inputs to construct buildings and modify the natural topography. For this reason, it seems justified to refer to Chavín de Huántar during the Early Horizon not only as a ceremonial center but also as an urban or "proto-urban" center (Burger 1984; Rowe 1963). Current scholarship utilizes functional and scalar definitions of urbanism that stress relative population size and heterogeneity (Cowgill 2004; Jennings 2016; Jennings and Earle 2016), variables that are clearly relevant to Chavín de Huántar. Consequently, we believe that Chavín de Huántar should be considered in contemporary discussions of the history and nature of Andean urbanism (D'Altroy 2001; Makowski 2008).

The Chavín Heartland

Urban centers have hinterlands (Yoffee 2005) and in this respect, it is important to stress that Chavín

de Huántar was one of many Initial Period/Early Horizon settlements in the Conchucos region. In "Archaeological Investigations of the Chavín Heartland: New Perspectives from Canchas Uckro," Jason Nesbitt discusses the results of his archaeological research at Canchas Uckro, a "secondary center" located along the Puccha River near Chavín de Huántar. Canchas Uckro is of special interest because the site was founded and occupied exclusively between 1100 and 800/750 BC and, therefore, provides a window into the early development of Chavín de Huántar. One of the important contributions of this chapter is the observation that Canchas Uckro was suddenly abandoned around 800/750 BC. This date is significant because it indicates that the abandonment corresponds with the rapid growth of Chavín de Huántar's urban settlement in the Chakinani and Janabarriu phases. As a result, Nesbitt hypothesizes that Canchas Uckro declined as the inhabitants of the site were increasingly drawn to the growing center of Chavín de Huántar.

In "Old Temples, New Substances: Emplacing and Replacing Chavín at Hualcayán, a Community Temple in Peru's North-Central Highlands," Rebecca E. Bria presents insights into the nature of Chavín influence in highland Ancash based on her work at Hualcayán, a site located in the northern Callejón de Huaylas. Hualcayán has a long history of occupation that begins in the Late Preceramic period and continues until the end of the first millennium BC. This long sequence allows Bria to consider local and foreign influences on the area over the longue durée. More specifically, Bria examines changes in ritual practices as they impacted the local population inhabiting the site. At some point between 800 and 500 BC, Hualcayán was incorporated into the sphere of long-distance interaction associated with Chavín de Huántar, as reflected by the influx of Janabarriu-related pottery and foreign materials, such as obsidian. Bria argues that the site's transformation into a Chavín temple did not occur vis-à-vis a swift or sweeping "conversion" to the Chavín religion but was instead part of a long history of shifting ritual engagement during the Initial Period—one that increasingly valued public performance in prominent, visible spaces. To paraphrase

Bria, "becoming Chavín" in places like Hualcayán was more of a process than an event. Bria illustrates how the Chavín Phenomenon influenced much more than material culture. It modified everyday life through the modification of public spaces and the rituals carried out in them.

The Chavín Phenomenon from a Pan-Regional Perspective

It is apparent that there were fundamental shifts in the character of interregional interaction between the highlands, coast, and tropical forest after 800 BC (Burger 2008). Archaeological investigation in both ceremonial and domestic contexts from Chavín de Huántar suggest a political and ritual economy that was, in part, based on access to exotic goods from distant sources such as strombus and spondylus shell from coastal Ecuador, cinnabar from Huancavelica, obsidian from Ayacucho and Arequipa, and foreign pottery from the coast and northern highlands (Burger 1984, 2008; Burger et al. 2006; Contreras 2011; Druc 2004; Lumbreras 1993, 2007; Matsumoto et al. 2018; Rick 2005, 2008; Sayre, Miller, and Rosenfeld 2016).

Chavín de Huántar already had extensive interaction with many centers throughout the Central Andes during the late Initial Period, as is evident from both the Ofrendas Gallery and the refuse associated with Urabarriu residences (Burger 1992; Burger and Salazar, this volume). Nonetheless, the presence of increasing amounts of exotic items after 800 BC points to the deepening of exchange relationships with contemporary centers like Campanayuq Rumi (Matsumoto 2010; Matsumoto and Cavero Palomino, this volume; Matsumoto et al. 2018) and Atalla (Burger and Matos Mendieta 2002; Young 2017; Young, this volume) in the south. These probably encouraged the spread of long-distance llama caravans (Burger 2013; Contreras 2011) and provided valued preciosities not only to Chavín de Huántar but also to centers such as Kuntur Wasi (Onuki 1995) and Pacopampa (Seki et al. 2010) in the north. At the same time, there is evidence for the emulation of Chavín material culture at many

highland and coastal centers as well as the appearance of intrusive Chavín iconography (Burger 1988, 1993, 2008, 2013). Collectively, this evidence speaks to the opening of long-distance networks, the establishment of new socioeconomic relationships, connections between elites, and the emergence of a more cosmopolitan sense of identity in what had traditionally been a highly balkanized cultural landscape (Burger 2012; Tantaleán 2021:111). Many of the chapters in this volume highlight the considerable diachronic variability in the character of these long-distance connections.

The Northern Highlands

In "The Establishment of Power in the Formative Period of the North Highlands of Peru," Yuji Seki presents data from a research project undertaken by Japanese and Peruvian scholars in the Department of Cajamarca in the northern highlands of Peru. By the late Initial Period, Cajamarca was a major locus of cultural transformation with the founding of civic ceremonial centers such as Pacopampa, Huacaloma, and Layzón in the highland valleys of the Department of Cajamarca as well as Kuntur Wasi in the upper reaches of the adjacent Jequetepeque drainage. It is also at this time that there is a dramatic increase in the number of sites in the Cajamarca Basin (Seki 2014). Two of the major centers, Pacopampa and Kuntur Wasi, are the subject of Seki's analysis. Both have been known since the heyday of Tello and Rafael Larco, but it is only as a result of the intensive multiyear focus of Japanese scholars that the complicated histories of these centers can now be appreciated. Both sites revealed long sequences of architectural change that have been documented in considerable detail (Inokuchi 2010, 2014; Seki et al. 2010). While early research emphasized the similarities of these sites to Chavín de Huántar, focusing on formal elements such as cut and polished masonry blocks, elaborate drainage canals, and stone sculpture, the new picture reveals that the contrasts with Chavín de Huántar are more impressive than the similarities.

Archaeological evidence from both sites demonstrates that by the end of the second millennium BC, these centers exhibited local traditions of monumental architecture. For example, one of the main public structures in the early portion of Pacopampa's architectural sequence is a large round masonry platform, a feature that has no known analogue at Chavín de Huántar. At this time, Kuntur Wasi and Pacopampa had close relationships with their Cupisnique neighbors along the north coast and other groups living in adjacent highland and ceja de selva regions (Seki, this volume).

During the first millennium BC, both sites witnessed sociopolitical and economic transformations, particularly in the realm of status inequality, a pattern that also characterized Chavín de Huántar. Kuntur Wasi and Pacopampa have elaborate burials with some of the richest materials documented in all of Peru for this time (Onuki 1995; Seki et al. 2010). Goods within these burials include gold ornaments that exhibit Chavín iconography, as well as exotic materials such as cinnabar and spondylus shell, which were acquired from the south-central highlands and Ecuadorian coast, respectively. The incorporation of these reflected the growing exchange networks in highland and coastal Peru that begin to intensify around 800 BC.

The Northern Tropical Forest

One of the most exciting aspects of the last decade of research on the Initial Period and Early Horizon is renewed archaeological research in the ceja de selva and Upper Amazon (Church 1996; Clasby and Nesbitt 2021; Olivera Nuñez 2014). The importance of this region was stressed early in the history of Andean archaeology by Julio C. Tello and later by Donald Lathrap (1970, 1971, 1973). For Lathrap, the Upper Amazon was an important locus of cultural evolution and influence from the second millennium BC onward. Unfortunately, most of the ceja de selva and tropical forest of Peru remain poorly explored (Church 1996). Exceptions to this lacuna are the Bagua and Jaén regions as well as adjacent parts of Ecuador. This area has witnessed a proliferation of archaeological investigation with exciting results (e.g., Olivera Nuñez 2014; Valdez 2008, 2021; Yamamoto 2010, 2021). Investigations of the borderlands of northeastern Peru and southern Ecuador demonstrate precocious occurrences of public

architecture as well as relatively dense settlement, beginning in the late second millennium BC.

In "From Jaguars to Harpy Eagles: Re-evaluating the Chavín Phenomenon and Its Relationship with the Tropical Forest," Ryan Clasby presents a synthesis of the research in this area. By comparing early coeval sites, Clasby makes the convincing case that cultural connections were highly variable. Some sites like Ingatambo were embedded within the Chavín Interaction Sphere (Yamamoto 2010), but others, like Huayurco, apparently had only indirect relationships with this sphere and exhibited different traditions of ritual activity, ceremonial architecture, and material culture during the Early Horizon. This is not to say that Huayurco was isolated; instead, it seems to have been more closely tied to other interaction networks in far northern Peru and less connected with Chavín de Huántar. Nonetheless, ritual stone platters from the Huayurco area somehow reached the temple of Chavín de Huántar and were recovered from the Ofrendas Gallery (Clasby, this volume; Lumbreras 1993:lam. 85, 672–672b).

The North Coast of Peru

The relation of the north coast to the Chavín Phenomenon has long been of interest and has been the subject of disagreements since the 1940s (Larco 1941; Tello 1943). Larco had concluded that Tello's identification of "coastal Chavín" had been mistaken and that the Nepeña sites he investigated predated the constructions at Chavín de Huántar and served as an inspiration for the developments there. These differences in opinion have survived into recent times (e.g., Burger 1992; Elera 1993, 1997, 1998; Toshiahara 2002), partly due to the lack of an adequate definition for the Cupisnique culture and the absence of intensive research at Cupisnique sites. Research by Chicoine and colleagues in the Nepeña Valley, located 180 km to the south of the Chicama Valley, where Larco identified the Cupisnique culture, draws upon settlement patterns, architecture, iconography, and pottery to argue for a high degree of complexity and heterogeneity in the local economic, social, and political landscapes in the valley. Chicoine, Ikehara-Tsukayama, and Shibata demonstrate "fluctuations" with respect to relationships between Nepeña, Chavín de Huántar, and the Cupisnique centers of the north coast. They argue that Nepeña has traditions of architecture with monumental mural art that are linked to both the highland Chavín and coastal Cupisnique religious complexes, and they refer to sites such as Huaca Partida and Cerro Blanco as part of a "Chavín-Cupisnique Religious Complex." Prior to 800 BC, some architectural elements at Huaca Partida, such as the hypostyle hall flanked by rooms to the north and south, recall Cupisnique constructions at sites such as Caballo Muerto, while the painted clay friezes decorating this temple depict a local version of the stone frieze that adorns the Circular Plaza at Chavín de Huántar. The Huaca Partida frieze presents a line of elaborately dressed priestly figures processing in the upper register with a band of profile jaguars below them; both the figures and felines are shown moving toward the mound's central staircase.

Chicoine and his colleagues believe that between 800 and 500 BC local elites in Nepeña became increasingly entangled with the Chavín Interaction Sphere. Part of the evidence for this is the presence of exotic goods such as obsidian and cinnabar. Chicoine and his colleagues observe that this pattern ends after 500 BC with a halt in the construction of public monuments, a phenomenon seen at other Cupisnique sites, such as Caballo Muerto (Nesbitt, Gutiérrez, and Vásquez 2010; Pozorski 1983). Coinciding with this change is a move toward increasingly nucleated settlements, new site layouts emphasizing multiple environments for banquets, an absence of massive platforms, and dramatic changes in pottery style. The investigators observe that in Nepeña, the increase in interactions with Chavín de Huántar was preceded and outlasted by enduring ties with neighboring communities on the north and central coast (Chicoine, Ikehara-Tsukayama, and Shibata, this volume).

Interestingly, according to their analysis, resistance to the Chavín Interaction Sphere began at least a century earlier in Nepeña's lower valley at Caylán and Huambacho, where populations stopped constructing pyramid mounds and megalithic structures and began building smaller, enclosed spaces within elite compounds that featured plazas decorated with geometric friezes. Elaborate iconography related to Chavín de Huántar or Caballo Muerto was shunned, and monochrome light clay plastering replaced the brightly colored clay adornment that had characterized sites like Cerro Blanco and Huaca Partida. According to Chicoine, Ikehara-Tsukayama, and Shibata, the occupation of Caylán and Huambacho was partially coeval with the appearance of proto-urban settlement at Chavín de Huántar during the Janabarriu phase, but they were fundamentally dissimilar, since the nucleation of population in Nepeña was not focused on a monumental temple complex but rather on a multiplicity of plaza settings that suggests a fragmentation of ritual practice and political power.

The Central Coast

In "Transformation and Continuity along the Central Coast of Peru during the First Millennium BC and the Impact of the Chavín Phenomenon," Richard L. Burger and Lucy C. Salazar examine the nature of socioeconomic and cultural change along the central coast during the late second through first millennia BC. During the Initial Period, the coastal valleys of Chancay, Chillón, Rimac, and Lurín boasted some of the most impressive monuments in Peru. These centers of the Manchay culture were characterized by what is sometimes referred to as the U-shaped architectural tradition (Williams 1985). Radiocarbon dating demonstrates that U-shaped buildings were being constructed by 1700 BC (Burger 2009; Burger and Salazar 2008; Patterson 1985) and predated the foundation of Chavín de Huántar by many centuries (Burger 2019b). Instead, as Burger and Salazar (2008) argued previously, elements of Manchay architecture, including the U-shaped layout, appear to have been adopted at Chavín de Huántar. Substantial evidence for contact with Chavín de Huántar includes the presence of late Initial Period vessels found in the Ofrendas Gallery that are imports from the central coast, possibly left as gifts from visiting pilgrims (Burger 1992, 2019b; Lumbreras 1993, 2007).

It is interesting to note, however, that on the central coast contact with Chavín de Huántar coincides with the gradual abandonment of the local monumental public centers after 900 BC. Rather than being stimulated by their incorporation into the Chavín Interaction Sphere, the societies of the central coast seem to have gone into decline (Burger 1992:184). The number of monumental centers in the central coast valleys diminishes drastically and the ability to mobilize labor for any purpose likewise seems to contract. By 800 BC, ceremonial sites, such as Pampa Chica, were established, but they are much smaller than the preceding Initial Period complexes. Nearby on the shoreline, small village sites like Ancón were actively emulating the ceramic styles associated with Chavín de Huántar and the south coast. Moreover, in contrast to the situation at Hualcayán described by Bria for the Callejón de Huaylas, during the Early Horizon in the Lurín Valley emphasis shifts from public ceremony carried out on the summit of pyramids and in large open plazas to intimate rituals in small rooms and narrow terraces; these focused on the physical remains of ancestors.

The South Coast: Paracas

Two chapters explore the relationship of Chavín de Huántar with Paracas culture on the south coast. Recent years have seen a renaissance of archaeological research on Paracas and its antecedents (Dulanto and Bachir Bacha 2013) as well as dramatic improvements linking absolute dates (Unkel et al. 2012) with a detailed ceramic sequence (Carmichael 2019; Menzel, Rowe, and Dawson 1964). This highly resolved chronology has enabled sophisticated perspectives on the complex relationship between Paracas and other localities in the highlands, including Chavín de Huántar.

In "From the Inside Looking Out: Paracas Perspectives on Chavín," Lisa DeLeonardis focuses on local processes by studying "how the Paracas interpreted and translated Chavín imagery and its attendant ideas" by incorporating them into their visual culture, especially textiles and pottery. DeLeonardis employs a materials-based approach that combines iconography and archaeometric analysis to examine change over time in patterns of influence. She notes that throughout its long sequence, Paracas was embedded in multiple interaction spheres that

aided in cementing social relationships with neighboring and more distant polities. One important element of her study is the examination of the origin of the pigments and binders used in Paracas pottery. Early Paracas ceramics have long been recognized as incorporating Chavín iconography in a distinctively local manner, so perhaps it is not surprising that some of the crucial raw materials used in this pottery come from tropical forest sources, as well as the highlands, suggesting the area's widespread exchange networks at this time.

Jalh Dulanto's chapter, "The Chavín Interaction Sphere and Peru's South Coast: Maritime Communities, Long-Distance Exchange Networks, and Prestige Economies during the Early Horizon in the Central Andes," discusses the nature of exchange and its relationship to the beginnings of a prestige economy on Peru's south coast and the appearance of individualized inequality. Elite tombs have been found at Paracas sites such as Coyungo, Karwa, Mollake Chico, and Puerto Nuevo. Radiocarbon dating places the beginning of elite burials in the eighth century BC, roughly the same time as the appearance of high-status burials in the northern highlands at Kuntur Wasi and Pacopampa. Dulanto asserts that the emergence of elites can be connected to the involvement of the south coast in long-distance interaction. Utilizing a series of compositional analyses on a large sample of pottery, Dulanto argues for the presence of paste-groups tied to the central and north coast. Like DeLeonardis, Dulanto also notes that the minerals for making pigments, including cinnabar, were acquired from distant sources in the south-central highlands (see Young, this volume). Furthermore, he argues that these exotic pigments were used by local potters to imitate foreign iconography.

It is important to emphasize, however, that according to Dulanto, other elements of daily life at this coastal community remained fundamentally local in character, including a self-sufficient subsistence economy. In this sense, Puerto Nuevo is similar to the fishing communities of the central coast, such as Ancón (Burger and Salazar, this volume). Taken together, DeLeonardis and Dulanto make a clear argument that Paracas culture was embedded in multiple long-distance spheres that fluctuated over time, only one of which was the Chavín Interaction Sphere.

The South-Central Highlands

The next two chapters provide much needed syntheses of the south-central highlands, a region once considered marginal to the Chavín Phenomenon (e.g., Lumbreras 1974). New work at sites like Atalla in Huancavelica (Young, this volume) and Campanayuq Rumi in Ayacucho (Matsumoto and Cavero Palomino, this volume) has transformed our understanding of the importance of this area and demonstrated that the Chavín Interaction Sphere was more extensive than previously assumed. In addition, the work by Michelle Young, Yuichi Matsumoto, and Yuri Cavero Palomino provide new perspectives regarding interaction between the highlands and the south coast, complementing the discussions by DeLeonardis and Dulanto.

Michelle Young's chapter, "Horizon, Interaction Sphere, Cult? A View of the Chavín Phenomenon from Huancavelica," details the results of her research at the impressive center of Atalla. Located in the Mantaro drainage near the city of Huancavelica, Atalla is situated close to the most important cinnabar (mercuric sulfide) source in the Central Andes and one of the largest mercury ore deposits in the world (Burger, Lane, and Cooke 2016; Burger and Matos Mendieta 2002; Cooke et al. 2013). As noted throughout this volume, cinnabar was a prized exotic commodity that was used in burials in northern Peru (Seki, this volume), for pigments in Paracas pottery (DeLeonardis, this volume; Dulanto, this volume), and for face and body painting during religious and civic ceremonies (Burger and Leikin 2018). For this reason, Young's investigations into Atalla and its potential role in the cinnabar trade are crucial for understanding interregional interaction.

Through a detailed diachronic study, Young observes that Atalla was embedded "in multiple nested and overlapping interaction networks through which residents took up new religious practices, exchanged resources, and adopted technological innovations in ceramics and metallurgy." During the late Initial Period, these linkages were particularly strong with the surrounding highland areas and the adjacent south coast. During the ensuing centuries of the Early Horizon, Atalla was strongly linked to Chavín de Huántar, a relationship that was exhibited in Janabarriu-related pottery and architecture. It is during this time that Atalla shows the strongest evidence for playing a central role in the organization and transport of cinnabar pigment to distant zones. Abundant obsidian at the site points to ties with the Quispisisa obsidian source in southwest Ayacucho (Burger and Glascock 2000) and pottery imported from the Paracas region was surprisingly common. Evidence for camelids being utilized for long-distance transport begins in the late Initial Period and continues into the Early Horizon. Isotopic analysis of llama bone at Atalla indicates that some camelids traveled between the Huancavelica highlands and the coast and/or eastern lowlands, probably as part of caravans moving goods, including cinnabar, between these different areas.

The penultimate chapter by Yuichi Matsumoto and Yuri Cavero Palomino, "Campanayuq Rumi and the Southern Periphery of the Chavín Phenomenon," offers an overview of recent research in the Ayacucho region of the south-central highlands. Matsumoto and Cavero Palomino note that the area around Vilcashuamán is home to many newly discovered late Initial Period and Early Horizon sites with monumental architecture. Of these, the best known is Campanayuq Rumi, which is the subject of much of their chapter. From approximately 950 BC, Campanayuq Rumi exhibits architectural traits, including a U-shaped layout, a circular plaza, a large stone-lined rectangular plaza, and interior gallery architecture, that indicate contact with and emulation of Chavín de Huántar, as do individual artifacts such as a snuff spoon virtually identical to one recovered from the Ofrendas Gallery (Matsumoto 2010). Chavín style galleries are also present at other sites such as Tukri-Apu Urqu that are located near Campanayuq Rumi.

During its earliest phase of public construction (Campanayuq I phase), the material culture has a local character and shares little in common with Urabarriu-phase pottery from Chavín de Huántar.

However, socioeconomic changes occur in the Campanayuq II phase, when there are transformations in interaction patterns, with a spike in imports of Paracas-related pottery as well as an influx of Janabarriu-related pottery. It is also at this time that Campanayuq Rumi probably became a major distributor of obsidian mined in the south-central highlands at the Quispisisa source to distant places such as Chavín de Huántar (Matsumoto et al. 2018). Significantly, a residential sector adjacent to the monumental architecture has been identified, and precious items suggesting socioeconomic inequality, such as gold earspools, have been recovered from it. Like Young's contribution, Matsumoto and Cavero Palomino outline different, and diachronically shifting, patterns of interaction during the first five centuries of the first millennium BC.

The Chavín Interaction Sphere and the Cuzco and the Titicaca Basin Regions

Current evidence suggests that the Chavín Interaction Sphere extended to the south at least to the Nazca drainage on the coast and Vilcashuamán in the highlands (Burger 1988; Matsumoto et al. 2018). The developments to the south of this boundary are frequently ignored in discussions of the Chavín Phenomenon, just as analyses of the emergence of complexity in the southern highlands and altiplano often fail to mention Chavín. Though systematic comparisons between these areas have yet to be undertaken, the southern Peruvian highlands and the Bolivian altiplano probably followed a largely independent historical trajectory that included broad swaths of the Southern Andes (Burger 1992; Stanish 2003).

In Cuzco, an expanded number of radiocarbon dates have helped to place early ceramic styles such as Marcavalle and Chanapata (Rowe 1944) within the late second and first millennia BC, respectively (Chávez 1980, 1981a, 1981b; Davis 2011). Yet this ceramic sequence still lacks precision and archaeologists refer to this period broadly as "Formative" (Bauer 2004; Covey 2014; Davis 2014). Because of this chronological imprecision, diachronic trends during the Formative period are difficult to discern. Settlement pattern research, as well as limited

excavation, imply that the populations of the Cuzco area were living in village-scale settlements and engaged in agropastoral economic systems (Covey 2014; Davis 2011, 2014). Obsidian sourcing from sites of this period demonstrate the consumption of southern highland obsidian deposits, primarily the Chivay and Alca sources (Burger et al. 2000). There is little overlap with the obsidian used by the people inhabiting sites within the Chavín Interaction Sphere (Burger et al. 2006; Matsumoto et al. 2018).

Further differences between Cuzco and the Central Andes are expressed in architecture and material culture. Sites in Cuzco lack the scale of monumental architecture that characterize highland Peru. Furthermore, the Marcavalle and Chanapata pottery styles do not appear to be related to known ceramic complexes in Ayacucho or southern Peru (see Matsumoto 2010). These differences prompted Karen Mohr Chávez (1981b:319) to state that the Formative period of Cuzco "remained outside the sphere of Chavín influence."

Scholars working in the Puno region of Peru and the Bolivian altiplano refer to a Formative period that dates between 1500 BC and AD 475 (Hastorf 2008). When compared with the Peruvian chronology, the Bolivian Formative period would encompass the Initial Period, Early Horizon, and much of the Early Intermediate Period (see Figure 1.2). By 1500 BC (or the Early Formative period), settled village life emerges in the Lake Titicaca region (Hastorf 2005, 2008) and by the Middle Formative period (800–250/200 BC) there is increased evidence for a ceremonial architecture tradition characterized by sunken courts associated with stepped platforms (Chávez 1988; Hastorf 1999; Stanish 2003). However, the organization and layout of these buildings are distinct from contemporary centers in the Central Andes, and their size is much smaller. Also beginning in the Middle Formative period there was a distinctive, long-lived sculptural and iconographic style referred to as Yaya-Mama (Chávez 1988). The early phases of Yaya-Mama stone sculpture exhibit low-relief depictions of religious imagery, including anthropomorphic beings, as well as amphibians and reptiles (Chávez 2018). Though the early phases of Yaya-Mama sculpture are contemporary with the

Peruvian Early Horizon, they are radically different from the Chavín sculptural and iconographic corpus described earlier in this chapter and clearly originated independently (Chávez 2018:18).

Thus, like Cuzco, the cultures of the Titicaca Basin appear to have developed with seemingly little direct influence from the polities embedded within the Chavín Interaction Sphere. That said, the southern highlands were not totally separated from the long-distance connections that characterize the Chavín Interaction Sphere. For instance, one of the rich burials from Kuntur Wasi (Seki, this volume) includes 496 non-local sodalite beads (Onuki 1995, 1997) that were geochemically sourced to Cerro Sapo (Kato 2014:168), located in the western part of the Department of Cochabamba in Bolivia (see Becerra et al. 2021; Petersen 2010). Sodalite from Cerro Sapo was widely circulated among the people living around Lake Titicaca during the Formative period (Bandy 2005; Browman 1998) and its appearance 1800 km to the north in Cajamarca speaks to a poorly understood long-distance exchange network. Moreover, the appearance of a small amount of Alca source obsidian in refuse at Chavín de Huántar raises the possibility that pilgrims from Arequipa and/or Cuzco visited the famous northern highland temple (Burger, Mohr Chávez, and Chávez 2000).

Reconsidering the Chavín Phenomenon

The preceding review illustrates some major points of agreement and disagreement regarding the Chavín Phenomenon. One of the points of consensus shared by virtually all contributors to this volume is the necessity of creating local sequences to disentangle indigenous developments from foreign impacts. This has been facilitated by much-improved local ceramic and radiocarbon chronologies that can be profitably compared at a pan-regional level. It is no longer assumed that external influences occurred at the same time throughout the Central Andes (an idea underlying the horizon concept) or that the nature of this influence and the way in which it was incorporated was similar in all cases. On the contrary, the timing and character of the

Chavín Phenomenon varies from site to site even within the same drainage. Thus, the pattern that emerges is more complex and nuanced than many had anticipated.

There is also agreement about the existence of multiple overlapping interaction networks that change over time. The broadest of the networks is the Chavín Interaction Sphere. However, there are several others. For instance, Matsumoto and Cavero Palomino describe a Cajamarca Sphere and an Ayacucho Sphere. The Cajamarca Sphere is characterized by sites like Pacopampa and Kuntur Wasi, which exhibit public architecture that is distinct from Chavín de Huántar. These sites seem to undergo radical transformations after 800 BC, when they feature elite burials that include gold objects with Chavín-related iconography and exotic items acquired from very distant sources. At the same time, changes in the architectural layout remain driven by local traditions and interests. In contrast, the Ayacucho Sphere, as represented at Campanayuq Rumi, shows strong links to Apurimac and the south coast. Like the Cajamarca Interaction Sphere, this network began before its incorporation into the Chavín Interaction Sphere. In both areas, a version of these regional spheres continued to operate even after the collapse of Chavín de Huántar and the relationships associated with it. Unlike the Cajamarca Sphere, the Ayacucho Sphere shows evidence of emulating Chavín architectural conventions (such as U-shaped layouts, galleries, and circular plazas) (see also Matsumoto et al. 2018). Similarly, one can posit a Central Coast Interaction Sphere that extends from the Chancay Valley to the Lurín Valley and expands to the south coast during the Early Horizon (see Burger and Salazar, this volume; Dulanto, this volume). These spheres often overlapped, and they could be represented in a Venn diagram that changes over time. Many were subsumed within the broader Chavín Interaction Sphere during the late Initial Period/Early Horizon, but this varied according to region and time. In addition, there appear to be some places that never were incorporated into the Chavín Interaction Sphere, such as the Otuzco–Quiruvilca–Santiago de Chuco region (Burger 1992:115). Other areas, such as the lower Casma Valley, initially participated in it but rejected it in the Early Horizon while the Chavín de Huántar temple was still flourishing.

The recognition of multiple interaction spheres has been greatly enhanced by the widespread adoption of archaeometric analyses of archaeological materials such as obsidian, pottery, pigments, and bone. Several of the chapters point out that in many areas interregional interaction began to intensify at the beginning of the first millennium BC, then reached its apex between 800 and 500 BC, when there was a clear expansion and intensification of long-distance networks that was reflected by notable increases in foreign goods (Burger 1988, 2013).

In her chapter, Young introduces the term "Chavín International Style," which she defines as "a stylistic vocabulary that includes a set of technological and decorative techniques accompanied by loosely bound sets of traits that are shared by a number of sites participating in the Chavín Interaction Sphere during the Early Horizon." This provides an alternative to earlier terms such as "Janabarriu-related pottery," which was introduced to describe a perceived relationship between the local ceramic assemblage at Chavín de Huántar and other sites. Young's term has the advantage of referring to a pan-regional pattern of similar stylistic traits without assuming their origin; to this end, her terminology may facilitate discussion by avoiding confusion introduced by inappropriate or unclear language.

In the end, debates over terminologies should not distract from the core theme. In a very real sense, the Chavín Phenomenon, the Chavín Interaction Sphere, and the Chavín horizon are all referring to a set of complex processes of culture contact, economic change, and identity transformation. Multiple interaction spheres shift through time and reach their apex in the first centuries of the first millennium BC. The Chavín Interaction Sphere is important, but it is by no means the only or even the major one for some areas. These shifting patterns must be analyzed diachronically since they evolve over time in different ways.

Fortunately, the nature of these exchanges is becoming clarified through empirical research. However, there are other topics that need to be studied. Regardless of perspective, the first millennium BC exhibits a high degree of cultural cosmopolitanism (Burger 2012), in which numerous ethnic and linguistic groups came into direct or indirect contact. Interestingly, these interactions throughout the period between 1000 and 500 BC were largely peaceful, with little evidence of conflict (Arkush and Tung 2013; Burger 1992; Contreras 2011). This observation supports notions discussed at the beginning of this chapter that maintain that shared religious beliefs were a crucial mechanism for structuring and facilitating culture contact between distant and alien cultural groups (Burger 1988, 1993, 2012, 2013; Willey 1951).

One of the other distinctive features of consensus in this volume is the support for a bottom-up rather than a top-down perspective when trying to understand the Chavín Phenomenon. Traditionally, scholars such as Tello and Willey adopted a pan-regional perspective based on the view from Chavín de Huántar, then asked how elements coming from this center transformed less developed sites or regions outside of its heartland. While recent research has not diminished our appreciation of Chavín de Huántar as a major center, a new generation of archaeologists has found it more productive to begin by focusing on the cultural, socioeconomic, and political characteristics of the area being studied and then attempting to understand how and why the group in question chose to engage with the distant pilgrimage center and its sphere of interaction and what impact the resulting entanglements had for the local inhabitants. This perspective emphasizes the agency of local centers and their inhabitants, and it views emulation and importation of alien elements as reflecting conscious actions to modify previous lifestyles and cultural identities. The bottom-up approach has proved productive, whether dealing with sites on the coast, highlands, or *ceja de selva*, and this volume's emphasis on a bottom-up perspective helps to explain its lack of attention to Chavín technology, style, and other elements that have traditionally dominated the academic discourse on the Chavín Phenomenon.

Another crucial area of study mentioned in some of the chapters is the "collapse" of the Chavín

Interaction Sphere. Collectively, the authors appear to agree that this was a largely synchronous event occurring after 500 BC and before 400 BC. A clearer estimate of the dating of this occurrence is hindered by imprecision in dating introduced by the Hallstatt Plateau. At Chavín de Huántar, there is evidence for massive architectural destruction possibly caused by an earthquake that is believed to have occurred around 500 BC (Rick 2008). According to the Stanford University team's interpretation, the monumental constructions of the post-disaster Support Construction Stage attest to the inability of Chavín society to mobilize the resources necessary to recover from this natural disaster (Kembel 2008; Rick 2008). Outside of Chavín de Huántar, the cosmopolitan spirit promoted by the Chavín Interaction Sphere diminishes after 500 BC, and with the abandonment of Chavín de Huántar, a pattern of sociopolitical balkanization and small-scale cultures returns.

Analogous rejections of Chavín cultural patterns after roughly 400 BC occurred at Reparín (Nesbitt, Ibarra Asencios, and Tokanai 2020) and at Hualcayán (Bria 2017, this volume) in the Chavín heartland. Huarás, a pottery style characterized by white-on-red pottery with geometrical designs, suddenly appears after 400 BC (cf. Bennett 1944; Lau 2004; Lumbreras 1974; Rick et al. 2010). At Chavín de Huántar and other highland sites, these changes seem to represent a spurning of Chavín culture and belief (Burger 1992; Lau 2011, 2016). Because of the radical cultural differences that appear at this time, it is possible that Huarás culture represents the movement of different cultural groups into the region. The question of population stability or replacement has yet to be systematically investigated, but the advent of ancient DNA analysis offers the potential for evaluating this issue.

A similar process of radical material culture change occurs on the north coast, where Chavín-influenced Cupisnique pottery styles are replaced with white-on-red Salinar pottery in the mid to late first millennium BC (Elera 1997, 1998; Millaire 2020) and previously sacred mounds are reoccupied by squatters and covered with domestic refuse (Brennan 1980; Chicoine, Ikehara-Tsukayama,

and Shibata, this volume; Pozorski and Pozorski 2018). On the central coast and the valleys immediately to the north (i.e., the Norte Chico), there is also a shift toward large agglutinated settlements (Chicoine, Ikehara-Tsukayama, and Shibata, this volume; Ikehara 2021; Millaire 2020; S. Pozorski and T. Pozorski 1987). However, these post-Chavín transformations and their implications for new kinds of sociopolitical organization remain a poorly understood topic that needs to be investigated in more detail. Given the interregional scope of disruption, a pan-regional causal explanation may exist that is poorly understood.

While the data remains limited, there is compelling evidence for an increase in interpersonal violence following the collapse of the Chavín Interaction Sphere. This has been documented in the northern highlands in late Early Horizon burials in Pacopampa (Nagaoka et al. 2017), and a similar pattern has been observed in a survey of settlement patterns and paleopathology throughout the Central Andes (Arkush and Tung 2013). On the other hand, despite the widespread evidence for increased violence, there is not the same degree of cultural disruption in all parts of the Central Andes. The cultures of some areas, such as those in the Upper Huallaga and the Peruvian south coast, display significant continuity while at the same time abandoning most Chavín-inspired elements (Matsumoto 2020).

Chavín in Comparative Perspective

We believe that the empirical data that the authors bring to this volume have significantly enriched our understanding of the late Initial Period and Early Horizon. One of the goals of this publication is to encourage archaeologists working in other areas of the world and time periods to consider Chavín in comparative studies of "complex societies" (see Graeber and Wengrow 2021:386–391). While we are confident that the contributions of this volume will be of wide interest to archaeologists working in the Central Andes, we also hope that it will reach a wider audience and that this will lead to the Chavín Phenomenon becoming integrated within a broader, global, and comparative framework. It is in that spirit that we invited Olmec specialist Christopher A. Pool to serve as the discussant for the conference and to prepare the volume's concluding chapter.

We are convinced that issues of interregional interaction and its role in the emergence of political complexity in ancient Peru will resonate with scholars working on similar problems in early Mesopotamia (Stein 1998), Formative Mesoamerica, or the process of "Mississippianization" in the North American Southeast (Pauketat 2007). We also believe that the role of pan-regional and regional oracular centers, religious pilgrimages, and trade caravans in the emergence of inequality likewise have analogs in the early civilizations of Mesoamerica, North America, and the Old World (Blomster and Cheetham 2017; Chang 1980; Pauketat 2007; Pool 2007; Stein 1998). Simply put, the time is right for archaeologists working on early complex societies at a global level to consider the Chavín Phenomenon as part of their analyses.

REFERENCES CITED

Alva, Walter

1988   Investigaciones en el complejo formativo con arquitectura monumental de Purulén, costa norte del Perú. *Beiträge zur Allgemeinen und Vergleichenden Archäologie* 8:283–300.

Arkush, Elizabeth, and Tiffany Tung

2013   Patterns of War in the Andes from the Archaic to the Late Horizon: Insights from Settlement Patterns and Cranial Trauma. *Journal of Archaeological Research* 21:307–369.

Bandy, Matthew S.

2005   Trade and Social Power in the Southern Titicaca Basin Formative. In *Foundations of Power in the Prehispanic Andes*, edited by Kevin J. Vaughn, Dennis Ogburn, and Christina A. Conlee, pp. 91–111. Archeological Papers of the American Anthropological Association 14. University of California Press, Berkeley.

Bauer, Brian S.

2004   *Ancient Cuzco: Heartland of the Inca.* University of Texas Press, Austin.

Becerra, María F., Beatriz N. Ventura, Patricia Solá, Mariana Rosenbusch, Guillermo Cozzi, and Andrea Romano

2021   Arqueomineralogía de cuentas de los valles orientales del norte de Salta, Argentina. *Boletín del Museo Chileno de Arte Precolombino* 26:93–112.

Bennett, Wendell C.

1944   *The North Highlands of Peru: Excavations in the Callejón de Huaylas and at Chavín de Huántar.* American Museum of Natural History, New York.

Benson, Elizabeth P. (editor)

1971   *Dumbarton Oaks Conference on Chavín.* Dumbarton Oaks Research Library and Collection, Washington, D.C.

Blomster, Jeffrey, and David Cheetham (editors)

2017   *The Early Olmec and Mesoamerica: The Material Record.* Cambridge University Press, New York.

Brennan, Curtis T.

1980   Cerro Arena: Early Cultural Complexity and Nucleation in North Coastal Peru. *Journal of Field Archaeology* 7:1–22.

Bria, Rebecca

2017   Ritual, Economy, and the Production of Community at Hualcayán, Peru. PhD dissertation, Vanderbilt University, Nashville.

Browman, David L.

1998   Lithic Provenience Analysis and Emerging Material Complexity at Formative Period Chiripa, Bolivia. *Andean Past* 5:301–324.

Burger, Richard L.

1981   The Radiocarbon Evidence for the Temporal Priority of Chavín de Huántar. *American Antiquity* 46:592–602.

| 1984 | *The Prehistoric Occupation of Chavín de Huántar, Peru*. University of California Press, Berkeley. |

1985 Concluding Remarks: Early Peruvian Civilization and Its Relation to the Chavín Horizon. In *Early Ceremonial Architecture in the Andes*, edited by Christopher B. Donnan, pp. 269–289. Dumbarton Oaks Research Library and Collection, Washington, D.C.

1988 Unity and Heterogeneity within the Chavín Horizon. In *Peruvian Prehistory*, edited by Richard Keatinge, pp. 99–144. Cambridge University Press, Cambridge.

1989 An Overview of Peruvian Archaeology (1976–1986). *Annual Review of Anthropology* 18:37–69.

1992 *Chavín and the Origins of Andean Civilization*. Thames and Hudson, London.

1993 The Chavín Horizon: Stylistic Chimera or Socioeconomic Metamorphosis? In *Latin American Horizons*, edited by Donald Rice, pp. 41–82. Dumbarton Oaks Research Library and Collection, Washington, D.C.

2008 Chavín de Huántar and Its Sphere of Influence. In *The Handbook of South American Archaeology*, edited by Helaine Silverman and William H. Isbell, pp. 681–703. Springer, New York.

2009 Los fundamentos sociales de la arquitectura monumental del período inicial en el valle de Lurín. In *Arqueología del período formativo en la cuenca baja de Lurín*, vol. 1, edited by Richard L. Burger and Krzysztof Makowski, pp. 17–36. Fondo Editorial Pontificia Universidad Católica del Perú, Lima.

2011 What Kind of Hallucinogenic Snuff Was Used at Chavín de Huántar? An Iconographic Identification. *Ñawpa Pacha: Journal of Andean Archaeology* 31(2):123–140.

2012 Central Andean Language Expansion and the Chavín Sphere of Interaction. *Proceedings of the British Academy* 173:133–159.

2013 In the Realm of the Incas: An Archaeological Reconsideration of Household

Exchange, Long-Distance Trade, and Marketplaces in the Pre-Hispanic Central Andes. In *Merchants, Markets and Exchange in the Pre-Columbian World*, edited by Kenneth G. Hirth and Joanne Pillsbury, pp. 319–334. Dumbarton Oaks Research Library and Collection, Washington, D.C.

2019a Changing Interpretations of Early Central Andean Civilization. In *Perspectives on Early Andean Civilization in Peru: Interaction, Authority, and Socioeconomic Organization during the First and Second Millennia BC*, edited by Richard L. Burger, Lucy C. Salazar, and Yuji Seki, pp. 189–200. Yale University Publications in Anthropology Number 94. Yale University Press, New Haven.

2019b Understanding the Socioeconomic Trajectory of Chavín de Huántar: A New Radiocarbon Sequence and Its Wider Implications. *Latin American Antiquity* 30:373–392.

2021 Evaluating the Architectural Sequence and Chronology of Chavín de Huántar: The Case of the Circular Plaza. *Peruvian Archaeology* 5:25–49.

Burger, Richard L., and Michael D. Glascock

2000 Locating the Quispisisa Obsidian Source in the Department of Ayacucho, Peru. *Latin American Antiquity* 11:258–268.

Burger, Richard L., Kris E. Lane, and Colin A. Cooke

2016 Ecuadorian Cinnabar and the Prehispanic Trade in Vermilion Pigment: Viable Hypothesis or Red Herring? *Latin American Antiquity* 27:22–35.

Burger, Richard L., George F. Lau, Víctor M. Ponte, and Michael D. Glascock

2006 The History of Prehispanic Obsidian Procurement in Highland Ancash. In *La complejidad social en la Sierra de Ancash*, edited by Alexander Herrera, Carolina Orsini, and Kevin Lane, pp. 103–120. Civiche Raccolte d'Arte Applicata del Castello Fozesco, Milan.

Burger, Richard L., and Jerrold Leikin

2018 Cinnabar Use in Prehispanic Peru and Its Possible Health Consequences. *Journal of Archaeological Science Reports* 17:730–734.

Burger, Richard L., and Ramiro Matos Mendieta

2002   Atalla: A Center on the Periphery of
the Chavín Horizon. *Latin American
Antiquity* 13:153–177.

Burger, Richard L., Karen Mohr Chávez, and Sergio J.
Chávez

2000   Through the Glass Darkly: Prehispanic
Obsidian Procurement and Exchange
in Southern Peru and Northern Bolivia.
Journal of World Prehistory 14:267–362.

Burger, Richard L., and Lucy C. Salazar

2008   The Manchay Culture and the Coastal
Inspiration for Highland Chavín
Civilization. In *Chavín: Art, Architecture,
and Culture*, edited by William J. Conklin
and Jeffrey Quilter, pp. 85–105. Cotsen
Institute of Archaeology, University of
California, Los Angeles.

Burger, Richard L., Lucy C. Salazar, and Yuji Seki
(editors)

2019   *Perspectives on Early Andean Civilization
in Peru: Interaction, Authority, and
Socioeconomic Organization during
the First and Second Millennia BC.* Yale
University Publications in Anthropology
Number 96. Yale University Press,
New Haven.

Burger, Richard L., and Nikolaas J. Van der Merwe

1990   Maize and the Origin of Highland
Chavín Civilization. *American Anthropologist* 92:85–95.

Caldwell, Joseph

1964   Interaction Spheres in Prehistory. In
Hopewellian Studies, edited by Joseph R.
Caldwell and Robert L. Hall, pp. 133–143.
Illinois State Museum, Springfield.

Carmichael, Patrick H.

2019   Stages, Periods, Epochs and Phases in
Paracas and Nasca Chronology: Another
Look at John Rowe's Ica Valley Master
Sequence. *Ñawpa Pacha: Journal of
Andean Archaeology* 39:145–179.

Carrión Cachot, Rebeca

1948   La cultura Chavín: Dos nuevas colonias,
Kuntur Wasi y Ancón. *Revista del Museo
Nacional de Antropología y Arqueología*
2:99–172.

Chang, Kwang-chih

1980   *Shang Civilization.* Yale University Press,
New Haven.

Chávez, Sergio J.

2018   Identification, Definition, and
Continuities of the Yaya-Mama Religious
Tradition in the Titicaca Basin. In
*Images in Action: The Southern Andean
Iconographic Series*, edited by William H.
Isbell, Mauricio I. Uribe, Anne Tiballi,
and Edward P. Zegarra, pp. 15–49. Cotsen
Institute of Archaeology Press, University
of California, Los Angeles.

Church, Warren

1996   Prehistoric Cultural Development and
Interregional Interaction in the Tropical
Montane Forests of Peru. PhD disserta-
tion, Yale University, New Haven.

Clasby, Ryan, and Jason Nesbitt

2021   Changing Perspectives on the Archae-
ology of the Upper Amazon. In *The
Archaeology of the Upper Amazon:
Complexity and Interaction in the Andean
Tropical Forest*, edited by Ryan Clasby
and Jason Nesbitt, pp. 1–22. University
Press of Florida, Gainesville.

Conklin, William J., and Jeffrey Quilter (editors)

2008   *Chavín: Art, Architecture, and Culture.*
Cotsen Institute of Archaeology,
University of California, Los Angeles.

Contreras, Daniel A.

2011   How Far to Conchucos? A GIS Approach
to Assessing the Implications of Exotic
Materials at Chavín de Huántar. *World
Archaeology* 43:380–397.

2015   Landscape Setting as Medium of
Communication at Chavín de Huántar,
Peru. *Cambridge Archaeological Journal*
25:513–530.

2017   (Re)constructing the Sacred: Landscape
Geoarchaeology at Chavín de Huántar,
Peru. *Archaeological and Anthropological
Sciences* 9:1045–1057.

Contreras, Daniel A., and David K. Keefer

2009   Implications of the Fluvial History
of the Wacheqsa River for Hydraulic
Engineering and Water Use at Chavín
de Huántar, Peru. *Geoarchaeology*
24:589–618.

Cooke, Colin A., Holger Hintelmann, Jay J. Ague, Richard L. Burger, Harald Biester, Julian P. Sachs, and Daniel R. Engstrom

2013   Use and Legacy of Mercury in the Andes. *Environmental Science & Technology* 47(9):4181–4188.

Cordy-Collins, Alana

1977   Chavín Art: Its Shamanic/Hallucinogenic Origins. In *Pre-Columbian Art History: Selected Readings*, vol. 1, edited by Alana Cordy-Collins and Jean Stern, pp. 353–362. Peek Publications, Palo Alto, Calif.

Covey, R. Alan

2014   Formative Period Settlement in the Sacred Valley. In *Regional Archaeology in the Inca Heartland: The Hanan Cuzco Surveys*, edited by R. Alan Covey, pp. 65–73. Museum of Anthropology, University of Michigan, Ann Arbor.

Cowgill, George L.

2004   Origins and Development of Urbanism: Archaeological Perspectives. *Annual Review of Anthropology* 33:525–549.

D'Altroy, Terence

2001   A View of the Plains from the Mountains: Commentary on Uruk by an Andeanist. In *Uruk Mesopotamia and Its Neighbors: Cross-Cultural Interactions in the Era of State Formation*, edited by Mitchell S. Rothwell, pp. 445–476. School of American Research Press, Santa Fe.

Davis, Allison R.

2011   *Yuthu: Community and Ritual in an Early Andean Village*. Museum of Anthropology, University of Michigan, Ann Arbor.

2014   Formative Period Settlement Patterns in the Xaquixaguana Region. In *Regional Archaeology in the Inca Heartland: The Hanan Cuzco Surveys*, edited by R. Alan Covey, pp. 53–64. Museum of Anthropology, University of Michigan, Ann Arbor.

Donnan, Christopher B. (editor)

1985   *Early Ceremonial Architecture in the Andes*. Dumbarton Oaks Research Library and Collection, Washington, D.C.

Druc, Isabelle C.

2004   Ceramic Diversity at Chavín de Huántar, Peru. *Latin American Antiquity* 15:344–363.

Dulanto, Jalh, and Aïcha Bachir Bacha

2013   Nuevas evidencias y nuevas perspectivas sobre la cultura Paracas: Una introducción. *Boletín de Arqueología PUCP* 17:5–8.

Elera, Carlos G.

1993   El complejo cultural Cupisnique: Antecedentes y desarrollo de su ideología religiosa. In *El mundo ceremonial andino*, edited by Luis Millones and Yoshio Onuki, pp. 229–257. National Museum of Ethnology, Osaka.

1997   Cupisnique y Salinar: Algunas reflexiones preliminares. In *Arqueología peruana 2*, edited by Elizabeth Bonnier and Henning Bischof, pp. 120–144. Sociedad Arqueológica Peruana–Alemana Reiss-Museum, Mannheim.

1998   The Puémape Site and the Cupisnique Culture: A Case Study on the Origin and Development of Complex Society in the Central Andes, Peru. PhD dissertation, University of Calgary, Calgary.

Fux, Peter (editor)

2013   *Chavín: Peru's Enigmatic Temple in the Andes*. Scheidegger and Speiss, Zurich.

Gamboa, Jorge

2016   Las ocupaciones formativas en La Banda: Excavaciones durante la construcción de la variante Chavín y su impacto socioeconómico en el Valle de Mosna. In *Arqueología de la Sierra de Ancash 2: Población y territorio*, edited by Bebel Ibarra Asencios, pp. 53–76. Instituto de Estudios Huarinos, Huari, Ancash.

González-Ramírez, Andrea

2014   Las representaciones figurativas como materialidad social: Producción y uso de las cabezas clavas del sitio Chavín de Huántar, Perú. PhD dissertation, Universidad Autónoma de Barcelona, Barcelona.

Graeber, David, and David Wengrow

2021   *The Dawn of Everything: A New History of Humanity*. Farrar, Straus and Giroux, New York.

Hastorf, Christine A.

2005   The Upper (Middle and Late) Formative in the Titicaca Region. In *Advances in Titicaca Basin Archaeology I*, edited by Charles Stanish, Amanda B. Cohen, and

Mark S. Aldenderfer, pp. 65–94. Cotsen Institute of Archaeology, University of California, Los Angeles.

2008 The Formative Period in the Titicaca Basin. In *Handbook of South American Archaeology*, edited by Helaine Silverman and William H. Isbell, pp. 545–561. Springer, New York.

Hastorf, Christine A. (editor)

1999 *Early Settlement at Chiripa, Bolivia.* Archaeological Research Facility, University of California, Berkeley.

Ikehara, Hugo

2021 Unfinished Monuments and Institutional Crisis in the Early Pre-Columbian Andes. *Journal of Anthropological Archaeology* 61:101–267.

Inokuchi, Kinya

2010 La arquitectura de Kuntur Wasi: Secuencia constructiva y cronología de un centro ceremonial del período formativo. *Boletín de Arqueología PUCP* 12:219–247.

2014 Cronología del período formativo de la Sierra Norte del Perú: Una consideración desde el punto de vista de la cronología local de Kuntur Wasi. *Senri Ethnological Studies* 89:123–158.

Izumi, Seiichi

1971 The Development of the Formative Culture in the Ceja de Montaña: A Viewpoint Based on the Materials from the Kotosh Site. In *Dumbarton Oaks Conference on Chavín*, edited by Elizabeth P. Benson, pp. 49–72. Dumbarton Oaks Research Library and Collection, Washington, D.C.

Jennings, Justin

2016 *Killing Civilization: A Reassessment of Early Urbanism and Its Consequences.* University of New Mexico Press, Albuquerque.

Jennings, Justin, and Timothy Earle

2016 Urbanization, State Formation, and Cooperation: A Reappraisal. *Current Anthropology* 57:474–493.

Kato, Yasutake

2014 Kuntur Wasi: Un centro ceremonial del período formativo tardío. In *El centro ceremonial andino: Nuevas perspectivas para los períodos arcaico y formativo*, edited by Yuji Seki, pp. 159–174. National Museum of Ethnology, Osaka.

Kaulicke, Peter

2010 *Las cronologías del formativo: 50 años de investigaciones japonesas en perspectiva.* Fondo Editorial, Pontificia Universidad Católica del Perú, Lima.

Kaulicke, Peter, and Yoshio Onuki (editors)

2010a El período formativo: Enfoques e evidencias recientes; Cincuenta años de la misión arqueológica japonesa y su vigencia (primera parte). Special issue, *Boletín de Arqueología PUCP* 12.

2010b El período formativo: Enfoques e evidencias recientes; Cincuenta años de la misión arqueológica japonesa y su vigencia (segunda parte). Special issue, *Boletín de Arqueología PUCP* 13.

Kembel, Silvia

2001 Architectural Sequence and Chronology at Chavín de Huántar, Peru. PhD dissertation, Stanford University, Stanford.

2008 The Architecture at the Monumental Center of Chavín de Huántar: Sequence, Transformations, and Chronology. In *Chavín: Art, Architecture and Culture*, edited by William J. Conklin and Jeffrey Quilter, pp. 35–81. Cotsen Institute of Archaeology, University of California, Los Angeles.

Kembel, Silvia, and Herbert Haas

2015 Radiocarbon Dates from the Monumental Architecture at Chavín de Huántar, Perú. *Journal of Archaeological Method and Theory* 22(2):345–427.

Kembel, Silvia, and John W. Rick

2004 Building Authority at Chavín de Huántar. In *Andean Archaeology*, edited by Helaine Silverman, pp. 51–75. Blackwell Publishing, Malden.

Kroeber, Alfred L.

1944 *Peruvian Archaeology in 1942.* The Viking Fund, New York.

Lagarde, Patricia G. A.

2022   Facing Pilgrimage: Tenon Head Sculptures at the Ceremonial Center of Chavín de Huántar. PhD dissertation, Tulane University, New Orleans.

Larco, Rafael

1941   *Los Cupisniques*. Casa editora "La Crónica" y "Variedades," Lima.

Lathrap, Donald W.

1970   *The Upper Amazon*. Thames and Hudson, New York.

1971   The Tropical Forest and the Cultural Context of Chavín. In *Dumbarton Oaks Conference on Chavín*, edited by Elizabeth P. Benson, pp. 73–100. Dumbarton Oaks Research Library and Collection, Washington, D.C.

1973   Gifts of the Cayman: Some Thoughts on the Subsistence Basis of Chavín. In *Variation in Anthropology: Essays in Honor of John C. McGregor*, edited by Donald W. Lathrap and Jody Douglas, pp. 91–105. Illinois Archaeological Survey, Urbana.

Lau, George F.

2004   The Recuay Culture of Peru's North-Central Highlands: A Reappraisal of Chronology and Its Implications. *Journal of Field Archaeology* 29:177–202.

2011   *Andean Expressions: Art and Archaeology of the Recuay Culture*. University of Iowa Press, Iowa City.

2016   *An Archaeology of Ancash: Stones, Ruins and Communities in Andean Peru*. Routledge, London.

Lumbreras, Luis G.

1971   Towards a Re-evaluation of Chavín. In *Dumbarton Oaks Conference on Chavín*, edited by Elizabeth P. Benson, pp. 1–28. Dumbarton Oaks Research Library and Collection, Washington, D.C.

1974   *The Peoples and Cultures of Ancient Peru*. Smithsonian Institution Press, Washington, D.C.

1977   Excavaciones en el Templo Antiguo de Chavín (Sector R): Informe de la sexta campaña. *Ñawpa Pacha: Journal of Andean Archaeology* 15:1–38.

1993   *Chavín de Huántar: Excavaciones en la Galería de las Ofrendas*. P. von Zabern, Mainz.

2007   *Chavín: Excavaciones arqueológicas*. 2 vols. Universidad Alas Peruanas, Lima.

Makowski, Krzysztof

2008   Andean Urbanism. In *The Handbook of South American Archaeology*, edited by Helaine Silverman and William H. Isbell, pp. 633–657. Springer, New York.

Matsumoto, Yuichi

2010   The Prehistoric Ceremonial Center of Campanayuq Rumi: Interregional Interactions in the South-Central Highlands of Peru. PhD dissertation, Yale University, New Haven.

2020   *Prehistoric Settlement Patterns in the Upper Huallaga Basin, Peru*. Yale University Publications in Anthropology Number 95. Yale University Press, New Haven.

Matsumoto, Yuichi, Jason Nesbitt, Michael D. Glascock, Yuri Cavero Palomino, and Richard L. Burger

2018   Interregional Obsidian Exchange during the Late Initial Period and Early Horizon: New Perspectives from Campanayuq Rumi. *Latin American Antiquity* 29:44–63.

Menzel, Dorothy, John H. Rowe, and Lawrence E. Dawson

1964   *The Paracas Pottery of Ica: A Study in Style and Time*. University of California Press, Berkeley.

Mesía, Cristian

2007   Intersite Spatial Organization at Chavín de Huántar during the Andean Formative: Three Dimensional Modeling, Stratigraphy and Ceramics. PhD dissertation, Stanford University, Stanford.

Middendorf, Ernst W.

(1893–1895)
1974   *Perú: Observaciones y estudios del país y sus habitantes durante una permanencia de 25 años*. Translated by Ernesto More. Universidad Nacional Mayor de San Marcos, Lima.

Millaire, Jean-François

2020   Dating the Occupation of Cerro Arena:
        A Defensive Salinar-Phase Settlement
        in the Moche Valley, Peru. *Journal of
        Anthropological Archaeology* 57:101–142.

Miller, George R., and Richard L. Burger

1995   Our Father the Cayman, Our Dinner
        the Llama: Animal Utilization at Chavín
        de Huántar, Peru. *American Antiquity*
        60:421–458.

Mohr Chávez, Karen

1980   The Archaeology of Marcavalle, an Early
        Horizon Site in the Valley of Cuzco, Peru:
        Part I. *Baessler-Archiv*, n.f., 28(2):203–329.

1981a   The Archaeology of Marcavalle, an Early
        Horizon Site in the Valley of Cuzco, Peru:
        Part II. *Baessler-Archiv*, n.f., 29(1):107–125.

1981b   The Archaeology of Marcavalle, an Early
        Horizon Site in the Valley of Cuzco,
        Peru: Part III. *Baessler-Archiv*, n.f.,
        29(1):241–386.

1988   The Significance of Chiripa in Lake
        Titicaca Basin Developments. *Expedition*
        30:17–26.

Moseley, Michael E.

2001   *The Incas and Their Ancestors*. 2nd ed.
        Thames and Hudson, London.

Nagaoka, Tomohito, Kazuhiro Uzawa, Yuji Seki, and
Daniel Morales

2017   Pacopampa: Early Evidence of Violence
        at a Ceremonial Site in the Northern
        Peruvian Highlands. *PLoS One* 12(9):
        e0185421.

Nesbitt, Jason

2012   Excavations at Caballo Muerto: An
        Investigation into the Origins of the
        Cupisnique Culture. PhD dissertation,
        Yale University, New Haven.

2019   Wealth in People: An Alternative
        Perspective on Initial Period Monumental
        Architecture from Huaca Cortada.
        In *Perspectives on Early Andean Civiliza-
        tion in Peru: Interaction, Authority, and
        Socioeconomic Organization during the
        First and Second Millennia BC*, edited
        by Richard L. Burger, Lucy C. Salazar,
        and Yuji Seki, pp. 1–17. Yale University
        Publications in Anthropology Number 96.
        Yale University Press, New Haven.

Nesbitt, Jason, Belkys Gutiérrez, and Segundo Vásquez

2010   Excavaciones en Huaca Cortada, com-
        plejo de Caballo Muerto, valle de Moche:
        Un informe preliminar. *Boletín de
        Arqueología PUCP* 12:261–286.

Nesbitt, Jason, Bebel Ibarra Asencios, and Fuyaki
Tokanai

2020   The Architecture and Chronology of
        Reparín, Eastern Ancash, Peru. *Ñawpa
        Pacha: Journal of Andean Archaeology*
        40(1):41–59.

Nesbitt, Jason, Yuichi Matsumoto, and Yuri Cavero
Palomino

2019   Campanayuq Rumi and Arpiri: Two
        Ceremonial Centers on the Periphery of
        the Chavín Interaction Sphere. *Ñawpa
        Pacha: Journal of Andean Archaeology*
        39:57–75.

Olivera Nuñez, Quirino

2014   *Arqueología alto amazónica: El origen de
        la civilización en el Perú*. Apus Graph,
        Lima.

Onuki, Yoshio

1997   Ocho tumbas especiales de Kuntur Wasi.
        Boletín de Arqueología PUCP 1:79–114.

Onuki, Yoshio (editor)

1995   *Kuntur Wasi y Cerro Blanco: Dos sitios del
        formativo en el norte del Perú*. Hokuesen-
        Sha, Tokyo.

Patterson, Thomas C.

1971   Chavín: An Interpretation of Its
        Spread and Influence. In *Dumbarton
        Oaks Conference on Chavín*, edited
        by Elizabeth P. Benson, pp. 29–48.
        Dumbarton Oaks Research Library
        and Collection, Washington, D.C.

1985   La Huaca La Florida, Rimac Valley, Perú.
        In *Early Ceremonial Architecture in the
        Andes*, edited by Christopher B. Donnan,
        pp. 59–69. Dumbarton Oaks Research
        Library and Collection, Washington, D.C.

Pauketat, Timothy

2007   *Ancient Cahokia and the Mississippians*.
        Cambridge University Press, Cambridge.

Petersen, Georg G.

2010   *Mining and Metallurgy in Ancient
        Peru*. Translated by William E. Brooks.
        Geological Society of America, Boulder,
        Colo.

Pool, Christopher

2007   *Olmec Archaeology and Early Meso-america*. Cambridge University Press, Cambridge.

Pozorski, Shelia, and Thomas Pozorski

1987   *Early Settlement and Subsistence in the Casma Valley, Peru*. University of Iowa Press, Iowa City.

2018   Insult to Veneration: The Evolution of Prehistoric Intrusiveness within the Casma Valley of Peru. *Journal of Anthropological Archaeology* 49:51–64.

Pozorski, Thomas

1983   The Caballo Muerto Complex and Its Place in the Andean Chronological Sequence. *Annals of the Carnegie Museum of Natural History* 52(1):1–40.

Pozorski, Thomas, and Shelia Pozorski

1987   Chavín, the Early Horizon and the Initial Period. In *The Origin and Development of the Andean State*, edited by Johnathan Haas, Shelia Pozorski, and Thomas Pozorski, pp. 36–46. Cambridge University Press, Cambridge.

Prieto, Gabriel, Isabelle Druc, Leonardo Arrelucea, Helen Chavarria, Julio Asencio, and Luis Flores de la Oliva

2022   La ocupación del período inicial tardío (1100/100-800 a.C.) y el horizonte temprano (800-500/400 a.C.) en Huanchaco, costa norte del Perú. *Arqueología y sociedad* 36:9–66.

Quilter, Jeffrey

2022   *The Ancient Central Andes*. 2nd ed. Routledge, London.

Rick, John W.

2005   The Evolution of Authority and Power at Chavín de Huántar, Peru. In *Foundations of Power in the Prehispanic Andes*, edited by Kevin J. Vaughn, Dennis Ogburn, and Christina A. Conlee, pp. 71–89. Archeological Papers of the American Anthropological Association 14. University of California Press, Berkeley.

2008   Context, Construction, and Ritual in the Development of Authority at Chavín de Huántar. In *Chavín: Art, Architecture, and Culture*, edited by William J. Conklin and Jeffrey Quilter, pp. 3–34. Cotsen Institute

of Archaeology, University of California, Los Angeles.

2013   Architectural and Ritual Space at Chavín de Huántar. In *Chavín: Peru's Enigmatic Temple in the Andes*, edited by Peter Fux, pp. 151–166. Scheidegger & Speiss, Zurich.

2017   The Nature of Ritual Space at Chavín de Huántar. In *Rituals of the Past: Prehispanic and Colonial Case Studies in Andean Archaeology*, edited by Silvana A. Rosenfeld and Stefanie Bautista, pp. 21–49. University Press of Colorado, Boulder.

Rick, John W., Christian Mesía, Daniel A. Contreras, Silvia Rodriguez Kembel, Rosa M. Rick, Matthew Paul Sayre, and John Wolf

2010   La cronología de Chavín de Huántar y sus implicancias para el período formativo. *Boletín de Arqueología PUCP* 13:87–132.

Rick, John W., Silvia Rodriguez Kembel, Rosa M. Rick, and John A. Kembel

1998   La arquitectura del complejo ceremonial de Chavín de Huántar: Documentación tridimensional y sus implicancias. *Boletín de Arqueología PUCP* 2:181–214.

Roe, Peter G.

2008   How to Build a Raptor: Why the Dumbarton Oaks "Scaled Cayman" Callango Textile Is Really a Chavín Jaguaroid Harpy Eagle. In *Chavín: Art, Architecture, and Culture*, edited by William J. Conklin and Jeffrey Quilter, pp. 181–216. Cotsen Institute of Archaeology, University of California, Los Angeles.

Rosenfeld, Silvana A., and Matthew P. Sayre

2016   Llamas on the Land: Production and Consumption of Meat at Chavín de Huántar, Peru. *Latin American Antiquity* 27:497–511.

Rowe, John H.

1944   *An Introduction to the Archaeology of Cuzco*. Papers of the Peabody Museum of American Archaeology and Ethnology 27, no. 2. The Museum, Cambridge, Mass.

1962a   *Chavín Art: An Inquiry into Its Form and Meaning*. Museum of Primitive Art, New York.

1962b Stages and Periods in Archaeological Interpretation. *Southwestern Journal of Anthropology* 18:40–54.

1963 Urban Settlements in Ancient Peru. *Ñawpa Pacha: Journal of Andean Archaeology* 1:1–27.

Sandweiss, Daniel H., Kirk A. Maasch, Richard L. Burger, James B. Richardson III, Harold B. Rollins, and Amy Clement

2001 Variations in Holocene El Niño Frequencies: Climate Records and Cultural Consequences in Ancient Peru. *Geology* 29:603–606.

Sayre, Matthew

2010 Life across the River: Agricultural, Ritual, and Production Practices at Chavín de Huántar, Peru. PhD dissertation, University of California, Berkeley.

2018 The Historicity of the "Early Horizon." In *Constructions of Time and History in the Pre-Columbian Andes*, edited by Edward Swenson and Andrew P. Roddick, pp. 44–64. University of Colorado Press, Boulder.

Sayre, Matthew, Melanie J. Miller, and Silvana Rosenfeld

2016 Isotopic Evidence for the Trade and Production of Exotic Marine Mammal Bone Artifacts at Chavín de Huántar, Peru. *Archaeological and Anthropological Sciences* 8:403–417.

Seki, Yuji

2014 La diversidad del poder en la sociedad del período formativo: Una perspectiva desde la Sierra Norte. In *El centro ceremonial andino: Nuevas perspectivas para los períodos arcaico y formativo*, edited by Yuji Seki, pp. 175–200. National Museum of Ethnology, Osaka.

Seki, Yuji, Juan Pablo Villanueva, Masato Sakai, Diana Alemán, Mauro Ordóñez, Walter Tosso, Araceli Espinoza, Kinya Inokuchi, and Daniel Morales

2010 Nuevas evidencias del sitio arqueológico de Pacopampa, en la Sierra Norte del Perú. *Boletín de Arqueología PUCP* 12:69–95.

Shibata, Koichiro

2010 Cerro Blanco de Nepeña dentro de la dinámica interactiva del período formativo. *Boletín de Arqueología PUCP* 12:287–315.

Stanish, Charles

2003 *Ancient Titicaca: The Evolution of Complex Society in Southern Peru and Northern Bolivia.* University of California Press, Berkeley.

Stein, Gil

1998 *Rethinking World-Systems: Diasporas, Colonies, and Interaction in Uruk Mesopotamia.* University of Arizona Press, Tucson.

Tantaleán, Henry

2021 *The Ancient Andean States: Political Landscapes in Pre-Hispanic Peru.* Routledge, London.

Tello, Julio C.

1930 Andean Civilization: Some Problems of Peruvian Archaeology. *Proceedings of the 23rd International Congress of the Americanists*, pp. 259–290. New York.

1934 Origen, desarrollo, y correlación de las antiguas culturas peruanas. *Revista de la Universidad Católica del Perú* 2(10):151–168.

1943 Discovery of the Chavín Culture in Peru. *American Antiquity* 9:135–160.

1960 *Chavín: Cultura matriz de la civilización andina.* Publicación Antropológica del Archivo "Julio C. Tello" de la Universidad Nacional Mayor de San Marcos, Lima.

Torres, Constantino M.

2008 Chavín's Psychoactive Pharmacopeia: The Iconographic Evidence. In *Art, Architecture, and Culture*, edited by William J. Conklin and Jeffrey Quilter, pp. 239–259. Cotsen Institute of Archaeology, University of California, Los Angeles.

Toshiahara, Kayoko

2002 The Cupisnique Culture in the Formative Period World. PhD dissertation, University of Illinois, Urbana-Champaign.

Turner, Robert J. W., Rosemary Knight, and John Rick

1999   The Geological Landscape of the Pre-Inca Archaeological Site at Chavín de Huántar, Perú. *Geological Survey of Canada, Current Research.*

Unkel, Ingmar, Markus Reindel, Hermann Gorbahn, Johny Isla, Bernd Kromer, and Volker Sossna

2012   A Comprehensive Numerical Chronology for the Pre-Columbian Cultures of the Palpa Valleys, South Coast of Peru. *Journal of Archaeological Science* 39:2294–2303.

Valdez, Francisco

2008   Inter-zonal Relationships in Ecuador. In *Handbook of South American Archaeology*, edited by Helaine Silverman and William H. Isbell, pp. 865–888. Springer, New York.

2021   The Mayo-Chinchipe-Marañón Complex: The Unexpected Spirits of the Ceja. In *The Archaeology of the Upper Amazon: Complexity and Interaction in the Andean Tropical Forest*, edited by Ryan Clasby and Jason Nesbitt, pp. 62–82. University Press of Florida, Gainesville.

Watanabe, Luis

1976   Sitios tempranos en el valle de Moche (costa norte del Perú). PhD dissertation, Universidad Nacional Mayor de San Marcos, Lima.

Weismantel, Mary

2015a   Seeing Like an Archaeologist: Viveiros de Castro at Chavín de Huántar. *Journal of Social Archaeology* 15:139–159.

2015b   Encounters with Dragons: The Stones of Chavín. *RES: Anthropology and Aesthetics* 65/66:37–54.

Willey, Gordon R.

1948   Functional Analysis of "Horizon Styles" in Peruvian Archaeology. In *A Reappraisal of Peruvian Archaeology*, edited by Wendell C. Bennett, pp. 8–15.

Memoirs of the Society for American Archaeology, no. 4. Society for American Archaeology and Institute of Andean Research, Menasha, Wis.

1951   The Chavín Problem: A Review and Critique. *Southwestern Journal of Anthropology* 7:103–144.

Willey, Gordon R., and Phillip Phillips

1958   *Method and Theory in American Archaeology.* University of Chicago Press, Chicago.

Williams, Carlos

1985   A Scheme for the Early Monumental Architecture of the Central Coast of Peru. In *Early Ceremonial Architecture in the Andes*, edited by Christopher B. Donnan, pp. 227–240. Dumbarton Oaks Research Library and Collection, Washington, D.C.

Yamamoto, Atsushi

2010   Ingatambo: Un sitio estratégico de contacto interregional en la zona norte del Perú. *Boletín de Arqueología PUCP* 12:25–52.

2021   Emergence of Sociopolitical Complexity in Northern Peru: A Diachronic Perspective from the Huancabamba Valley. In *The Archaeology of the Upper Amazon: Complexity and Interaction in the Andean Tropical Forest*, edited by Ryan Clasby and Jason Nesbitt, pp. 83–105. University Press of Florida, Gainesville.

Yoffee, Norman

2005   *Myths of the Archaic State: Evolution of the Earliest Cities, States, and Civilizations.* Cambridge University Press, Cambridge.

Young, Michelle

2017   De la montaña al mar: Intercambio entre la sierra centro-sur y la costa sur durante el horizonte temprano. *Boletín de Arqueología PUCP* 22:9–34

New Galleries at Chavín de Huántar

An Exploration of Chavín Underground Architecture and Organization

JOHN W. RICK

As a central Californian child fascinated with building underground spaces, what we termed "underground forts," the exotic ambience of restricted, dark, cool, and otherwise well-removed-from-outer-reality spaces was more than apparent. As I turned into an archaeologist, the presence of similar spaces known as galleries in the central Andean site of Chavín de Huántar intrinsically attracted me and others with an air of mystery—how were they built, used, and particularly, conceived and perceived by Formative peoples? The possibility of strange rituality, perhaps in some way like that of the little troglodyte boys of my own past, carried an undeniable fascination.

Answers to these questions were not quickly forthcoming for Chavín de Huántar, largely because there seemed to be little in situ data, in some cases due to limited investigation or poor gallery conditions, but most commonly because they were presumably emptied of any original content across the millennia since their original use. The early historical record suggests that galleries have been known

at Chavín since the time of the Spanish conquest (Vásquez de Espinoza [1620] 1948:458), and we have clear evidence that galleries were accessible and visited throughout the nineteenth century, leaving ample opportunity for clearing them and removing sediments and artifacts.

Having spent nearly a quarter century in Chavín with a sizable program of investigations, my colleagues and I have had the fortunate opportunity to add significant new knowledge on the topic of galleries, which itself has a multiplying effect of making sense of what seemed like an untidy subject matter (Kembel 2008; Rick 2008). The diversity of gallery location, form, age, and content seemed daunting and almost random, but I think our new information forms a threshold, allowing both a forward vision into new realms of understanding and an ability to reorder the rear vision of the accumulated experience of one hundred years of investigations in Chavín de Huántar, among the many contributing projects and investigators (Lumbreras 1989). My proposition here is to create a synthetic, if still necessarily incomplete, vision of how the variability of the galleries and their contents speak to a deep, structural importance of these spaces within Chavín religious and ritual practice. I will argue that they offer a clue to many seemingly unrelated aspects of the site, a vision of the interrelatedness of spaces within the Chavín ritual worldview that composed their major center.

What Is a Gallery?

Chavín de Huántar has a number of clear classes of "underground" spaces, of which galleries are but one. But to clarify—most galleries probably were not initially designed to have the deeply buried feel that they have today (although they may have gained this over centuries of additional construction), and, in fact, they were never truly underground. Something abundantly apparent is that Chavín constructed deeply—very little of the ground surface of the monumental site of Chavín is, in fact, anywhere near the original natural topographic surface of the landscape (Rick 2013). All known galleries are within constructed masses, and none intrude into underlying sub-construction natural sediments. This is generally true of other subsurface structures, most notably the canal systems. While it may be that the earliest canals within the site were open and possibly partially intruding into sediments (Bustamante and Crousillat 1974; Bustamante, Crousillat, and Rick 2021), and even cut into underlying bedrock, they were rapidly converted into constructions within a constantly rising cultural ground surface. The differences between canals and galleries are notorious. Canals have a clear, directional gradient, are in most cases somewhat smaller in cross-section than galleries, are dendritic in organization, often involve long and straight or more often irregularly curvilinear trajectories, usually have flagged floors, and otherwise obey drainage logic. There is a rarer category of gallery-like spaces more easily seen as chambers and simple corridors: smaller in section and generally non-extensive, usually roofed lightly if at all, but rather clearly subsurface in character and distinguishable from surface constructions.

Galleries, then, have rectilinear layouts that never involve curved passages, are almost always of a size allowing upright human posture, and never have stone floors. Their floor segments are quite level, although multiple levels may exist connected by staircases, never by ramps. While canals frequently have sloping and even vertical ducts leading to the surface of their epoch, galleries almost without exception have only very strictly horizontal ducts, which always lead to further galleries or to exterior walls and facades. I have previously noted that ducts tend to point down long passages, or aim through rooms, and not infrequently coordinate between features of rather distant galleries (Rick 2008). They tend toward symmetrical layouts, although sometimes the symmetry encompasses more than one apparent gallery—in cases allowing gallery groups to be defined within the extent of the quite apparent symmetrical organization. Galleries may include entranceway segments, corridors and passages, full-height alcoves the size of closets, rooms with entrance passages, and rather occasionally wall niches, usually rectangular in landscape disposition. Corbels are often seen, especially in large cross-section galleries, and in common with some canals, the crossing of gallery segments almost always involves an increase in roof height to achieve the necessary crossing beams. In galleries, it appears to have been unacceptable to use even a few lower height beams to achieve the crossing roof structure.

Chavín Gallery Background

Galleries have been the subject of various investigations for nearly one hundred years. Excavations were carried out in galleries prior to the late 1960s (Lumbreras and Amat Olazábal 1965–1966), but documentation is scant or absent prior to the well-documented excavation by Luis G. Lumbreras in the Ofrendas Gallery in 1966–1967 (Lumbreras 1993, 2007). There is occasional mention of excavations of a Gallery of the Giants (Lumbreras 1989), but the exact location of the gallery and its contents remain a matter of rumor. Lumbreras very briefly began an excavation in the Caracolas Gallery in 1972, which

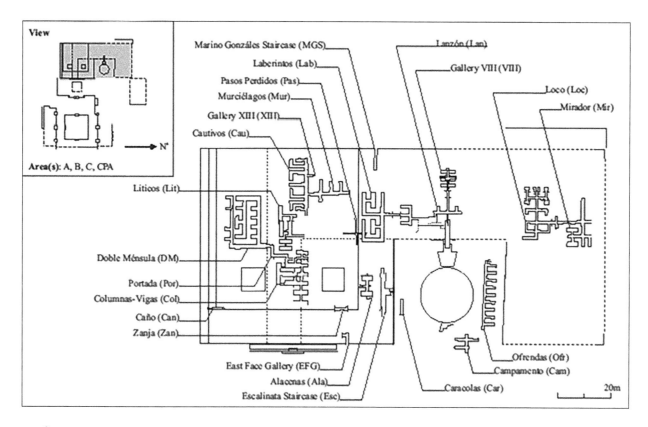

View

Area(s): A, B, C, CPA

Marino Gonzáles Staircase (MGS)
Laberintos (Lab)
Pasos Perdidos (Pas)
Murciélagos (Mur)
Gallery XIII (XIII)
Cautivos (Cau)

Liticos (Lit)

Doble Ménsula (DM)

Portada (Por)
Columnas-Vigas (Col)
Caño (Can)
Zanja (Zan)

East Face Gallery (EFG)
Alacenas (Ala)
Escalinata Staircase (Esc)

Lanzón (Lan)
Gallery VIII (VIII)

Loco (Loc)
Mirador (Mir)

Ofrendas (Ofr)
Campamento (Cam)
Caracolas (Car)

20m

figure 2.1
Overall map of galleries at Chavín de Huántar. Map by Silvia Kembel.

I completed in 2001. Various maps have been created, for the moment culminating with the total-station-based mapping project carried out by Silvia Kembel in the late 1990s (Figure 2.1) (Kembel 2001). She uses details related to gallery construction and expansion to develop a sophisticated vision of the architectural growth of the site, thus demonstrating how gallery growth occurred within and across building segments. On a specific level, Kembel details the origin and growth of the Lanzón Gallery, containing the famous monolithic sculpture, and shows how the gallery and its expansions maintained access to a space and object of continued importance within the Chavín cult during the growth of the building around and above the location. Her work further suggests a strong motivation during the Chavín period to extend and interconnect a number of galleries to permit their continued use across centuries of architectural growth. A simple rule I have induced from this pattern is that Chavín conserved access to as many early galleries as possible, even at the cost of

considerable time and energy invested in architecture designed to maintain access.

The number of galleries known at Chavín de Huántar has evolved in complex ways. Julio C. Tello (1960) created a list of eighteen galleries sometime in the 1940s, but these include a number of galleries lying outside the monumental core architecture that have not been seen since, along with a number since destroyed or lumped together. Lumbreras and Hernán Amat Olazábal (1965–1966) list seventeen galleries, but of these, two are actually canals. Kembel (2008) recognizes twenty-six galleries using a rather broad definition for the form. Since 2010, we have added five new galleries to the list, all of which have been excavated. We believe we know the location of an additional five galleries, bringing the number known to between thirty-one and thirty-six. Given our recent success in locating new galleries, it is reasonable to believe that Chavín probably has at least double the number now known, making them a very common and widely used architectural form in the site.

Structural Aspects of Galleries

A great deal has been learned about galleries over the last decades, including patterns of construction and use. Galleries seem to have been a regular part of the Chavín architectural grammar, and their structural requirements condition other aspects of the "sentences" composing the various areas of construction. Here are some examples:

Modular Height Issues

Galleries generally have the same heights, ranging between 1.8 and 2.2 m from floor to ceiling, with only a few exceptions. If ceiling beam thickness is taken into account, then the modular constructive height of galleries is very close to 2.5 m. It is striking that in multiple instances, including the Circular Plaza, Plaza Mayor, a number of the primary terraces, the North Esplanade, and Building C, an increase of major buildings and surfaces (which occurs at least once and sometimes twice during the Chavín epoch) very close to 2.5 m in height is consistent, and in most cases, galleries are inserted into the architectural mass of the rise. Thus, the way in which Chavín de Huántar grew vertically may be a product of the intent to build new galleries into a given space.

Lateral Growth Issues

Chavín de Huántar, more than many early New World centers, grew laterally rather independently from its vertical growth. Because many galleries would be easily made inaccessible by new lateral architecture, builders were faced with losing galleries unless complex accommodations were made to extend corridors or provide new entrances (see Kembel 2001 for details on the architectural logic involved). It appears that Chavín planners and builders were reticent to abandon old galleries, and the connection made by keeping access to highly important but aged spaces and the justification of authority based on tradition (Rick 2008) seem intrinsic to Chavín growth strategies. Galleries are thus spaces that can be continually reconnected with growing architectural masses in ways that horizontal surfaces cannot.

Location Retention

There is a tendency, of unknown pervasiveness, for galleries to superimpose other galleries or prior versions of the same gallery. The four known superimpositions may greatly underestimate this pattern because very few excavations have been attempted beneath galleries. In the case of the Lanzón Gallery, Tello reported the presence of the remains of a gallery largely removed by the 1945 *aluvión* (Gallery VIII in Tello 1960), directly if not exactly conforming to the same outline, immediately above the Lanzón. Given that the Lanzón Gallery remained accessible until historic times, it is unlikely that Gallery VIII directly replaced it. In the Laberintos Gallery, there is a short segment of a corridor that runs above another one, a minor case of overlay. Perhaps more informative, in the cases of the Loco and Capilla Galleries, there is immediate superposition over lower gallery segments. In the case of the Capilla Gallery, part of the gallery walls immediately cover a lower gallery that had clearly been de-roofed and intentionally filled with clean fill; the superimposed walls were only separated by a few centimeters of intervening non-wall fill. In the outermost Loco Gallery, a lower gallery had been similarly filled to support the installation of the Loco Gallery, but the galleries were not completely spatially congruent. These latter two cases clearly indicate a sequence of galleries built in the same space, a pattern that may prove very common, and may correspond to situations where it was architecturally impossible to maintain the earlier gallery, but it was effectively replicated at a 2.5 m higher level (Rick et al. 2016).

Preexisting Floor and Wall Incorporation

If previously external spaces (such as surfaces, rooms, small plazas, etc.) are partially or wholly being preserved or "remembered" by "gallery-izing" them, then an interesting question is what becomes of the walls associated with such original spaces. In the Lanzón chamber, it is notable that the north, west, and south ends of the gallery that is installed around the idol are composed of strikingly different stonework—because they are wall segments of the rectangular small plaza that once surrounded the sculpture. In fact, it could be argued that the size of the cruciform

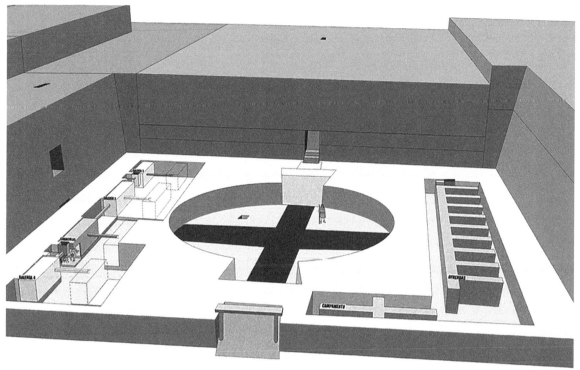

figure 2.2

Map of Circular Plaza Atrium (CPA) Galleries. Illustration by Miguel Ortiz, courtesy of the Programa de Investigación Arqueológica y Conservación Chavín de Huántar (PIACCH).

gallery around the Lanzón was as much a way of displaying these earlier walls as being limited by them or as simply taking advantage of the small amount of labor their adoption saved. Similarly, several walls of the Gallery of the Esplanade (Rick et al. 2016) are clearly double-sided walls of surface structures that predated the overall gallery construction from the time the surrounding surface was raised.

The Case of the Circular Plaza Atrium Galleries

Although no set of galleries within the monumental limits of Chavín de Huántar can be seen as typical or representative—so many factors are involved, and the record has proved exceptionally and structurally diverse—the galleries of the atrium—the flat area, or landing, surrounding the Circular Plaza Atrium (CPA)—have provided the richest, best preserved, and most investigated data on galleries in Chavín de Huántar (Figure 2.2). Certainly, the attention

focused on this core area of the site has contributed to this high data density, but it is yet unclear whether similar attention paid to other sectors would yield equivalently dense distributions of galleries. I suspect the truth is somewhere between the extremes—the CPA probably always was a focus of gallery-related ceremonialism, but explorations outside this sector have revealed galleries in unsuspected architectural contexts. Most notably, very few excavations in this monumental center have gone below the stratigraphically highest Chavín surface—without doing this, finding galleries will be difficult.

Relevant Architectural History of the CPA

Although the CPA and the plaza itself were long thought to be associated with an "Old Temple"—that is, the earliest archaeological stage of monumental Chavín de Huántar—substantial investigations in this sector over the last twenty years have decisively shown that the construction and use of these

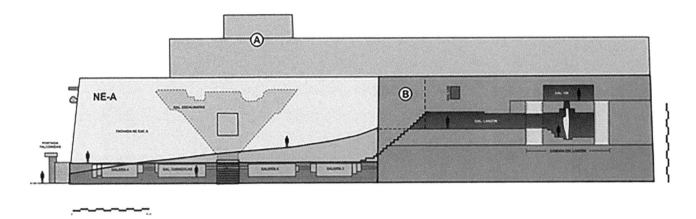

figure 2.3
Locational relationships of the Circular Plaza Atrium with the atrium, Lanzón Gallery, and Escalinata Gallery.
Illustration by Miguel Ortiz, courtesy of the Programa de Investigación Arqueológica y Conservación Chavín
de Huántar (PIACCH).

particular features is from the last major phase of architectural development, the Black and White phase dating from 850 to 550 BC (Kembel 2008; Rick et al. 2010). Carbon samples from key locations in this sector support this conclusion, as does the intensive architectural analysis provided by Kembel (Kembel and Haas 2015; Rick 2008). The construction of this final configuration is conceptually simple—as Lumbreras (1989) long ago observed, the roughly 45 × 45 m area surrounding what was to become the Circular Plaza was raised about 2.5 m in height, as was a former, possible plaza floor lying more than 2 m below the floor of the Circular Plaza. The Circular Plaza was a large circular space left open within that square slab of nuclear core "fill" (which is actually not a fill but rather a highly organized and consolidated construction mass). In a similar way, the galleries underlying the CPA surface were built into this core—it is quite apparent that both the Circular Plaza and the gallery structures, all occupying space within the slab, were installed as the slab was constructed upward, rather than imposed after the slab was finished (Figure 2.3). This is an exceptional case of perhaps the primary Chavín gallery construction context—a jump upward of the use surfaces in the modular 2.5 m height mentioned previously. What is exceptional is the extensive space in the CPA that was created, apparently in a single, uninterrupted massive construction event—something akin to a large

blank slate, within a key ritual area, surrounding what was designed to be the most elaborate, ornate, and labor-intensive architecture at the site.

Therefore, it is not surprising that this quite precious ceremonial real estate would be highly designed and intensively used. In the intricate sequence of construction events projected by Kembel (2008) for Chavín de Huántar, it is relatively rare to have a clearly defined, extensive, and relatively uninterrupted space symmetrically arranged around a central feature, particularly one that is still near the surface and well-preserved for research access. These aspects make the setting unique within the site. In short, it was an exceptional opportunity to organize an extensive space according to important aspects of anticipated use.

The galleries known in the CPA until 2017 were the Lumbreras-excavated Ofrendas Gallery, the Rick-excavated Caracolas Gallery, and the little-known Campamento Gallery. From my observations, the latter was nearly fully excavated but in an unknown (to me) moment by unknown personnel. The non-CPA galleries of the Lanzón and Laberintos are spatially and perhaps functionally linked to the CPA, and the Escalinata Gallery (a dual staircase and entryway that is generally classified as a gallery, although this could be questioned) is linked to the CPA, in whatever configuration it might have had in the prior architectural stage (this

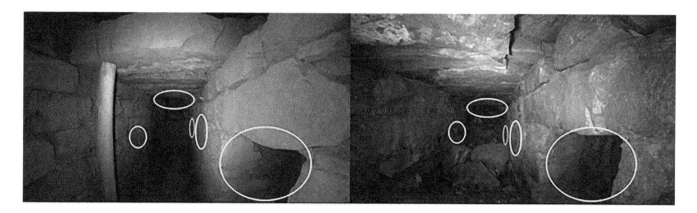

figure 2.4

The discovery of Gallery X. On the right side is a remotely filmed, mirrored image of Galería del Fuego / Gallery X from a camera inserted into the gallery through a 6 m long duct from Caracolas Gallery, which was photographed with the same camera under similar conditions (left side). The green circles indicate the position of major gallery features, showing their identical position. In this way, it was clear that Galería del Fuego / Gallery X had the same dimensions as the Caracolas Gallery. Photographs by Andrew Lesh, courtesy of the Programa de Investigación Arqueológica y Conservación Chavín de Huántar (PIACCH).

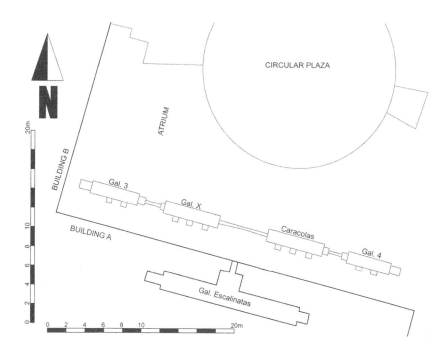

figure 2.5
Layout of Caracolas Gallery series. Illustration courtesy of the Programa de Investigación Arqueológica y Conservación Chavín de Huántar (PIACCH).

latter configuration is proving to be rather complex, and suggests to be notably different from the Black and White CPA situation) (Figure 2.3). As such, the CPA in 2017 was already gallery-rich, considering its limited surface area.

In 2017, a creative group of Stanford University engineering students took the first steps toward a program of underground, video-based exploration techniques, beginning auspiciously with the immediate discovery of a previously unknown symmetrically disposed gallery well to the west of Caracolas, heavily overlain by deep, mostly post-Chavín cultural deposits (Figure 2.4). Clever simulation work by an engineering student determined that the new gallery had dimensions and features identical to the Caracolas Gallery (1.2 m wide by slightly more than

6 m long). A deep perforation put to the west of the new Gallery X (temporary names were assigned to galleries until their contents could help determine appropriate names), in part to search for a "lost" canal segment, unexpectedly struck the beams of a further gallery to the west of Gallery X. In 2017, it was possible to enter the new Gallery 3 (letters continuing from X were now deemed ineffective given the multiplying quantity of new galleries) and to determine that it was in-line with both the Caracolas Gallery and Gallery X and was apparently identical in its dimensions and features, taking into account linear mirroring symmetry between adjacent galleries. Originally, we had thought that the Caracolas Gallery and Gallery X would be a symmetrical pair, but now the same situation existed bilaterally for Gallery X and Gallery 3. The obvious implication is that there should be, following Chavín patterns of symmetry, a fourth gallery, this time to the east of the Caracolas Gallery—blocked ducting between the known and potential gallery spaces helped build this supposition (Figure 2.5). Unlike the area to the west, overlain by deep deposits, the eastern area is eroded or otherwise lowered to the point that the roof could be projected as now absent, assuming that the galleries were all at a common level. Surface evidence was ambiguous, leaving Gallery 4 as a hypothetical match to the Caracolas Gallery.

CPA Excavation Results

In 2018, we returned to excavate the three new galleries (one hypothetical) from 2017. Reviewing these galleries and their contents, I first begin with a synopsis of the 2001 Caracolas Gallery excavations, then end with a further discussion of the Ofrendas Gallery. As the contents will support, we have given the name Galería del Fuego for Gallery X, Galería de los Inhaladores for Gallery 3, and Galería de las Visitantes for Gallery 4.

Caracolas Gallery Excavated in 1972 (Lumbreras) and 2001 (Rick)

The Caracolas Gallery had been revealed by the gap left by a fallen roof beam sometime prior to 1972,

and brief trial excavations that year by Lumbreras (1989) uncovered the presence of pottery of Chavín and post-Chavín age, along with fragments of large sea mollusks of the genus *Strombus* or *Lobatus* (the current genus name is *Lobatus*, but I will use the more commonly used *Strombus*). Some of these fragments were in the process of being made into small engraved ornament-like objects. The gallery layout itself proved iconic of the Caracolas Gallery series—three large rectangular niches in the south wall, ducts aiming to the east and west in the ends of the gallery, and one duct going north from the north wall. An entrance-like feature consists of a number of stair-like elevations leading into a reduced-width terminal gallery segment capped by shorter beams with some evidence that the beams had been removed in the past, perhaps multiple times. This entrance configuration at only one end is the most diagnostic and asymmetric feature of the Caracolas Gallery series (Figure 2.6).

In the intervening years prior to our 2001 research, the Caracolas Gallery had suffered a virtual deluge of material from the surface, ranging from additional post-Chavín pottery to modern-day detritus. The gallery proved to have three differentiable strata overlying its floor: Layer 1, consisting of a detrital cone centered on the beam gap on the western side, with a mix of modern and mostly post-Chavín material; and Layer 2, with a slight admixture of post-Chavín ceramics, but predominantly stamped and lightly incised polished black wares referred to as Janabarroide, in reference to similarities with Richard L. Burger's illustrations of Janabarriu materials (Burger 1984). The lack of a formal, quantitative definition of Janabarriu makes it inappropriate to assign this assemblage to that entity. The amount of this material was moderate in Layer 2, predominantly bowl forms, with very little pottery outside this description. Some strombus fragments were present, as well as blackened animal bone, whose coloration is common in damp gallery deposits and probably represents mineralization from calcic and other salts rather than burning. Layer 3 was relatively thin, consisting of grainy clay deposits resting on a thin sheet of pure fine clay, which is typical of the floors of galleries in

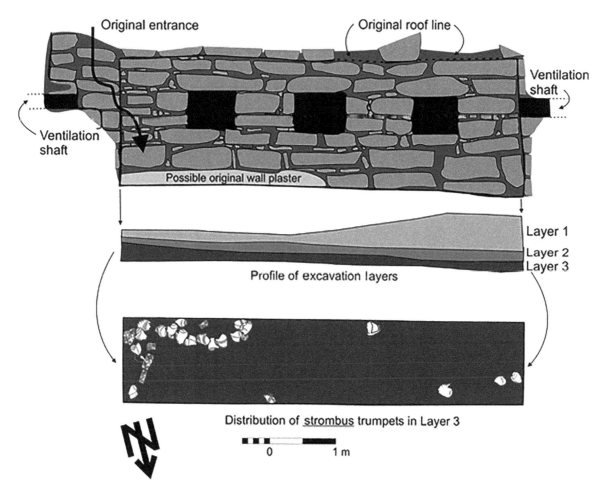

Original entrance

Original roof line

Ventilation shaft

Ventilation shaft

Possible original wall plaster

Profile of excavation layers

Layer 1
Layer 2
Layer 3

Distribution of <u>strombus</u> trumpets in Layer 3

N

0   1 m

figure 2.6

The Caracolas Gallery east–west longitudinal section, south wall stonework, stratigraphic layering, and find location of the twenty *pututus*. Illustration by John W. Rick, courtesy of the Programa de Investigación Arqueológica y Conservación Chavín de Huántar (PIACCH).

our experience. The immediately over-floor deposit consists of the plastering materials from the gallery walls, which sloughed off relatively rapidly after abandonment, and which all galleries show evidence of near the wall bases. Underlying the floor deposit is a subfloor of micro-gravel and clay in a layer ranging up to 5 cm, a consistent feature across all known galleries, below which lie deep, layered nuclear fills.

In Layer 3, the primary finds were generally large fragments of strombus shell, but more notably twenty complete shell trumpets or *pututus* of *Strombus galeatus* were found resting directly on the gallery floor (Figure 2.7). Described elsewhere (Rick 2005, 2008), these mostly showed engraving with a variety of designs, many of which had been partially

or nearly completely erased by the polish of lengthy usage. The clear evidence of breakage of many of these trumpets and partially made shell ornaments was found throughout Layer 2 (Figure 2.8). The remaining intact trumpets were mostly in areas where incoming sediments or collapsed wall plastering materials were deep (Figure 2.7). Little pottery was found in and around the undisturbed trumpets. Most pottery present was characterized by Janabarroide styles and was associated with soft spots in Layer 3, where shells or other materials had been removed. A few other pottery fragments were found, outside the Janabarroide range, including some plainware vessels (mostly jar forms, relatively few neckless jars, a few fragments of Chavín

figure 2.7
Pututus (strombus trumpets) on the floor of the Caracolas Gallery (left), with the most detailed engraved trumpet (right). Photographs courtesy of the Programa de Investigación Arqueológica y Conservación Chavín de Huántar (PIACCH).

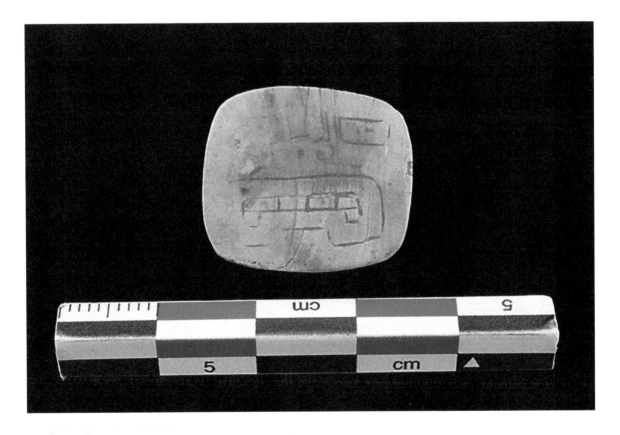

figure 2.8
Strombus ornament made from fragmented *pututus* in very late Chavín times. Photograph courtesy of the Programa de Investigación Arqueológica y Conservación Chavín de Huántar (PIACCH).

Grueso, and a variety of very large jars generally ranging from 30–50 cm mouth diameter). In general, the pottery from Layers 2 and 3 of recognizable Chavín period was of small fragment size and often shows considerable rounding, which is consistent with it originating from outside the gallery and undergoing considerable reworking en route to its resting place. A few ground stone items were recovered, mostly small beads of diverse and colorful raw materials; obsidian was relatively rare in the gallery. Two radiocarbon dates were obtained from charcoal from Layer 3: 2522±34 BP (795–538 BC [95.4 percent confidence interval]) and 2573±33 BP (811–566 BC [95.4 percent confidence interval]). These dates from sediments accumulating above the original use floor are consistent with gallery construction quite early in the Black and White phase (ca. 850 BC) and subsequent sediment accumulation during the same phase between 850 and 550 BC.

Galería del Fuego / Gallery X Excavated in 2018 (Rick)

Galería del Fuego is located immediately west of the Caracolas Gallery, connected to it by an approximately 6 m duct (see Figure 2.5). Perforation to the gallery was achieved by a small excavation that descended through about 2.5 m of overlying cultural deposits, mostly fills, of the Mariash-Recuay period (0–AD 700). Surprisingly, these fills as well as some structures ended just short of the neatly sealed CPA floor—a fine white level surface lying 10–20 cm above the beam tops of the gallery below (Figure 2.9). The gallery's entrance had been sealed with exclusively Chavín-epoch sediments, thus confirming the general observation that the gallery contains no evidence of human presence after Chavín times. The gallery, although structurally intact, shows signs of subsidence in its north wall, evidently due to compaction of the fill of a roofless canal running parallel to the gallery, but some distance below. This has led to the distortion of the north wall of the gallery and caused the beams to rest at a downward angle toward the north, to the point of shearing two beams without causing their collapse. The floor of the gallery was noted, even in the previous year's remote video documentation, to

have a layer of quite large wall-stone-sized blocks lying irregularly on top of the highest sediments. Notably there are no similarly sized stones lost from the walls or ceiling, and eventually it became clear that the stones had been brought in through the gallery's entrance as perhaps the last human action to take place within it. The same forces that led to the wall and beam damage also jarred loose a corbel-like stone from the extreme northeast corner of the gallery ceiling, opening a roughly 20 × 20 cm upward orifice through the roof. Immediately below this was a conical deposit of soil and cultural material that had drained into the gallery after its closure, and not surprisingly this material is from the Mariash-Recuay period. The orifice, reaching some distance upward, had been used as a convenient way of downwardly disposing of unwanted cultural material; fortunately, it was quite easy to clear this stratified cone completely prior to excavation of the gallery's Chavín-period deposits.

Two primary strata of the Chavín period were found—an upper, thick, and internally stratified layer that increases in thickness toward the entrance, is loaded with large stones, and contains a small amount of cultural material of Chavín age, judging from the exclusively Chavín pottery (Figure 2.10). Layer 2 rests on the floor of the gallery, defined as noted for the Caracolas Gallery. The amount of cultural material declines even more in this floor contact layer, becoming quite scarce, and interestingly becoming predominantly *compoteras*—a ceramic form composed of a cylindrical base, on top of which is mounted a broad, dish-like bowl. Although the squat cylindrical base is apparently not perforated, there is clear evidence of burning within the cylinder, as if these vessels were used as censers or for heating some sort of substances. The remainder of the ceramics from Chavín layers are polished blackwares of the Janabarroide tradition, but with a diversity of engraved and stamped designs; they do not seem to be fragments of locally broken vessels, with the exception of the *compoteras*, which have large fragments with sharp broken edges. The floor of the gallery is more notable than its contents—it has a light color and might have been white originally; it is flat except for countersunk, lightly

figure 2.9
Galería del Fuego /
Gallery X entrance,
adjacent to preserved
atrium floor surface
(below bucket). Visible
stone walls are part of a
Mariash-Recuay structure.
Photograph courtesy
of the Programa de
Investigación Arqueológica
y Conservación Chavín de
Huántar (PIACCH).

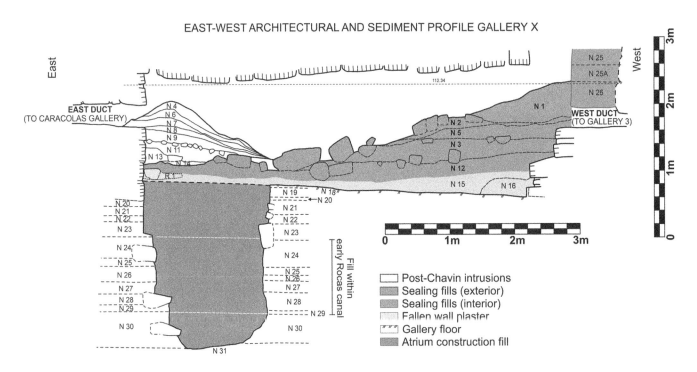

EAST-WEST ARCHITECTURAL AND SEDIMENT PROFILE GALLERY X

figure 2.10
Longitudinal section of the Galería del Fuego / Gallery X, showing excavated stratigraphy. Illustration by Erick Acero, courtesy of the Programa de Investigación Arqueológica y Conservación Chavín de Huántar (PIACCH).

trenched depressions near some of the walls. The light-colored floor is heavily stained with two distinct reddish colors—one is the result of the burning of the floor surface, apparently repeatedly and in multiple locations. The other well-defined areas of bright, cherry-red coloration is identical to the tones we have previously chemically identified as cinnabar. The content of charcoal in Layer 2 is quite high right above the floor, becoming a substantial proportion of the soil volume.

Although it is of limited relevance here, we perforated the eastern third of the gallery floor to determine the nature of subfloor sediments, and to intentionally search for evidence of an early route of the main trunk of the Rocas Canal, the primary canal draining the central parts of the monumental center. In doing so, we found the subfloor layers of selected but unworked blocks of quartzite that characterize the construction nucleus used to establish and raise construction surfaces, interspersed with occasional and significant objects, including a complete quadrilateral shaped and highly polished metamorphic stone anvil with fine edges known in Formative sites as a tool for working sheet metal, primarily gold (Grossman 1972). This fully functional and unbroken tool represents considerable labor investment in its shaping and polishing, and its significant size suggests that it was unlikely to have been lost and is probably an intentional offering not uncommon to the formal, organized, and constructed fills of the Chavín period.

Galería de los Inhaladores / Gallery 3 Excavated in 2018 (Rick)

This gallery is in the far west position of the four galleries, interconnected by a short duct of around 2 m with Gallery X. Entry to the gallery required perforating more than 3 m through thick, loose refuse-charged fills of Mariash-Recuay date to encounter the poorly preserved atrium surface. Directly below this, the beams of the gallery were apparent, and by lifting one we gained access to the gallery chamber (Figure 2.11). While the size, form, and features of the gallery initially appeared identical to the Caracolas Gallery and a mirror image of Galería del Fuego / Gallery X, it was impossible to be sure because the

figure 2.11
Entry into the Galería de los Inhaladores / Gallery 3; one ceiling stone beam (at bottom) has been lifted to allow entry. Photograph courtesy of the Programa de Investigación Arqueológica y Conservación Chavín de Huántar (PIACCH).

gallery had a fill of clean, moderate, and small-sized stones forming a slope up from east to west, reaching the roof of the gallery and blocking visibility of its far west end. The entranceway feature on the east end of the gallery generally conforms to that of the Caracolas Gallery, with the exception that the placement of the roof beams and the size of the entrance beams suggest that they would have been very difficult to open in their final position. As excavations lowered the rock slope to the west, a number of finds and features were discerned.

First, a series of ceramic vessels had been broken on top of this rock slope, ostensibly the last act prior to the sealing of the gallery. This closure apparently occurred in very late Chavín times, since the gallery shows no post-Chavín material and its entrance was immediately covered by later cultural materials. Second, shortly after we initiated the removal of the rock mass, a human skeleton was encountered under the few rocks that accumulated at the east (lower) end of the talus-like slope. This individual was not a real burial in that the flexed, face-down body had been placed on the surface of about 35 cm of accumulated over-floor gallery sediments, and three large stones had been placed directly on top of the head, torso, and pelvic areas. No burial accompaniments were apparent, nor is there evidence that sediments were piled on the body, beyond the stones mentioned. The burial apparently precedes the placement of the stone gallery fill but lies immediately beneath it. Initial analysis of the skeleton shows it to be a male of twenty-five to thirty-five years in apparent good health but with exceptionally short, lightly muscled arms. His legs, feet, and hands are robust in size and muscle development. The cranium shows a bilobal deformation of moderate degree, and a clean, aligned, and linear fracture of both the maxilla/palate and mandible suggests some form of trauma to the lower face.

Third, the talus itself represents an event of considerable complexity. Because it is well below the repose angle, it is not easily explained as a rock flow from the west end of the gallery, perhaps through its roof. Yet, the roof beams of the eastern entrance constriction (see Figure 2.13) are interlocked in a pattern that disallows entry there late in the use sequence. When the ceiling was cleared on the west side, at least two beams were found to be missing, which suggests that although the talus is not likely an unintentional rock flow, it might well be the result of rocks intentionally brought through these gaps in the roof. A further clue of importance is that part of the western ceiling was reconstituted, albeit in precarious form, in part with a large slab of granite, a material very unusual for roof beams. This flat granite stone had been worked to provide a facing angle typical of the fine granite stonework of the superior courses of Buildings A, B, and C at Chavín. The presence of this stone, together with the extensive talus

rubble and the blocks present in Gallery X, strongly suggest that these two galleries were used, to different degrees, to dispose of architectural remnants of a major wall. The presence of the worked granite stone from high in the courses of Chavín de Huántar's major architecture further indicates that this stone mass may have come from the collapse of the nearby west wall of the CPA, something that was linked to a major seismic event around 550 BC (Lumbreras 1989; Rick 2008). In the 550–500 BC Support phase, it was clearly the builders' intent to hide the evidence of damage by doing rapid and uncharacteristically informal repairs, as well as building support walls and platforms covering wall fall, probably to avoid the appearance that Chavín de Huántar's architecture had suffered damage. A logical corollary action would be to hide any excess rubble by pushing it into the two galleries nearest the collapse and to seal the galleries at that time.

After the talus of rocks was removed, it was clear that a major series of fine sediments was present above the floor of Gallery 3, also angling up toward the west. These clearly had been in place prior to the intrusion of the rock talus and had a very different character and content. While the rock layer had surface material of smashed ceramic vessels, the fine sediment Layers 4–6 had several concentrations of multiple smashed ceramic vessels, constituting a large corpus of pottery that had been broken in situ. Many of the vessels were complete or nearly complete when the fragments were visually reconstructed, many using photogrammetric reconstruction (Figure 2.12). Fragments were large, with sharp broken edges, and in many cases found in discernible concentrations. These actions do not seem to have happened on sediment surfaces of any duration, but during an uninterrupted process of sediment accumulation. The vessels are surprisingly uniform, consisting of bowls with everted rim segments for pouring spouts; the decoration is overwhelmingly Janabarroide with S-stamps predominating, representing many vessels with a wide variety of sizes of S's—the S is rarely seen in large numbers in other Chavín contexts (Rick 2014). This emphasis on stamped bowls is characteristic of Gallery 3 in all its layers.

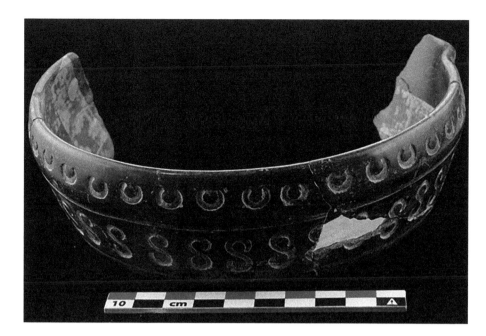

figure 2.12
Reconstructed typical
Janabarroide vessel
from the Galería de los
Inhaladores / Gallery 3.
Note the pouring spout in
the upper right. Photograph
courtesy of the Programa de
Investigación Arqueológica
y Conservación Chavín de
Huántar (PIACCH).

Two other features of the gallery in Layers 4–6 stand out. First is the presence of two additional individuals, found associated with one another, and also with a number of the aforementioned smashed vessels. Both are sub-adults—they are of approximately one and twelve to fourteen years of age, may be secondary burials, and show no evidence of a significant grave excavation. Instead, they were probably placed together with the vessels as a tight mass of bones in a bundle-like formation. Although their bones were relatively poorly preserved, it is reasonable to believe they were substantially complete individuals at the time of their placement.

The final characteristic of these above-floor layers is clear evidence of modification of the gallery's structure on the far west end (Figure 2.13), corresponding to the area lacking beams. About 1 m of the gallery's southern and northern walls had been dismantled (including almost all of the westernmost niche of the original three), apparently to allow the installation, on each side of the gallery, of a vertical stone, from an igneous columnar formation; at Chavín de Huántar, a small proportion of architectural detrital rubble consists of very short segments of these columns, which range 10–20 cm in diameter and have between four and six length-spanning facets. These are the first known columns in an original architectural location, and their placement

adjacent to and slightly impinging within the original wall line of the gallery evidently required the wall dismantling. We refer to them as *huancas*, a term for vertical stones fully incorporated into walls of Huarás (500–0 BC) and Recuay (AD 0–700) constructions (see also Nesbitt, this volume). Given the lack of post-Chavín materials in the gallery and the stratigraphic context of the pillars' imposition, it is clear that the *huancas* were installed in the gallery during the late, perhaps terminal, Black and White phase (850–550 BC), or possibly in the brief post-seismic Support phase (550–500 BC), a very striking deviation from Chavín's very orderly and regular horizontally coursed wall construction. It is probable that this construction event involved the partial de-roofing of the gallery and that the rebuilding of the west end involved a switching of the entranceway from the eastern to the western extremes of the gallery; it seems likely that the apparent missing north and south wall segments were actually filled in with unsubstantial, lighter masonry patches. The *huanca* placement was made at the eastern edge of a step-like raised floor segment that clearly but shortly preceded the placement of the two immature burials in their immediate vicinity.

Like other galleries, the Galería de los Inhaladores has a thin floor of clay with relatively little material directly associated with the floor itself. This

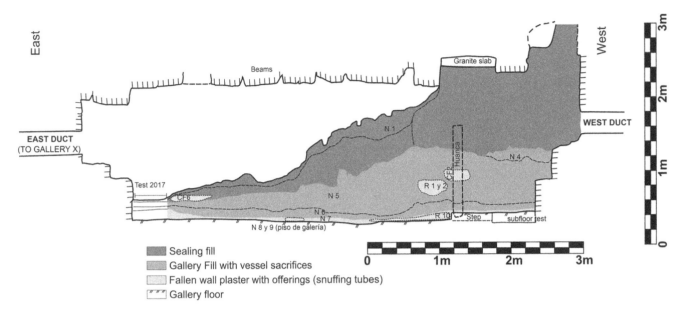

■ Sealing fill
■ Gallery Fill with vessel sacrifices
▨ Fallen wall plaster with offerings (snuffing tubes)
▨ Gallery floor

figure 2.13
Longitudinal section of the Galería de los Inhaladores / Gallery 3, showing excavated stratigraphy. Illustration by Giuseppe Alva, courtesy of the Programa de Investigación Arqueológica y Conservación Chavín de Huántar (PIACCH).

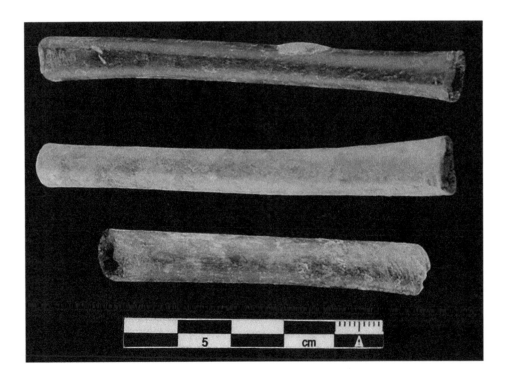

figure 2.14
The Galería de los Inhaladores / Gallery 3 bird wing bone tubes, likely for inhalation of psychoactive substances. Photograph courtesy of the Programa de Investigación Arqueológica y Conservación Chavín de Huántar (PIACCH).

includes the continued presence of Janabarroide pottery, some animal bone, and a few beads manufactured from spondylus and other shell remains—but notably no fragments of strombus. Most importantly, directly resting on the floor itself are nineteen small prepared bird wing bone tubes, cut and polished on their ends (Figure 2.14). These are distributed over much of the floor and in cases were found broken in situ—they are of quite thin bone that would easily break with trampling. They are notably *not* cut by grooving and snapping—a common Chavín bone-working method—but rather show end irregularities as if they had been nibbled away, with the sharp points of the small edge breaks rounded and eventually polished. It is clear that these are not the byproduct of bead making, in the way of many larger bone tubes found elsewhere. The tubular form probably was used as such and thus can be tentatively suggested to be for the inhalation of substances such as psychoactive snuffs.

Galería de las Visitantes / Gallery 4 Excavated in 2018 (Rick)

The Galería de las Visitantes / Gallery 4 is the easternmost of the four Caracolas Galleries, interconnected to the Caracolas Gallery by a roughly 2 m duct, identical to the connection between Galería de los Inhaladores / Gallery 3 and Galería del Fuego / Gallery X. Near-surface excavation revealed evidence of a number of Mariash-Recuay structures, including some that had adopted the alignment and nearly the position of underlying (but not stratigraphically continuous) Chavín walls that indeed turned out to be a gallery in line with the other three (Figure 2.15). The vertical position of these walls showed that by the Mariash-Recuay period, the Galería de las Visitantes / Gallery 4 had already lost all but one of its stone beams, and the walls of the gallery were increasingly incomplete toward the eastern end of the gallery, either through erosion or demolition.

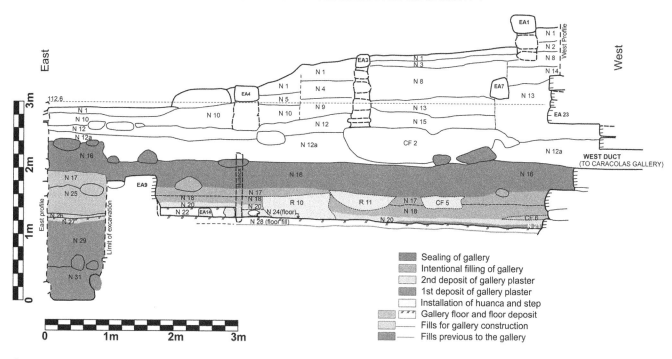

figure 2.15

The Galería de las Visitantes / Gallery 4 longitudinal section, showing excavated layers and later architecture. Illustration by Patricia Flores, courtesy of the Programa de Investigación Arqueológica y Conservación Chavín de Huántar (PIACCH).

figure 2.16
Overall view of the Galería de las Visitantes / Gallery 4; note the *huancas* visible on the extreme right. The layer
shown is the major part of Feature 10, ceramic concentration. Photograph courtesy of the Programa de Investigación
Arqueológica y Conservación Chavín de Huántar (PIACCH).

While excavating within the walls of the Mariash-Recuay structures, we encountered evidence of later intrusion, probably an excavation, into the western side of this space in the form of abundant loose stones of fairly uniform 20–40 cm size. Removing these, and proceeding below the level of the Mariash-Recuay structures and their assumed floor level, we encountered a large amount of human skeletal material, partially organized in discernible individuals in loosely fetal positions (which might be either primary or secondary), now within the upper wall definitions of the gallery. The overall bone mass showed disturbance, evidently from the continued placement of new burials, and possibly to minor, relatively modern intrusion, but not apparently to any activity of the Mariash-Recuay

period. There were clear associations of Huarás-period pottery, both fragmented and complete, with the approximately eighteen individuals excavated.

Upon removal of these human skeletons, a further stratum of soil was removed, and subsequently another group of four human individuals was encountered. All adults, these individuals are differentiated from the stratigraphically higher skeletons in showing tubular erect cranial deformation of moderate degree, a dark coloration typical of gallery bone in general (and most notably the human remains from the Ofrendas Gallery), and association only with Chavín-period pottery, all fragmented. If these remains are of the Chavín period, they represent the last activity from that period in the gallery.

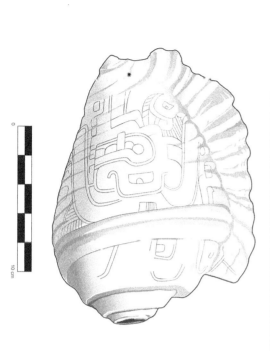

figure 2.17
Strombus trumpet from the Galería de las Visitantes / Gallery 4 on right, with drawing of engraving that is barely visible due to use polish. Illustration by Miguel Ortiz, courtesy of the Programa de Investigación Arqueológica y Conservación Chavín de Huántar (PIACCH).

The Chavín-period deposits in the Galería de las Visitantes / Gallery 4 with the most content is below the potential Chavín funerary deposits mentioned above. These consist of animal bone, fragments of strombus shell, and dense ceramic concentrations representing many vessels, some of which are nearly complete and clearly broken in situ (Figure 2.16). The nature of the ceramic assemblage is strikingly different from the other three galleries, containing many plates and bottles and fewer bowl forms. Even more striking are the decorative types represented. Janabarroide decoration is rare; instead, there are a wide variety of types described by Lumbreras and others as non-local (Lumbreras 1993). These are diverse, including styles related to the Cupisnique, Cajamarca, and Jaén areas, and include kaolin pastes, high relief sculpting, modeling, and various forms of painted vessels. The strombus fragments include several partially complete ornaments similar to those observed in the Caracolas Gallery. The densest layer of pottery and other remains was removed as a separate unit in ¼ m² sub-units, in the hope of aiding in vessel reconstruction. Unlike

the other galleries, the floor deposit materials were effectively the same as those in a number of layers immediately above, although the frequency of materials declines somewhat toward the floor itself, especially the case for strombus fragments.

In a nearly identical situation to the Galería de los Inhaladores / Gallery 3, the Galería de las Visitantes / Gallery 4 suffered modifications to its entrance consisting of the closure of the original western entrance, the dismantling of about a meter of the eastern walls, the installation of two matching *huancas* of the same columnar rock as in Gallery 3, and the patching of the narrowed walls of the eastern entrance with inferior, unstable masonry. Framed by the *huancas* and backed up against a step-like, raised floor segment, a complete, engraved strombus trumpet was found resting exactly on the gallery floor along its center line (Figure 2.17). The far eastern section of the gallery had been significantly modified by intrusive activity conducted during Mariash-Recuay times, making it impossible to determine with confidence if a second or replacement entrance had been installed in symmetry with the second entrance installed in the Galería de los Inhaladores / Gallery 3, but many fragmentary late features of the galley argue in favor of this theory.

Ofrendas Gallery Excavated in 1966–1967 (Lumbreras)

The Ofrendas Gallery has been extensively published by Lumbreras (1993, 2007) and so only a brief summary will be given to note the differences with the other CPA galleries. There is every reason to believe that the Ofrendas Gallery, in spite of its placement across the Circular Plaza from the Caracolas Gallery series as well as its strikingly different form, was built in the same massive construction event. Although it could be argued that the scale of this event is great, involving the construction of about 6000 m² of highly organized and carefully placed constructive nucleus, plus massive amounts of fully faced and at times engraved granite, any pattern other than full construction would have left the plaza unfinished and nonfunctional. It is further unlikely that either the north or south atrium areas were finished long before the other. This would have left a strange, half-circular plaza that would break many Chavín canons of symmetry and form.

The Ofrendas Gallery has a comb-like layout, quite different from the rather simple rectangular-with-modifications form of the Caracolas Gallery series. Yet the general construction pattern is very similar, resulting in passages that are about 1 m in width with a ceiling height just under 2 m. Although the entranceway is not in-line with the main axis of the gallery, the general sense of stepping up to the surface by quite large steps is similar. The Ofrendas Gallery is well-known for the spectacular ceramic assemblage of approximately 681 vessels, mostly deposited intact on the floor of the gallery but subsequently crushed and fragmented under an overlayer of sediments, presumably by pressures including those of people walking through the gallery. The assemblage includes a wide range of forms and decorative styles, including some rarely seen in other contexts at Chavín de Huántar. A total of 18,275 ceramic sherds were recovered over all gallery surfaces (Lumbreras 2007), suggesting that each ceramic vessel was, on average, reduced

to about twenty-seven fragments. In comparison, the excavations of Galería del Fuego / Gallery X, Galería de los Inhaladores / Gallery 3, and Galería de las Visitantes / Gallery 4 produced 7,933 ceramic fragments from Chavín contexts, which at the same fragmentation rate would indicate the presence of around 290 ceramic vessels. Intuitively, this is not reasonable—because relatively few vessels are indicated by identifiably similar fragments and because the fragments are small enough on average that many more than twenty-seven fragments of their size would be necessary to constitute a single vessel. Thus, the Ofrendas Gallery has very large fragments in comparison, which is confirmed by published photographs (Lumbreras 2007). Although many site formation processes need to be taken into account, it is likely that whole vessels were predominantly deposited in the Ofrendas Gallery but usually not in the Caracolas Gallery series.

A wide range of additional remains, including animal and human bone, bone tools, and ground stone of both grinding and ornamental function, were found in the gallery. Shell is present, but in small objects such as beads or fragments of reduced size. There is no indication of the presence of strombus shell, much less fragments that might indicate the presence of trumpets—although one bone pin and at least one ceramic vessel have depictions of strombus included in their decoration.

The Ofrendas Gallery has roughly double the surface area of all four of the Caracolas Galleries combined (approximately 56 m² versus approximately 30 m²). Sampling issues may partially explain the greater variety of remains in the Ofrendas Gallery, but not the very different quantity, character, and quality of many ceramic vessels. The dense distribution of ceramic vessels on the floor of the gallery (Figure 2.18) suggests that when fully populated with ceramics, activity in the gallery would have been highly constrained. This is not the case with the Caracolas Gallery series, where most floor areas were relatively clear, at least the basal floor used immediately after construction. This raises an issue that may provide a further contrast within the CPA galleries. The Ofrendas Gallery, in the interpretation of Lumbreras, held a monumental offering, placed on

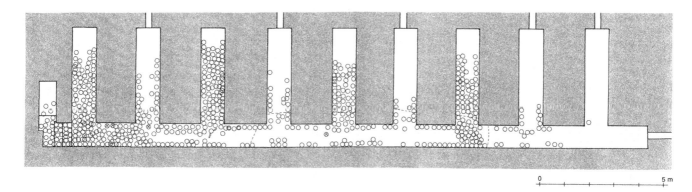

0   5 m

figure 2.18
Distribution of ceramic vessels over the floor plan of the Ofrendas Gallery. Illustration courtesy of Luis G. Lumbreras.

a one-time basis, after which the gallery was sealed. The stratigraphy of the gallery seems to support this idea, having a massive floor-level artifact (primarily pottery) distribution, followed by a lengthy period of deposition of fine sediments, probably from sediment infiltration. Although there may be similar sedimentation in the Caracolas Gallery, there is clear evidence of gallery reuse during Chavín times; the other three Caracolas Galleries show abundant evidence of continued Chavín-period use after the laying of floor deposits. This suggests that the Ofrendas Gallery may well have been sealed after the deposition of the major offering (probably early in the Black and White phase), while the Caracolas Gallery series may have been used repetitively throughout much of that phase. This suggests a structurally different use pattern and function, which possibly correlates with the planned and highly contrastive gallery layouts between the simple Caracolas Gallery series with diverse usage and the large single-use Ofrendas Gallery.

Summary and Conclusions

Although the analysis of the Caracolas Gallery series is still in its initial phase, there are a number of striking patterns in this data.

1 Within the context of the CPA, the known galleries are as contemporary as the data quality can specify, and in the case of the Caracolas Gallery series, they contain deposits that clearly span the Black and White, and perhaps the Support, phase in a parallel fashion. Although this gives a period of around three hundred years for the construction, use, and abandonment of these galleries, it is a strong architectural supposition that all were constructed within a unified construction event. The apparent seismic evidence (Rick 2008) in at least two and perhaps three of the galleries toward the end of their use frames time in a similar way; at this point, the variability in use patterns cannot easily be attributed to sequential changes, and a good part is roughly if not exactly contemporary. Thus, there is no reason to suspect that the contents of the galleries vary significantly in temporal coverage, arguing that variability between them is effectively contemporary.

2 At a macro scale, the differences between the forms and, where present, the contents of the CPA galleries are striking. With Chavín's general tendency toward symmetry in layout, the placement and layout of the Caracolas Gallery series, Ofrendas Gallery, and Campamento Gallery suggest strong reasons for not maintaining some version of symmetry around the main east–west axis of the Circular Plaza. This suggests either functional or social differences between them, and the data support that. Leaving the Campamento Gallery aside because of its lack of known contents, the architectural history and condition of contents

differ markedly between the Ofrendas Gallery and the Caracolas Gallery series. The Ofrendas Gallery is proposed to have been used primarily, if not exclusively, to house a large volume of offerings, sealed in place fairly early as a possible dedicatory act for the plaza area. The Ofrendas Gallery lacks the apparent complexity of stratigraphic record, as well as any significant history of modification that is so prominent in the Caracolas Gallery series, which is more consistent with the former having been sealed early in the Black and White phase. At least the western Galería del Fuego / Gallery X and Galería de los Inhaladores / Gallery 3 seem to have been available up to and after the 550 BC seismic event, incorporating materials from the event inside their chambers. The diversity is even more striking if the nearby Lanzón Gallery is added, which seems to have had an image-centric ritual focus that was totally lacking in the CPA galleries.

Notable in this regard is the evidence that use of the Lanzón Gallery seems to have involved visual and auditory manipulation provided through channeled light and sound (Kolar et al. 2012; Rick 2008). Could it be that we are starting to get a functional sorting of gallery forms, with the architecturally simplest and uniform galleries being rather function, and possibly personnel, specific, but multiuse across their multiplicity and perhaps over time (perhaps like blank slates capable of accepting dynamically assigned functions) with the cell-heavy (or comb-like) galleries used as vaults for major offerings and the labyrinthine galleries aimed at complex ceremonialism? The Lanzón Gallery is an example of image-centric activity; the Gallery of the Esplanade is an example of a complex gallery apparently used as a type of isolation chamber. Studies of archaeoacoustics in the Laberintos Gallery, Gallery of the Esplanade, and Doble Mensula Gallery suggest sound manipulation along the lines of the Lanzón Gallery, hinting at members of a set with commonalities beyond just their layout. These observations constitute reasonable hypotheses

to test, especially if further intact galleries are found in the near future. It is notable, in this regard, that there is tantalizing evidence that the four galleries of the Caracolas Gallery series may be matched by another row of four galleries just to their north (Figure 2.2).

3 Looking specifically at the Caracolas Gallery series, a more concerted attempt toward symmetry can be seen, as if these galleries were meant to be like a unit in some sense. The first major symmetry is that the east and west gallery pairs are precisely symmetrical around the centerline of the Escalinata Gallery entrance (Figure 2.19), the major pre–Black and White phase manner of reaching the heights of at least the major Building A. Given the perfection of this symmetry with respect to a major site entrance that was closed off by the very architectural mass that made the Caracolas Gallery series possible, it is likely that this placement was intentional and an act of remembering or at least respecting this prominent feature—undoubtedly a ceremonial pathway of early Chavín. This is all the more evident when we consider that the placement of the galleries apparently forces a rerouting of Rocas Canal from underneath the location where the galleries were being built to underneath the to-be-built Circular Plaza. The most long-lasting symmetry of these four galleries is the pairing of the Caracolas Gallery and the Galería del Fuego / Gallery X, which are near-perfect mirror images of each other. It seems likely, however, that the eastern and western pairs of galleries were originally equally striking in their match, but this was subverted by the late entranceway reversals in the Galería de los Inhaladores / Gallery 3 and the Galería de las Visitantes / Gallery 4, which made these end galleries more specifically mirror-imaged to each other—and given the exact replication of constructive actions taken, and architectural features achieved, a complex, evolving symmetric motivation cannot be more clear. Perhaps this is more evidence for the "blank slate" hypothesis—not only were gallery functions assignable within a sense of symmetry, but

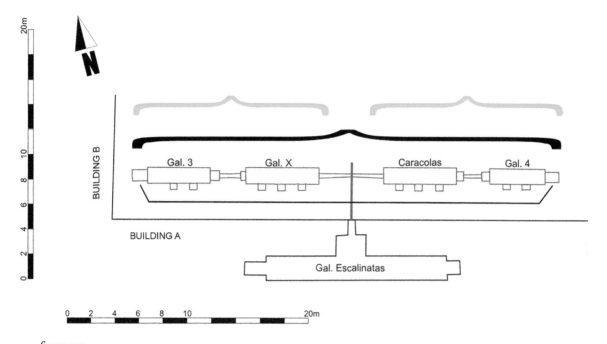

figure 2.19

Symmetry of the Caracolas Gallery series, showing the axis of the site's earlier north entrance (red line), the overall symmetry around that axis (black bracket), the dual incorporated bilateral symmetry of the lateral gallery pairs (green brackets), and the extremity-specific symmetry of the late-modified entrances of the Galería de los Inhaladores / Gallery 3 and Galería de las Visitantes / Gallery 4 (thin black lines). Illustration courtesy of the Programa de Investigación Arqueológica y Conservación Chavín de Huántar (PIACCH).

the sense of symmetry itself evolved, probably reflecting changing ideas and directions of the leadership(s).

4 If the evidence of contents is added in, the situation becomes much more complex at various levels. First, some galleries seem to change both form and function over time, while others apparently do not. There is no evidence for the early Black and White phase presence of mortuary function anywhere in the series, but this apparently is added to the Galería de los Inhaladores / Gallery 3 and the Galería de las Visitantes / Gallery 4, about the time their entrances are rebuilt and *huancas* installed. The mortuary function is notable for its apparent lack of attention to preserved accompaniments for these individuals, suggesting that the galleries were not turned into tombs but rather may have become contexts for which the presence of human bodies was appropriate. The contrast of cranial deformations between Gallery 3 and Gallery 4 is potentially meaningful and might

point to some identity differences in the directors and/or users of these galleries.

This could, in turn, be related to the most numerically significant difference of all—the segregation of ceramic form and style between the Galería de los Inhaladores / Gallery 3 and the Galería de las Visitantes / Gallery 4 (these data are not yet available for the Caracolas Gallery). The predominant pottery forms (Figure 2.20) are distributed quite differentially among these three galleries, as confirmed by a p-value of .00 on the chi-square test, with bottles and based bowls (*compoteras*) being much more common in the Galería de las Visitantes / Gallery 4, with a corresponding predominance of bowls in the Galería de los Inhaladores / Gallery 3 (Table 2.1). These forms are likely to have functional differences, but additional work, including starch analysis, should be completed to understand the distribution. Decorative techniques are probably more stylistic in origin, and their even greater differential distribution

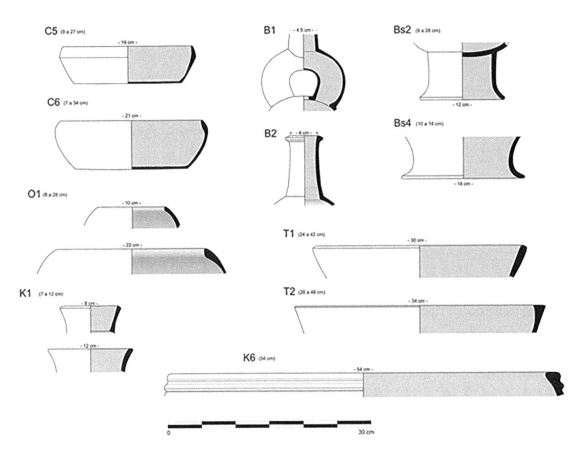

figure 2.20
Predominant pottery forms found in the Caracolas Gallery Series; Bs2 and Bs4 are *compotera* forms. (C's: bowls; B's: bottles; O's: neckless jars; K1: necked jars; and T's and K6: very large bowls and jars). Illustration by Erick Acero, courtesy of the Programa de Investigación Arqueológica y Conservación Chavín de Huántar (PIACCH

table 2.1
Pottery form percentages found in the Galería del Fuego / Gallery X, the Galería de los Inhaladores / Gallery 3, and the Galería de las Visitantes / Gallery 4.

POTTERY FORM PERCENTAGES							
	BASED BOWLS	BOTTLE	NECKED JARS	BOWLS	NECKLESS JARS	VERY LARGE BOWLS AND JARS	TOTAL DIAGNOSTIC
Gallery X main levels	15.3	6.3	12.6	57.7	3.6	4.5	111
Gallery 3 main levels	14.6	4	6.2	61.1	11.7	12.4	274
Gallery 4 main levels	31.3	10.9	17.7	32.3	3.6	4.2	192
Gallery 4 Feature 10	25.4	30.7	4.8	25.4	2.6	11.1	189

table 2.2

Pottery decoration percentages found in the Galería del Fuego / Gallery X, the Galería de los Inhaladores / Gallery 3, and the Galería de las Visitantes / Gallery 4.

	INCISED	O's	S's AND C's	COMPLEX	STAMPED	PUNCTATE	RELIEF AND MODELLED	TEXTURED /TOTALLY DECORATED / HIGH INVESTMENT	PAINTED	TOTAL DECORATED
Gallery X main levels	56.3	26.6	12	8.9	47.5	3.8	5.7	49.4	11.4	158
Gallery 3 main levels	66	31.5	14.7	4.6	50.8	15.1	14.3	69.3	6.7	238
Gallery 4 main levels	56.9	11.7	1.7	6.7	20.1	3.3	16.3	50.6	20.9	239
Gallery 4 Feature 10	64.7	4.6	0.2	4.3	9.1	4.6	16.3	62.9	37.1	606

between these spaces (chi-square is not appropriate for the overlapping nature of these categories [Table 2.2]) clearly points to a local–distant issue. Stamped Janabarroide pottery is mostly a local production, while the Galería de las Visitantes / Gallery 4 ceramic diversity and character, including painting, points to distant origins. These differences contrast with the unbalanced presence of strombus in only the eastern galleries; there may be a tendency to complement that with a greater or perhaps nearly unique presence of spondylus in the western galleries, but that is not as clear, especially numerically. The different cranial deformations from the Galería de los Inhaladores / Gallery 3 and the Galería de las Visitantes / Gallery 4 offer tantalizing challenges for further, perhaps isotopic analyses.

5 Specific ritualistic activities have yet other patterns, it would seem, and the patterns become gallery specific. Galería del Fuego / Gallery X's emphasis on fire, both on the floor and in relation to the *compotera* pottery, and the presence of cinnabar, together with the very restricted amount of pottery, suggest certain aspects of ritual. The Galería de los Inhaladores / Gallery 3 shows a distinctive pattern of probable snuffing tubes early in its use and more generalized pattern of in-gallery vessel destruction and some funerary or mortuary activity later. The same

later pattern seems to come to the Galería de las Visitantes / Gallery 4. The Caracolas Gallery seems to have a storage or sacristy-like function for the strombus trumpets; perhaps something similar is found in the Galería de las Visitantes / Gallery 4, but by very late Chavín times the "sacred" trumpets are being broken up for ornaments.

6 Finally, the imposition of *huancas* during final Chavín use hints at some striking changes. A willingness to implement major change, especially toward a culturally unusual pattern, suggests that something is changing rather sharply. The coupling of this architectural change with the seismic evidence may be significant, and it might be that the major challenge of seismic damage, together with a possibly looming presence of an alternative cultural entity—Huarás is apparently rapidly expanding—may be leading to emulation in hopes of greater efficacy under a difficult series of events. It is notable that the inhabitants of Chavín de Huántar chose to emplace *huancas* in a rather tight and out-of-sight location; this could speak toward a location of recourse, a place where appeals could be made.

Overall, galleries should be seen as a "deep" pattern of Chavín de Huántar, not a passing or trivial architectural whim. Dimensions and patterns of growth include threshold costs for architectural expansion, raw material demands (especially beams), "container-ized" contexts capable of definitive partitioning, and underworld linkages where over time these spaces get deeper and more difficult to maintain access to. Yet it is for these very reasons the galleries might have been doorways into the past in multiple senses. These are potential gallery associations worthy of exploration. Something unexpected, perhaps because of our Ofrendas-influenced view of the galleries, is that these container contexts were in many cases used in different manners across time, and because of their way of holding sediments and materials without easy escape, they are ideal archaeological contexts for witnessing a very specialized but important series of activities and actions with high chronological resolution.

Galleries are a genre at Chavín, such that most individuals associated with them, particularly novitiates in the Chavín cult(s),

would have recognized them as a broad category of space. They were appropriate locations for a wide variety of cultural activities, perhaps nearly all ritually related, but a series of resource spaces with forms appropriate for different ranges of activities. They were designed in intra- and inter-gallery patterns—their form and placement were undoubtedly significant, but usually constrained as to where they could be placed in a site that grew horizontally and vertically. The CPA is a special case where those restraints are somewhat relaxed, perhaps enhancing the potential or even necessity for a "perfect storm" of meaningful arrangement. It is likely that when we have a full map of galleries and their growth over time we will observe many levels of structural and spatial meaning that evolved in complex and dynamic ways. Taking galleries into deep account at Chavín is utterly essential to understanding this key Formative site.

REFERENCES CITED

Burger, Richard L.
1984   *The Prehistoric Occupation of Chavín de Huántar, Peru.* University of California Press, Berkeley.

Bustamante, Julio, and Enrique Crousillat
1974   Análisis hidráulico del sitio arqueológico de Chavín de Huántar. Undergraduate thesis, National Engineering University, Lima.

Bustamante, Julio, Enrique Crousillat, and John W. Rick
2021   Nuevos conceptos sobre la secuencia constructiva y usos de la red de canales de Chavín de Huántar. *De venir: Revista de estudios sobre patrimonio edificado* 8(15):75–94.

Grossman, Joel W.
1972   An Ancient Gold Worker's Tool Kit: The Earliest Metal Technology in Peru. *Archaeology* 25:270–275.

Kembel, Silvia
2001   Architectural Sequence and Chronology at Chavín de Huántar, Peru. PhD dissertation, Stanford University, Stanford.

2008   The Architecture at the Monumental Center of Chavín de Huántar: Sequence, Transformations, and Chronology. In *Chavín: Art, Architecture, and Culture*, edited by William J. Conklin and Jeffrey Quilter, pp. 35–81. Cotsen Institute of Archaeology, University of California, Los Angeles.

Kembel, Silvia, and Herbert Haas
2015   Radiocarbon Dates from the Monumental Architecture at Chavín de Huántar, Perú. *Journal of Archaeological Method and Theory* 22(2):345–427.

Kolar, Miriam A., John W. Rick, Perry R. Cook, and Jonathan S. Abel

2012   Ancient Pututus Contextualized: Integrative Archaeoacoustics at Chavin de Huantar, Peru. In *Flower World— Music Archaeology of the Americas*, edited by Mathias Stöckli and Arnd Adje Both, pp. 23–53. Ekho Verlag, Berlin.

Lumbreras, Luis G.

1989   *Chavín de Huántar en el nacimiento de la civilización andina*. Instituto Andino de Estudios Arqueológicos, Lima.

1993   *Chavín de Huántar: Excavaciones en la Galería de las Ofrendas*. P. von Zabern, Mainz.

2007   *Chavín: Excavaciones arqueológicas*. 2 vols. Universidad Alas Peruanas, Lima.

Lumbreras, Luis G., and Hernán Amat Olazábal

1965–1966   Informe preliminar sobre las galerías interiores de Chavín (primera temporada de trabajos). *Revista del Museo Nacional* 34:143–197.

Rick, John W.

2005   The Evolution of Authority and Power at Chavín de Huántar, Peru. In *Foundations of Power in the Prehispanic Andes*, edited by Kevin J. Vaughn, Dennis Ogburn, and Christina A. Conlee, pp. 71–89. Archeological Papers of the American Anthropological Association 14. University of California Press, Berkeley.

2008   Context, Construction, and Ritual in the Development of Authority at Chavín de Huántar. In *Chavín Art, Architecture, and Culture*, edited by William J. Conklin and Jeffrey Quilter, pp. 3–34. Cotsen Institute of Archaeology, University of California, Los Angeles.

2013   Architectural and Ritual Space at Chavín de Huántar. In *Chavín: Peru's Enigmatic Temple in the Andes*, edited by Peter Fux, pp. 151–166. Scheidegger & Spiess, Zurich.

2014   Cambio y continuidad, diversidad y coherencia: Perspectivas sobre variabilidad en Chavín de Huántar y el período formativo. In *El centro ceremonial andino: Nuevas perspectivas para los períodos arcaico y formativo*, edited by Yuji Seki, pp. 261–289. National Museum of Ethnology, Osaka.

2017   The Nature of Ritual Space at Chavín de Huántar. In *Rituals of the Past: Prehispanic and Colonial Case Studies in Andean Archaeology*, edited by Silvana A. Rosenfeld and Stefanie Bautista, pp. 21–49. University Press of Colorado, Boulder.

Rick, John W., Luis G. Lumbreras, Augusto E. Bazán, and Rosa M. Rick

2016   Cambiando la percepción sobre Chavín: Las últimas campañas del proyecto de investigación arqueológica y conservación en Chavín de Huántar. *Actas del I Congreso Nacional de Arqueología* 2:5–19.

Rick, John W., Christian Mesía, Daniel A. Contreras, Silvia Rodriguez Kembel, Rosa M. Rick, Matthew Sayre, and John Wolf

2010   La cronología de Chavín de Huántar y sus implicancias para el período formativo. *Boletín de Arqueología PUCP* 13:87–132.

Tello, Julio C.

1960   *Chavín: Cultura matriz de la civilización andina*. Publicación Antropológica del Archivo "Julio C. Tello" de la Universidad Nacional Mayor de San Marcos, Lima.

Vásquez de Espinoza, Antonio

(1620) 1948   *Compendium and Descriptions of the West Indies*. Translated by C. Upton Clark. Smithsonian Institution, Washington, D.C.

A River Runs through It

Ritual and Inequality in the La Banda Sector of Chavín de Huántar

MATTHEW P. SAYRE AND SILVANA A. ROSENFELD

Chavín de Huántar is an important Formative-period site located in the Conchucos region of north-central Peru (Figure 3.1). It is characterized by unique monumental architecture, which includes a series of temples with complex passageways and finely crafted stone sculptures (Burger 1984, 1992; Burger and Nesbitt, this volume; Lumbreras 1989, 1993; Rick 2006, this volume). The site is located at 3150 masl, roughly halfway between the Amazon rainforest and the Pacific coast and was built and occupied between 1200 and 500 BC (cf. Burger 2019; Kembel and Haas 2015; Rick et al. 2010 for discussions of the chronology). Based on artistic depictions and its elaborate architecture, it is believed that Chavín de Huántar had strong leaders who manipulated sound and light and used psychoactive plants to influence small groups of pilgrims from local and distant origins (Kembel and Rick 2004; Kolar et al. 2012; Rick 2005, 2006, 2008). Although substantial research has been conducted on Chavín iconography and architecture (e.g., Burger 1992; Rick 2008, 2014), much less is known about the people who lived and worked outside of, and presumably for, the monumental core (Burger 1984). As a result, the socioeconomic organization of Chavín society is still poorly understood. This chapter investigates the intersection between inequality, ritual, and daily life through a discussion of our work in the residential sector of La Banda.

While the traditional approach of studying status through burials and accompanied artifacts would be an ideal starting point, no cemeteries of Chavín age have been found at the site. Instead, the study of artifact and food production, distribution, and consumption, along with the analysis of architecture (including room size analysis), can reveal key aspects of how social differentiation was materialized at La Banda, as well as the daily activities that underwrote the ritual performances of the ceremonial center.

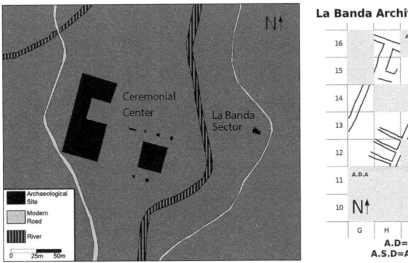
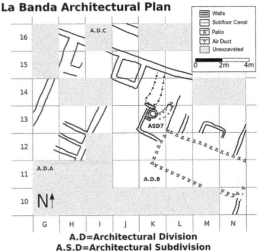

figure 3.1

Map of Chavín de Huántar. Illustration by Matthew P. Sayre, modified by Nick Rader.

Ritual

The changing nature of ritual practice has long fascinated anthropologists, as it can explain a set of social practices involving supernatural beings that has repercussions in many dimensions of a society, including the political, economic, and cosmological spheres. Though ritual has long been important to anthropologists (e.g., Bell 1992; Geertz 1973; Rappaport 1999; Turner 1967), archaeologists have only recently focused on the importance of studying ritual and its role in past societies (e.g., Bauer and Stanish 2001; Cook and Benco 2000; Insoll 2004; Kyriakidis 2007; Rosenfeld and Bautista 2017). Many scholars considered ritual to be a key factor in the growth, maintenance, and change of some ancient sociopolitical systems (DeMarrais, Castillo, and Earle 1996; Flannery and Marcus 2012; Hastorf 2007; Hodder 2010; Marcus and Flannery 2004; Moore 1996; Pauketat et al. 2002). It has been argued that ritual has been a motor of transformation in the past and present Andes in a variety of ways (e.g., Bauer and Stanish 2001; Hastorf 2003; Moore 1996; Rosenfeld and Bautista 2017).

Christine A. Hastorf (2007) has discussed two types of rituals that are relevant to our interest in the intersection of ritual and inequality in the Andes.

One type of ritual is inclusive, and one is exclusive. The inclusive type of ritual can be conceptualized as communally oriented, and it often included spaces for gathering, feasting, and ancestor veneration. This type of ritual highlighted performance and participation to build and maintain a sense of community. Another type of ritual highlights and displays exclusion through the use of architecture and artifacts that only some could access. This type of ritual created and maintained social hierarchy and inequality (Hastorf 2007:84).

At Chavín de Huántar, the labyrinth-like galleries and the placement of most of the images high on walls and around columns suggest restricted access to the experiences occurring in many areas of the monumental core (Burger 1992; Rick 2005). John W. Rick (2005) argued that the ceremonial center at Chavín de Huántar was a place where cult information was given by and to a privileged group of people. In this sense, there is evidence that points to the use of ritual in creating and supporting social inequality at Chavín de Huántar. However, there are also large public spaces (such as the Square Plaza) that could have held large numbers of pilgrims visiting the site (Burger 2013). The presence of elite or commoner pilgrims in the open spaces was probably visible by the people in La Banda, a sector located across the river from the monumental center. Here, we seek to investigate the La Banda community's involvement with the ritual activities and the people performing and participating at the center.

Inequality

Inequality, at least in the form of age and sex, is ubiquitous in human societies. The debate is over when and how status differentiation became formalized or institutionalized in society. Institutionalized inequality refers to status differences that are inherited and socially reproduced and maintained over time. The appearance of formalized inequality provided the foundation for the development of more complex hierarchical forms of organization (Price and Feinman 1995). Some scholars have drawn direct connections between early temples and ritual, credit economies, and surplus food storage in ancient Mesopotamia (Graeber 2011; Scott 2017). In the ancient Americas, research on the origins of socioeconomic inequality has mostly been approached through the analysis of settlement patterns, ceramic styles, monumental construction, and human burials (e.g., Flannery and Marcus 2012; Garraty and Stark 2010; Kohler et al. 2017; Papadopoulos and Urton 2012; Stanish 2001). While the transition from egalitarian to ranked societies may have begun as early as 3000 BC in the Central Andes (Shady Solís 2006), the Formative period (1500–200 BC) is considered a time when social, political, and economic inequality qualitatively increased and became institutionalized (e.g., Burger 1992; Dulanto, this volume; Kaulicke 2010; Onuki 1995; Rick 2006, 2008; Sayre 2018; see Seki, this volume).

The empirical evidence for the existence of strong asymmetrical relations can be materialized by the presence of highly elaborated architecture, carved stones, and refined ceramics. Certain sites show facilities that were costly in terms of the resources and labor required to build them. The conclusion is that this indicates the presence of some type of asymmetric power with enough authority to organize and carry out such endeavors. In particular, Chavín de Huántar, with its complex architecture and intricate sculptural art, has been the focus of research on the evolution of authority and power (Rick 2005, 2008), as the scale of building (platforms, galleries, plazas, and canals) implies the ability by some to mobilize labor and resources. Chavín de Huántar appears to be a good example of an early concentration of power in a religious elite with continuity across time. While research is being conducted on understanding the development of a convincing system by the religious leaders of Chavín de Huántar (Rick 2005), less research has been done on those who were on the lower end of the power spectrum and who lived their daily lives outside of the temple. One exception to this is Richard L. Burger's (1984) excavations of residential occupations underneath the contemporary town of Chavín de Huántar. This bottom-up perspective has been missing from much research on the origins of social inequality (see Schortman and Urban 2004 for a summary on different models). This area of inquiry is important because recent research shows that at least some of the people living in La Banda and elsewhere outside of Chavín de Huántar's monumental core were involved in manufacturing prestige and utilitarian artifacts to be used in the temple as well as by the inhabitants of the site (Burger 1984; Sayre, Miller, and Rosenfeld 2016).

Edward M. Schortman and Patricia A. Urban (2004:187) have already drawn attention to the connections between the production, distribution, and use of specific crafts and the processes of social differentiation and inequality. Since rituals can form the basis of ideological power (*sensu* Earle 1997), those items produced for ritual practices can be key for authority building and power continuity (DeMarrais, Castillo, and Earle 1996; Vaughn 2006). The paraphernalia used during ceremonies and rituals at Chavín de Huántar most probably had ideological content, such as signifying individual social position and political power. The restriction in their production and circulation can be a way to maintain the value and exclusive associations of these artifacts (DeMarrais, Castillo, and Earle 1996). In this sense, understanding the production, distribution, consumption, and access of skillfully crafted artifacts—including artifacts made of bone and shell, like those recovered in La Banda—can shed light on social differentiation and inequality at Chavín de Huántar.

Archaeological Background

The occupations in La Banda are roughly contemporary with the Black and White phase. The Black and White phase is a chronological term for one of the architectural stages in the monumental core of Chavín de Huántar and dates between 1000 and 550 BC (all dates presented in this chapter are calibrated) (Kembel and Haas 2015; Rick 2008:11). During this phase, all or portions of the galleries in Buildings A and B as well as in the East Area, were apparently constructed (Kembel 2008:44). Kembel writes that "in the final monumental stage, the Black and White Stage, site-wide additions, including plazas, terraces, and open staircases, are built with high levels of symmetry, decorated fine stonework, and standardized galleries" (Kembel 2008:45). This phase occurs when the site was at its peak and when many previously open gallery patios are covered. This change in the spatial layout of the site reflects an increasing importance in controlling how visitors experienced the temple. Importantly, the broad span of time encompassed by the Black and White phase corresponds to the chronology of occupation in the La Banda sector (Sayre 2010). The La Banda occupation has also been associated with abundant Janabarriu-style ceramics, which have been dated to 700–400 BC (cf. Burger 2019; Rick et al. 2010). As defined by Burger (1984, 1992), the Janabarriu style includes polished red and black wares with designs made by stamps and seals, circles, stamped circles and dots, and S-shaped forms.

Previous Excavations in the La Banda Sector

There is a long history of excavations at the site of Chavín de Huántar (Burger 1984, 1992; Contreras 2007:14; Lumbreras 1989; Rick et al. 2010; Tello 1943). Much of the previous research focused on the ceremonial core of the monument (e.g., Kembel 2008; Lumbreras 1977, 1993; Mesía Montenegro 2007; Rick 2008; Rowe 1963). Other foci of research include the West Field (Contreras 2007, 2010, 2015), the area

underneath the modern town (Burger 1984), and the area of La Banda (Burger 2013; Gamboa 2016; Rick et al. 2010; Sayre 2010). Most pertinent to this chapter is Burger's excavations to the west of the ceremonial core, where household foundations and refuse were recovered (Burger 1984, 1992; Miller and Burger 1995; see discussion below).

In 2003, the construction of a road through the La Banda sector uncovered extensive settlements. The Peruvian Ministry of Culture and a Stanford University team conducted rescue excavations (Rick et al. 2010). The course of the road was eventually changed to avoid the destruction of the archaeologically significant area. As an intact Formative-period domestic sector close to the monumental center, it offers an opportunity to investigate the lives of Chavín de Huántar's inhabitants. Remains of domestic settlements were found in the La Banda sector that date from the same time as the height of temple activity at Chavín de Huántar (ca. 900–500 BC; see Rick et al. 2010; Sayre 2010). Until the excavations at La Banda, it was presumed that the residential areas connected to the temple were located beneath the modern town of Chavín de Huántar (Burger 1984, 1992). With the La Banda discovery, it became clear that there were significant Chavín-era residential sectors other than the constructions under modern Chavín de Huántar (see also Gamboa 2016). The La Banda occupations revealed a diverse array of artifacts, including Janabarriu-style ceramics, elaborate lithic technology, and artifacts manufactured from animal bone.

The 2003 rescue work in La Banda led to a detailed stratigraphic record of occupations in the region. One area in particular—Sector 3, Unit 5A, excavated by John Wolf—revealed eighteen stratigraphic layers. Six radiocarbon dates demonstrate that these layers date between 1300 and 400 BC and showed a heightened occupational presence between 800 and 400 BC (Rick et al. 2010:118–119). These portions of the La Banda sector also revealed the best evidence for status differentiation visible in the ceramic finds and architectural remains.

Systematic excavations in La Banda since 2005 have investigated the domestic areas (Sayre 2010). This sector is located directly east and slightly north

figure 3.2
Radiocarbon dates from La Banda. Chart by Matthew P. Sayre.

SAMPLE #	MEASURED RADIOCARBON AGE	CONVENTIONAL RADIOCARBON AGE	CALIBRATED DATE, 2 SIGMA
Beta-224479	2430 +/- 40 BP	2450 +/- 40 BP	Cal BC 760 to 400
Beta-224480	2630 +/- 40 BP	2660 +/- 40 BP	Cal BC 900 to 790
Beta-224481	2710 +/- 40 BP	2760 +/- 40 BP	Cal BC 1000 to 820
Beta-224482	2420 +/- 40 BP	2420 +/- 40 BP	Cal BC 750 to 680 and 670 to 610, and 600 to 400
Beta-224483	2590 +/- 50 BP	2620 +/- 50 BP	Cal BC 840 to 760
Beta-224484	2610 +/- 40 BP	2620 +/- 40 BP	Cal BC 830 to 770

of the Square Plaza of the monumental sector. During the dry season, the river is low enough to walk across in certain sections, and the ancient residents of La Banda could see and hear rituals and activities that took place in some parts of the ceremonial core of the site, such as the Square Plaza and the White and Black Portal. There are six radiocarbon samples from the 2005 excavations in the La Banda sector (Rick et al. 2010:100–101, table 2; Sayre 2010). The six dates overlap significantly (Sayre 2010:98, table 6.2) with a mean date of 755 BC. There is variation in these dates as they come from different stratigraphic contexts (Figure 3.2). Nevertheless, the mean date falls within the 95.4 percent confidence interval of nearly all radiocarbon samples from the sector. The occupation of La Banda is contemporaneous with the period associated with the height of activity at the monumental zone at Chavín de Huántar (900–500 BC) (Rick et al. 2010:100–101; Sayre 2010:97–98). This is also a period when the radiocarbon curve rests on a dating plateau.

There have been further excavations in the La Banda sector in 2003, 2005, 2012, 2013, and 2015 (see Figure 3.3). The areas between N400 and N500, and between E600 and 700, have revealed little evidence for Chavín-period occupations. While there are constructions, such as retaining walls from that time, there is no substantial domestic architecture (see Contreras 2007). The 2012 field excavations directed by Matthew P. Sayre confirmed the lack of domestic occupations in this area. Instead, the majority of the Chavín-period occupations have

been uncovered in the sectors from N500–700 and E600–800. These four hectares, along with the area from N300–400 E600–700, are the centers of clear Chavín-period domestic occupations. Further excavations around N700–800 E600–700 and N300–500 E700–800 will confirm the intensity of occupations in this sector of the site. At this point, it seems most appropriate to state that there was likely 6 ha of occupied land in La Banda.

The finding that there was approximately 6 ha of domestic occupation space led to an attempt to define the ancient population size of the sector. Population estimates are challenging, and different parameters for the estimates can lead to divergent outcomes. Estimates range from 30 people per hectare for highland agricultural villages in Mexico (De Roche 1983, cited in Chamberlain 2006:128) to 130 people per hectare for preindustrial urban centers (Storey 1997, cited in Chamberlain 2006:128). These numbers would lead to estimates of anywhere from 180 to 780 people in the La Banda sector. Burger estimates that during the Janabarriu phase there were 42 ha of inhabited land on the western bank of the Mosna River for a total population of 2,000–3,000 people (Burger 1984). This estimate assumes that there were roughly 50–70 people per hectare; if we apply these numbers to La Banda, then we are left with a population estimate of 300–420 people for this sector. Further excavation will refine the estimates on the number of households, which will allow us to state with greater confidence our approximations of the

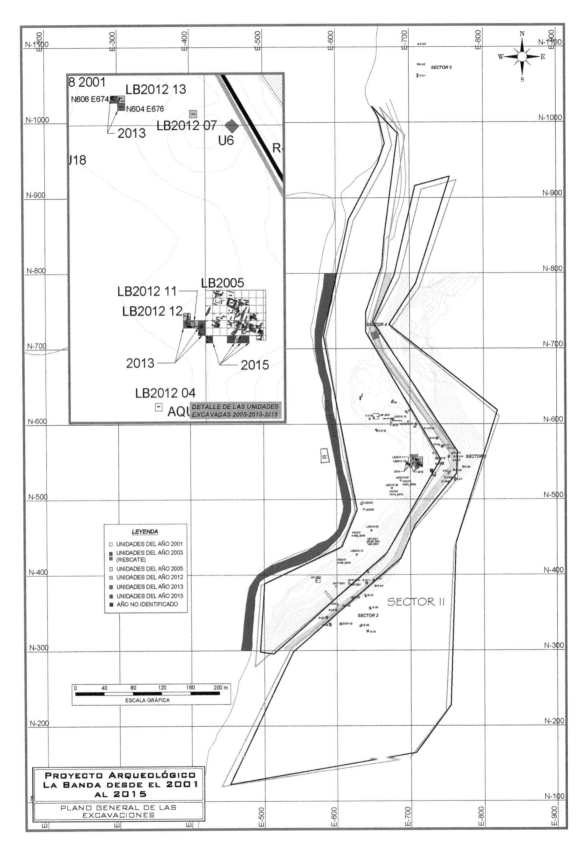

figure 3.3
Map of La Banda. Illustration by Diana Mogrovejo.

ancient population of La Banda. However, even that additional evidence is dependent upon our certainty of the contemporaneity of the houses and their numbers of inhabitants.

The finds in La Banda also revealed many types of materials of local and non-local origin (Figure 3.4), including marine shells and bone from the Pacific Ocean (Sayre and Aldave Lopez 2010; Sayre, Miller, and Rosenfeld 2016) and obsidian predominantly from the Quispisisa source (Burger, Mohr Chávez, and Chávez 2000; Tripcevich and Contreras 2013). Thus far, it appears that only La Banda and the areas underneath the modern town of Chavín de Huántar (Burger 1984) contain evidence for the production of goods. While the West Field contained evidence of ceremonial architecture (Contreras 2010) and the Wacheqsa sector revealed stone rooms and midden deposits (Mesía Montenegro 2007, 2014, 2022), there were no other sectors that contained units with extensive evidence of elite goods production. However, further excavations outside of the main temple area are needed to verify if there is differentiation in goods production by sectors across the settlement.

Excavations in La Banda uncovered a domestic group organized into at least three major architectural divisions (AD), which were subdivided into architectural subdivisions (ASD). The largest division in this area, ADB, was the space that expanded out from the stone patio (Figure 3.1). The patio group revealed living spaces north of the patio and a workshop to produce goods located off the patio. The workshop, predominantly uncovered in unit K-13 (ASD 7, Figure 3.1), covered an extension of at least 4 m², and it included distinct objects, such as artifacts manufactured of shell and bone (Figure 3.5). These artifacts were found surrounding a stone hearth feature that had an air duct leading into it (Figure 3.6). This feature may have been used for heat-tempering materials as well as heating water and other elements used to transform the raw materials encountered in the unit. Marine shells (*Argopecten purpuratus*) covered with red pigment (presumably cinnabar) were recovered in this area. These shells had holes drilled in their lower center portion, which would have enabled people to hang the pieces on clothing or to use them as adornments (Sayre, Miller, and Rosenfeld 2016).

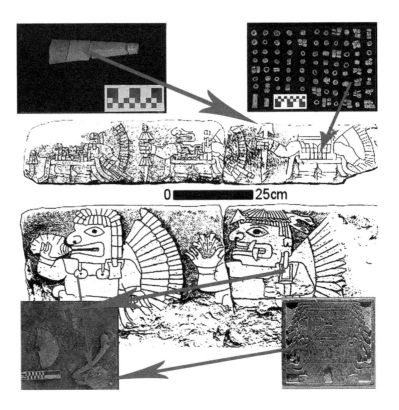

figure 3.5
Artifacts in relation to site iconography. Photographs by Nick Weiland, line drawing courtesy of John W. Rick.

0 ▬▬▬ 25cm

figure 3.6
Artistic depiction of hearth and artifact production. Illustration by Kathryn Killackey.

Inequality at Chavín de Huántar

Ritual Architecture and Inequality

Chavín de Huántar has long been understood as a religious center in which ceremonies occurred in various contexts (e.g., Burger 1992; Contreras 2010, 2017; Rick 2008, 2017; Tello 1960). The ceremonial function of the site is based on several elements: clean and open plazas, underground galleries, massive platforms, supernatural depictions on carved stones, and the presence of ceremonial paraphernalia such as spoons and tubes related to psychotropic consumption (Burger 2013; Rick 2017; Rowe 1963).

Rick (2017) has argued that the design and configuration of Chavín architecture emphasizes the presence of high-ranked individuals who had specific strategies to enhance and manipulate the experience of the ritual participants. While the Lanzón monolith, the circular and square plazas, and the Black and White Portal were probably some of the foci of ceremonies, Rick also details a variety of less conspicuous ritual locations, including pits, construction fills, and underground galleries and canals. In this sense, Rick interprets the complex design and content of part of the canals as places where water-related rituals took place. The concentration of complete, but smashed, vessels at the intersection of canals is understood as an indication of possible locations of ritual sacrifice or offerings. These water-related rituals were perhaps performed to control the risks and outcomes involving water's energy, which would have been part of the complex belief system at the temple of Chavín. Rick (2017:46) concludes that ritual would have integrated those who participated in the ritual process and differentiated them from those who did not participate.

Daniel A. Contreras (2017) argues that a diversity in ritual architecture demonstrates that a variety of social and religious sources existed contemporaneously at Chavín. Contreras (2010) analyzes the Mito-style architecture in the West Field sector at the margins of the site of Chavín de Huántar and evaluates its relationship to the contemporaneous use of monumental structures in the core of the Chavín landscape. Most of the main features of the Mito Tradition found at the site of Kotosh—the quadrangular room, the central hearth, the split-level floor, the niches, and the use of plaster (Bonnier 1997:137, fig. 111)—are present in the Chavín de Huántar example (Contreras 2017:55). A hearth similar to Mito-style constructions was also excavated in 2002 in the La Banda sector, in an area removed from the domestic excavations (Rick et al. 2010). Contreras (2017) argues that diversity in ritual architecture allowed authorities to reinforce different ritual practices at this early ceremonial complex.

The above research reveals some of the arguments in favor of the presence of ritual in a variety of contexts in the ceremonial center and in the West Field. Neither of these two areas had any remains of domestic dwellings. In contrast, in the La Banda sector, domestic dwellings have been excavated, but no obvious ritual activity or ritual architecture associated with domestic occupations has been detected to date. However, exotic objects probably used for ritual paraphernalia in the ceremonial area were recovered.

Exotics, Crafts, and Inequality

Julio C. Tello (1943, 1960), the father of Peruvian archaeology, was the first to systematically relate the iconography of Chavín de Huántar and its depictions of exotic plants and animals to similar iconography in various media at other sites throughout Peru. The Tello Obelisk likely depicts caimans, tropical plants, and animals that live across the Andes and in the jungle. The clear depiction of Amazonian, or tropical Ecuadorian, imagery led to further debate surrounding Chavín's connections to the tropical lowlands (see Clasby, this volume). Donald W. Lathrap (1973) posits that the origins of the civilization itself might lie in the eastern jungles, but as stated by Burger (1992:154), there is little material evidence to support this claim.

Much research has been conducted on the implications of Chavín de Huántar's interaction with distant regions (Burger and Nesbitt, this volume; Contreras 2011; Lumbreras 1989; Matsumoto et al. 2018; Rick et al. 2010). These studies are based on the known provenience of non-local material found at the site, such as cinnabar (Burger and Matos Mendieta 2002; Young, this volume), marine

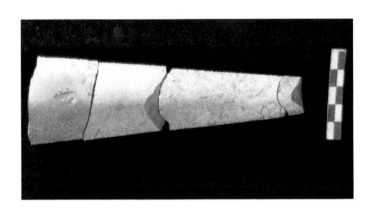

figure 3.7
Finely polished lithic
piece recovered from four
separate units. Photograph
by Nick Weiland.

shells (Rick 2008; Sayre and Aldave Lopez 2010), obsidian (Burger 1992), and marine mammal bones (Sayre, Miller, and Rosenfeld 2016). Marine mammal bones were transported to Chavín and probably worked at La Banda, where they were found along with bone tools in different stages of production. Many objects uncovered in La Banda were found in the process of manufacture, thus providing greater insight into the production of value in Chavín times (Rosenfeld and Sayre 2016). Because the marine mammal bones were recovered from a workshop area, they could have been transported unmodified, or as preforms, from the coast and carved on site. If these bones had been transported as finished artifacts, they would likely be found in a use location context rather than in a manufacturing area. The lack of unfinished ceremonial artifacts in the main temple suggests that these processes were intentionally separated from the ritual space. Other crafts, such as objects made from the marine shells spondylus and strombus, have been found in completed form in offering contexts in the Ofrendas and Caracolas Gallery at the main temple (Lumbreras 1989; Rick 2005).

From a ritual economy perspective, Patricia A. McAnany and E. Christian Wells (2008) emphasize provision and consumption, practice materialization, and the important role of ritual in giving meaning and shaping the interpretation of the experience. Provision and consumption are part of the reproduction of social relationships. The provision of certain crafts by the people living in La Banda emphasized their status in the society as well as with the consumers of those artifacts who organized and

experienced ritual in the ceremonial center. Many of the objects produced probably carried meaning beyond a utilitarian purpose. Chavín-era priests may have encouraged the production of the materials that they would wear, thus indirectly increasing the prestige codified in these artifacts as used in their religious practices. Some of the materials, such as the worked marine mammal bone artifacts and a large lithic staff found broken in four pieces (Figure 3.7), clearly required extensive specialized knowledge to produce. Similar objects to those found in the process of production in La Banda were excavated as finished objects in the monumental center, and some also appear to have correlates in the iconography. The marine ornamental pieces, camelid bone beads, elaborate lithic piece, and marine shells all have visual correlates to the main temple stone iconography depicting priests marching in processions (Sayre, Miller, and Rosenfeld 2016:413). These objects materialized some of the practices and relationships that (at least some) Chavínos and pilgrims had during ritual. The elaborate architecture and iconography undoubtedly provided a particular meaning to the ritual and a specific worldview that selected people were able to consume and perhaps later share when they returned home (Burger 2013).

Food and Inequality

Looking at disparities in access to food resources offers one approach to social differentiation in the past (e.g., Cuéllar 2013; Curet and Pestle 2010; De France 2009). Zooarchaeology can provide insight into the differential consumption of animal species, meat cuts, and cooking practices (such as boiling,

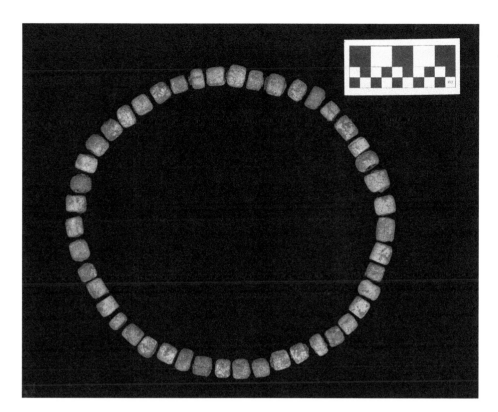

figure 3.8
Bone beads recovered in
La Banda. Photograph
courtesy of Nick Weiland.

roasting, etc.) across a site. George Miller and Burger (1995) studied faunal evidence from a unit underlying the modern town of Chavín de Huántar and two units on the southwest edge of the archaeological site to argue for a pattern of imported dried camelid meat (*chʾarki*). While there are critiques of this model, separate research has revealed alternative possibilities (Stahl 1999; Valdez 2000). Extensive faunal analysis from thirty-two excavation units in La Banda (Rosenfeld and Sayre 2016) has started to shed light on the cultural complexity of the resident population of Chavín de Huántar in terms of meat acquisition and consumption. Results from the skeletal part analysis, the food utility index, and the high presence of podials at La Banda suggest that whole camelids were transported to this sector of Chavín de Huántar (Rosenfeld and Sayre 2016:fig. 5, tables 3–4). La Banda inhabitants used most of the camelid carcass and selected different parts for meat consumption and tool manufacture. The people who worked in the La Banda workshop appear to have cooked their own food, as indicated by high fresh bone fragmentation. This was possibly done to extract marrow or to make the bones fit in cooking

pots. Bones also showed cutmarks and evidence for burning, suggesting food preparation and discard. The people who inhabited La Banda had access to whole camelid carcasses, possibly in connection with their activity as craft producers. The presence of a workshop is evident, given the specimens of different stages in the manufacture of bone artifacts (Figure 3.8) (Rosenfeld and Sayre 2016). Perhaps the La Banda residents, as a group involved in manufacturing artifacts, were interested in receiving full carcasses, including less meaty bones (lower extremities) suitable for craft activities.

It is possible that the activity and status of different groups in Chavín de Huántar influenced differential access to food resources (Miller and Burger 1995). In sectors like La Banda, discarded bone remains may have subsequently been used for crafting. The people from the La Banda sector had access to all camelid skeletal elements, and they used metapodials to manufacture elaborate objects, such as beads and tablets. An alternative explanation is that people at La Banda ate *chʾarki* (thus the presence of the meatier bones) and that they received through other means the less meaty bones used for artifact manufacture. It is obviously difficult to prove that different skeletal elements belonged to the same carcass, especially when they were highly fragmented, as in this case. Nonetheless, if the La Banda people were solely receiving metapodials for bone manufacture (already de-fleshed somewhere else), then the presence of a large quantity of podials at the site remains unexplained (Rosenfeld and Sayre 2016).

Perhaps social differentiation within Chavín de Huántar influenced meat consumption patterns, as has been hypothesized by Miller and Burger (1995). It is possible that, in other areas of La Banda and in other sectors of Chavín de Huántar, local *ch'arki* preparation played a role in extending the availability of meat during certain parts of the year. Evaluation of this hypothesis entails further analysis in those sectors where data may show *ch'arki* consumption, which was not the case in the La Banda sector excavated to date. The current zooarchaeological evidence (Miller and Burger 1995; Rosenfeld and Sayre 2016) shows that multiple production strategies probably occurred at Chavín de Huántar, demonstrating the socioeconomic complexity of the people who lived and worked around the monumental center.

There is a need for further paleoethnobotanical work to answer more social questions about plant use at the site (Sayre and Bruno 2017). The macrobotanical remains revealed a diet focused on local goods such as quinoa (*Chenopodium quinoa*), tubers (*Solanum* sp., and others), and maize (*Zea mays*) (Sayre 2010, 2023). Phytolith analysis revealed local goods such as maize as well as the presence of some non-local plants, such as bottle gourd (*Lagenaria* sp.) (Sayre 2010, 2023). Preliminary starch grain analysis has revealed the presence of local plants as well as some non-local plants such as manioc (*Manihot esculenta*) and sweet potato (*Ipomea batatas*) (Sadie Weber, personal communication 2018). This raises important questions about the status of exotic foods in the ritual economy. Also, if further excavations reveal that the plant remains solely contain species of local origins with limited evidence of long-term storage, with a slight presence of non-local plants, this is more evidence for answering the questions about which types of pilgrims were visiting the La Banda sector. Were these visitors capable of arranging for the large-scale transportation of food goods? The presence of exotic plants can be considered a form of wealth exchange or luxury food exchange (Hastorf 2003).

Discussion and Conclusion

There are tensions between the inclusive/communal rituals and exclusive/individualized rituals (Hastorf 2007) discussed above. Research to date has not fully resolved which of these types better describes the ritual activity at Chavín de Huántar. The Formative period in the Andes is considered a time when social, political, and economic inequality increased (e.g., Kaulicke 1998; Onuki 1995; Rick 2006, 2008). It could certainly be the case that there was an ongoing change in ritual practice that coincided with economic transformations that were occurring in the Formative period. The production of goods for priests, as seen in the La Banda sector (Rosenfeld and Sayre 2016; Sayre, Miller, and Rosenfeld 2016), can be indicative of both inclusive and exclusive ritual. This paraphernalia would be a powerful symbol of status in both open, large-scale events as well as in more intimate events where elite participants were face-to-face with Chavín priests in small, enclosed spaces.

Ritual at Chavín de Huántar can be interpreted as inclusive if it was communally oriented or if it included spaces for gathering, feasting, and ancestor veneration. Inclusive ritual at Chavín highlighted performances for local and non-local audiences to build and maintain a sense of "Chavín" community. Burger (2013:325–326) has suggested that the La Banda region was where pilgrims likely stayed during their visit to the temple. These common people would engage in market-like activities and communal rituals in the ceremonial center. If ritual at the site was more inclusive, then we would expect further investigations to find evidence for common goods (i.e., lower status foods and raw materials) being brought as tribute and/or exchanged for Chavín-style artifacts. Continued investigations in the sector will help to resolve this issue.

figure 3.9
The Lanzón. Photograph
courtesy of Nick Weiland.

The argument that ritual at Chavín de Huántar was exclusive and limited to a small number of elite pilgrims has primarily been advanced by Rick (2007) and Luis G. Lumbreras (1989). Evidence for this claim is visible in the main temple area, as the occupation sequence reveals that the temple increasingly emphasized the segregated and tight spaces of the galleries over those of more public ceremonial spaces (Kembel 2008). Pilgrims gained knowledge that permitted them to enhance their differences in their home communities. These exclusive pilgrims did not gather in La Banda but rather brought with them exotic raw materials that would be transformed into paraphernalia by the La Banda residents.

It seems apparent that ritual at Chavín could have been both inclusive and exclusive (Contreras 2010). The La Banda sector would serve as a gathering and production area for pilgrims of all statuses. The architecture of the main temple area certainly lends itself to the idea that ritual practices at the site were both exclusive and inclusive. The Square Plaza was a later addition to the site; its construction involved the movement of the Mosna River, and its large open space would certainly have been capable of fitting large numbers of pilgrims or visitors (Kembel 2008; Turner, Knight, and Rick 1999). However, the confined spaces of the galleries meant that only limited numbers of people could have entered these spaces at a specific point in time. This is also the case for the most famous gallery and sculpture found at the site, the Lanzón (Figure 3.9). The transition from large open spaces, through the more enclosed Circular Plaza, into the tightly confined spaces of the galleries was a transition across liminal spaces into more marked and enclosed domains of the few.

The nature of the ritual and economic practices at Chavín de Huántar has implications beyond the site; it helps to reveal broader trends that were occurring in the Central Andes during the Formative period. This paper has focused on the La Banda sector of the site, which unlike the main ceremonial temple, has evidence to support the idea that people lived and worked in the area (Burger 1984). The location where goods were produced can inform us of how the people of Chavín de Huántar and La Banda conceived space. Many objects uncovered in La Banda were found in the process of manufacture, thus providing a greater insight into the production of value in Chavín times. The marine mammal bones were uncovered near other artifacts that were being modified for final use. If these pieces had been transported as finished artifacts, then they would likely be found in a location of use, not in a manufacturing area. This contrasts with the camelid bone beads mentioned earlier that were found whole and in different stages of production in the same workshop area. The absence of unfinished ceremonial artifacts in the main temple suggests that these processes were intentionally separated from this ceremonial space. Other crafts, such as the objects made from the marine shells spondylus and strombus, have been found in completed form in offering contexts in the Ofrendas and Caracolas Gallery at the main temple (Lumbreras 1989; Rick 2005). The artifacts to be worn by the priests were not found in sufficient quantity to make a solid conclusion about whether common goods were being produced in massive quantities for lower-status pilgrims. The evidence is clearer that elite goods were being produced in this sector and that these goods were likely worn by priests in the ceremonial center. These results complement earlier work on the residential populations living to the west of the monumental core. In this area, Burger (1984) identified evidence for craft specialization and the production of bone tools, beads, and spondylus jewelry, as well as evidence for hide working. There is now clear evidence that the people who lived and worked in the La Banda sector were engaged in the exchange of lightweight but high-status goods. In contrast, there is little evidence for the trade and exchange of commodities, such as maize, potatoes, or ch'arki, during this time period in this sector. This evidence coincides with other arguments that emphasize that the movement of large quantities of commodities is only possible once greater regional integration has occurred (D'Altroy et al. 1985; Jennings 2006). The research in La Banda has revealed a local economy embedded in regional exchange networks. The trade of exotic goods and the production of material goods for the ceremonial center clarify how the sacred and the profane could be physically separated yet connected through social and cultural relationships.

Bauer, Brian S., and Charles Stanish

2001   *Ritual and Pilgrimage in the Ancient Andes: The Islands of the Sun and the Moon.* University of Texas Press, Austin.

Bell, Catherine M.

1992   *Ritual Theory, Ritual Practice.* Oxford University Press, New York.

Benson, Elizabeth P., and Anita G. Cook (editors)

2001   *Ritual Sacrifice in Ancient Peru.* University of Texas Press, Austin.

Bonnier, Elizabeth

1997   Preceramic Architecture in the Andes: The Mito Tradition. In *Archaeologica peruana 2,* edited by Elizabeth Bonnier and Henning Bischof, pp. 120–144. Sociedad Arqueológica Peruano-Alemana, Mannheim.

Burger, Richard L.

1984   *The Prehistoric Occupation of Chavín de Huántar, Peru.* University of California Press, Berkeley.

1992   *Chavín and the Origins of Andean Civilization.* Thames and Hudson, London.

2013   In the Realm of the Incas: An Archaeological Reconsideration of Household Exchange, Long-Distance Trade, and Marketplaces in the Pre-Hispanic Central Andes. In *Merchants, Markets, and Exchange in the Pre-Columbian World,* edited by Kenneth G. Hirth and Joanne Pillsbury, pp. 321–336. Dumbarton Oaks Research Library and Collection, Washington, D.C.

2019   Understanding the Socioeconomic Trajectory of Chavín de Huántar: A New Radiocarbon Sequence and Its Wider Implications. *Latin American Antiquity* 30(2):373–392.

Burger, Richard L., and Ramiro Matos Mendieta

2002   Atalla: A Center on the Periphery of the Chavín Horizon. *Latin American Antiquity* 13:153–177.

Burger, Richard L., Karen Mohr Chávez, and Sergio J. Chávez

2000   Through the Glass Darkly: Prehispanic Obsidian Procurement and Exchange in Southern Peru and Northern Bolivia. *Journal of World Prehistory* 14:267–362.

Chamberlain, Andrew T.

2006   *Demography in Archaeology.* Cambridge University Press, Cambridge.

Contreras, Daniel A.

2007   Sociopolitical and Geomorphologic Dynamics at Chavín de Huántar, Peru. PhD dissertation, Stanford University, Stanford.

2010   A Mito-Style Structure at Chavín de Huántar: Dating and Implications. *Latin American Antiquity* 21(1):3–21.

2011   How Far to Conchucos? A GIS Approach to Assessing the Implications of Exotic Materials at Chavín de Huántar. *World Archaeology* 43 (3):380–397.

2015   Landscape Setting as Medium of Communication at Chavín de Huántar, Peru. *Cambridge Archaeological Journal* 25:513–530.

2017   Not Just a Pyramid Scheme? Diversity in Ritual Architecture at Chavín de Huántar. In *Rituals of the Past: Prehispanic and Colonial Case Studies in Andean Archaeology,* edited by Silvana Rosenfeld and Stefanie Bautista, pp. 51–78. University of Colorado Press, Boulder.

Cook, Anita, and Nicole Benco

2000   Vasijas para la fiesta y la fama: Producción artesanal en un centro urbano huari. *Boletín de Arqueología PUCP* 4:489–504.

Cuéllar, Ana M.

2013   The Archaeology of Food and Social Inequality in the Andes. *Journal of Archaeological Research* 21:123–174.

Curet, Antonio L., and William J. Pestle

2010   Identifying High-Status Foods in the Archaological Record. *Journal of Anthropological Archaeology* 29:413–431.

D'Altroy, Terence N., Timothy K. Earle, David L. Browman, Darrell La Lone, Michael E. Moseley, John V. Murra, Thomas P. Myers, Frank Salomon, Katharina J. Schreiber, and John R. Topic

    1985   Staple Finance, Wealth Finance, and Storage in the Inka Political Economy [and Comments and Reply]. *Current Anthropology* 26(2):187–206.

De France, Susan

    2009   Zooarchaeology in Complex Societies: Political Economy, Status, and Ideology. *Journal of Archaeological Research* 17:105–168.

DeMarrais, Elizabeth, Luis Jaime Castillo, and Timothy Earle

    1996   Ideology, Materialization, and Power Strategies. *Current Anthropology* 37:15–31.

De Roche, Charles D.

    1983   Population Estimates from Settlement Area and Number of Residences. *Journal of Field Archaeology* 10:187–192.

Earle, Timothy K.

    1997   *How Chiefs Come to Power: The Political Economy in Prehistory*. Stanford University Press, Stanford.

Flannery, Kent, and Joyce Marcus

    2012   *The Creation of Inequality: How Our Prehistoric Ancestors Set the Stage for Monarchy, Slavery, and Empire*. Harvard University Press, Cambridge, Mass.

Gamboa, Jorge

    2016   Las ocupaciones formativas en La Banda: Excavaciones durante la construcción de la cariante Chavín y su impacto socioeconómico en el Valle del Mosna. In *Arqueología de la Sierra de Ancash 2: Población y territorio*, edited by Bebel Ibarra Asencios, pp. 53–76. Instituto de Estudios Huarinos, Huari, Ancash.

Garraty, Charles P., and Barbara Stark

    2010   *Archaeological Approaches to Market Exchange in Ancient Societies*. University Press of Colorado, Boulder.

Geertz, Clifford

    1973   *The Interpretation of Cultures: Selected Essays*. Basic Books, New York.

Graeber, David

    2011   *Debt: The First 5,000 Years*. Melville House Publishing, Brooklyn.

Hastorf, Christine A.

    2003   Community with the Ancestors: Ceremonies and Social Memory in the Middle Formative at Chiripa, Bolivia. *Journal of Anthropological Archaeology* 22:305–332.

    2007   Archaeological Andean Rituals: Performance, Liturgy, and Meaning. In *The Archaeology of Ritual*, edited by Evangelos Kyriakidis, pp. 77–108. Cotsen Institute of Archaeology, University of California, Los Angeles.

Hodder, Ian

    2010   *Religion in the Emergence of Civilization: Çatalhöyük as a Case Study*. Cambridge University Press, Cambridge.

Insoll, Timothy

    2004   *Archaeology, Ritual, Religion*. Routledge, London.

Jennings, Justin

    2006   Understanding Middle Horizon Peru: Hermeneutic Spirals, Interpretative Traditions, and Wari Administrative Centers. *Latin American Antiquity* 17:265–285.

Kaulicke, Peter

    1998   *Max Uhle y el Perú antiguo*. Fondo Editorial, Pontificia Universidad Católica del Perú, Lima.

    2010   *Las cronologías del formativo: 50 años de investigaciones japonesas en perspectiva*. Fondo Editorial, Pontificia Universidad Católica del Perú, Lima.

Kembel, Silvia R.

    2008   The Architecture at the Monumental Center of Chavín de Huántar: Sequence, Transformations, and Chronology. In *Chavín: Art, Architecture, and Culture*, edited by William J. Conklin and Jeffrey Quilter, pp. 35–81. Cotsen Institute of Archaeology, University of California, Los Angeles.

Kembel, Silvia R., and Herbert Haas

    2015   Radiocarbon Dates from the Monumental Architecture at Chavín de Huántar, Perú. *Journal of Archaeological Method and Theory* 22(2):345–427.

Kembel, Silvia R., and John W. Rick

2004   Building Authority at Chavín de Huántar:
        Models of Social Organization and
        Developments in the Initial Period and
        Early Horizon. In *Andean Archaeology*,
        edited by Helaine Silverman, pp. 51–76.
        Blackwell Publishing, Malden, Mass.

Kohler, Timothy A., Michael E. Smith, Amy Bogaard,
Gary M. Feinman, Christian E. Peterson, Alleen
Betzenhauser, and Matthew Pailes, et al.

2017   Greater Post-Neolithic Wealth Disparities
        in Eurasia than in North America and
        Mesoamerica. *Nature* 551:619–622.

Kolar, Miriam, John W. Rick, Perry R. Cook, and
Jonathan Abel

2012   Ancient *Pututus* Contextualized:
        Integrative Archaeoacoustics at Chavín
        de Huántar, Peru. In *Flower World: Music
        Archaeology of the Americas*, vol. 1, edited
        by Mathias Stöckli and Arnd Adje Both,
        pp. 23–53. Ekho Verlag, Berlin.

Kyriakidis, Evangelos (editor)

2007   *The Archaeology of Ritual*. Cotsen
        Institute of Archaeology, University
        of California, Los Angeles.

Lathrap, Donald W.

1973   Gifts of the Cayman: Some Thoughts
        on the Subsistence Basis of Chavín. In
        *Variations in Anthropology: Essays in
        Honor of John C. McGregor*, edited by
        Donald W. Lathrap and Jody Douglas,
        pp. 91–105. Illinois Archaeological Survey,
        Urbana.

Lumbreras, Luis G.

1977   Excavaciones en el Templo Antiguo de
        Chavin (Sector R): Informe de la sexta
        campaña. *Ñawpa Pacha: Journal of
        Andean Archaeology* 15:1–38.

1989   *Chavín de Huántar en el nacimiento de la
        civilización andina*. Instituto Andino de
        Estudios Arqueológicos, Lima.

1993   *Chavín de Huántar: Excavaciones en la
        Galería de las Ofrendas*. P. von Zabern,
        Mainz.

Marcus, Joyce, and Kent Flannery

2004   The Coevolution of Ritual and Society:
        New 14 C Dates from Ancient Mexico.
        *Proceedings of the National Academy of
        Sciences of the United States of America*
        101:18257–18261.

Matsumoto, Yuichi, Jason Nesbitt, Michael D.
Glascock, Yuri Cavero Palomino, and Richard L.
Burger

2018   Interregional Obsidian Exchange during
        the Late Initial Period and Early Horizon:
        New Perspectives from Campanayuq
        Rumi, Peru. *Latin American Antiquity*
        29:44–63.

McAnany, Patricia A., and E. Christian Wells

2008   Toward a Theory of Ritual Economy. In
        Dimensions of Ritual Economy, edited by
        Patricia A. McAnany and E. Christian
        Well, pp. 1–16. Emerald Group Publish-
        ing, Bingley.

Mesía Montenegro, Christian

2007   Intrasite Spatial Organization at Chavín
        de Huántar during the Andean Forma-
        tive: Three-Dimensional Modeling,
        Stratigraphy and Ceramics. PhD disserta-
        tion, Stanford University, Stanford.

2014   Festines y poder en Chavín de Huántar
        durante el período formativo tardío
        en los Andes Centrales. *Chungara*
        46:313–343.

2022   Social Complexity and Core-Periphery
        Relationships in an Andean Formative
        Ceremonial Centre: Domestic Occupa-
        tion at Chavín de Huántar. *Antiquity*
        96(388):883–902.

Miller, George, and Richard L. Burger

1995   Our Father the Cayman, Our Dinner
        the Llama: Animal Utilization at Chavín
        de Huántar, Peru. *American Antiquity*
        60:421–458.

Moore, Jerry D.

1996   *Architecture and Power in the Ancient
        Andes: The Archaeology of Public
        Buildings*. Cambridge University Press,
        Cambridge.

Onuki, Yoshio (editor)

1995   *Kuntur Wasi y Cerro Blanco: Dos sitios
        del formativo en el norte del Peru*.
        Hokusensha, Tokyo.

Papadopoulos, John K., and Gary Urton (editors)

2012   *The Construction of Value in the Ancient
        World*. Cotsen Institute of Archaeology,
        University of California, Los Angeles.

Pauketat, Timothy R., Lucretia S. Kelly, Gayle J. Fritz, Neal H. Lopinot, Scott Elias, and Eve Hargrave

2002   The Residues of Feasting and Public Ritual at Early Cahokia. *American Antiquity* 67:257–279.

Price, T. Douglas, and Gary M. Feinman

1995   Foundations of Prehistoric Social Inequality. In *Foundations of Social Inequality*, edited by T. Douglas Price and Gary M. Feinman, pp. 3–11. Springer, Boston.

Rappaport, Roy A.

1999   *Ritual and Religion in the Making of Humanity*. Cambridge University Press, Cambridge.

Rick, John W.

2005   The Evolution of Authority and Power at Chavín de Huántar, Peru. In *Foundations of Power in the Prehispanic Andes*, edited by Kevin J. Vaughn, Dennis Ogburn, and Christina A. Conlee, pp. 71–89. Archeological Papers of the American Anthropological Association 14. University of California Press, Berkeley.

2006   Chavín de Huántar: Evidence for an Evolved Shamanism. In *Mesas and Cosmologies in the Central Andes*, edited by Douglas Sharon, pp. 101–112. San Diego Museum of Man, San Diego.

2008   Context, Construction, and Ritual in the Development of Authority at Chavín de Huántar. In *Chavín: Art, Architecture, and Culture*, edited by William J. Conklin and Jeffrey Quilter, pp. 3–34. Cotsen Institute of Archaeology, University of California, Los Angeles.

2012   Realizing the Illustration Potential of Digital Models and Images: Beyond Visualization. In *Past Presented: Archaeological Illustration and the Ancient Americas*, edited by Joanne Pillsbury, pp. 413–438. Dumbarton Oaks Research Library and Collection, Washington, D.C.

2014   Cambio y continuidad, diversidad y coherencia: Perspectivas sobre variabilidad en Chavín de Huántar y el período formativo. In *El Centro ceremonial andino: Nuevas perspectivas para los períodos arcaico y formativo*, edited by

Yuji Seki, pp. 261–289. National Museum of Ethnology, Osaka.

2017   The Nature of Ritual Space at Chavín de Huántar. In *Rituals of the Past: Prehispanic and Colonial Case Studies in Andean Archaeology*, edited by Silvana A. Rosenfeld and Stefanie L. Bautista, pp. 21–50. University Press of Colorado, Boulder.

Rick, John W., Rosa Rick, Silvia Kembel, Daniel Contreras, Matthew P. Sayre, and John Wolf

2010   La cronología de Chavín de Huántar y sus implicancias para el período formativo. *Boletín de Arqueología PUCP* 13:87–132.

Rosenfeld, Silvana A., and Stefanie Bautista (editors)

2017   *Rituals of the Past: Prehispanic and Colonial Case Studies in Andean Archaeology*. University Press of Colorado, Boulder.

Rosenfeld, Silvana A., and Matthew P. Sayre

2016   Llamas on the Land: Production and Consumption of Meat at Chavín de Huántar, Peru. *Latin American Antiquity* 27:497–511.

Rowe, John H.

1963   Urban Settlements in Ancient Peru. *Ñawpa Pacha: Journal of Andean Archaeology* 1:1–27.

Sayre, Matthew P.

2010   Life across the River: Agricultural, Ritual, and Production Practices at Chavín de Huántar, Perú. PhD dissertation, University of California, Berkeley.

2018   The Historicity of the "Early Horizon." In *Constructions of Time and History in the Pre-Columbian Andes*, edited by Edward Swenson and Andrew Roddick, pp. 44–73. University Press of Colorado, Boulder.

2023   Plants and the Political Economy of Chavín de Huántar. *Senri Ethnological Studies* 112:107–125.

Sayre, Matthew P., and Natali Aldave Lopez

2010   Exchange at Chavín de Huántar: Insights from Shell Data. *Andean Past* 9:340–345.

Sayre, Matthew P., and Maria Bruno (editors)

2017   *Social Perspectives on Ancient Lives from Paleoethnobotanical Data*. Springer Press, New York.

Sayre, Matthew P., Melanie J. Miller, and Silvana A. Rosenfeld

    2016   Isotopic Evidence for the Trade and Production of Exotic Marine Mammal Bone Artifacts at Chavín de Huántar, Peru. *Archaeological and Anthropological Sciences* 8:403–417.

Scott, James C.

    2017   *Against the Grain: A Deep History of the Earliest States.* Yale University Press, New Haven.

Schortman, Edward M., and Patricia A. Urban

    2004   Modeling the Roles of Craft Production in Ancient Political Economies. *Journal of Archaeological Research* 12:185–226.

Shady Solís, Ruth

    2006   America's First City? The Case of Late Archaic Caral. In *Andean Archaeology III*, edited by William H. Isbell and Helaine Silverman, pp. 28–66. Springer, New York.

Stahl, Peter

    1999   Structural Density of Domesticated South American Camelid Skeletal Elements and the Archaeological Investigations of Prehistoric Andean Ch'arki. *Journal of Archaeological Science* 26:1347–1368.

Stanish, Charles

    2001   The Origins of State Societies in South America. *Annual Review of Anthropology* 30:41–64.

Storey, Glenn R.

    1997   Estimating the Population of Ancient Roman Cities. In *Integrating Archaeological Demography: Multidisciplinary Approaches to Prehistoric Population*, edited by Richard R. Paine, pp. 101–130. Center for Archaeological Investigations, Southern Illinois University, Carbondale.

Tello, Julio C.

    1943   Discovery of the Chavín Culture in Peru. *American Antiquity* 9:135–160.

    1960   *Chavín: Cultura matriz de la civilización andina.* Publicación Antropológica del Archivo "Julio C. Tello" de la Universidad Nacional Mayor de San Marcos, Lima.

Tripcevich, Nicholas, and Daniel A. Contreras

    2013   Archaeological Approaches to Obsidian Quarries: Investigations at the Quispisisa Source. In *Mining and Quarrying in the Ancient Andes: Sociopolitical, Economic and Symbolic Dimensions*, edited by Nicholas Tripcevich and Kevin Vaughn, pp. 23–44. Springer, New York.

Turner, Robert, Rosemary Knight, and John W. Rick

    1999   Geological Landscape of the Pre-Inca Archaeological Site at Chavín de Huántar, Peru. *Geological Survey of Canada Current Research* 1999-D:47–56.

Turner, Victor

    1967   *The Forest of Symbols: Aspects of Ndembu Ritual.* Cornell University Press, Ithaca, N.Y.

Valdez, Lidio M.

    2000   On Ch'arki Consumption in the Ancient Central Andes: A Cautionary Note. *American Antiquity* 65:567–572.

Vaughn, Kevin J.

    2006   Crafts and the Materialization of Chiefly Power in Nasca. *Archeological Papers of the American Anthropological Association* 14:113–130.

4

Archaeological Investigations of the Chavín Heartland

New Perspectives from Canchas Uckro

JASON NESBITT

A century of archaeological research at Chavín de Huántar has demonstrated its unique nature in comparison with its contemporaries (Tantaleán 2009). The distinctiveness of this center is seen in the scale and elaboration of the monumental core, which includes galleries, large plazas, and stone sculpture (Burger and Nesbitt, this volume; Rick this volume). For this reason, a great deal of scholarship emphasizes the ritual and ceremonial aspects of Chavín de Huántar (e.g., Burger 1992; Lumbreras 1989; Rick 2017). Recent investigation reveals a complex building history that transformed the temple between the late second and middle part of the first millennia BC (Kembel 2001, 2008; Kembel and Haas 2015; Rick 2008, this volume; Rick et al. 2010).

Despite a focus on the monumental architecture of the site, scholars studying the areas outside of the temple identified an extensive residential settlement (Burger 1984; Gamboa 2016; Sayre 2010; Sayre and Rosenfeld, this volume). Radiocarbon dating (all dates presented in this chapter are calibrated) indicates that this settlement was founded in the

Urabarriu phase (950–800 BC) and expanded in conjunction with the overall growth of the monumental sector of Chavín de Huántar (Burger 2019; Mesía-Montenegro 2022). By the Janabarriu phase (700–400 BC), residential occupations covered an area of 30–40 ha (Burger 1984, 2008a; Gamboa 2016; Sayre 2010). Furthermore, over the site's history, there was a dramatic population increase, from five hundred people in the Urabarriu phase to at least three thousand people in the Janabarriu phase, making Chavín de Huántar the largest highland center of its time (Burger 1984:247). By the Janabarriu phase, the residential zones housed a heterogenous population in terms of the social status and production activities of its inhabitants. An analysis of household contents reveals evidence for specialized craft production of quotidian and ceremonial objects that formed vital components of the political economy and ritual economy (Burger 1984; Rosenfeld and Sayre 2016; Sayre 2010; Sayre and Rosenfeld, this volume). Variation in the materials recovered from the houses also suggests social differentiation among the site's inhabitants (Burger 1984; Miller and Burger 1995; Sayre and Rosenfeld, this volume). Taken as a whole, this type of social and economic heterogeneity is a defining characteristic of preindustrial urbanism (e.g., Cowgill 2004; Jennings 2016); it supports descriptions of Chavín de Huántar as an urban or "proto-urban" center by 750/700 BC (Burger 1984; Burger and Nesbitt, this volume; Rowe 1963).

But how was Chavín de Huántar created in the first place? Like ancient urban centers in other parts of the world (Algaze 2018; Yoffee 2005), its origin and expansion were the partial result of people who moved into this center from the outside. From its inception around 1000 BC, a cosmopolitan ethos contributed to the formation of Chavín de Huántar, as exemplified by the adoption of foreign architectural elements (Burger and Salazar 2008), the existence of exotic artifacts (such as pottery, marine shell, and obsidian) in the temple core and residential sector (Burger 1984; Druc 2004; Lumbreras 1993, 2007; Sayre 2010; Sayre and López Aldave 2009; Sayre, Miller, and Rosenfeld 2016), and the presence of Amazonian-related imagery in the stone sculpture (Lathrap 1973).

Additionally, much of the substantial labor required to build the monumental center and to transform its immediate landscape required greater numbers of people than would have lived at the site (Contreras 2015; Contreras and Keefer 2009). A key question, therefore, centers on the origin of this labor and the nature of the communities that helped support Chavín de Huántar's growth and create its unique culture. Answering this question requires an examination of the "outer landscapes" (Smith 2014) of settlement that were dispersed throughout Chavín's heartland in the Conchucos[1] region of eastern Ancash. Yet, until recently few of these sites have been subjected to detailed research (but see Burger 1982; Nesbitt, Ibarra Asencios, and Tokanai 2020; Orsini 2014).

To that end, this chapter presents the results of recent archaeological investigations of Canchas Uckro, a site located above the Puccha River, just to the north of Chavín de Huántar. Canchas Uckro is significant because it dates between 1100 and 800/750 BC, thus providing a window into the period when Chavín de Huántar was coalescing as a major center (Kembel and Haas 2015). Research suggests that during the late Initial Period, Canchas Uckro functioned as a village and ceremonial center. During this time, the site displays some connections with the architecture and material culture of Chavín de Huántar. Nevertheless, there is other evidence, both architectural and ceramic, that suggests that Canchas Uckro was also embedded in interaction networks with the peoples inhabiting adjacent parts of the Eastern Andes and *ceja de selva*. Importantly, the site's abandonment occurred around 800–750 BC and corresponded to a time of settlement growth at Chavín de Huántar, as well as the expansion of the Chavín Interaction Sphere (Burger and Nesbitt, this volume). This chapter concludes with a discussion of the implications of the research at Canchas Uckro for understanding the socioeconomic conditions underlying the formation of Chavín de Huántar in the late second and early first millennia BC. I argue that Canchas Uckro, and sites like it, were instrumental in the process of creating Chavín de Huántar.

The Chavín Heartland

In *Chavín: Cultura matriz de la civilización andina,* Julio C. Tello (1960:147–157) reports the results of a pioneering survey undertaken in 1919 that followed the Puccha River on a route that connected Chavín de Huántar with the Upper Marañon. Along this transect, Tello and his colleagues record at least twenty-three archaeological sites that were related to Chavín. Sites such as Gotush, Runtu, Olayán, Matibamba, and Uchku-machay exhibited megalithic architecture, galleries, and stone sculpture with Chavín iconography (Espejo 1951, 1955; Rojas Ponce 1958; Tello 1960:147–157). As a result, Tello was the first to recognize that Chavín de Huántar was surrounded by a landscape of "secondary settlements" (Figure 4.1).

Tello's findings were bolstered by subsequent surveys in other parts of the Conchucos region, in which even greater numbers of contemporary sites

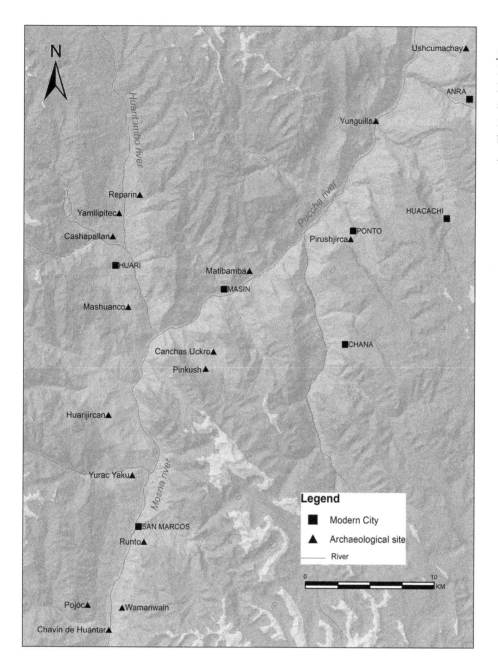

figure 4.1
Map of the Chavín heartland, showing sites mentioned in the text. Map by Bebel Ibarra Asencios.

were recorded (Amat 1971, 1976; Burger 1982, 2008a, 2008b; Diessl 2004; Espejo 1951, 1955; Herrera 2003; Ibarra Asencios 2003; Nesbitt, Ibarra Asencios, and Tokanai 2020; Orsini 2014). Secondary sites are characterized by small platform mounds that were rounded or rectangular in form (Diessl 2004). A survey of a sample of these sites in the Puccha drainage by Ibarra Asencios and Nesbitt indicates that those dating to the Initial Period and Early Horizon were 1–5 ha in size (Figure 4.2), making them considerably smaller than Chavín de Huántar

at its apex. While the survey of the region is still ongoing, most of the identified sites are in the mid-elevation *quechua* (3000–3500 masl) and high-elevation *puna* (3500–4000 masl) production zones. Preliminary surveys also demonstrate that some sites, such as Matibamba, as well as rock art sites with Initial Period iconography near Yunguilla and Allpash, were in the lower *yungas* situated on the valley floor of the Puccha River (1900–2200 masl) (Ibarra Asencios 2003; Nesbitt, Johnson, and Ibarra Asencios 2021; Tello 1960:156).

figure 4.2
The site of Pinkush, an Initial Period/ Early Horizon site near Canchas Uckro. Photograph by Jason Nesbitt.

Past prospection in the Puccha drainage (Diessl 2004; Ibarra Asencios 2003; Tello 1960), coupled with our more recent work, leads to an estimate of at least forty sites contemporary with Chavín de Huántar in this region. Yet it should be stressed that this estimate is conservative for several reasons. First, there are large stretches of land, particularly along the valley floors and in parts of the *puna*, that remain unexplored. In addition, the area between Masin and the Marañon, which connects with the Upper Amazon (Herrera Wassilowsky 2021), is also poorly studied, though Tello (1960; Rojas Ponce 1958) recorded some sites, suggesting that it was occupied during Chavín times (see also Nesbitt, Johnson, and Ibarra Asencios 2021:121). A second challenge in estimating settlement number is the recognition that many sites in the Conchucos region were occupied for long periods of time. Analysis of surface collections from sites surveyed along the Huaritambo and Puccha drainages has documented pottery styles

that date between the Initial Period/Early Horizon until, in some cases, the Late Intermediate Period (AD 1000–1450) (see also Ibarra Asencios 2003; Orsini 2014). The longevity of some of these sites is exemplified by excavations at Reparín, a site with Chavín-related architecture dating between 700 and 400 BC, which was subsequently covered by a large platform that was constructed in early Recuay times (AD 100–200) (Nesbitt, Ibarra Asencios, and Tokanai 2020). Without excavation, the deeply buried Early Horizon component of the site would not have been identified. Similar patterns of reoccupation have also been observed at Pojóc and Waman Wain, two Early Horizon village settlements located above Chavín de Huántar (Burger 1982).

These kinds of multi-component sites illustrate the difficulty of analyzing settlement patterns during Chavín times based on surface indications alone. That said, what is clear is that by just after 800 BC, Chavín de Huántar was between ten and forty times larger than its surrounding settlements. Surveys throughout the Conchucos region have failed to find sites of equivalent size, which reinforces the notion that Chavín de Huántar was radically different from these nearby settlements (Burger 2008a:697; Rick 2017:45). In overall terms, the extant information from these regional surveys support John Rowe's (1963) characterization of Chavín de Huántar as a "synchoritic city," an urban center that was surrounded by dispersed communities.

Thus, there is an emerging picture of a Chavín hinterland that consists of smaller sites distributed along the intermontane valleys of the Mosna and Puccha Rivers as well as other drainages within the Conchucos region of eastern Ancash. A great number of sites have been found in this region, but they have not been problematized with respect to their relationship with Chavín de Huántar. While these sites have been characterized as simple rural communities (Rick 2017:45), my research suggests that they were more complex. In the remainder of this chapter, I discuss the results of research at one of these sites: Canchas Uckro. Dating to the period

between 1100/1050 and 800/750 BC, Canchas Uckro was both a village and ceremonial center that was contemporary with the earliest phases of Chavín de Huántar. Excavations suggest that during the late second and early first millennia BC, Canchas Uckro might have been a peer center with early Chavín de Huántar, rather than simply a village-scale community.

The Landscape Setting of Canchas Uckro

At an altitude of 3190 masl, Canchas Uckro is located above the Puccha drainage near the town of Huachis, 22 km to the northeast of Chavín de Huántar. Canchas Uckro is situated on an earth-flow formation incised by two steep quebradas that border the site to the east and north–northwest (Figure 4.3). The positioning of Canchas Uckro recalls the concept of *tinkuy*, a place where two supernatural forces on the landscape converge. Interestingly, Chavín de Huántar is also placed within a similar landscape context at the juncture of

figure 4.3

The geographic location of Canchas Uckro atop a prominent earthflow that is incised on both sides by steep quebradas. Photograph by Jason Nesbitt.

the Huachecsa and Mosna Rivers (Burger 1992:130). Canchas Uckro has a direct view of the snowcapped peaks of the Cordillera Blanca to the west, as well as proximity to Cerro Pan de Azúcar, a prominent peak in the region. This positioning was probably part of the builder's intention to locate the site in a place that references several features within a ritually charged and animated landscape (*sensu* Contreras 2015).

Canchas Uckro was also in an economically propitious location, with access to the vertically stacked production zones that characterize the Andean highlands. The site is within the mid-elevation *quechua*, which today is an agriculturally rich production area where crops like maize can be cultivated. Above the site is the high-elevation *puna* grasslands, as well as the low-elevation *yungus* in the valley floor of the Puccha River. Archaeological evidence shows that each of these zones was within the catchment area of Canchas Uckro in terms of the subsistence economy. For instance, starch-grain analysis of pottery residues and isotopic analysis of human skeletal remains demonstrate that the people living at Canchas Uckro consumed manioc (*Manihot esculenta*), potato (*Solanum tuberosum*), and low quantities of maize (*Zea mays*) (Nesbitt et al. n.d.). Canchas Uckro's position along the Puccha River also places the site along natural routes into the eastern slopes and tropical forest regions of the *ceja de selva* (Nesbitt, Johnson, and Ibarra Asencios 2021).

Excavations of Canchas Uckro

Canchas Uckro consists of a two-tiered platform that measures approximately 60 (north–south) × 35 (east–west) m and at least 3 m in height (Figure 4.4). Surveys in the agricultural fields surrounding the platform have documented pottery scatters, suggesting that the site may have extended over an area of 4–5 ha. Platform revetment walls are visible on the surface and manufactured from large sandstone blocks. While a specific quarry has not yet been identified, sandstone outcrops are found in the immediate vicinity of Canchas Uckro and nearby parts of the Mosna River (Turner, Knight, and Rick 1999).

To date, excavations have focused on different parts of the platform, including the main facade, the summit, and the retaining walls along the northwest side of the building (Figures 4.5 and 4.6). These excavations have established that Canchas Uckro was built in two construction phases in which the platform was remodeled and enlarged horizontally. In the following sections, I outline this building sequence and its absolute chronology, which is based on thirteen radiocarbon measurements (Figure 4.7).

figure 4.4
Canchas Uckro in relation to the nearby Cerro Pan de Azúcar. Photograph by Jason Nesbitt.

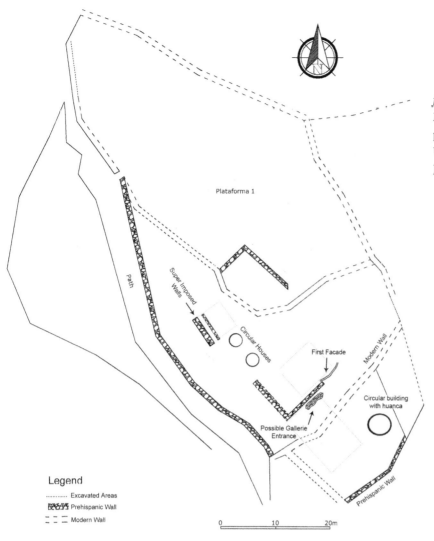

figure 4.5
Map of the main platform at Canchas Uckro. Illustration by Jason Nesbitt.

Plataforma 1

Path

Super Imposed Walls

Circular Houses

First Facade

Modern Wall

Circular building with huanca

Possible Gallerie Entrance

Prehispanic Wall

Legend

.... Excavated Areas

Prehispanic Wall

‒ ‒ ‒ Modern Wall

0   10   20m

figure 4.6
Drone image showing the main platform and areas of excavation. Photograph by Jason Nesbitt.

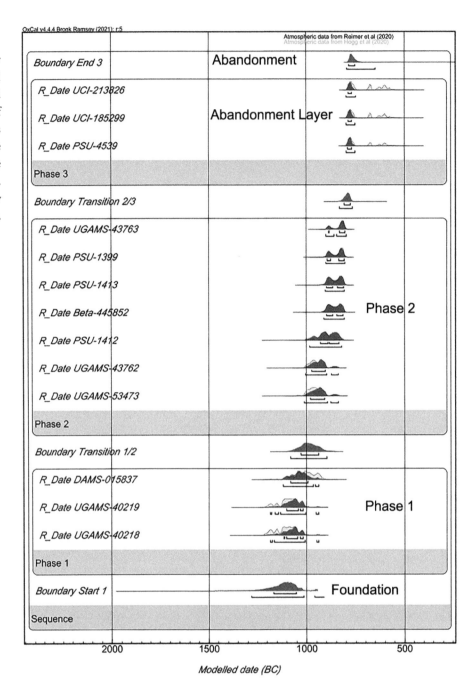

figure 4.7
Chronological model of the construction and occupation history of Canchas Uckro. Dates were calibrated using the mixed calibration curve (Marsh et al. 2018). Image produced by Jason Nesbitt.

The First Architectural Phase

Canchas Uckro was founded around 1100–1050 BC. The first phase of the building sequence consisted of the construction of the original platform, which served both ceremonial and domestic functions. At present, there is only limited data on the form of the platform during this time. Archaeological excavations on the southeast side of the platform exposed the site's main facade. The facade wall, which corresponds to the upper terrace of the platform, was approximately 1 m in height and was built from large rectangular sandstone blocks that were set in mud mortar (Figure 4.8a). The clearing of a section of this wall revealed curved walls; therefore, it is plausible that the original configuration of the platform is rounded (Figure 4.8b). Rounded platforms are not known from any phase of architecture at Chavín de Huántar (Kembel 2001, 2008), but

a

figure 4.8

a) Facade wall associated with the first phase of the Canchas Uckro platform, showing the presence of the boulder fill; and b) the curved shape of the Canchas Uckro platform. Photographs by Jason Nesbitt.

b

there are possible examples from the Mosna/Puccha River (Diessl 2004) and at the site of Chupán in the Upper Marañon to the east (Paredes Olvera 2002). The rounded form of the Canchas Uckro platform may signify connections with architectural traditions from regions to the east.

Excavations directly behind this facade wall yielded insight into the considerable effort that went into the building of the original platform. In this area, a large section of the fill of the platform was exposed (Figure 4.8a). This fill consisted of a deep layer of quarried sandstone blocks, the largest of which measured more than 1.5 m in length and would have weighed over a ton. Within this fill, there was abundant ceramic and faunal refuse.

Excavations along the base of the facade uncovered the remnants of a megalithic feature, which was a destroyed, or poorly preserved, gallery. The intact segment consists of a massive rectangular roofing slab measuring 3.36 m in length (Figure 4.9a) that runs below the main facade. Clearing underneath this stone suggests that the gallery was roughly 1.4 m in height. Following its use, the interior of this structure was intentionally filled with smaller, light-colored sandstone rocks (Figure 4.9b), which may have been part of sealing and burying this structure in the second construction phase. In front of the megalith was a series of collapsed flat stone slabs, which run on a southwest bearing (Figure 4.10). In the excavation profiles there were some additional large slabs, resting horizontally, suggesting that they were roofing stones for the gallery.

figure 4.9
a) Roofing slab
associated with the
destroyed gallery/
megalithic feature; and
b) the white rocks that
were used to seal the
interior. Photographs
by Jason Nesbitt.

a

b

figure 4.10
The alignment of
collapsed sandstone slabs
that comprise part of
the roof of the destroyed
gallery/megalithic
feature. Photograph by
Jason Nesbitt.

First Architectural Phase:
Domestic Occupation on the Platform Summit

Excavations on the platform summit exposed two circular buildings referred to as Structures 1 and 2 (Figure 4.11 and 4.12), both of which were completely excavated. Building foundations consisted of small boulders and cobbles, which supported a perishable superstructure with thatch roofing. The two structures are found in the same stratigraphic layer and are likely contemporary. Two radiocarbon dates from Structure 1 indicate that the buildings date to 1100–1030 BC and correspond with the first building phase at Canchas Uckro. Features and artifacts within both buildings suggest that they were domestic spaces. Each room contained abundant refuse, including pottery, grinding stones, and small quantities of animal bone, on the floors. Moreover, Structure 1 had an interior hearth and a small drainage canal on the outside of the building.

While most of the artifacts were of a quotidian nature, Structure 2 had one artifact that indicated ritual activity. A unique stone figurine (Figure 4.13) manufactured from a fine-grained volcanic rock was intentionally placed face down near the room's entrance. Though the figurine comes from late Initial Period contexts, it bears no resemblance to

figure 4.11
Structure 1 and associated drainage canal found on the platform summit. Note the monumental stone fill underlying this building. Photograph by Jason Nesbitt.

figure 4.12
Structure 2. Photograph by Jason Nesbitt.

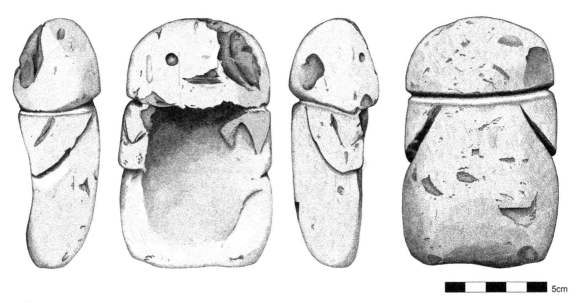

5cm

figure 4.13
Stone figurine associated with Structure 2. Drawing by Alana Garvey.

examples of Chavín sculpture or figurative art. On one side, the piece resembles the shape of a ground-stone axe, while on the other, it has a face, arms, and a destroyed body. It is possible that this figurine was utilized in domestic rituals.

Each building is relatively small, measuring 2.5 m (Structure 1) and 3 m (Structure 2) in diameter, with estimated floor areas of 5 and 7 m², respectively. These are comparable in size to contemporary buildings from the Mantaro region in the central highlands (Browman 1970) and to circular structure from Atalla in Huancavelica (Young, this volume). Cross-cultural studies suggest that each of these dwellings may have housed as many as three people (Flannery 2002). While these structures are quite small, it is likely that most activities were undertaken outside (see Quilter 1989:18). Based on the proximity and contemporaneity of these buildings, it is probable that they formed part of a cluster of structures around an open space, similar to the patio groups known for the Late Intermediate Period (AD 1000–1450) in the central highlands (DeMarrais 2001).

The circular dwellings at Canchas Uckro contrast with the domestic structures in the residential sectors of Chavín de Huántar, which are square or rectangular buildings associated with patio spaces (Burger 1984; Gamboa 2016; Mesía-Montenegro 2022; Rick 2005; Sayre 2010; Sayre and Rosenfeld, this volume). The best-excavated examples at Chavín de Huántar date between 800 and 400 BC (Burger 2019; Sayre 2010) and are, thus, later than the examples from Canchas Uckro. Within this context, the circular houses at Canchas Uckro are noteworthy. Circular houses are known from early and late Initial Period contexts at the site of Piruru in the Tantamayo Valley of the Upper Marañon (Bonnier and Rozenberg 1988). Radiocarbon dates and pottery styles from Piruru suggest that these houses dated from the middle part of the second millennium BC to approximately 1000–800 BC, which would make them contemporary with Canchas Uckro.

Second Architectural Phase

The second phase of the building sequence dates between 950 and 800 BC. During this phase, the original facade wall, as well as the associated gallery, were covered over in a thick layer of dark soil that contained abundant pottery, animal bone, bone tools, and marine shell, which were deposited in a single event. On top of this layer, a second facade wall was built that expanded the platform outward. The masonry of this later facade wall is different from the earlier one, and it exhibits techniques that used stone blocks that were separated by chinking

figure 4.14
The facade wall associated with the second phase of construction and its relationship with the first building phase. Photograph by Jason Nesbitt.

figure 4.15
Structure 4 and its *huanca*. Photograph by Jason Nesbitt.

stones (Figure 4.14). Associated with this second building phase was a series of constructions, most of which was badly damaged.

The best-preserved architecture from this phase is a circular building (Structure 4) measuring 3 m in diameter and positioned just off the midline of the platform (Figure 4.15). Though this building resembles the circular dwellings on the summit discussed earlier, it also has important differences. Part of this structure's masonry is of higher quality, with some quarried stones. Yet what sets this structure apart as unique is a large unworked sandstone boulder resting near the building's center. This stone, which measures 2 m in height and 1 m in diameter at its base, was quarried and dragged to Canchas Uckro, then set upright in antiquity. In this sense, the stone is reminiscent of a *huanca*, a sacred stone that represented a petrified, animated ancestor and that was also used as a symbolic territorial marker (Dean 2010, 2015; Duviols 1979; Lau 2021). Excavations at the base of this stone uncovered abundant material remains that were placed as offerings. While the analysis of this context is still ongoing, disarticulated animal and human bone, as well as a large quantity of pottery, were identified. The association of offerings with *huancas* has been documented for the later Recuay culture (AD 100–800) in the north-central highlands (Bazán 2007; Lau 2011:85–86, 2016:163–164; Nesbitt, Ibarra Asencios, and Tokanai 2020). For these reasons, it is probable that Structure 4 was some form of ceremonial building associated with the second architectural phase of Canchas Uckro.

Excavations of the Retaining Walls

Further insight into the construction of Canchas Uckro came from the excavation of the retaining walls on the northwest side of the platform. Here, two walls representing two separate building phases were encountered (Figure 4.16). Radiocarbon dating from these contexts shows that the construction of the retaining walls was contemporary with that of the main facade. In contrast to the facade, the retaining walls are much simpler constructions, consisting of a single course of stones built using much simpler masonry techniques than the platform facade described above. Importantly, in the fills separating the two walls were dark midden deposits with abundant pottery, as well as faunal remains that consisted mostly of the bones of wild

deer. As will be elaborated later in this chapter, these refuse deposits were probably formed from feasting, or communal consumption, events associated with the building of Canchas Uckro.

Abandonment of Canchas Uckro

Canchas Uckro was abandoned just after 800 BC. Much of the second phase of architecture was buried at this time. In the upper layers covering the main facade was a single, partially preserved, secondary human interment. This individual had no associated cultural materials. Three radiocarbon samples from this skeletal material yielded measurements that place the abandonment of Canchas Uckro between 800 and 750 BC (Nesbitt and Ibarra Asencios 2023).

The Significance of the Chronology of Canchas Uckro

The chronological data from Canchas Uckro is crucial to understanding aspects of the social processes occurring in the Chavín heartland during the late second and early part of the first millennia BC. This

figure 4.16
The two phases of retaining wall constructions from the northwest side of the platform. Photograph by Jason Nesbitt.

chronology is supported by thirteen radiocarbon dates, as well as a large pottery assemblage that exhibits stylistic traits characteristic of late Initial Period ceramics in the north-central highlands.

Radiocarbon Dates

The chronological model presented in Figure 4.7 suggests that Canchas Uckro was founded between 1100 and 1050 BC (see Nesbitt and Ibarra Asencios 2023 for details on the radiocarbon chronology). It was during this time that the platform of Canchas Uckro was first constructed. Deep stratigraphic excavations have thus far failed to find earlier construction phases or pottery styles that point to an early Initial Period occupation. Collectively, the chronological data strongly indicate that Canchas Uckro appeared suddenly at the end of the second millennium BC. The dates associated with the foundation of Canchas Uckro are crucial for understanding the site's regional importance because they are contemporary with the early phases of monumental construction at Chavín de Huántar (cf. Kembel 2001; Kembel and Haas 2015; Rick et al. 2010; see discussion below).

Radiocarbon measurements of organic remains from refuse contexts date the second phase of construction between 950 and 800 BC. It is during this time that the original facade walls were covered with the second construction episode. In comparison with the first architectural phase, the expansion of the platform required smaller labor inputs. Finally, three dates from contexts associated with the abandonment of the site suggest that Canchas Uckro ceased to function between 800 and 750 BC. Importantly, the abandonment of Canchas Uckro coincides with the rapid increase in the size of Chavín de Huántar's residential settlement as well as the apogee of the Chavín Interaction Sphere (Burger 2019). The suite of radiocarbon dates indicates that Canchas Uckro was occupied for approximately 300–350 years. As will be detailed later in this chapter, this relatively short period of occupation contrasts with the longer chronological sequence at Chavín de Huántar, as well as with other highland centers that become entangled in the Chavín Interaction Sphere.

Archaeological Evidence for Exchange and Interaction

The inhabitants of Canchas Uckro had limited access to exotic goods, particularly when compared to Chavín de Huántar. Non-local items included a small quantity of marine mollusks, primarily *Choromytilus chorus*, that were obtained from the central coast. Moreover, a single perforated *Spondylus* sp. bead was recovered from midden contexts associated with the facade and represents one of the only examples of personal adornment. This species of shell originated from the warm tropical waters of the far north coast of Peru or Ecuador (Carter 2011). Finally, a single obsidian flake was found in refuse deposits outside of Structures 1 and 2 on the platform summit. This piece was sourced to the Quispisisa quarry located in the south-central highlands (Nesbitt, Johnson, and Ibarra Asencios 2021:116–117), approximately 600 km to the south of Canchas Uckro.

Though the presence of these exotics could indicate direct connections with distant regions, their scarcity suggests that they were acquired via down-the-line exchange, possibly from Chavín de Huántar, where much higher quantities of both marine shell and obsidian were found in ceremonial and domestic contexts dating to the Urabarriu phase or late Initial Period (Burger 1984; Lumbreras 1993, 2007; Sandweiss and Carmen Rodríguez 1993).

Pottery Style as an Indicator of Interaction

Further insight into interaction comes from the study of the Canchas Uckro pottery assemblage. In general terms, the collection is dominated by neckless ollas, short-neck jars, and open bowls (Figure 4.17). Decoration includes incision, zoned punctation, cane-stamped circles, appliqué bands, and rare instances of rocker stamping. Taken as a whole, much of the pottery from Canchas Uckro appears closely related to the Urabarriu-phase (950–800 BC) assemblage from Chavín de Huántar (Burger 1984), which is partially contemporary with Canchas Uckro. Stylistic similarities can also be found with other late Initial Period pottery complexes from the north-central highlands, including Huaricoto in the

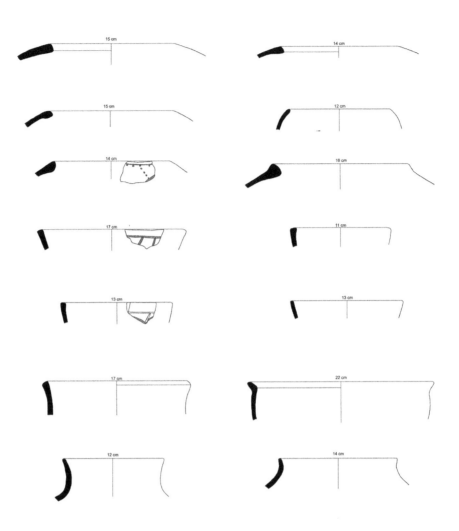

figure 4.18
Waira-jirca pottery
from Canchas
Uckro. Photograph
by Jason Nesbitt.

Callejón de Huaylas (Burger 1985:510–517), as well as the site of Piruru in the Upper Marañon (Rozenberg and Picon 1990).

The local character of most of the Canchas Uckro pottery is supported by preliminary paste analysis of a small sample of sherds (n=121) (Nesbitt, Johnson, and Ibarra Asencios 2021). Pastes included sand (comprised of quartz, feldspars, and mafic minerals), granodiorite, schist, and sandstone tempers. These raw materials are available within the local geology of the region surrounding Canchas Uckro (Turner, Knight, and Rick 1999). The temper types identified at Canchas Uckro are also technologically similar to the locally made pottery from the Urabarriu phase of Chavín de Huántar (Druc 2004).

Though the majority of the pottery was locally circulated, the Canchas Uckro assemblage also includes an important collection of clear imports. Most notable is Waira-jirca pottery, which makes up roughly 26 percent (minimum number of vessels [MNV=27]) of the decorated pottery (MNV=104) and was present in most excavated contexts at Canchas Uckro (Nesbitt, Johnson, and Ibarra Asencios 2021). Waira-jirca pottery is characterized by dark monochrome vessels, with distinctive zone-hatching, diamond patterned grooved designs, excision, and carinated forms (Figure 4.18). This pottery style was first described from the sites of Kotosh and Shillacoto, and it is widely distributed throughout

the Huánuco Basin of the Upper Huallaga in the *ceja de selva* region of the Eastern Andes (Izumi 1971; Izumi, Cuculiza, and Kano 1972:77; Izumi and Terada 1972:196, pls. 122–123; Kanezaki, Omori, and Tsurumi 2021; Kano 1979; Matsumoto 2020; Tello 1943:pl. XIX; Villar Quintana and Zuñiga Tapia 2020), as well as parts of the Upper Marañon (Nesbitt, Johnson, and Ibarra Asencios 2021:121). Stylistically, Waira-jirca is quite different from contemporary highland assemblages (DeBoer 2003) and is related to pottery complexes from the Upper Amazon of central and north-central Peru (Kanezaki, Omori, and Tsurumi 2021; Lathrap 1970, 1971).

The ubiquity of Waira-jirca pottery implies that Canchas Uckro was partially embedded within an interaction network oriented toward the eastern slopes (Nesbitt, Johnson, and Ibarra Asencios 2021) (Figure 4.19). Notably, zone-hatched pottery has not yet been found at Chavín de Huántar (Burger 1992:154). Consequently, Canchas Uckro may have been part of down-the-line (*sensu* Renfrew 1975) networks that connected portions of the Upper Huallaga and Upper Marañon to places in the Upper Amazon. Conceivably, it is through these exchange networks that tropical forest products and ideas were brought to the Chavín heartland region of Conchucos in the late Initial Period (Nesbitt, Johnson, and Ibarra Asencios 2021). While speculative, these types of connections can provide insight into long-standing

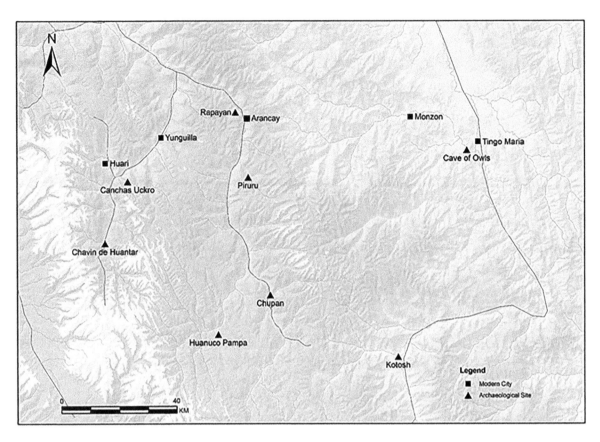

figure 4.19

Map showing the spatial relationships between Canchas Uckro and important sites in the Upper Huallaga. Illustration by Jason Nesbitt.

debates about the role that interaction with the *ceja de selva*/Upper Amazon played in Chavín religious ideology (Clasby, this volume; Lathrap 1971, 1973).

Discussion

Because Canchas Uckro emerged around 1100/1050 BC and lasted until just after 800 BC, it provides considerable insight into some of the historical processes that led to the formation of Chavín de Huántar and early Chavín culture. Though radiocarbon evidence demonstrates that the monumental core of Chavín de Huántar dates to the late second millennium BC (Kembel and Haas 2015; Rick et al. 2010), investigators have had difficulties exposing the earliest architectural phases because they are generally buried by later structures (Rick 2017:26–27). As a result, the beginning stages of development in

which Chavín de Huántar was consolidating itself into a major center remain poorly understood. Accordingly, the information gained from Canchas Uckro can provide new perspectives on this formative moment of Chavín culture history. In this section, I describe how Canchas Uckro can inform scholars on the early phases of culture making at Chavín de Huántar through comparison of architecture, chronology, labor mobilization, interaction, and abandonment.

Monumental Architecture and Labor Organization

Based on the platform's dimensions, the volume of Canchas Uckro is roughly 6300 m³, which is much smaller than the most conservative estimates for Chavín de Huántar's monumental core in its final form (Contreras 2015; see also Rick, this volume). Nevertheless, buildings like the gallery, the quarried stones of the facade walls, and the large boulders used for the platform fill reveal a high degree of monumentality at Canchas Uckro. Many of the largest sandstone blocks used for construction weighed several tons and would have required supra-community coordination and labor investment to move. Individually, it is possible to quarry and move such stones with relatively small groups of people (e.g., Lipo, Hunt, and Rapua Haoa 2013) using fiber ropes to drag these stones from nearby quarries. However, the quantity of large stones would have necessitated coordination among groups of people that would have exceeded the small population that inhabited Canchas Uckro, raising the problem of how this labor was mobilized.

I argue that one of the primary mechanisms for recruiting labor was feasting, an activity that was sponsored and organized by incipient community leaders. As mentioned earlier, archaeological evidence for feasting comes from the refuse layers associated with the construction phases of the platform. The fill layers that separated different building phases contained abundant refuse, including grinding stones, pottery, and fauna, that are indicative of food preparation and consumption. Analysis of the faunal assemblage is particularly informative in this regard. The animal bone assemblage is dominated by deer (taruca [*Hippocamelus antisensis*] and white-tailed deer [*Odocoileus virginianus*]), while camelid remains were very rare (Nesbitt et al. n.d.). This prevalence of wild animals reflects the widespread importance of hunting in the north-central and northern highlands prior to 800 BC (Miller and Burger 1995; Uzawa 2010). An analysis of the elements suggests that choice cuts of meat, such as the leg and trunk, were consumed. Other fauna in the midden included guinea pig (*Cavia porcellus*), a highly valued, fatty food that is consumed in contemporary and ancient feasts in the Andes (Bolton 1979; Rosenfeld 2008).

Other artifacts in the refuse deposits associated with the two construction phases point to other ritual practices. For example, there are incised bones, snuff tubes, and spoons that are correlates for the use of hallucinogenic plants such as *Anadenanthera* (Burger 2011; Torres 2008). Similar objects have been found in feasting contexts at Chavín de Huántar (Mesía-Montenegro 2014) and other contemporary sites such as Campanayuq Rumi (Matsumoto 2012). There was also a single spondylus shell bead that was part of a necklace or other kind of personal ornamentation. Non-local species were also found, including a small quantity of marine mollusks from the central Peruvian coast, which were valued for their exotic provenience.

In sum, the residues of the consumption of high-value foods, exotic goods, and ritual paraphernalia co-occurred with the process of monument building. This relationship between feasting and construction recalls similar associations of refuse deposition and building events at the Late Preceramic civic-ceremonial center of Cerro Lampay (2400–2200 BC) from the central coast of Peru (Vega-Centeno 2007). Following Rafael Vega-Centeno (2007), I hypothesize that the inhabitants of Canchas Uckro engaged in "work feasts" (e.g., Dietler and Herbich 2001; see also Dietrich, Notroff, and Schmidt 2017), in which leaders provisioned workers with food and other valued items in ceremonial events in return for participation in communal labor projects. Scholars observe that this kind of feasting is often used as a means of recruiting labor in societies in which positions of formal leadership are weak or absent (Dietler and Herbich 2001; Vega-Centeno 2007). Leaders at Canchas Uckro gained some of their prestige and authority through access to exotic materials. In this sense, leaders at Canchas Uckro may have exerted more persuasive power, which involved ritual consumption and the accumulation of networks of social relationships (Nesbitt 2019). Work feasts also created reciprocal social relationships between individuals and communities to undertake collective activities. That said, the relatively small size of Canchas Uckro suggests limited labor recruitment that was probably drawn from the nearby populations.

Comparisons between Canchas Uckro and Early Chavín de Huántar

Archaeological research at Canchas Uckro is yielding important data to help comprehend some of the cultural dynamics that occurred in the Chavín

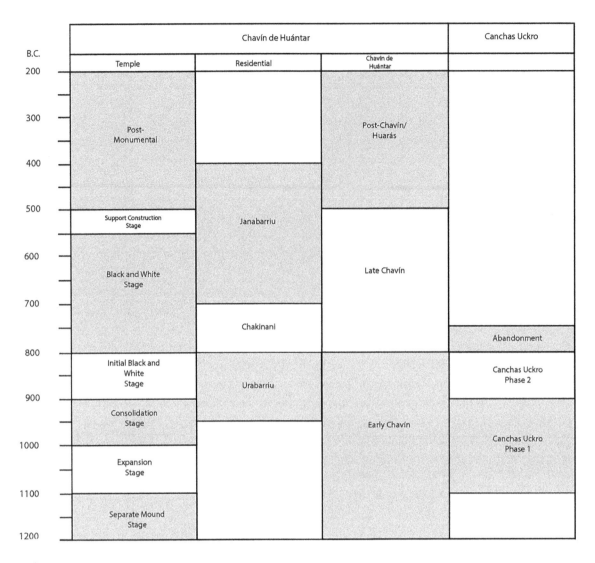

figure 4.20

A comparison of the chronologies of Canchas Uckro and Chavín de Huántar. Dates from Chavín de Huántar are based on Burger 2019; Kembel 2008; Kembel and Haas 2015; Rick et al. 2010.

heartland during the late second and early first millennia BC. Canchas Uckro was founded around 1100–1050 BC; at this time, it consisted of a platform that measured 60 × 35 m at its base and 3 m in height. As highlighted earlier in this chapter, the foundation date of Canchas Uckro is contemporary with the earliest known phases of monument building and settlement at Chavín de Huántar, which began around 1100–950 BC (cf. Burger 2019; Kembel and Haas 2015; Rick et al. 2010). More broadly, Canchas Uckro was one of several highland centers that was founded during the late second millennium BC, including Campanayuq Rumi, Atalla, Kuntur Wasi,

and Pacopampa (Inokuchi 2010; Matsumoto 2010; Matsumoto and Cavero Palomino, this volume; Onuki 1995; Seki, this volume; Seki et al. 2010; Young, this volume), as well as Ingatambo in the *ceja de selva* of northern Peru (Yamamoto 2010, 2021).

Based on the results of my investigations, I hypothesize that during its occupation between 1100 and 800 BC, Canchas Uckro may have been a peer center to Chavín de Huántar *during its earliest phases*. Silvia Kembel's (2001, 2008) detailed analysis of the building sequence suggests that in the "Separate Mound Stage" Chavín de Huántar apparently consisted of a group of two small platforms and a few galleries, along with a small village settlement (e.g., Burger 1984; Mesía-Montenegro 2022). Associated radiocarbon dates obtained from architectural mortars suggest a date of approximately 1100/1000–900 BC for this period of early temple building (Kembel and Haas 2015:376, fig. 17). Though the exact size of the platforms during the Separate Mound Stage is not clear, it seems that early Chavín de Huántar was not much larger than the estimated size of Canchas Uckro. During this period, the two sites shared some elements of material culture and architectural features and techniques, while also differing in others.

Yet, unlike Chavín de Huántar, Canchas Uckro was seemingly short-lived. Chronological data presented in this chapter specify an occupation span at Canchas Uckro of approximately three to four hundred years before the site was suddenly abandoned in 800–750 BC. This argument is supported not only by radiocarbon measurements but also by the absence of later Chavín ceramic styles referred to as Janabarriu (Burger 1984; Rick et al. 2010), which date between 750/700 and 400 BC (Burger 2019). In contrast to Canchas Uckro, radiocarbon dating shows that Chavín de Huántar was occupied for between six and seven centuries, lasting until 500–400 BC (cf. Burger 2019; Kembel and Haas 2015; Rick et al. 2010) (Figure 4.20).

The Implications of Abandonment

The abandonment of Canchas Uckro between 800 and 750 BC was sudden and coincides with significant transformations at Chavín de Huántar. At this time, "two major plazas were added, monumental constructions were formalized and expanded to reach their fullest known extent, a river was rechanneled, and an extensive network of subterranean canals was greatly expanded" (Mesía-Montenegro 2022:895). Furthermore, after 800 BC the residential sector of Chavín de Huántar grew, from 7 ha in the Urabarriu phase to at least 40 ha in the Janabarriu phase (Burger 1984, 2019; Gamboa 2016; Sayre 2010). Lastly, there is increasing evidence for Chavín influence over distant localities, with Janabarriu, or Chavín International Style (Young, this volume) pottery appearing over a wide region,

which is indicative of the expansion of the Chavín Interaction Sphere that connected much of the Peruvian highlands and coast (Burger 2008a, 2013; Burger and Nesbitt, this volume; Contreras 2011; Matsumoto et al. 2018; Nesbitt, Matsumoto, and Cavero Palomino 2019).

Why would Canchas Uckro be abandoned during such a period of prosperity over such a wide region? There is, for example, no evidence that the site was subjected to violent destruction. Instead, an alternative explanation can be found in the rapid urbanization that was occurring at Chavín de Huántar after 800 BC. It is conceivable that as Chavín de Huántar's residential population was increasing, places like Canchas Uckro were abandoned as part of a process of ruralization (Yoffee 2005), in which the inhabitants of neighboring sites were attracted to Chavín de Huántar. Part of the draw of Chavín de Huántar at the time was its emerging prestige as a religious and cosmopolitan center at the beginnings of the first millennium BC. While Chavín de Huántar and Canchas Uckro may have been nearly the same size around 1000 BC, Chavín de Huántar was a rapidly growing residential and ceremonial center of pan-regional importance by 800 BC. Evidence from late Initial Period contexts like the Ofrendas Gallery points to contacts with the central and north coast of Peru, as well as the highlands of Cajamarca (Lumbreras 1993, 2007). These exotic vessels arrived alongside visitors that came to the site in long-distance pilgrimages, a testament to the importance of Chavín de Huántar from its inception. In contrast, Canchas Uckro never had this degree of direct contact with distant regions. I, therefore, hypothesize that peoples from Canchas Uckro, and elsewhere in the heartland region, around 800 BC were attracted by Chavín's "spiritual magnetism" (*sensu* Preston 1992), as well as access to important trade networks. Yet at the same time, the people that moved to Chavín de Huántar during this period of fluorescence contributed to its cosmopolitan identity (Burger 2012). Migrants from the hinterlands brought new ideas and people that helped make and create Chavín cultural order (*sensu* Pauketat 2003).

This is not to say that the Mosna/Puccha drainage was completely, or even largely, abandoned after

800 BC. For example, excavations at the nearby site of Reparín, located above the Huaritambo River, reveal that it was occupied between 700 BC and 400 BC. The dates from Reparín provide evidence that this site was founded sometime after the abandonment of Canchas Uckro and may signal changes in regional settlement in the Early Horizon (Nesbitt, Ibarra Asencios, and Tokanai 2020), though this remains a hypothesis to be evaluated by future investigation.

Conclusions

One of the goals of this chapter is to problematize the populations inhabiting the outer landscapes of the Chavín heartland. While this region has been "largely characterized by scattered, small-scale, modest dwellings and communities that seem largely to have remained much as they were over time" (Rick 2017:45), the research presented in this chapter shows a highly dynamic landscape with sites that were more complex and varied than previously thought. Though research is still in a nascent stage, archaeological investigations in Conchucos suggest variation in settlement size, function, and chronology. For instance, research at Pojóc and Waman Wain indicates that these two sites functioned as small-scale hamlets that were involved in economically integrated relationships with Chavín de Huántar (Burger 1982; Miller and Burger 1995). Conversely, sites like Canchas Uckro exhibit evidence that it functioned as a ceremonial center and small village community. Tello (1960:147–157) also describes sites along the Puccha River that may also have functioned as secondary public centers. Settlement heterogeneity in the Chavín heartland raises the possibility of the kinds of multitiered site hierarchies and diverse functions that characterize urban landscapes in other parts of the ancient world (Wright and Johnson 1975; see Isbell and Schreiber 1978 for an Andean example). Verifying this pattern will require much more research.

The data obtained from Canchas Uckro illustrates the value that a detailed study of one of these settlements can provide to understanding the social, political, economic, and religious changes that were occurring in the Chavín heartland during the late Initial Period. I maintain that Canchas Uckro was instrumental in contributing to the formation of Chavín de Huántar during the formative stage of the site's history. One factor that warrants attention is the abandonment and inferred movement of peoples out of centers like Canchas Uckro. Confirming population movements will require more detailed types of analysis, including isotopic investigation of human remains (Washburn et al. 2021). Regardless, people from Canchas Uckro and other contemporary settlements in Conchucos contributed labor, ideas, and myths that helped promote Chavín de Huántar's growth and importance and, in a very real sense, created Chavín culture.

Acknowledgments

I would like to thank Colin McEwan for his efforts in helping to organize the symposium on which this book is based. The research presented in this chapter was supported by grants from the Roger Thayer Stone Center for Latin American Studies, the Provost's Office, and the Tulane-Xavier Center for Bioenvironmental Research. Archaeological research at Canchas Uckro and Reparín was co-directed by Bebel Ibarra Asencios, who also aided in the preparation of some of the maps in this chapter. The contents of this chapter benefitted from conversations and critical commentary provided by Alina Álvarez Larrain, Nick Brown, Richard Burger, Marcello Canuto, Ryan Clasby, Melisa Galván, Bebel Ibarra Asencios, Yuichi Matsumoto, Rosa Mendoza Rick, Tatsuya Murakami, John Rick, Christopher Rodning, Lucy Salazar, Sara Taylor, John Verano, and Michelle Young. Restoration of the vessel illustrated in Figure 4.18 was undertaken by Alison Salazar of the Museo Larco in Lima.

NOTE

1 The Conchucos region is defined as a series of inter-montane valleys, located on the southeastern side of the Cordillera Blanca, that drain into the Upper Marañon.

REFERENCES CITED

Algaze, Guillermo
2018   Entropic Cities: The Paradox of Urbanism in Ancient Mesopotamia. *Current Anthropology* 59:23–54.

Amat, Hernán
1971   Informe preliminar de exploraciones arqueológicas PAEA. *Arqueología y sociedad* 5:36–56.
1976   Estudios arqueológicos en la Cuenca del Rio del Mosna y en el Alto Marañon. *Actas del XLI Congreso Internacional de Americanistas* 3:532–546.

Bazán, Francisco
2007   Las ceremonias especializadas de veneración a los huancas. *SIAN: Revista arqueológica* 18:3–20.

Bolton, Ralph
1979   Guinea Pigs, Protein, and Ritual. *Ethnology* 18:229–252.

Bonnier, Elisabeth, and Catherine Rozenberg
1988   Del santuario al caserío: Acerca de la neolitización en la cordillera de los Andes centrales. *Bulletin de L'Institut Français d'Études Andines* 17(2):23–40.

Browman, David L.
1970   Early Peruvian Peasants: The Culture History of a Central Higlands Valley. PhD dissertation, Harvard University, Cambridge, Mass.

Burger, Richard L.
1982   Pojóc and Waman Wain: Two Early Horizon Villages in the Chavín Heartland. *Ñawpa Pacha: Journal of Andean Archaeology* 20:3–40.
1984   *The Prehistoric Occupation of Chavín de Huántar, Peru*. University of California Press, Berkeley.
1985   Prehistoric Stylistic Change and Cultural Development at Huaricoto, Peru. *National Geographic Research* 1:505–534.
1992   *Chavín and the Origins of Andean Civilization*. Thames and Hudson, London.
2008a   Chavín de Huántar and Its Sphere of Influence. In *Handbook of South American Archaeology*, edited by Helaine Silverman and William H. Isbell, pp. 681–703. Springer, New York.
2008b   The Original Context of the Yauya Stela. In *Chavín: Art, Architecture, and Culture*, edited by William J. Conklin and Jeffrey Quilter, pp. 163–179. Cotsen Institute of Archaeology, University of California, Los Angeles.
2011   What Kind of Hallucinogenic Snuff Was Used at Chavín de Huántar? *Ñawpa Pacha: Journal of Andean Archaeology* 31:123–140.
2012   Central Andean Language Expansion and the Chavín Sphere of Interaction. *Proceedings of the British Academy* 173:133–159.
2013   In the Realm of the Incas: An Archaeological Reconsideration of Household Exchange, Long-Distance Trade, and Marketplaces in the Pre-Hispanic Central Andes. In *Merchants, Markets, and Exchange in the Pre-Columbian World*, edited by Kenneth G. Hirth and Joanne Pillsbury, pp. 319–334. Dumbarton Oaks Research Library and Collection, Washington, D.C.
2019   Understanding the Socioeconomic Trajectory of Chavín de Huántar: A New Radiocarbon Sequence and Its Wider Implications. *Latin American Antiquity* 30:373–392.

Burger, Richard L., and Lucy C. Salazar

2008   The Manchay Culture and the Coastal
Inspiration for Highland Chavín
Civilization. In *Chavín: Art, Architecture,
and Culture*, edited by William J. Conklin
and Jeffrey Quilter, pp. 85–105. Cotsen
Institute of Archaeology, University of
California, Los Angeles.

Carter, Benjamin P.

2011   *Spondylus* in South American Prehistory.
In *Spondylus in Prehistory: New Data
and Approaches: Contributions to the
Archaeology of Shell Technologies*,
edited by Fotis Ifantidis and Marianna
Nikolaidou, pp. 63–89. Bar International
Series, Oxford.

Contreras, Daniel A.

2011   How Far to Conchucos? A GIS Approach
to Assessing the Implications of Exotic
Materials at Chavín de Huántar. *World
Archaeology* 43:380–397.

2015   Landscape Setting as Medium of Communication at Chavín de Huántar,
Peru. *Cambridge Archaeological Journal*
25:513–530.

Contreras, Daniel A., and David K. Keefer

2009   Implications of the Fluvial History
of the Wacheqsa River for Hydraulic
Engineering and Water Uses at Chavín
de Huántar, Peru. *Geoarchaeology*
24:589–618.

Cowgill, George L.

2004   Origins and Development of Urbanism:
Archaeological Perspectives. *Annual
Review of Anthropology* 33:525–549.

Dean, Carolyn

2010   *A Culture of Stone: Inka Perspectives
on Rock*. Duke University Press,
Durham, N.C.

2015   Men Who Would Be Rocks: The Inka
Wank'a. In *The Archaeology of Wak'as:
Explorations of the Sacred in the Pre-
Columbian Andes*, edited by Tamara L.
Bray, pp. 213–238. University of Colorado
Press, Boulder.

DeBoer, Warren R.

2003   Ceramic Assemblage Variability
in the Formative of Ecuador and
Peru. In *Archaeology of Formative
Ecuador*, edited by J. Scott Raymond

and Richard L. Burger, pp. 289–336.
Dumbarton Oaks Research Library and
Collection, Washington, D.C.

DeMarrais, Elizabeth

2001   The Architecture and Organization
of Xauxa Settlements. In *Empires and
Domestic Economy*, edited by Terence N.
D'Altroy and Christine Hastorf, pp. 115–
153. Springer, New York.

Diessl, Wilhelm

2004   *Sitios arqueológicos en los Distritos
Huántar, San Marcos, Chavín*. Instituto
Cultural Runa, Lima.

Dietler, Michael, and Ingrid Herbich

2001   Feasts and Labor Mobilization: Dissect-
ing a Fundamental Economic Practice. In
*Feasts: Archaeological and Ethnographic
Perspectives on Food, Politics, and Power*,
edited by Michael Dietler and Brian
Hayden, pp. 240–264. Smithsonian
Institution Press, Washington, D.C.

Dietrich, Oliver, Jens Notroff, and Klaus Schmidt

2017   Feasting, Social Complexity, and the
Emergence of the Early Neolithic of
Upper Mesopotamia: A View from
Göbekli Tepe. In *Feast, Famine, or
Fighting? Multiple Pathways to Social
Complexity*, edited by Richard J. Chacon
and Ruben G. Mendoza, pp. 91–132.
Springer International Publishing,
New York.

Druc, Isabelle C.

2004   Ceramic Diversity in Chavín de Huántar,
Peru. *Latin American Antiquity* 15:344–363.

Duviols, Pierre

1979   Un simbolisme de l'occupation, de l'amé-
nagement et de l'exploitation de l'espace:
Le monolithe "Huanca" et sa fonction
dans les Andes préhispaniques. *L'Homme*
19(2):7–31.

Espejo, Julio

1951   Exploraciones arqueológicas en las
cabeceras del Pukcha (Perú). *Cuadernos
americanos* 56:139–152.

1955   Gotush: Nuevos descubrimientos en
Chavín. *Baessler-Archiv*, n.s., 3:123–136.

Flannery, Kent V.

2002   The Origins of the Village Revisited:
From Nuclear to Extended Households.
American Antiquity 67:417–433.

Gamboa, Jorge

2016   Las ocupaciones formativas en La Banda: Excavaciones durante la construcción de la variante Chavín y su impacto socioeconómico en el Valle de Mosna. In *Arqueología de la Sierra de Ancash 2: Población y territorio*, edited by Bebel Ibarra Asencios, pp. 53–76. Instituto de Estudios Huarinos, Huari, Ancash.

Herrera Wassilowsky, Alexander

2003   Patrones de asentamiento y cambios en las strategias de ocupación en la cuenca del Rio Yanamayo, Callejón de Conchucos. In *Arqueología de la Sierra de Ancash: Propuestas y perspectivas*, edited by Bebel Ibarra Asencios, pp. 221–250. Instituto Cultural Runa, Lima.

2021   Changing Andes-Amazonia Dynamics: *El Chuncho* Meets *El Inca* at the End of the Marañón Corridor. In *Rethinking the Andes-Amazonia Divide: A Cross-Disciplinary Exploration*, edited by Adrian J. Pearce, David G. Beresford-Jones, and Paul Heggarty, pp. 115–126. UCL Press, London.

Ibarra Asencios, Bebel

2003   Arqueología del valle del Puccha: Economía, cosmovisión y secuencia estilística. In *Arqueología de la Sierra de Ancash: Propuestas y perspectivas*, edited by Bebel Ibarra Asencios, pp. 251–330. Instituto Cultural Runa, Lima.

Inokuchi, Kinya

2010   La arquitectura de Kuntur Wasi: Secuencia constructiva y cronología de un centro ceremonial del período formativo. *Boletín de Arqueología PUCP* 12:219–247.

Isbell, William H., and Katharina Schreiber

1978   Was Huari a State? *American Antiquity* 43:372–389.

Izumi, Seiichi

1971   The Development of the Formative Culture in the Ceja de Montaña: A Viewpoint Based on the Materials from the Kotosh Site. In *Dumbarton Oaks Conference on Chavín*, edited by Elizabeth P. Benson, pp. 49–72. Dumbarton Oaks Research Library and Collection, Washington, D.C.

Izumi, Seiichi, Pedro J. Cuculiza, and Chiaki Kano

1972   *Excavations at Shillacoto, Huánuco, Peru.* The University Museum, University of Tokyo, Tokyo.

Izumi, Seiichi, and Kazuo Terada

1972   *Excavations at Kotosh, Peru. A Report on the Third and Fourth Expeditions.* University of Tokyo Press, Tokyo.

Jennings, Justin

2016   *Killing Civilization: A Reassessment of Early Urbanism and Its Consequences.* University of New Mexico Press, Albuquerque.

Kanezaki, Yuko, Takayuki Omori, and Eisei Tsurumi

2021   Emergence and Development of Pottery in the Andean Early Formative Period: New Insights from an Improved Wairajirca Pottery Chronology at the Jancao Site in the Huánuco Region, Peru. *Latin American Antiquity* 32:239–254.

Kano, Chiaki

1979   *The Origins of the Chavín Culture.* Dumbarton Oaks Research Library and Collection, Washington, D.C.

Kembel, Silvia

2001   Architectural Sequence and Chronology at Chavín de Huántar, Peru. PhD dissertation, Stanford University, Stanford.

2008   The Architecture at the Monumental Center of Chavín de Huántar: Sequence, Transformations, and Chronology. In *Chavín: Art, Architecture, and Culture*, edited by William J. Conklin and Jeffrey Quilter, pp. 35–81. Cotsen Institute of Archaeology, University of California, Los Angeles.

Kembel, Silvia, and Herbert Haas

2015   Radiocarbon Dates from the Monumental Architecture at Chavín de Huántar, Peru. *Journal of Archaeological Method and Theory* 22:345–427.

Lathrap, Donald W.

1958   The Cultural Sequence of Yarinacocha, Eastern Peru. *American Antiquity* 23:379–388.

1970   *The Upper Amazon.* Thames and Hudson, London.

1971   The Tropical Forest and the Cultural Context of Chavín. In *Dumbarton Oaks*

Conference on Chavín, edited by Elizabeth P. Benson, pp. 73–100. Dumbarton Oaks Research Library and Collection, Washington, D.C.

1973 Gifts of the Cayman: Some Thoughts on the Subsistence Basis of Chavín. In *Variation in Anthropology: Essays in Honor of John C. McGregor*, edited by Donald W. Lathrap and J. Douglas, pp. 91–105. Illinois Archaeological Survey, Urbana.

Lau, George F.

2011 *Andean Expressions: Art and Archaeology of the Recuay Culture*. University of Iowa Press, Iowa City.

2016 *An Archaeology of Ancash: Stones, Ruins, and Communities in Andean Peru*. Routledge, London.

2021 Animating Idolatry: Making Ancestral Kin and Personhood in Ancient Peru. *Religions* 12(5):287, https://doi.org/10.3390/rel12050287.

Lipo, Carl P., Terry L. Hunt, and Sergio Rapu Haoa

2013 The "Walking" Megalithic Statues (Moai) of Easter Island. *Journal of Archaeological Science* 40:2859–2866.

Lumbreras, Luis G.

1989 *Chavín de Huántar en el nacimiento de la civilización Andina*. Instituto Andino de Estudios Arqueológicos, Lima.

1993 *Chavín de Huántar: Excavaciones en la Galería de las Ofrendas*. P. von Zabern, Mainz.

2007 *Chavín: Excavaciones arqueológicas*. 2 vols. Universidad Alas Peruanas, Lima.

Marsh, Erik J., Maria C. Bruno, Sherilyn C. Fritz, Paul Baker, José M. Capriles, and Christine A. Hastorf

2018 IntCal, SHCal, or a Mixed Curve? Choosing a 14C Calibration Curve for Archaeological and Paleoenvironmental Records from Tropical South America. *Radiocarbon* 60:925–940.

Matsumoto, Yuichi

2010 The Prehistoric Ceremonial Center of Campanayuq Rumi: Interregional Interactions in the South-Central Highlands of Peru. PhD dissertation, Yale University, New Haven.

2012 Recognizing Ritual: The Case from Campanayuq Rumi. *Antiquity* 86:746–759.

2020 *Prehistoric Settlement Patterns in the Upper Huallaga Basin, Peru*. Yale University Department of Anthropology, New Haven.

Matsumoto, Yuichi, Jason Nesbitt, Michael D. Glascock, Yuri I. Cavero Palomino, and Richard L. Burger

2018 Interregional Obsidian Exchange during the Late Initial Period and Early Horizon: New Perspectives from Campanayuq Rumi. *Latin American Antiquity* 29:44–63.

Mesía-Montenegro, Christian

2014 Festines y poder en Chavín de Huántar durante el período formativo tardío en los Andes centrales. *Chungara: Revista de antropología chilena* 46:313–343.

2022 Social Complexity and Core–Periphery Relationships in an Andean Formative Ceremonial Centre: Domestic Occupation at Chavín de Huántar. *Antiquity* 96:883–902.

Miller, George R., and Richard L. Burger

1995 Our Father the Cayman, Our Dinner the Llama: Animal Utilization at Chavín de Huántar, Peru. *American Antiquity* 60:421–458.

Nesbitt, Jason

2019 Wealth in People: An Alternative Perspective on Initial Period Monumental Architecture from Huaca Cortada. In *Perspectives on Early Andean Civilization in Peru: Interaction, Authority, and Socioeconomic Organization during the First and Second Millennia BC*, edited by Richard L. Burger, Lucy C. Salazar, and Yuji Seki, pp. 1–17. Yale University Publications in Anthropology Number 96. Yale University Press, New Haven.

Nesbitt, Jason, and Bebel Ibarra Asencios

2023 The Radiocarbon Chronology of Canchao Uckro: Implications for Understanding the Late Initial Period (1100–800 BC) in the Chavín Heartland. *Senri Ethnological Studies* 112:169–196.

Nesbitt, Jason, Bebel Ibarra Asencios, and Fuyaki Tokanai

2020   The Architecture and Chronology of Reparín, Eastern Ancash, Peru. *Ñawpa Pacha: Journal of Andean Archaeology* 40:41–59.

Nesbitt, Jason, Rachel Johnson, and Bebel Ibarra Asencios

2021   Connections between the Chavín Heartland and the Upper Amazon: New Perspectives from Canchas Uckro (1100–850 BC). In *The Archaeology of the Upper Amazon: Complexity and Interaction in the Andean Tropical Forest*, edited by Ryan Clasby and Jason Nesbitt, pp. 106–128. University Press of Florida, Gainesville.

Nesbitt, Jason, Yuichi Matsumoto, and Yuri Cavero Palomino

2019   Campanayuq Rumi and Arpiri: Two Ceremonial Centers on the Periphery of the Chavín Interaction Sphere. *Ñawpa Pacha: Journal of Andean Archaeology* 39:57–75.

Nesbitt, Jason, Sadie Weber, Eden Washburn, Bebel Ibarra Asencios, Anne R. Titelbaum, Andrew Schroll, and Lars Fehren-Schmitz

n.d.   Ancient Diet during the Late Initial Period (c. 1100–800 cal BC) in the Chavín Heartland: New Data from Canchas Uckro (North-Central Peru). *Ethnobiology*, in press.

Onuki, Yoshio (editor)

1995   *Kuntur Wasi y Cerro Blanco: Dos sitios del formativo en el norte del Perú.* Hokusen-Sha, Tokyo.

Orsini, Carolina

2014   *Arqueología de Chacas: Comunidades, asentamientos y paisaje en un valle de los Andes ventrales del Perú.* Pendragon, Bologna.

Paredes Olvera, Juan

2002   El templo de Chupan en los orígenes de la civilización Andina. *Arkinka* 83:92–99.

Pauketat, Timothy

2003   Resettled Farmers and the Making of a Mississippian Polity. *American Antiquity* 68:39–66.

Preston, James

1992   Spiritual Magnetism: An Organizing Principle for the Study of Pilgrimage. In *Sacred Journeys*, edited by A. Morinis, pp. 31–46. Greenwood Press, Westport, Conn.

Quilter, Jeffrey

1989   *Life and Death at Paloma: Society and Mortuary Practices in a Preceramic Peruvian Village.* University of Iowa Press, Iowa City.

Renfrew, Colin

1975   Trade as Action at a Distance: Questions of Integration and Communication. In *Ancient Civilization and Trade*, edited by Jeremy A. Sabloff and C. C. Lamberg-Karlovsky, pp. 3–59. University of New Mexico Press, Albuquerque.

Rick, John W.

2005   The Evolution of Authority and Power at Chavín de Huántar, Peru. In *Foundations of Power in the Prehispanic Andes*, edited by Kevin Vaughn, Dennis Ogburn, and Christina A. Conlee, pp. 71–89. Archeological Papers of the American Anthropological Association 14. University of California Press, Berkeley.

2008   Context, Construction, and Ritual in the Development of Authority at Chavín de Huántar. In *Chavín: Art, Architecture, and Culture*, edited by William J. Conklin and Jeffrey Quilter, pp. 3–34. Cotsen Institute of Archaeology, University of California, Los Angeles.

2017   The Nature of Ritual Space at Chavín de Huántar. In *Rituals of the Past: Prehispanic and Colonial Case Studies in Andean Archaeology*, edited by Silvana A. Rosenfeld and Stefanie Bautista, pp. 21–49. University Press of Colorado, Boulder.

Rick, John W., Silvia R. Kembel, Rosa Mendoza Rick, and John Kembel

1998   La arquitectura del complejo ceremonial de Chavín de Huántar: Documentación tridimensional y sus implicancias. *Boletín de Arqueología PUCP* 2:181–214.

Rick, John W., Christian Mesía, Daniel A. Contreras, Silvia Rodríguez Kembel, Rosa M. Rick, Matthew Paul Sayre, and John Wolf

 2010 La cronología de Chavín de Huántar y sus implicancias por el período formativo. *Boletín de Arqueología PUCP* 13:87–132.

Rojas Ponce, Pedro

 1958 *Exploración arqueológica a la cuenca del Río Puccha y Alto Marañón*. Wenner Gren Foundation, New York.

Rosenfeld, Silvana A.

 2008 Delicious Guinea Pigs: Seasonality Studies and the Use of Fat in the Pre-Columbian Andean Diet. *Quaternary International* 180:127–134.

Rosenfeld, Silvana A., and Matthew Sayre

 2016 Llamas on the Land: Production and Consumption of Meat at Chavín de Huántar, Peru. *Latin American Antiquity* 27:497–511.

Rowe, John H.

 1963 Urban Settlements in Ancient Peru. *Ñawpa Pacha: Journal of Andean Archaeology* 1:1–27.

Rozenberg, Catherine, and Maurice Picon

 1990 Circulation, échange et production de poteries dan les Andes centrales au deuxième millénaire av. J.-C. *Bulletin de L'Institut Français d'Études Andines* 19:1–14.

Sandweiss, Daniel H., and María del Carmen Rodríguez

 1993 Apéndice IV: Restos malacológicos de la Galería de las Ofrendas. In *Excavaciones en la Galería de las Ofrendas*, edited by Luis G. Lumbreras, pp. 406–413. P. von Zabern, Mainz.

Sayre, Matthew

 2010 Life Across the River: Agricultural, Ritual, and Production Practices at Chavín de Huántar, Peru. PhD dissertation, University of California, Berkeley.

Sayre, Matthew, and N. L. López Aldave

 2009 Exchange at Chavín de Huántar: Insights from Shell Data. *Andean Past* 9:340–345.

Sayre, Matthew, Melanie J. Miller, and Silvana Rosenfeld

 2016 Isotopic Evidence for the Trade and Production of Exotic Marine Mammal Bone Artifacts at Chavín de Huántar, Peru. *Archaeological and Anthropological Sciences* 8:403–417.

Seki, Yuji, Juan Pablo Villanueva, Diana Alemán, Mauro Ordoñez, Masato Sakai, Walter Tosso, Kinya Inokuchi, Araceli Espinoza, and Daniel Morales

 2010 Nuevas evidencias del sitio arqueológico Pacopampa en la Sierra Norte del Peru. *Boletín de Arqueología PUCP* 12:69–95.

Smith, Monica L.

 2014 The Archaeology of Urban Landscapes. *Annual Review of Anthropology* 43:307–323.

Tantaleán, Henry

 2009 Chavín de Huántar y la definición arqueológica de un estado teocrático andino. *Boletín de antropología americana* 45:99–168.

Tello, Julio C.

 1943 Discovery of the Chavín Culture in Peru. *American Antiquity* 9:135–160.

 1960 *Chavín: Cultura matriz de la civilización andina*. Publicación Antropológica del Archivo "Julio C. Tello" de la Universidad Nacional Mayor de San Marcos, Lima.

Torres, Constantino M.

 2008 Chavín's Psychoactive Pharmacopoeia: The Iconographic Evidence. In *Chavín: Art, Architecture, and Culture*, edited by William J. Conklin and Jeffrey Quilter, pp. 239–259. Cotsen Institute of Archaeology, University of California, Los Angeles.

Turner, Robert J. W., Rosemary J. Knight, and John W. Rick

 1999 The Geological Landscape of the Pre-Inca Archaeological Site of Chavín de Huántar, Perú. *Current Research 1999-D, Geological Survey of Canada*: 47–56.

Uzawa, Kazuhiro

 2010 La difusión de los camélidos domesticados en el norte del Perú durante el período formativo. *Boletín de Arqueología PUCP* 12:249–260.

Vega-Centeno, Rafael

 2007 Construction, Labor Organization, and Feasting during the Late Archaic Period in the Central Andes. *Journal of Anthropological Archaeology* 26:150–171.

Villar Quintana, Anthony, and Jhon Zuñiga Tapia

2020   Guellayhuasin: Un sitio formativo en la cuenca del Río Tingo (Pallanchacra-Pasco). *Arkinka* 296:72–87.

Washburn, Eden, Jason Nesbitt, Bebel Ibarra Asencios, Lars Fehren-Schmitz, and Vicky M. Oelze

2021   A Strontium Isoscape for the Conchucos Region of Highland Peru and Its Application to Andean Archaeology. *PLOS One* 16(3), https://doi.org/10.1371/journal.pone.0248209.

Wright, Henry, and Gregory A. Johnson

1975   Population, Exchange, and Early State Formation in Southwestern Iran. *American Anthropologist* 77:267–289.

Yamamoto, Atsushi

2010   Ingatambo: Un sitio estratégico de contacto interregional en la zona norte del Perú. *Boletín de Arqueología PUCP* 12:25–51.

2021   Emergence of Sociopolitical Complexity in Northern Peru: A Diachronic Perspective from the Huancabamba Valley. In *The Archaeology of the Upper Amazon: Complexity and Interaction in the Andean Tropical Forest*, edited by Ryan Clasby and Jason Nesbitt, pp. 83–105. University Press of Florida, Gainesville.

Yoffee, Norman

2005   *Myths of the Archaic State: Evolution of the Earliest Cities, States, and Civilizations.* Cambridge University Press, Cambridge.

Old Temples, New Substances

Emplacing and Replacing Chavín at Hualcayán, a Community Temple in Peru's North-Central Highlands

REBECCA E. BRIA

To understand Chavín's social impact in the ancient Andes is to inquire into how institutions, practices, and even material substances introduced during the Early Horizon influenced or conditioned the possibility for later social developments, as well as how earlier traditions shaped Chavín ideas and practices in local places. As for other early cultural phenomena in the Americas (see Pool, this volume), archaeologists may understand Chavín's influence in one of two ways: as the foundation for later and largely continuous landscapes and beliefs, or as part of many widespread cultural transformations that created a myriad of different and discontinuous political and aesthetic traditions. This chapter considers a more local point of view by providing evidence and a theoretical orientation for understanding the impact of Chavín on a longstanding community temple at Hualcayán, located in the Chavín heartland of highland Ancash in north-central Peru (Figure 5.1). In particular, it traces the ongoing changes in space, material, and practice in Hualcayán's principal temple called

"Perolcoto" (Figures 5.2 and 5.3), which was maintained as a collective ritual space between 2400 and 1 BC, to explore the social consequences of interweaving Chavín ritual practices and concretized local traditions over the longue durée.

Adopting and Replacing Chavín in Highland Ancash

Chavín de Huántar's social and cultural impact on its contemporaries, as well as on subsequent Andean societies, is indisputable. During the Early Horizon, the temple community at Chavín de Huántar set itself apart from others and drew pilgrims from near and far through a cosmopolitan mix of traditional and novel forms of architecture, art, religious leadership, and ritual experience, which was bolstered by an extensive system of trade to acquire and produce rare ritual goods (Burger 1992a, 2008a; Burger and Nesbitt, this volume; Burger and Salazar 2008; Contreras

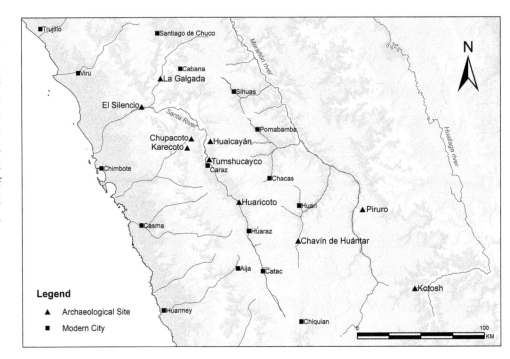

figure 5.1
Map of north-central Peru, showing Hualcayán's location and geographical proximity to several Formative-period temple sites within and beyond the region of Ancash. Map by Bebel Ibarra Asencios.

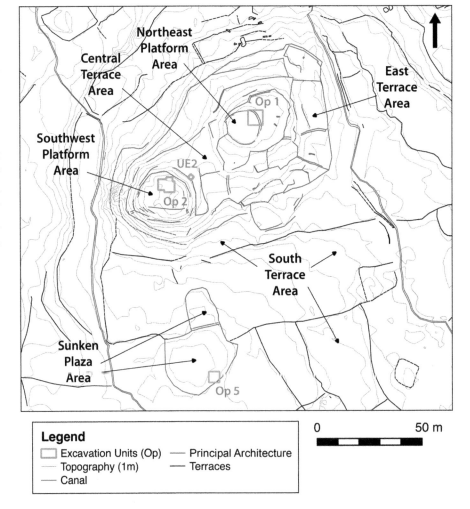

figure 5.2
Map of the Perolcoto mound and plaza complex at Hualcayán, indicating the location of architectural areas and excavation units discussed in the text. Surface architecture is a palimpsest of building and reuse over approximately four thousand years, with the majority occurring between 2400 and 1 BC. Map by Rebecca E. Bria.

Southwest Platform Area

Central Terrace Area

Northeast Platform Area

East Terrace Area

South Terrace Area

Sunken Plaza Area

figure 5.3
Photograph facing northwest of the Perolcoto mound and plaza complex at Hualcayán. Labels indicate major architectural areas. Photograph by Rebecca E. Bria.

2011; Kembel and Rick 2004; Matsumoto et al. 2018; Rick 2005, 2008a, 2008b, 2013, this volume; Sayre 2010; Sayre and López Aldave 2010; Sayre, Miller, and Rosenfeld 2016; Sayre and Rosenfeld, this volume). As Chavín's influence spread, it opened up new social, economic, and political possibilities across the Central Andes. Scholars have moved beyond the idea that Chavín was the "mother culture" of Andean complex society (Tello 1960), which has led to intensive explorations of how it grew out of and built upon earlier societies, such as coastal Cupisnique or Manchay religious and political systems (Burger 1992a; Burger and Salazar 1986, 2008; Nesbitt 2012; Rick 2008b). Yet scholarship has paid insufficient attention to the long-term social changes of the particular communities that existed before, then adopted, and later replaced Chavín. How did existing communities, with their

own local traditions and temple spaces, come to adopt Chavín ideology and emplace its practices? What impact did these local histories have on how a community later rejected Chavín or built a new community in its wake?

To address these questions, we must understand what Chavín became to the people already assembled through the community practices of ritual and labor, who were deeply invested in the temple of their forefathers, and we must examine how this community subsequently rejected Chavín. I thus suggest that the answer to the broader question of "what was Chavín" lies between these ruptures and continuities of Chavín's emergence and waning. This chapter concentrates on the long-term social developments in highland Ancash across the Formative period (3000–1 BC), with attention to how communities like Hualcayán experienced and performed social changes as they sought to maintain certain traditions or to reinvent themselves anew. In this section, I review the major cultural transitions that occurred in Ancash during the Formative period, first as the Kotosh Religious Tradition (3000–500/400 BC) was replaced by, or in some cases combined with, Chavín (900–500/400 BC), and then as people turned away from Chavín and developed a novel cultural identity called Huarás (400/300 BC–AD 100).

The Kotosh Religious Tradition before and during Chavín

Many pre-Chavín temples in highland Ancash were part of the Kotosh Religious Tradition. In Kotosh ceremonies, participants gathered in platform mound temples to perform rituals in which they burned a variety of materials, such as plants, meats, and shells, in sacred hearths within walled chambers (Burger 1992a; Burger and Salazar 1980; see also Bonnier 1997; Burger and Salazar 1986; Contreras 2010; Grieder and Bueno Mendoza 1985; Grieder et al. 1988; Izumi, Cuculiza, and Kano 1972; Izumi and Sono 1963; Izumi and Terada 1972).[1] Communities practicing Kotosh rituals rebuilt these ceremonial spaces many times over hundreds of years by superimposing new floors, hearths, and entire temples over old ones. The multiplicity of intimate hearth enclosures atop one or more mounds points to how particular groups, perhaps kin, likely maintained distinct hearths within an otherwise shared temple complex (Burger 1992a; Burger and Salazar 1980, 1986). The near ubiquity of these architectural features and practices in the north-central highlands, along with the evidence for long-distance trade of valued or ritual goods (e.g., Pacific mussels or rare stones), suggests that there was a strong regional social network and perhaps even direct interactions between communities who practiced this tradition (Burger 1992a:121, 2012; Burger and Salazar 1980).

The variation in the Kotosh Religious Tradition temple forms across north-central Peru points to how each community uniquely materialized a broad set of shared ideas and practices. Elisabeth Bonnier (1997) divides Kotosh Religious Tradition temples into two overarching groups: the Mito Tradition, named after a construction phase at the site of Kotosh, and the non-Mito Tradition. She identifies Mito Tradition temples as having tall standing walls built in a rectangular or sub-rectangular shape and featuring interior plaster, niches, and a split-level interior floor or "altar" with a central hearth—a building sequence and style that she views as a prescribed liturgical form (see also Contreras 2010).

Highland communities in Ancash turned away from Kotosh practices in distinct ways and at different times, before or along with Chavín's fluorescence and demise. People abandoned or covered Kotosh temples with new kinds of ritual architecture within a few centuries of the appearance of pottery during the early Initial Period between 1800 and 1500 BC (e.g., Grieder et al. 1988; Izumi and Sono 1963; Izumi and Terada 1972). The Kotosh Religious Tradition maintained relevance throughout the Early Horizon at other sites, even at Chavín de Huántar, where Daniel A. Contreras (2010) uncovered a Chavín-era Mito-style enclosure and hearth a short distance from Chavín de Huántar's monumental core. This evidence bolsters the earlier findings of Richard L. Burger and Lucy C. Salazar (1980, 1986) from the site of Huaricoto, which demonstrates how some Ancash communities not only practiced Kotosh rituals throughout the Early Horizon but also maintained Kotosh as their dominant religion even while Chavín influenced their artifact styles, building practices, and perhaps, certain beliefs (Burger 1992a:194–195; Burger and Salazar 1980:31). Together, the studies at Huaricoto and Chavín de Huántar reveal the sometimes selective and syncretic aspects of Kotosh and Chavín religious practices during the Early Horizon. They also point to how Ancash communities incorporated Chavín ideas and rituals, either in accordance with or against deep-rooted histories of practice, belief, and tradition—histories that were tied to local spaces, people, and lands.

Huarás Society after Chavín

After Chavín de Huántar's influence waned between 500 and 400 BC (Rick et al. 2010), people in highland Ancash shaped a new kind of culture and society called Huarás, coalescing by 300 BC. The Huarás emergence is marked by the appearance of distinct kinds of materials, especially the characteristic white-on-red painted ceramics that replaced Chavín's incised designs (Amat Olazábal 2004; Bennett 1944; Burger 1985; Gero 1990, 1991; Lau 2004, 2011; Lumbreras 2007). There are, nonetheless, subtle threads of continuity between Chavín and Huarás styles, such as in how Huarás groups embedded Chavín motifs, like circles and S-shapes, into their painted pottery, although this may reflect some archaistic appropriation or transformation of the ideas these symbols represent as opposed to continuity. Beyond pottery, Huarás settlements are quotidian compared to those associated with Chavín, as they are characterized by modest domestic units of agglutinated patio groups, subterranean tombs, and plaza spaces (Gero 1990, 1991; Lau 2011; Ponte Rosalino 2014).

Many archaeologists consider Huarás to be an intentional rejection of Chavín values and its religious authority (Amat Olazábal 2004; Burger 1992a:228; Lau 2011:244; Lumbreras 2007; Rick et al. 2010; Terada 1979). They largely base this on evidence from Chavín de Huántar, where Huarás groups—likely the descendants of Chavín devotees—partially dismantled, deposited trash inside, and/or built houses within previously sacred spaces (Lumbreras 2007). John W. Rick (2008a) and the Stanford team's (Kembel 2001, 2008; Rick et al. 2010) recent evidence suggests that an earthquake may have undermined the power of Chavín's oracle and the religious elites' ability to control natural and supernatural forces. Within one hundred years, the complex became a quotidian Huarás village, though recent evidence for Huarás activities in Chavín's galleries reveals a more complex picture of Chavín to Huarás transitional practices than previously understood.

Some scholars see the Huarás emergence less as a rejection of Chavín and more as a set of cultural and political practices that arose organically in the political vacuum that followed Chavín's collapse. For example, Joan M. Gero (1991, 1992) and George F. Lau (2011, 2016) have considered how the absence of Chavín political structures provided opportunities for new kinds of leadership, based not in exclusive ritual knowledge but in lineage, warfare, and labor—values that grew in importance, along

with ancestor veneration, within subsequent Recuay societies after AD 100 (Lau 2011:248–249). Based on mortuary evidence, hierarchical divisions within Huarás communities were not pronounced, but perhaps growing (Lau 2011:117, 136, fig. 26). Gero (1990, 1991) proposes that Huarás communities increasingly emphasized social hierarchies during ritual feasts, whereby lineage heads sponsored consumption events to demonstrate both their generosity and their ability to organize the labor of their kin to ensure group success.

The Chavín to Huarás transition thus marks a dramatic juncture in Ancash prehistory, in which authority and social organization became more rooted in the people and places of one's kin and community (Bria 2017; Lau 2011). The breakdown of Chavín's vast political and economic networks, which had been fueled by pilgrimage and the need for exotic ritual goods, along with the growing value of community-focused economic activities like agropastoralism in the post-Chavín era, seem to have together heightened the value of more localized social connections in Huarás society. That is, people in Ancash seem to have turned away from Chavín's universalizing views of the supernatural world and toward the local and the familiar. With this, they abandoned or repurposed the sacred temples their predecessors had revered for centuries or millennia.

Evaluating the Chavín Phenomenon through the Lens of Community

My approach to understanding the Chavín Phenomenon is through the lens of community. In particular, I am interested in how a history of ritual practice and the ongoing processes of community formation shaped how people adopted and rejected Chavín in local places like Hualcayán. I move away from the assumption that Early Horizon communities emerged or changed only in reaction to the external influences of Chavín, as such an assumption can obscure the agency that people had in shaping their own communities as well as how "peripheral" communities might have contributed to Chavín's rise and demise as a regional phenomenon.

In using community to discuss Formative-period temple societies, I do not refer exclusively to the people who dwelled next to a temple but instead to the collective of interacting and potentially diverse participants who came together to practice their rituals in, to provide labor and resources to, or to identify with a particular temple and its deities. At comparatively smaller temples like Perolcoto, the community of participants was likely to be more localized than at larger centers, drawing people from nearby villages who may have been simultaneously linked to other temple communities in asymmetrical and overlapping ways, whether through social ties or economic relationships.

My principal focus is to consider what Chavín was to people in communities like Hualcayán. In this, I circumvent interpretations that would explain the widespread adoption of Chavín as either a pathway for belonging to a broader social community through participation in a shared religion or as the web of practices and relationships of an aspiring elite to gain power and bolster their status position vis-à-vis their association with the religion (Durkheimian and Marxian premises, respectively). Certainly, decades of research support the notion that these social, religious, and political forces were significant, even central, to the spread and growth of Chavín at the magnitude it achieved (Burger 1992a, 1992b; Rick 2005, 2013). But I argue that, while recognizing these dynamics, we must not lose sight of the value and meaning that Chavín held for the diverse peoples who adopted it, to whom Chavín would have been more than an instrument for advancing their interests and positions. From this perspective, we can also consider how the Huarás emergence, in the wake of Chavín's breakdown, was forged as much by the desire to shape a new kind of society as it was driven by a loss of faith or an opportunistic competition between emergent elites in the absence of Chavín authority.

We must, therefore, ask how and why people would begin to subscribe to and reconfigure Chavín in local settings, while being careful not to assume that the agency of a person or community in the Chavín world was firmly structured by the overarching principles of a broader religion. What was it that attracted people to this set of beliefs and practices, particularly in settings beyond Chavín de Huántar and other major Chavín ritual centers? Were these practices adopted wholesale or selectively, and how did these decisions inform their later movement away from Chavín? To explore answers to these questions, I focus on Chavín's impact at the temple of Perolcoto at Hualcayán, which was not a major religious center in the Chavín world but instead a focal point of community life that persisted for thousands of years.

Hualcayán's Perolcoto Temple during the Andean Formative Period

Hualcayán is a large multi-component archaeological site located in the northern Callejón de Huaylas valley and situated on a broad sloping plateau below the Santa Cruz and Alpamayo glaciers in the Cordillera Blanca mountain range. My team's excavations at Hualcayán documented a long sequence of building and reuse spanning approximately 2400 BC to AD 1450 (Bria 2017; Cruzado Carranza and Bria 2014; Livora Castillo, Bria, and Cruzado Carranza 2012, 2013; Rivas Otaíza and Bria 2010). The focus of my present analysis is the site's Formative-period occupation (2400–1 BC), during which most temple construction occurred, which spanned the Kotosh, Chavín, and Huarás phases.[2] The extent of this Formative-period construction is difficult to calculate given the amount of later building, but the area of monumental construction, which comprised at least four platform mounds[3] and several plazas, covered at least 17 ha.

Perolcoto is the largest of the four Formative-period mounds at Hualcayán and is the only mound associated with a sunken plaza. The base of the Perolcoto mound covers approximately 1 ha and has a length of approximately 130 m and a height of 12–16 m; its associated sunken plaza measures approximately 30 m wide. The mound has two prominent platform areas—the higher Southwest Platform Area and the lower Northeast Platform Area (Figure 5.3). Immediately south of the Southwest Platform Area is the sunken plaza, which is

figure 5.4

Photograph facing southeast of the Sunken Plaza Area (right foreground) and the surrounding broad bench terraces that make up the South Terrace Area. Excavation unit (Operation 5) that was placed on the southern margin of the sunken plaza is marked in white. A hilltop habitation area is visible in the background. Photograph by Rebecca E. Bria.

irregularly shaped, likely because of later modifications. The plaza is offset from the center of the dual-platform mound, placed in front of its most prominent platform. This temple arrangement is reminiscent of the dual mound and plaza layout at La Galgada (see Grieder and Bueno Mendoza 1985:fig. 2; Grieder et al. 1988:figs. 14, 19), a coeval temple about 60 km northwest of Hualcayán, which may reflect relationships between Perolcoto's builders and people in other temple communities.

Hualcayán's Kotosh Religious Tradition Origins

The earliest and lowest cultural layer we recovered above sterile in the Perolcoto complex was below the sunken plaza, and a radiocarbon date from this layer revealed that activity in the temple was underway by the middle Late Preceramic period, between 2462 and 2295 cal BC (Figure 5.4).[4] The specific practices of this initial occupation are somewhat unclear (see Bria 2017:188–196 for a discussion), but our excavations in the Southwest Platform Area revealed greater precision with the discovery of a Late Preceramic, Mito-style Kotosh enclosure named PC-A. A radiocarbon measurement from an early modification of PC-A's interior (although perhaps

not the initial construction) indicates that the enclosure was built sometime around or perhaps before 2140–1901 cal BC (Figure 5.5). PC-A was built atop at least 12 m of buried, still unexcavated architecture, which likely contains hundreds of years of construction history in the Southwest Platform Area. We also dated carbon from the fill below PC-A's final interior floor, which revealed that Kotosh-related construction waned during or shortly after 1616–1506 cal BC. This date corresponds to the early Initial Period and is coeval with the final Mito-style constructions at La Galgada (Grieder et al. 1988).

The PC-A enclosure is the highest, most prominent, and presumably last Kotosh enclosure to be built on the Perolcoto mound; therefore, it provides the greatest insight into early pre-Chavín activities at Hualcayán during the Late Preceramic period and the early Initial Period. Though more than half of the structure is still buried below 4 m of construction fill, the architecture we uncovered has distinctive features that identifies it as a Mito-style Kotosh enclosure, including tall walls with rounded corners, a split-level floor, and a narrow inner ledge covered with thick plaster. Excavations exposed PC-A inside a looters' trench that had destroyed

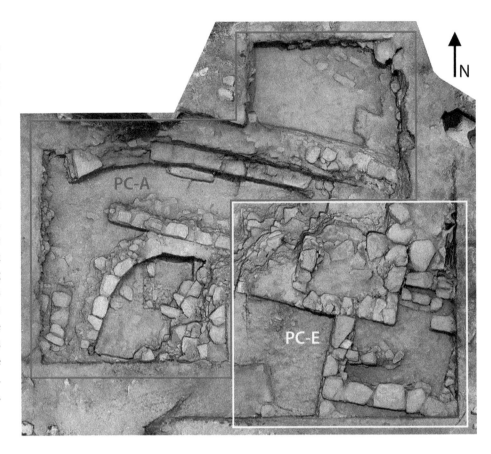

figure 5.5

Orthophoto of the architecture uncovered in the Southwest Platform Area (Operation 2). The Late Preceramic and early Initial Period temple enclosure PC-A (red box) is superimposed below the Early Horizon PC-E platform and room complex (yellow box). A looters' trench cut the western extent of both architectural areas, with greater damage to PC-E. Note that the two inner/southernmost walls inside PC-A are retaining walls for platforms whose surfaces and fills (which extended to the north and west of the stone faces) were excavated prior to this photograph. PC-C architecture is buried beneath PC-E. Photograph by Rebecca E. Bria.

much of PC-A's western wall but left the rest of the structure and its interior floors intact. Based on the curvature of PC-A's external wall and its location in the Southwest Platform Area, I estimate that its full extent is 12 m in diameter (Figure 5.6). It is possible that PC-A was not, in fact, a Kotosh temple, given that excavations have yet to reach the structure's center to confirm a hearth was the enclosure's focal point. Yet the Perolcoto mound's architectural form and overall temple layout at the time of PC-A is reminiscent of the contemporaneous temple at La Galgada, including in how PC-A was built atop and near the center of the most prominent of two platform mounds (see Figure 5.7; also compare Figures 5.2 and 5.3 to Grieder et al. 1988, figs. 14, 19).

During the early Initial Period, PC-A's interior was modified with at least three major constructions (Figure 5.8, A2–A4) after its creation (A1), with additional modifications occurring outside the structure (A6–A7) and some perhaps occurring during a period of later reuse (A5). Each of these construction events altered the proxemics

of ritual engagement in ways that appear to foreshadow a trend toward spatially separating individuals, such as ritual specialists, from other ritual participants—a distinction that became common during the subsequent Chavín era. Each modification to PC-A's interior involved altering the upper/outer and lower/inner sections of its split-level floor (designated by Bonnier [1997] as the epicaust and pericaust of a Mito Tradition temple, respectively). The outer floor, which was constructed by building a flanking platform against the temple wall's interior face, increased from an estimated 15 m² to 50 m² by the final modification. As each modification increased the surface area of the upper floor, the sunken inner floor became smaller, reduced from an estimated 90 m² in its original form to 40 m² in its final form. The outer floor, which was at first a low step, was refashioned into a 1 m flanking platform, making it difficult for someone to move freely between the upper and lower floors without having to scale a short ladder, to climb, or more likely, to use a designated stairway that may have been located

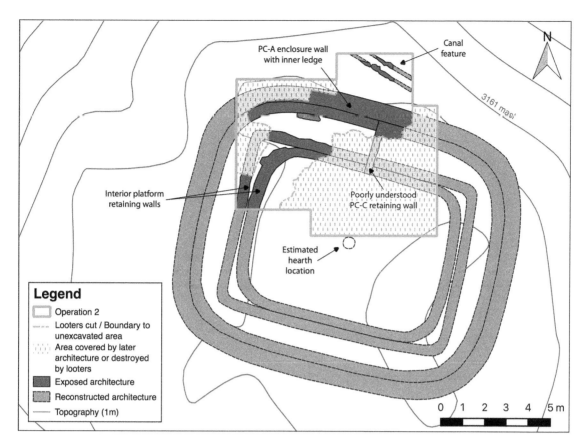

figure 5.6

Map of the exposed (dark gray) and projected/hypothesized (light gray) walls and features in the PC-A ritual enclosure, Southwest Platform Area (Operation 2). The entrance to PC-A is likely at the center of its southern wall. Map by Rebecca E. Bria.

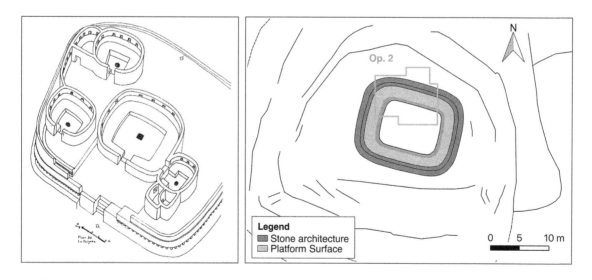

figure 5.7

A visual comparison of the final Mito temple complex at La Galgada (left, North Mound; redrawn from Grieder and Bueno Mendoza 1985:103, fig. 10) and a reconstruction of Hualcayán's PC-A temple (right, Southwest Platform Area), both constructed during the Late Preceramic period. Illustration by Rebecca E. Bria.

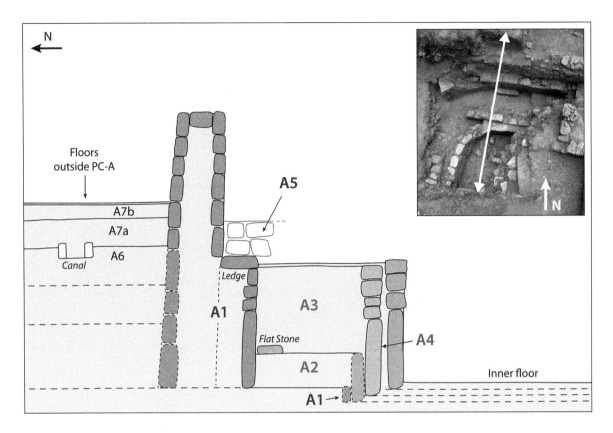

figure 5.8
Schematic cross section of PC-A, showing the relative associations of its architectural features and phases of construction. The exterior floors were higher than the interior floors and laid in successive stages. Several iterations of the interior floor exist as well, and their extents have been visualized here. Labels A1–A7 provide a possible construction order, with A1 being the earliest, original enclosure. However, exterior floors A6 and A7 were likely placed when interior floors were also laid down and A5 is likely associated with a reconstruction that postdates PC-A's original use (PC-C). Illustration by Rebecca E. Bria.

near the structure's entrance—all of these options would have restricted and directed movement more strictly than in earlier periods. Each modification also included notable aesthetic changes. At first, the retaining wall for the upper floor had curved corners that shadowed the temple's subrectangular form. The next reconstruction built the retaining wall with angular corners that contrasted the outer form, and the third and final reconstruction returned the upper floor to curved corners (see Figure 5.6).

These changes to PC-A would have restructured how people performed rituals inside it through time. Many have suggested that the upper, outer floors of Mito-style Kotosh temples provided a bench-like space (Burger 1992a:45; Grieder et al. 1988) for sitting or standing while viewing and venerating the

central fire below, or perhaps for performances around it (Bonnier 1997:124). Their building of the taller and wider platforms in PC-A may have materialized distinctions between the ritual practitioners who tended to the fire and the other individuals present, altering the ways they watched and contributed to a ceremonial event. In short, each change increasingly marked distinction between participants, even while eliciting their mutual interaction in an intimate space. The builders' choice to incrementally increase PC-A's flanking platforms inside a subrectangular enclosure reflects a development that, based on existing data, is unique to Hualcayán and is perhaps only associated with these final centuries of Kotosh practice before people eventually turned away from it.

The proposed trend of increasing spatial and social distinctions at Hualcayán between the end of the Late Preceramic period and the early Initial Period nonetheless parallels Terence Grieder and Alberto Bueno Mendoza's (1985) suggestion that community organization at La Galgada was becoming more centralized over time. In particular, they observed that, before abandoning Kotosh by constructing a U-shaped space, the La Galgada builders redesigned the temple layout in order to give prominence to a single central enclosure (Grieder et al. 1988:figs. 19, 38, 39). Although we have yet to uncover much of the early areas of ritual activity in Perolcoto for a full comparison, PC-A's monumentality and placement near the center of the Southwest Platform points to how the people of Hualcayán gave similar prominence to the PC-A enclosure. This seems to reflect a process of social reorganization at Hualcayán, particularly of the roles that distinct corporate or kin groups, who Burger and Salazar (1980, 1986) believe to have built and used distinct Kotosh enclosures, played in the community.

In particular, the spatial dominance of a certain Kotosh enclosure reflects a strong consensus among the community of people who built it, whereby they chose to collectively emphasize one temple enclosure over others on the mound. This may also point to the

ability of some groups to pool more corporate labor, as suggested by Burger and Salazar (1986:76–77) and Seiichi Izumi and Kazuo Terada (1972:306). The Hualcayán and La Galgada data together may indicate a pivotal moment during the transition between the Late Preceramic and Initial Period, in which new ideas about community and social order emerged in highland Ancash, particularly those that more comfortably allowed for hierarchical distinctions and that may have led to the eventual abandonment of the Kotosh Religious Tradition in many places.

Between Traditions: Turning Away from the Kotosh Religious Tradition before Chavín

The pivotal moment in which the people of Hualcayán abandoned the Kotosh Religious Tradition was during the middle Initial Period, when they filled the PC-A enclosure in order to construct a prominent platform, named PC-C, in the Southwest Platform Area. Displaced stones and eroded plaster, which was found intact only on top of the building's inner ledge, suggest that PC-A was either in disrepair or partially dismantled when people filled and covered it. Before the fill event, they placed a human cranium, which we found poorly preserved and fragmented, on PC-A's inner floor near its northwest corner (Figure 5.9) and then laid down alternating

figure 5.9
Photograph facing north showing the locations of the fragmented cranium placed on the surface of PC-A's final inner floor before filling to construct PC-C (A), and a carbon sample from the fill immediately below this floor (B). The PC-C stony fill used to cover the PC-A enclosure is visible at right. Photograph by Rebecca E. Bria.

figure 5.10
Photograph facing east, taken from the lowest point in the excavated looters' trench and showing PC-C's layered construction fill, indicated by white dotted lines, placed inside the PC-A enclosure. The fill included carefully placed stones along the face of the interior wall (toward the left of the image) but these stones were mostly removed prior to the photograph (see Figure 5.11). Architecture above the uppermost white line dates to the Chavín era (PC-E). The white asterisk indicates where a carbon sample was recovered within an in situ deposit of cooking pots and grinding stones (see Figure 5.11). Photograph by Rebecca E. Bria.

figure 5.11
Photographs facing north showing the careful stacking of PC-C's stone fill against the interior face of PC-A's outer wall (left), over which soil was laid that contained an in situ deposit of food preparation and consumption materials, including charred cooking pot fragments and two grinding stones, one visible here (right). Photograph by Rebecca E. Bria.

layers of stone and fairly clean soil throughout the structure (Figure 5.10). They may have placed other human remains on the eastern side of the structure, but this area remains unexcavated.

One AMS date of 1413–1277 cal BC obtained from an in situ context with food remains near the top of the PC-C fill (Figures 5.10 and 5.11) indicates that people covered PC-A one to two hundred years after they laid down the last PC-A floor. This context included a group of neckless cooking pot fragments and two grinding stones deposited approximately 30 cm below the top of the PC-A wall. We found the ceramic fragments between the two grinding stones, each of which was laid flat, revealing their intentional

figure 5.12
Artifacts from the PC-A and PC-C construction phases of the Perolcoto mound (Southwest Platform Area). PC-A materials span the Late Preceramic and early Initial Period and include marine mollusks, deer bone, and antler implements, such as an atlatl hook, a stone axe, a white and green stone bead (perhaps chrysocolla), and early ceramics. PC-C materials date to the middle Initial Period and include bone, shell, and stone (perhaps sodalite and chrysocolla) adornments, anthracite fragments, ceramic tubes, and ceramics vessels with similarity to Urabarriu styles. The black ware fragment with a drawn profile is a bottle with an undulating body and X incisions that likely depict cactus spines. Image by Rebecca E. Bria.

placement. I interpret this context as the probable evidence of a consumption event to recognize the collective labor pooled to fill PC-A and construct a new platform. Microbotanical analysis of residues from seven cooking pot fragments and the two grinding stones revealed the preparation and consumption of maize (*Zea mays*) and potato (*Solanum tuberosum*). This was the only exposed concentration of artifacts reflecting an activity area within the fill, fortunately secured below undisturbed later architecture, and it thus provides the most secure context for dating the fill event. There were likely other areas with similar food consumption deposits near the top of PC-C, but these were either destroyed by looters or remain buried under later architecture. Other PC-C fill materials include beads carved from bone, shell, and stone (perhaps sodalite), marine mollusks, polished anthracite, and ceramics, which point to individuals with personal adornments and ritual paraphernalia, food and drink consumption on the mound, and exchange beyond the temple walls (Figure 5.12). Decorated ceramics bear similarity to the Urabarriu style from the late Initial Period (Burger 1998; see Nesbitt, this volume). These vessels are primarily burnished and have incisions, rocker stamping, dentate punctuation, zoned textures, and/or circular nubbins. More unique vessel forms and designs were also present, such as a black bottle with an undulating body and rows of an incised X motif that may depict a cactus. The filling of the PC-A enclosure was clearly intended to transform the area into a platform complex, but PC-C's form is currently unclear due to a combination of the looting activities and the subsequent constructions that cover much of it beyond the excavated area. Moreover, there is a likelihood that the construction I am calling PC-C, which remains mostly buried below later constructions, occurred in two building phases, for near the eastern extent of our excavations we found a small segment of a buried retaining wall built immediately over PC-A's internal ledge (see Figure 5.6). This early PC-C construction would predate the food consumption remains that produced a date of 1413–1277 cal BC.

The PC-C constructions that transformed the PC-A temple into a platform complex changed the Southwest Platform Area from a space for intimate group activities that were hidden from the view of onlookers to a space for exclusive but highly visible performances. An individual who stood on top of the PC-C platform would have been visible from most locations on and around the mound. Later, people erected another platform complex atop PC-C, which is named PC-E (Figures 5.5 and 5.13). Carbon from within the PC-E fill revealed it was likely first built between 1385–1057 cal BC, or the late Initial Period. Builders later expanded and reused PC-E during the Early Horizon, when it became a focal point of temple activities.

The Chavín-Era Temple

Four lines of evidence suggest that the people of Hualcayán incorporated Chavín rituals and/or the widely held values of the Chavín era: (1) the extensive reconstruction of the Perolcoto complex in order to increase its monumentality and to enhance rituals of performance; (2) the acquisition of foreign materials like obsidian and Pacific marine resources; (3) the appearance of Janabarriu-style ceramics; and (4) the use of hallucinogenic substances. Potential auxiliary evidence comes from a fragment of a sculpted architectural panel with complex Chavín iconography[5] that was reportedly recovered by a collector from the District of Santa Cruz (Querevalú Ulloa 2014); survey indicates that Hualcayán is the only known major Early Horizon site with high densities of Janabarriu ceramics (Bria 2017). Although the monolith does not help to precisely identify Perolcoto as a formally converted or sanctioned "Chavín" temple during the Early Horizon, it helps to substantiate the evidence that local people in the northern Callejón de Huaylas, such as at Hualcayán, were part of the Chavín network or interacting with its practitioners. Regardless, foreign materials such as obsidian, which likely originated in south-central Peru (Burger et al. 2006:108), and mollusks from the Pacific Ocean, including a spondylus bead, reveal active participation in these networks and a shared value of such objects (Figure 5.18).

The filling in of the PC-A enclosure with the construction of the PC-C platform and the initial building of the PC-E platform complex in the Southwest Platform Area, both of which occurred during the Initial Period, suggest that Perolcoto's process of becoming a "Chavín" temple began not as a major conversion that turned local people away from the Kotosh Religious Tradition but as a localized process of transformation beginning four to five hundred years before the temple of Chavín de Huántar became a pan-Andean pilgrimage center. Moreover, Chavín-related ritual elements were emplaced within highly localized ritual traditions that are unknown to Chavín, such as the secondary burial of children (see PC-H, below).

After its initial construction and first amplification during the Initial Period (1385–1057 cal BC), the PC-E complex was used and modified several times between 898 and 425 cal BC—a range based on six dates that mostly overlap in time due to the atmospheric plateau that spans the Chavín era. Excavations indicate the following constructions in the PC-E complex (Figure 5.13). First, builders constructed a small platform and later expanded it to rectangular form with a narrow sunken stairway on its south side (1385–1057 cal BC). They subsequently covered the stairs with a raised stairway leading to the platform (811–548 cal BC) but left exposed the stones that framed the original stairway, as if to keep it marked.

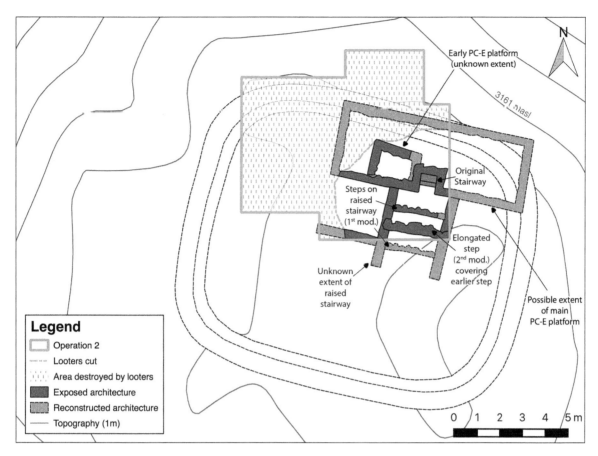

figure 5.13

Map of excavated of PC-E architectural features in Operation 2 (Southwest Platform Area), including the possible extent of these features in light gray. A dotted outline of the PC-A enclosure below PC-E illustrates the spatial relationship between the two building phases. Map by Rebecca E. Bria.

A major construction event later used ashy, rocky fill to bury the lower portion of PC-E's architecture (777–544 cal BC) and converted the raised stairway into a single elongated step (801–543 cal BC), although looting made it difficult to determine if these were from a single remodeling event or two distinct moments in time. Regardless, it was only during these constructions that Janabarriu ceramics appeared within PC-E contexts. A final construction event covered much of this exposed architecture, yet PC-E's upper structure remained exposed. Thus, although PC-E was partially destroyed due to looting and only partially excavated, the evidence indicates quite clearly that, throughout all Early Horizon building events, it remained important to preserve the top of PC-E's early platform.

Beyond the Southwest Platform Area of the mound, Chavín-era constructions were extensive,

including the creation of broad terraces around the base and sunken plaza of Perolcoto, which could accommodate large groups of people (see Figure 5.4). The prominent PC-E platform thus became an area where individuals could demonstrate their ritual knowledge through performances that were viewed by potentially large groups below. In short, these constructions created a prominent space that would have heightened the religious authority of specific individuals. Prominent but exclusive spaces and performances in mound complexes were key to both Chavín and Cupisnique ritual practices during the Early Horizon. However, the data suggest that such activities, along with long-distance exchange relationships, begin much earlier at Hualcayán and are simply enhanced during the Chavín era.

figure 5.14

Annotated photograph, facing north, of a test pit within Operation 1 (Northeast Platform Area). The profile shows the Early Horizon PC-H sequence of alternating ash floors over brown fills. Circular pits were cut into the top of each ash floor. A large vessel was set in clay and left in situ within the lowest pit (shown removed, except in profile). This may suggest other pits once held ceramic vessels. The ash and fill layers likely continue below the lowest level excavated. Illustration by Rebecca E. Bria.

Juxtaposed against the authoritative spaces of the PC-E platform are the coeval building episodes of PC-H in the Northeast Platform Area, which tell an alternative version of Chavín-era ritual engagement in the Perolcoto complex. These unique activities involved the repetitive building of platforms featuring superimposed rustic rooms and the repeated laying down of ashy floors and brown soil fills (Figure 5.14). The floors were informal in that they were mounded against a platform, thinning out as they extended away from it. These mounded soils were special despite their unevenness, for within them were the primary and secondary remains of deceased children. Pits were cut into the ashy floors,

likely to stabilize ceramic pots. The sequence of soil layers, cuts, and materials reveals that during a given ritual event, participants first excavated pits into an existing ash floor (which was laid during a prior ritual event) and then deposited brown soil fill that interred child remains. Following this, they sealed the area with a new layer of ash flooring that became the new surface of the mound until the subsequent burial event. Three radiocarbon dates spanning 805–544 cal BC and Janabarriu-style ceramic fragments distributed throughout the PC-H fills confirm these burial and building practices date to the Early Horizon. Similar practices are unknown in other Chavín-era temples, with the closest example being

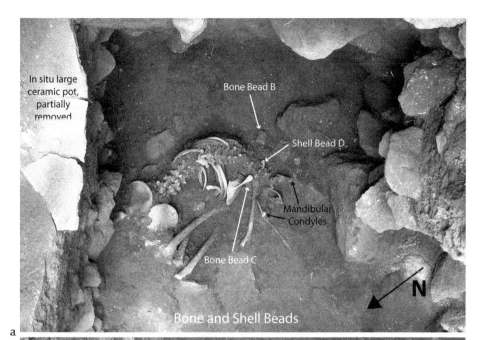

In situ large ceramic pot, partially removed

Bone Bead B

Shell Bead D

Mandibular Condyles

Bone Bead C

N

Bone and Shell Beads

a

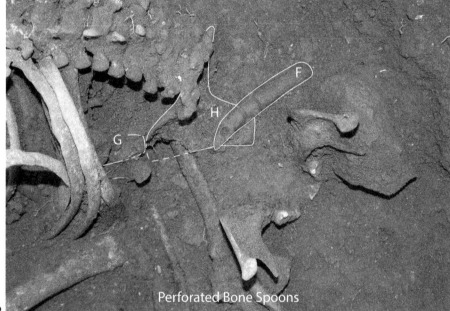

F

H

G

Perforated Bone Spoons

b

figure 5.15
Photographs facing southeast of the most complete child burial found in the PC-H complex of the Northeast Platform Area. Both images show the child remains after the cranium was removed during excavation to expose the position of objects below the neck. The prone position of the mandible reveals the head was face down while the body was flexed and facing west. a) The location of bone and shell beads around and below the cervical vertebrae; and b) detail of the bone spoons positioned below and on the anterior side of the removed cervical vertebrae and right scapula. Photographs by Rebecca E. Bria.

the Early Horizon burials of children in large vessels atop the Late Preceramic mound at Kareycoto in the upper Nepeña Valley (Munro 2018). I interpret the recurrent practices in PC-H as rites of renewal, in that, by coming together periodically to grieve and bury the deceased members of the next generation, people renewed their collective commitment to both their temple and their community.

The human remains in the PC-H layers included a near complete child, aged five to seven years, whose body was mixed with bone elements and teeth from one or more other juveniles (Figure 5.15). In another level, we encountered the disarticulated remains, including ribs, vertebrae, and cranial fragments, of one or more children aged four or younger (Sharp 2017). Given that we recovered these remains within a restricted 2 m² excavation area (within Operation 1), it is probable that more juvenile remains are buried in the surrounding and lower soils.

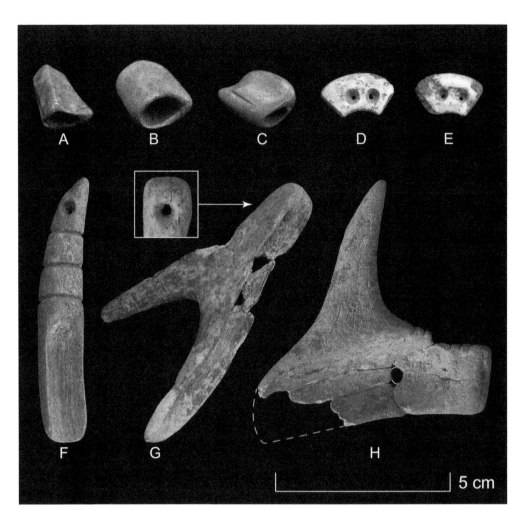

figure 5.16
Perforated objects, likely strung together, found below the neck of the interred child in PC-H (Operation 1, Northeast Platform Area; see Figure 5.15). Top: three worked, polished bone beads (A–C) and two shell beads (D and E). Bottom: three bone or antler spoons likely used for inhaling hallucinogenic snuff (F–H). Each spoon has a perforated hole. The lower left edge of spoon H was found highly fragmented (see Figure 5.15) and is therefore missing. Illustration by Rebecca E. Bria.

Materials from this unique child burial practice included the ritual paraphernalia used for achieving hallucinogenic states, pointing to how the people of Hualcayán enmeshed Chavín rituals—or at least those practices that became emblematic to Chavín during the Early Horizon—within a highly localized tradition. This paraphernalia consisted of three perforated shallow bone or antler spoons (Figure 5.16) believed to be used for ingesting snuff, similar to the spoon-type spatulas found at Chavín de Huántar (Burger 1998:195) and those used during the Sajara-patac phase at Kotosh (Izumi and Terada 1972:pl. 62a-17). We recovered these worked bone/antler objects, along with two shell and three bone beads, close to the anterior side of the C7 vertebra of the near complete child burial. The child was positioned face down and flexed (see Figure 5.15). The objects' perforations and their location at the front of the

neck is firm evidence that they were strung on a necklace and worn by the child at the time of burial. Regardless of whether the child ingested any hallucinogenic substances when alive, the association may reflect a relationship between the experience of shamanic transformation and the transformative experience of death. The evidence may alternatively suggest that the ongoing renovation of the mound through building and burial—practices that altered its shape, size, and internal substance—complemented or materialized the ability to transcend and transform through mind-altering substances.

Sometime during the latter centuries of the Chavín era, people abruptly abandoned these recurring building and child-burial ritual practices when they constructed a formal platform complex over the Northeast Platform Area, labeled PC-J (Figure 5.17). Flanking rooms around the main platform

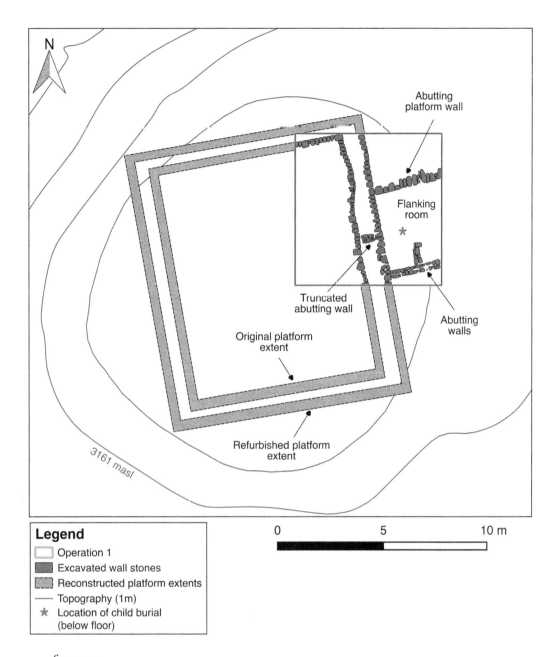

Legend

- ☐ Operation 1
- ▨ Excavated wall stones
- ▨ Reconstructed platform extents
- — Topography (1m)
- ✳ Location of child burial (below floor)

0   5   10 m

figure 5.17

Map showing the estimated size and shape of the original and refurbished main platform of the
PC-J platform complex in the Northeast Platform Area. The size and shape of the platform, which
was buried under later architecture, was determined by the wall sections exposed in Operation 1
in combination with the mound's shape in unexcavated areas. Abutting walls to the east of the PC-J
platform create flanking rooms. Map by Rebecca E. Bria.

permanently covered the mounded ashy soils where
people had once buried children. Carbon recovered from behind the main platform's retaining wall
dated this construction event to 756–409 cal BC. The
event may reflect an intensification of Chavín values
at Hualcayán, for it involved people turning away
from a more idiosyncratic local tradition of repetitive burning, burial, and building in order to create a fixed and formal platform structure. Analysis
of architectural alignments also suggests that many

figure 5.18
Artifacts from the PC-E (Southwest Platform Area) and PCE-H and PC-J (Northeast Platform Area) construction phases of the Perolcoto mound and dating to the early and middle Early Horizon. Artifacts include marine mollusks, bone implements, lithics made from obsidian, chert, crystal, and slate materials, a spondylus bead, and ceramics that include Janabarriu styles. The face fragment is likely part of a figurine. Image by Rebecca E. Bria.

of Perolcoto's flanking terraces were simultaneously rebuilt around the same time as the new platform in the Northeast Platform Area, likely to create a more cohesive temple space. In particular, while the majority of late Chavín-era architecture is aligned to one orientation, between 65° and 77° (for example, the terraces in Figure 5.4 were built at the same orientation as the PC-J platform in the Northeast Platform Area, as seen in Figure 5.17), earlier subsurface architecture, which was exposed through excavation, was built facing a number of different and constantly changing orientations (Bria 2017:504–507, figs. 7.12–7.13). These construction events undoubtedly

required intense negotiations over whether and how to end long-standing community traditions in the face of new or changing ideas.

When viewed together, the distinct histories of ritual and building in the Northeast and Southwest Platform Areas reveal local people did not "convert" to the Chavín religion in a swift or sweeping way. For the first few hundred years of Chavín influence, the displays of ritual authority on formal platforms in the Southwest Platform Area of the Perolcoto mound were paired with, if not intentionally complemented by, the architecturally informal and recurrent mortuary practices in the Northeast

Platform Area. Moreover, while the soils and spaces of the Southwest Platform Area were largely clean, soils in the Northeast Platform Area contained evidence of the consumption of a range of local food products, including maize (*Zea mays*), potato (*Solanum tuberosum*), beans (*Phaseolus vulgaris*), and camelids (*Lama sp.*); the ash floors in PC-H were presumably made from the burned refuse of these consumption events. These differences in remains point to how the value of local foods and people was defined and celebrated on one side of the mound while the value of foreign connections and rare and exotic objects such as obsidian, crystal, and marine mollusks was elevated on the other side (Figure 5.18). These distinct practices on opposite sides of the Perolcoto mound may have been seen as complementary, but they may also have

been viewed by the corporate groups affiliated with each—whether priests or community collectives— as incompatible. Disagreements over how community rituals should be performed could have contributed to the eventual efforts made to create a more unified space during the construction events associated with PC-J, presumably to shape a common ritual purpose vis-à-vis the Chavín religion.

Becoming Huarás after Chavín

These unifying efforts, however, were undermined when the people of Hualcayán turned away from the rituals and temple spaces that had defined their community for hundreds of years during the late Early Horizon. Excavations and radiocarbon dates suggest that intensive decommissioning activities began in the Southwest Platform Area between 500

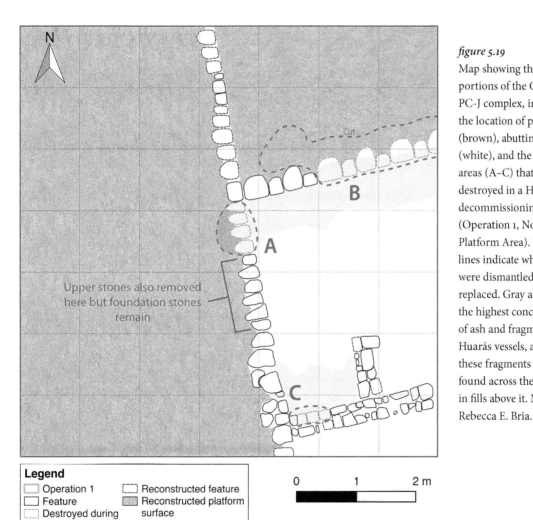

figure 5.19
Map showing the excavated portions of the Chavín-era PC-J complex, indicating the location of platforms (brown), abutting rooms (white), and the three areas (A–C) that were destroyed in a Huarás decommissioning ritual (Operation 1, Northeast Platform Area). Red dotted lines indicate where stones were dismantled and then replaced. Gray areas indicate the highest concentrations of ash and fragmented Huarás vessels, although these fragments were also found across the floor and in fills above it. Map by Rebecca E. Bria.

Upper stones also removed here but foundation stones remain

Legend
Operation 1
Feature
Destroyed during Huarás phase
Reconstructed feature
Reconstructed platform surface

0   1   2 m

figure 5.20

White-on-red painted and plain red burnished Huarás ceramics recovered from Destruction Areas A–C and found smashed atop the adjacent floors of the PC-J complex. One of these vessels, shown at the top right, is a rare Huarás polychrome bowl, reconstructed from fragments that were recovered in a thin layer of ash that extended across the PC-J floor and beneath the Destruction Areas. All decoration is painted except for the bowl in the lower right, which shows a cross etched onto its base. Photographs by Rebecca E. Bria.

and 400 BC, followed by the appearance of Huarás ceramic styles by 300 BC. In the Northeast Platform Area, excavations uncovered striking evidence for Huarás decommissioning activities, which involved an elaborate process of dismantling and then re-dedicating the PC-J platform, sometime between 200 and 50 BC.

In the PC-J platform complex of the Northeast Platform Area (Operation 1), we exposed three areas of dismantled walls, labeled Destruction Areas A through C (Figure 5.19). We found a similar sequence of events in each Destruction Area, which began when people first dismantled a section of wall stones before feasting within the platform complex using Huarás-style white-on-red vessels (Figure

5.20). They then strategically placed their refuse and ash from these feasts in the destroyed wall cavities before haphazardly rebuilding the walls by stacking stones. Finally, they also used stones to smash decorated Huarás vessels atop the Chavín-era floor, then sealed these contexts with more soil and stone.

Several lines of evidence reveal that the three Destruction Areas were intentionally dismantled rather than simply in disrepair during the Huarás phase. For example, in Destruction Area A, we found a dense concentration of Huarás-style decorated bowls and a large broken jar within a destroyed wall section and its abutting floor. A stack of somewhat dressed stones, presumably from the now-dismantled retaining wall, were placed directly upon

figure 5.21

Photographs of PC-J Destruction Area B facing north–northwest and presented in reverse order of their excavation to demonstrate the sequence of Huarás-era practices of wall destruction and reconstruction. 1) A section of the Chavín-era retaining wall was dismantled down to its foundation, after which a Huarás vessel fragment, a lithic core, and a marine mollusk shell were deposited at the base of the dismantled wall (these objects are visible atop the loose soil). 2) Parallel stacked stones were then placed in the wall cavity without mortar. 3) Feasting remains and soil were then deposited over the stacked stones, followed by more stones and soil. 4) Detail of part of the deposit visible in 3, showing how the feasting contents included nearly complete but fragmented ceramic vessels and in situ guinea pig remains. Photographs by Rebecca E. Bria.

the broken and burned feasting remains. Destruction Areas B and C were destroyed and rebuilt in a similar fashion. In Destruction Area B (Figure 5.21), between the coursings of loosely stacked stones we found the in situ remains of consumption, which included guinea pig (*Cavia porcellus*) and camelid (*Lama sp.*) bones and several nearly complete Huarás bowls containing the residues of maize (*Zea mays*), potato (*Solanum tuberosum*), and quinoa (*Chenopodium quinoa*). Of these plant remains, maize was the most

prevalent, found also on large jars perhaps used for fermenting and serving chicha beer. A marine mollusk shell (*Semele solida*), lithic core, and Huarás ceramic sherd were intentionally placed in the loose soil at the base of the destroyed wall section before rebuilding it (see Figure 5.21). Given the lack of evidence for long-distance trade during this period, it is likely that the Huarás decommissioners encountered the mollusk as they destroyed the PC-J complex. No other foreign foods or objects were present within the Huarás Destruction Areas, pointing to a simultaneous breakdown in interregional trade and an increased valuation of the things and foods that were locally produced.

Together, the late Early Horizon remains suggest that Huarás ritual events on the Perolcoto mound were defined by the need to infuse Chavín spaces with new materials and meanings. Huarás painted pottery and maize, perhaps in the form of chicha, were essential to the acts of recommissioning. By depositing these distinctly new materials inside the walls of the Chavín structure, they effectively transformed its substance from the inside out. These events thus manifested and marked the change from the previous to the new era. It is surely no coincidence, though perhaps counterintuitive, that these intensive Huarás decommissioning practices occurred in the Northeast Platform Area and not the Southwest Platform Area, the latter of which was a more prominent and persistent symbol of Chavín-era religious authority. Instead, Huarás groups were intensely focused on converting the mound in spaces where Chavín's authority had been more recently emplaced—not long before it diminished—vis-à-vis the platforms that were built over the spaces used for the rites of cyclical building and collective burial.

Chavín Communities over the Longue Durée: Emplacing and Replacing Chavín in Peru's North-Central Highlands

Hualcayán presents an interesting case for studying Chavín's rise and fall from the perspective of community, revealing how one community selectively employed and then rejected Chavín's rituals and values according to their own history, social tensions, and perhaps even vision of community. The Hualcayán evidence suggests that Perolcoto's transformation into a "Chavín temple"—or more precisely, a temple that shared many of Chavín's materials, ideas, and practices of ritual performance—did not occur with a swift or sweeping conversion at the beginning of the Early Horizon. Instead, the temple platforms that endured throughout the Early Horizon were first constructed during

the Initial Period, indicating a process of change that began hundreds of years before Chavín coalesced as a regional phenomenon. We can perhaps even see the origins of the social transformations that led to this new platform-building tradition in how, during the transition from the Late Preceramic to the early Initial Period, people began changing Perolcoto's Kotosh chambers to create greater spatial divisions between ritual participants—before eventually rejecting Kotosh altogether. The subsequent construction of platforms (PC-C and PC-E) atop these Kotosh spaces (PC-A) indicates that Initial Period ritual shifted to community-scale performances that would have further defined the social boundaries between religious practitioners on restricted platforms and other participants in surrounding spaces. These Initial Period rituals on platforms featured individuals wearing fine stone beads, involved "exotic" traded objects like anthracite mirrors and marine mollusks, and featured the consumption of food and drink from ceramics crafted in the "Urabarriu" style similar to those also seen at Chavín de Huántar and elsewhere during the late Initial Period and early Early Horizon.

During the Early Horizon, Chavín-affiliated practices and materials, including consumption activities involving the display of Janabarriu ceramics, were carried out in formal platform complexes and plazas. But these rituals were performed alongside the highly localized rituals of building and child burial, which created uneven and frequently changing temple forms on one side of the mound. It was not until the second half of the Chavín era that local people may have turned to the Chavín religion in an effort to unify community practices on the mound. This moment may have been somewhat fleeting, however, for within a few hundred years of starting this extensive construction project, the Hualcayán community, like others across the Chavín world, abandoned the Chavín religion and rejected many of the social positions and relationships that supported it.

These data from Perolcoto point to how "becoming Chavín" was a localized, meandering, and even contested process. The evidence also supports that Initial Period communities in highland Ancash were already shifting toward new ritual practices and structures of community organization that foreshadow and may have laid the foundation for the Early Horizon society we attribute to Chavín de Huántar's religion. We might, therefore, more strongly consider the role of late Initial Period communities across highland Ancash in determining what became Chavín (see Nesbitt, this volume), seeing them as producers and not just consumers of new ideas in the already strong regional network that Chavín de Huántar built upon toward the end of the second millennium BC.

In this chapter, I propose that we attempt to explain Chavín not only in terms of its regional spread or its elite–commoner relationships but also by considering whether and how collective groups sought out or emphasized Chavín ideas and practices as a way to enhance or reorganize the relationships that composed their community. The Perolcoto data support the perspective that, when we consider the evidence for Chavín influence within the long-term history of a "Chavín community," Chavín is revealed as a set of ideas and practices that people used selectively, according to or juxtaposed against existing practices (see also Burger and Salazar 1980). Later, Huarás groups demarcated a rupture from the old ways of doing things as they decommissioned Chavín structures and emplaced Huarás materials, effectively transforming the mound's substance and, in so doing, themselves.

Interrogating Chavín through the lens of community also helps us to consider how local factions within Hualcayán may have had differing commitments to the Chavín religion or distinct interpretations of how to implement its practices. This is visible in the contrasting Chavín-era rituals performed on opposite ends of the Perolcoto mound, which simultaneously emphasized permanence and/or priestly authority in the Southwest Platform Area and community renewal and regeneration in the Northeast Platform Area. Tensions between these practices may have led to the ultimate decision to rebuild the entire Perolcoto mound and plaza complex during the late Chavín era, refashioning it to align more closely with the formal temples associated with Chavín.

To understand Chavín's impact during the Early Horizon, we might thus consider not only how the Chavín religion influenced local practices in communities across the Central Andes but also how Chavín became, whether through its emplacement or rejection, the means through which people in places like Hualcayán reconfigured who they were, how they interacted, and what they valued as a community. This was a constant process that unfolded throughout the Formative period, and Chavín played an important, but not absolute, role in this process. Local politics, such as tensions between corporate groups and the ritual traditions they emphasized, likely had as much an influence on what Hualcayán became during the Chavín era as the ideas and practices of Chavín itself. Each reconstruction of the Perolcoto mound not only transformed the temple's physical substances but also generated new, locally oriented meanings of what it meant to be part of the Hualcayán community.

1 Variations of Kotosh enclosures are also present at some coastal sites (Montoya Vera 2007; Piscitelli 2014; Pozorski and Pozorski 1996; Shady, Machacuay, and López 2003).

2 During the post-Formative period, Recuay groups (AD 1–700) built low platforms on Perolcoto's summit and converted some its flanking platforms into mortuary areas that were continuously used or later reused during the Middle Horizon (AD 700–1000; Bria 2017) and Late Intermediate Period (AD 1000–1450; Sharp 2022:485, sample 35747).

3 Three other Formative-period mounds at Hualcayán are significantly smaller both in height and area and have been more heavily altered or destroyed by modern occupation (Bria 2017).

4 All radiocarbon (AMS) dates were calibrated using OxCal, IntCal20. Date ranges presented are with the 95.4 percent confidence interval.

5 A comparison to known Chavín iconography (Bria 2017:527–530) indicates that the sculptural fragment may depict or be related to the so-called Master of the Fishes deity (Lathrap 1985:246) found on the Yauya stela and discussed by Burger (2008b:166, fig. 6.4). However, Jorge Gamboa (2016) and José Samuel Querevalú Ulloa (2014) offer other possible interpretations.

REFERENCES CITED

Amat Olazábal, Hernán

2004 Huarás y Recuay en la sequencia cultural del Callejón de Conchucos: Valle del Mosna. In *Arqueología de la Sierra de Ancash: Propuestas y perspectivas*, edited by Bebel Ibarra Asencios, pp. 97–120. Instituto Cultural Runa, Lima.

Bennett, Wendell C.

1944 *The North Highlands of Peru: Excavations in the Callejón de Huaylas and at Chavín de Huántar*. Anthropological Papers of the American Museum of Natural History 39, no. 1. American Museum of Natural History, New York.

Bonnier, Elisabeth

1997 Preceramic Architecture in the Andes: The Mito Tradition. In *Archaeológica peruana 2: Prehispanic Architecture and Civilization in the Andes*, edited by Elisabeth Bonnier and Henning Bischof, pp. 120–144. Sociedad Archaeológica Peruano Alemana, Reiss Museum, Mannheim.

Bria, Rebecca E.

2017 Ritual, Economy, and the Production of Community at Hualcayán, Peru. PhD dissertation, Vanderbilt University, Nashville.

Burger, Richard L.

1985 Prehistoric Stylistic Change and Cultural Development at Huaricoto, Peru. *National Geographic Research* 1:505–534.

1992a *Chavín and the Origins of Andean Civilization*. Thames and Hudson, London.

1992b The Sacred Center of Chavín de Huántar. In *The Ancient Americas: Art from Sacred Landscapes*, edited by Richard F. Townsend, pp. 265–277. Art Institute of Chicago, Chicago.

2008a Chavín de Huántar and Its Sphere of Influence. In *Handbook of South American Archaeology*, edited by Helaine Silverman and William H. Isbell, pp. 681–704. Springer, New York.

2008b The Original Context of the Yauya Stela. In *Chavín: Art, Architecture, and Culture*, edited by William J. Conklin and Jeffrey Quilter, pp. 163–179. Cotsen Institute of Archaeology, University of California, Los Angeles.

2012 The Construction of Values during the Peruvian Formative. In *The Construction of Value in the Ancient World*, edited by John K. Papadopoulos and Gary Urton, pp. 288–305. Cotsen Institute of Archaeology, University of California, Los Angeles.

Burger, Richard L., George F. Lau, Victor M. Ponte, and Michael D. Glascock.

2006   The History of Prehispanic Obsidian Procurement in Highland Ancash. *La complejidad social en la Sierra de Ancash*, pp. 103–120. Civiche Raccolte d'Arte Aplicada del Castello Sforzesco, Milan.

Burger, Richard L., and Lucy C. Salazar

1980   Ritual and Religion at Huaricoto: A New Religious Tradition Defined in the Peruvian Highlands. *Archaeology* 33: 26–32.

1986   Early Organizational Diversity in the Peruvian Highlands: Huaricoto and Kotosh. In *Andean Archaeology: Papers in Memory of Clifford Evans*, edited by Ramiro Matos Mendieta, Solveig A. Turpin, and Herbert H. Eling, pp. 65–82. Cotsen Institute of Archaeology, University of California, Los Angeles.

1998   *Excavaciones en Chavín de Huántar*. Pontifica Universidad Católica del Perú, Lima.

2008   The Manchay Culture and the Coastal Inspiration for Highland Chavín Civilization. In *Chavín: Art, Architecture, and Culture*, edited by William J. Conklin and Jeffrey Quilter, pp. 85–106. Cotsen Institute of Archaeology, University of California, Los Angeles.

Contreras, Daniel A.

2010   A Mito-Style Structure at Chavín de Huántar: Dating and Implications. *Latin American Antiquity* 21:1–19.

2011   How Far to Conchucos? A GIS Approach to Assessing the Implications of Exotic Materials at Chavín de Huántar. *World Archaeology* 43:380–397.

Cruzado Carranza, Elizabeth K., and Rebecca E. Bria

2014   *Proyecto de Investigación Bioarqueológico Regional Ancash: Informe final de las labores realizadas durante la Temporada de Campo 2013*. Instituto Nacional de Cultura, Lima.

Gamboa, Jorge

2016   Una escultura lítica del formativo temprano (1600–1000 aC) de Caraz, Callejón de Huaylas, Perú. *Boletín del Museo Chileno de Arte Precolombino* 21(2):9–24.

Gero, Joan M.

1990   Pottery, Power, and . . . Parties! *Archaeology* 43:52–56.

1991   Who Experienced What in Prehistory? A Narrative Explanation from Queyash, Peru. In *Processual and Postprocessual Archaeologies: Multiple Ways of Knowing the Past*, edited by Robert W. Preucel, pp. 126–139. Center for Archaeological Investigations, Southern Illinois University, Carbondale.

1992   Feasts and Females: Gender Ideology and Political Meals in the Andes. *Norwegian Archaeological Review* 25:17–30.

Grieder, Terence, and Alberto Bueno Mendoza

1985   Ceremonial Architecture at La Galgada. In *Early Ceremonial Architecture in the Andes*, edited by Christopher B. Donnan, pp. 93–109. Dumbarton Oaks Research Library and Collection, Washington, D.C.

Grieder, Terence E., Alberto Bueno Mendoza, C. Earle Smith Jr., and Robert M. Malina

1988   *La Galgada, Peru: A Preceramic Culture in Transition*. University of Texas Press, Austin.

Izumi, Seiichi, Pedro J. Cuculiza, and Chiaki Kano

1972   *Excavations at Shillacoto, Huánuco, Peru*. University of Tokyo Press, Tokyo.

Izumi, Seiichi, and Toshihiko Sono

1963   *Andes 2: Excavations at Kotosh, Peru 1960*. Kadokawa Publishing, Tokyo.

Izumi, Seiichi, and Kazuo Terada

1972   *Andes 4: Excavations at Kotosh, Peru 1963 and 1966*. University of Tokyo Press, Tokyo.

Kembel, Silvia R.

2001   Architectural Sequence and Chronology at Chavín De Huántar, Peru. PhD dissertation, Stanford University, Stanford.

2008   The Architecture at the Monumental Center of Chavín de Huántar: Sequence, Transformations, and Chronology. In *Chavín: Art, Architecture, and Culture*, edited by William J. Conklin and Jeffrey Quilter, pp. 35–81. Cotsen Institute of Archaeology, University of California, Los Angeles.

Kembel, Silvia R., and John W. Rick

2004   Building Authority at Chavín de Huántar:
        Models of Social Organization and
        Development in the Initial Period and
        Early Horizon. In *Andean Archaeology*,
        edited by Helaine Silverman, pp. 51–76.
        Blackwell, Oxford.

Lathrap, Donald W.

1985   Jaws: The Control of Power in the Early
        Nuclear American Ceremonial Center.
        In *Early Ceremonial Architecture in the
        Andes*, edited by Christopher B. Donnan,
        pp. 241–267. Dumbarton Oaks Research
        Library and Collection, Washington, D.C.

Lau, George F.

2004   The Recuay Culture of Peru's North-
        Central Highlands: A Reappraisal of
        Chronology and Its Implications. *Journal
        of Field Archaeology* 29:177–202.

2011   *Andean Expressions: Art and Archaeology
        of the Recuay Culture.* University of Iowa
        Press, Iowa City.

2016   *An Archaeology of Ancash: Stones, Ruins,
        and Communities in Andean Peru.*
        Routledge, New York.

Livora Castillo, Felipe F., Rebecca E. Bria, and
Elizabeth K. Cruzado Carranza

2012   *Proyecto de Investigación Arqueológico
        Regional Ancash: Informe final de las
        labores realizadas durante la Temporada
        de Campo 2011.* Instituto Nacional de
        Cultura, Lima.

2013   *Proyecto de Investigación Arqueológico
        Regional Ancash: Informe final de las
        labores realizadas durante la Temporada
        de Campo 2012.* Instituto Nacional de
        Cultura, Lima.

Lumbreras, Luis G.

2007   *Chavín: Excavaciones arqueológicas.*
        2 vols. Universidad Alas Peruanas, Lima.

Matsumoto, Yuichi, Jason Nesbitt, Michael D. Glascock,
Yuri I. Cavero Palomino, and Richard L. Burger

2018   Interregional Obsidian Exchange during
        the Late Initial Period and Early Horizon:
        New Perspectives from Campanayuq
        Rumi, Peru. *Latin American Antiquity* 29:
        44–63.

Montoya Vera, María

2007   Arquitectura de la tradición mito en el
        valle medio del Santa: Sitio El Silencio.
        *Bulletin de l'Institut Français d'Études
        Andines* 36:199–219.

Munro, Kimberly E.

2018   Landscapes of Persistence and Ritual
        Architecture at the Cosma Complex,
        Upper Nepeña Valley, Peru. PhD dis-
        sertation, Louisiana State University,
        Baton Rouge.

Nesbitt, Jason

2012   Excavations at Caballo Muerto: An
        Investigation into the Origins of the
        Cupisnique Culture. PhD dissertation,
        Yale University, New Haven.

Piscitelli, Matthew

2014   Ritual Is Power? Late Archaic Small-Scale
        Ceremonial Architecture in the Central
        Andes. PhD dissertation, University of
        Illinois, Chicago.

Ponte Rosalino, Victor M.

2014   *Arqueologia en la Cordillera Negra del
        Callejón de Huaylas Perú: Área de influen-
        cia Mina Pierina.* Barrick, Surco.

Pozorski, Thomas, and Shelia Pozorski

1996   Ventilated Hearth Structures in the
        Casma Valley, Peru. *Latin American
        Antiquity* 7:341–353.

Querevalú Ulloa, José Samuel

2014   *Análisis comparativo de la arquitectura
        temprana de los sitios de Tumshukayko y
        Chupacoto distritos de Caraz y Huaylas,
        provincia de Huaylas.* Universidad
        Nacional Mayor de San Marcos, Lima.

Rick, John W.

2005   The Evolution of Authority and Power at
        Chavín de Huántar, Peru. In *Foundations
        of Power in the Prehispanic Andes*, edited
        by Kevin J. Vaughn, Dennis Ogburn,
        and Christina Conlee, pp. 71–89.
        American Anthropological Association,
        Washington, D.C.

2008a   Context, Construction, and Ritual in the
        Development of Authority at Chavín de
        Huántar. In *Chavín: Art, Architecture, and
        Culture*, edited by William J. Conklin and
        Jeffrey Quilter, pp. 3–34. Cotsen Institute
        of Archaeology, University of California,
        Los Angeles.

2008b   Un análisis de los centros ceremoniales del período formativo a partir de los estudios en Chavín de Huántar. *Boletín de Arqueología PUCP* 10:201–214.

2013   Architecture and Ritual Space at Chavín de Huántar. In *Chavín: Peru's Enigmatic Temple in the Andes*, edited by Peter Fux, pp. 151–166. Scheidegger & Spiess, Zurich.

Rick, John W., Christian Mesía, Daniel A. Contreras, Silvia Rodríguez Kembel, Rosa M. Rick, Matthew Sayre, and John Wolf

2010   La cronología de Chavín de Huántar y sus implicancias para el período formativo. *Boletín de Arqueología PUCP* 13:87–132.

Rivas Otaíza, Cora A., and Rebecca E. Bria

2010   *Proyecto de Investigación Arqueológico Regional Ancash—Huaylas: Informe final de las labores realizadas durante la Temporada de Campo 2009.* Instituto Nacional de Cultura, Peru.

Sayre, Matthew P.

2010   Life across the River: Agricultural, Ritual, and Production Practices at Chavín de Huantar, Peru. PhD dissertion, University of California, Berkeley.

Sayre, Matthew P., and N. López Aldave

2010   Exchange at Chavín de Huántar: Insights from Shell Data. *Andean Past* 9:340–345.

Sayre, Matthew P., Melanie J. Miller, and Silvana A. Rosenfeld

2016   Isotopic Evidence for the Trade and Production of Exotic Marine Mammal Bone Artifacts at Chavín de Huántar, Peru. *Archaeological and Anthropological Sciences* 8:403–417.

Shady, Ruth, Marco Machacuay, and Sonia López

2003   Recuperando la historia del Altar del Fuego Sagrado. In *La ciudad sagrada de Caral-Supe: Los orígenes de la civilización andina y la formación del estado prístino en el antiguo Perú*, edited by Ruth Shady and Carlos Leyva, pp. 237–253. Instituto Nacional de Cultura, Lima.

Sharp, Emily A.

2017   Appendix H: Human Remains. In *Ritual, Economy, and the Production of Community at Hualcayán, Peru*, by Rebecca E. Bria, pp. 853–858. PhD dissertation, Vanderbilt University, Nashville.

2022   Precarious Lives in the Late Prehispanic Andes: A Bioarchaeological Study of Physical Violence and Its Legacies in the North-Central Highlands. PhD dissertation, Arizona State University, Tempe.

Tello, Julio C.

1960   *Chavín: Cultura matriz de la civilización andina.* Publicación Antropológica del Archivo "Julio C. Tello" de la Universidad Nacional Mayor de San Marcos, Lima.

Terada, Kazuo

1979   *Excavations at La Pampa in the North Highlands of Peru, 1975: Report 1 of the Japanese Scientific Expedition to Nuclear America.* University of Tokyo Press, Tokyo.

The Establishment of Power in the Formative Period of the North Highlands of Peru

YUJI SEKI

Recent research on the north-highlands ceremonial centers of Kuntur Wasi and Pacopampa presents clear evidence for the emergence of institutionalized leaders in the Late Formative period (800–250 BC) (Seki 2014). Previously, the emergence of leaders and social differentiation was interpreted as the result of cultural or religious diffusion of the Chavín culture or cult (Carrión Cachot 1948:16; Tello 1960:36–41). However, subsequent studies have suggested that the leaders' basis of power and the process of social differentiation varied from region to region. These characteristics should not be understood as the result of one-sided influence and interaction with Chavín de Huántar.

Many researchers now emphasize not only the political and cultural independence of each ceremonial center but also the establishment of a coalition—loose or firm—between ceremonial centers by employing peer polity models (Burger 1993:74, 2008:698; Matsumoto and Cavero Palomino, this volume; Renfew 1982). It is now clear that interaction between ceremonial centers significantly intensified during the Late Formative period through the widespread trade of precious materials such as obsidian, cinnabar, pottery, and marine shell (Burger 2008). However, this discussion frequently ignores the relationship among earlier societies that developed in the preceding Middle Formative period (ca. 1100–800 BC).

In this chapter, I discuss the relationship between the establishment of power in the Formative period and the Chavín Phenomenon, especially through the analysis of data recovered from two large ceremonial centers in the north highlands of Peru: Pacopampa and Kuntur Wasi. I focus not only on the interaction between ceremonial centers but also on the diachronic transformations of architectural components and mortuary practice from the Middle to Late Formative periods as a means to understand the power bases that the leaders exploited, such as control over long-distance trade and access to memory. Through this analysis,

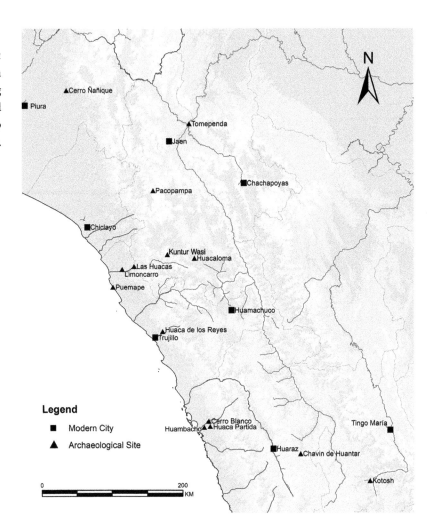

figure 6.1
Map of the northern region of Peru, showing the locations of Middle and Late Formative sites. Map by Bebel Ibarra Asencios.

Legend

■ Modern City

▲ Archaeological Site

0   200
                      KM

figure 6.2
Topographical map of the Pacopampa archaeological site and its surrounding sites. © Pacopampa Archaeological Project.

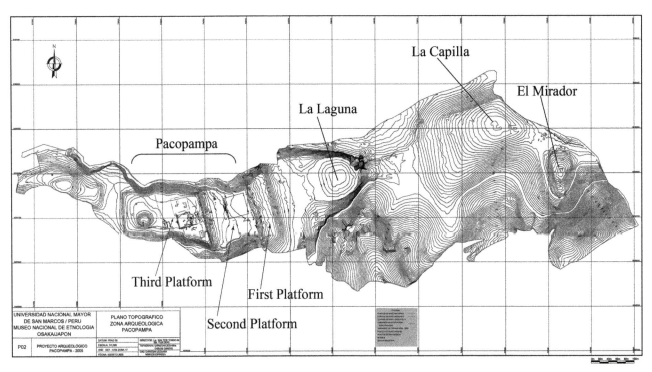

La Capilla

El Mirador

La Laguna

Pacopampa

Third Platform

First Platform

Second Platform

I would like to contribute to a more nuanced understanding of the Chavín Phenomenon. I begin this chapter with a discussion of Pacopampa, before moving on to related research at the site of Kuntur Wasi.

Archaeological Investigations of Pacopampa

Pacopampa is situated on the eastern slopes of the Andes Mountains in the north highlands of Peru. It is located next to the village of Pacopampa in Querocoto District, Chota Province, Cajamarca Region (Figure 6.1). The site is found at 2500 masl, on the left bank of the Chotano River, one of the tributaries of the Marañon River. It is composed of three large platforms (Figure 6.2) with the main masonry constructions located on the third (or uppermost) platform. The site was previously investigated by several archaeologists (Fung Pineda 1975; Morales Chocano 1980; Rosas and Shady 1970), but these efforts were limited in scale and duration. This chapter is based primarily on the results of the Pacopampa Archaeological Project, organized through an agreement between the Universidad Nacional Mayor de San Marcos and the National Museum of Ethnology of Japan. Our long-term project has investigated Pacopampa since 2005.

Based on stratigraphic data recovered from these excavations and radiocarbon dating, our project has established the existence of two sequential phases (Seki et al. 2010): Pacopampa I (1200–700 BC) and Pacopampa II (700—400 BC) (all dates are calibrated). Each of these phases is subdivided into two sub-phases: IA and IB, IIA and IIB, respectively (Seki et al. 2010) (Table 6.1). During the excavations, we found a layer overlying sterile soil containing exclusively Pandanche pottery, an Early Formative (Initial Period) style thought to be among the earliest ceramic complexes in the north highlands of Peru (Kaulicke 1981). Unfortunately, no evidence of building activity has been found associated with this pottery. Furthermore, traces of activities after sub-phase IIB have been confirmed by recent excavations, but since this is the phase when activities as a ceremonial center ceased, they

will not be further discussed in this chapter. In the following section, I will summarize the architectural sequence of Pacopampa (Seki et al. 2019; Seki et al. 2016, 2017; Seki et al. 2010).

Sub-Phase IA

Most of the architecture from sub-phase IA can be observed along the western portion of the Third Platform. A stepped platform dating to this sub-phase was identified, and in the north portion there is a staircase. During sub-phase IA, several platforms and small patios were built in front of that platform (Seki et al. 2010:figs. 5–7). Nevertheless, we have no clear evidence of how the access was organized or controlled.

Sub-Phase IB

During sub-phase IB, the architectural plan of the site was drastically changed (Figure 6.3). According to radiocarbon dating, this event occurred around 900 BC. Recent studies demonstrate that the large-scale retaining walls of the First, Second, and Third Platforms, along with staircases between the platforms, may have been built at that time.

Along the western portion of the Third Platform, the previous structures of sub-phase IA were sealed and the new platform (Western Platform) was built. On the Western Platform, the Circular Building (28.50 m in diameter and 1.4 m in height) was constructed, along with a lower square platform at the eastern front of the building. It is unknown if this was the access to the top of the structure. However, on a low square platform attached to the Circular Building, three benches covered by a fine plaster were found and, in front of them, hearths with evidence of burning were exposed (Figure 6.4). Around the same moment, at the eastern part of the Third Platform, a square Sunken Court measuring 30 m in length and 1.20 m in depth was constructed (Figures 6.3 and 6.5). This court has four axial stairs in the middle of each wall.

The Sunken Court was surrounded with three low platforms forming a U-shape. A series of rooms was constructed on top of each platform. Looking from above, it can be seen that these rooms were arranged in a stepped design (Figure 6.3).

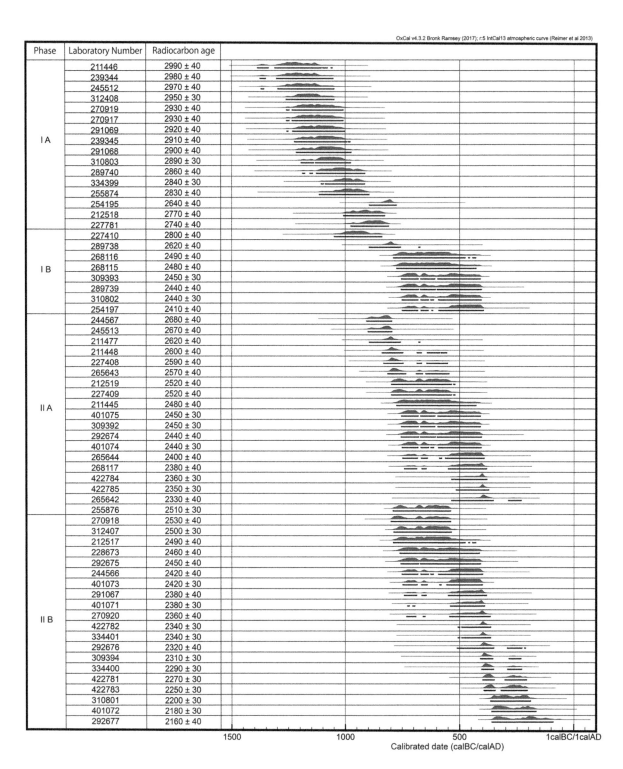

Phase	Laboratory Number	Radiocarbon age	
I A	211446	2990 ± 40	
	239344	2980 ± 40	
	245512	2970 ± 40	
	312408	2950 ± 30	
	270919	2930 ± 40	
	270917	2930 ± 40	
	291069	2920 ± 40	
	239345	2910 ± 40	
	291068	2900 ± 40	
	310803	2890 ± 30	
	289740	2860 ± 40	
	334399	2840 ± 30	
	255874	2830 ± 40	
	254195	2640 ± 40	
	212518	2770 ± 40	
	227781	2740 ± 40	
I B	227410	2800 ± 40	
	289738	2620 ± 40	
	268116	2490 ± 40	
	268115	2480 ± 40	
	309393	2450 ± 30	
	289739	2440 ± 40	
	310802	2440 ± 30	
	254197	2410 ± 40	
II A	244567	2680 ± 40	
	245513	2670 ± 40	
	211477	2620 ± 40	
	211448	2600 ± 40	
	227408	2590 ± 40	
	265643	2570 ± 40	
	212519	2520 ± 40	
	227409	2520 ± 40	
	211445	2480 ± 40	
	401075	2450 ± 30	
	309392	2450 ± 30	
	292674	2440 ± 40	
	401074	2440 ± 30	
	265644	2400 ± 40	
	268117	2380 ± 40	
	422784	2360 ± 30	
	422785	2350 ± 30	
	265642	2330 ± 40	
	255876	2510 ± 30	
II B	270918	2530 ± 40	
	312407	2500 ± 30	
	212517	2490 ± 40	
	228673	2460 ± 40	
	292675	2450 ± 40	
	244566	2420 ± 40	
	401073	2420 ± 30	
	291067	2380 ± 40	
	401071	2380 ± 40	
	270920	2360 ± 40	
	422782	2340 ± 30	
	334401	2340 ± 30	
	292676	2320 ± 40	
	309394	2310 ± 30	
	334400	2290 ± 30	
	422781	2270 ± 30	
	422783	2250 ± 30	
	310801	2200 ± 30	
	401072	2180 ± 30	
	292677	2160 ± 40	

table 6.1

Radiocarbon dates of the Pacopampa archaeological site. For the bottom ten samples, it may be considered to be the time when the site suspended the function as a ceremonial center.

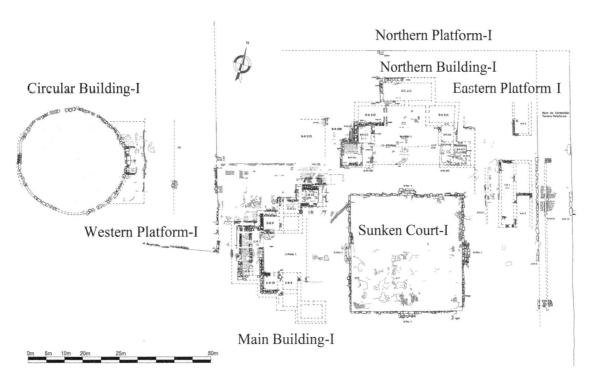

figure 6.3
Architectural plan of sub-phase IB. © Pacopampa Archaeological Project.

figure 6.4
Three benches attached to Circular Building-I. © Pacopampa Archaeological Project.

figure 6.5
a) The Sunken Court after the conservation work. The stairs are visible in the center of the two lateral walls running in parallel. The stairs of other walls were sealed in sub-phase IIB. b) A staircase located at the western wall of the Sunken Court. © Pacopampa Archaeological Project.

a

b

The rooms located at the center of the western platform are called Main Building-I. Main Building-I is composed of five rooms; the access to these rooms was located along the main axis of Main Building-I, except for a room located at the extreme west that has two symmetric entrances (Figure 6.6).

At the first room on the east side, hearths with evidence of burning were found dug into the floor and later covered with gray plaster. The floor was modified at least four times. After the first and second floors were used, several small pits were excavated and filled with soil prior to making the next floor. The variety of size and location of the holes are inconsistent with post holes, particularly since their location would have obstructed the access. Therefore, it is likely that these holes were related to a religious activity linked with the abandonment of each floor. Interestingly, the floor associated with the second

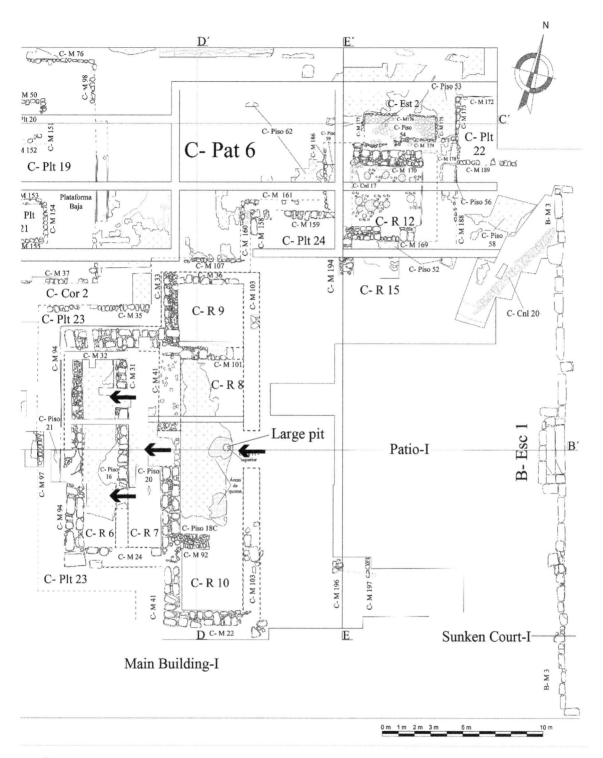

figure 6.6
Main Building-I and its access in sub-phase IB. © Pacopampa Archaeological Project.

figure 6.7
Renovation for a second time of the floor in the first room of the Main Building. The large hole in the center is a possible tomb in sub-phase IB, which was cut by the later tomb of the "Lady of Pacopampa." © Pacopampa Archaeological Project.

renovation moment features a large pit (10PC-C-Hoyo-11) with a diameter of around 1 m and a depth of 1 m (Figure 6.7). Most of the pit was destroyed by a later pit belonging to the next sub-phase (IIA) that contained the tomb of the "Lady of Pacopampa" (C-Entierro 09-02), which will be discussed later in this chapter. In the fill of the earlier pit, we recovered two stone vessels, one of them made of anthracite. These unusual artifacts and the shape and scale of the pit suggest that the early pit was a tomb.

The axis of Main Building-I also passes through the center of the stairs at the Sunken Court and the center of the staircases between the First, Second, and Third Platforms. Because the axis also passes through the middle of another sunken court on the Second Platform, we suspect that the court may have also been constructed during this sub-phase. As a consequence, almost all structures of this sub-phase were arranged along the axis. This axis crosses the Pacopampa site and passes through the middle of La Laguna, another mound, where we discovered an access toward the uppermost platform (see Figure 6.2). This axis also leads to another mound called La Capilla, where we also identified architectural activity like the retaining wall belonging to sub-phase IB.

Sub-Phase IIA

In sub-phase IIA, the architectural components of the previous sub-phase were modified by means of

covering or re-utilization, though certain elements of the earlier architectural organization were preserved (Figure 6.8). An entrance to the east facade of the Circular Building was added although the rectangular platform attached to the building was covered with a thick fill. Furthermore, the retaining wall was raised in height, and we found a clear use of the space on the top of the building for the first time, as new architectural components were constructed there.

The Sunken Court was reused without major changes. The stairs located between the First and Second Platforms, and between the Second and Third Platforms, were also reused. Interestingly, a pair of stone carvings was unearthed from the layer that covered the stairs located between the First and Second Platforms. Although we do not know their original position, it seems likely that these stone carvings were set on both sides of the stairs. One stone carving had a height of 1.6 m and a width of 0.4 m (Figure 6.9). The carving is an anthropomorphic representation using shallow relief techniques. Its face represents a feline with fangs, but from the neck to the bottom it shows a standing human. Both hands were carved together at the chest and tied up; it also has a loincloth at its waist.

The other stone carving was 1.9 m in height and 40 cm in width; it was discovered in a partially fragmented condition. Much of the face was severely damaged, so its expression could not be determined, but broad lines indicate a representation of hair that

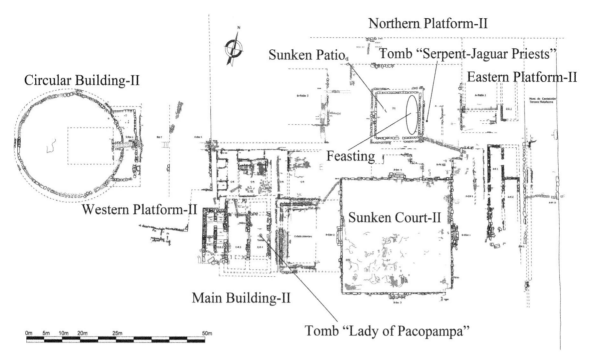

figure 6.8
Architectural plan of sub-phase IIA. © Pacopampa Archaeological Project.

figure 6.9
A stone carving with an anthropomorphic representation made in sub-phase IIA. © Pacopampa Archaeological Project.

was engraved on the back of the head, a feature absent in the previously mentioned stone carving. Both hands were put together at the chest, but no representation of a loincloth at the waist could be found. Judging from the presence or absence of hair, the former stone carving could represent a male, while the latter one could depict a female.

The stone carvings had been intentionally pushed over. Interestingly, miniature pots were placed around the head of the male stone carving just below the face. This context is similar to that of the Sunken Court. There are many miniature pots around the structures built during the Early Cajamarca period (AD 200–400), after the abandonment of the ritual

figure 6.10
A stone carving representing a feline animal exhibited at the Pacopampa village. © Pacopampa Archaeological Project.

space of the Formative period (Seki et al. 2016). Therefore, it is highly possible that people of the Early Cajamarca period dismantled the stone carvings and buried them with the stairs.

Besides the examples mentioned before, there are five other stone carvings recovered from the Pacopampa site. Two are exhibited at the Museo Larco in Lima, two are at the site itself, and one is located in a plaza at the Pacopampa village. The two carvings in Lima were discovered in 1939 by Rafael Larco Hoyle during a six-day excavation. One of them has a human body and a feline face (Roe 1974:fig. 24a); it is similar to the stone carving we uncovered during our excavation. The other one is a round engraved carving representing a feline animal in three dimensions (Roe 1974:fig. 24b); it is thought to be part of the pair of the one located at the plaza of the Pacopampa village (Figure 6.10). The original location of these carvings is unknown, and it is difficult to judge whether they were made during the Pacopampa I or II phase, or even a later date. However, in the stone carvings of feline animals at the Museo Larco and in the plaza at Pacopampa village, circle and dot designs made by incision can be observed. These patterns are generally recognized as spots of jaguars, and they are also characteristic of the pottery of the Pacopampa II

phase. Therefore, we think these stone carvings can be dated to Pacopampa II.

During sub-phase IIA, Main Platform-I was sealed with construction fill, then used as the base for another platform (Main Platform-II). This latter platform supported Main Building-II with its eight square rooms (Figure 6.11). The access and entrances to these rooms maintained the same axis as in the previous sub-phase IB, except for the last room located at the extreme west. The route to reach the last room was indirect, following a zigzag path that suggests a degree of control and the importance of access to it. It should be noted that the Sunken Court was reused during this subphase. An open patio stretched across the front of the Main Building, surrounded by an open canal.

Excavations at Pacopampa conducted from 2005 to the present day have uncovered more than sixty burials on the Third Platform, where the most important buildings are concentrated. Except for a few cases, most of them correspond to sub-phase IIA or later. The majority of these were burials set in simple pits. Only two burials, described below, had the special feature of a shaft-shaped hole deep underground. In 2009, a tomb (C-Entierro 09-02) located along the main axis of Main Building-II was found

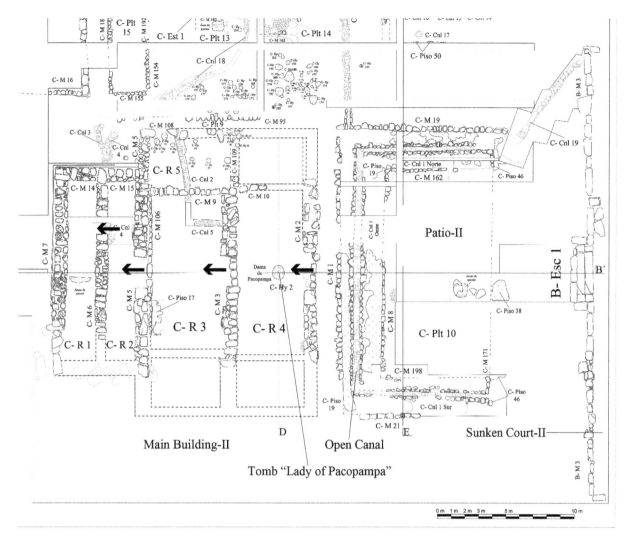

figure 6.11
Main Building-II and its access in sub-phase IIA. © Pacopampa Archaeological Project.

and named the tomb of the "Lady of Pacopampa." The tomb had been built after the abandonment of Main Building-I and before the constructions of sub-phase IIA. Tomb C-Entierro 09–02 is a deep shaft in a cylindrical shape, with an oval opening approximately 1 m in diameter and reaching a depth of 2 m (Figure 6.12). At a depth of 1.5 m, plain slabs of andesite rock were found piled one over the other within the tomb shaft. After removing them, we found five ceramic vessels. A small long-necked bottle was found in the northern part of the tomb and three vessels were unearthed in the southern part of the tomb (Figure 6.13). A small bowl with concave walls and a flat base was found overlying

a pedestal dish (*compotera*). There were signs of burning on the interior base of the *compotera*, and this evidence suggests that a funerary ritual was performed when burying the individual. Between the two groups of ceramics, the tomb diameter was reduced. A large slab was left leaning against the wall of the tomb. After removing this slab and excavating 0.50 m below the ceramic vessels, skeletal remains of a buried individual were found at the bottom of the tomb (Figure 6.14).

A series of offerings were found accompanying the individual, including a pair of gold earplugs measuring 6 cm in diameter, a pair of gold earrings with dimensions of 25 × 11 cm (Figure 6.15), and objects

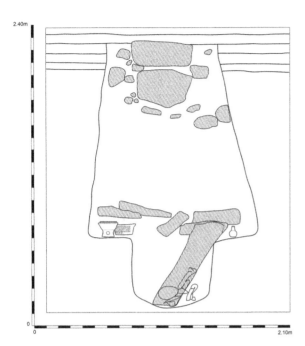

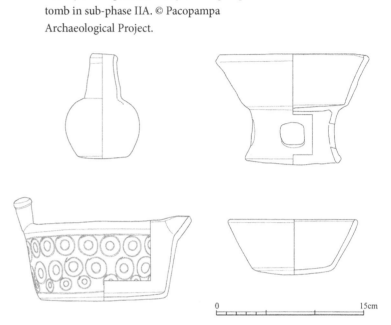

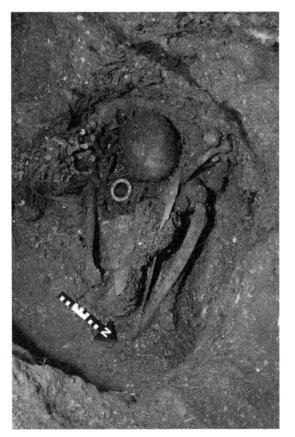

made with marine shells identified as *Pteriidae* (Vásquez and Tham 2010). A radiocarbon measurement of 2330±40 BP (Beta–265642) was taken from a bone of the buried individual. The buried individual was an adult female aged twenty to thirty-nine years with a height of 1.62 m (Nagaoka et al. 2012). Based on the data obtained at the Kuntur Wasi site, the average height for men and women at this time was 1.58 m and 1.46 m, respectively. Therefore, the woman buried in the elaborate tomb at Pacopampa was taller than most men and women of her time. Her head showed signs of cranial deformation and was surrounded with red (cinnabar) and blue (azurite) pigments. Around the mandible, a small stone disk made of chrysocolla was found. The disk was

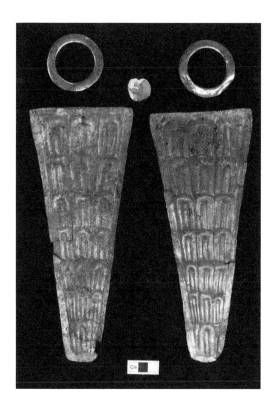

figure 6.15
Gold earplugs and
earrings as offerings
at the "Lady of
Pacopampa" tomb.
© Pacopampa
Archaeological Project

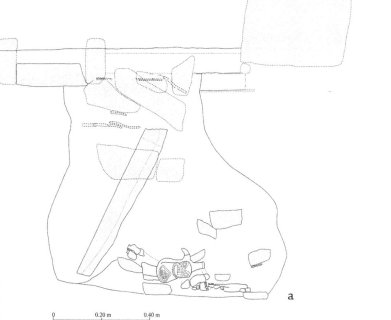

probably placed in the mouth, as we have observed
in other funerary contexts at Pacopampa.

In front of Main Building-II, a patio surrounded
by an open canal was constructed. On the Northern
Platform, the Sunken Patio was unearthed. The
patio measured 14 m on each side and was bounded
by two walls of different levels at each side. In sub-
phase IIA, there was a direct access to the patio from
the Sunken Court.

At the end of sub-phase IIA, some evidence
of feasting was found at the Sunken Patio on the
Northern Platform (Seki et al. 2016). Several pottery fragments; lithic, bone, and metal artifacts;
and animal and human bones were unearthed here
(see Figure 6.8). Interestingly, several pottery vessels were found broken by intentional destruction.
Therefore, this feasting can be identified as a ritual
act. Simultaneously, a tomb was installed close to
the eastern wall of the patio (Seki et al. 2017). These
two events likely occurred at the same time.

This second tomb is in a pit with a diameter of
55 cm and a depth of approximately 1 m. The base
of the shaft is larger than the upper part. It is a little
smaller than the tomb of the "Lady of Pacopampa"

figure 6.16
a) Cross section of the "Serpent-Jaguar Priests"
tomb in sub-phase IIA; and b) burials at the
"Serpent-Jaguar Priests" tomb. © Pacopampa
Archaeological Project.

(Figure 6.16). However, the two tombs have some characteristics in common. In the fill of the tomb, several large slabs were placed over the individuals. The individual found at the bottom was a young male aged fifteen to thirty-four years (Nagaoka et al. 2020) and was associated with a gold necklace (Figure 6.17). Near the cranium, six kinds of minerals, including cinnabar, hematite, azurite, barite, magnetite, and malachite, were observed in powder form. The other individual found over the young male was an adult woman aged thirty-five to fifty-four years (Nagaoka et al. 2020). A stirrup bottle in the shape of a serpent or feline was positioned over the body (Figure 6.18) and, for this reason, we refer to this feature as the tomb of the "Serpent-Jaguar Priests." It is interesting that the right foot was not found in its original position, but near the cranium. It probably indicates that this female individual had a special role of guarding the male individual, though it is unknown if the woman was sacrificed because examination of the bone failed to identify cut marks (Nagaoka et al. 2020).

Sub-Phase IIB

Following the feasting event and the installation of the tomb of the "Serpent-Jaguar Priests," two

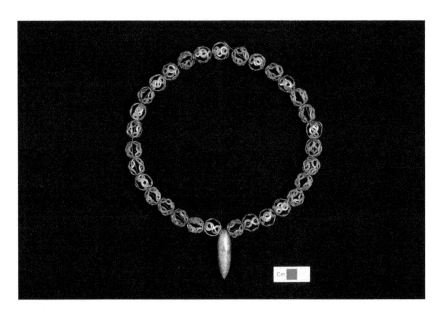

figure 6.17
A gold necklace recovered from the "Serpent-Jaguar Priests" tomb. © Pacopampa Archaeological Project.

figure 6.18
A stirrup bottle in the shape of a serpent with a feline head. © Pacopampa Archaeological Project.

consecutive feasting events were held at the same place in sub-phase IIB. These feasts were accompanied by the construction of small platforms inside and outside of the patio. It is probable that the first feasting event was related to the installation of the tomb—that is, to the death of the individuals. If so, the second and the third feasting events held at the same place could have been made to commemorate their deaths.

However, feasting has another characteristic. Brian Hayden has observed that funeral feasts are arenas for reconfirming and creating socioeconomic and political alliances and ties among the community members because the death of important leaders "creates uncertainties as to the ability of surviving members to maintain previous social, production and political roles" (Hayden 2009:40). Feasting at Pacopampa may have been held not only for keeping the death of the "Serpent-Jaguar Priests" in memory but also for the purpose of recreating the relationship with the group that supports the ceremonial center.

The access to the Sunken Patio from the Sunken Court was sealed after the second feasting event, with a small platform constructed directly over it. In place of the older access, a new one was built at the north side of the Sunken Patio. Like the closing at the entrance to the Sunken Patio, the north stairs in the Sunken Court connecting the patio were sealed. It is likely that the other three staircases were also sealed. In place of these sealed stairs, two new stairs were built at the northwestern and the southeastern corners of the Sunken Court. In this way, the Sunken Court changed its function and no longer followed the architectonic axis.

Main Building-II was also modified in sub-phase IIB but was kept functioning as before. However, the space probably functioned as a patio in front of the building surrounded by an open canal, which was totally covered with soil. After the filling, deep pits were dug. These pits contained burned organic materials, including animal bone, and copper objects, which seemed to be indicators for religious activities analogous to a *pago* (or *pagapu*). *Pago* refers to ceremonial dedications, or offerings, to supernatural beings that were traditionally performed by Indigenous peoples in the Andes (Benson and Cook 2001:156, 161; Chacaltana Cortez and Nash 2009:159). It is generally an act to establish a reciprocal relationship between ritual participants and the supernatural world. At Pacopampa, even after its function as a ceremonial center changed, people continued to perform *pagos* by remembering the existence of the "Lady of Pacopampa" buried in the central platform. Bone and metal objects, including needles and pins that might be related to female activities, were recovered from the pits, indicating that people must have been commemorating her. Radiocarbon measurements of the samples recovered from the pits demonstrated that the events associated with the pits probably occurred at the end of, or just after, sub-phase IIB.

The Emergence of Power in the North Highlands

The data from Pacopampa show the process of power generation during the Formative period. Power is often viewed within the framework of political economy (Earle 1987). However, I prefer to think of power as a broader concept. Following Charles Stanish and Kevin J. Haley (2005:56), I define power as the ability of one person or group to coerce or persuade another person or group. According to this perspective, power also existed in the Early and Middle Formative period (or Late Preceramic period and Initial Period). However, in such cases, it was not coercive power as recognized at the state level, but rather persuasive power. The existence of this persuasive power can be seen in the corporate architectures that were built for ritual purposes through voluntary, cooperative labor (Burger and Salazar 2014; Stanish and Haley 2005:63–64).

This perspective is consistent with the ideas presented by the Japanese archaeological team. We pointed out that the large public buildings belonging to the Middle Formative period at the Huacaloma site in the Cajamarca Valley were constructed by voluntary corporate labor of the local people who supported a leader who could only wield weak levels of power (Kato and Seki 1998; Seki 2014). In the

Pacopampa I phase (or Middle Formative period), it is also assumed that the construction of the large platform and the orderly arrangement of the buildings, which also embedded the surrounding landscape, were built by similar kinds of decentralized political groups. It is likely that there were leaders who directed this construction activity and performed the rituals, but they would have held only persuasive power.

In addition to architecture, what other perspectives should we pay attention to when discussing power in the Formative period? In the case for a state-level society, social hierarchy and power are often identified through settlement hierarchies and the presence of royal palaces, areas of priestly activity, and elite tombs (Flannery 1998). Although there are studies that have discussed palaces (Wester La Torre 2016), Andean archaeology has particularly focused on the relationship between burial patterns and the development of social ranking and stratification (Dillehay 1995a:11). In studies on the Moche state, the existence of elites such as warrior-priests and female priests was identified, and the differences among the elite were discussed by combining analysis of burial patterns, offerings associated with the individuals, and iconography (Alva and Donnan 1993; Castillo 2001).

Yet recent studies of burial patterns have not been limited to these approaches. The focus of research has shifted from the dead to the living. Many studies have pointed out that the rituals of mourning and praying for the dead create unity and order in the world of the living (Dillehay 1995b; Hastorf 2003). It is the connection with the dead through kinship (such as lineages) that helps explain the inequality of the world of the living. In other words, the specially constructed tombs, or the individual and offerings buried in them, not only represent the social status of the deceased but also provide a source of power for the leaders of the living world.

The large pit dug in Pacopampa I was a tomb and the individual buried in it may have been a leader in the Middle Formative period. However, the clearest evidence of leaders should be attributed to the tombs of the "Lady of Pacopampa" and the "Serpent-Jaguar Priests" in sub-phase IIA (or the Late Formative period). These tombs are markedly different from other tombs in terms of their shape, individual cranial deformations, and burial offerings. Such differences not only indicate the social status of the person buried but also suggest the social status of the people who orchestrated this burial and performed the subsequent rituals. As already mentioned, rituals in front of the tombs of the "Lady of Pacopampa" were still performed in sub-phase IIB to remember the female burials. Several feasting rituals were also held in connection with the tomb of the "Serpent-Jaguar Priests." From a stratigraphic perspective, the tomb of the "Serpent-Jaguar Priests" was built later than the tomb of the "Lady of Pacopampa." The individuals in the tomb of the "Serpent-Jaguar Priests" were probably leaders who built the tomb of the "Lady of Pacopampa" or conducted the rituals related to her.

In addition to these traces of burial rituals, skeletal evidence for violence and decapitation has been detected (Nagaoka et al. 2018; Nagaoka et al. 2017). All of these are based on the analysis of human burial remains, and the power of Late Formative period leaders appears to be a less persuasive aspect than that of the Middle Formative period. The power base of these leaders will be discussed in a later section, but before that, I would like to examine whether similar data have been obtained from other Late Formative sites in the north highlands.

Kuntur Wasi

Kuntur Wasi was excavated by the Japanese archaeological team between 1988 and 2003 (see Figures 6.1 and 6.19, Table 6.2). As a result of their investigations, a detailed chronological sequence was established: Idolo phase (1000 BC–800 BC), Kuntur Wasi phase (800 BC–550 BC), Copa phase (550 BC–250 BC), and Sotera phase (250 BC–50 BC) (Inokuchi 2014; Onuki, Kato, and Inokuchi 1995). Although some masonry constructions were installed at the uppermost part of the mountain ridge in the Idolo phase, the totality of the architectural plan at that time is unknown because the constructions were deeply buried. In the subsequent Kuntur Wasi phase (early half of the Late Formative period), the site was completely

figure 6.19
The Main Platform of
the Kuntur Wasi site.
© Kuntur Wasi Project.

transformed (Inokuchi 2014:134–137; Onuki, Kato, and Inokuchi 1995:8–10). At least three terraces were built, and on the uppermost terrace, a large stepped platform, referred to as the Main Platform, was built. Staircases were built between terraces and on the Main Platform (Figure 6.20). On the Main Platform, a Sunken Square Court measuring 23 m on each side was constructed, and stairs were built in the center of each side. Stone carvings depicting supernatural beings that combined the faces of a jaguar and a snake were placed in the steps at the top of these stairs. Apart from these stone carvings, several stone stelae of a standing anthropomorphic figure have also been reported (Onuki, Kato, and Inokuchi 1995:21–22). The sculptures date to the Kuntur Wasi phase and were reused during the Copa phase. Around the Sunken Square Court, three lower platforms were placed forming a U-shape, creating a plan that is similar to that of Pacopampa. However, a difference from Pacopampa can be observed at the rear part of the lower platforms. A Sunken Circular Court was unearthed during the excavations at Kuntur Wasi. It originally could have had two wedge-shaped staircases along the central axis, but

only one of them was identified. This feature closely resembles the Sunken Circular Court of the Old Temple of Chavín de Huántar (Burger 1992:133–135; Lumbreras 1974; see also Matsumoto and Cavero Palomino, this volume).

In the subsequent Copa phase (latter half of the Late Formative period) at Kuntur Wasi, the northeastern part of the Main Platform continued to be used without major transformations (Figure 6.21). However, along the southwestern part of the Main Platform, a series of square architectural complexes was constructed and piled up one over the other, but with a different axis from that of the northeastern part (Inokuchi 2014:137–144). The difference in the axis at the southwestern part was related to a newly installed staircase at the southwestern retaining wall of the Main Platform.

During the Copa phase, which was composed of at least three sub-phases, ritual activity was active. The number of square architectural complexes, or units constituted by a small patio surrounded by small rooms, increased. There were thirteen of these units in the Kuntur Wasi phase; the number increased to twenty-two in the first sub-phase

table 6.2
Chronological chart of
the northern highlands
of Peru during the
Middle and Late
Formative periods.

BC		Period	Pacopampa	Kuntur Wasi	Huacaloma
50	Formative			Sotera	Layzón
250		Late		Copa	EL
400			Pacopampa II		
500					
700				Kuntur Wasi	Late Huacaloma
800		Middle	Pacopampa I	Idolo	
1000					
1200					Early Huacaloma
		Early	Pandanche ?		
1500					

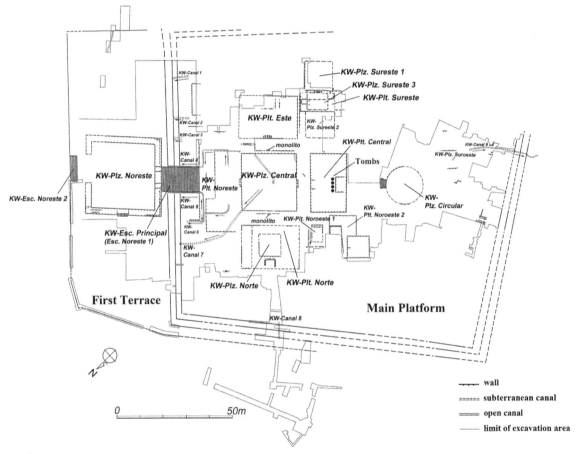

figure 6.20
Architectural plan of the Kuntur Wasi phase. © Kuntur Wasi Project.

of the Copa phase and seventy-eight in the second sub-phase (Inokuchi 2017:341). The floor and wall of the patio and room were decorated with thick white plaster. Several tubed beads of spondylus shell were recovered from the plaster of a room wall. At the center of the patio, a canal or drainage for overflow was found. These data suggest that this unit was used for ritual rather than residential purposes. After the Copa phase, some pottery evidence of a later occupation associated with the Sotera phase (Final Formative period) was found in a limited area, but the space as a ceremonial center ceased to function.

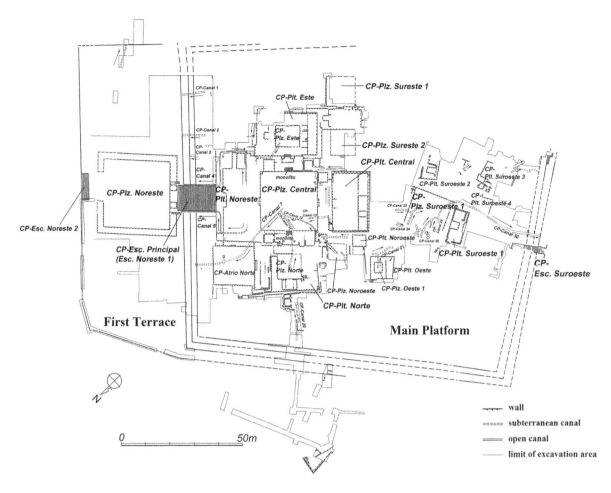

figure 6.21
Architectural plan of the Copa phase. © Kuntur Wasi Project.

Tombs of the Kuntur Wasi Phase

In the Kuntur Wasi phase, three boot-shaped tombs containing gold objects such as a crown, nose ornaments, earplugs, and other offerings were discovered at the Main Platform close to the Sunken Square Court (Onuki, Kato, and Inokuchi 1995:15–19). These tombs were approximately contemporaneous with the Pacopampa II phase. They were placed after the abandonment of the small platform constructed in the previous Idolo phase and, later, they were covered with clay fill to construct a new platform (see Figure 6.20). The stratigraphic position of the tombs is similar to the tomb of the "Lady of Pacopampa."

The tombs have a depth of 2.5 m. A lateral hole was excavated at the bottom of the shaft, where the individual was placed, and a partition made by a wall of poorly piled small stones was placed between the shaft and hole. Gold objects were found only in the boot-shaped tombs. Another tomb was found nearby, made of a simple pit and associated with copper and bone objects. These individuals were buried with special treatment in space, structure, and offerings.

The special treatment can also be identified in the physical characteristics of the associated human skeletal remains. Evidence for cranial deformation was reported only from the individuals buried in the boot-shaped tombs (Matsumura et al. 1997:15). As at Pacopampa, cranial deformation must have been decided at infancy (Ricci et al. 2008:384) and, therefore, the individual of the tomb was destined to become a high-status person since childhood.

This situation of Kuntur Wasi is very similar to that of Pacopampa. Even at the Kuntur Wasi site, there is no clear evidence of stratification of the settlement, so we pay attention to the tomb. To be sure, the Kuntur Wasi tombs mentioned above are not evidence of society after the ritual space was completed, in that the individual was buried during the construction of the building. However, even after the completion of the ritual space, special tombs associated with gold objects were found not only in the Kuntur Wasi phase but also in the Copa phase (Onuki and Inokuchi 2011). No doubt those interred were leaders who played special roles in society.

Moreover, a recent analysis of the gold objects through x-ray fluorescence revealed differences in the relative ratio of gold and silver at the tombs (Hidaka et al. 2014:156–157). The forgoing suggests that there may have been differences in status between the leaders of Kuntur Wasi.

Although the source of power for these leaders will be discussed in the next section, I would like to point out that the manifestation of social differences in Kuntur Wasi was not due to gradual changes from the Middle Formative period. Japanese researchers think that the individuals of the tombs mentioned before were brought from outside the site, probably from the coast, because of offerings like sea shells (like strombus shells) and Cupisnique-style ceramics (Kato 2014:162). Furthermore, clear evidence of exostosis of the external auditory canal, a pathology usually found in divers who swim in deep water (Standen et al. 1997:125), was identified in an individual from a tomb (Matsumura, personal communication 1997), showing that the individual could have come from the coast.

Finally, it is worth mentioning the society of the Copa phase. Even during the Copa phase, burials associated with gold objects were found in boot-shaped tombs. In that sense, the activities of the leader continued. However, it is interesting that cranial deformation is not limited to those special burials; cranial deformation is more common. This situation, if linked to the increase in ritual architectural units during the Copa phase mentioned before, may indicate that the social leaders increased and differentiation within the leaders began to emerge in this phase.

Comparative Analysis between Pacopampa, Kuntur Wasi, and Chavín de Huántar

In this section, I will analyze the source of power of Pacopampa and Kuntur Wasi. As the data show so far, there is no doubt that institutionalized leaders became apparent at both around 800–700 BC. "Leader" here refers to the person who built the tomb and performed the rituals related to the dead, as well as to the person who is buried in the tomb. We have already noted that at both Pacopampa and Kuntur Wasi, the burials were embedded inside a main construction on a central axis. Judging from the fact that the burials were unearthed in a ritual space, rather than in a place dedicated to burial, such as a cemetery, it is clear that they were the targets of the rites performed by the living. Thus, the rituals associated with burials were related to the construction of the social order of the living, including the power structure. In the north highlands, these rituals related to the burials did not appear until the Late Formative period.

In addition to gold, exotic goods such as spondylus shell beads, a conch (*Strombus galeatus*) trumpet, and sodalite beads were reported from the boot-shaped tombs at Kuntur Wasi. Obsidian artifacts were also recovered from other ritual spaces. As we know, *Spondylus* and *Strombus* inhabit the warm waters along the Ecuadorian coast, which is more than 350 km to the north of the north highlands. According to sourcing studies, sodalite was obtained from the Bolivian highlands (Burger and Nesbitt, this volume; Kato 2014:168). Similarly, obsidian was brought from the famous Quispisisa mine (Burger and Glascock 2009:25), roughly 900 km to the south.

It is difficult to determine if these exotic objects were worn by the deceased during their lifetime or if they were collected and offered by the person who buried them. In any case, the data indicate that leaders at Kuntur Wasi gained their power through controlling access to these exotic goods using ritual activities as their base of power (Seki 2014:194–195), as well as the long-distance interaction networks through which they were acquired.

In Pacopampa, earplugs, ear ornaments, and necklaces made of gold were unearthed from the tombs belonging to sub-phase IIA. Many beads made of marine shell, including spondylus and feather oyster shell (*Pteriidae*), were reported from the tombs (Vásquez and Tham 2010). A strombus trumpet and gold objects, probably belonging to phase II, were also discovered at the Coche Corral site, located at the foot of the Pacopampa site during a rescue excavation undertaken by the Minister of Culture-Cajamarca (Seki 2013). This information indicates that sub-phase IIA of Pacopampa also had close contact with the coastal area.

Some obsidian flakes and objects were found in the layers of sub-phase II at Pacopampa, although their quantity is limited in comparison with Kuntur Wasi. Provenience studies of an obsidian sample indicate that they were brought from the Quispisisa and Alca mines in the south-central highlands (Burger and Glascock 2009:25). These data suggest to us that the leaders of Pacopampa, like those of Kuntur Wasi, controlled the access of exotic goods gained by long-distance trade.

Besides precious and exotic goods, other evidence informs us about Pacopampa's interaction sphere. Pottery from Pacopampa I shares common characteristics (Figure 6.22a), such as polychrome and post-firing types that are similar to those from the northeastern part of the Andes, especially from the eastern slope or lowlands of Peru (Clasby, this volume; Olivera Nuñez 1998:105–112; Shady and Rosas 1980; Yamamoto 2010). Meanwhile, the pottery of Pacopampa II presents characteristics similar to that of the north coast and the highlands (Figure 6.22b). These data coincide with the results of an analysis of the settlement pattern in the upper part of the Chotano River (Yamamoto 2015:547–552). The settlement pattern in Pacopampa I indicates that the route of interaction extending from Pacopampa to the east or northeast was important. In Pacopampa II, in addition to these routes, routes to the coastal regions to the west were newly established.

Moreover, the analysis of starch grains adhering to the pottery indicates that manioc (*Manihot esculenta*), cultivated in the lowlands, was identified only in the Pacopampa I phase and disappeared in the following Pacopampa II phase, when maize (*Zea mays*) replaced manioc (Vásquez and Tham 2007, 2009). Potato (*Solanum tuberosum*) continued to appear from phase I to II. Analysis based on carbon and nitrogen stable isotopes using samples from the human and animal bones also indicates that the consumption of C4 plant—probably maize—appears from phase II, although the dependence of maize on food or ritual consumption was unrepresentative (Takigami and Yoneda 2017:298). The data suggest that in phase II, the relationship to the lowlands or eastern part of Peru was replaced by that of the highlands or the coast.

The analysis of the animal bones recovered from Pacopampa adds further insight. Kazuhiro Uzawa notes the drastic increase in the utilization of camelids in Pacopampa II (Uzawa 2017). Similarly in Kuntur Wasi, the use of camelids increases from the Late Formative period (Uzawa 2010). Since the Andean camelids are raised in a high ecological zone in general, it can be interpreted that the interest in phase II shifted from the eastern lowlands to the highlands. In the case of the Pacopampa site, however, a recent isotopic analysis of animal bones indicates that camelids were kept in the vicinity of the site rather than being brought from higher altitudes (Takigami et al. 2019). In any case, in addition to their value as a source of meat and hair, camelids can be used for transportation, which could be related to the development of the growth of long-distance interregional interaction (Matsumoto et al. 2018).

Therefore, the emergence of power in the north highlands of Peru was not only related to the rituals for the dead but also associated with the long-distance trade of materials and objects related to the ritual. The prosperity of long-distance trade in the north highlands coincides with the time of the establishment of the Chavín Interaction Sphere, at least in the central and south highlands as well as in some areas of the coast (Burger 2008; Burger and Nesbitt, this volume; Matsumoto and Cavero Palomino 2010, 2012, this volume; Matsumoto et al. 2018; Young, this volume). In this sense, it can be said that the power source of the social leaders at Kuntur Wasi and Pacopampa would be influenced from this phenomenon. The production of

a

b

stone carvings found at Pacopampa and Kuntur Wasi could be imported from the north-central highlands because this tradition is unknown in the north highlands or the north coast during the Middle Formative period. The breeding camelids also had been introduced from the south, although it is unknown where the consumption of maize in the northern highlands originates from. There is no doubt that the interaction had increased by 800–700 BC.

However, it is also necessary to consider the differences between the north-highlands sites and Chavín de Huántar and related sites. Both Pacopampa and Kuntur Wasi are located at a mountain ridge and are composed of terraces or platforms using the natural topography. Furthermore, the location of Pacopampa, in particular, seems to have been decided by the direction where the Pleiades constellation appears in subphase IA (Sakai et al. 2019). This feature contrasts with Chavín de Huántar, a site located in the bottom of a valley between two rivers. This location would have been related to the cosmology of each local community. Moreover, while the ceremonial architecture is isolated from residential dwellings at Pacopampa and Kuntur Wasi sites, traces of elite residences are confirmed around the core ceremonial area of Chavín de Huántar (Burger 2008:696; Rick 2005; Sayre and Rosenfeld, this volume). There were differences in the use of rituals and residential spaces between the north-highlands sites and Chavín de Huántar.

Platforms at both Kuntur Wasi and Pacopampa were constructed solidly and did not have any inner galleries, like those at Chavín de Huántar, although previous archaeologists misidentified subterranean canals as galleries at Pacopampa (Rosas and Shady 1970). At Chavín de Huántar, the inner galleries are generally related to special ritual activities (Burger 2008:689–690; Rick 2017:43, this volume). The difference in architectural characteristics between the north-highlands sites and Chavín de Huántar could be interpreted as differences in the use of space and in a cosmology created by ritual activities.

Another difference is that the tombs of important individuals are located under the floor of a central building at Pacopampa and Kuntur Wasi. It is probable that the installation of these tombs at the central building would have been related to the special rite dedicated to them. Such elite funerary contexts have not been reported at Chavín de Huántar, although there is the possibility that some tombs of social leaders may be recovered in the future. These different views of the universe, inferred from different spaces and locations, lead us to speculate on the different strategies of the leaders who used rituals as their power base.

So far, we have examined the sites of the north highlands together and also compared them with Chavín de Huántar. But are there any differences between the north-highlands sites? Similar architectural patterns can be found at Pacopampa and Kuntur Wasi. However, differences can also be observed in the north-highlands sites. The Sunken Court of Pacopampa can be traced back to the Middle Formative period, before the construction

of the sunken court at Kuntur Wasi (Seki 2014). At Pacopampa, a circular building was constructed at the central space; a similar structure is absent and instead a Sunken Circular Court was constructed at Kuntur Wasi. Besides these characteristics, the shape of the tombs is different between both sites.

Moreover, differences can also be found in cultural remains. While copper objects, slag, and instruments such as chisels and crucibles used to produce these objects were unearthed at Pacopampa, there was little evidence of them at Kuntur Wasi (Seki 2014:191). In addition, according to a general survey around Pacopampa conducted by the geologists of our team, a mine of secondary copper—chrysocolla, azurite, and malachite—was discovered. We have not confirmed that this mine was used during the Formative period, but according to experiments conducted at the laboratory using samples collected from the mine, copper production was possible (Arata, Shimizu, and Shimizu 2017:172–173). We can suppose that the control of access to metalworking functioned as an important source of power at Pacopampa.

Apart from the structures and cultural remains, differences between these sites can also be observed in how spaces and materials for ritual are used and how spaces are defined. Special attention should be paid to this relationship between the Middle Formative and the Late Formative periods at both sites, as the following indicates.

Inheriting Social Memory from the Middle Formative to the Late Formative

In sub-phase IIA at Pacopampa, almost all structures built in the previous sub-phase IB were reused. As mentioned earlier, the Circular Building, the Sunken Court, and the staircases between platforms continued to be used. Main Building-I and the other small rooms around the Sunken Court were covered with clay fill to construct new rooms on them, but the new rooms stood in the same place as before. This means that the previous architectural disposition was taken over. The new architectural elements are only some sunken patios on the Northern Platform. Probably the new ritual space in sub-phase IIA was not strange to the visitors who were accustomed

figure 6.23
The retaining wall that supports the Third Platform. The stone materials in the lower part were placed in sub-phase IB, while those in the upper part were placed in sub-phase IIA. © Pacopampa Archaeological Project.

to the previous ritual circumstances, though it is unknown if architectural surface decorations were similar or not.

The continuity or succession from the previous phase can also be observed in architectural materials. The retaining wall that supports the Third Platform consists of limestone blocks (Figure 6.23). However, at the lower part of the wall, we can observe large stones carefully cut, and at the upper part of the wall, fragile and coarse stones were placed (Seki et al. 2019:125, fig. 8.17). According to a geological analysis conducted by our team, these two types of stone materials have different origins (Shimizu et al. 2012). The stratigraphic analysis during excavations indicates that the lower part of the wall was constructed in sub-phase IB and it was reused in the following phase. The upper part of the wall was modified in sub-phase IIA, adding stone blocks brought from another quarry. Previously, we thought that the placement of new materials might be caused by the exhaustion of the stone resource. However, I now believe that the stacking of stones from different phases was an intentional choice. To understand it, we must observe another archaeological context.

In the small rooms around the Sunken Court, we found evidence for stone materials being reused.

Some walls built of large limestone in sub-phase IB were partially dismantled and the stone blocks were carefully removed to be reused for the walls of the following phase. The number and scale of the rooms in sub-phase IIA are larger than those in the previous phase, and more stone materials were needed, but only a part of the previous wall was dismantled. Considering this situation, social leaders had the intention of combining two types of stone blocks belonging to different phases rather than saving on materials.

It is difficult to know the real reason why they reused space and access or showed the materials of different phases in their architecture. I hypothesize that social leaders were showing themselves not only as innovators (in sub-phase IIA) but also as successors to the previous society (in sub-phase IB). If the visitors used the same access and looked at the same architecture and materials, then these experiences would remind them of familiar feelings and memories. The addition of new elements was limited. The partial reuse of materials and spaces was a measure to prevent visitors to Pacopampa from feeling changes in leaders or society. The term "visitors" also refers to commoners in the area who had been involved in maintaining this ceremonial center. It is highly possible that the leaders of sub-phase IIA migrated from other places, as in the case of the Kuntur Wasi phase at Kuntur Wasi, but it is unlikely that the commoner who visited this ceremonial center and participated in the rituals were also replaced. It could be a strategy conducted by the leaders at Pacopampa to persuade their audience and supporters, as the source of power for the leaders at Pacopampa was an invocation of the past.

In addition, we can observe through the burial process that the leaders of the Pacopampa II phase paid attention to inheriting social memory. The tomb of the "Serpent-Jaguar Priests" was placed after the tomb of the "Lady of Pacopampa." Both tombs share the use of andesite stones that were stuffed inside the tomb shaft. In addition, the placement of a large slab obliquely over the body is similar. It is presumed that those who made the tomb of the "Serpent-Jaguar Priests" had remembered and memorialized the burial process of the tomb of the "Lady of Pacopampa." It is also possible to assume that the leaders tried emphasizing the role of the buried person, especially a masculine individual, as a successor of a powerful woman (a founder).

In contrast, at Kuntur Wasi, almost all structures from the previous Idolo phase were destroyed and totally covered with thick fill to establish a new architectural plan (Inokuchi 2014:134; Onuki, Kato, and Inokuchi 1995:11). The invisibility, or the concealment, of any evidence of the past was a choice taken by new leaders in the Kuntur Wasi phase. Meanwhile, in the Copa phase, new elements were added while following the main part of the architectural plan of the Kuntur Wasi phase. Thus, whether the culture and memories of the past were inherited or denied depended on the leaders of each phase or site. As to how to use the past, many researchers have shown interesting examples using the concept of social memory. I take up the issue of social memory at the end of this chapter because I believe that by introducing this perspective, the diversity of power in the Formative period can be clarified.

Social memory refers to a collective, not a personal, view of the meaning of a material (Connerton 1989:1; Van Dyke and Alcock 2003:2). While social memory is the sum of individuals with disparate memories, it "is not a simple reflection of the past, but a social construct through which the past is brought to bear on the present" (Nielsen 2008:207). This point indicates that social memory is necessary for the reproduction of the current social order, including power relations (Connerton 1989).

Tom Dillehay (1990, 1995b) argues that the renewal of the mounds constructed by the Mapuche people in detachment from burials is an enactment of social ties on many levels. Christine A. Hastorf (2003) also discusses the formation of social memory related to ancestor worship by relating burials and the expansion of public buildings to the Formative sites in the southeast lakeshore region of Lake Titicaca in Bolivia. Alternatively, as Jerry D. Moore (2010) highlights, there is certainly a problem in explaining the repeated use of a single site within the framework of social memory, even ignoring historical rupture, and it is a concept that requires careful discussion. In any case, the construction of social memory can also be said to be "in progress," as it is necessary to repeat actions and practices. To be more specific, the repetition of commemorative ceremonies, bodily practices, narratives, and materials (such as artifacts, monuments, and landscape) is often cited as a way in which societies share, maintain, and transmit knowledge and values (Connerton 1989; Nielsen 2008). Moreover, the ways in which these social memories are formed are intertwined and interdependent.

Michael Rowlands has also stated that social memory is built by various practices, which can be divided into two broad categories—"inscribed memory practices" and "incorporated memory practices" (Rowlands 1993:142). The former refers to the construction and use of visible substances such as monumental buildings, and the latter refers to archaeologically invisible acts such as ritual acts or oral tradition. However, even in the latter ceremony, many cases are observed that used visible materials such as mural paintings, stone statues, pottery, and stone and bone objects, so it can be archeologically known as a part of the act of building social memory.

With these perspectives in mind, I return to the Pacopampa data. The traces of repeated rituals (or *pagos*) in front of the tomb of the "Lady of Pacopampa" can probably be understood as the formation of social memory, which Rowlands called "incorporated memory practices." Here, however, I would like to focus on the "inscribed memory practices," or the reuse of buildings and wall stones that we can see at Pacopampa.

A similar example has been verified by data from Maya archaeology. It is common in classic Maya sites to see the continuing use of older building elements incorporated into new architectural designs, similar to the case of Pacopampa. Rosemary A. Joyce suggests that the persistence of the visible was not an accident but rather an intentional way to create long-term social memory (Joyce 2003:112). She points out that a monumental building set with older components—such as famous Maya stone stelae and altars associated with inscriptions—could provide information about the person, date, and events to privileged visitors. Representations, like statues or stelas, can be occasionally identified as important media for commemorative functions. Joyce recognizes the construction of social memory as a source of political power in Maya society. Furthermore, the fact that the layout of architecture and architectural axes is inherited is also related to building social memory. Joyce points out that the route and access by visitors and ceremonial executors in Maya ritual space are devices that encourage the construction of social memory. It is an opportunity to build collective and social memories of visitors and executors by using the same route repeatedly, encountering and participating in rituals in each space.

In view of that, it is important to note that access had not fundamentally changed from sub-phase IB to sub-phase IIA of Pacopampa, thus suggesting that the construction of social memory did not change significantly. Thus, in Pacopampa, continuity is recognized in the construction of social memory in various elements, including the place of construction, materials, and access, from sub-phase IB to sub-phase IIA. In this way, there is no doubt that the new leaders of Pacopampa were conscious of the connection with past social memory in terms of building materials, routes, and the arrangement of buildings. This point again reminds us that images of the past legitimize the social order of the present (Connerton 1989:3). On the other hand, the

leaders of the Kuntur Wasi phase were seeking the formation of power while remaining conscious of the disconnection from the past in the Idolo phase. By destroying and filling up the buildings, the leaders of the Kuntur Wasi phase forced people to forget the social memories associated with the place (Connerton 2009) and sought to generate new social memories in new ritual spaces. Thus, even at the ceremonial centers in the north highlands, there was a difference in the leaders' strategies to gain power.

Conclusions

The contrast between the strategies used at different centers in the north highlands during the Formative period indicates that there were various ways to establish power. Leaders of each site would use different strategies, including long-distance trade, the production of metal, and the control of social memory. Thus, long-distance trade related to the Chavín Interaction Sphere was just one source of power—though this does not mean that long-distance trade was unimportant to the formation of power. Indeed, the acquisition of foreign materials was crucial to the ritual and political economy of both Pacopampa and Kuntur Wasi. There is no doubt that the network of trade revitalized interregional exchanges through the distribution of goods related to ceremonies. Even if regional diversity is recognized in the formation of power, the knowledge of rituals and ideas circulated mutually among these networks and possibly gave a mutual stimulation.

In this sense, it seems completely possible to apply the peer polity model to the Late Formative period (Burger 2008:698; Renfrew 1982). This model considers that each regional group had a center; they competed, but they also shared ideas through the distribution of rare and valuable goods. Our data from the north highlands fully coincide with this model. However, researchers who promote the model mostly rely on data from Chavín de Huántar, emphasizing its complexity (Burger 2008; Rick 2005). Certainly, a variety of pottery styles unearthed from the Ofrendas Gallery at Chavín de Huántar, as well as the architectural style, seem to come from various areas of the Andes. In this respect, Chavín de Huántar had a high centripetal force. Many researchers place great emphasis on this site as the center of a pilgrimage system that received people from regional centers all over the Andes (Burger 1992; Rick 2005). These pilgrims would have learned the Chavín cult and brought new knowledge and ideas back to their regional centers. However, the evidence of the pilgrims has not been shown archaeologically beyond pottery and architectural style. The high centripetal force does not mean a superiority of the Chavín de Huántar site over other ceremonial centers, such as Kuntur Wasi and Pacopampa. The variety of earthenware for pottery found in Chavín de Huántar can also be explained as objects obtained from Chavín's leaders through their own network system. In contrast, the leaders of Kuntur Wasi and Pacopampa seem to have taken elements from other places that had more important value for the formation of power in their own land. None of these examples demonstrate centrality, making it difficult to explain the superiority between Chavín de Huántar and the north highlands sites.

At Chavín de Huántar, an occupation in the Middle Formative period has been inferred from pottery and the architectural sequence (Burger 1992:159–164; Rick et al. 2010), but the relationship between the Middle Formative and the Late Formative is still unclear. Because of that, Chavín de Huántar has been placed in the phenomenon of the Late Formative period. Regional interaction has, moreover, been emphasized as the main feature of that period. However, in addition to the north highlands discussed in this paper, traces of occupation before the Late Formative period have been reported in the south highlands, and the need to understand the Chavín Phenomenon diachronically is increasing (Matsumoto and Cavero Palomino 2010, this volume).

I would like to add that careful consideration of this view is desirable in the future. In 2022, the Pacopampa Archaeological Project led by the author discovered a burial that corresponds to the Middle Formative period (Pacopampa I phase) at the La Capilla site, located about 600 m east of the Pacopampa site. It is known that this site was constructed in the Middle Formative period together with the Pacopampa site and that it functioned as an integral part of the Pacopampa site. The tomb was 1 m deep and sealed with several tons of large stone. The body was placed on top of twenty strombus shells and was decorated with blue stones (probably chrysocolla), blue-purple stones (possibly sodalite), and white shell necklaces. The strombus shells were put with large amounts of cinnabar. This situation indicates the presence of leaders and long-distance trade, even in the Middle Formative period, although the provenance of these materials has not yet been identified. In this sense, we can no longer deny the possibility that the characteristics of Late Formative period society described in this paper can be traced back to the Middle Formative period. Nevertheless, the overwhelming archaeological evidence is unequivocal that they appeared in the Late Formative period.

In any case, if we pay attention to the diachronic change in architecture and other cultural components of the site, we can find new aspects of power exercised by past leaders, as introduced in this chapter. We should collect more archaeological information to elaborate models and hypotheses to understand the Late Formative period. How did local communities or their social leaders face the new situation of increased interaction? How did they incorporate new components into their traditional cosmology? There are still many topics that remain to be discussed.

Acknowledgments

The archaeological studies at Pacopampa presented in this article were supported by JSPS KAKENHI Grant Number JP14101003, JP19202028, JP19251013, JP23222003, 16H05639, 16H02729. The studies were also supported by research grants from the Mitsubishi Foundation and Heiwa Nakajima Foundation. We gratefully acknowledge the collaboration of the Universidad Nacional Mayor de San Marcos, Ministry of Culture of Peru, and various colleagues who have helped to organize and develop the project, including Daniel Morales Chocano, Juan Pablo Villanueva, Diana Alemán Paredes, Mauro Ordoñez Livia, Percy Santiago Andía Roldán, José Samuel Querevalú, Walter Tosso Morales, Kinya Inokuchi, Masato Sakai, Kazuhiro Uzawa, Tomohito Nagaoka, Minoru Yoneda, Wataru Morita, Atsushi Yamamoto, Mai Takigami, Masaaki Shimizu, Marina Shimizu, Shingo Hidaka, Sachi Hashimoto, Megumi Arata, Nagisa Nakagawa, and the people of the Pacopampa village.

REFERENCES CITED

Alva, Walter, and Christopher Donnan

1993 *Royal Tombs of Sipán*. Fowler Museum of Cultural History, University of California, Los Angeles.

Arata, Megumi, Masaaki Shimizu, and Marina Shimizu

2017 Metallurgy at Pacopampa: Technical Innovation Occurred at the Formative Site. In *Andean Civilization: The World of Power through the Analysis of the Archaeological Data Recovered from the Temple*, edited by Yuji Seki, pp. 161–189. Rinsen-Shoten, Kyoto.

Benson, Elizabeth P., and Anita G. Cook (editors)

2001 *Ritual Sacrifice in Ancient Peru*. University of Texas Press, Austin.

Burger, Richard L.

1992 *Chavín and the Origins of Andean Civilization*. Thames and Hudson, London.

1993 The Chavín Horizon: Stylistic Chimera or Socioeconomic Metamorphosis? In *Latin American Horizons*, edited by Don S. Rice, pp. 41–82. Dumbarton Oaks Research Library and Collection, Washington, D.C.

2008 Chavín de Huántar and Its Sphere of Influence. In *Handbook of South American Archaeology*, edited by Helaine Silverman and William H. Isbell, pp. 681–703. Springer, New York.

Burger, Richard L., and Michael D. Glascock

2009 Intercambio prehistórico de obsidiana a larga distancia en el norte peruano. *Revisita del Museo de Arqueología, Antropología e Historia* 11:17–50.

Burger, Richard L., and Lucy C. Salazar

2014 ¿Centro de que? Los sitios con arquitectura pública de la cultura Manchay en la costa central del Perú. In *El centro ceremonial andino: Nuevas perspectivas para los períodos arcaico y formativo*, edited by Yuji Seki, pp. 291–313. National Museum of Ethnology, Osaka.

Carrión Cachot, Rebeca

1948 *Julio C. Tello y la arqueología peruana*. Tipografía Peruana, Lima.

Castillo, Luis Jaime

2001 The Last of the Mochicas. In *Moche Art and Archaeology in Ancient Peru*, edited by Joanne Pillsbury, pp. 307–332. Yale University Press, New Haven.

Chacaltana Cortez, Sofía, and Donna Nash

2009 Análisis de las ofrendas en los Andes sur centrales: Las ofrendas como tradición de orígen prehispánico; El caso de Cerro Baúl, Valle Alto de Moquegua. *Andes* 7:155–179.

Connerton, Paul

1989 *How Societies Remember*. Cambridge University Press, Cambridge.

2009 *How Modernity Forgets*. Cambridge University Press, Cambridge.

Dillehay, Tom

1990 Mapuche Ceremonial Landscape: Social Recruitment and Resource Rights. *World Archaeology* 22(2):223–241.

1995a Introduction. In *Tombs for the Living: Andean Mortuary Practices*, edited by Tom Dillehay, pp. 1–26. Dumbarton Oaks Research Library and Collection, Washington, D.C.

1995b   Mounds of Social Death: Araucanian
         Funerary Rites and Political Succession.
         In *Tombs for the Living: Andean Mortuary
         Practices*, edited by Tom Dillehay,
         pp. 281–313. Dumbarton Oaks Research
         Library and Collection, Washington, D.C.

Earle, Timothy

1987   *How Chiefs Come to Power: The Political
         Economy in Prehistory*. Stanford Univer-
         sity Press, Stanford.

Flannery, Kent

1998   The Ground Plans of Archaic States.
         In *Archaic States*, edited by Gary M.
         Feinman and Joyce Marcus, pp. 15–57.
         School for Advanced Research Press,
         Santa Fe.

Fung Pineda, Rosa

1975   Excavaciones en Pacopampa, Cajamarca.
         Revista del Museo Nacional 41:129–207.

Hastorf, Christine A.

2003   Community with the Ancestors: Ceremo-
         nies and Social Memory in the Middle
         Formative at Chiripa, Bolivia. *Journal of
         Anthropological Archaeology* 22:305–332.

Hayden, Brian

2009   Funerals as Feasts: Why Are They So
         Important? *Cambridge Archaeological
         Journal* 19(1):29–52.

Hidaka, Shingo, Yuji Seki, Sachi Hashimoto, and
Hiroshi Shiino

2014   A Study of the Production of Metal
         Objects during the Formative Stage of the
         Andean Civilization: From the Results
         of X-Ray Fluorescence Analysis of Metal
         Objects Unearthed from the Kuntur Wasi
         and Pacopampa Sites in Peru. *Bulletin
         of the National Museum of Ethnology*
         38(2):125–185.

Inokuchi, Kinya

2014   Cronología del período formativo de
         la sierra del Perú: Una reconsideración
         desde el punto de vista de la cronología
         local de Kuntur Wasi. In *El centro cere-
         monial andino: Nuevas perspectivas para
         los períodos arcaico y formativo*, edited by
         Yuji Seki, pp. 123–158. National Museum
         of Ethnology, Osaka.

2017   Transformation Process of the Kuntur
         Wasi Temple and Generation of Power:
         What Brought about the Temple

Innovation during the Formative Period?
In *Andean Civilization: The World
of Power through the Analysis of the
Archaeological Data Recovered from the
Temple*, edited by Yuji Seki, pp. 321–354.
Rinsen-Shoten, Kyoto.

Joyce, Rosemary A.

2003   Concrete Memories: Fragments of the
         Past in the Classic Maya Present (500–
         1000 AD). In *Archaeologies of Memory*,
         edited by Ruth M. Van Dyke and Susan E.
         Alcock, pp. 104–125. Blackwell, Malden.

Kato, Yasutake

2014   Kuntur Wasi: Un centro ceremonial del
         período formativo tardío. In *El centro ere-
         monial andino: Nuevas perspectivas para
         los períodos arcaico y formativo*, edited by
         Yuji Seki, pp. 159–174. National Museum
         of Ethnology, Osaka.

Kato, Yasutake, and Yuji Seki (editors)

1998   *Bunmei no souzouryoku* (Creativity of the
         Civilization). Kadokawa Shoten, Tokyo.

Kaulicke, Peter

1981   Kermik der frühen Initialperode aus
         Pandanche, Dpto. Cajamarca, Peru.
         *Beiträge zur allgemeinen und vergleichen-
         den Archäologie* 3:363–389.

Lumbreras, Luis G.

1974   Informe de labores del proyecto
         Chavín. *Arqueológicas* 15:37–55.

Matsumoto, Yuichi, and Yuri I. Cavero Palomino

2010   Una aproximación cronológica del cen-
         tro ceremonial de Campanayuq Rumi,
         Ayacucho. *Boletín de Arqueología PUCP*
         13:323–346.

2012   Early Horizon Metallurgy from
         Campanayuq Rumi in the Peruvian
         South-Central Highlands. *Ñawpa
         Pacha: Journal of Andean Archaeology*
         32(1):115–129.

Matsumoto, Yuichi, Jason Nesbitt, Michael D.
Glascock, Yuri I. Cavero Palomino, and Richard L.
Burger

2018   Interregional Obsidian Exchange during
         the Late Initial Period and Early Horizon:
         New Perspectives from Campanayuq
         Rumi, Peru. *Latin American Antiquity*
         29(1):44–63.

Matsumura, Hirofumi, Yoshio Onuki, Yasutake Kato, Ryozo Matsumoto, Tsuyoshi Ushino, Yuji Seki, Kinya Inokuchi, and Hiroko Hashimoto

1997   Human Remains from the Kuntur Wasi, Huacaloma, Loma Redonda and Kolgitin Sites in the Cajamarca Region, Peru. *Bulletin of the National Science Museum, Tokyo, Series D, Anthropology* 23:1–28.

Moore, Jerry D.

2010   Making a Huaca: Memory and Praxis in Prehispanic Far Northern Peru. *Journal of Social Archaeology* 10:398–422.

Morales Chocano, Daniel

1980   *El dios felino en Pacopampa*. Seminario de Historia Ruarl Andina, Universidad Nacional Mayor de San Marcos, Lima.

Nagaoka, Tomohito, Yuji Seki, Wataru Morita, Kazuhiro Uzawa, Diana Alemán Paredes, and Daniel Morales Chocano

2012   A Case Study of a High-Status Human Skeleton from Pacopampa in Formative Period Peru. *Anatomical Science International* 87:234–237.

Nagaoka, Tomohito, Yuji Seki, Juan Pablo Villanueva Hidalgo, and Daniel Morales Chocano

2020   Bioarchaeology of Human Skeletons from an Elite Tomb at Pacopampa in Peru's Northern Highlands. *Anthropological Science* 128(1):11–17.

Nagaoka, Tomohito, Mai Takigami, Yuji Seki, Kazuhiro Uzawa, Diana Alemán Paredes, Percy Santiago Andía Roldán, and Daniel Morales Chocano

2018   Bioarchaeological Evidence of Decapitation from Pacopampa in the Northern Peruvian Highlands. *PLOS ONE*, https://doi.org/10.1371/journal.pone.0210458.

Nagaoka, Tomohito, Kazuhiro Uzawa, Yuji Seki, and Daniel Morales Chocano

2017   Pacopampa: Early Evidence of Violence at a Ceremonial Site in the Northern Peruvian Highlands. *PLOS ONE*, https://doi.org/10.1371/journal.pone.0185421.

Nielsen, Axel E.

2008   Materiality of Ancestors: Chullpas and Social Memory in the Late Prehispanic History of the South Andes. In *Memory Work: Archaeologies of Material Practices*, edited by Barbara J. Mills and William H. Walker, pp. 207–231. School for Advanced Research Press, Santa Fe.

Olivera Nuñez, Quirino

1998   Evidencias arqueológicas del período formativo en la cuenca baja del Río Utcubamba y Chinchipe. *Boletín de Arqueología PUCP* 2:105–112.

Onuki, Yoshio, and Kinya Inokuchi

2011   *Gemelos prístinos: El tesoro del templo Kuntur Wasi*. Fondo Editorial Congreso del Perú, Lima.

Onuki, Yoshio, Yasutake Kato, and Kinya Inokuchi

1995   La primera parte: Las excavaciones en Kuntur Wasi, la primera etapa, 1988–1990. In *Kuntur Wasi y Cerro Blanco: Dos sitios del formativo en el norte del Perú*, edited by Yoshio Onuki, pp. 1–125. Hokusen-sya, Tokyo.

Renfrew, Colin

1982   Polity and Power: Interaction, Intensification, and Exploitation. In *An Island Polity: The Archaeology of Exploitation in Melos*, edited by Colin Renfrew and J. Malcolm Wagastaff, pp. 264–290. Cambridge University Press, Cambridge.

Ricci, Francesca, Cinzia Forani, Vera Tiesler Blos, Olga Rickards, Sabino Di Lernia, and Giorgio Manzi

2008   Evidence of Artificial Cranial Deformation from the Later Prehistory of the Acacus Mts. (Southwestern Libya, Central Sahara). *International Journal of Osteoarchaeology* 18:372–391.

Rick, John W.

2005   The Evolution of Authority and Power at Chavín de Huántar, Peru. In *Foundation of Power in the Prehispanic Andes*, edited by Kevin J. Vaughn, Dennis Ogburn, and Christina A. Conlee, pp. 71–89. American Anthropological Association, Washington D.C.

2017   The Nature of Ritual Space at Chavín de Huántar. In *Prehistoric and Colonial Case Studies in Andean Archaeology*, edited Silvana A. Rosenfeld and Stefanie L. Bautista, pp. 21–49. University Press of Colorado, Denver.

Rick, John W., Christian Mesía, Daniel Contreras, Silvia R. Kembel, Rosa M. Rick, Matthew Sayre, and John Wolf

2010   La cronología de Chavín de Huántar y sus implicancias para el período formativo. *Boletín de Arqueología PUCP* 13:87–132.

Roe, Peter

    1974   *A Further Exploration of the Rowe Chavín Seriation and Its Implications for North Central Coast Chronology*. Dumbarton Oaks, Washington, D.C.

Rosas, Hermilio, and Ruth Shady

    1970   *Pacopampa: Un centro formativo en la sierra nor.-peruana*. Seminario de Historia Rural Andina, Universidad Nacional Mayor de San Marcos, Lima.

Rowlands, Michael

    1993   The Role of Memory in the Transmission of Culture. *World Archaeology* 25(2):141–151.

Sakai, Masato, Shinpei Shibata, Toshihiro Takasaki, Juan Pablo Villanueva, and Yuji Seki

    2019   Monument, Stars, and Mounds at the Temple of Pacopampa: Changing Recognition of Landscape and a Secular Change of the Rising Azimuth of Pleiades. In *Perspectives on Early Andean Civilization in Peru: Interaction, Authority, and Socioeconomic Organization during the 1st and 2nd Millennia BC.*, edited by Richard L. Burger, Lucy C. Salazar, and Yuji Seki, pp. 129–148. Yale University Press, New Haven.

Seki, Yuji

    2013   Informe final del rescate emergencia del sitio arqueológico Coche Corral, Pacopampa. Report presented to the DDC-Cajamarca. Proyecto Arqueológico Pacopampa, Lima.

    2014   La diversidad del poder en la sociedad del período formativo: Una perspectiva desde la Sierra Norte. In *El centro ceremonial andino: Nuevas perspectivas para los períodos arcaico y formativo*, edited by Yuji Seki, pp. 175–200. National Museum of Ethnology, Osaka.

Seki, Yuji, Diana Alemán, Mauro Ordoñez, and Daniel Morales

    2019   Emergence of Power during the Formative Period at the Pacopampa Site. In *Perspectives on Early Andean Civilization in Peru: Interaction, Authority, and Socioeconomic Organization during the 1st and 2nd Millennia BC.*, edited by Richard L. Burger, Lucy C. Salazar, and Yuji Seki, pp. 107–127. Yale University Press, New Haven.

Seki, Yuji, Juan Pablo Villanueva, Diana Alemán, Mauro Ordoñez, and Daniel Morales

    2016   La tumba de los sacerdotes de la Serpiente-Jaguar de Pacopampa: Nuevos hallazgos en el complejo arqueológico más antiguo y extenso de la Sierra Norte. *Gaceta cultural* 53:12–15. Ministerio de Cultura, Lima.

    2017   The Formation of Power from an Architectural Perspective. In *Andean Civilization: The World of Power through the Analysis of the Archaeological Data Recovered from the Temple*, edited by Yuji Seki, pp. 27–52. Rinsen-Shoten, Kyoto.

Seki, Yuji, Juan Pablo Villanueva, Masato Sakai, Diana Alemán, Mauro Ordóñez, Walter Tosso, Araceli Espinoza, Kinya Inokuchi, and Daniel Morales.

    2010   Nuevas evidencias del sitio arqueológico de Pacopampa, en la Sierra Norte del Perú. *Boletín de Arqueología PUCP* 12:69–95.

Shady, Ruth, and Hermilio Rosas

    1980   El complejo Bagua y el sistema de establecimientos durante el formativo en la Sierra Norte del Perú. *Ñawpa Pacha: Journal of Andean Archaeology* 17:109–142.

Shimizu, Masaaki, Mami Nakajima, Marina Shimizu, Megumi Arata, and Yuji Seki

    2012   The Pacopampa Archaeological Site: The Oldest Smelting Site in South America? In *Abstracts Issue of the Annual Meeting of the Korean Society for Geosystem Engineering*, p. 53. Jeju Island, South Korea.

Standen, Vivien G., Bernard T. Arriaza, and Calogero M. Santoro

    1997   External Auditory Exostosis in Prehistoric Chilean Populations: A Test of the Cold Water Hypothesis. *American Journal of Physical Anthropology* 103:119–129.

Stanish, Charles, and Kevin J. Haley

    2005   Power, Fairness, and Architecture: Modeling Early Chiefdom Development in the Central Andes. In *Foundation of Power in the Prehispanic Andes*, edited by Kevin J. Vaughn, Dennis Ogburn, and Christina A. Conlee, pp. 53–70. American Anthropological Association, Washington D.C.

Takigami, Mai, Kazuo Uzawa, Yuji Seki, Daniel Morales Chocano, and Minoru Yoneda

    2019   Isotopic Evidence for Camelid Husbandry during the Formative Period at the Pacopampa Site, Peru. *Environmental Archaeology* 25:262–278.

Takigami, Mai, and Minoru Yoneda

    2017   The Access to the Foods and the Formation of Power. In *Andean Civilization: The World of Power through the Analysis of the Archaeological Data Recovered from the Temple*, edited by Yuji Seki, pp. 291–317. Rinsen-Shoten, Kyoto.

Tello, Julio C.

    1960   *Chavín: Cultura matriz de la civilización andina*. Publicación antropología del archivo "Julio C. Tello" de la Universidad Nacional Mayor de San Marcos, Lima.

Uzawa, Kazuhiro

    2010   La difusión de los camélidos domesticados en el norte del Perú durante el período formativo. *Boletín de Arqueología PUCP* 12:249–259.

    2017   The Use of Animals in Pacopampa. In *Andean Civilization: The World of Power through the Analysis of the Archaeological Data Recovered from the Temple*, edited by Yuji Seki, pp. 223–245. Rinsen-Shoten, Kyoto.

Van Dyke, Ruth M., and Susan E. Alcock

    2003   Archaeology of Memory: An Introduction. In *Archaeologies of Memory*, edited by Ruth M. Van Dyke and Susan E. Alcock, pp. 1–13. Blackwell, Malden, Mass.

Vásquez, Victor, and Teresa R. Tham

    2007   Análisis microscópios de granos de almidón antiguos en fragmentos de cerámica de Pacopampa. Report prepared for the Pacopampa Archaeological Project. Arqueobios: Centro de Investigaciones Arqueobiológicas y Paleoecológicas Andinas, Trujillo.

    2009   Análisis microscópios de granos de almidón antiguos en fragmentos de cerámica de Pacopampa, temporada 2008. Report prepared for the Pacopampa Archaeological Project. Arqueobios: Centro de Investigaciones Arqueobiológicas y Paleoecológicas Andinas, Trujillo.

    2010   Análisis e identificación taxonómica de muestras de moluscos de Pacopampa. Report prepared for the Pacopampa Archaeological Project. Arqueobios: Centro de Investigaciones Arqueobiológicas y Paleoecológicas Andinas, Trujillo.

Wester La Torre, Carlos

    2016   *Chornancap: Palacio de una gobernante y sacerdotisa de la cultura Lambayeque*. Proyecto Especial Nayamp-Lambayeque Unidad Ejectora No 005, Museo Arqueológico Nacional Brüning, Ministerio de Cultura del Perú, Chiclayo.

Yamamoto, Atsushi

    2010   Ingatambo: Un sitio estratégico de contacto interregional en la zona norte del Perú. *Boletín de Arqueología PUCP* 12:25–51.

    2015   Social Dynamics in the Chotano Basin, Northern Peru: Formation and Change in a Prehistoric Andean Society. *Bulletin of the National Museum of Ethnology* 39(4):511–573.

From Jaguars to Harpy Eagles

Re-evaluating the Chavín Phenomenon and Its Relationship with the Tropical Forest

RYAN CLASBY

In attempting to examine the rise of the Chavín Phenomenon, scholars have long considered the role and influence of the tropical forest, a culture area typically regarded as peripheral to the development of Andean civilization. Despite the highland location of the principal ceremonial center of Chavín de Huántar, the apparent prevalence of tropical lowland animal and plant imagery within Chavín art, including the use of jaguars, harpy eagles, and caimans, has led scholars to consider the tropical forest as critical to explaining the ideological and cosmological underpinnings of Chavín culture and its widespread manifestation throughout the Andes (Burger 1992, 2009; Clasby and Nesbitt 2021; Lathrap 1971, 1973, 1985; Roe 1982; Tello 1921, 1940). Indeed, as early as the 1920s, this emphasis on tropical forest imagery prompted Julio C. Tello (1921, 1940) to argue that Chavín culture originated in the eastern Andean tropical montane forest (also known as the *ceja de selva*), before later crystallizing in the highlands. For Tello, this process was the result of the westward migration of tropical forest peoples.

While Tello's emphasis on the tropical forest was contested at the time by Rafael Larco Hoyle (1941) in favor of coastal-centric models for the beginnings of Andean civilization, his ideas would find support with later generations of archaeologists, albeit in a modified form. Setting aside the idea of direct migration, these scholars instead have viewed the presence of tropical forest imagery within Chavín art as the result of Chavín's adoption of foreign elements and ideas (Burger 1992). Ethnographic comparisons to modern Amazonian religious systems have suggested that Chavín's emphasis on tropical forest imagery drew on shared symbols and cosmological frameworks that had deep histories within the tropical lowlands (Lathrap 1971, 1973; Roe 1982), such as the triple tier cosmology of sky, earth, and subaquatic worlds that is commonly found among lowland societies (Roe 2008). In fact, many scholars have attempted to demonstrate these connections by pinpointing both cosmic deities and tropical forest plant and animal species within Chavín art (Burger 1992, 2011; Lathrap 1973; Roe 2008; Rowe 1962, 1967).

A prominent theme of the first Chavín symposium at Dumbarton Oaks in 1968 was the meaning behind Chavín art (Benson 1971). Most notably, Donald Lathrap (1971) argued that the iconography and conventions behind Chavín art partially stemmed from the growth and expansion of Initial Period interregional exchange networks between certain areas of the coast, highlands, and tropical forest, in which elements of tropical forest culture pushed westward (Nesbitt, this volume; Nesbitt, Johnson, and Ibarra Asencios 2021). Lathrap identifies these Initial Period interaction networks through both the identification of tropical forest symbols within Chavín iconography as well as a comparison of tropical forest ceramic assemblages with contemporary traditions from the coast and highlands of Ecuador and Peru, particularly focusing on the close stylistic relationships between the central Ucayali and the Huánuco Basin. Lathrap (1973) would later argue that many of the iconographic depictions within Chavín art stemmed from the spread of agricultural systems from the tropical lowlands into the highlands, with the "Great Caiman" as a primordial being and principal deity.

In recent years, the question of Chavín's relationship to the tropical forest has been altered even further, as scholars have recognized that interregional interaction and exchange during the Initial Period and Early Horizon were likely multidirectional and that Chavín appears to have drawn on antecedent coastal and highland traditions as well as those of the tropical forest (Bischof 2008; Burger 1992, 2008, 2012; Burger and Salazar 2008, this volume; Fung Pineda 1983). A major proponent of this idea, Richard L. Burger (1992, 2008, 2012, 2013a, 2013b; Burger and Salazar 2008) has argued that the Chavín Phenomenon was a religious cult that spread throughout the Andes via a series of branch oracles and pilgrimage sites. The cult grew in popularity as it adopted and reconfigured coastal, highland, and tropical forest ideas into a new, but familiar, ideological system that made it attractive to societies across the different environments of the Andean landscape. The widespread adoption of the cult allowed for new advances in technologies such as gold working and textile production. It also facilitated the increased exchange of exotic items

such as spondylus and strombus marine shell from the Ecuadorian coast and obsidian and cinnabar from the southern Peruvian highlands, a process that was likely aided by camelid caravans (Burger 1992; Matsumoto et al. 2018).

The expansion of interregional exchange also included the tropical forest. However, despite the longstanding prominence of the tropical forest within debates concerning the Chavín Phenomenon, concrete evidence of these relationships has remained relatively scarce, apart from similarities in ceramic styles and interpretations of tropical forest imagery within early coastal and highland art. The absence of other evidence is largely due to a general lack of investigation within the tropical forest as well as the fact that many of the "products" that are suspected to have come from this environmental zone are either specialized knowledge or perishable organic goods (Burger 1992:115–116; Raymond 1988). Among the types of products that are suspected to have been traded to the highlands and coast, but that are unlikely to have been preserved within the archaeological record, are animal pelts, wood, bird feathers, salt, dyes, and psychotropic and medicinal plant products (Raymond 1988; Wilkinson 2018). Beyond the simple exchange of material goods and esoteric knowledge, other types of relationships may have also existed that would be difficult to confirm in the archaeological record. For example, a study of the ethnographic and historical record suggests that people could have also been moved as part of these highland–lowland networks, possibly as intended marriage partners (see Uzendoski 2004) for the purpose of establishing bonds between communities or ethnic groups, which would have helped to solidify continued exchange. In addition, ethnographic reports suggest that aspiring coastal and highland shamans often traveled to tropical forest areas to train with and to obtain ritual and magical paraphernalia from lowland shamans who were perceived as having access to greater esoteric knowledge and power (Burger 2011; see also Harner 1972; Helms 1979, 1988; Langdon 1981; Lyon 1974:345; Oberem 1974).

As a result of these practical issues in identifying tropical forest products, archaeologists have often had to rely on indirect evidence regarding Chavín's

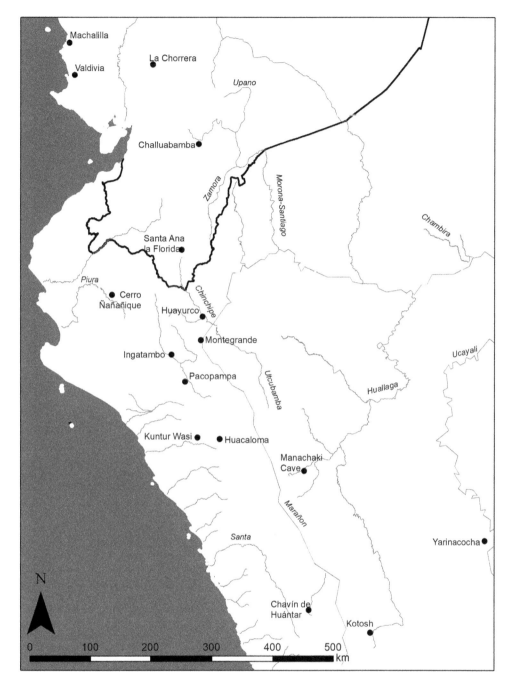

figure 7.1
Map of northern
Peru and Ecuador,
with sites and regions
mentioned in the
text. Map by Bebel
Ibarra Asencios.

connections to the tropical forest. For example, it has been argued that the presence of snuff trays, tubes, spatulas, small spoons, and elaborate stone mortars at Chavín and other formative highland and coastal sites is likely indicative of the use of *Anadenanthera* sp. (*vilca*), a psychotropic plant only grown within the *ceja de selva* and tropical lowlands (Burger 2011; Torres 2008; Zeidler 1988). In addition, Burger (2011:figs. 2–3) has shown that at least

one instance of Chavín art, a stone frieze now held at the Museo Nacional Chavín in Chavín de Huántar, depicts naturalistic representations of the *vilca* plant and its seeds. Unfortunately, physical evidence of the plant has yet to be positively identified at Chavín or Chavín-affiliated sites (Sayre 2018; Torres 2008).

Despite a general lack of primary evidence within coastal and highland sites, and the fact that archaeological research in both the eastern Andean

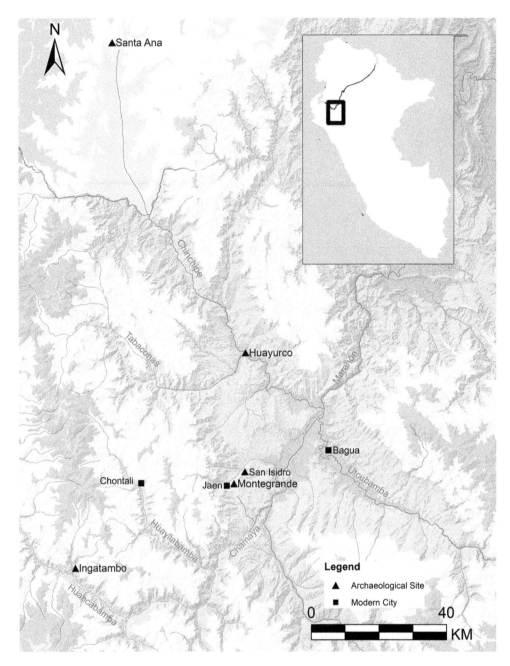

figure 7.2
Map of the Jaén
region, with sites and
regions mentioned in
the text. Map by Bebel
Ibarra Asencios.

montane forest and western Amazonian lowlands still lags behind the Andean coast and highlands, recent years have seen renewed interest in these regions, particularly with respect to the Chavín Phenomenon and the Andean Formative period. These studies have allowed scholars to better contextualize the relationship of Chavín and other Andean interaction networks to the tropical forest. In this chapter, I will synthesize this research to present a clearer picture of earlier sociopolitical developments in the tropical forest (including both the tropical lowlands and the *ceja de selva*) and their relationship to Chavín, focusing not only on the origins of tropical forest integration within Andean exchange networks but also on the role of the region within the development and fluorescence of Chavín culture. In particular, this chapter will focus on the Jaén region (Figures 7.1 and 7.2) in the northeastern Peruvian Andes. Recent investigations in this region have led to a general reconstruction of sociopolitical developments from the Late Preceramic period through the Early Horizon. The results of this research have shown a unique cultural trajectory in comparison to archaeological studies of other areas of the tropical forest (Clasby 2014a, 2014b, 2019; Clasby and Meneses Bartra 2013; Olivera Núñez 2013, 2014; Valdez 2007, 2008, 2011, 2013a, 2013b, 2021; Yamamoto 2007, 2008, 2011, 2013, 2021).

Early Sociopolitical Developments in the Tropical Forest

Archaeological evidence increasingly suggests that domesticated plants were moved between the coast, highlands, and tropical rainforest as far back as the Archaic period (8000–6000 BC) (Dillehay 2020; Pearsall 2008). In fact, many of the earliest domesticated crops within the Andes were first domesticated in the tropical forest, including arrowroot, peanuts, sweet potatoes, manioc, chili peppers, cacao, and various types of fruit (Pearsall 2008; Zarillo et al. 2018). Notwithstanding the preference for community self-sufficiency (Murra 1972) that has been canonized in the Andean literature, these relationships were likely based on factors such as migration or exchange between autonomous social groups rather than the result of early vertical archipelago systems.

Apart from the introduction of domesticated crop species, however, little is understood about the nature of tropical forest interaction with the coast and highlands during this time and the evidence remains scarce for the Late Preceramic period. Nevertheless, Lathrap (1970:66–67, 1973; Lathrap, Pino, and Zeidler 1977) has argued that the Formative-period Valdivia culture (4400–1450 BC) on the Ecuadorian coast was the expression of a tropical forest culture that had moved westward. This argument is largely based on the similarity of Valdivia ceramics to known tropical forest assemblages, the possible iconographic depictions of jaguars within Valdivia art, and the fact that the Real Alto settlement features a circular village plan, a type of settlement pattern that is commonly found within different parts of the Amazon, both historically and ethnographically.

By the Initial Period, the connections between the Andean coast and highlands and the tropical forest become clearer, as several cultures including Cupisnique, Casma, and Manchay exhibit representations of tropical forest plants and animals in ceramics, wall murals, and other media (Bischof 2008; Burger 1992; Larco Hoyle 1941). While some scholars have argued that coastal and highland familiarity with tropical forest animals comes from contact with coastal Ecuador, where the habitat of certain tropical forest species (e.g., caimans, snakes, and jaguars) may have extended into the western side of the Andes (see Bischof 2008:136; Dillehay, McCray, and Netherly 2020:231), evidence increasingly suggests that these connections also derived from first-hand contact with the Eastern Andes and western Amazon. As mentioned above, some of the earliest pottery within ancient Peru is found along the central Ucayali River and aspects of that ceramic tradition notably appear as elements in the Upper Huallaga Kotosh-Wairajirca style as early as 1200 BC (Kanezaki, Omori, and Tsurumi 2021; Lathrap 1970:106, 1971, 1974; Nesbitt, Johnson, and Ibarra Asencios 2021). This idea is further supported by representations of tropical forest imagery such as monkeys in Kotosh pottery of the late Initial Period (Burger 1992:fig. 110; Kano 1972:fig. 1).

Warren Church (1996; Church and von Hagen 2008) has argued that the Manachaqui Cave site, located further to the north in the Chachapoyas region at the upper limits of the cloud forest, functioned as an important way station between the Late Preceramic period and the Early Horizon on a route that connected the highlands to the tropical lowlands. Indeed, Initial Period ceramics from this site, which date to as early as 1300 BC (Church 1996, 2021; Church and von Hagen 2008), show strong similarities in form and decoration to contemporary assemblages from sites located in the northern Peruvian highlands and eastern Andean slopes, including Huacaloma in Cajamarca, Pacopampa, and the Bagua area along the lower Utcubamba River. People from the Chachapoyas area also appear to have been growing maize by this point, as documented at Laguna Pomacochas (Church and Guengerich 2017). Manachaqui Cave would continue to maintain long-distance ties during the Early Horizon with ceramics sharing stylistic attributes with Bagua, Chorrera in coastal Ecuador, and the Upano region of the Ecuadorian eastern slopes.

To the east, several small-scale investigations by scholars such as Daniel Morales Chocano (1992, 1998), Thomas Myers (1972–1974, 1981; Myers and Dean 1999; Myers and Rivas Panduro 2005), Scott Raymond (1982), Rogger Ravines (1989), and Santiago Rivas Panduro (2003; Rivas Panduro et al. 2008) have been undertaken along the Huallaga, Marañon, and Santiago-Morona drainages. While none of these projects have led to extensive excavation or survey, they have provided information as to the diversity of pottery traditions along the eastern edge of the Andes and the western Amazon, many of which can be compared stylistically to coastal and highland Initial Period and Early Horizon assemblages in Peru or Ecuador. Most notably, Warren DeBoer (2003) has argued for the existence of an Upper Amazonian flash horizon dating to around 800 BC that extends north to south from Quito to the upper Ucayali and as far east as the Chambira drainage in the Loreto province of Peru. This flash horizon is centered around the widespread appearance of the double-spout-and-bridge bottle with asymmetrical spouts in highland, *ceja de selva*, and tropical lowland sites. While many of the specimens (and their associated styles) within DeBoer's flash horizon lack radiocarbon dates and cannot be securely tied together chronologically, the ubiquitous presence of these unique vessel forms over vast distances is suggestive of shared traditions and possible riverine exchange routes that developed throughout the Upper Amazon, branching deep into the Peruvian and Ecuadorian tropical lowlands. These ideas cannot yet be proven but hopefully further investigations along the Ucayali, Huallaga, Marañon, and Santiago-Morona drainages will help to shed light on the existence of these networks and their underlying mechanisms.

The Jaén Region

Notwithstanding the evidence brought forth in the preceding section, an understanding of Chavín's

relationship with the tropical forest might best be explained through an examination of the Jaén region. The Jaén region (see Figure 7.2) is located south of the Peruvian–Ecuadorian frontier with Loja and forms the eastern half of the transitional zone (along with the far north coast of Peru) that has traditionally been used to separate the northern and central Andean culture areas. Unlike most areas of the *ceja de selva* and western Amazon, which remain poorly known archaeologically, the Jaén region has a relatively long history of investigation, albeit mostly in the form of small-scale excavations and reconnaissance projects. However, these studies together provide a broad understanding of the general culture history of the region as well as some of the social developments that occurred.

Much of this archaeological interest stems from the favorable geographical conditions of the Jaén region for exploring coastal and highland contact with the tropical forest. Situated in the Huancabamba Depression, Jaén is in an area of the Andes that is relatively low and narrow due to the fragmentation of the central and eastern cordilleras into multiple ranges of less than 3500 masl (Raymond 1988; Wiegend 2002; Young 2021; Young and Reynel 1997), a factor that blurs the geographical division between coast, highlands, and tropical forest. Environmentally, the Jaén region is characterized by montane forest and can be broadly divided into high altitude *páramo* (above 3200 masl), montane cloud forest (1700–3300 masl), and dry forest (1700–300 masl) (Young and Reynel 1997), the latter of which makes up many of the lower river valleys in Jaén and which often features thick xerophytic scrub vegetation (Figure 7.3). Several tributaries of the Marañon River flow through this area, creating natural corridors that, in combination with the low elevations of the cordilleras, would have promoted movement and exchange between coastal, highland, and tropical forest populations.

Indeed, as early as the 1960s, archaeologists had begun to recognize that the geography of the Jaén region made it an ideal area for understanding tropical forest influence on Chavín. In 1961, Pedro Rojas Ponce, a protégé of Julio Tello, conducted small-scale test excavations at the site of

figure 7.3
Dry forest near the
Chinchipe-Tabaconas
confluence. Photograph
by Ryan Clasby.

Huayurco along the Chinchipe-Tabaconas confluence to expand on his mentor's ideas that Chavín
had its origins in the Eastern Andes (1961, 1985;
see also Lathrap 1970:107–108). Test excavations of
the site led to the discovery of a burial cache featuring a variety of offerings, including exotic sea-
shell necklaces, strombus shell trumpets, a ceramic
bottle (Figure 7.4a), and numerous finely carved
stone vessels and stone vessel fragments (Figure
7.4b–d), some of which depicted figurative imagery
along the exterior (Figure 7.4d). These findings not
only demonstrated clear evidence of exchange with
the Pacific coast, but the unique style of the carved
stone bowls and numerous associated fragments led
Rojas and Lathrap to argue that Huayurco may have
been the source for some of the finely carved stone
bowls that were found at Chavín and other early
sites in the Andes. Lathrap (1971:92) also noted the
similarity of the stone vessel decoration to his Early
Shakimu ceramic phase from the central Ucayali
River Valley.

Geoffrey Bushnell (1966) would later report
on similar lithic and ceramic artifacts that had
been recovered from the surfaces of Jaén region
sites including Huayurco. A photograph published
by Bushnell (1966:fig. 10) shows several stone vessels collected by a man living near the site. Around
this time, Henry and Paule Reichlen (Musée du
Quai Branly-Jacques Chirac n.d.) would also visit
Huayurco and the Jaén region. They photographed
and collected several stone bowls from Huayurco
along with other lithic and ceramic artifacts (see
also Valdez 2014).[1] These materials were donated
by the Reichlens to the Musée de l'Homme in Paris
before being moved to the Musée du Quai Branly-
Jacques Chirac. This early research would soon be
followed by Jaime Miasta Gutiérrez (1979) and Ruth
Shady Solís (1973, 1987, 1999; Shady Solís and Rosas
La Noire 1979), who conducted small-scale survey and excavation along the lower Tabaconas and
lower Utcubamba Rivers, respectively. Each of these
investigations identified early ceramic styles that
showed broad stylistic similarities to Chavín pottery and other late Initial Period and Early Horizon
highland and coastal assemblages. Motifs like those
found on Chavín ceramics include concentric circles and serpents (Figure 7.5). Beyond these investigations, the discovery of a stone stela near the
town of Chontalí (Figure 7.6a–b) may provide further indication of Jaén's engagement with the coast

figure 7.4
Artifacts excavated by
Pedro Rojas Ponce at
the site of Huayurco
in 1961: a) brown ware
ceramic bottle; and
b–d) stone vessels.
Museo Nacional
de Arqueología,
Antropología e Historia
del Perú. Photographs
by Ryan Clasby.

figure 7.5
Ceramic sherds
recovered from the
Bagua region by
Ruth Shady Solís,
Centro Cultural de la
Universidad Nacional
Mayor de San Marcos,
Lima. Photograph
by Ryan Clasby.

a

b

figure 7.6
a) The Stela of Chontalí and iconographic comparisons (photograph courtesy of Ulises Gamonal), b) inverse image of the iconography present on the Stela of Chontalí (redrawn by Ryan Clasby, after photograph taken by Ulises Gamonal; c) petroglyph at Tolón, Jequetepeque Valley (redrawn by Ryan Clasby, after Bischof 2008:fig. 4.15a); and d) stone lintel from La Pampa, Santa Valley (redrawn by Ryan Clasby, after Bischof 2008:4.15b).

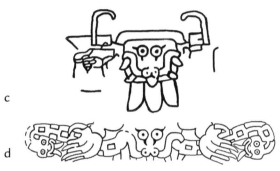
c

d

and highlands, as the complex design patterns are reminiscent of Initial Period iconographic patterns depicting agnathic mouths found on petroglyphs and lintels from the Jequetepeque Valley (Figure 7.6c) (Pimentel Spissu 1986:fig. 13; see also Bischof 2008:fig. 4.15a) and the La Pampa site in Ancash (Figure 7.6d) (Terada 1979:pl. 129; see also Bischof 2008:fig. 4.15b).

In more recent years, the Jaén region has seen multiple large-scale survey and excavation projects led by Peruvian, Ecuadorian, American, and Japanese scholars (Clasby 2014a, 2014b, 2019; Clasby and Meneses Bartra 2013; Olivera Núñez 2013, 2014; Valdez 2007, 2008, 2011, 2013a, 2013b, 2014, 2021; Yamamoto 2007, 2008, 2011, 2012, 2013, 2021). Together, these investigations have helped to establish a general chronology for the Late Preceramic period, Initial Period, and Early Horizon, providing

insight into early eastern slope cultural developments and their relationship to Chavín. Indeed, archaeological research suggests that Jaén benefited from interregional exchange routes moving between the coast and tropical lowlands at an early date. By the Late Preceramic period, the people of Jaén already were constructing ceremonial architecture in the form of spiral-shaped stone structures made of river cobbles, built along artificially modified hills and terraces (Figures 7.7 and 7.9).

Excavations by Francisco Valdez (2007, 2008, 2011, 2013a, 2013b, 2021) at the site of Santa Ana–La Florida recovered a series of ritual offerings that had been placed within the center of the spiral architecture (Figure 7.7), including finely carved stone bowls, green stone objects possibly made of turquoise, ceramic vessels, and marine shell (*Strombus* sp.). While only the strombus shell is of clear exotic

figure 7.7
Spiral architecture,
Santa Ana–La Florida.
Photograph courtesy
of Francisco Valdez.

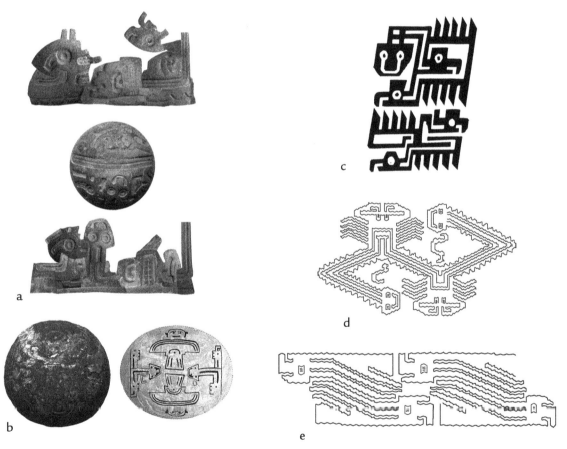

a

b

c

d

e

figure 7.8
Dualism and bicephalous imagery: a–b) stone vessels recovered from Santa Ana–La Florida (image courtesy of
Francisco Valdez); c) looped bag from La Galgada (redrawn by Ryan Clasby, after Grieder 1988:fig. 130); d) twined
fabric from Huaca Prieta (redrawn by Ryan Clasby, after Bird 1963:fig. 4); and e) reconstructed textile design from
Huaca Prieta (redrawn by Ryan Clasby, after Bird 1963:fig. 7b).

figure 7.9
Spiral architecture,
Montegrande. Photograph
courtesy of Quirino
Olivera Núñez.

origin, the offerings found at Santa Ana–La Florida are suggestive of a site that was well engaged within established coastal and highland exchange networks at this time. In fact, multiple ceramic vessels pertain to stirrup-spout forms (Valdez 2013a:fig. 9), making them the earliest dated examples of stirrup-spout vessels in the Andes, preceding the Ecuadorian Machalilla and Cotocollao styles by at least five hundred years (see DeBoer 2003) and providing support for Lathrap's idea that at least some of the cultural traits found in early coastal Ecuadorian cultures had their antecedents in the tropical forest. Most notably, one of these stirrup-spout vessels depicted a face within a bivalve shell, likely depicting *Spondylus* sp. (Valdez 2008:881–882, fig. 43.8, 2013a:fig. 7), suggesting that marine shell was central to the ritual and ideological underpinnings of this early eastern slope culture.

As Valdez (2013a) has shown, Santa Ana–La Florida's interregional relationships can also be inferred from the iconography present on the stone vessels and other lithic artifacts, much of which shows broad similarities to conventions and designs found on textiles and gourds from coastal and highland Late Preceramic sites, including La Galgada (Grieder 1988:figs. 130–132, 138–140) and Huaca Prieta (Bird 1963:figs. 1, 4, 7a–b). Most notable among

these designs are the bicephalous serpent and avian imagery that appears at all three sites (Figure 7.8). These similarities provide support for earlier ideas that viewed the gourd from Huaca Prieta (Bird 1963:fig. 1) as an import from the Ecuadorian coast based on its similarity to Valdivian ceramic designs (Lathrap 1974). While the stylistic comparisons are not direct evidence of exchange, they do suggest that each of these sites was part of a broader ideological sphere that extended between each of the major geographical zones during the Late Preceramic period.

Beyond possible exchange relationships, the evidence from Santa Ana–La Florida also indicates that Late Preceramic populations within the region were cultivating plants, such as maize, cacao, and chili peppers, which were found within the stirrup vessels recovered from the site (Zarillo and Valdez 2013; Zarillo et al. 2018), lending support to the idea that these were agricultural societies.

The spiral architecture at Montegrande (Figure 7.9) has yet to be securely dated and is still awaiting further investigation, but its similarity in form to Santa Ana–La Florida suggests that similar items of ritual importance and exotic origins may also be found once excavation of the structure is carried out. Maintaining somewhat of a different layout from Santa Ana–La Florida, Montegrande features a small staircase leading into the spiral-shaped architecture (Olivera Núñez 2013, 2014:72–73). In addition, some of the stone footings were plastered yellow on the exterior (Olivera Núñez 2014:78, figs. 37–38), a trait that would be commonly applied to footings associated with ceremonial architecture at the Early Horizon site of Huayurco. Overall, early results from Montegrande, in combination with the findings from Santa Ana–La Florida, suggest that the Jaén region was home to a unique style of ceremonial architecture during the Late Preceramic period, with river cobbles used to form spiral-shaped structures that contained offerings or hearths at the center. While further investigation is needed to understand the significance of this architectural pattern to early Jaén region sociopolitical formations, the spiral shape (with its central orienting direction) recalls concepts of axis mundi and pathways between the sacred and the profane (see Eliade 1959) that may have served as a physical manifestation of local cosmological frameworks centered at transition points between the physical and spiritual worlds.

The Jaén Region and Chavín: Observations from Ingatambo and Huayurco

The major developments in sociopolitical complexity, technology, and interregional interaction that first arose during the Late Preceramic period saw little disruption during the subsequent Initial Period, with local populations continuing to inhabit the natural terraces along the edges of river valleys (Shady Solís 1987, 1999; Yamamoto 2007, 2008, 2013) while also engaging in the construction of ceremonial centers at sites such as San Isidro (Olivera Núñez 2014) near the city of Jaén and Ingatambo (Yamamoto 2008, 2013) along the Huancabamba River. Although the spiral-shaped architecture of the Late Preceramic period appears to have fallen out of use in favor of rectangular-shaped construction forms, inhabitants would continue to employ river cobbles in their masonry, at least in part due to the abundance of these stones lining the beds of the many rivers within the area. Interregional interaction continued during

this period as well with Initial Period ceramics, primarily characterized by bowls and short neck jar forms featuring polychrome painting and incision, showing strong similarities to assemblages from the southern Ecuadorian highlands, the northern Peruvian highlands, and the far north coast of Peru (Yamamoto 2013).

Jaén's interaction with other areas only appears to have increased during the late Initial Period and Early Horizon, coinciding with the expansion of interregional exchange throughout the Andes. Yet Jaén was not uniform from a cultural perspective, and a comparison of the sites of Ingatambo and Huayurco, located roughly 83 km apart as the crow flies, suggest that responses to the intensification of exchange during this period differed as autonomous polities or sociopolitical units within the Jaén region sought different resources and relationships from these interaction networks.

At Ingatambo, a large site located roughly 100 km west of the modern city of Jaén, participation with the Chavín Interaction Sphere appears to have been much stronger. Investigated by Japanese archaeologist Atsushi Yamamoto (2007, 2008, 2011, 2012, 2013, 2021), Ingatambo gradually expanded during the late Initial Period and Early Horizon into an important ceremonial center along the Huancabamba River, taking advantage of a major interregional exchange route that connected the Piura drainage and the northern coast of Peru to Jaén. In fact, as indicated by Ingatambo's name, reports from the *Cápac Ñan* indicate that Inca roads passed through this area (Espinosa Reyes 2002), likely capitalizing on ancient routes that were constructed to provide passage between the Pacific coast and tropical forest.

The architectural layout of the site is characterized by at least four platform mounds around the central plaza (Yamamoto 2012, 2013). Ingatambo's growth during the late Initial Period and Early Horizon, which can be observed in multiple phases of platform construction, appears to coincide with a depopulation of earlier sites located on the Huancabamba River. In terms of architecture, Ingatambo shared similar types of stone river cobble masonry, as seen at the Late Preceramic sites of

a

Principal Platform

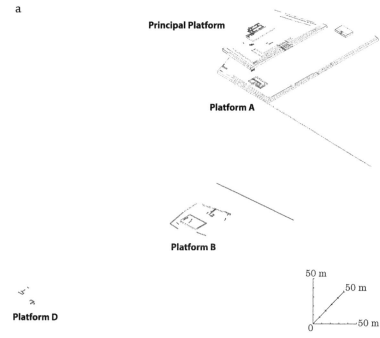

Platform A

Platform B

Platform D

50 m

50 m

50 m

0

figure 7.10

a) Ingatambo site with major platforms during the Early Horizon / Ingatambo phase (drawing courtesy of Atsushi Yamamoto); and b) view of principal platform mound at Ingatambo showing the central staircase (photograph courtesy of Atsushi Yamamoto).

b

Santa Ana–La Florida and Montegrande. However, while those sites were characterized by spiral-shaped architecture, the principal platform mound at Ingatambo featured rectangular stone structures at the top of the mounds and a central staircase leading down to the plaza (Figure 7.10). From a stylistic perspective, the associated architecture at Ingatambo closely resembles late Initial Period and Early Horizon ceremonial centers identified in the northern highlands of Peru at sites such as Pacopampa (Seki et al. 2010), Huacaloma (Terada and Onuki 1982, 1985), and Kuntur Wasi (Onuki and Inokuchi 2011; Seki, this volume).

In addition to the architecture, Ingatambo's interregional relationships can be seen in late Initial Period and Early Horizon pottery assemblages,

figure 7.11
Early Horizon (Ingatambo II) ceramics from Ingatambo. Photograph by Atsushi Yamamoto.

which are characterized by bowls with straight or convex walls, short neck jars, and decorative techniques such as incision, polychrome painting, line burnishing, and punctation (Yamamoto 2008). Yamamoto (2008, 2021) has argued that the pottery shows broad stylistic similarities to contemporary assemblages from Jaén and highland sites such as Cerro Ñañañique (Guffroy 1989), Challuabamba (Grieder et al. 2009), Kuntur Wasi (Onuki 1995), and Pacopampa (Rosas La Noire and Shady Solís 2005) and thus may be reflective of a broader northern sphere of interaction during the Initial Period. Additional influences are seen during the Early Horizon Ingatambo phases I and II, when Janabarriu-like pottery in the form of black monochrome vessels with circle-and-dot motifs (Figure 7.11; see Yamamoto 2008:figs. 23–24) also appear in the archaeological record, suggesting that Ingatambo adopted different elements of the Chavín cult in order to more directly participate within

these newly reconfigured long-distance exchange networks that now extended well beyond the northern highlands and that enveloped major ceremonial centers (such as the neighboring Pacopampa) previously tied to Ingatambo during the Initial Period.

Beyond the pottery, evidence of interregional exchange and possible interaction with Chavín includes the introduction of exotic items such as marine shell (including spondylus) and camelid bone during the late Initial Period, as well as obsidian during the Early Horizon (Yamamoto 2013). In fact, the obsidian was sourced to the Quispisisa mine in the southern highlands of Peru despite Ingatambo's closer proximity to Ecuadorian sources. As noted by Burger (1984, 1992, 2003, 2008), the increased frequency and distribution of these materials coincide with the spread of the Chavín cult, which in combination with Chavín-style pottery would suggest that Ingatambo was involved within the Chavín Interaction Sphere. Ingatambo's

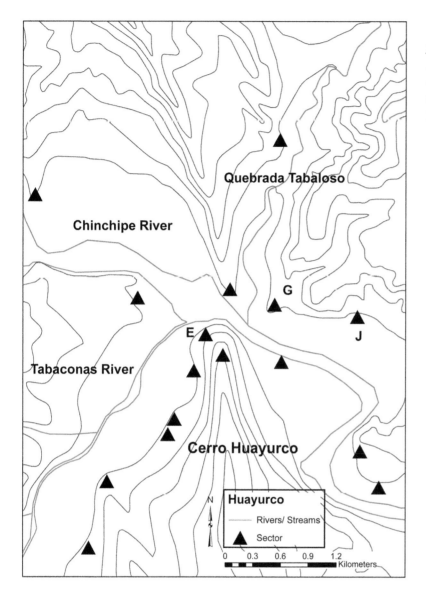

figure 7.12
Map of Huayurco, with
corresponding sectors
mentioned in the text.
Map by Ryan Clasby.

participation within the Chavín Interaction Sphere
may have been partially due to its location along a
major east–west corridor near the western entrance
to the Jaén region, allowing the site to become a
primary contributor of tropical forest products to
coastal and highland societies, a role that it had perhaps already filled during the Initial Period with
its participation in exchange networks involving
major northern highland ceremonial centers like
Pacopampa and Kuntur Wasi (Seki, this volume).
Ingatambo would eventually be abandoned by
around 550 BC, roughly coinciding with the fall of
Chavín de Huántar—a result that may reflect the

dissolution or decline of some coastal and highland
exchange networks, particularly those networks oriented south of the Huancabamba Depression.

An investigation of the Huayurco site, however,
presents a slightly different picture, one that entails
a more indirect relationship with Chavín. Located
along the Chinchipe-Tabaconas confluence, roughly
50 km north of the modern city of Jaén, Huayurco
is a large site complex comprised of at least sixteen
sectors (Figure 7.12) (Clasby 2014a, 2014b, 2019,
2021; Clasby and Menses Bartra 2013). Extensive
excavation and survey show that Huayurco was
occupied without interruption between 800 BC and

figure 7.13

Huayurco, Sector G: a) location of Sector G along the north bank of the Chinchipe River; and b) topographic map of Sector G with location of Early Horizon structure. Photograph and topographic map by Ryan Clasby.

AD 550, with people living along the river terraces that make up the edge of the confluence. Although gradual changes occur in terms of architecture, settlement patterns, subsistence, and material culture, the site maintained a remarkable degree of cultural continuity from the beginning of the Early Horizon to the end of the Early Intermediate Period, with the inhabitants engaging in agriculture and a mixed game hunting economy.

Three distinct phases have been noted for the Early Horizon between 800 and 1 BC. The earliest and least-known phase, Ambato, which dates between 800 and 600 BC, was identified only in Sector E on the eastern side of the Tabaconas River. However, excavations revealed small rectangular stone structures made of river cobbles packed in a mud-based mortar. While further investigation is needed, these structures likely served domestic purposes, as at least two hearths were found along the interiors of the walls.

By 600 BC, Huayurco shows clear evidence of ceremonial architecture, in the form of a large rectangular stone structure built on an artificially terraced hill (corresponding to Sector G) just north of the Chinchipe River (Figure 7.13). The structure was built in two major phases, Tabaloso (600–400 BC) and Las Juntas (400–1 BC), and consists of multiple rooms (Figure 7.14). The architecture is composed of river cobble footings set in mortar, a method of construction that closely follows the masonry techniques identified at earlier and contemporary Jaén sites such as Montegrande, Santa Ana–La Florida, and Ingatambo. Also notable is the use of yellow plaster on the footings (Figure 7.15), which is present at the Late Preceramic site of Montegrande (Olivera Núñez 2014:78, figs. 37–38), suggesting that the color may have been symbolically important within the architecture of the Jaén region. The architecture associated with the earlier Tabaloso-phase structure was only partially exposed along the eastern side of the hill; however, limited horizontal excavation suggests that the original architectural plan closely mirrored the subsequent Las Juntas structure, which

<figure>
figure 7.14
Huayurco, Sector G:
a) structure facing
north; and b) plan
map of structure.
Photograph and plan
map by Ryan Clasby.
</figure>

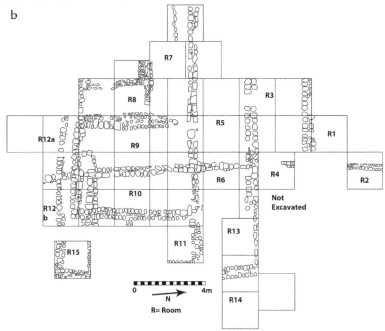

featured at least fifteen rooms split into two halves
(Figure 7.14b).

The ceremonial function of the Sector G structure is evident through several pieces of evidence.
First, underneath the foundations of the earliest
phase, Tabaloso, excavation identified the partial
remains of at least twenty-four individuals, of which
nineteen were infants and young children (Toyne
2012). As most individual skeletons were incomplete

(Figure 7.16), it seems probable that these were secondary burials laid down as part of the ritual activities associated with the construction of ceremonial
architecture to sanctify the activities inside. As
Burger (1992:74) has noted, the re-burial of children
underneath the foundation of ceremonial architecture has a long tradition in the Andes. These activities would be repeated with the reconstruction
efforts of the Las Juntas phase, as the burial of a child

figure 7.15
Interior of the structure in Sector G (Room 3), showing a stone footing with yellow plaster in the background and firepits in the foreground. Photograph by Ryan Clasby.

figure 7.16
Burial remains underneath the foundations of the Tabaloso-phase architecture in Sector G. Photograph by Ryan Clasby.

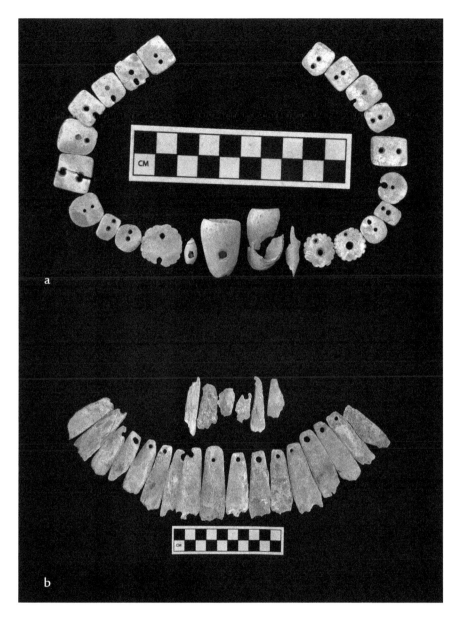

figure 7.17
Las Juntas–phase
ritual deposits in
Sector G: a) marine
shell necklace, and
b) rose-colored quartz
necklace. Photographs
by Ryan Clasby.

and an adult were placed under the floor and one of the footings of the structure, respectively.

Several of the rooms in the later Las Juntas structure also contained multiple hearths, many of which were found superimposed (Figure 7.15). A few of the hearths contained evidence of marine shell from the Pacific coast and animal bone, the latter corresponding to a medium-sized feline species (*Felis cf. tigrine*) (Vásquez Sánchez and Rosales Tham 2012). These felines are non-native to the area around Huayurco and are typically found in tropical lowland areas far to the east with a range that only slightly extends into Peru. The disposal of these

items suggest that the hearths were used primarily for ritual activities centered around the disposal of exotic goods. The presence of marine shell pendants within the Las Juntas–phase hearths followed a pattern that was persistent through three phases of the Early Horizon concerning the importation of small, easily portable species (such as pearl oyster and strombus) for the production of ornamental or ritual items (Paz Flores 2011). In fact, offerings of two mostly complete marine shell necklaces were found along the interior of the structure (Figure 7.17a). Notably, spondylus was not found at Huayurco despite its presence at Ingatambo, although further

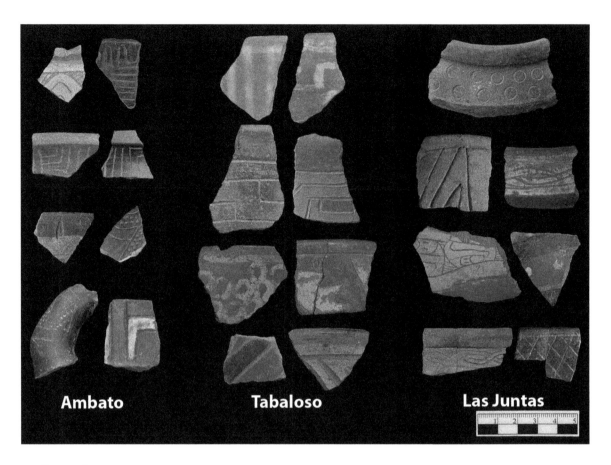

figure 7.18
Sample of Early Horizon ceramics from Huayurco. Photograph by Ryan Clasby.

investigation may yet reveal evidence of the shell. Other types of offerings found within the interior rooms were a necklace made of rose-colored quartz (Figure 7.17b) and two large ceramic jars, one of which was placed inside the other.

Huayurco's engagement in long-distance inter-action networks during the Early Horizon is also evident by local subsistence strategies and ceramic styles. While the subsistence patterns primar-ily relied on agriculture and mixed game hunting of local forest and riverine species, Huayurco also shows evidence of contact with the coast, highlands, and tropical forest in the form of marine fish and crab, guinea pig and camelids, and capybara, respec-tively (Vásquez Sánchez and Rosales Tham 2012). As mentioned, the spread of domesticated camelids into the northern highlands has been attributed to the expansion of the Chavín Interaction Sphere (Burger 1984, 1992, 2003), and the appearance of camelids

during the Early Horizon mirrors results from Ingatambo, suggesting that Huayurco also benefitted from Chavín's pan-Andean influence by exploiting these newly available species. While identified in low percentages during the Ambato phase, these animals (along with deer) would become a significant part of the overall diet by the end of the Early Horizon and beginning of the Early Intermediate Period.

The Early Horizon ceramics at Huayurco are dominated by convex and straight-walled bowls and short neck jars, many of which were decorated with incised and/or painted geometric and figurative designs (Figure 7.18). The neckless olla, a vessel form characteristic of Initial Period and Early Horizon assemblages, is either rare or absent within each of the three Early Horizon phases. As with Ingatambo and the Bagua sites, strong similarities can be drawn between the Huayurco ceramics and local assem-blages from the northern Peruvian highlands, the far north coast of Peru, and southern Ecuador, reinforcing the idea that Huayurco was well connected within broader interregional exchange networks straddling both sides of the transitional zone between the Northern and Central Andes. However, unlike Ingatambo and Bagua, Huayurco revealed scant evidence for Janabarriu-like ceramics. There is a preference during the Ambato phase (800–600 BC) for black or dark gray reduced ware and fine incision. Likewise, small quantities of stirrup-spout vessels are also present in this phase before eventually giving way to double-spout-and-bridge vessels. These characteristics could indicate that Chavín influence was greater in the Jaén region during this period and that even sites that did not fully adopt the religion were still impacted by the broader stylistic trends occurring in the central Andes.

Overall, the evidence suggests that Huayurco's relationship with Chavín was primarily indirect. Despite extensive excavation and survey, investigations have so far failed to yield the type of products associated with the spread of Chavín influence, such as Chavín-style art, Janabarriu-style pottery, spondylus shell, cinnabar, or obsidian. Nevertheless, Huayurco was clearly engaged in interregional exchange with the coast, highlands, and tropical forest during the Early Horizon, likely benefitting from exchange routes and networks that began in the Late Preceramic period and Initial Period and that were intensified or altered with the widespread adoption of the Chavín Interaction Sphere.

The Jaén Stone Bowl Tradition within the Context of the Chavín Interaction Sphere

Chavín's connection to the Jaén region can also be demonstrated through a comparison of lithic materials, most notably that of the finely carved stone vessels that have become characteristic of the region's material culture. Since Rojas Ponce's initial investigations at Huayurco, numerous specimens have been recovered from sites located around Jaén (Clasby 2022). While most of these vessels come from

figure 7.19
Stone vessel fragment during surface survey of Sector J. Photography by Ryan Clasby. Drawing by Edwin Silva de la Roca.

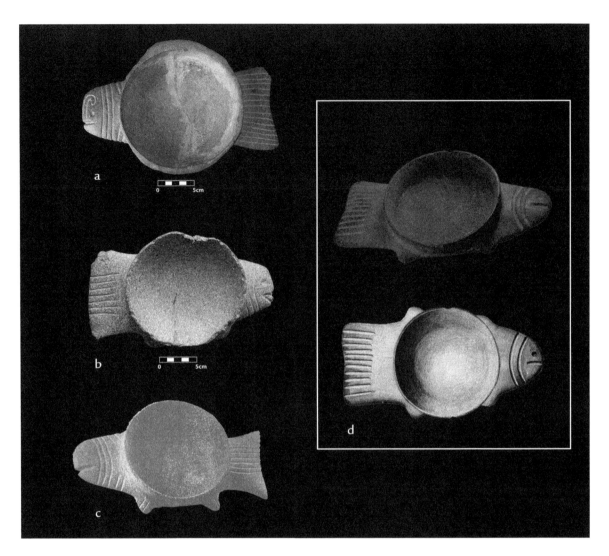

figure 7.20
Stone fish platters: a) unprovenienced example recovered along the Chamaya River, Museo Hermógenes Mejia Solf (photograph by Ryan Clasby); b) unprovenienced example recovered near the modern town of Pomahuaca, Museo Hermógenes Mejia Solf (photograph by Ryan Clasby); c) vessel depicted by Amat Olazábal (1997:246), likely recovered near the site of Huayurco along the lower Tabaconas River; and d) example recovered from the Ofrendas Gallery, Chavín de Huántar (Lumbreras 2007:fig. 199 and fig. 216, sp. 672).

unprovenienced contexts, a few examples have been located through excavation and survey. Remarkably, excavations at Huayurco did not yield any stone vessels, although a fragment of a finely covered stone bowl was recovered during surface survey of Sector J on the north side of the Chinchipe (Figure 7.19) (Clasby 2014b). Nevertheless, Valdez's recent finds at Santa Ana–La Florida along with Rojas Ponce's initial discoveries suggests that these vessels were produced from the Late Preceramic period through

the late Initial Period, and possibly into the Early Horizon with vessel forms primarily corresponding to convex-curved bowls, straight walled bowls, and zoomorphic effigy vessels. Based on stylistic comparisons of excavated and unprovenienced stone vessels found throughout the Andes, most of the Jaén vessels were likely produced for local ritual use. However, at least some of these vessels appear to have been exported to other areas of the Andes, including the far north coast and the central highlands of

figure 7.21
Stone figurine of an
individual sitting on a stool,
which features a feline
motif on the front. The
figurine was discovered
near Chontalí. Museo
Hermógenes Mejia Solf.
Photograph by Ryan Clasby.

Peru (see Clasby 2014b), providing support for Rojas Ponce's and Lathrap's idea.

In fact, the stone fish platter discovered by Luis G. Lumbreras (2007:figs. 199, 201a) in the Ofrendas Gallery at Chavín de Huántar is nearly identical to at least three other examples now known from the Jaén region, including one specimen supposedly recovered near the site of Huayurco (Figure 7.20) (Bushnell 1966:fig.10; see also Amat Olazábal 1997:246).[2] This likely provenience is significant, as the Ofrendas Gallery is thought to have been a depository for exotic ceramic and stone artifacts brought by pilgrims to the site during the late Initial Period (Burger 2013b). Thus, the presence of a Jaén vessel within the gallery would appear to indicate participation by the Jaén region in the Chavín Interaction Sphere. While various analyses could more fully address the question of the fish platter's original provenience, at least some of the stone vessel fragments discovered by Tello (1960:figs. 130b, 132) at Chavín de Huántar also show stylistic similarities

to documented vessels from the Jaén region, suggesting it was not an isolated occurrence.

Apart from stone vessels, within the Jaén region, a black stone figurine (Figure 7.21) housed in the Museo Hermógenes Mejia Solf may be contemporary with Chavín art (Clasby 2014b). While there is some question of its provenience and authenticity, the figurine depicts a shaman or chief-like figure sitting on a decorated stool. The design on the front of the stool features a stylized, jaguar-like face with downward pointed jaws, similar to figures carved on Chavín stone sculpture.

Discussion

In the fifty years since the 1968 Dumbarton Oaks symposium on Chavín, scholars have made significant strides in their efforts to understand the emergence of the first pan-Andean cultural phenomenon. Numerous investigations during this time at Chavín and other Formative sites on the Andean coast and in the highlands have helped to clarify the nature and geographical extent of the Chavín Phenomenon and to contextualize its role within the broader historical processes that led to the development of Andean civilization.

Yet, despite these advances, Chavín's relationship to the tropical forest remains an enigma. Investigations within the tropical forest still lag behind research conducted on the coast and in the highlands. Most areas of the Eastern Andes and western Amazon, except for a few key regions such as Chachapoyas and the central Ucayali, remain completely unknown archaeologically. Of those areas that have seen research, they tend to be understood only on a cursory level, as the scope of the investigations were small scale and non-sustained. Furthermore, archaeologists have yet to overcome many of the hurdles that exist in finding concrete evidence of tropical forest products within coastal and highland sites. This problem is not only reflective of preservation issues but also a general lack of knowledge concerning tropical forest ceramic and lithic artifact styles. Thus, despite significant advances in Andean archaeology over the last fifty years, interpretations of Chavín art and iconography remain the primary means for exploring Chavín's relationship to the tropical forest.

Recent investigations within the Jaén region have provided a glimpse into the complex interregional relationships that existed between tropical forest societies and their contemporaries in the coast and highlands during the Late Preceramic period, Initial Period, and Early Horizon. The results suggest that not only did these networks have considerable time depth, stretching back as early as 3000 BC, but that many of them continued to expand over time and eventually realigned themselves with the widespread adoption of the Chavín Interaction Sphere. The Jaén region was well situated to take advantage of these shifts in interregional exchange, as not only was it located on an east–west axis between the tropical forest and Andean highlands but the natural corridors that exist within the region would have also made it a favored interior route for the southward importation of warm water marine

shell into the Peruvian Andes, allowing travelers to bypass the harsh conditions of the Sechura Desert (see Hocquenghem et al. 1993) while also simultaneously gaining more immediate access to tropical forest products. This idea has been born out through the frequent documentation of marine shell within Jaén region sites and the close similarities between ceramic styles on both sides of the Transitional Zone, suggesting that movement was fluid between these different areas.

The sites of Ingatambo and Huayurco help to demonstrate the impact of these networks on the Jaén region, as each settlement benefited from the increased interregional interaction that occurred during the Early Horizon with the arrival of Chavín influence. In fact, the presence of the stone fish platter in the Ofrendas Gallery at Chavín is a strong indication that the Jaén region was important to the broader expansion of the Chavín Interaction Sphere. Yet, a close comparison of Ingatambo and Huayurco suggests that each site engaged with Chavín in a slightly different manner. For Ingatambo, this interaction appears to have been direct, with Ingatambo producing or adopting Chavín-style pottery alongside local styles while also mimicking architectural patterns common to the highlands of Cajamarca and importing exotic goods that came to be affiliated with Chavín, such as spondylus and obsidian. For Huayurco, the local populations imported marine shell from the Pacific coast such as strombus, rice shell, and pearl oyster and would eventually take advantage of the influx of camelids into the northern highlands of the Central Andes—but they do not appear to have adopted Chavín-style pottery or any of the conventions or iconography associated with the Chavín art style, nor did they appear to seek out spondylus or obsidian. While further investigation of Huayurco's settlement may yet find evidence of these materials, their absence from the archaeological record may also symbolize a conscious rejection of the ideology behind the Chavín cult.

Unfortunately, an understanding of Chavín's relationship to the Jaén region is still in its infancy, and the mechanisms that underlined the exchange networks that connected them have yet to be determined. The varied patterns of interaction demonstrated by Ingatambo and Huayurco suggest that Chavín's connection to the tropical forest was not uniform and that scholars should explore the relationship between Chavín and the tropical forest in much the same way that they have examined its relationship with other parts of the highlands and coast, recognizing that the tropical forest was a heterogenous environment and that peoples living within this zone would have had access to different types of resources, knowledge, and ideas based on both location and sociopolitical organization. Indeed, historical evidence suggests that trade networks within western Amazonia and the Eastern Andes were extensive and that variation existed within these networks, with products such as salt, curare, and other types of plant products playing major roles within their organization (Taylor 1999). Utilizing Jaén and nearby Chachapoyas as an example, Henry Wassen (1979) has noted that the area was known historically for producing *espingo* seeds. Highly desired as an additive to chicha during the colonial period, the seeds were exported via small wooden or stone *conopas* to the highlands and coast. Jaén also forms part of what is known as the central Andean "Health Axis," an area recognized ethnographically and historically for its strong basis in traditional healing and access to desired medicinal plants (Bussmann and Sharon 2006). While the idea of a central Andean "Health Axis" cannot necessarily be projected to the Early Horizon (or earlier), it reasserts the idea that certain areas of the tropical forest may have been recognized for particular products or ideas.

Archaeologically, this is much more difficult to examine, but greater emphasis on analyzing Formative-period material culture within the eastern slopes and western Amazon, along with studying the preferred natural ranges of desired plant and animal products by Andean populations, may help clarify these regional distinctions and allow archaeologists to examine Chavín's relationship more fully with the tropical forest. For example, the Jaén region appears to have been precocious in its production of finely carved stone vessels, even in comparison to highland and coastal societies. As some of these vessels found their way to different areas of the Andes, including Piura and the site of Chavín

de Huántar, it suggests that they were highly desired as ritual objects with outsiders recognizing the skill of the Jaén region in producing them (Clasby 2014b). Similar types of products—both perishable and nonperishable—may have also been characteristic of other areas of the Eastern Andes and may have helped Chavín grow as an interaction sphere, a point that is underscored by its seeming interaction with the montane forest east of Chavín (Nesbitt, this volume; Nesbitt, Johnson, and Ibarra Asencios 2021) as well as the Upper Huallaga, the central Ucayali (Lathrap 1971), and Jaén.

Thus, while much remains unknown regarding Chavín's relationship to the tropical forest, recent advances are beginning to demonstrate that certain areas of the tropical forest were actively participating within the broader networks of interregional interaction that arose before and alongside the spread of Chavín. These relationships were likely multidirectional, with products, ideas, and technologies going in each direction. Chavín appears to have incorporated specific tropical forest elements into its culture, as it did with elements from the coast and highlands, using its firsthand knowledge of the region to build an ideological system that could be widely adopted across each of the major environments of the Andes. Continued investigation within the eastern tropical forest is a necessity then to fully understand the scale of the Chavín cult and its geographical reach.

Acknowledgments

I would like to thank the organizers of the symposium, Richard Burger, Jason Nesbitt, and Colin McEwan, for inviting me to contribute to this volume and for their helpful editorial comments. Research for the investigations at Huayurco were supported by the National Science Foundation Doctoral Dissertation Improvement Grant and the Yale University MacMillan Grant. I would also like to thank Christopher Milan for his preparation of the maps and Ulises Gamonal, Quirino Olivera, Francisco Valdez, and Atsushi Yamamoto for their generosity in sharing images and illustrations related to their work.

1 The date of the Reichlens' visit to Jaén is uncertain as they did not publish on these collections nor make mention of travel to the region. In fact, their publication on the nearby Utcubamba River (Reichlen and Reichlen 1950) lacks mention of travel to Jaén. Inventory lists of the collections from the Musée du Quai Branly suggest they were first donated to the Musée de l'Homme in 1965. An examination of the Reichlen collection suggests that some of the stone and ceramic vessels belonged to the same private collection from Huayurco that appears in a photograph published by Bushnell (1966:fig. 10), who himself was reporting information gathered by graduate students from the University of Cambridge. Thus, it appears likely that the Reichlens' visit to Huayurco postdates the reporting by Bushnell's graduate students.

2 Amat Olazábal (1997:246) published a stone fish vessel, noting the similarities between the Ofrendas specimen and an example recorded by the Reichlens (unpublished) along the Chinchipe. Comparisons suggest that the Amat Olazábal vessel, mislabeled as the Ofrendas specimen, is actually the same vessel recorded by Bushnell (1996:fig. 10) and the Reichlens near Huayurco.

REFERENCES CITED

Amat Olazábal, Hernán

1997 Formación y desarrollo de las sociedades teocráticas en los Andes centrales. In *XI Congreso Peruano del Hombre y la Cultura Andina "Augusto Cardich": Actas y trabajos científicos*, vol. 1, edited by Hernán Amat Olazábal and Luis Guzmán Palomino, pp. 241–252. Universidad Nacional "Hermilio Valdizán" de Huánuco, Huánuco.

Benson, Elizabeth P. (editor)

1971 *Dumbarton Oaks Conference on Chavín.* Dumbarton Oaks Research Library and Collection, Washington, D.C.

Bird, Junius B.

1963 Pre-Ceramic Art from Huaca Prieta, Chicama Valley. *Ñawpa Pacha: Journal of Andean Archaeology* 1:29–34.

Bischof, Henning

2008 Context and Contents of Early Chavín Art. In *Chavín: Art, Architecture, and Culture*, edited by William J. Conklin and Jeffrey Quilter, pp. 107–142. Cotsen Institute of Archaeology, University of California, Los Angeles.

Burger, Richard L.

1984 Archaeological Areas and Prehistoric Frontiers: The Case of Formative Peru and Ecuador. In *Social and Economic Organization in the Pre-Hispanic Andes*, edited by David L. Browman, Richard L. Burger, and Mario A. Rivera, pp. 33–71. BAR International Series, Oxford.

1992 *Chavín and the Origins of Andean Civilization.* Thames and Hudson, New York.

2003 Conclusions: Cultures of the Ecuadorian Formative in Their Andean Contexts. In *Archaeology of Formative Ecuador*, edited by J. Scott Raymond and Richard L. Burger, pp. 465–486. Dumbarton Oaks Research Library and Collection, Washington, D.C.

2008 Chavín de Huántar and Its Sphere of Influence. In *Handbook of South American Archaeology*, edited by Helaine Silverman and William H. Isbell, pp. 681–703. Springer, New York.

2009 The Intellectual Legacy of Julio C. Tello. In *The Life and Writing of Julio C. Tello: America's First Indigenous Archaeologist*, edited by Richard L. Burger, pp. 65–88. University of Iowa Press, Iowa City.

2011 What Kind of Hallucinogenic Snuff Was Used at Chavín de Huántar? An Iconographic Identification. *Ñawpa*

Pacha: Journal of Andean Archaeology 31(2):123–140.

2012   The Construction of Values during the Peruvian Formative. In *The Construction of Value in the Ancient World*, edited by John K. Papadopoulos and Gary Urton, pp. 288–305. Cotsen Institute of Archaeology, University of California, Los Angeles.

2013a   Central Andean Language Expansion and the Chavín Sphere of Interaction. In *Archaeology and Language in the Andes: A Cross-Disciplinary Exploration of Prehistory*, edited by Paul Heggarty and David Beresford-Jones, pp. 133–159. The British Academy, Oxford.

2013b   In the Realm of the Incas: An Archaeological Reconsideration of Household Exchange, Long-Distance Trade, and Marketplaces in the Pre-Hispanic Andes. In *Merchants, Markets, and Exchange in the Pre-Columbian World*, edited by Kenneth G. Hirth and Joanne Pillsbury, pp. 319–334. Dumbarton Oaks Research Library and Collection, Washington, D.C.

Burger, Richard L., and Lucy C. Salazar

2008   The Manchay Culture and the Coastal Inspiration for Highland Chavín Civilization. In *Chavín: Art, Architecture, and Culture*, edited by William J. Conklin and Jeffrey Quilter, pp. 85–105. Cotsen Institute of Archaeology, University of California, Los Angeles.

Bushnell, Geoffrey H. S.

1966   Some Archaeological Discoveries from the Frontier Region of Perú and Ecuador near Jaén. *Actas y memorias de XXXVI Congreso Internacional de Americanistas* 1964(1):501–507. Seville.

Bussmann, Rainer W., and Douglas Sharon

2006   Traditional Medicinal Plant Use in Northern Peru: Tracking Two Thousand Years of Healing Culture. *Journal of Ethnobiology and Ethnomedicine* 2:47.

Church, Warren B.

1996   Prehistoric Cultural Development and Interregional Interaction in the Tropical Montane Forests of Peru. PhD dissertation, Yale University, New Haven.

2021   A Record of Early Long-Distance Societal Interaction from Manachaqui Cave in Peru's Northeastern Andes. In *The Archaeology of the Upper Amazon: Complexity and Interaction in the Andean Tropical Forest*, edited by Ryan Clasby and Jason Nesbitt, pp. 38–61. University Press of Florida, Gainesville.

Church, Warren B., and Anna Guengerich

2017   Introducción: La (re)construcción de Chachapoyas a través de la historia e hstoriografía (1532–2000 d.C.). *Boletín de Arqueología PUCP* 23(2):5–38.

Church, Warren B., and Adriana von Hagen

2008   Chachapoyas: Cultural Development at an Andean Cloud Forest Crossroad. In *Handbook of South American Archaeology*, edited by Helaine Silverman and William H. Isbell, pp. 903–926. Springer, New York.

Clasby, Ryan

2014a   Early Ceremonial Architecture in the *Ceja de Selva* (800–100 BC): A Case Study from Huayurco, Jaén Region, Peru. In *Antes de Orellana: Actas del 3er Encuentro Internacional de Arqueología Amazónica*, edited by Stéphen Rostain, pp. 233–242. Instituto Francés de Estudios Andinos, Quito.

2014b   Exploring Long Term Cultural Developments and Interregional Interaction in the Eastern Slopes of the Andes: A Case Study from the Site of Huayurco, Jaén Region, Peru. PhD dissertation, Yale University, New Haven.

2019   Diachronic Changes in Sociopolitical Developments and Interregional Interaction in the Early Horizon Eastern Montane Forest. In *Perspectives on Early Andean Civilization in Peru: Interaction, Authority, and Socioeconomic Organization during the First and Second Millennia BC*, edited by Richard L. Burger, Lucy C. Salazar, and Yuji Seki, pp. 149–171. Yale University Press, New Haven.

2021   Continuity and Interaction along the Eastern Edge of the Andes during the Central Andean Early Intermediate Period. In *The Archaeology of the Upper Amazon: Complexity and Interaction in the Andean Tropical Forest*, edited by Ryan Clasby and Jason Nesbitt, pp. 148–167. University Press of Florida, Gainesville.

2022   The Jaén Stone Bowl Tradition and Ceja de Selva Contributions to Early Andean Exchange Networks. *Latin American Antiquity*, https://doi.org/10.1017/laq.2022.9.

Clasby, Ryan, and Jorge Meneses Bartra

2013   Nuevas investigaciones en Huayurco: Resultados iniciales de las excavaciones de un sitio de la *ceja de selva* de los Andes peruanos. *Arqueología y sociedad* 25:303–326.

Clasby, Ryan, and Jason Nesbitt

2021   Introduction: New Perspectives on the Archaeology of the Upper Amazon. In *The Archaeology of the Upper Amazon: Complexity and Interaction in the Andean Tropical Forest*, edited by Ryan Clasby and Jason Nesbitt, pp. 1–22. University Press of Florida, Gainesville.

DeBoer, Warren R.

2003   Ceramic Assemblage Variability in the Formative of Ecuador and Peru. In *Archaeology of Formative Ecuador*, edited by J. Scott Raymond and Richard L. Burger, pp. 465–486. Dumbarton Oaks Research Library and Collection, Washington, D.C.

Dillehay, Tom D.

2020   Initial East and West Connections Across South America. In *Rethinking the Andes-Amazonia Divide: A Cross-Disciplinary Exploration*, edited by Adrian J. Pearce, David G. Beresford-Jones, and Paul Heggarty, pp. 77–86. UCL Press, London.

Dillehay, Tom D., Brian McCray, and Patricia J. Netherly

2020   The Pacific Coast and Andean Highlands/Amazonia. In *Rethinking the Andes-Amazonia Divide: A Cross-Disciplinary Exploration*, edited by Adrian J. Pearce, David G. Beresford-Jones, and Paul Heggarty, pp. 221–238. UCL Press, London.

Eliade, Mircea

1959   *The Sacred and the Profane: The Nature of Religion*. Translated by Willard R. Trask. Harcourt, Brace and World, New York.

Espinosa Reyes, Ricardo

2002   *La gran ruta Inca: El Cápaq Ñan*. Petróleos del Perú, Lima.

Fung Pineda, Rosa

1983   Sobre el origen selvático de la civilización Chavín. *Amazonía peruana* 4:77–92.

Grieder, Terence E.

1988   Burial Patterns and Offerings. In *La Galgada, Peru: A Preceramic Culture in Tradition*, by Terrence Grieder, Alberto Bueno Mendoza, C. Earle Smith Jr., and Robert M. Malina, pp. 73–102. University of Texas Press, Austin.

Grieder, Terence E., James D. Farmer, David V. Hill, Peter W. Stahl, and Douglas H. Ubelaker

2009   *Art and Archaeology of Challuabamba, Ecuador*. University of Texas Press, Austin.

Guffroy, Jean

1989   Un centro ceremonial formativo en el Alto Piura. *Bulletin de l'Institut Français d'Études Andines* 18(2):161–207.

Harner, Michael J.

1972   *The Jivaro*. Doubleday, Garden City.

Helms, Mary W.

1979   *Ancient Panama: Chiefs in Search of Power*. University of Texas Press, Austin.

1988   *Ulysses' Sail: An Ethnographic Odyssey of Power, Knowledge, and Geographical Distance*. Princeton University Press, Princeton.

Hocquenghem, Anne-Marie, Jaime Idrovo Urigüen, Peter Kaulicke, and Dominique Gomis

1993   Bases del intercambio entre las sociedades norperuanas y surecuatorianas: Una zona de transición entre 1500 AC y 600 DC. *Bulletin del'Institut Français d'Études Andines* 22(3):701–719.

Kanezaki, Yuko, Takayuki Omori, and Eisei Tsurumi

2021   Emergence and Development of Pottery in the Early Andean Formative Period: New Insights from an Improved Wairajirca Pottery Chronology at the Jancao Site in the Huánuco Regin, Peru. *Latin American Antiquity* 32:239–254.

Kano, Chiaki

1972   Pre-Chavín Cultures in the Central Highlands of Peru: New Evidence from Shillacoto, Huánuco. In *Cult of the Feline*, edited by Elizabeth P. Benson, pp. 139–152. Dumbarton Oaks Research Library and Collection, Washington, D.C.

Langdon, E. Jean

    1981   Cultural Bases for Trading of Visions and Spiritual Knowledge in the Colombian and Ecuadorian Montaña. In *Networks of the Past: Regional Interaction in Archaeology*, edited by Peter Francis, François Kense, and P. G. Duke, pp. 101–116. Department of Archaeology, University of Calgary, Calgary.

Larco Hoyle, Rafael

    1941   *Los cupisniques*. Casa editora "La Crónica" y "Variedades" S.A., Lima.

Lathrap, Donald W.

    1970   *The Upper Amazon*. Thames and Hudson, New York.

    1971   The Tropical Forest and the Cultural Context of Chavín. In *Dumbarton Oaks Conference on Chavín*, edited by Elizabeth P. Benson, pp. 73–100. Dumbarton Oaks Research Library and Collection, Washington, D.C.

    1973   Gifts of the Cayman: Some Thoughts on the Subsistence Basis of Chavín. In *Variation in Anthropology: Essays in Honor of John C. McGregor*, edited by Donald W. Lathrap and Jody Douglas, pp. 91–105. Illinois Archaeological Survey, Urbana.

    1974   The Moist Tropics, the Arid Lands, and the Appearance of Great Art Styles in the New World. In *Art and Environment in Native America*, edited by Mary E. King and Idris Traylor, pp. 115–158. Special Publications of The Museum No. 7, Texas Tech University, Lubbock.

    1985   Jaws: The Control of Power in the Early Nuclear American Ceremonial Center. In *Early Ceremonial Architecture in the Andes*, edited by Christopher B. Donnan, pp. 241–267. Dumbarton Oaks Research Library and Collection, Washington, D.C.

Lathrap, Donald W., Jorge Marcos Pino, and James A. Zeidler

    1977   Real Alto: An Ancient Ceremonial Center. *Archaeology* 30(1):2–13.

Lumbreras Salcedo, Luis G.

    2007   *Chavín: Excavaciones arqueológicas*. Universidad ALAS Peruanas, Lima.

Lyon, Patricia J.

    1974   *Native South Americans: Ethnology of the Least Known Continent*. Little, Brown and Company, Boston.

Matsumoto, Yuichi, Jason Nesbitt, Michael D. Glascock, Yuri I. Cavero Palomino, and Richard L. Burger

    2018   Interregional Obsidian Exchange during the Late Initial Period and Early Horizon: New Perspectives from Campanayuq Rumi, Peru. *Latin American Antiquity* 29(1):44–63.

Miasta Gutiérrez, Jaime

    1979   *El Alto Amazonas, arqueología de Jaén y San Ignacio, Perú*. Universidad Nacional Mayor de San Marcos, Dirección de Proyección Social, Seminario de Historia Rural Andina, Lima.

Morales Chocano, Daniel

    1992   Chambira: Alfareros tempranos de la Amazonia peruana. In *Estudios de arqueología peruana*, edited by Duccio Bonavia, pp. 149–176. Fomciencias, Lima.

    1998   Chambira: Una cultura de sabana árida en la Amazonía peruana. *Investigaciones sociales* 2(2):61–75.

Murra, John V.

    1972   El control vertical de un máximo de pisos ecológicos en la economía de las sociedades andinas. In *Visita de la provincia de León de Huánuco*, edited by John V. Murra, pp. 429–476. Universidad Nacional Hermilio Valdizán, Huánuco.

Musée du Quai Branly-Jacques Chirac

    n.d.   Musée du Quai Branly-Jacques Chirac. L'unité patrimoniale des collections des Amériques. Electronic document, http://www.quaibranly.fr/en/explore-collections/, accessed August 9, 2021.

Myers, Thomas P.

    1972–1974   Archaeological Survey of the Lower Aguaytía River, Eastern Peru. *Ñawpa Pacha: Journal of Andean Archaeology* 10/12:61–89.

    1981   Ceramics from the Hacienda Tarapoto, Department of San Martin, Peru. *Ñawpa Pacha: Journal of Andean Archaeology* 19:155–163, 165–166.

Myers, Thomas P., and Bartholomew Dean

    1999   Cerámica prehispánica del Río Chambira, Loreto. *Amazonía peruana* 13(26):255–288.

Myers, Thomas P., and Santiago Rivas Panduro

    2005   Evidencias arqueológicas en el Alto Amazonas: Explorando las cuencas de los Ríos Aichiyacu y Morona, Loreto. *Unay Runa* 7:83–122.

Nesbitt, Jason, Rachel Johnson, and Bebel Ibarra Asencios

    2021   Connections between the Chavín Heartland and the Upper Amazon: New Perspectives from Canchas Uckro (1100–850 BC). In *The Archaeology of the Upper Amazon: Complexity and Interaction in the Andean Tropical Forest*, edited by Ryan Clasby and Jason Nesbitt, pp. 106–128. University Press of Florida, Gainesville.

Oberem, Udo

    1974   Trade and Trade Goods in the Ecuadorian Montaña. In *Native South Americans: Ethnology of the Least Known Continent*, edited by Patricia J. Lyon, pp. 346–357. Little, Brown and Company, Boston.

Olivera Núñez, Quirino

    2013   Avance de las investigaciones arqueológicas en la Alta Amazonía, nororiente de Perú. In *Arqueología amazónica: Las civilizaciones ocultas del bosque tropical*, edited by Francisco Valdez, pp. 173–203. Instituto francés de estudios andinos, Lima.

    2014   *Arqueología alto amazónica: El origen de la civilización en el Perú*. Apus Graph, Lima.

Onuki, Yoshio (editor)

    1995   *Dos sitios del formativo en el norte del Perú*. Hokusen-sha, Tokyo.

Onuki, Yoshio, and Kinya Inokuchi

    2011   *Gemelos prístinos: El tesoro del templo de Kuntur Wasi*. Fondo Editorial del Congreso del Perú / Minera Yanacocha, Lima.

Paz Flores, Gladys

    2011   *Análisis malacológico: Proyecto de Investigación Arqueológico Huayurco; Bellavista, Jaén-Huarango, San Ignacio Cajamarca*. Unpublished field report.

Pearsall, Deborah M.

    2008   Plant Domestication and the Shift to Agriculture in the Andes. In *Handbook of South American Archaeology*, edited by Helaine Silverman and William H. Isbell, pp. 105–120. Springer, New York.

Pimentel Spissu, Victor

    1986   *Petroglifos en el valle medio y bajo de Jequetepeque, norte del Perú*. Materialien zur allgemeinen und vergleichenden, Archäologie 31. Verlag C. H. Beck, Munich.

Ravines, Rogger

    1989   Cerámica del Río Morona, alto amazonas, Loreto. *Boletín de Lima* 66:14–18.

Raymond, J. Scott

    1982   Quimpiri, a Ceramic Style from the Peruvian Montaña. *Ñawpa Pacha: Journal of Andean Archaeology* 20:121–146.

    1988   A View from the Tropical Forest. In *Peruvian Prehistory*, edited by Richard W. Keatinge, pp. 279–300. Cambridge University Press, Cambridge.

Reichlen, Henry, and Paule Reichlen

    1950   Recherches archéologiques dans les Andes du Haut Utcubamba. *Journal de la Société des Américanistes* 39:219–246.

Rivas Panduro, Santiago

    2003   *Asentamientos prehispánicos de la cuenca del Río Cachiyacu-Amazonia Peruana*. Instituto Cultural RVNA, Lima.

Rivas Panduro, Santiago, Ada Medina Mendoza, Julio Abanto Llaque, Richer Rios Zumaeta, and Corina Caldas Carillo

    2008   Arqueología de las cuencas del Pastaza y Morona: Reporte de Zonificación Ecológica Económica. *Amazonia Peruana* 15(31):269–302.

Roe, Peter

    1982   *The Cosmic Zygote: Cosmology in the Amazon Basin*. Rutgers University Press, New Brunswick, N.J.

    2008   How to Build a Raptor: Why the Dumbarton Oaks "Scaled Cayman" Callango Textile Is Really a Jaguaroid Harpy Eagle. In *Chavín: Art, Architecture, and Culture*, edited by William J. Conklin and Jeffrey Quilter, pp. 181–216. Cotsen Institute of Archaeology, University of California, Los Angeles.

Rojas Ponce, Pedro

1961 *Informe preliminar de la explora-ción arqueológica al Alto Marañon: Exploración arqueológica al Alto Marañon*, vol. 3. Unpublished field report. Wenner-Gren Foundation, New York.

1985 La "Huaca" Huayurco, Jaén. In *Historia de Cajamarca I: Arqueología*, edited by Fernando Silva Santiesteban, Waldemar Espinoza Soriano, and Rogger Ravines, pp. 181–186. Instituto Nacional de Cultura-Cajamarca, Cajamarca.

Rosas La Noire, Hermilio, and Ruth Shady Solís

2005 Pacopampa: Un centro formativo en la Sierra Nor-Peruana; Arqueología de pacopampa. *Arqueología y socie-dad* 16:11–62. Museo de Arqueología y Antropología, Centro Cultural de San Marcos, Universidad Nacional Mayor de San Marcos, Lima.

Rowe, John H.

1962 *Chavín Art: An Inquiry into Its Form and Meaning*. Museum of Primitive Art, New York.

1967 Form and Meaning in Chavín Art. In *Peruvian Archaeology: Selected Readings*, edited by John H. Rowe and Dorothy Menzel, pp. 72–103. Peek Publications, Palo Alto.

Sayre, Matthew P.

2018 A Synonym for Sacred: Vilca Use in the Preconquest Andes. In *Ancient Psychoactive Substances*, edited by Scott M. Fitzpatrick. pp. 265–285. University Press of Florida, Gainesville.

Seki, Yuji, Juan Pablo Villanueva, Masato Sakai, Diana Alemán, Mauro Ordoñez, Walter Tosso, Araceli Espinoza, Kinya Inokuchi, and Daniel Morales Chocano.

2010 Nuevas evidencias del sitio arqueoló-gico de Pacopampa, en la Sierra Norte del Perú. *Boletín de Arqueología PUCP* 12:69–95.

Shady Solís, Ruth

1973 La arqueología de la cuenca inferior del Utcubamba. PhD dissertation, Universidad Nacional Mayor de San Marcos, Lima.

1987 Tradición y cambio en las sociedades formativas de Bagua, Amazonas, Perú. *Revista andina* 5(2):457–488.

1999 Sociedades formativas de Bagua-Jaén y sus relaciones andinas y amazónicas. In *Formativo sudamericano*, edited by Paulina Ledergerber-Crespo, pp. 201–211. Abya-Yala, Quito.

Shady Solís, Ruth, and Hermilio Rosas LaNoire

1979 El Complejo Bagua y el sistema desde establecimiento durante el Formativo en la Sierra Norte del Perú. *Ñawpa Pacha: Journal of Andean Archaeology* 10:109–154.

Taylor, Anne Christine

1999 The Western Margins of Amazonia from the Early Sixteenth to the Early Nineteenth Century. In *The Cambridge History of the Native Peoples of the Americas*, vol. 3, *South America*, pt. 1, edited by Frank Salomon and Stuart Schwartz, pp. 188–256. Cambridge University Press, Cambridge.

Tello, Julio C.

1921 *Introducción a la historia antigua del Peru*. Editorial Euforion, Lima.

1940 *Origen y desarrollo de las civilizacio-nes prehistóricas andinas*. Proceedings of the 27th International Congress of Americanists 1:589–720. Lima.

1960 *Chavín: Cultura matriz de la civiliza-ción andina (primera arte)*. Publicación Antropológica del Archivo "Julio C. Tello" de la Universidad Nacional Mayor de San Marcos, Lima.

Terada, Kazuo

1979 *Excavations at La Pampa in the North Highlands of Peru, 1975*. Japanese Scientific Expedition to Nuclear America, Report 1. University of Tokyo Press, Tokyo.

Terada, Kazuo, and Yoshio Onuki

1982 *Excavations at Huacaloma in the Caja-marca Valley, Peru, 1979*. University of Tokyo Press, Tokyo.

1985 *The Formative Period in the Cajamarca Basin, Peru: Excavations at Huacaloma and Layzón, 1982*. Report 3 of the Japanese Scientific Expedition to Nuclear America. University of Tokyo Press, Tokyo.

Torres, Constantino Manuel

2008   Chavín's Psychoactive Pharmacopoeia: The Iconographic Evidence. In *Chavín: Art, Architecture, and Culture*, edited by William J. Conklin and Jeffrey Quilter, pp. 239–259. Cotsen Institute of Archaeology, University of California, Los Angeles.

Toyne, J. Marla

2012   Final Report of the Human Osteological Analysis from the Huayurco Archaeological Project, Jaén-Peru. Unpublished field report.

Uzendoski, Michael A.

2004   The Horizontal Archipelago: The Quijos/Upper Napo Regional System. *Ethnohistory* 51(2):317–357.

Valdez, Francisco

2007   Mayo-Chinchipe: The Half-Open Door. In *Ecuador: The Secret Art of Precolumbian Ecuador*, edited by Daniel Klein, Ivan Cruz Cevallos, and Leon Doyon, pp. 320–349. 5 Continentes, Milan.

2008   Inter-Zonal Relationships in Ecuador. In *Handbook of South American Archaeology*, edited by Helaine Silverman and William H. Isbell, pp. 865–888. Springer, New York.

2011   La cerámica mayo chinchipe, el Formativo Temprano de la ceja de selva oriental. In *Revista nacional de cultura: Letras, artes, y ciencias del Ecuador* 15–16, vol. 3, edited by Francisco Valdez, pp. 685–708. Consejo Nacional de Cultura de Ecuador, Quito.

2013a   Mayo Chinchipe: Hacia un replanteamiento del origen de las sociedades complejas en la civilización andina. In *Arqueología amazónica: Las civilizaciones ocultas del bosque tropical*, edited by Francisco Valdez, pp. 99–146. Instituto Francés de Estudios Andinos, Lima.

2013b   *Primeras sociedades de la alta amazonía: La cultura mayo Chinchipe-Marañón*. Institut de Recherche pour le Développement, Quito.

2014   Investigaciones arqueológicas en Palanda, Santa Ana-La Florida. In *Arqueología alto amazónica: El origen de la civilización en el Perú*, edited by Quirino Olivera Nuñez, pp. 222–245. Apus Graph, Lima.

2021   The Mayo-Chinchipe-Marañon Complex: The Unexpected Spirits of the *Ceja*. In *The Archaeology of the Upper Amazon: Complexity and Interaction in the Andean Tropical Forest*, edited by Ryan Clasby and Jason Nesbitt, pp. 62–82. University Press of Florida, Gainesville.

Vásquez Sánchez, Víctor, and Teresa Rosales Tham

2012   Análisis de los restos de fauna de Huayurco. Unpublished field report.

Wassen, S. Henry

1979   Was Espingo (Ispincu) of Psychotropic and Intoxicating Importance for the Shamans in Peru? In *Spirits, Shamans, and Stars: Perspectives from South America*, edited by David Browman and Ronald Schwarz, pp. 55–62. Mouton, The Hague.

Wiegend, Maximilian

2002   Observations on the Biogeography of the Amotape-Huancabamba Zone in Northern Peru. *Botanical Review* 68(1):38–54.

Wilkinson, Darryl

2018   The Influence of Amazonia on State Formation in the Andes. *Antiquity* 92:1362–1376.

Yamamoto, Atsushi

2007   *El reconocimiento del valle de Huancabamba, Jaén, Cajamarca, Perú*. ARKEOS, Lima.

2008   Ingatambo: Un sitio estratégico de contacto interregional en la zona norte del Perú. *Boletín de Arqueología PUCP* 12:25–52.

2011   Contacto intercultural entre el sur de Ecuador y el norte del Perú. *Revista nacional de cultura* 15–16(2):399–408. Consejo Nacional de Cultura del Ecuador.

2012   Dinámica social en el Formativo de los Andes: Desde el punto de la vista de actividades y estrategias de sociedades del valle de Huancabamba, norte del Perú. PhD dissertation, The Graduate University for Advanced Studies, Japan.

2013   Las rutas interregionales en el período formativo para el norte del Perú y el sur de Ecuador: Una perspectiva desde el sitio Ingatambo, valle de Huancabamba. *Arqueología y sociedad* 25:9–34.

2021   Emergence of Sociopolitical Complexity in Northern Peru: A Diachronic Perspective from the Huancabamba Valley. In *The Archaeology of the Upper Amazon: Complexity and Interaction in the Andean Tropical Forest*, edited by Ryan Clasby and Jason Nesbitt, pp. 83–105. University Press of Florida, Gainesville.

Young, Kenneth R.

2021   Ecology and Human Habitation of Andean Forests. In *The Archaeology of the Upper Amazon: Complexity and Interaction in the Andean Tropical Forest*, edited by Ryan Clasby and Jason Nesbitt, pp. 23–37. University Press of Florida, Gainesville.

Young, Kenneth R., and Carlos Reynel

1997   *Huancabamba Region, Peru and Ecuador: Centers of Plant Diversity; A Guide and Strategy for Their Conservation*, vol. 3, *The Americas*, edited by Stephen Davis, Vernon Heywood, Olga Herrera-MacBryde, Jane Villa-Lobos, and Alan Hamilton, pp. 465–469. WWF and IUCN, London.

Zarillo, Sonia, and Francisco Valdez

2013   Evidencias del cultivo de maíz y de otra plantas en la ceja de selva oriental ecuatoriana. In *Arqueología amazónica: Las civilizaciones ocultas del bosque tropical*, edited by Francisco Valdez, pp. 147–171. Instituto Francés de Estudios Andinos, Lima.

Zarillo, Sonia, Nilesh Gaikwad, Claire Lanaud, Terry Powis, Christoper Viot, Isabelle Lesur, Olivier Fouet, Xavier Argout, Erwan Guichoux, Franck Salin, Rey Loor Solorzano, Olivier Bouchez, Helene Vignes, Patrick Severts, Julio Hurtado, Alexandra Yepez, Louis Grivetti, Michael Blake, and Francisco Valdez

2018   The Use and Domestication of the *Theobroma* Cacao during the Mid-Holocene in the Upper Amazon. *Nature Ecology and Evolution* 2:1879–1888.

Zeidler, James A.

1988   Feline Imagery, Stone Mortars, and Formative Period Interaction Spheres in the Northern Andean Area. *Journal of Latin American Lore* 14(2):243–283.

Beyond Chavín

The First Millennium BC in Nepeña

DAVID CHICOINE, HUGO IKEHARA-TSUKAYAMA, AND KOICHIRO SHIBATA

Since the discovery of spectacular architectural friezes and sculptures at Punkurí and Cerro Blanco in the first decades of the twentieth century, the Nepeña Valley has occupied a special place in Chavín studies and broader narratives about the first millennium BC in Peru (Tello 1943, 1960). The region has been central in articulating discussions about stylistic similarities and temporal priority between coastal and highlands developments (e.g., Burger 1992), and its location on the western Andean slopes of Ancash makes it highly suitable to study interactions between the Cupisnique (Larco 1941), Chavín (Rowe 1962), and Manchay cultures (Burger and Salazar 2008) (Figure 8.1).

Sustained scientific excavations at several archaeological sites in Nepeña since 2002 have produced a firmer chronological control over the first millennium BC, and the wealth of new data makes the valley one of the best documented regions of northern Peru to study local developments during Chavín times. Perhaps more importantly, integrating the analysis of multiple kinds of archaeological remains now permits us to supplement traditional studies on public monuments, ritual paraphernalia, and their related imageries. Combined, these new data help to reveal the complexity and heterogeneity of local economic, social, and political landscapes as well as their longitudinal transformations.

This chapter offers a synthesis of recent archaeological research from the Nepeña Valley with the objective of reconsidering the multiple and diverse ways through which local groups engaged with broader regional processes. A database of sixty-three calibrated radiocarbon measurements falling within the first millennium BC helps to explore the complex and changing relationships between key archaeological datasets, including monumental architecture, mural art, material culture, and faunal and botanical remains (all dates presented in this chapter are calibrated). In particular, we analyze settlement patterns; ritual settings, practices, and mural art; pottery for everyday and special occasions; and exchange networks to shed light on the evolution of local leadership. We suggest that

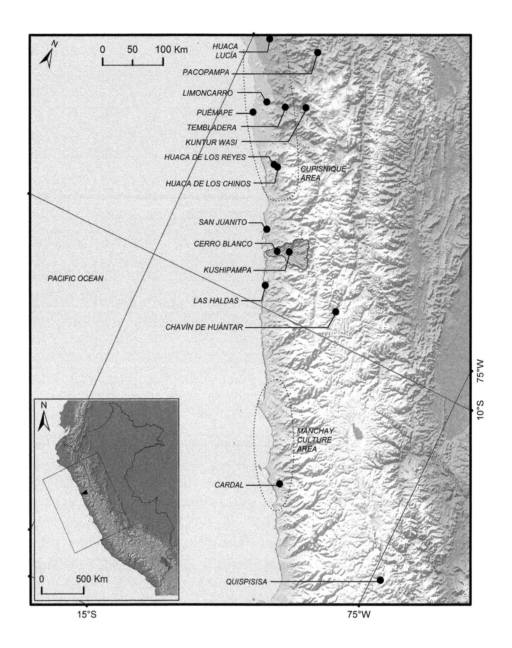

figure 8.1
Map of Peru, showing the location of the Nepeña Valley (inset) and the archaeological sites and places mentioned in the text. ALOS DSM data originally provided by JAXA. Map by Hugo Ikehara-Tsukayama.

people in Nepeña engaged in complex, fluctuating relations with Chavín de Huántar and other coeval religious centers. This increase in interactions with the adjacent highlands was preceded and outlasted by enduring ties with neighboring communities on the north and central coasts.

Antecedents

In September 1928, workers of the Hacienda San Jacinto sugar company were excavating a ditch in the vicinity of Cerro Blanco de Nepeña (Figure 8.2) when they inadvertently uncovered portions of an ancient building decorated with striking painted murals. Curious about the discovery, John B. Harrison, the manager of the estate, instructed the employees to clear portions of what we today call the South Platform of the U-shaped complex. Five years later, Julio C. Tello visited Nepeña, and, after seeing photographs of the 1928 clearing efforts and painted murals at Cerro Blanco, he was struck by their similarities with stone sculptures discovered at Chavín de Huántar, some 140 km away in highland Ancash.

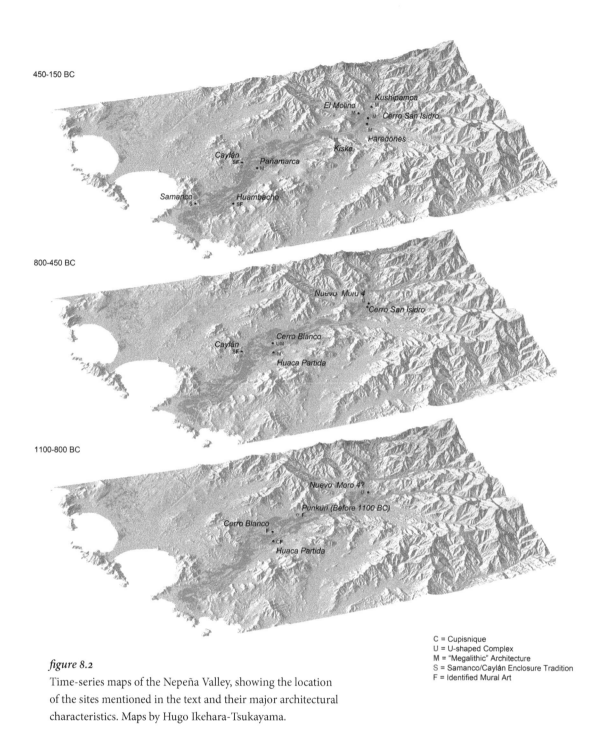

450-150 BC

Kushipampa
El Molino
M
Cerro San Isidro
M
Paredones
Kiske
Caylán
SF
Pañamarca
M
Samanco
Huambacho
SF

800-450 BC

Nuevo Moro 4
Cerro San Isidro
Caylán
SF
Cerro Blanco
UM
Huaca Partida
M

1100-800 BC

Nuevo Moro 4?
U
Punkurí (Before 1100 BC)
F
Cerro Blanco
F
CF
Huaca Partida

C = Cupisnique
U = U-shaped Complex
M = "Megalithic" Architecture
S = Samanco/Caylán Enclosure Tradition
F = Identified Mural Art

figure 8.2
Time-series maps of the Nepeña Valley, showing the location
of the sites mentioned in the text and their major architectural
characteristics. Maps by Hugo Ikehara-Tsukayama.

Tello would return to lead additional clearing efforts
on Cerro Blanco's South Platform, with the help of
Rebeca Carrión Cachot, Toribio Mejía Xesspe, and
Pedro Benvenutto. In 1934, excavations were also
undertaken at the neighboring mound of Punkurí,
located 4 km upriver, where the team uncovered
a burial accompanied by a large stone mortar and

pestle as well as several other grave goods (Bischof
1997:203; Daggett 1987:111–112; Vega-Centeno 2005).

During the 1933–1934 fieldwork season in
Nepeña, Tello sent various letters to the press and
was interviewed on many occasions, resulting in
the broadcasting of the findings and their relation
to Chavín de Huántar. As noted by Richard Daggett

(2016:56), "the Nepeña story was clearly good for circulation and the newspapers in Lima were obviously battling one another to get the most interesting details," many asking if the Nepeña ruins belonged to the Maya civilization. On October 3, 1934, Tello was in Chimbote and presented a diorite mortar similar to the one excavated at Punkurí. He bought the artifact and took it with him to Lima on his flight the next day. On October 5, Tello ordered for the excavations in Nepeña to stop. For him, there was now sufficient data to support his theory of an early Chavín culture and its expansion, one that was indigenous to the Andes and that preceded later civilizations. Tello's efforts in Nepeña also contributed to his view that Chavín de Huántar preceded the development of "coastal Chavín."

At the same time, Rafael Larco, who had visited Tello's excavations in Nepeña, suggested a stronger stylistic connection with materials of the coastal Cupisnique culture, which he had documented through the excavation of mortuary contexts in the Chicama region, 180 km to the north. For Larco (1941, 1963), the Nepeña monuments predated the foundation of Chavín de Huántar. From his perspective, the art style at Chavín was more mature than the coarser Cupisnique style. Larco suggests that Punkurí and Cerro Blanco were the models upon which the builders of Chavín de Huántar drew, contributing to the spread of the Cupisnique style to the highlands. For decades, Larco's and Tello's interpretations of the Nepeña findings would serve as the centerpiece in the narratives about Chavín and Cupisnique and would help polarize the debate about the coastal or highland primacy of early Andean cultural developments. Despite the widespread national and international fame of the Nepeña sites, however, very little archaeology was carried out in the valley until the turn of the twenty-first century.

Several scholars, including Wendell C. Bennett, Paul Kosok, Richard Schaedel, Frédéric Engel, Duccio Bonavia, and Henning Bischof, visited the valley following Tello's discoveries, but problem-oriented archaeology was scarce. Between 1967 and 1981, Donald Proulx (1968, 1973, 1985) and Richard Daggett (1984) realized the first systematic regional survey to collect surface materials, producing an inventory and preliminary sequencing of almost four hundred archaeological sites. Combined, the work of Proulx and Daggett allowed for the creation of the first pottery seriation and sequencing of early settlements for the Nepeña Valley. Credit also has to go to Daggett (1987), as well as to Bischof (1997) and Rafael Vega-Centeno (2000), for clarifying the chronological placement of Punkurí and Cerro Blanco. In 1998 and 1999, Lorenzo Samaniego (2006, 2012) reopened Punkurí and confirmed Tello's assertion that the temple was the result of three construction phases. Samaniego's work did not yield pottery, but it added weight to the greater antiquity of Punkurí and its potential occupation during the Late Preceramic period.

Since the turn of the twenty-first century, more than a dozen distinct field projects have been carried out in Nepeña. In 2001 and 2002, rescue efforts by members of the CHINECAS irrigation project uncovered remains of small colonnaded structures near Sute Bajo on the southern margin of the lower valley (Cotrina et al. 2003). Between 1999 and 2003, Alexander Herrera (2005) and Kevin Lane (2005) surveyed the Loco and Chaclancayo basins in the highlands of Nepeña. In 2002, Koichiro Shibata (2004, 2010, 2011a) returned to Cerro Blanco with the objectives of clarifying its construction sequence and chronological implications as well as testing its relation to Chavín de Huántar. A few years later, he expanded excavations to Huaca Partida. In 2003, David Chicoine began a long-term investigation in the lower Nepeña Valley, focusing on Early Horizon architecture at Huambacho (Chicoine 2006a) and the development of urban forms of living at Caylán (Chicoine and Ikehara 2014; Chicoine, Ikehara, and Ortiz 2021; Chicoine and Whitten 2019).

Since then, several scholars, including Hugo Ikehara (2010a, 2015), Lisa Trever (2017), Carlos Rengifo (2014), Matthew Helmer (2015), and Kimberly Munro (2018), have focused on Nepeña for their doctoral dissertation fieldwork. These field projects have emphasized stratigraphic excavations and radiocarbon measurements as major tools of chronological control. Twenty-first-century archaeology has also developed more overt collaborations

(Chicoine et al. 2017; Helmer et al. 2018), critical reassessment of cultural-historical constructs (Ikehara and Chicoine 2011), and interdisciplinary efforts in paleoethnobotany (Chicoine, Clement, and Stich 2016; Ikehara, Paipay, and Shibata 2013) and zooarchaeology (Chicoine and Rojas 2013). This chapter provides a synthesis of our various field projects since 2002, particularly as they pertain to the development of societies in Nepeña and their relations to Chavín and other regional phenomena.

Cultural History of the Nepeña Valley during the First Millennium BC

Excavations of stratified contexts at Cerro Blanco allowed for the creation of the first chronological sequence supported by radiocarbon measurements for the Nepeña Valley. Based on changes in architecture, building materials, pottery styles, and radiocarbon assays, excavations at Cerro Blanco enabled the creation of the following sequence: Huambocayán phase (1500–1100 BC), Cerro Blanco phase (1100–800 BC), Nepeña phase (800–450 BC), and Samanco phase (450–150 BC) (Shibata 2011b). Since 2002, archaeological projects at other sites have complemented this original sequence, yielding more than one hundred radiocarbon measurements. Most assays (n=63) fall between 2750±50 BP and 2090±40 BP. Their calibration and analysis permit a detailed consideration of the history of the Nepeña Valley during the first millennium BC. Figure 8.3 presents the calibrated calendar ranges for sixty-three assays and helps visualize the correspondences in the occupational sequences at various sites in Nepeña. It is significant to note that many dates fall within the Hallstatt Plateau (ca. 800–400 BC) and will require more sophisticated statistical treatment.

Not much is known of the Huambocayán phase at Cerro Blanco. Pottery is analogous to the Las Haldas type from Casma (Pozorski and Pozorski 2006:45, fig. 7) and the Tizal Temple in the Chao Valley (Cárdenas Martin 1998:72–73). The earliest documented monumental constructions at Cerro Blanco and Huaca Partida were built during the following Cerro Blanco phase (Figure 8.4).

The Nepeña phase is defined by the drastic remodeling of ceremonial structures at Cerro Blanco. New buildings were erected, some of them using large-size ashlar-type masonry, a technique referred to as "megalithic" (Daggett 1983; Proulx 1985; Tello 1930). Assemblages are also marked by the appearance of exotic materials, such as obsidian. Pottery, meanwhile, compares favorably with that of the Ofrendas Gallery at Chavín de Huántar (Lumbreras 1993). Overall, the Nepeña phase, in particular its beginning, appears to mark the height of interregional interactions at Cerro Blanco and in the lower Nepeña Valley more broadly. The end of the monumental renovations, and the closure of the structure, are dated to around 416 BC (2σ) at the latest.

Between 800 and 600 BC, new forms of community arrangements developed on the margins of the lower valley. Radiometric data from Caylán, although ranging back to the eighth century BC (2σ), indicate less statistical probability for an occupation prior to 600 BC. A similar situation is observed at Huambacho, where radiocarbon ranges go back to 781 BC (2σ), but where most ranges fall later than 600 BC (see Chicoine 2010a). At Huambacho, radiocarbon dates cluster between 2370±70 BP and 2250 ±40 BP. This suggests that the bulk of the occupation of these two sites was roughly contemporary, starting before 600 BC (2σ) and ending by 150 BC (2σ). Closer to the shoreline, the settlement of Samanco appears to have been founded after the initial impetus to settle at Caylán and Huambacho. Eight AMS measurements from Samanco cluster between 2270±28 BP and 2139±29 BP, which yield a range of 398–51 BC (2σ). In the middle valley, meanwhile, two dates from Kushipampa show considerable overlap with Samanco and the latter parts of the occupations at Caylán and Huambacho, between 395 and 171 BC (2σ). By 500 BC, both lower and middle valley communities had changed their stylistic preferences. While some pottery designs appear similar to those classified by archaeologists as Salinar (see Ikehara and Chicoine 2011), strong isolationist trends can be observed.

At Cerro Blanco, following the abandonment of the ceremonial mounds, subsequent human presence is dated to 406–208 BC (2σ) and associated

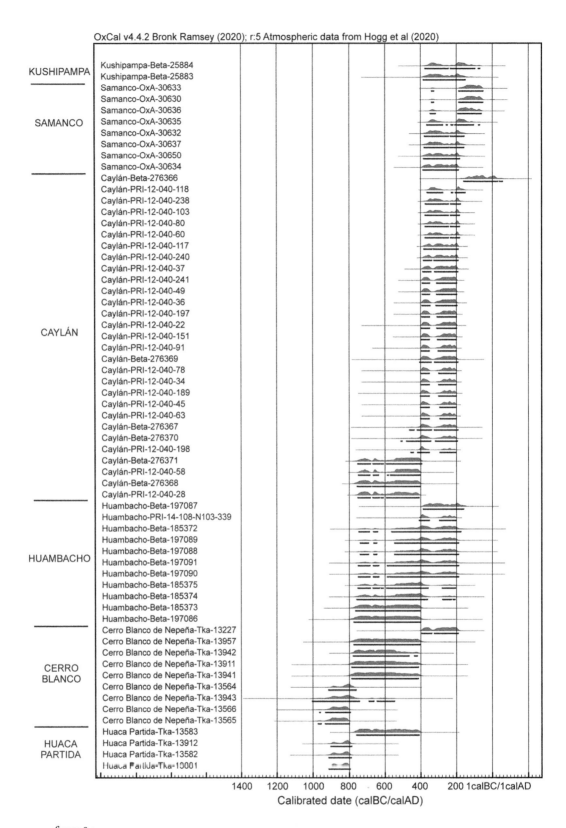

OxCal v4.4.2 Bronk Ramsey (2020); r:5 Atmospheric data from Hogg et al (2020)

KUSHIPAMPA
- Kushipampa-Beta-25884
- Kushipampa-Beta-25883

SAMANCO
- Samanco-OxA-30633
- Samanco-OxA-30630
- Samanco-OxA-30636
- Samanco-OxA-30635
- Samanco-OxA-30632
- Samanco-OxA-30637
- Samanco-OxA-30650
- Samanco-OxA-30634

CAYLÁN
- Caylán-Beta-276366
- Caylán-PRI-12-040-118
- Caylán-PRI-12-040-238
- Caylán-PRI-12-040-103
- Caylán-PRI-12-040-80
- Caylán-PRI-12-040-60
- Caylán-PRI-12-040-117
- Caylán-PRI-12-040-240
- Caylán-PRI-12-040-37
- Caylán-PRI-12-040-241
- Caylán-PRI-12-040-49
- Caylán-PRI-12-040-36
- Caylán-PRI-12-040-197
- Caylán-PRI-12-040-22
- Caylán-PRI-12-040-151
- Caylán-PRI-12-040-91
- Caylán-Beta-276369
- Caylán-PRI-12-040-78
- Caylán-PRI-12-040-34
- Caylán-PRI-12-040-189
- Caylán-PRI-12-040-45
- Caylán-PRI-12-040-63
- Caylán-Beta-276367
- Caylán-Beta-276370
- Caylán-PRI-12-040-198
- Caylán-Beta-276371
- Caylán-PRI-12-040-58
- Caylán-Beta-276368
- Caylán-PRI-12-040-28

HUAMBACHO
- Huambacho-Beta-197087
- Huambacho-PRI-14-108-N103-339
- Huambacho-Beta-185372
- Huambacho-Beta-197089
- Huambacho-Beta-197088
- Huambacho-Beta-197091
- Huambacho-Beta-197090
- Huambacho-Beta-185375
- Huambacho-Beta-185374
- Huambacho-Beta-185373
- Huambacho-Beta-197086

CERRO BLANCO
- Cerro Blanco de Nepeña-Tka-13227
- Cerro Blanco de Nepeña-Tka-13957
- Cerro Blanco de Nepeña-Tka-13942
- Cerro Blanco de Nepeña-Tka-13911
- Cerro Blanco de Nepeña-Tka-13941
- Cerro Blanco de Nepeña-Tka-13564
- Cerro Blanco de Nepeña-Tka-13943
- Cerro Blanco de Nepeña-Tka-13566
- Cerro Blanco de Nepeña-Tka-13565

HUACA PARTIDA
- Huaca Partida-Tka-13583
- Huaca Partida-Tka-13912
- Huaca Partida-Tka-13582
- Huaca Partida-Tka-10001

1400   1200   1000   800   600   400   200 1calBC/1calAD

Calibrated date (calBC/calAD)

figure 8.3

Multiple plot diagram showing the calibrated ranges (2σ [95.4%]) for the sixty-three radiocarbon assays discussed in the text (OxCal 4.4 [curve = SHCal 20]; see Bronk Ramsey 2009, 2020; Hogg et al. 2020). Illustration by David Chicoine and Hugo Ikehara-Tsukayama.

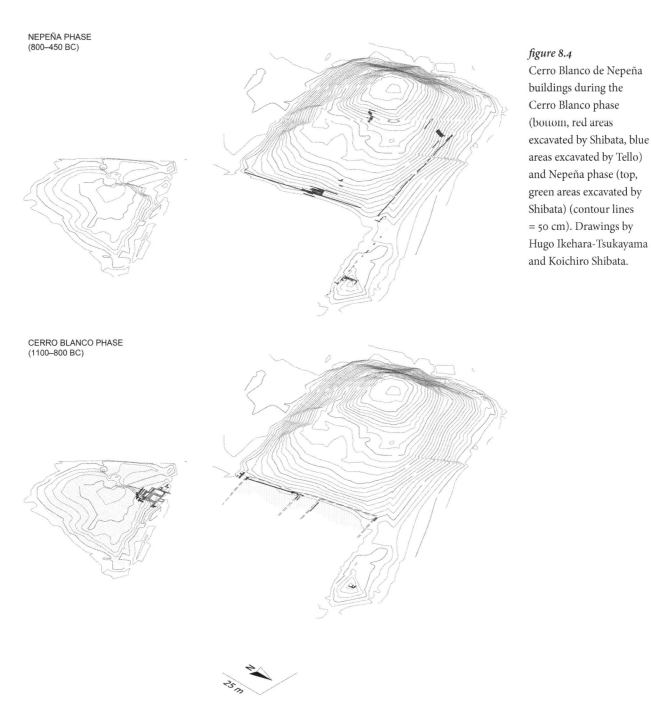

NEPEÑA PHASE
(800–450 BC)

CERRO BLANCO PHASE
(1100–800 BC)

25 m

figure 8.4
Cerro Blanco de Nepeña buildings during the Cerro Blanco phase (bottom, red areas excavated by Shibata, blue areas excavated by Tello) and Nepeña phase (top, green areas excavated by Shibata) (contour lines = 50 cm). Drawings by Hugo Ikehara-Tsukayama and Koichiro Shibata.

with the reuse of the Central Platform. Here, domestic and ceremonial refuse accumulated on the outside of the perimeter wall of the Central Platform. AMS measurements from Huaca Partida are consistent with Cerro Blanco, ranging between 922 and 424 BC (2σ). Builders at Huaca Partida paralleled Cerro Blanco and renovated mud brick structures with megalithic, ashlar-type masonry.

The remainder of our chapter synthesizes datasets from our various field projects with the objective of providing an updated perspective of social processes in play in Nepeña before, during, and after the development of Chavín de Huántar. While detailed descriptions of field procedures, empirical datasets, archaeological contexts, and analytical protocols have been published at length elsewhere (see

Chicoine 2006a; Chicoine and Ikehara 2010, 2014; Helmer 2015; Helmer and Chicoine 2015; Ikehara 2010a, 2015; Shibata 2010, 2011a), this essay weaves key lines of evidence into an interpretive narrative of the complex relationships between Nepeña communities and broader regional phenomena during the first millennium BC.

Historical Processes and Material Trends during the First Millennium BC in Nepeña

Datasets from our respective projects in Nepeña provide a nuanced understanding of the materiality of historical processes during the first millennium BC. Here, we focus on settlement patterns, ritual settings and public art, pottery assemblages, and exchange goods. Our objective is to shed light on the developments of Nepeña communities and their relation to regional phenomena, including Chavín and Cupisnique. We organize our presentation geographically and distinguish between the lower and middle sections of the valley.

Settlement Patterns

To analyze settlement patterns in Nepeña, we rely on three different kinds of datasets: Proulx and Daggett's comprehensive pedestrian surveys; research at specific sites; and the full coverage and intensive survey of the middle valley (also known as the "Moro Pocket" [Daggett 1984; Proulx 1968]). Methodological differences between those field initiatives place limitations on our understanding of settlement patterns and demographic trends. For instance, in the Moro Pocket, Ikehara (2015) carried out a non-site survey and systematically sampled surface artifacts rather than identifying discrete sites (Proulx 1968).

In the lower Nepeña Valley, we know little of settlement patterns prior to 1100 BC. Some groups do appear to have lived on the coast near the modern town of Los Chimús, perhaps as early as five thousand years ago. The earliest site from which excavation data are available is Punkurí. Based on comparative evidence, including recent excavations by Claude Chapdelaine at San Juanito in the Santa

Valley (Chapdelaine and Gagné 2015), Punkurí can be interpreted as perhaps dating back to 1500 BC (Vega-Centeno 2005:15) or even earlier (Samaniego 2012). The earliest levels at Cerro Blanco appear coeval with, or slightly later than, this time frame. By 800 BC, Cerro Blanco was a small ceremonial center with painted and sculpted walls. It appears to have reached its U-shaped layout only after 800 BC.

Cerro Blanco and the coeval Huaca Partida are located near the Nepeña River, perhaps at the limit of the archaic flood plain prior to its anthropogenic modification. Very little is known about residential patterns in the lower valley at the time. It is likely that people lived in small hamlets or villages scattered around the cultivable zone within and/or at the edges of the floodplain. Starting around 800 BC, both Cerro Blanco and Huaca Partida would see megalithic renovations for about three hundred years. By 500 BC, monumental constructions at both centers had stopped. The ruins would be reoccupied for the next four hundred years, as indicated by domestic and ceremonial refuse.

Coeval with the megalithic renovations of Cerro Blanco and Huaca Partida, people colonized the valley margins, at the edge of modern cultivated fields. The sites of VN-35 and VN-36 (referred to as Sute Bajo), Huambacho on the southern margin, and Caylán and Samanco on the northern margin of the floodplain, represent the best documented cases of this new type of settlement. Based on radiocarbon assays, Caylán and Huambacho emerged as the earliest, between 800 and 600 BC. Those changes in settlement patterns appear linked to an increased concern with defense, as indicated by the proximity of residential architecture to adjacent hills, lookouts, and fortresses (Figure 8.5).

In contrast to the lower valley, information from the middle valley enables us to reconstruct settlement patterns and demographic shifts (see Ikehara 2015) (Figure 8.6). Before 500 BC, it is estimated that approximately one thousand five hundred people lived in the Moro Pocket. Cerro San Isidro, the largest settlement in the Moro Pocket at that time, is estimated to have had four hundred people. It was likely the center of a supra-local community (see Peterson and Drennan 2005).[1] A smaller community

figure 8.5
Fortress at Caylán (a), Kiske
(b), and Cerro San Juan 3 (c),
in the second half of the first
millennium BC. Photographs by
David Chicoine (a) and Hugo
Ikehara-Tsukayama (b and c).

was located a few kilometers to the west. Its residents appear to have engaged in more intensive pottery production. Higher ranked households (defined by higher-than-average proportions of fineware pottery) were living in both Cerro San Isidro and the peripheral hamlets before 500 BC. The possible relationships between middle valley communities and Chavín and Cupisnique are unclear. A possible U-shaped ceremonial center has been reported at Nuevo Moro 4, and fineware with decorative styles similar to those found in Cerro Blanco and Huaca Partida have been found, suggesting that these communities participated in Chavín and Cupisnique networks.

After 500 BC, the population in the Moro Pocket surged to around ten thousand people. This is seen in the continuing growth of existing hamlets as well as in the establishment of new settlements. Departing from the previous phase, the Moro Pocket became fragmented into multiple supra-local communities or districts, each one with its own demographic center and at least one ceremonial center. The demographic center of gravity moved eastward, and the town of Kushipampa became the largest population cluster of the middle valley with around one thousand five hundred people or three hundred households. Cerro San Isidro, while still important and the center of its own district, lost its regional centrality during this epoch.

By 500 BC, groups around the Moro Pocket started the construction of several megalithic

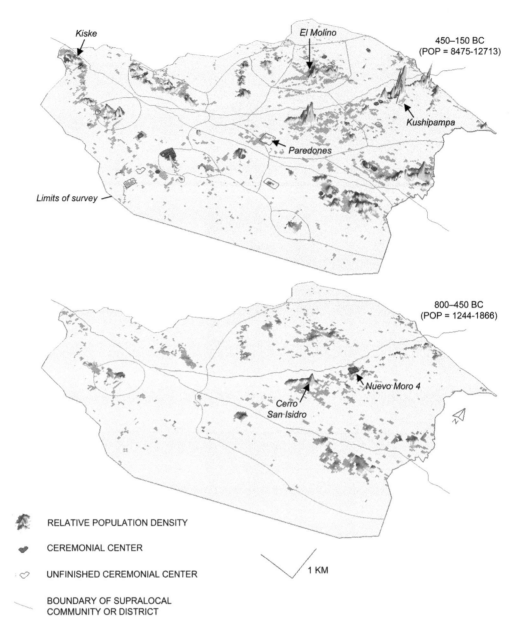

figure 8.6
Maps of the middle Nepeña Valley (Moro Pocket), showing relative population concentrations and the location of major ceremonial centers during the first half (bottom) and second half (top) of the first millennium BC. Ceremonial centers in red and unfinished buildings in black. Map by Hugo Ikehara-Tsukayama.

ceremonial centers with some features reminiscent of earlier traditions (Ikehara 2015). Overall, observations from the middle valley support the hypothesis of increasing demographic and political fragmentation. This aligns well with the construction of dozens of fortresses and outlooks, the location of which indicates a concern over attacks coming from both

neighboring groups as well as from a larger enemy from outside the Moro Pocket (Ikehara 2016). In sum, there were major disruptions in the patterning of human settlements in Nepeña between 600 and 500 BC. This shift is visible in both the lower and middle valley and concomitant with the waning of Chavín influence and the rise in armed conflicts.

Ritual Settings, Practices, and Mural Art

Other publications have tackled in detail ancient ritual life in Nepeña (Chicoine 2010b; Chicoine et al. 2017; Helmer et al. 2018; Shibata 2017). This chapter focuses only on a few key relevant patterns. In the lower valley by 1100 BC, people mobilized to build and renovate small ceremonial complexes. At Cerro Blanco, between 1000 and 800 BC, a conical adobe platform stood in the eastern portion of what is identified as the central plaza. Evidence for additional conical adobe and stone buildings dated to this period exists on the North and South Platforms. The South Platform, excavated by Tello in the 1930s, consisted of a series of contiguous rooms decorated with elaborated polychrome mural sculptures depicting stylized carnivorous beings resembling Cupisnique friezes and Chavín stone sculptures (Larco 1941; Nesbitt 2012; Pozorski 1980; Rowe 1962).

During the Cerro Blanco phase, Huaca Partida was formed by multiple platforms built with adobes and stones. The middle platform contained a hypostyle hall surrounded by two rooms to the north and south, the upper platform to the west, and an opening to the east. This configuration is very similar to the temple mounds of the Cupisnique tradition on the north coast (Shibata 2020:40–41) (Figure 8.7). Additionally, excavations by Shibata (2017) have shown the presence of figures organized in a manner that is reminiscent of the Circular Plaza at Chavín de Huántar (Burger 1992:133). In the second upper level, a procession of polychrome winged anthropomorphic beings with a rope in hand is moving toward, in other words facing, the main facade and entrance. Below these, a 3 m high band depicting beige and white felines follows the same direction (Figure 8.8).

Between 800 and 500 BC, ceremonial structures at both Cerro Blanco and Huaca Partida

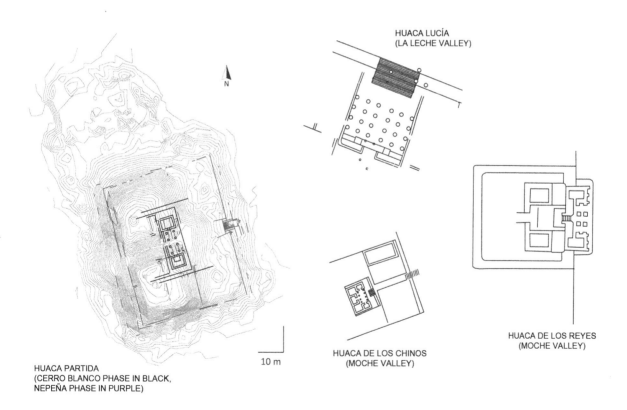

HUACA PARTIDA
(CERRO BLANCO PHASE IN BLACK,
NEPEÑA PHASE IN PURPLE)

10 m

HUACA LUCÍA
(LA LECHE VALLEY)

HUACA DE LOS CHINOS
(MOCHE VALLEY)

HUACA DE LOS REYES
(MOCHE VALLEY)

figure 8.7

Plan reconstruction of the mound with hypostyle hall at Huaca Partida during the Cerro Blanco phase (black) and similar hypostyle hall structures at Cupisnique ceremonial spaces in the La Leche and Moche Valleys. Drawings by Hugo Ikehara-Tsukayama and Koichiro Shibata, based on Pleasants 2009; Pozorski 1980; Shimada, Elera, and Shimada 1982.

figure 8.8
Frieze AM-208 at Huaca Partida, depicting a stylized feline. Height = 2.8 m. Photograph by Koichiro Shibata.

were renovated following the megalithic tradition (Figure 8.9). Older conical adobe and stone structures were covered with platforms supported by retaining walls of large ashlars. At Cerro Blanco, the main mound was placed above and west of the previous building. The main staircase was placed in the middle of the main facade and painted red and white in the northern half and white in the southern half. On top of the mound, a smaller platform was built; its entrance was defined by finely dressed stones and a large lintel. During this time, Cerro Blanco acquired its distinctive U shape. Excavations on the North Platform uncovered middens of feasting events that may have been occurring in the central plaza (Ikehara, Paipay, and Shibata 2013; Ikehara and Shibata 2008). These middens contained obsidian, remains of marine and terrestrial animals (including camelids, cervids, and dogs), and pottery that resembles assemblages found at other coetaneous sites in Nepeña and elsewhere.

In the middle valley, the possible U-shaped temple of Nuevo Moro 4 may have been the only ceremonial center of the area. Comparisons with approximations of plaza audiences and demographic estimates suggest that the whole middle valley population may have gathered there (see Ikehara 2015 for methods). A brief comparative analysis of architectural layouts of different Andean ceremonial centers in 1000–500 BC hints at the high degree of heterogeneity in Nepeña (Figure 8.10). While the building of the Cerro Blanco phase at Huaca Partida is very similar to north coast centers, the final configurations of Cerro Blanco and Nuevo Moro 4 resemble architectural layouts found at Chavín de Huántar (wide main mound, short arms) and U-shaped temples found on the central coast (narrow main mound, long arms), respectively.

By 500 BC, monumental renovations ceased at Cerro Blanco and Huaca Partida. Data from Caylán and Huambacho suggest that lower valley groups sponsored the constructions of smaller, enclosed ceremonial spaces nested within residential elite compounds perhaps a century earlier. Some of the plazas were ornamented with geometric friezes (Figure 8.11). While their building techniques are reminiscent of earlier architectural sculptures (e.g., sculpted unfired clay cones, columns, hypostyle galleries), their imagery contrasts markedly with previous forms. The geometric designs of plaza art at Caylán and Huambacho suggest significant ideological changes.

Clearing of plaza architecture at Huambacho and Caylán indicates that the spaces were decorated with elaborate arrangements of built-in friezes, sculpted cones, and reliefs (Chicoine 2006b, 2022; Chicoine and Ikehara 2014). The location of the designs suggests exclusive target audiences, perhaps linked to initiation rites (Helmer et al. 2018). The multiplicity of plaza settings suggests a fragmentation of ritual practices, as well as a continuation of perhaps century-old factional competition. Mapping operations at Caylán, for instance, suggest the existence of more than forty distinct plazas located in separate compounds or neighborhoods (Chicoine and Whitten 2019).

figure 8.9
Megalithic, ashlar-type masonry
from sites in Nepeña, including
Cerro Blanco (a–b) in the
lower valley and Paredones (c),
El Molino (d), and Kushipampa (e)
in the middle valley. Photographs
by Koichiro Shibata (a and b) and
Hugo Ikehara-Tsukayama (c–e).

Following the demise of Cerro Blanco and Huaca Partida, the shedding of zoomorphic and supernatural imagery from public contexts likely reflects ideological shifts as the depictions of the Chavín and Cupisnique religious traditions fell out of favor (Ikehara 2020). At Huambacho and Caylán, mural artists focused on creating dazzling displays of light and shadow through arrangements of geometric forms. Another indicator of change is the use of color in the murals. Excavations at Huambacho and Caylán did not yield in situ examples of polychrome sculptures (although fragments of red, yellow, and black painted plaster were discovered). From that standpoint, colors do not appear to have been a major emphasis following the demise of the Cerro Blanco and Huaca Partida temples (Figure 8.12).

Around 500 BC in the middle valley, several ceremonial centers with megalithic features were designed and their foundations laid out, but they were never completed (Ikehara 2015, 2021). While most of these incomplete projects are located on the floodplain, the centers that were finished and used during the following centuries were placed in elevated and easily defendable terrain. Kushipampa

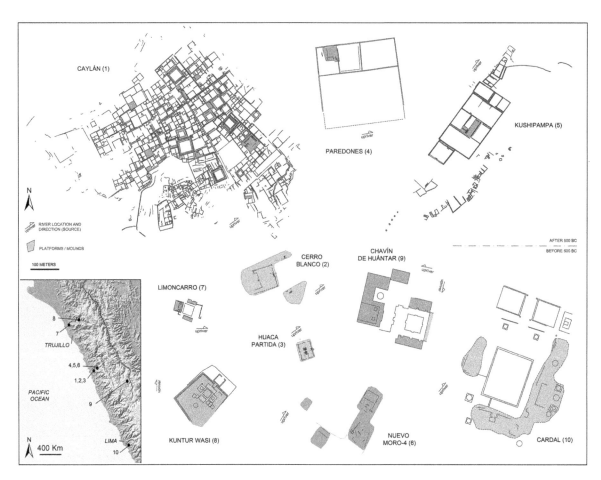

figure 8.10

Comparison of the architectural and spatial organization of the Nepeña sites discussed in the text, as well as a comparative sample from coeval sites. Drawing by Hugo Ikehara-Tsukayama, based on Burger 1992; Inokuchi 2010; Kembel and Haas 2015; Sakai and Martinez 2010.

figure 8.11
Architectural
sculptures at Caylán
(Plaza-A). Scale = 1 m.
Photograph by
David Chicoine.

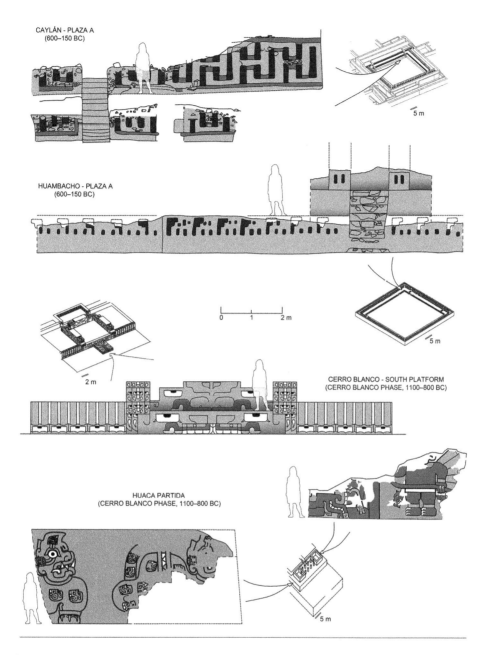

CAYLÁN - PLAZA A
(600–150 BC)

5 m

HUAMBACHO - PLAZA A
(600–150 BC)

5 m

0   1   2 m

2 m

CERRO BLANCO - SOUTH PLATFORM
(CERRO BLANCO PHASE, 1100–800 BC)

HUACA PARTIDA
(CERRO BLANCO PHASE, 1100–800 BC)

5 m

figure 8.12
Comparison of mural artworks and their architectural contexts at Caylán, Huambacho, Cerro Blanco, and Huaca Partida. Drawings by Hugo Ikehara-Tsukayama, Koichiro Shibata, and David Chicoine, based on Bischof 1997; Vega-Centeno 2000.

and Paredones exemplify these new centers, where builders emphasized large spaces for communal ceremonies.

Pottery for Everyday and Special Occasions
Excavations at Cerro Blanco and Huaca Partida allow a glimpse into changes in pottery assemblages between 1500 and 150 BC. Neckless ollas represent the only vessel shape identified so far for the Huambocayán occupation at Cerro Blanco. Those multipurpose storage and cooking vessels were sometimes decorated with elongated punctations similar to those of the contemporary Las Haldas style of the Casma Valley (Pozorski and Pozorski

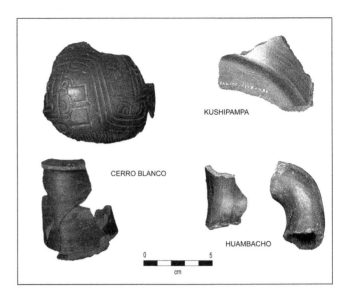

figure 8.13
Graphite black pottery sherds from some of the sites discussed in the text. Illustration by David Chicoine, Hugo Ikehara-Tsukayama, and Koichiro Shibata.

KUSHIPAMPA

CERRO BLANCO

HUAMBACHO

0 5
cm

CERRO BLANCO

HUAMBACHO

MORO

KUSHIPAMPA

CAYLÁN

SAMANCO

0 5
cm

figure 8.14
Pattern-burnished pottery sherds from some of the sites discussed in the text. Illustration by David Chicoine, Hugo Ikehara-Tsukayama, Koichiro Shibata, and Matt Helmer.

MORO

CAYLÁN

HUAMBACHO

SAMANCO

0 5
cm

figure 8.15
Stamped circle-and-dot pottery sherds from some of the sites discussed in the text. Illustration by David Chicoine, Hugo Ikehara-Tsukayama, and Matt Helmer

2006:45, fig. 7). During the subsequent Cerro Blanco phase, small and fine serving vessels share many traits with the Middle Cupisnique style of the Chicama Valley (Elera 1997:195, fig. 11). Fine-line incising appears diagnostic of this phase, while graphite-like[2] painting persists into the following Nepeña phase (Figure 8.13). Around 800 BC, local artisans began to rely on a broader repertoire of decorative techniques, some of which are believed to be imported, such as graphite-on-red and red-on-orange. Broad-line incisions are common decorations. Pattern-burnished and circle-and-dot stamping are for the first time documented in the region; they would endure until the end of the first millennium BC (Figures 8.14–8.15). Rocker stamping and circle-and-dot stamping filled with red pigment appear exclusively in and diagnostic of the Nepeña phase.

The Cerro Blanco assemblages also documented subtle changes in the shape of the lips of neckless ollas. From 1500 to 800 BC, most neckless ollas are brownware and show inner-beveled lips. In contrast, around 800 BC, some potters begin shaping the lips of neckless ollas in an outer-beveled fashion. This change in modeling technique is concomitant with the appearance of better fired and harder redwares. At Cerro Blanco, such pottery is associated with the megalithic renovations of the Central Platform.

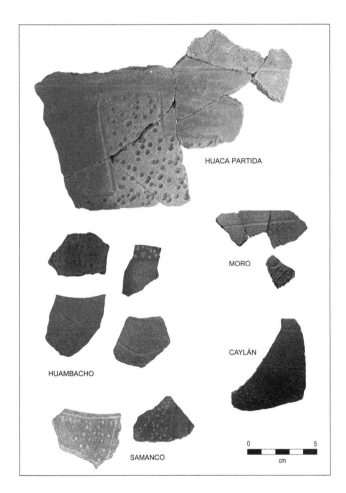

figure 8.16
Zoned punctate pottery sherds from some of the sites discussed in the text. Illustration by David Chicoine, Hugo Ikehara-Tsukayama, Matt Helmer, and Koichiro Shibata.

figure 8.17
Zoned textile-impressed pottery sherds from some of the sites discussed in the text. Illustration by David Chicoine, Hugo Ikehara-Tsukayama, and Matt Helmer.

The redware and outer-beveled neckless ollas would become staples of local assemblages until at least the end of the first millennium BC.

Combined with excavation data from Caylán, Huambacho, and Samanco, the Cerro Blanco sequence sheds light on the endurance and transformation of craftsmanship. The transition into urban forms of living on the valley margins between 800 and 600 BC did not correspond with a break in pottery-making traditions in the lower valley. Earlier publications have emphasized the gradual increase in popularity of closed or necked jars, and the concomitant decrease in the prevalence of open buckets, perhaps linked to changes in *chicha* production techniques (Chicoine 2011; Ikehara 2010b; Ikehara, Paipay, and Shibata 2013). The basic vessel shapes persist, however, suggesting the continuation of culinary habits. For instance, blackware stirrup-spout bottles and redware carinated bowls represent the serving vessels par excellence in the lower valley during the first millennium BC. Some blackware stirrup-spout bottles from Huambacho resemble those of the Late Cupisnique style and are comparable to findings from Cerro Blanco. (Although many archaeologists think that there is some kind of transition from the trapezoidal stirrup-spout bottles common at Huaca de los Reyes [Pozorski 1983] and Huaca Cortada [Nesbitt, Gutiérrez, and Vásquez 2010] in the late Initial Period, toward the thick, rounded stirrup-spout bottles like the one illustrated here [Figure 8.13].) At Huambacho, those are decorated with rocker-stamping techniques using a small marine bivalve (e.g., *Donax* sp.) but also impressed with woven textiles. Both the bivalve rocker and the textile-impressed styles of decoration were used in conjunction with burnishing techniques to create alternating zones of matte and shiny effects. Such "zoning" techniques of decoration are also prominent at Caylán, as both zoned punctate and zoned textile-impressed styles are reported here (Figures 8.16–8.17). The carinated bowls, meanwhile, are typically decorated with stamped circle-and-dot designs, banded lozenge, and sinuous/ linear designs.

The Caylán pottery assemblage also contains fragments of incised and zoned stirrup-spout bottles, both in black and redware. More data are needed from stratified contexts, but it appears that toward the end of Caylán's occupational sequence, potters also produced white-on-red styles associated with the Salinar style. The decorative technique and its visual effects resemble the style of the Tembladera hollow figurines (see "Tembladera Flutists" [Burtenshaw-Zumstein 2013]). It is also significant to note that fragments of blackware human sculptures have been reported at Huambacho (Chicoine 2006a). The remains are very fragmentary but resemble the Cupisnique style of sculpted bottles (see "Puémape Contortionist" [Elera 2009:77–79]).

Excavations at Kushipampa show that ceramic vessel shapes are similar to those found in the lower valley. Examples of circle-and-dot designs have been found in the Moro Pocket. At Kushipampa, pattern-burnished and post-fire scratching are the common types of decoration (Ikehara 2010a). Survey efforts in the Moro Pocket have also documented a fragment of a fine black stirrup-spout bottle with stamped circle-and-dot motifs similar to vessels from the highland Janabarriu style (Burger 1984), as well as graphite redware similar to the Wacheqsa style from Chavín de Huántar (Ikehara 2015).

Exchange Networks

As published elsewhere (Shibata 2010), fieldwork at Cerro Blanco and Huaca Partida has revealed evidence for interregional interactions, especially during the Nepeña phase. Prior to 800 BC, similarities with areas beyond coastal Ancash appear limited to architectural features (e.g., hypostyle halls) and mural art (e.g., felines and winged anthropomorphs). During the period between 800 and 500 BC, however, local elites at Cerro Blanco and Huaca Partida acquired obsidian (most likely from Quispisisa [Burger and Glascock 2000, 2009:26; Contreras, Tripcevich, and Cavero Palomino 2012; Shibata 2011a:217]), cinnabar (likely from Huancavelica [Burger and Matos Mendieta 2002; Cooke et al. 2013; Young, this volume]), and perhaps exotic pottery from the north highlands (red-on-orange) and north coast (graphite-on-red) (Shibata 2014) (Figure 8.18).

In the lower valley, the settlement shift to the valley margins between 800 and 600 BC was

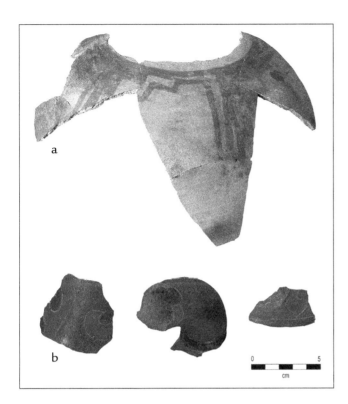

figure 8.18
Red-on-orange (Mosna-like) pottery fragment
from Huaca Partida (a) and graphite-on-red
(Wascheqsa-like) pottery sherds from Cerro
Blanco (b). Illustration by David Chicoine,
Hugo Ikehara-Tsukayama, and Koichiro Shibata.

concomitant with the collapse of elite interaction networks, increased armed conflicts, and factional competition. The most obvious effect of this reorganization appears to have been the breakdown of the long-distance, elite-centered networks in which ritually significant objects circulated—in particular, obsidian, cinnabar, metalwork, and other ritual paraphernalia. For instance, despite extensive and systematic excavations at Caylán, Huambacho, and Samanco, no obsidian has yet to be discovered. Elite ceremonial contexts at Huambacho have yielded yellow and red mineral pigments, perhaps cinnabar. No clear case of exotic pottery has been documented following the waning of the Chavín and Cupisnique influences in the region. In contrast, remains of camelids are more ubiquitous during the Samanco phase. Excavations at Samanco have even documented a camelid corral with piled dung (Helmer and Chicoine 2015:636, fig. 10). Comparative morphometric analyses carried out by ARQUEOBIOS on the Caylán camelid remains suggest that they belong to domesticated llamas (*Llama glama*) (Chicoine, Vásquez, and Rosales 2022). Meanwhile, isotopic analyses of camelid remains

from Caylán and Huambacho (Szpak et al. 2016) indicate that the animals likely transited between the coast and the highlands. These data might point to the persistence of llama caravans and bulk subsistence exchange following the demise of Chavín and Cupisnique influences and enduring through the tense few centuries that followed. This assertion is further supported by the ubiquitous presence of remains of marine mollusks in the Moro Pocket, including Kushipampa (Ikehara 2015). This suggests that subsistence exchange networks ran parallel to the political spheres characterized by rivalry and armed conflicts.

In sum, the procurement of quotidian pottery and exotics was carried out by different economic systems. In Nepeña, pottery manufacture during the first millennium BC was never highly centralized or specialized; current evidence does not demonstrate central workshops or attached production. From that standpoint, pottery making could be seen as a household-level domestic activity that perdured through the ebbs and flows of political and ritual life. Following the demise of Chavín and Cupisnique networks, the Nepeña landscape fragmented, eroding the resilience of long-distance exchange networks and limiting the movement of exotic prestige items.

Discussion: Reconsidering the First Millennium BC

The data synthesized in this chapter allow us to fill gaps in the archaeological understanding of the first millennium BC in Nepeña. Not surprisingly, one of the major conclusions of recent field research and material analyses is that societies were more diverse and complex than previously envisioned. Based on the data presented in this chapter, at least three patterns of monumental architecture and associated mural art can be delineated in Nepeña, including ceremonial centers with painted friezes depicting supernatural beings that share stylistic and symbolic affinities with the Cupisnique and Chavín religious complexes; megalithic, ashlar-type architecture; and walled enclosures with built-in clay geometric friezes and nested plazas with outer wall platforms.

Based on the current evidence from Nepeña, we are now in a position to better control time and move "beyond chronology" (Sayre 2018; Swenson and Roddick 2018). On the one hand, the classification of time is instrumental in comparing distinct moments of the past. On the other, chronological schemes can reduce time to a uniform, linear phenomenon that can potentially lead to historical constructions that homogenize the passage of artificially bounded events. By producing a more nuanced historical narrative on the transformations of settlement patterns, ritual architecture, pottery, and exchange networks in Nepeña during the first millennium BC, we suggest that Andeanists could move "beyond Chavín" and the traditional emphasis on "cultural horizon markers." We make our case by further comparing the historical processes at play in Nepeña and northern Peru with recent advances in the archaeological record at Chavín de Huántar.

Recent advances in the radiometric dating of the occupation of Chavín de Huántar enable a reconsideration of its potential relations to groups in Nepeña. For instance, renewed fieldwork at Chavín

de Huántar by a team of Stanford-based archaeologists (Rick, this volume; Sayre and Rosenfeld, this volume), as well as a new set of AMS dates from the bone collagen of camelids (Burger 2019), allows for a more precise grasp of the site's three-phase ceramic sequence developed by Richard L. Burger (1984). Burger (2019) now dates the three phases as follows: Urabarriu (950–800 BC), Chakinani (800–700 BC), and Janabarriu (700–400 BC). While John Rick and colleagues have suggested that the foundations of Chavín de Huántar might date back to 1200 BC or even earlier (Kembel and Haas 2015; Rick et al. 2010), as pointed out by Burger (2019), there is limited statistical evidence to suggest that monumental constructions at Chavín de Huántar were built prior to 900 BC. One major revision to our initial chronological positioning of Chavín's occupation has been the realization that monumental constructions had stopped by 500 BC (Kembel and Haas 2015). This chronological refinement has significant implications for reconsidering the relationships between local Nepeña communities and the development and regional impact of Chavín de Huántar.

In Nepeña, architectural sculptures resembling Chavín and/or Cupisnique canons are found at the sites of Cerro Blanco and Huaca Partida (Figure 8.19). While their constructions began during the local Cerro Blanco phase and could predate the foundation of Chavín de Huántar, their use, as well as the associated megalithic renovations of monuments around 800 BC, overlaps with the early occupation of the monumental core at the highland center. By 500 BC and the following Samanco phase, the Cerro Blanco and Huaca Partida centers were abandoned, most likely around the same time that monumental constructions stopped at Chavín de Huántar.

A stylistic analysis carried out by Shibata (2010:304) identified parallels between Cerro Blanco and Chavín de Huántar as visible in the following iconographic elements: tooth/bone kenning, foot/head; and anthropomorphic figures with wings found on felines. These features in Nepeña date to 850–800 BC. Remains of feasting associated with this time have been found on the North Platform (Ikehara and Shibata 2008). The festive middens contain the first evidence of maize (*Zea mays*) at Cerro Blanco

figure 8.19
Polychrome frieze
AM–52 at Huaca Partida,
depicting a raptorial bird.
Current height = 1 m (but
original height = 2.53 m).
Note that the row of
adobes was placed by
conservators to protect the
sculptures. Photograph by
Koichiro Shibata.

(Shibata 2010:294). Little building effort has been documented on the North and South Platforms during the following Nepeña phase, but the Central Platform witnessed megalithic renovations. Circle-and-dot and pattern-burnished pottery fragments are found in association with the megalithic, ashlar type of architecture. No monumental constructions have so far been documented after 500 BC at Cerro Blanco, as the ceremonial center appears to have fallen in disuse. Stylistically, circle-and-dot pottery continued to be produced, and artisans also added textile-impressed forms to their repertoire.

Groups in Nepeña were also enmeshed with developments traditionally associated with the Cupisnique style, including the platform complex of Caballo Muerto. This relation was enduring and materialized in architecture, mural art, pottery, and ritual life. The ramifications of this millennia-old cultural tradition appear distributed along the coast from Manchay centers on the central coast to Cupisnique sites on the north coast. In a complex, synthetic, innovative, and transformative fashion, groups in Nepeña were caught in those broader regional networks. The period between 800 and 500 BC appears to have been particularly vibrant, as local elites became increasingly entangled in Chavín

de Huántar's growing influence, as visible in monumental renovations, mural art, and exotic prestige goods. The rise of Chavín de Huántar, however, does not appear to have marked any significant "break" in local ideologies and/or ritual practices. Considering this continuity and the enduring depiction of supernatural images in Nepeña and more broadly in northern Peru between 1500 and 500 BC, we suggest the term "Chavín-Cupisnique Religious Complex" (see also Ikehara 2015).

The integration of communities of the Chavín-Cupisnique Religious Complex was reproduced over a period of a thousand years by rituals carried out in specifically designed architectural spaces. These centers were formed by the combination of rectangular platforms with decorated facades, squared plazas, and hypostyle halls, arranged symmetrically or with a U-shaped layout. From this perspective, we consider Chavín de Huántar as one center among many, albeit with impressive masonry, architectural settings, and stone sculptures, whose leaders eventually gained increasing influence and support through factional competition and other aggrandizing mechanisms. In Nepeña, the growth of Chavín de Huántar and its apex during the Janabarriu phase (700–400 BC) was felt in the presence of more exotic goods, megalithic renovations, and long-distance exchange goods, especially obsidian and cinnabar. Here, the Chavín-Cupisnique Religious Complex is most visible in the mural art of Cerro Blanco and Huaca Partida during the Cerro Blanco phase, while material evidence for highland connections is more ubiquitous during the following Nepeña phase.

By 500 BC, the Chavín-Cupisnique Religious Complex suddenly lost popularity on the coast and in the highlands. In Nepeña and neighboring valleys, the subsequent Samanco phase somewhat echoes broader regional processes at the time, including the reduction in the scale of monuments and associated ritual gatherings, shifts in settlement patterns and a marked preference for defensive locations, the construction of fortifications, an increase in physical violence, the depiction of violence in visual arts, the adoption of new types of pottery, a political balkanization, and the emergence of regional corporate styles such as Salinar, Puerto Moorin, and Huarás. In the Callejón de Huaylas, Burger (1992:228–229) suggests that change in context from Janabarriu to Huarás at Chavín de Huántar indicates a major "cultural break" (see Bria, this volume). In Nepeña, potters and artisans continued to produce incised, stamped circle-and-dot, and pattern-burnished vessels, while masons and architectural sculptors steered clear of Chavín-Cupisnique images.

After the collapse of the Chavín-Cupisnique Religious Complex, local populations continued to diverge and take different historical trajectories. In coastal Ancash, the waning of this religious complex appears linked to a failure to reproduce non-coercive religious ideology. In the Moche Valley, Brian Billman (1999) suggests a shift in leadership from mound building to water management, irrigation, and defensive strategies. In the Casma Valley, local groups followed a similar trajectory as Nepeña, where ceremonial mounds were abandoned and groups nucleated in clustered settlements, including Pampa Rosario and San Diego (Pozorski and Pozorski 1987). In Nepeña, continuities in pottery technology, architectural building techniques, and foodways, combined with the explicit rejection and/or avoidance of the visual culture at Cerro Blanco

and Huaca Partida, suggest the existence of dissident factions moving away from traditional leadership (see also Shibata 2014). After a few centuries of fragmentation, some regions witnessed higher degrees of integration. In the Moche, Virú, and Santa Valleys, large-scale polities emerge in association with extensive agricultural infrastructures and hierarchical settlement systems (Chapdelaine 2010; Millaire 2010). In Nepeña, these processes appear to have materialized in the vicinity of the Pañamarca complex, including the adjacent mound cluster known as Tres Marias.

Concluding Thoughts

In this chapter, we have attempted to move beyond the traditional consideration of typical "horizon markers" (e.g., Chavín-related supernatural beings depicted on stone sculpture) and examine the complex and intertwined aspects of first millennium BC societies. Figure 8.20 represents an attempt at summarizing the data that was presented and discussed. In the Nepeña Valley, groups thrived through mixed strategies of marine exploitation and farming. They built and renovated ceremonial spaces, decorated them with murals and friezes, produced pottery for different daily and special occasions, and engaged in regional exchange networks. Our field projects since 2002 have produced rich datasets that allow a reconsideration of the transformation, persistence, and alteration of key aspects of societies during the first millennium BC.

This chapter has focused on settlement patterns, ritual settings and public buildings, pottery, and exchange networks. We attempted to go beyond some of the limitations of the use of chronological schemes by using data from sixty-three calibrated radiocarbon assays. Analyses reveal major changes in settlement patterns between 800 and 600 BC. This observation parallels broader regional processes in the Central Andes when, around 500 BC, many monumental centers were abandoned. Centuries-old forms of social arrangement and leadership based on esoteric knowledge and regional elite networks appear to erode. Intercommunal violence

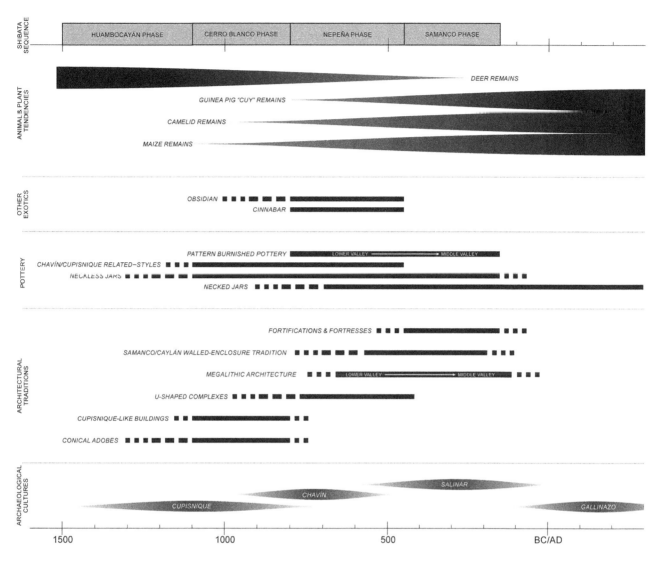

figure 8.20
Diagram summarizing the occupation sequences and historical processes in Nepeña during the first millennium BC. Drawing by Hugo Ikehara-Tsukayama.

and armed conflicts, as well as high levels of socio-economic inequality, developed. In coastal Ancash, those transformations appear closely tied to the waning of what we refer to as the Chavín-Cupisnique Religious Complex.

Engagement with Chavín de Huántar is most visible in monumental architecture, sculptures, and paintings documented at the sites of Cerro Blanco and Huaca Partida. Stylistic and architectural analyses suggest a complex web of entanglement between the Nepeña groups and the broader Cupisnique, Chavín, and Manchay phenomena

between 1100 and 500 BC. While the U-shaped layout at Nuevo Moro 4 resembles the U-shaped temples of the central coast (Williams 1980), including those of the Manchay culture (Burger and Salazar 2008), the U-shaped layout at Cerro Blanco resembles more closely the spatial proportions seen at Chavín de Huántar (Bischof 1997). Huaca Partida, meanwhile, appears more closely aligned with the Cupisnique architectural tradition of the north coast. We observe a similar complexity in the iconographic content of murals, which hints at multiple autonomous communities whose leaders competed for status through heterogeneous networks of long-distance interactions (see also Shibata 2020).

Following the waning of Chavín, Cupisnique, and Manchay influences in the valley, the rise in armed conflicts and defensive architecture, as well as concomitant changes in settlement patterns, murals, and exchange networks, indicate significant transformations in the nature of authority. By 500 BC, foreign influences in Nepeña, including contacts with the adjacent highlands and Chavín de Huántar, had weakened. As we continue to investigate the impact of Chavín in the Central Andes, scholars of the twenty-first century will need to pay close attention to the centuries that followed its demise and the ways different people remembered, reshaped, and revived its rich and enduring legacy.

Acknowledgments

We sincerely thank Richard Burger and Jason Nesbitt for the kind invitation to contribute to the volume. Since 2002, our respective field projects have benefited from the help and support of several different people and institutions. Our warm appreciation also goes to the people of Nepeña for their hospitality, continued support, and interest. George Lau's insightful comments, as well as suggestions from two anonymous reviewers and the volume editors, greatly helped in shaping the final version of this text. Thanks to Sara Taylor for her editorial prowess. Finally, we would like to dedicate this chapter to the memory of Colin McEwan and his invaluable contribution to Pre-Columbian studies.

NOTES

1 A supra-local community is defined here as a group of households that interacts more with each other than with other people in the region. The degree of interaction is measured by the distance between these households. The delineation of supra-local communities was made using tridimensional surfaces created by the interpolation (inverse distance weighting) of population density and distance (see Ikehara 2015 for methods).

2 What archaeologists typically refer to as graphite paint does not necessarily contain graphite. In the particular case of graphite-on-red (*rojo grafitado*) discussed here, SEM–EDXRF analyses carried out by Druc (2015) suggest the use of manganese.

REFERENCES CITED

Billman, Brian R.

1999 Reconstructing Prehistoric Economies and Cycles of Political Power in the Moche Valley, Peru. In *Settlement Pattern Studies in the Americas: Fifty Years since Virú*, edited by Brian R. Billman and Gary M. Feinman, pp. 131–159. Smithsonian Institution Press, Washington, D.C.

Bischof, Henning

1997 Cerro Blanco, valle de Nepeña, Perú: Un sitio del horizonte temprano en emergencia. In *Archaeologica peruana 2: Arquitectura y civilización en los Andes prehispánicos*, edited by Elizabeth Bonnier and Henning Bischof, pp. 202–234. Sociedad Arqueológica Peruana-Alemana, Mannheim.

Bronk Ramsey, Christopher

2009 Bayesian Analysis of Radiocarbon Dates. *Radiocarbon* 51(1):337–360.

2020 OxCal Software Version 4.4 (online version). University of Oxford Radiocarbon Accelerator Unit, Oxford.

Burger, Richard L.

1981   The Radiocarbon Evidence of the Temporal Priority of Chavín de Huántar. *American Antiquity* 46(3):592–601.

1984   *The Prehistoric Occupation of Chavín de Huantar, Peru*. University of California Press, Berkeley.

1992   *Chavín and the Origins of Andean Civilization*. Thames and Hudson, New York.

2019   Understanding the Socioeconomic Trajectory of Chavín de Huántar: A New Radiocarbon Sequence and Its Wider Implications. *Latin American Antiquity* 30(2):373–392.

Burger, Richard L., and Michael D. Glascock

2000   Locating the Quispisisa Obsidian Source in the Department of Ayacucho, Peru. *Latin American Antiquity* 11:258–268.

2009   Intercambio prehistórico de obsidiana a larga distancia en el norte peruano. *Revista del Museo de Arqueología, Antropología e Historia* 11:17–50.

Burger, Richard L., and Ramiro Matos Mendieta

2002   Atalla: A Center on the Periphery of the Chavín Horizon. *Latin American Antiquity* 13(2):153–177.

Burger, Richard L., and Lucy C. Salazar

2008   The Manchay Culture and the Coastal Inspiration for Highland Chavín Civilization. In *Chavín: Art, Architecture, and Culture*, edited by William J. Conklin and Jeffrey Quilter, pp. 85–105. Cotsen Institute of Archaeology, University of California, Los Angeles.

Burtenshaw-Zumstein, Julia T.

2013   The "Tembladera" Figurines: Ritual, Music, and Elite Identity in Formative Period North Peru, circa 1800–200 BC. *Ñawpa Pacha: Journal of Andean Archaeology* 33(2):119–148.

Cárdenas Martin, Mercedes

1998   Material diagnóstico del período formativo en los valles de Chao y Santa, costa norte del Perú. *Boletín de Arqueología PUCP* 2:61–81.

Chapdelaine, Claude

2010   Moche Political Organization in the Santa Valley: A Case of Direct Rule through Gradual Control of the Local Population. In *New Perspectives on Moche Political Organization*, edited by Jeffrey Quilter and Luis Jaime Castillo, pp. 252–279. Dumbarton Oaks Research Library and Collection, Washington, D.C.

Chapdelaine, Claude, and Gérard Gagné

2015   A Temple for the Dead at San Juanito, Lower Santa Valley, during the Initial Period. In *Funerary Practices and Models in the Ancient Andes: The Return of the Living Dead*, edited by Peter Eeckhout and Lawrence S. Owens, pp. 34–54. Cambridge University Press, Cambridge.

Chicoine, David

2006a   Architecture and Society at Huambacho (800–200 B.C.), Nepeña Valley, Peru. PhD dissertation, Sainsbury Research Unit, University of East Anglia, Norwich.

2006b   Early Horizon Architecture at Huambacho, Nepeña Valley, Peru. *Journal of Field Archaeology* 31(1):1–22.

2010a   Cronología y secuencias en Huambacho, valle de Nepeña, costa de Ancash. *Boletín de Arqueología PUCP* 12:317–348.

2010b   Elite Strategies and Ritual Settings in Coastal Peru during the 1st Millennium BC. In *Comparative Perspectives in the Archaeology of Coastal South America*, edited by Robyn Cutright, Enrique López-Hurtado, and Alexander C. Martin, pp. 191–212. Fondo Editorial PUCP, Lima; Center for Comparative Archaeology, University of Pittsburgh, Pittsburgh; and Ministerio de Cultura de Ecuador, Quito.

2011   Feasting Landscapes and Political Economy at the Early Horizon Center of Huambacho, Nepeña Valley, Peru. *Journal of Anthropological Archaeology* 30(3):432–453.

2022   Enchantment in Ancient Peru: Salinar Period Murals and Architecture. *World Art* 12(1):67–94.

Chicoine, David, Beverly Clement, and Kyle Stich

2016   Macrobotanical Remains from the 2009 Season at Caylán: Preliminary Insights into Early Horizon Plant Use in the Nepeña Valley, North-Central Coast of Peru. *Andean Past* 12:155–161.

Chicoine, David, and Hugo Ikehara

2010 Nuevas evidencias sobre el período formativo del valle de Nepeña: Resultados preliminares de la primera temporada de investigaciones en Caylán. *Boletín de Arqueología PUCP* 12:349–370.

2014 Ancient Urban Life at the Early Horizon Center of Caylán, Peru. *Journal of Field Archaeology* 39(4):336–352.

Chicoine, David, Hugo Ikehara, and Jessica Ortiz

2021 Cercaduras and Domestic Urban Life in Early Horizon Nepeña, Coastal Ancash. In *Ancient Households on the North Coast of Peru*, edited by Ilana Johnson, David Pacifico, and Robyn E. Cutright, pp. 68–102. University Press of Colorado, Boulder.

Chicoine, David, Hugo Ikehara, Koichiro Shibata, and Matthew Helmer

2017 Territoriality, Monumentality, and Religion in Formative Nepeña, Coastal Ancash. In *Rituals of the Past: Prehispanic and Colonial Case Studies in Andean Archaeology*, edited by Silvana A. Rosenfeld and Stefanie L. Bautista, pp. 123–149. University Press of Colorado, Boulder.

Chicoine, David, and Carol Rojas

2013 Shellfish Resources and Maritime Economy at Caylán, Coastal Ancash, Peru. *Journal of Island and Coastal Archaeology* 8(3):336–360.

Chicoine, David, Víctor Vásquez, and Teresa Rosales

2022 Taxonomic Analyses of the Vertebrate Faunal Remains from Caylán, Peru. *Andean Past* 13:452–466.

Chicoine, David, and Ashley Whitten

2019 Gated Communities, Neighborhoods, and Modular Living at the Early Horizon Urban Center of Caylán, Peru. *Archaeological Papers of the American Anthropological Association* 30(1):84–99.

Contreras, Daniel A., Nicholas Tripcevich, and Yuri I. Cavero Palomino

2012 Investigaciones en la fuente de la obsidiana tipo Quispisisa, Huancasancos-Ayacucho. *Investigaciones sociales* 16(28):185–195.

Cooke, Colin A., Holger Hintelmann, Jay J. Ague, Richard L. Burger, Harald Biesler, Julian P. Sachs, and Daniel R. Engstrom

2013 Use and Legacy of Mercury in the Andes. *Environmental Science and Technology* 47:4181–4188.

Cotrina, Jorge, Victor Peña, Arturo Tandaypan, and Elvia Pretell

2003 Evidencias Salinar: Sitios VN-35 y VN-36, Sector Sute Bajo, valle de Nepeña. *Revista Arqueológica SIAN* 14:7–12.

Daggett, Richard E.

1983 Megalithic Sites in the Nepeña Valley, Peru. In *Investigations of the Andean Past*, edited by Daniel H. Sandweiss, pp. 75–97. Cornell University Latin American Program, Ithaca, N.Y.

1984 The Early Horizon Occupation of the Nepeña Valley, North Central Coast of Peru. PhD dissertation, University of Massachusetts, Amherst.

1987 Reconstructing the Evidence for Cerro Blanco and Punkurí. *Andean Past* 1(1):111–132.

2016 *Julio C. Tello, Politics, and Peruvian Archaeology*. Andean Past Monograph 1. University of Maine, Orono.

Druc, Isabelle

2015 Rojo Grafitado Is Not Graphite: A Slow-Science Interpretation of the Production of an Andean Ceramic Style. Paper presented at the 80th Annual Meeting of the Society for American Archaeology, San Francisco.

Elera, Carlos G.

1997 Cupisnique y Salinar: Algunas reflexiones preliminares. In *Arqueología peruana 2*, edited by Elizabeth Bonnier and Henning Bischof, pp. 177–201. Sociedad Arqueológica Peruana-Alemana Reiss-Museum, Mannheim.

2009 La cultura Cupisnique a partir de los datos arqueológicos de Puémape. In *De Cupisnique a los Incas: El arte del valle de Jequetepeque*, edited by Luis Jaime Castillo and Cecilia Pardo, pp. 68–111. Museo de Arte de Lima, Lima.

Helmer, Matthew

2015   *The Archaeology of an Ancient Seaside Town: Performance and Community at Samanco, Nepeña Valley, Peru (ca. 500–1 BC)*. Archaeopress, Oxford.

Helmer, Matthew, and David Chicoine

2015   Seaside Life in Early Horizon Peru: Preliminary Insights from Samanco, Nepeña Valley. *Journal of Field Archaeology* 40(6):626–643.

Helmer, Matthew, David Chicoine, Hugo Ikehara, and Koichiro Shibata

2018   Plaza Settings and Public Interactions in Formative Nepeña, North-Central Coast of Peru. *Americae: European Journal of Americanist Archaeology* 3:7–31.

Herrera, Alexander

2005   Territory and Identity in the Pre-Columbian Andes of Northern Peru. PhD dissertation, University of Cambridge, Cambridge.

Hogg, Alan G., Timothy J. Heaton, Quan Hua, Jonathan G. Palmer, Chris S. M. Turney, John Southon, Alex Bayliss, Paul G. Blackwell, Gretel Boswijk, Christopher Bronk Ramsey, Charlotte Pearson, Fiona Petchey, Paula Reimer, Ron Reimer, and Lukas Wacker

2020   SHCal20 Southern Hemisphere Calibration, 0–55,000 Years cal BP. *Radiocarbon* 62(4):759–778.

Ikehara [-Tsukayama], Hugo C.

2010a   Kushipampa: El final del período formativo en el valle de Nepeña. *Boletín de Arqueología PUCP* 12:371–404.

2010b   Social Organization, Technology of Production, and the Function of Utilitarian Ceramics for Feasting during the Middle and Late Formative Periods in the Central Andes. In *Comparative Perspectives on the Archaeology of Coastal South America*, edited by Robyn E. Cutright, Enrique López-Hurtado, and Alexander J. Martin, pp. 45–62. Center for Comparative Archaeology, University of Pittsburgh, Pittsburgh; Pontificia Universidad Católica del Perú, Lima; and Ministerio de Cultura de Ecuador, Quito.

2015   Leadership, Crisis and Political Change: The End of the Formative Period in the Nepeña Valley, Peru. PhD dissertation, University of Pittsburgh, Pittsburgh.

2016   The Final Formative Period in the North Coast of Peru: Cooperation during Violent Times. *World Archaeology* 48(1):70–86.

2020   Multinaturalismo y perspectivismo en los centros ceremoniales formativos. In *Los desafíos del tiempo, el espacio y la memoria*, edited by Rafael Vega-Centeno and Jalh Dulanto, pp. 339–373. Pontificia Universidad Católica del Perú, Fondo Editorial, Lima.

2021   Unfinished Monuments and Institutional Crisis in the Early Pre-Columbian Andes. *Journal of Anthropological Archaeology* 61:101–267.

Ikehara, Hugo, and David Chicoine

2011   Hacia una revaluación de Salinar desde la perspectiva del valle de Nepeña, costa de Ancash. In *Arqueologia de la Costa de Ancash*, edited by Milosz Giersz and Ivan Ghezzi, pp. 153–184. ANDES Boletín del Centro de Estudios Precolombinos de la Universidad de Varsovia 8. Centro de Estudios Precolombinos de la Universidad de Varsovia, Warsaw; and Institut Français d'Études Andines, Lima.

Ikehara, Hugo, Fiorella Paipay, and Koichiro Shibata

2013   Feasting with *Zea mays* in the Middle and Late Formative North Coast of Peru. *Latin American Antiquity* 24(2):217–231.

Ikehara, Hugo, and Koichiro Shibata

2008   Festines e integración social en el período formativo: Nuevas evidencias de Cerro Blanco, valle bajo de Nepeña. *Boletín de Arqueología PUCP* 9:123–159.

Inokuchi, Kinya

2010   La arquitectura de Kuntur Wasi: Secuencia constructiva y cronología de un centro ceremonial del período formativo. *Boletín de Arqueología* PUCP 12:219–247.

Kembel, Silvia Rodríguez, and Herbert Haas

2015   Radiocarbon Dates from the Monumental Architecture at Chavín de Huántar, Perú. *Journal of Archaeological Method and Theory* 22(2):345–427.

Lane, Kevin

2005   Engineering the Puna: The Hydraulics of Agro-Pastoral Communities in a North-Central Peruvian Valley. PhD dissertation, University of Cambridge, Cambridge.

Larco, Rafael

    1941   *Los Cupisniques*. Casa Editorial La Cró-
nica y Variedades, Lima.

    1963   A Culture Sequence for the North Coast
of Perú. In *Handbook of South American
Indians*, vol. 2, *The Andean Civilizations*,
edited by Julian H. Steward, pp. 149–
175. Smithsonian Institution, Bureau
of American Ethnology 143. Cooper
Square Publishers, New York.

Lumbreras, Luis G.

    1993   *Chavín de Huántar: Excavaciones en
la Galería de las Ofrendas*. Materialien
zur allgemeinen und vergleichenden
Archäologie 51. P. von Zabern, Mainz.

Millaire, Jean-François

    2010   Primary State Formation in the Virú
Valley, North Coast of Peru. *Proceedings
of the National Academy of Sciences*
107(14):6186–6191.

Munro, Kimberly

    2018   Landscapes of Persistence and Ritual
Architecture at the Cosma Complex,
Upper Nepeña Valley, Peru. PhD dis-
sertation, Louisiana State University,
Baton Rouge.

Nesbitt, Jason

    2012   Excavations at Caballo Muerto: An
Investigation into the Origins of the
Cupisnique Culture. PhD dissertation,
Yale University, New Haven.

Nesbitt, Jason, Belkys Gutiérrez, and Segundo Vásquez

    2010   Excavaciones en Huaca Cortada, com-
plejo de Caballo Muerto, valle de Moche:
Un informe preliminar. *Boletín de
Arqueología PUCP* 12:261–286.

Peterson, Christian E., and Robert D. Drennan

    2005   Communities, Settlements, Sites, and
Surveys: Regional-Scale Analysis of
Prehistoric Human Interaction. *American
Antiquity* 70(1):5–30.

Pleasants, John G.

    2009   Huaca de los Chinos: The Archaeology of
a Formative Period Ceremonial Mound in
the Moche Valley, Peru. PhD dissertation,
University of North Carolina, Chapel Hill.

Pozorski, Shelia, and Thomas Pozorski

    1987   *Early Settlement and Subsistence in the
Casma Valley, Peru*. University of Iowa
Press, Iowa City.

    2006   Las Haldas: An Expanding Initial
Period Polity of Coastal Peru. *Journal
of Anthropological Research* 62:27–52.

Pozorski, Thomas

    1980   The Early Horizon Site of Huaca de los
Reyes: Societal Implications. *American
Antiquity* 45(1):100–110.

    1983   The Caballo Muerto Complex and Its
Place in the Andean Chronological
Sequence. *Annals of Carnegie Museum*
52:1–40.

Proulx, Donald A.

    1968   *An Archaeological Survey of the Nepeña
Valley, Peru*. Research Report 2. Depart-
ment of Anthropology, University of
Massachusetts, Amherst.

    1973   *Archaeological Investigations in the
Nepeña Valley, Peru*. Research Report 13.
Department of Anthropology, University
of Massachusetts, Amherst.

    1985   *An Analysis of the Early Cultural Sequence
in the Nepeña Valley, Peru*. Research
Report 25. Department of Anthropology,
University of Massachusetts, Amherst.

Rengifo, Carlos

    2014   Moche Social Boundaries and Settlement
Dynamics at Cerro Castillo (c. AD 600–
1000), Nepeña Valley, Peru. PhD dissertation, Sainsbury Research Unit for the Arts
of Africa, Oceania, and the Americas,
University of East Anglia, Norwich.

Rick, John W., Christian Mesía, Daniel A. Contreras,
Silvia Rodriguez Kembel, Rosa M. Rick, Matthew Paul
Sayre, and John Wolf

    2010   La cronología de Chavín de Huántar y sus
implicancias para el período formativo.
Boletín de Arqueología PUCP 13:87–132.

Rowe, John H.

    1962   *Chavín Art; An Inquiry into Its Form
and Meaning*. Museum of Primitive Art,
New York.

Sakai, Masato, and Juan José Martinez

    2010   Excavaciones en el Templete de
Limoncarro, valle bajo de Jequetepeque.
Boletín de Arqueología PUCP 12:171–201.

Samaniego, Lorenzo

2006   *Punkurí: Proyecto cultural.* Universidad Nacional del Santa, Chimbote.

2012   Arte mural de Punkurí, Nepeña, Ancash. *Investigaciones sociales* 16(28):15–33.

Sayre, Matthew P.

2018   The Historicity of the "Early Horizon." In *Constructions of Time and History in the Pre-Columbian Andes*, edited by Edward R. Swenson and Andrew P. Roddick, pp. 44–64. University Press of Colorado, Boulder.

Shibata, Koichiro

2004   Nueva cronología tentativa del período formativo—aproximación a la arquitectura ceremonial. *Desarollo arqueológico costa norte del Perú* 1:79–98.

2010   Cerro Blanco de Nepeña dentro de la dinámica interactiva del período formativo. *Boletín de Arqueología PUCP* 12:287–315.

2011a   A Model for Competitive Complex Societies as Viewed from the Formative Lower Nepeña Valley, North-Central Coast of Peru—Temples, Gathering People and Traveling Leaders. PhD dissertation, University of Tokyo, Tokyo.

2011b   Cronología, relaciones interregionales y organización social en el formativo: Esencia y perspectiva del valle bajo de Nepeña. In *Arqueologia de la Costa de Ancash*, edited by Milosz Giersz and Ivan Ghezzi, pp. 113–134. ANDES Boletin del Centro de Estudios Precolombinos de la Universidad de Varsovia 8. Centro de Estudios Precolombinos de la Universidad de Varsovia, Warsaw; and Institut Français d'Études Andines, Lima.

2014   Centros de "reorganización costeña" durante el período formativo tardío: Un ensayo sobre la competencia faccional en el valle bajo de Nepeña, costa nor-central peruana. *Senri Ethnological Studies* 89:245–260.

2017   Cosmología tripartita en Huaca Partida, valle bajo de Nepeña. *Indiana* 34(1):13–29.

2020   Intraregional Competition and Interregional Reciprocity: Formative Social Organization in the Lower Nepeña Valley on the North-Central Coast. In *Perspectives on Early Andean Civilization in Peru: Interaction, Authority, and Socioeconomic Organization during the First and Second Millennia BC*, edited by Richard L. Burger, Lucy C. Salazar, and Yuji Seki, pp. 35–47. Yale University Press, New Haven.

Shimada, Izumi, Carlos Elera, and Melody Shimada

1982   Excavaciones efectuadas en el centro de Huaca Lucía-Chólope, del horizonte temprano, Batán Grande, costa norte del Perú: 1979–1981. *Arqueologicas* 19:109–210.

Szpak, Paul, David Chicoine, Jean-François Millaire, Christine D. White, Rebecca Parry, and Fred J. Longstaffe

2016   Early Horizon Camelid Management Practices in the Nepeña Valley, North-Central Coast of Peru. *Environmental Archaeology: The Journal of Human Palaeoecology* 21(3):230–245.

Swenson, Edward R., and Andrew P. Roddick

2018   Introduction: Rethinking Temporality and Historicity from the Perspective of Andean Archaeology. In *Constructions of Time and History in the Pre-Columbian Andes*, edited by Edward R. Swenson and Andrew P. Roddick, pp. 3–43. University Press of Colorado, Boulder.

Tello, Julio C.

1930   Andean Civilization: Some Problem of Peruvian Archaeology. *Proceedings of the 23rd International Congress of Americanists* 1928:259–290.

1943   Discovery of the Chavín Culture in Peru. *American Antiquity* 9(1):135–160.

1960   *Chavín: Cultura matriz de la civilización andina.* Universidad Nacional Mayor de San Marcos, Lima.

Trever, Lisa

2017   *The Archaeology of Mural Paintings at Pañamarca, Peru.* Dumbarton Oaks Research Library and Collection, Washington, D.C.

Vega-Centeno, Rafael

2000   Imagen y simbolismo en la arquitectura de Cerro Blanco, costa norcentral peruana. *Bulletin de l'Institut Français d'Études Andines* 29(2):139–159.

2005   *Arqueología del valle de Nepeña: Excavaciones en Cerro Blanco y Punkurí.* Museo de Arqueología y Antropología, Universidad Nacional Mayor de San Marcos, Lima.

Williams, Carlos

1980   Complejos de pirámides con planta de U: Patrón arquitectónico de la costa central. *Revista del Museo Nacional* 44:95–110.

Transformation and Continuity along the Central Coast of Peru during the First Millennium BC and the Impact of the Chavín Phenomenon

RICHARD L. BURGER AND LUCY C. SALAZAR

At the Dumbarton Oaks Chavín Conference in 1968, Thomas Patterson (1971) presented a paper that attempted to explicate the spread of the Chavín Phenomenon to the central coast. The essay drew upon a decade of research by Patterson, his collaborators, and his students. He focused on extensive excavations at a shell midden known as the Tank Site at Ancón, as well as valley surveys and small-scale excavations at inland sites in several valleys (Lanning 1960, 1961, 1963, 1967; Patterson and Lanning 1964; Patterson and Moseley 1968; Scheele 1970).

Since Patterson's article, little has been written about Chavín's impact on the central coast. This is surprising, because earlier in the twentieth century scholars used the archaeological record of the central coast, especially from Ancón, to demonstrate the existence of a pan-regional phenomenon sometimes referred to as the Chavín horizon (Burger and Nesbitt, this volume). Noteworthy among these were Julio C. Tello (1943), Alfred Kroeber (1944), Rebeca Carrión Cachot (1948), and Gordon Willey (1948,

1951). Their tentative identification of Chavín culture at Ancón led investigators to continue excavations at the site during the following decades; among these investigators were Jorge Muelle (Muelle and Ravines 1973), Ernesto Tabío (1957), Hermilio Rosas (2007), Rogger Ravines, Edward Lanning (1960), Michael Moseley (1968; Moseley and Barrett 1969) and, of course, Tom Patterson (1971).

In this chapter, we review some of what has been learned about the central coast during the Initial Period and Early Horizon since Patterson's presentation at Dumbarton Oaks, and we reflect on how these advances require a reconsideration of some of the earlier interpretations of Ancón and the monumental U-shaped pyramid complexes contemporary with it. Our goal is to consider how central coast society was organized during the first and second millennia BC and how its culture changed during this period of time in order to evaluate what impact, if any, the Chavín Phenomenon had on this region. For the purpose of this chapter, the central coast will be defined as consisting of the lower and middle valley sections of the Chancay, Chillón, Rimac, and Lurín drainages.

The Manchay Culture and the Central Coast during the Initial Period

Until the 1980s, discussions of the Chavín Phenomenon on the central coast were hampered by an inability to distinguish between the area's Initial Period culture, now known as the Manchay culture, and the Chavín-related cultural elements associated with the Early Horizon occupation of this region (Burger and Salazar 2008). Neckless cooking pots and dark monochrome pottery decorated with incised designs were common along much of the central coast during the Initial Period (1800–800 BC; all dates presented in this chapter are calibrated) and scholars such as Carrión Cachot (1948), Jose Casafranca (1960), and Duccio Bonavia (1965) have assumed that these ceramic features indicated a close relationship with Chavín culture. Similarly, John Rowe (1962:5) and Edward Lanning (1967) believe the U-shaped center of Garagay to be a major Chavín center on the central coast. In his unpublished 1970 doctoral dissertation, "The Chavín Occupation of the Central Coast of Peru," Harry Scheele concludes that the multiple U-shaped civic-ceremonial centers in the Lurín Valley were the result of Chavín influence, even after weighing evidence to the contrary (Scheele 1970).

However, as the early pottery assemblages and monumental architectural complexes of the central coast began to be studied in more detail, their local character became increasingly obvious. For example, Patterson (1971) demonstrates that a late Initial Period style known as Colinas, with its geometric incisions and zoned punctation, developed from still earlier local Initial Period styles such as the one found at Huaca La Florida (Patterson 1985). The Peruvian architect Carlos Williams (1971, 1980a, 1985) likewise argued that the U-shaped complexes developed locally long before the pattern appeared at Chavín de Huántar. This reevaluation of the chronological position of central coast ceramics and public architecture received support from radiocarbon

measurements recovered from Huaca La Florida that demonstrated that public constructions of this monumental complex began during the early Initial Period (Patterson 1985; see also Burger 1981, 2019).

At the present time, some forty U-shaped civic-ceremonial complexes characteristic of the Manchay culture are known from the four major valleys of the central coast (Figure 9.1); additional ones have been documented in Huaura, Supe, Fortaleza, and Pativilica (Tantaleán and Leyva 2011; Williams 1980a, 1985). The larger examples of U-shaped centers cover up to 30 ha, and the terraced platforms in the ceremonial core of these complexes sometimes rise to over 25 m in height. In terms of area and volume, many of the monumental public complexes on the central coast are larger than the highland center at Chavín de Huántar (Williams 1980b:412, 1985) and they are also more extensive and massive than contemporary highland sites such as Pacopampa and Kuntur Wasi (Burger 1992).

Most of the civic-ceremonial centers of the Manchay culture were founded during the Initial Period, several centuries before the establishment of Chavín de Huántar. The earliest public constructions at two of the largest U-shaped centers, La Florida in the Rimac Valley and Mina Perdida in the Lurín Valley, were under construction by 1700 BC. Other civic-ceremonial complexes, such as Garagay in lower Rimac and Manchay Bajo in lower Lurín, were functioning by 1500 BC (Burger and Salazar 2012), as was Malpaso in the middle Lurín Valley (Milan 2014).

In contrast, based on a recent set of AMS measurements run on mammal bones from excavations at Chavín de Huántar, the Urabarriu phase can be estimated as running from 950 to 800 BC, the Chakinani phase can be estimated as lasting from 800 to 700 BC, and the Janabarriu phase can be estimated as running from 700 to 400 BC (Burger 2019). At the present time, there is no unambiguous evidence that the temple at Chavín de Huántar was established prior to the Urabarriu phase. If this is the case, the pan-regional Chavín Phenomenon related to the temple at Chavín de Huántar dates roughly to between 950 and 400 BC. Given this chronological understanding, some of the U-shaped centers

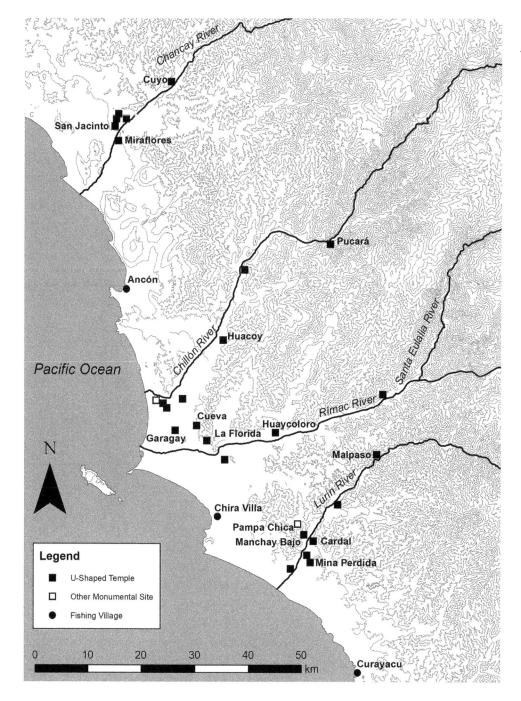

figure 9.1
Map of the key
U-shaped centers on
the central coast. Map
by Christopher Milan.

of the Manchay culture on the central coast, such as Huaca La Florida and Mina Perdida, had been flourishing for seven centuries prior to the establishment of Chavín de Huántar (Figure 9.2) (Burger 2019; Patterson 1985); consequently, many of the formal similarities observed between the Manchay and Chavín cultures are better understood as the result of coastal inspiration rather than as an expression

of Chavín influence on the coast (Burger 1981, 1988, 1992; Burger and Salazar 2008).

The site of Cardal is the civic-ceremonial center of the Manchay culture that has been studied in most detail (Burger 1987; Burger and Makowski 2009; Burger and Salazar 1991, 2012, 2014). Located in the lower Lurín Valley (Figure 9.3), Cardal illustrates how different the U-shaped centers of the Manchay

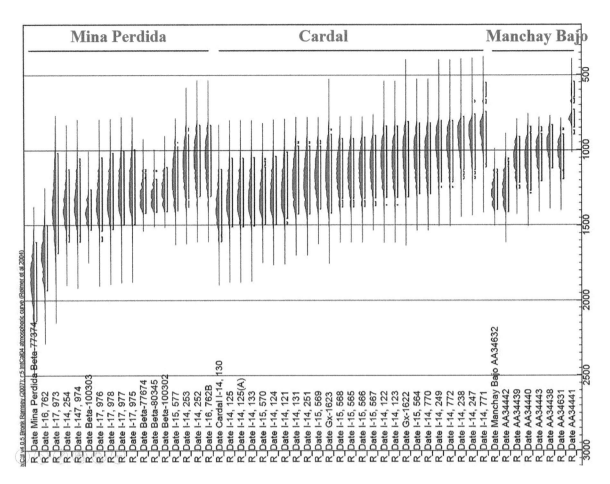

figure 9.2a
Multiplot of radiocarbon dates from Mina Perdida, Cardal, and Manchay Bajo. Illustration by Jason Nesbitt.

culture are from Chavín de Huántar. Based on aerial photographs and surface reconnaissance, Williams recognized ten sunken circular courtyards at Cardal, eight of which are situated along the outer margins of the terraced platforms that constitute the core of the site. Two circular courtyards flank the site's centerline, underscoring the pattern of dual organization that pervades Cardal (Burger and Salazar 1994). Chavín de Huántar, in contrast, features only a single circular courtyard, and it is located directly on the centerline of what Rowe referred to as the Old Temple (Lumbreras 1977; Rowe 1962). Many other differences exist with Chavín de Huántar, and these have become increasingly evident from the fieldwork carried out at Cardal (Figure 9.4).

To illustrate how a limited knowledge of Manchay public architecture produced a false

impression of strong similarity to the monumental architecture at Chavín de Huántar, we can use a discovery made on Cardal's main mound during the 2018 excavations. Based on our investigations in 1987, we believed that the central mound was dominated by a massive cream-colored stairway leading up to a narrow landing decorated with the sculpted polychrome frieze of a mouth band with large fangs (Burger and Salazar 1991). This was consistent with the original generic description of the architecture of U-shaped complexes by Williams and his hypothetical reconstruction of Cardal (Figure 9.5) (Williams 1980b, 1985). To our surprise, the 2018 excavations on the highest portion of Cardal's central pyramid unearthed a round summit chamber with a burned clay feature in the center of its floor (Figure 9.6). The summit feature was linked to

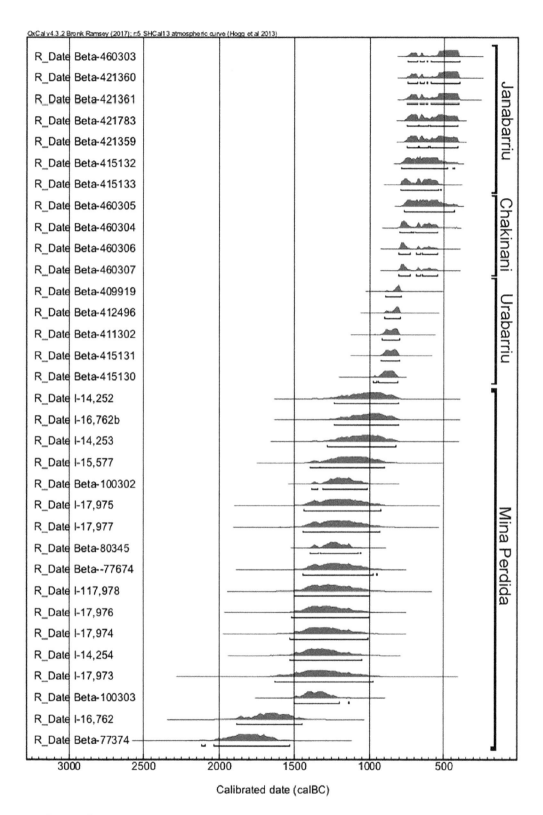

Calibrated date (calBC)

figure 9.2b
Multiplot comparing radiocarbon dates from Mina Perdida and Chavín de Huántar. Illustration by Jason Nesbitt.

figure 9.3
Map of Initial Period and Early Horizon sites in the Lurín Valley. Map by Christopher Milan.

figure 9.4
Oblique aerial photograph of Cardal. Photograph by Richard L. Burger and Lucy C. Salazar.

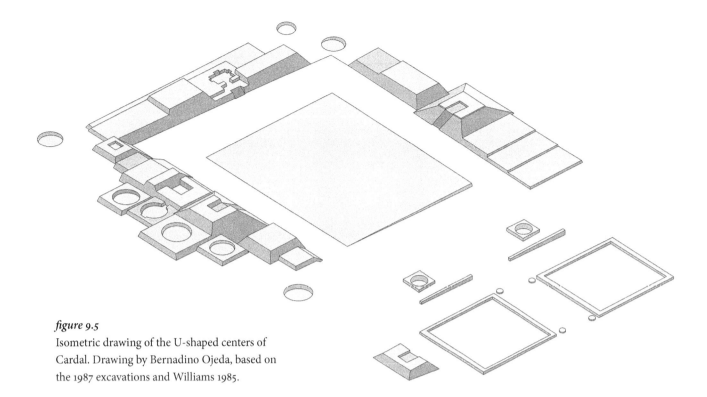

figure 9.5
Isometric drawing of the U-shaped centers of
Cardal. Drawing by Bernadino Ojeda, based on
the 1987 excavations and Williams 1985.

the central plaza by way of a large yellow staircase
(Figure 9.7). Its stairs were different in size, layout,
and color from those of the central staircase excavated in 1987. Three superimposed versions of the
second massive staircase were identified, suggesting
the long-standing role of the second staircase in the
site's history and organization. Thus, we now know
that throughout much or all of its history the main
mound at Cardal featured contrasting dual staircases, a pattern more reminiscent of the Templo
Mayor of Tenochtitlán than of Chavín de Huántar.
The latter site has a single narrow staircase leading
down along the Old Temple's centerline to the site's
sunken circular plaza.

Perhaps the aspect of Manchay culture that
has drawn the most attention from scholars interested in the Chavín Phenomenon is its religious
iconography. Manchay imagery features monstrous
creatures sporting prominent upper fangs (Burger
1992; Ravines 1984). As noted, a massive mouth
band with these characteristic canines adorned the
landing outside of Cardal's penultimate atrium, and
this same motif appears in a clay frieze on the outer
terrace wall of the atrium on the summit of Cardal's

left arm (Burger and Salazar 2014, 2019). This iconographic theme is, likewise, popular at the coeval
Manchay center of Garagay in the Rimac Valley
(Figure 9.8) (Ravines and Isbell 1976; Hector Walde,
personal communication 2018). It seems likely that
some features of Chavín iconography, such as the
fanged mouth bands on the Tello Obelisk and other
stone sculptures, may have been inspired by the
iconographic conventions of the Manchay culture.

However, when fanged mouths appear as a part
of larger images in Manchay representations, the
non-Chavín character of the religious iconography
becomes apparent. While Chavín religious iconography features creatures inspired by the fauna of
the tropical forest, the motifs of the Manchay culture have a more coastal inspiration. For example,
a blackware bowl from Ancón shows a mouth band
on a supernatural turtle (Burger 1992:fig. 47), and
the prominent mouth bands in the atrium mural at
Garagay are associated with arachnid supernaturals
(Burger 1992:fig. 43; Ravines and Isbell 1976). Neither
the turtle nor the spider theme appears in the hundreds of sculptures at Chavín de Huántar (Figure 9.9)
(Salazar and Burger 1983; see also Ravines et al. 1984).

figure 9.6
Round building
on the summit of
the main mound at
Cardal. Photograph
by Richard L. Burger
and Lucy C. Salazar.

figure 9.7
Dual staircase at
Cardal. Photograph by
Richard L. Burger and
Lucy C. Salazar, 2018.

figure 9.8
Mouth band from
Garagay. Photograph
courtesy of
Hector Walde.

Unfortunately, the ceramics of the central coast during the Initial Period were mostly undecorated or adorned with only geometric motifs; religious iconography was rare. When more elaborate decoration occurs, the fragmentation of the pottery makes the images difficult to reconstruct. As a result, we are largely dependent on the few known cases of wall paintings and low relief sculptures that decorate the public architecture of the U-shaped centers for much of our knowledge of Manchay religious iconography (see Burger and Salazar 1998 for an exception). Fortunately, the 2018 and 2019 excavations at Cardal unearthed additional examples of Manchay sacred images. On the outer terrace of the right arm of the U, a sunken circular courtyard dating to approximately 1000 BC was built on top of an earlier semi-subterranean circular courtyard. The surviving segment of the courtyard was buried within the fill of a platform forming the later courtyard. The interior of the earlier courtyard had been decorated with an incised polychrome frieze. Subsequently, a new floor was added and the frieze was covered by a thick layer of red-painted clay plaster sometime during its use life. This outer monochrome layer concealed the frieze and helped to protect it from damage by post-abandonment forces.

During the 2018 field season, we were able to uncover and conserve two small sections of the new mural, and much of the remainder was revealed during the 2019 field season. It is divided into segments by a set of black-and-white diagonal bands that extend lattice-like across the wall, forming a series of diamond-shaped spaces. The bi-color treatment of the bands suggests that it represents an open-meshed textile or net. The 2018 investigations showed that two of the diamond-shaped spaces were filled with profile images of fanged monstrous supernaturals (Figure 9.10). These differed from one another in detail, but both consisted of a combination of feline, avian, arachnid, and insect elements. The closest comparison of this wall decoration is with the atrium frieze from Garagay, which shares some stylistic conventions, including prominent upper fangs and eyes with eccentric pupils (Burger 1992:fig. 43). The 2019 investigations of the Cardal frieze revealed that other spaces in the interstices of the net or net-bag contained the images of spider legs and other severed limbs of supernaturals. A complete supernatural creature with the features of a bat appeared in another of the diamond-shaped spaces. None of the images from the new Cardal frieze matches the ones at Garagay or the earlier

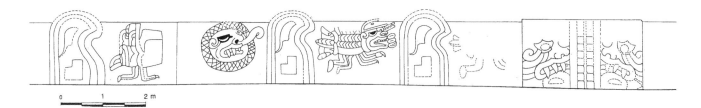

0   1   2 m

figure 9.9
Atrium frieze at Garagay. Drawing by Richard L. Burger and Lucy C. Salazar.

figure 9.10
Circular courtyard frieze at Cardal; insect monster, from the 2019 excavations. Photograph by Richard L. Burger and Lucy C. Salazar.

murals from Cardal in detail. Based on the available radiocarbon measurements, we estimate the age of the new Cardal frieze to be approximately 1100 BC. If so, it was created at least a century before the Lanzón at Chavín de Huántar.

None of the major Chavín stylistic conventions—kennings, double profiles, anatropic designs, and modular widths—are present in the Cardal frieze (Burger 1992:148–149). Outside of the central coast, the closest parallels are on the north coast, with Cupisnique iconographic representations on stone ritual vessels and architecture from Limoncarro in the lower Jequetepeque drainage (Burger 1992:fig. 82; Sakai and Martínez 2010; Salazar and Burger 1983) and the polychrome frieze

from Collud in the Lambayeque drainage (Alva 2010:fig. 18). The net motif is found in both areas, and the presence of dismembered limbs appears on Cupisnique vessels and on the clay frieze and stone sculpture from Cerro Sechín in the lower Casma Valley (Burger 1992:fig. 58). However, despite their shared features, the Manchay and Cupisnique iconographies are quite distinct from each other in style and content.

The geographically restricted character of Manchay public art and architecture is consistent with the evidence of the localized nature of the subsistence economy and the circumscribed patterns of social interaction. Independent archaeobotanical studies of household refuse from the U-shaped civic-ceremonial centers of Cardal by Marcelle Umlauf and Mina Perdida by Alexander Chevalier both conclude that almost all the agricultural and wild plant resources encountered in the domestic zone of these centers could have been acquired without leaving the Lurín drainage (Chevalier 2002; Umlauf 2009). The faunal remains, likewise, showed input from the nearby Pacific shore, as well as adjacent riverine and *lomas* environments, but nothing suggested exploitation of more distant resources (Gorriti 2009; Ali Altamirano, personal communication 2019; George Miller, personal communication 2018). Neutron activation analysis of pottery from Cardal by Trisha Thorme focusing on the composition of clay pastes likewise confirms exchange between the lower and middle valley centers in Lurín, as well as those on the nearby shoreline such as Curayacu, but none with sites beyond the drainage (Burger and Salazar 2014:309–310, fig. 12-12; Thorme 1999).

The pattern of valley self-sufficiency and strong local identity seen at the large inland sites such as Cardal and Mina Perdida is repeated at the small fishing villages. A petrographic study of ceramics from the Ancón shell middens identified a pattern of local pottery production at workshops near the shoreline site and in the lower Chillón Valley, but there is no evidence of exchange between Ancón and the major U-shaped complex of Garagay located in the neighboring Rimac Valley (Druc et al. 2001) or more distant Initial Period centers on the central coast.

In terms of subsistence activities, the Manchay culture appears to have been dominated by farmers who supported themselves with canal-based intensive agriculture that produced a wide range of cultigens, including manioc (*Manihot esculenta*), sweet potato (*Ipomoea batatas*), potatoes (*Solanum tuberosum*), maize (*Zea mays*), squash (*Cucurbita* sp.), peanuts (*Arachis hypogea*), and chili pepper (*Capsicum* sp.), as well as native fruits such as guava (*Psidium guajava*) and pacay (*Inga feuilleei*). These were supplemented by wild foods, such as cactus fruit, and hunted animals, such as deer from the *lomas*. Maize was present but remained a minor crop (Tykot, van der Merwe, and Burger 2006). The main source of protein came from fish and seafood brought to the inland valley communities from the Pacific shores. The stability of this lifeway is attested to by the longevity of the Manchay centers, most of which were occupied for several centuries and some of which flourished for almost a thousand years.

The success of these central coast populations can be inferred from a gradual increase in the number of the centers in each valley during the Initial Period. For example, in Lurín, the number of civic-ceremonial centers appears to have grown from a single center at Mina Perdida to eight centers by the end of the Initial Period. In the Rimac Valley, Huaca La Florida seems to have been the sole founding center, but the total number of U-shaped civic-ceremonial centers eventually reached sixteen by 900 BC (Fuentes 2012). This rise in the number of centers in each valley is interpreted as a result of an increasing population that produced social discord and eventually resulted in the fissioning of communities. It is hypothesized that the establishment of a new community required the founding of a new U-shaped civic-ceremonial center as well as the construction of a new gravity canal; the latter would have increased the amount of agricultural land and the valley's carrying capacity (Burger 2009; Burger and Salazar 2012).

The Manchay culture belongs to what Patterson (1983) has referred to as the La Florida Social Formation. This is an organizational pattern based on economically specialized farming villages that were established in ecological locations suitable for the production of food crops and the establishment of water management systems. The civic-ceremonial centers with U-shaped pyramids served as the environment for rituals, predictions, and offerings. These ceremonies maintained the conditions for successful farming while also providing a social context for planning canal maintenance and repair, finding mates, and sharing agricultural and other practical knowledge. Like Patterson, we believe that there is no compelling evidence for significant economic inequalities among the people living at the centers or for class-based distinctions between those residing at the centers and those in the countryside. Besides an ecologically based contrast

figure 9.11

Three superimposed circular plazas, from the 2019 excavations of the right arm of Cardal. Photograph by Richard L. Burger and Lucy C. Salazar.

between farmers, such as those living at Cardal, and fisherfolk, such as those living at Curayacu or Ancón, there is a conspicuous absence of contrasting consumption patterns that would suggest differences in wealth or privilege. Similarly, there are no examples of elaborate burials or goods produced by craft specialists in the refuse or burials. Most of the artifacts recovered in the domestic refuse, such as bone and stone tools, were manufactured at the household level, and the by-products of these activities were frequently discarded in the residential garbage (Burger 1987).

There is likewise no indication of sociopolitical centralization or settlement hierarchies on the central coast during the Initial Period (Burger and Salazar 2012, 2014; cf. Silva 1998). Any surplus that was produced seems to have gone to the community as a whole in the form of new construction of features such as huge check dams (Burger 2003) and the annual renewal of the public architecture as well

as the yearly cleaning and repair of the canal systems that supported these sociopolitical units. It is likely that all of these group activities were accompanied by drinking and feasting. In the Marxist terminology favored by Patterson, the Manchay society would have been characterized by social relations dominated by a communal, kin-based mode of production, one in which exploitation of one group by another was absent (Patterson 1983).

The cultural conservatism of the Manchay culture is impressive and pervasive. It is expressed in many ways, perhaps most notably by the repeated construction of public buildings one above the other often without change in form or orientation. The six superimposed central staircases documented for Mina Perdida are a vivid example of this, as are the many examples of superimposed staircases at Cardal (Burger and Salazar 1991, 2012:figs. 14.5 and 14.8). Similarly, the 2019 excavations revealed a series of three superimposed circular courtyards near the northern extreme of the right lateral arm (Figure 9.11).

Given the absence of strong political and economic ties linking the valleys of the central coast, the principal factor responsible for the coherence of the Manchay culture appears to have been a shared ideology and its associated religious and civic rituals. These are expressed through the similar layouts of the civic-ceremonial centers and the building complexes on the summits of the stepped platforms that dominated the sites. The decoration of these buildings with similar symbols, such as wave-mountain icons, supernatural beings with arachnid features, and disembodied fanged mouth bands at Garagay in Rimac and Cardal in Lurín, is evidence in support of this interpretation.

The Appearance of the Chavín Phenomenon on the Central Coast

When did the Chavín Phenomenon reach the central coast and how can it be identified? Traditionally, this has been accomplished through an analysis of pottery style (Patterson 1971). At the end of the Initial Period, the ceramic style of the central coast experienced changes in the decoration and forms of its ceramic vessels. New techniques of surface texturing were introduced; these included rocker stamping, dentate rocker stamping, rouletting, appliqué nubbins, and combing. The production of contrasting matte and reflective surfaces likewise proliferated, as did the frequency of highly polished black vessels. There also was an increase in elaborate incised motifs, including many with fangs. Some of these can be linked with the iconography of Chavín de Huántar, but often, due to their fragmentary nature, it is hard to determine whether the design is related to images characteristic of Manchay or Chavín iconography. New vessel forms, most notably bottles with stirrup spouts, appeared at the same time as these changes in vessel decoration. Prior to this, the bottles of the central coast were single-necked bottles or, more rarely, spout-and-bridge bottles (Burger 1987; Engel 1956).

The new decorative elements and shapes have parallels in the oldest pottery style known from Chavín de Huántar and other sites interacting with it. Given that pattern, archaeologists have often interpreted their appearance on the central coast as an indicator that the region had been incorporated into the Chavín Interaction Sphere (e.g., Lanning 1967; Patterson 1971). The parochial character of the Manchay culture, including its ceramics, makes the incorporation of alien elements into the local pottery style all the more noteworthy. Most of the pottery vessels with these new stylistic elements were intended for daily use in the households of common fisherfolk or farmers rather than for special purposes such as burials, elite displays, or public religious rituals. Moreover, since pottery was created at the community level, these innovative elements were being produced locally by potters who consciously emulated exotic style elements associated with more northern centers, including Chavín de Huántar (Druc et al. 2001).

The sheer number of new elements raises the possibility that the ceramics could have been made by itinerant potters using local raw materials. Such a model for pottery production has been proposed by Gabriel Ramón (2011) based on historic and ethnographic analogy, and this model should be considered for Ancón and other sites on the central coast. Nonetheless, even if "swallow" potters played a role in producing the Chavín-related style of local pottery, this would not significantly affect the argument presented here, since ethnographically itinerant potters produce their wares in response to local tastes. Thus, the intentional act of abandoning local ceramic conventions in favor of ones popular among alien populations would still need to be explained.

The adoption of these novel elements on the central coast is coeval with the emergence of Chavín de Huántar as a major Andean religious center during the final centuries of the Initial Period. In addition, the appearance of these elements is contemporary with the intensification of sociopolitical problems along the central coast. Around 950 BC, the centers of the Manchay culture began to experience difficulties in mobilizing labor, and some complexes, such as Mina Perdida and Cardal, appear to

figure 9.12
Ancón. Photograph by Richard L. Burger and Lucy C. Salazar.

have been abandoned by 900 BC. At both centers, the final episodes of public construction consisted of buildings constructed using poorly built masonry or flimsy composite wattle-and-daub walls.

Other changes in the Manchay civic-ceremonial centers were also noteworthy at the end of the Initial Period. At Cardal, a group of individuals was disinterred and reburied beneath the thick layer of sterile gravel fill sustaining the final atrium (Burger and Salazar 1991). Traditionally on the central coast, going back as far as the Middle Preceramic (Quilter 1989), burials were placed under and around the residences and, consistent with this, at Cardal most interments were found beneath floors in the residential zone behind the pyramid complex (Burger 1987). The transfer of the mummy bundles of some individuals to a sacred location on the pyramid summit can be interpreted as a late attempt to reinforce the authority of religious leaders in response to the emerging crisis. It may also reflect the increasingly important roles that Cardal's ancestors played in the public ceremonies. Subsequently, near the northern edge of Cardal, the building of a set of twin rectangular plazas was initiated but never completed

(Burger and Salazar 1991:fig. 5), presumably because of an inability to mobilize sufficient labor.

At least one U-shaped center in the Lurín Valley, Manchay Bajo, seems to have lasted longer than its neighboring centers, but it apparently failed to survive beyond the beginning of the Early Horizon (Burger 2003). A radiocarbon measurement (AA34441) from one of its final constructions falls within the Hallstatt Plateau and, thus, yielded a calibrated 2-sigma range of 822–513 BC. Significantly, unlike Cardal, some ceramic elements known from Ancón and traditionally associated with Chavín influence have been found at Manchay Bajo.

The problems identified for the central coast at the end of the Initial Period appear to have been part of a larger crisis that engulfed much of the north, north-central, and central coast (Chicoine, Ikehara-Tsukayama, and Shibata, this volume). First recognized in 1981, this hypothesis has been reinforced by investigations over the last two decades (Burger 1981, 1992, 2019). Judging from the observations of archaeologists working in the lower and middle Rimac Valley (Fuentes 2012; Palacios 1988, 2017; Ravines et al. 1984; Silva and García 1997), the Chillón Valley

figure 9.13
Ceramics from Ancón
exhibiting the Chavín
International Style.
Photographs courtesy
of Nicholas Brown.

0 cm   5 cm   10 cm

(Silva 1998), and the Chancay drainage (Cancho 2017; Carrión 1998, 2000), the abandonment of the U-shaped centers during the final centuries of the Initial Period (ca. 950–800 BC) in the Lurín Valley also occurred throughout the central coast.

At Garagay, some Early Horizon pottery was recovered, but the most recent radiocarbon measurement (CU-09) from the site when calibrated is 911–799 BC (Ravines et al. 1984). Ravines has suggested that one of the painted stone offerings in the penultimate atrium at Garagay was linked to anthropomorphic representations of the main deity at Chavín de Huántar because of its large upper fangs and the use of San Pedro cactus spines to represent a pair of staffs attached to this small image. Yet if we consider the images represented at both Garagay and Cardal on public constructions dating to the end of the sites' use as civic-ceremonial centers, it is unequivocal that these depict Manchay religious symbols rather than those characteristic of Chavín de Huántar. Additional excavation at Manchay sites will be needed to better distinguish between the prolonged survival of centers with monumental architecture as the foci of civic and ceremonial activity as opposed to a reoccupation of these complexes by Early Horizon squatters. The latter pattern has been documented in the Casma Valley at Las Haldas (Pozorski and Pozorski 1987) and may also occur in the Rimac Valley at Garagay and La Florida.

Of the Initial Period sites on the central coast, Ancón in the Chillón drainage and Curayacu on the southern shores of the Lurín Valley are the only documented examples of settlements that continued to flourish during the Early Horizon (Figure 9.12) (Engel 1956; Lanning 1960, 1967; Patterson 1971; Scheele 1970). It is probably not coincidental that both are shoreline fishing villages rather than civic-ceremonial centers. Moreover, it is at these two shoreline sites that the adoption of Chavín elements into the ceramic assemblage has been most clearly identified.

At Ancón and Curayacu, the decision of the central coast potters to emulate the pottery elements of the Chavín Interaction Sphere continued over the next four centuries, including the period of Chavín de Huántar's greatest prosperity and pan-regional influence. From 800 to 500 BC, the pottery at Ancón and Curayacu reflected the changing ceramic styles at Chavín de Huántar and other related sites. New elements were incorporated, including vessel forms such as stirrup-spouted bottles with strongly flanged rims and straight or convex-curved spouts, flat-bottomed bowls with beveled rims and pouring lips, and jars with strap handles. Decorative elements similar to the Janabarriu-phase assemblage at Chavín de Huántar also appear, most notably rows of repetitive circle-dots and concentric circles (Figure 9.13) (Burger 1993:fig. 8). This suite of ceramic elements suggests that the shoreline residents identified with the Chavín Interaction Sphere and that this identification lasted for several centuries. We hypothesize that the motivation behind this may have been a desire to shape a more cosmopolitan identity that transcended the narrow regional character of the preceding centuries.

Were the changes in the local ceramic style part of an effort to look for solutions to their problems outside of their region? Elsewhere it has been suggested that it might be appropriate to think of the expansive Chavín cult as an example of the general phenomena sometimes referred to as "crisis cults" or "revitalization movements" (Burger 1988, 1993:69–70; La Barre 1971; Wallace 1956). Crisis cults are often adopted to alleviate the stress produced by the contrast between the unfavorable reality and the explanations and claims offered by traditional religious ideology. This interpretation seems possible for the central coast, given the evidence that sociopolitical problems were undermining traditional religious centers when Chavín influence appeared in the region. In order to understand how the people of the central coast became aware of the Chavín cult and entered into the Chavín Interaction Sphere, it is necessary to consider archaeological evidence recovered at the famous center in the northern highlands.

Pilgrimages to Chavín de Huántar from the Central Coast during the Late Initial Period

There is compelling evidence that representatives from the central coast visited the pan-regional highland center at Chavín de Huántar as religious pilgrims. In 1967, Luis Lumbreras was excavating in Chavín de Huántar's ceremonial core when he discovered the Ofrendas Gallery, a subterranean complex built within the stone hearting of the platform surrounding the sunken circular plaza. The gallery complex consisted of cells and a central passageway filled with ritual paraphernalia, including hundreds of complete ceramic bottles, plates, bowls, and jars. Most of these had apparently been brought to Chavín de Huántar as gifts by pilgrims visiting the site from distant lands in the highlands, coast, and cloud forest (Burger 1984, 1992; Lumbreras 2007). Several of the radiocarbon measurements coming from the gallery suggested an Urabarriu-phase date for the architectural features, and most of the ceramics found there appear to date to the late Initial Period (Burger 1981, 1984, 1992; Lumbreras 2007).

Many of the vessels in the Ofrendas Gallery have a style that is quite different than the local Urabarriu-phase pottery of Chavín de Huántar. There are pieces that appear to be from the Moche, Chicama, and Jequetepeque Valleys of the north coast that are crafted in several different styles traditionally linked to the Cupisnique culture (Alva 1986; Lumbreras 1971:fig. 24, fig. 25a–b). There are also incised bowls with fine cross-hatching typical of Piura on the far north coast (Lumbreras 2007:fig. 654), bichrome bottles with curvilinear slip-painted motifs popular in the Cajamarca highlands (Lumbreras 1971:fig. 25d–e), and stone platters from the forested eastern slopes of Jaén near the current Peruvian–Ecuadorian border (Clasby 2019, this volume; Lumbreras 1971:fig. 27a). Most importantly, for this chapter, there also were numerous dark incised bowls and bottles that appear to have come from the central coast (Lumbreras 1971:figs. 17–23). These vessels are among the most common imports in the Ofrendas Gallery.

Ofrendas Gallery ceramics with a likely central coast origin were subdivided into a series of styles referred to as Dragoniano, Ofrendas, and Floral (Lumbreras 1971, 2007). As already noted, during the late Initial Period, potters on the central coast began to decorate their household pottery with religious images. Among the favored locations for these images were the interior of bowls and plates; more rarely, this decoration extended to the underside of the vessels. Interior decoration and adornment of the underside of bowls and plates are rare in the Central Andes, but it is common at the shoreline sites of Ancón and Curayacu. At Ancón during the late Initial Period, about 13 percent of the decorated bowls and plates had interior incision and the percentage was even higher at the shoreline site of Curayacu (Lanning 1960). Interior decoration was also common at inland sites of the Manchay culture such as Garagay in Rimac and Huacoy in Chillón (Ludeña 1970, 1973; Ravines et al. 1984).

The presence of this unusual decorative convention alone would be enough to make an argument for the central coast origin for some of the Ofrendas Gallery pieces; additionally, some of the vessels in the Ofrendas Gallery display Manchay iconography. Although the pottery in question occurs in a gallery next to Chavín de Huántar's circular courtyard, few of the motifs on the plates and bowls resemble the images on the stone sculptures there. Several of the Dragoniano vessels show a profile head with an eccentric eye and a nasal extrusion (e.g., Lumbreras 2007:fig. 314). This image is well-known from the atrium frieze at Garagay and is also found on pottery from Ancón (Burger 1992:43–46). Other Ofrendas Gallery vessels show elements of style common on Manchay culture pottery but absent elsewhere. For example, several Ofrendas Gallery vessels display an element consisting of a series of three or four parallel diagonal lines incised near the base of fang-like elements (Lumbreras 1971:figs.18, 20, 21). This unusual convention is widely used in the religious images on central coast pottery from Ancón, Curayacu, and other Manchay culture sites but is absent in the pottery assemblages from Chavín de Huántar and elsewhere (Burger 1992:fig. 46; Rosas 2007:drawing 39c). When these elements are combined with other distinctive ceramic features, it is hard to avoid the conclusion that a significant portion of the decorated pottery from the Ofrendas Gallery was produced on the central coast.

The pattern of bringing elaborately decorated pottery from the central coast to Chavín de Huántar was not limited to the bowls and plates but also includes elaborately incised bottles. In contrast to the evidence from Chavín de Huántar, pottery similar to the ceramics from the central coast has not been encountered during the extensive excavations at the northern highland monumental centers of Kuntur Wasi and Pacopampa (Inokuchi 2010; Onuki and Kato 1995; Seki et al. 2010).

The hypothesis that the pottery vessels found in the Ofrendas Gallery were brought by pilgrims from the central coast is consistent with a petrographic study by Isabelle Druc of sherds recovered at Chavín de Huántar (Druc 1998; Druc et al. 2001). In a relatively small sample from the ceremonial core and the residential area, she identified evidence for a bowl, a jar, and two bottles that, based on a study of the paste, had been brought to Chavín de Huántar from Ancón. She also found a dozen other vessels that had similar paste and may have been brought from another yet unlocated central coast area near Ancón. Interestingly, all of the sherds identified as coming from Ancón date to the Urabarriu and Chakinani phases at Chavín de Huántar.

The presence of Manchay-style pottery in a gallery of the Old Temple at Chavín de Huántar and in the residences nearby is important for various reasons. First, assuming the ceramics were brought by pilgrims, it indicates direct contact between individuals from the central coast and the religious authorities and residents of Chavín de Huántar. The exotic pottery confirms that this began in the late Initial Period and continued into the Early Horizon. Second, because many of the pottery pieces in the Ofrendas Gallery could be restored, it is possible to identify the motifs represented on the complex incised bottles, bowls, and plates believed to come from the central coast and, as we have noted, many of them display symbols of the Manchay culture (e.g., Lumbreras 1971:fig. 19, 21, 2007:figs. 297–320). This implies that objects with Manchay culture religious themes were acceptable as gifts or at the very least as containers of gifted food and drink at the highland temple. A pattern of coexisting compatible religious traditions, none claiming sole validity, is foreign to contemporary Western society, but it was widespread in the Andes during Inca times.

A few of the vessels of possible central coast origin from the Ofrendas Gallery show versions of the monstrous felines, birds, and other supernaturals known from the Chavín de Huántar stone sculptures (e.g., Lumbreras 1971:figs. 11–13, 18). Pottery recovered from the late Initial Period and Early Horizon refuse at Ancón includes incised decoration illustrating the felines and birds of Chavín de Huántar iconography as well as images and symbols more typical of the Manchay culture. This suggests an acceptance by some of the central coast population of the power of the Chavín de Huántar temple and its pantheon.

The flow of pilgrims returning to their homes from Chavín de Huántar offers a mechanism by which Chavín-style decorative elements and vessel shapes could have been introduced into the central coast during the late Initial Period, a process that continued over the following centuries of the Early Horizon. It is likely that pilgrims arriving back on the central coast brought news of the remarkable pan-regional center to their homeland and, perhaps as a result of the experiences of these pilgrims,

potters on the central coast began to emulate new decorative techniques from Chavín de Huántar and other sites in contact with it. Pottery with Chavín-related decorative techniques such as plain rocker stamping, dentate rocker stamping, and appliqué modeling eventually displaced vessels with zoned red-and-beige bichrome painting, cane stamping, geometric motifs, and zoned punctations that had been characteristic of local late Initial Period styles on the central coast.

As noted, one of the new vessel forms adopted was the stirrup-spouted bottle, a form that had no local antecedent but had appeared earlier in the northern highlands and north coast. Judging from residue analysis of samples from Ancón, some of these stirrup-spout bottles were used for holding a corn beverage, probably maize beer (or chicha). At Ancón, this drink was sometimes enhanced with flavoring from the algarroba tree (Sadie Weber, personal communication 2018). Given the traditional importance of corn beer in Andean ceremonial life during later times and the impracticality of the stirrup-spouted vessel form, it is possible that the bottles may have played a role in the household religious rituals of the fisherfolk at sites like Curayacu and Ancón.

This model of the spread of the Chavín religious system and its impact on the Early Horizon culture of the central coast assumes that it was the agency of residents of the central coast valleys that was ultimately responsible for this change in behavior. There is no evidence that the ideology was imposed by coercion, nor is there evidence that there would have been powerful economic advantages to becoming part of the Chavín Interaction Sphere. Why Chavín de Huántar became an attractive sacred destination to distant coastal populations is unknown. Was it a growing dissatisfaction with the local religious system and its leaders, or was it the expanding pan-regional reputation of the highland temple's ceremonies and, perhaps, its oracular predictions? Did Chavín de Huántar ever establish a branch oracle or cult center on the center coast, as Burger speculated in 1988? So little fieldwork has been carried out on the central coast for this time period that it remains impossible to evaluate this idea. And even if a formal branch oracle of the Chavín cult was not established, its beliefs could still have been brought back to the central coast by pilgrims returning from their visit to the unique highland site.

The Transformation of the Central Coast during the Early Horizon

It is remarkable that although the valleys of the central coast have been surveyed on multiple occasions by Peruvian and foreign scholars, no evidence has been found of large settlements or monumental constructions during the Early Horizon. The Peruvian government air photography service (SAN) and satellite imagery provide total coverage of this region, and these images have been combed in vain for evidence of major Early Horizon centers. There were, however, two small shoreline communities, Ancón and Curayacu, that continued to be occupied during the Early Horizon and a third fishing village, Chira-Villa, that was abandoned toward the end of the Initial Period (Escarcena 2010; Lanning 1960).

Similarly, by the beginning of the Early Horizon, circa 800 BC, all of the U-shaped centers appear to have fallen into disuse. In a few cases, such as La Florida, Garagay, and San Jacinto, some Early Horizon pottery has been recovered, but it seems likely that this material was the result of ephemeral reoccupations or squatter settlements. At Garagay, the public architecture on the summit of the main mound dates to the late Initial Period, so reoccupation seems the most plausible explanation for the Early Horizon refuse.

As noted, there is no evidence on the central coast for the founding of large Early Horizon public centers or major residential sites, and the evidence for small villages is limited. Yet it does not seem likely that the large agricultural population that existed during the late Initial Period disappeared completely during the Early Horizon. At the shoreline villages of Ancón and Curayacu, a diet of domesticated cultigens continued to be consumed regularly, implying the existence of inland farming communities from whom these foodstuffs could

have been obtained (Cohen 1978; Sadie Weber, personal communication 2018).

Moreover, it should be recalled that despite the numerous Initial Period public centers on the central coast discussed previously, no coeval hamlets or villages had been located in the lower valley. While the excavations at Cardal, Mina Perdida, and Manchay Bajo encountered residential areas adjacent to the public architecture at all three sites, the number of people living there would have been insufficient to build and maintain the adjacent U-shaped monumental complexes (Burger 1987, 1992). Therefore, it would seem likely that most of the Initial Period population lived on the valley floor in small hamlets and villages that were scattered among the agricultural fields. This settlement pattern would be archaeologically invisible using conventional surface surveys or aerial and satellite reconnaissance. If a pattern of dispersed population existed in the Initial Period, it probably persisted into the Early Horizon. Unfortunately, these habitation sites have either been destroyed or currently lie beneath several meters of alluvial and colluvial deposits.

Evidence of Early Horizon habitation has survived in rocky ravines, particularly in the mid-valley locations of Rimac and Lurín, but most of these sites have been badly damaged by rockslides and modern development. Jonathan Palacios (2017) reports the remains of modest Early Horizon houses, hearths, pits, and garbage deposits in erosional cuts made by the Huaycoloro River, a tributary of the Rimac. The Early Horizon cultural materials encountered by Palacios near Chosica usually alternate ceramics and other refuse with layers of clay. These mixed clay and archaeological deposits have been exploited to make unbaked adobes and fired bricks for contemporary Lima. The stratigraphic context of these Early Horizon materials constitutes evidence of destructive flooding caused by a series of El Niño events. This finding seems to confirm that, as has been suggested on the basis of other evidence, localized climatic disturbances from El Niño were common during the Early Horizon in comparison with earlier times (Sandweiss et al. 2001).

The absence of large public constructions during the Early Horizon on the central coast contrasts

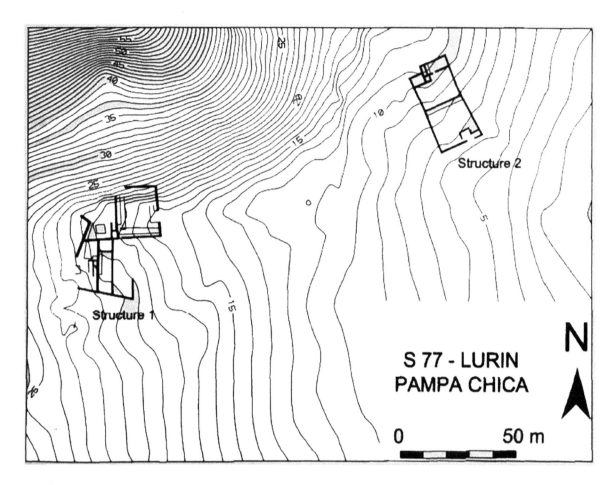

figure 9.14
The architectural layout of Pampa Chica. Drawing by Jalh Dulanto.

sharply with the pattern in these valleys during the Initial Period. Apparently, the centuries following the abandonment of the Manchay civic-ceremonial centers were characterized by a society that was organized very differently than during the Initial Period, and it seems evident that this new form of sociopolitical organization lacked the ability or motivation to mobilize public labor on a large scale.

Nonetheless, judging from the archaeological site of Pampa Chica in the Lurín Valley, not all group activity was discontinued. In 1992, a PUCP team led by Krzysztof Makowski encountered a site in a rocky ravine near the U-shaped civic-ceremonial center of Manchay Bajo. After extensive excavations directed by Jalh Dulanto, Pampa Chica was interpreted as a public site with a focus on ancestor veneration (Dulanto 2002, 2009). Judging from a suite of radiocarbon dates, Pampa Chica appears to have

been used between 700 and 400 BC, and the pottery recovered there is consistent with this estimate.

Pampa Chica is located 17 km inland from the Pacific shores, midway between the valley bottom and the Lomas de Atacongo. It consists of two small building complexes, the larger of which measures 45 × 37 m and includes patios, terraces, and orthogonal rooms (Figure 9.14). The lower portion of the structure has open spaces that favor public displays, while the upper zone consists of numerous small rooms and closed spaces (Figure 9.15). The terraces are crudely made and take advantage of local stone and the natural topography. The amount of labor that would have been required for the constructions is modest.

There is evidence for large-scale preparation and storage of food, areas for food consumption, and spaces for ritual activity involving repeated burial,

figure 9.15
The architecture at Pampa Chica. Photograph by Jalh Dulanto.

removal, manipulation, and reinterment of human remains. Judging from the built environments, the number of people involved in these activities would not have been large. The open spaces are not comparable to those of the U-shaped centers, where centrally located open plaza areas frequently cover several hectares. Judging from the size and layout of Pampa Chica, it could have served only a fraction of the population that had once been involved in the activities at the nearby U-shaped centers. This suggests that during the Early Horizon the population in the Lurín Valley had diminished in size or that it had become more fragmented, with smaller groups worshipping at a greater number of yet undiscovered small ritual centers.

Based on the radiocarbon assays, Pampa Chica is contemporary with the zenith of Chavín de Huántar (Burger 2019), but no evidence of stone sculpture or any other feature or artifact associated with the Chavín cult was found there. The concept

of making ancestor veneration the central focus of ritual marks a departure from the religious system of the Manchay culture, and it is also alien to Chavín religious practice. Makowski has observed that the inhabitants of Pampa Chica appear to have mined building materials from the nearby U-shaped center of Manchay Bajo, thus reinforcing the impression that an ideological break had occurred with the Manchay culture ceremonial system of the Initial Period. It is also significant that the ceramics recovered from Pampa Chica show more similarities to pottery from the south coast of Peru than northern centers such as Chavín de Huántar. For example, bowls with resist-painted motifs similar to those from Cerrillos in Ica and Puerto Nuevo in Paracas (Figure 9.16) (Dulanto 2013; Wallace 1962) are particularly common in the assemblage from Pampa Chica (Jalh Dulanto, personal communication 2018).

However, it would be a mistake to conclude, based on evidence from a single small ritual center

figure 9.16
Resist painted
pottery from Pampa
Chica. Photograph
by Jalh Dulanto.

such as Pampa Chica, that the Chavín Phenomenon had little impact on the central coast during the Early Horizon or that a total cultural rupture occurred. It is important to balance the insights gained from Pampa Chica with the contrasting and complementary understanding that can be gained by considering the Early Horizon deposits at Ancón and Curayacu. In contrast to Pampa Chica, the data from the two shoreline sites suggest a significant degree of continuity between 1800 and 450 BC, with little indication of disruption at the end of the Initial Period. Technical analyses of the textile and ceramic collections from Ancón show evidence not only of cultural continuity but also of a population that was deeply conservative in most respects. After a study of 1,436 fragments of textiles from the Initial Period and Early Horizon at Ancón, Dwight Wallace was able to identify differences between the Early Horizon textiles of Ancón and those of the Supe Valley on the north-central coast as well as those those valleys further to the north (Wallace, personal communication 1991). He could also delineate contrasts in textile-production technique between Ancón and those from Cerrillos in the Ica Valley of the south coast. The regional differences that existed in textile traditions during the Early Horizon can be traced to local weaving practices beginning in the Initial Period. Wallace concludes that the degree of change in Ancón's textiles during the Early Horizon was small in comparison with other areas. At Ancón, the textiles were made entirely of cotton, and the lack of exotic techniques from other zones convinced him that there had been limited contact between the weavers of Ancón and those of the highlands. This impression was reinforced by the complete absence of camelid fiber from the large sample of cloth from Ancón.

Wallace's conclusions concerning the textiles are paralleled by those of Isabelle Druc in her technical analysis of Initial Period and Early Horizon ceramics (Druc 1998; Druc et al. 2001). She concludes that, despite the shifts in style mentioned earlier, the technological tradition and the ceramic resources used at Ancón did not change during the Initial Period and Early Horizon. During the Early Horizon, 92 percent of the ceramics were locally produced and the clays and tempers employed were drawn from deposits near Ancón and from an outcrop 10 km inland. These were the same sources that had been used during the Initial Period. According to Druc, "the type, size angularity of the rock fragments stay the same from the early Initial Period to the Early Horizon attesting to the transmission of knowledge and recipes across generations of craft people" (Druc et al. 2001). The evidence in unbroken traditions of textile and pottery production suggests a long-term occupation by a stable population that was not disrupted or replaced by outsiders.

Similarly, Mark Nathan Cohen's review of food remains recovered from Ancón and other early sites on the central coast does not reveal the introduction of new crops during the Early Horizon. The cultigens grown and consumed during the Early Horizon were basically the same as those during the Initial Period (Cohen 1978). In 1986, a more quantitatively oriented study was carried out at Ancón focusing on hypothetical crises in the subsistence system during the Initial Period and Early Horizon. Peruvian archaeologist Alberto Miller sampled the deep refuse at the site in order to systematically collect and measure food remains from the entire sequence (Miller 1986). He has concluded that there was remarkable continuity in Ancón's subsistence system, with no indication of major shifts or transformations produced either by ecological or demographic crises. The main source of protein consistently came from fish, particularly small species such as anchovy and pejerrey (silverside). Some of these were dried and preserved using a procedure developed by the end of the Preceramic period. In addition, twenty-four species of shellfish were collected, including six species of bivalves. Miller found almost no variation in the types or sizes of fish and shellfish being exploited during the one thousand four hundred years that Ancón was occupied. There also was evidence of bones from birds such as cormorants, gannets, and sea gulls as well as from mammals such as sea lions, sea turtles, guinea pigs, llamas, and dogs. However, these animals never constituted major elements in the diet (Miller 1986). Significantly, like Cohen, Miller found no indication at Ancón of a shift to a diet rich in maize or camelid meat during the Early Horizon occupation.

While many of the aspects of daily life at Ancón showed little evidence of change, the style of the pottery reflected shifts in community identity and the increased involvement of the shoreline residents with groups outside the drainage. The potters at Ancón abandoned or diminished many of the conventions that had made central coast pottery distinctive and, as already noted, they began creating pottery that was similar to that being crafted at Chavín de Huántar and other highland and coastal centers tied to that preeminent center during the Chakinani and Janabarriu phases. The introduction of forms and decoration characteristic of Janabarriu-related ceramic assemblages into Ancón is particularly noteworthy (see Figure 9.13). Assemblages in this style are found throughout much of northern and central Peru during the Early Horizon, and they have

figure 9.17
Modeled
anthropomorphic
head on a bottle spout
from Ancón, possibly
showing influence from
Jequetepeque on the
north coast. Photograph
by Nicholas Brown.

0 cm   5 cm   10 cm

been referred to as the Chavín International Style by Michelle Young (this volume). They have been interpreted as conscious expressions of an emerging pan-regional identity in local communities (Burger 1988, 1992, 1993). If this interpretation is correct, then the occupants of Ancón and other shoreline communities were intentionally signaling their desire to be considered part of the Chavín Interaction Sphere through the style of the pottery they produced and consumed. In many cases, this pottery, a product of local emulation, is difficult to distinguish from coeval pottery at Chavín de Huántar. In some cases, the iconography on the vessels can be linked directly with the religious iconography of the Chavín temple; thus, it is likely that pilgrims from Ancón continued

to visit that site during the first three hundred years of the Early Horizon.

Ancón's involvement in the pan-regional sphere of interaction linked to Chavín de Huántar is also indicated by an increase in the number of ceramics with exotic styles. In Patterson's collections from the Early Horizon occupation at Ancón, there are sherds related to the Cupisnique style, probably from the Moche or Chicama Valleys, and from the far north coast, perhaps Piura (see also Rosas 2007:drawing 26). One bottle neck from Ancón has the form of an anthropomorphic head, and it resembles vessels said to come from Jequetepeque (Figure 9.17) (Alva 1986). In these cases, further analysis is needed to determine if the pieces are imports or products of

figure 9.18
Ancón decorated sherds
with influence from
the Ica Valley and the
Paracas Peninsula,
judging from decorative
techniques such as resist
painting, post-fire resin
painting, and crenellated
rims. Photograph by
Nicholas Brown.

0 cm   5 cm   10 cm

emulation. Their rarity suggests imports, but this needs to be confirmed using scientific methods.

More common in the Early Horizon layers at Ancón are materials apparently brought from the south coast, including a small number of Paracas-style sherds with post-fire resin painting and others with resist painting (Figure 9.18). There are also bowl fragments with crenellated rims. These alien stylistic features resemble ceramics excavated at Cerrillos in Ica and at Puerto Nuevo in Paracas (Dulanto 2009, this volume; Wallace 1962). They are quite rare, well

under 1 percent of the Ancón assemblage, and given the exotic character and complexity of the decorative techniques employed, emulation seems an unlikely explanation.

These possible imports from the north and south coast suggest that the world in which Ancón's occupants lived was a more cosmopolitan one than that of their Initial Period ancestors, despite the collapse of the U-shaped centers. The occasional presence at Ancón of cinnabar pigment on pottery and obsidian flakes from the south-central highlands

figure 9.19
Ancón oxidized
sherds that may
reflect influence from
the southern central
coast (e.g., Cañete).
Photograph by
Nicholas Brown.

0 cm   5 cm   10 cm

confirms that the Early Horizon world was more
conducive to movement and exchange than that of
the Initial Period. The pottery evidence also suggests
that contacts with the south coast had intensified.
Significantly, at Puerto Nuevo, numerous fragments
were recovered that strongly resemble the Early
Horizon ceramics from Ancón (Dulanto 2009);
these could represent imports from Ancón or emulations of pottery from the Ancón area.

The Early Horizon assemblage from Ancón also
shows evidence of influences that Edward Lanning

and Tom Patterson believed came from the northern portion of the south coast (i.e., Cañete, Topará,
and Chincha drainages), a zone associated with the
poorly defined Topará style that is usually dated
to the late Early Horizon and Early Intermediate
Period (Lanning 1967). Patterson (1971) interprets
the increase at Ancón in thin orange oxidized pottery as a reflection of this southern influence. The
surface of these vessels is often brushed, combed,
or left undecorated and generally lacks the decorative techniques associated with Chavín de Huántar.

There are also thin orange versions of new forms such as spout-and-bridge bottles (Figure 9.19). These same trends were detected by Palacios in the mid-valley sites of Rimac (Palacios 1987:figs. 19–21), and while many or all of these oxidized ceramics may have been locally produced, the decision to emulate this alien style reinforces the impression of increased involvement by the Early Horizon communities of the central coast with their neighbors to the south.

Discussion and Conclusions

As seen in this overview, the relation of the central coast to the Chavín Phenomenon is a complex one. It does not easily fit into traditional narratives of the Chavín horizon or Chavín civilization. While the Initial Period culture of the central coast, known as the Manchay culture, may have been a source of inspiration for highland Chavín civilization, no major Early Horizon Chavín-related center has been identified on the central coast. And while some communities of the central coast chose to participate in the Chavín Interaction Sphere, their integration into this sphere was not sufficient to save the troubled civic-ceremonial centers that had flourished in the lower and middle valleys of the central coast during the Initial Period.

Participation in the Chavín Interaction Sphere did, however, produce a more cosmopolitan sense of identity than the one that had existed during the Initial Period. It also resulted in increased contact with distant societies, including those in highland Ancash, the north coast, and the south coast. It is likely that some of these interactions involved the Chavín religious cult and pilgrimages by individuals from the central coast to the oracular center at Chavín de Huántar. The impact of these visits on pilgrims led potters to emulate the exotic styles they encountered there. It also seems to have stimulated the occasional importation of foreign pottery and small amounts of other exotic materials. Nonetheless, this interaction and broadening of identity appears to have had only limited impact. It did not produce changes in the local subsistence economy, nor did it

result in the introduction or adoption of new technologies, cultigens, or craft products.

Chavín civilization has been justly credited with the development and dissemination of a host of revolutionary technologies (Burger 1988, 1992; Conklin 1978; Lechtman 1980). The apparent failure of the Chavín Phenomenon to introduce them to the sites on the central coast probably should not come as a shock. Most of the Early Horizon technological innovations were not intended to produce any clear-cut savings of energy. On the contrary, surpluses would have been required to allow these technologies to exist. What the new technologies did provide was a means of creating objects that were immediately distinguishable from other items. These items were especially suitable and effective as emblems of religious and political authority (Burger 1988:130). Given the lack of evidence on the central coast for social stratification and the apparent absence of major religious centers during the Early Horizon, it is understandable that awe-inspiring items, such as brightly dyed wool textiles, gold jewelry, or sculpted stone tenon heads, are lacking. On the contrary, following the collapse of the Manchay-culture centers at the end of Initial Period, the central coast appears to have experienced a period of social fragmentation and possible population decline. During this time of troubles, old civic-ceremonial centers were abandoned and new centers were created for ritual practices focusing on ancestor veneration to serve a dispersed agricultural population. These new foci of social life were small in scale and required little group labor compared to the Initial Period antecedents.

Life continued uninterrupted in shoreline fishing communities such as Ancón, although judging from the style and iconography of their pottery, they appear to have participated in the Chavín cult and the pan-regional sphere of interaction that it generated. But while their sense of identity transformed into one that was less provincial and more inclusive, there seems to have been little change in everyday existence. The population living on the central coast did not change into a more complex and stratified society as a result of being incorporated into the Chavín Interaction Sphere, as could be argued for Peru's south coast or south-central highlands

(DeLeonardis, this volume; Matsumoto and Cavero Palomino, this volume; Young, this volume), nor did it resist alien influence by developing its own distinctive and dynamic alternative to Chavín culture, such as occurred in some valleys of the north coast (see Chicoine, Ikehara-Tsukayama, and Shibata, this volume). Given the lack of large centers, it would not be unreasonable to suggest that the central coast may have devolved into what might be regarded as a cultural backwater during the Early Horizon. The Chavín-related innovations touted by archaeologists were probably more relevant to those living in regions characterized by stratified societies with large civic-ceremonial centers and powerful elites than they were to the populations of the central coast.

Between 500 and 400 BC, Ancón, Curayacu, Pampa Chica, and other settlements on the central coast seem to have been abandoned. This is roughly the same time that Chavín de Huántar, Pacopampa, and many of the other large highland centers also experienced disruptions. The pan-regional interaction sphere centered around Chavín de Huántar ceased to exist, and judging from the disappearance of its distinctive iconography throughout much of Peru, there also appears to have been a crisis of faith among those who had embraced the Chavín cult.

What produced this disruption over such a vast and varied area, one that includes the central coast, remains one of the vexing problems in Andean archaeology. Factors such as catastrophic earthquakes, environmental downturns, and the emergence of a culture of violence have all been mentioned as possible factors, but the cause or causes remains uncertain. What is clear from the archaeological record of the central coast, however, is that the cultures and societies that emerged from this process were radically different than those of its ancestors. The sociocultural transformation seen during the final centuries of the Early Horizon at sites such as the Tablada de Lurín and Villa Salvador is reflected in changes in the foodways, technology, architecture, ceramic style, paleopathology, and other aspects of the culture (Burger and Makowski 2009). Along the central coast, these transformations appear to have been even more profound than those produced centuries before by the appearance of the Chavín Phenomenon.

Acknowledgments

We are grateful to Nicholas Brown, Jalh Dulanto, Christopher Milan, Jeffrey Quilter, and Samantha Ware for their assistance. This essay is dedicated to Thomas C. Patterson and the inspiration he has provided as teacher, investigator, and friend.

REFERENCES CITED

Alva, Ignacio
    2010   Los complejos de Cerro Ventarrón y Collud-Zarpán: Del Precerámico al Formativo en el valle de Lambayeque. *Boletín de Arqueología PUCP* 12:97–117.

Alva, Walter
    1986   *Cerámica temprana en el valle de Jequetepeque, norte del Perú.* Materialen fur allgemeinen und vergleichenden Archaeologie 32. KAVA, Bonn.

Bonavia, Duccio
    1965   *Arqueología de Lurín: Seis sitios de ocupación en la parte inferior del valle.* Tesis Antropológicas 4. Instituto de Estudios Etnológicos del Museo Nacional de la Cultura Peruana y el Departamento de Antropología de UNMSM, Lima.

Burger, Richard L.
    1981   The Radiocarbon Evidence for the Temporal Priority of Chavín de Huántar. *American Antiquity* 46(3):562–602.

    1984   *The Prehistoric Occupation of Chavín de Huántar, Peru.* University of California Press, Berkeley.

1987   The U-Shaped Pyramid Complex, Cardal, Perú. *National Geographic Research* 3(3):363–375.

1988   Unity and Heterogeneity within the Chavín Horizon. In *Peruvian Prehistory: An Overview of Pre-Inca and Inca Society*, edited by Richard Keatinge, pp. 99–144. Cambridge University Press, Cambridge.

1992   *Chavín and the Origins of Andean Civilization*. Thames and Hudson, New York.

1993   The Chavín Horizon: Stylistic Chimera or Socioeconomic Metamorphosis? In *Latin American Horizons*, edited by Don Rice, pp. 41–82. Dumbarton Oaks Research Library and Collection, Washington, D.C.

2003   El Niño, Civilizational Origins and Human Agency: Some Thoughts from the Lurín Valley. *Fieldiana Botany New Series* 43:90–107.

2008   Chavín de Huántar and Its Sphere of Influence. In *Handbook of South American Archaeology*, edited by Helaine Silverman and William Isbell, pp. 681–703. Springer, New York.

2009   Los fundamentos sociales de la arquitectura monumental del período inicial en el valle de Lurín. In *Arqueología del período formativo en la Cuenca Baja de Lurín*, vol. I, edited by Richard L. Burger and Krzysztof Makowski, pp. 17–36. Fondo Editorial, Pontificia Universidad Católica del Perú, Lima.

2019   Understanding the Socioeconomic Trajectory of Chavín de Huántar: A New Radiocarbon Sequence and Its Wider Implications. *Latin American Antiquity* 30(2):373–392.

2022   Evaluating the Architectural Sequence and Chronology of Chavín de Huántar: The Case of the Circular Plaza. *Peruvian Archaeology* 5:24–49. University of Yamagata, Japan.

Burger, Richard L., and Krzysztof Makowski (editors)

2009   *Arqueología del período formativo en la Cuenca Baja de Lurín*. Fondo Editorial, Pontificia Universidad Católica del Perú, Lima.

Burger, Richard L., and Ramiro Matos Mendieta

2002   Atalla: A Center on the Periphery of the Chavín Horizon. *Latin American Antiquity* 13(2):153–177.

Burger, Richard L., and Lucy C. Salazar

1991   The Second Season of Investigation at the Initial Period Center of Cardal, Peru. *Journal of Field Archaeology* 18:275–296.

1994   La organización dual en el ceremonial andino temprano: Un repaso comparativo. In *El mundo ceremonial andino*, edited by Luis Millones and Yoshio Onuki, pp. 97–116. Editorial Horizonte, Lima.

1998   A Sacred Effigy from Mina Perdida and the Unseen Ceremonies of the Peruvian Formative. *Res: Anthropology and Aesthetics* 33:28–53.

2008   The Manchay Culture and the Coastal Inspiration for Highland Chavín Civilization. In *Chavín: Art, Architecture, and Culture*, edited by William J. Conklin and Jeffrey Quilter, pp. 85–105. Cotsen Institute of Archaeology, University of California, Los Angeles.

2012   Monumental Public Complexes and Agricultural Expansion on Peru's Central Coast during the Second Millennium BC. In *Early New World Monumentality*, edited by Richard L. Burger and Robert Rosenswig, pp. 399–430. University of Press of Florida, Gainesville.

2014   ¿Centro de qué? Los sitios con arquitectura pública de la cultura Manchay en la Costa Central del Perú. In *El centro ceremonial andino: Nuevas perspectivas para los periodos arcaico y formativo*, edited by Yuji Seki, pp. 291–313. National Museum of Ethnology, Osaka.

2019   New Insights into the Architecture and Organization of Cardal. In *New Perspectives on the Socioeconomic Organization of Formative Peru*, edited by Richard L. Burger, Lucy C. Salazar, and Yuji Seki, pp. 49–65. Yale University Publications in Anthropology 94. Yale University Press, New Haven.

Cancho, Christian G.

2017   Hacia un modelo de organización espacial dual tras la prácticas constructivas en Huando "B," un complejo en "U" del formativo medio del valle de Chancay. Unpublished thesis, Pontificia Universidad Católica del Perú, Lima.

Carrión, Lucénida

1998   Excavaciones en San Jacinto, templo en U en el valle de Chancay. *Boletín de Arqueología PUCP* 2:239–250.

2000   Análisis e interpretación de la ceramica formativa del centro ceremonial en "U" de San Jacinto. *Arqueológicas* 24:195–262.

Carrión Cachot, Rebeca

1948   La cultura Chavín: Dos nuevas colonias Kuntur Wasi y Ancón. *Revista del Museo Nacional de Antropología y Arqueología* 2(1):99–172.

Casafranca, Jose

1960   Los nuevos sitios arqueológicos chavinoides en el Departamento de Ayacucho. In *Antiguo Perú espacio y tiempo*, edited by Ramiro Matos Mendieta, pp. 325–334. Librería Editorial Juan Mejia Baca, Lima.

Chevalier, Alexander

2002   L'exploitation de plantes sur la cote péruvienne en context foratif. Unpublished thesis, Geneva University, Geneva.

Clasby, Ryan

2019   Perspectives on Early Andean Civilization Diachronic Changes in Sociopolitical Developments and Interregional Interaction in the Early Horizon Eastern Montane Forest. In *Perspectives on Early Andean Civilization in Peru: Interaction, Authority and Socioeconomic Organization during the First and Second Millennia BC*, edited by Richard L. Burger, Lucy C. Salazar, and Yuji Seki, pp. 149–171. Yale University Press, New Haven.

Cohen, Mark Nathan

1979   Archaeological Plant Remains from the Central Coast of Peru. *Nawpa Pacha: Journal of Andean Archaeology* 16:23–50.

Conklin, William

1978   Revolutionary Weaving Inventions of the Early Horizon. *Ñawpa Pacha: Journal of Andean Archaeology* 16:1–12.

Druc, Isabelle C.

1998   *Ceramic Production and Distribution in the Chavín Sphere of Influence, North-Central Andes*. BAR International Series 731. Hadrian Books, Oxford.

Druc, Isabelle C., Richard L. Burger, Regina Zamojska, and Pierre Magny

2001   Ancón and Garagay Ceramic Production at the Time of Chavín de Huántar. *Journal of Archaeological Science* 28(1):29–43.

Dulanto, Jalh

2002   The Archaeological Study of Ancestor Cult Practices: The Case of Pampa Chica, a Late Initial Period and Early Horizon Site on the Central Coast of Peru. In *The Space and Place of Death*, edited by Helaine Silverman and D. B. Small, pp. 97–117. Archaeological Papers of the American Anthropological Association, Chicago.

2009   Pampa Chica? Que sucedió en la costa central después del abandono de los templos en "U"? In *Arqueología del período formativo en la Cuenca Baja de Lurín*, edited by Richard L. Burger and Krzysztof Makowski, pp. 377–399. Pontificia Universidad Católica del Perú, Lima.

2013   Puerto Nuevo: Redes de intercambio a larga distancia durante la primera mitad del primer mileno antes de nuestra era. *Boletín de Arqueología PUCP* 17:103–132.

Engel, Frédéric

1956   Curayacu, a Chavinoid Site. *Archaeology* 9(2):98–105.

Escarcena, Pablo Augusto

2010   Investigaciones arqueológicas en Chira-Villa. Licenciatura thesis, Universidad Nacional Mayor de San Marcos, Lima.

Fuentes, Jose Luis

2012   Huaca La Florida: La secuencia cronológica de un templo en U en el valle del Rimac. *Arqueología y sociedad* 24:191–226.

Gorriti, Manuel Martin

2009   Una primera aproximación al consumo de moluscos en el sitio formativo de Mina Perdida. In *Arqueología del período formativo en la Cuenca Baja de Lurín*, edited by Richard L. Burger and

Krzysztof Makowski, pp. 111–117. Fondo Editorial, Pontificia Universidad Católica del Perú, Lima.

Inokuchi, Kinya

2010   La arquitectura de Kuntur Wasi: Secuencia constructiva y cronología de un centro ceremonial del período formativo. *Boletín de Arqueología PUCP* 12:219–247.

Kroeber, Alfred

1944   *Peruvian Archaeology in 1942.* Viking Fund Publications in Anthropology 4. Wenner Gren Foundation, New York.

La Barre, Weston

1971   Materials for a History of Crisis Cults: A Bibliographic Essay. *Current Anthropology* 12(1):3-44.

Lanning, Edward P.

1960   Chronological and Cultural Relationships of Early Pottery Styles in Ancient Peru. PhD dissertation, University of California, Berkeley.

1961   Cerámica pintada pre-Chavín de la costa central del Perú. *Revista del Museo Nacional* 30:78–83.

1963   An Early Ceramic Style from Ancón, Central Coast of Peru. *Ñawpa Pacha: Journal of Andean Archaeology* 1:47–59.

1967   *Peru before the Incas.* Prentice-Hall, Englewood.

Lechtman, Heather

1980   The Central Andes: Metallurgy without Iron. In *The Coming of the Age of Iron*, edited by T. Wertime and J. Muhly, pp. 267–334. Yale University Press, New Haven.

Ludeña, Hugo

1970   San Humberto, un sitio formativo en el valle de Chillón (informe preliminar). *Arqueología y sociedad* 2:36–45.

1973   Investigaciones arqueológicas en el sitio de Huacoy, valle de Chillón. PhD dissertation, Universidad Nacional Mayor de San Marcos, Lima.

Lumbreras, Luis G.

1971   Towards a Re-evaluation of Chavín. In *Dumbarton Oaks Conference on Chavín*, edited by Elizabeth P. Benson, pp. 1–28.

Dumbarton Oaks Research Library and Collection, Washington, D.C.

1977   Excavaciones en el Templo Antiguo de Chavín (sector R): Informe de la sexta campaña. *Ñawpa Pacha: Journal of Andean Archaeology* 15:1–38.

2007   *Chavín de Huántar: Excavaciones arqueológicas.* 2 vols. Universidad Alas Peruanas, Lima.

Milan, Christopher

2014   The Initial Period (1800–800 BC) Occupation of the Middle Lurín Valley: A Discussion on the Interactions Between Early Civic Ceremonial Centers on the Central Coast of Peru and Nearby Hamlets. PhD dissertation, Yale University, New Haven.

Miller, Alberto

1986   Economic Prehistory at the Ancón Tank Site: A Test of Demographic Explanations of Agricultural Origins in the Ancón-Chillón Region, Central Peruvian Coast. PhD dissertation, State University of New York, Binghamton.

Moseley, Michael

1968   Late Preceramic and Early Ceramic Cultures of the Central Coast of Peru. *Ñawpa Pacha: Journal of Andean Archaeology* 6:115–133.

Moseley, Michael, and Linda Barrett

1969   Change in Preceramic Twined Textiles from the Central Peruvian Coast. *American Antiquity* 34(2):162–165.

Muelle, Jorge, and Rogger Ravines

1973   Los estratos precerámicos de Ancón. *Revista del Museo Nacional* 39:49–70.

Onuki, Yoshio, and Y. Kato

1995   *Las excavaciones en Kuntur Wasi, Peru: La primera etapa 1988–1990.* University of Tokyo Press, Tokyo.

Palacios, Jonathan

1988   La secuencia de la cerámica temprana del valle de Lima en Huachipa. *Gaceta arqueológica andina* 16:13–24.

2017   *Agua: Ritual y culto en Yañac (Ñaña); La motaña sagrada.* Universidad Peruana Union, Centro de Aplicación Editorial, Lima.

Patterson, Thomas C.

1971   Chavín: An Interpretation of Its Spread and Influence. In *Dumbarton Oaks Conference on Chavín*, edited by Elizabeth P. Benson, pp. 29–48. Dumbarton Oaks Research Library and Collection, Washington, D.C.

1983   The Historical Development of a Coastal Andean Social Formation in Central Peru, 6000 to 500 BC. In *Understanding the Andean Past: Papers from the First Annual Northeast Conference on Andean Archaeology and Ethnohistory*, edited by Daniel Sandweiss, pp. 21–38. Latin American Studies Program, Cornell University, Ithaca.

1985   La Huaca La Florida, Rimac Valley, Perú. In *Early Ceremonial Architecture in the Andes*, edited by Christopher B. Donnan, pp. 59–69. Dumbarton Oaks Research Library and Collection, Washington, D.C.

Patterson, Thomas C., and Edward Lanning

1964   Changing Settlement Patterns on the Central Peruvian Coast. *Ñawpa Pacha: Journal of Andean Archaeology* 2: 113–123.

Patterson, Thomas C., and Michael Moseley

1968   Late Preceramic and Early Ceramic Cultures of the Central Coast of Peru. *Ñawpa Pacha: Journal of Andean Archaeology* 6:115–133.

Pozorski, Shelia, and Thomas Pozorski

1987   *Early Settlement and Subsistence in the Casma Valley, Peru.* University of Iowa Press, Iowa City.

Quilter, Jeffrey

1989   *Life and Death at Paloma: Society and Mortuary Practice at a Preceramic Peruvian Village.* University of Iowa Press, Iowa City.

Ramón, Gabriel

2011   The Swallow Potters: Seasonally Migratory Styles in the Andes. In *Archaeological Ceramics: A Review of Current Research*, edited by Simona Scarcella, pp. 160–175. BAR International Series, Oxford.

Ravines, Rogger

1984   Sobre la formación de Chavín: Imágenes y símbolos. *Boletín de Lima* 35:27–45.

Ravines, Rogger, and William Isbell

1976   Garagay: Sitio ceremonial temprano en el valle de Lima. *Revista del Museo Nacional* 41:253–275.

Ravines, Rogger, Helen Engelstad, Victoria Palomino, and Daniel Sandweiss

1984   Materiales arqueológicos de Garagay. *Revista del Museo Nacional* 46:135–233.

Rosas, Hermilio

2007   *La secuencia cultural del período formativo en Ancón.* Avqi Edición, Lima.

Rowe, John Howland

1962   *Chavín Art: An Inquiry into Its Form and Meaning.* The Museum of Primitive Art, New York.

Sakai, Masato, and Juan Martínez

2010   Excavaciones en el Templete de Limoncarro, valle de Jequetepeque. *Boletín de Arqueología PUCP* 12:171–201.

Salazar, Lucy C., and Richard L. Burger

1983   La araña en la iconografía del horizonte temprano en la costa norte del Perú. *Beitrage zur allgemeinen und vergleichenden Archaeologie* 4:213–253.

Sandweiss, Daniel, Richard Burger, Kirk Maasch, James Richardson III, and Harold Rollins

2001   Variation in Holocene El Niño Frequencies: Climate Records and Cultural Consequences in Ancient Peru. *Geology* 29(7):603–606.

Scheele, Harry

1970   The Chavín Occupation of the Central Coast of Peru. PhD dissertation, Harvard University, Cambridge, Mass.

Seki, Yuji, Juan Pablo Villanueva, Masato Sakai, Diana Aleman, Mauro Ordoñez, Walter Tosso, Aracela Espinoza, Kinya Inokuchi, and Daniel Morales

2010   Nuevas evidencias del sitio arqueológico de Pacopampa en la Sierra Norte del Perú. *Boletín de Arqueología PUCP* 12:69–95.

Silva, Jorge Elias

1998   Una aproximación del formativo en el valle del Chillón. *Boletín de Arqueología PUCP* 2:251–268.

Silva, Jorge Elias, and Rubén García

1997   Huachipa-Jicamarca: Cronología y desarrollo sociopolítico en el Rímac. *Bulletin de l'Institut Français d'Études Andines* 2(26):195–228.

Tabío, Ernesto

1957   *Excavaciones en la costa central del Perú (1955–1958)*. Academia de Ciencias, La Habana, Cuba.

Tantaleán, Henry, and María Ysela Leyva

2011   Los "Templos en U" del valle de Huaura, costa norcentral: Una aproximación preliminar a un problema monumental. *Bulletin de l'Institut Français d'Études Andines* 40(3):459–493.

Tello, Julio C.

1943   Discovery of the Chavín Culture in Peru. *American Antiquity* 9(1):135–160.

Thorme, Trisha

1999   Patterns of Commerce in the Valley of Lurín in the Initial Period. Paper presented at the Annual Meeting of the Society of American Archaeology, Chicago.

Tykot, Robert, Nicholas van der Merwe, and Richard L. Burger

2006   The Importance of Maize in Initial Period and Early Horizon Peru. In *Histories of Maize: Multidisciplinary Approaches to the Prehistory, Linguistics, Biogeography, Domestication and Evolution of Maize*, edited by John Staller, Robert Tykot, and Bruce Benz, pp. 187–197. Elsevier, New York.

Umlauf, Marcelle

2009   Restos botánicos de Cardal durante el período inicial. In *Arqueología del período formativo en la Cuenca Baja de Lurín*, edited by Richard L. Burger and Krzysztof Makowski, pp. 95–110. Fondo Editorial, Pontificia Universidad Católica del Perú, Lima.

Wallace, Anthony

1956   Revitalization Movements. *American Anthropologist* 58:264–281.

Wallace, Dwight

1962   Cerrillos, an Early Paracas Site in Ica. *American Antiquity* 27:303–314.

Willey, Gordon

1948   Functional Analysis of "Horizon Style" in Peruvian Archaeology. In *A Reappraisal of Peruvian Archaeology*, edited by Wendell Bennett, pp. 8–15. Memoirs of the Society for American Archaeology, no. 4. Society for American Archaeology and the Institute of Andean Research, Menasha, Wisc.

1951   The Chavín Problem: A Review and Critique. *Southwestern Journal of Anthropology* 7(2):103–144.

Williams, Carlos

1971   Centros ceremoniales tempranos en el valle de Chillón, Rimac y Lurín. *Apuntes arqueológicos* 1:1–4.

1980a   Complejos de pirámides con planta en U, patrón arquitectónico de la costa central. *Revista del Museo Nacional* 44:95–110.

1980b   Arquitectura y urbanismo en el antiguo Perú. In *Historia del Perú*, vol. 8, pp. 369–585. Mejía Baca, Lima.

1985   A Scheme for the Early Monumental Architecture of the Central Coast of Peru. In *Early Ceremonial Architecture in the Andes*, edited by Christopher B. Donnan, pp. 227–240. Dumbarton Oaks Research Library and Collection, Washington, D.C.

From the Inside Looking Out

Paracas Perspectives on Chavín

LISA DeLEONARDIS

There is a long-standing consensus that Chavín de Huántar influenced a wide geography of the ancient Andes through the expansion of religious ideology and the intensification of long-distance interaction. These influences are clearly evident in works of art produced by the Paracas culture (ca. 800–200 BC) of south coastal Peru. Nearly a century after Julio C. Tello's work in both regions, questions continue to loom about the relationship. With chronological refinements, better analytical techniques, and the discoveries of new highland and coastal centers, adjustments to our research questions are necessary. How and when the interactions occurred are still of interest, and whether Chavín was the sole impetus for increased interaction or one of many forces factors into our analyses.

Questions about the Chavín–Paracas relationship speak to larger research concerns about how complex ideology is transmitted, received, and materially manifested by its intended audiences. These issues have been addressed primarily through frameworks that position Chavín as the hegemonic purveyor of a persuasive ideology. Arresting images of supernaturals apparent in the visual programs of both led early studies to consider Paracas as a regional or branch cult of Chavín religion (Figure 10.1) (Burger 1995, 2008a; Cordy-Collins 1976; Patterson 1971). Lacking in these models is the matter of agency on the part of the Paracas or the recognition of an established interaction sphere before the advent of Chavín. Yet a compatible ideological environment and shared cultural practices are precisely the factors that would explain Chavín's success in the south, especially in the absence of coercion.

My research offers insight into how the Paracas interpreted and translated Chavín imagery and its attendant ideas. In this essay, I approach the related questions of transmission, reception, and materialization through the lenses of iconographic, technical, and contextual analyses. I examine trends in iconography and design practices and highlight the problems faced in the interpretation of Chavín visual culture on the south coast. Techné is an important factor in these analyses. Paracas artists went to great

271

lengths to acquire materials to practice their craft (DeLeonardis 2016). I am interested in how the preference for materials may have stimulated interaction in local and long-distance exchange networks. The role played by Chavín in this arena is questioned. I also consider contextual analysis of painted textiles. This corpus consists of orthodox Chavín imagery that is reinterpreted and distributed in fragmentary form across tombs. Drawing from my research on fragmentation (DeLeonardis 2013), my concern is with the act itself and how this practice figures in the power of the images that so forcefully impacted Paracas visual culture.

The Paracas Landscape and Its Spheres of Social Valuables

Paracas cultural remains are found in the coastal river valleys and adjacent highlands of the south-central coast (Figure 10.2). Julio C. Tello was the first scholar to call international attention to the spectacular materials found with hundreds of mummy bundles on the Paracas Peninsula in the Wari Kayan ("Necrópolis") and Cavern ("Cavernas") tombs (Tello 1929, 1959; Tello and Mejía Xesspe 1979). The elaborately embroidered textiles that enveloped the mummies received acclaim and became emblematic of Paracas culture. So too were the curious post-fired painted ceramics that accompanied the cavern burials and the finely sculpted, monochromatic wares (now recognized as Topará) found with the Wari Kayan bundles. As the mummies were unwrapped, sometimes at society events, Tello, who was trained as a physician, celebrated

the deformed and trepanned skulls as the work of a highly advanced society (Daggett 1991, 2009). Tello's experiences on the Paracas Peninsula and at Chavín de Huántar, as well as his rigorous field research across the Andes, led him to link the two in his Andean-wide cultural matrix, privileging Chavín as America's first civilization (Burger 1984, 2009; Daggett 2009) (Figure 10.3).

Nearly a century later, scholars recognize Paracas as a powerful polity whose roots were established earlier than Tello had predicted and in few places that resembled the Paracas Peninsula sites. The late-period temple at Animas Altas (ca. 250 BC), renowned for its intricate plastered relief, is now understood to be one of many (Bachir 2017). Distinct radial shapes characterize the configuration of some settlements (Reindel and Isla 2017:fig. 9), while others are void of surface architecture (see Cook 1999). Celestial alignments of buildings and landscape features are notable for Tajahuana (Gundrum 1996) and Cerrillos (Splitstoser 2009:90) and are seen between large complexes in Pisco (Peters 2013) and Chincha (Canziani 1992, 2013; Stanish and Tantaleán 2018) (Figures 10.4–10.5). Mountain peaks and key *cerros* shadow sacred places at Karwa and Callango.

A long-held reverence for the landscape by ancient Andeans is manifest in geoglyphs that cover the Chincha, Palpa, and Ica Valleys and the areas adjacent to the Paracas Peninsula (Cook 1992; Garcia 2013; More More 2018; Reindel and Isla 2013:fig. 20; Stanish and Tantaleán 2018, 2020). These permanent constructions anticipate the Nasca lines by almost two centuries. Petroglyphs provide the earliest instances of place-marking in stone (Fux 2011:fig. 4; Reindel and Isla 2013:fig. 19a).[1]

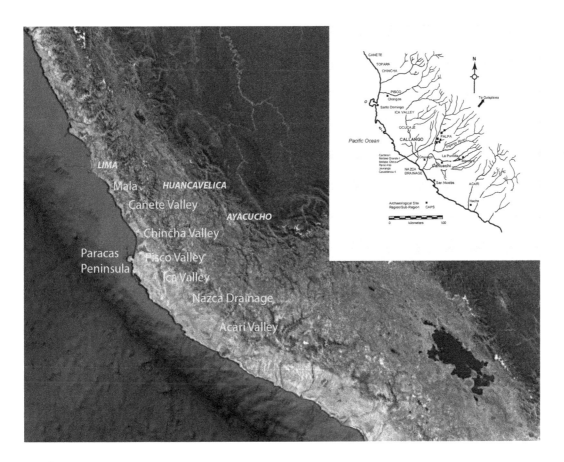

figure 10.2
Map of south coastal Peru. Map by Lisa DeLeonardis.

figure 10.3
Frontispiece to Pablo Soldi, "Chavín en Ica," *Voz de Ica*, 1956. Soldi was inspired by the work of Julio C. Tello and believed that Chavín peoples had migrated from Ancash to the south coast. Erroneously, he attributed the full temporal spectrum of Paracas material culture to Chavín. Photograph by Lisa DeLeonardis.

figure 10.4
The middle Ica Valley
site of Tajahuana.
Photograph by
Lisa DeLeonardis.

figure 10.5
View of Teojate and
Juan Pablo from the
summit of Cerrillos,
upper Ica Valley.
Photograph by
Lisa DeLeonardis.

As Tello had initially demonstrated, the Paracas placed great attention on the human body, modifying its appearance through cranial deformation and attending to its traumas and pathologies (Tello 1929; Tello and Mejía Xesspe 1979). They were the first to successfully trepan the human skull, a surgical procedure that was not repeated again in the Andes for almost five hundred years (Verano 2016:140). Such skill was duly manifest in the mummification of the head, a practice later emulated by the Nasca. The enveloped mummy is now understood to be but one form in a range of body treatments. Study of the body as a living organism has advanced our perspective of the Paracas beyond the concerns of death (Tomasto Cagiga 2009).

Objects in Motion

The Paracas interaction sphere in exotic and quotidian materials was well established by the first millennium and it was geographically pan-Andean in scope. As early as 3800 BC, intervalley and coastal exchanges of obsidian and shell are evident (Reindel 2009:442; Reindel and Isla 2009).[2] This trend continues in the late Initial Period (1200–800 BC), during which time intervalley exchange in ceramics, maize, and other domestic material is apparent, as are materials imported from distant regions (García 2009:fig. 6). Post-fired painted and incised ceramics bearing an iconography more akin to the central and north coast are found at sites such as Disco Verde and Puerto Nuevo (Dulanto, this volume). In turn, coastal ceramics and shell are found to the south, in Paracas domestic contexts (DeLeonardis 1997:310, 2005:38) (Figure 10.6).

By 800 BC, both valley-wide and long-distance exchange in ceramics, feathers, pigments, obsidian, and other luxury goods accelerates. These materials are found in various Paracas contexts across the south coast. Obsidian, a highly valued material, is worked, cached, and fashioned into tools and weapons (Figure 10.7). To date, all of the obsidian from the Ica Valley has been traced to a single source, Quispisisa, near Huancasancos in the Department of Ayacucho (Burger and Asaro 1979; DeLeonardis and Glascock 2013:174). Coeval with the earliest exchanges (ca. 800 BC) are Chavín-influenced portable objects, found primarily in sumptuous graves and elite contexts (Kaulicke et al. 2009:fig. 16; Reindel 2009:fig. 25.4; Splitstoser, Wallace, and Delgado 2009:figs. 3–6). Late-phase Paracas ceramics are found as far south as Moquegua in elite tombs (Goldstein 2000).[3] Cotton became a predominant industrial crop along with the comestibles maize, beans, and squash (Beresford-Jones et al. 2009:table 1, 244–246; DeLeonardis 1997; Wallace 1962:312; Zorogastúa, Ávila, and Jones 2017:table 10.1, fig. 10.1) (Figure 10.8). Materials used in the production of ceramics and textiles were also in circulation and are exchanged among coastal, highland, and Amazonian regions of the Andes (DeLeonardis 2016).

We can be sure that social alliances—the invisible aspects of exchange and the larger social world

figure 10.6
View of PV62D13 in Callango, lower Ica Valley. One of seven in a cluster of early Paracas occupations on the west bank, the site remains one of the few Paracas domestic sites excavated to date. Photograph by Lisa DeLeonardis.

a

b

figure 10.7

a) Obsidian from PV62D13 has been chemically sourced to the Quispisisa quarry near Ayacucho (photograph by James T. Van Rensselaer); and b) points and other stones and crystals were valued for their color and transparency (photograph by Lisa DeLeonardis).

figure 10.8
Cotton (*Gossypium barbadense*) became an industrial crop during the first millennium BC and continues to be cultivated on the south coast, one of the two centers of cotton production in Peru. Photograph by Lisa DeLeonardis.

embodied in these objects—were cemented between groups and individuals, including Chavín and its affiliates, over this long period. Logistically, Paracas leaders may have held a special relationship with the Chavín–Ayacucho sphere, including Campanayuq Rumi, for its proximity to Quispisisa and the long term use of the obsidian quarry by both groups (Matsumoto and Cavero Palomino, this volume; Matsumoto et al. 2018:54–55).[4] The Chavín-affiliated Atalla in Huancavelica figured in the Paracas sphere for the key resource of cinnabar (Burger and Matos Mendieta 2002; Young 2017; see also Dulanto, this volume; Matsumoto and Cavero Palomino, this volume; Young, this volume).

Consideration of the nature and extent of these networks, including pilgrimage to Chavín de Huántar, is critical to defining the nodes of interaction in which the Paracas and Chavín intersected. Multiple Paracas spheres of exchange—and by extension, social interaction spheres—were established before the proposed spread of Chavín influence to the south coast. Potentially, the relationships embedded in these spheres would provide a rapid exchange structure for the transmission and dissemination of Chavín ideology. They may also explain the differential regional exposure and reception of Chavín in the south.

Implicit in this discussion is engagement with the "outside," a strategy in which the Paracas materialized the presence of distant peoples and places through the acquisition of things. Objects and materials embodied a larger social world whose presence conferred a degree of worldliness upon them. Early on, this penchant for the exotic was demonstrated on the Paracas Peninsula, where the mummy, itself a "museum in miniature," provided stunning concentrations of materials (DeLeonardis 2012; Paul 1990; Tello and Mejía Xesspe 1979). These early discoveries have been validated since Tello's time by veritable caches of objects, gold ornaments, and masks, attesting to Paracas leaders' proclivities for ostentation in bodily ornamentation and attire (DeLeonardis 2016:fig. 5.11). The theatrics of display inferred by such practices would have appealed to their performance-conscious neighbors.

Portable Objects and the Circulation of Ideas

Despite the numerous projects undertaken on the south coast in the last twenty years, investigators have not identified architectural configurations or stone bas reliefs comparable to those of Chavín de Huántar or its related centers (Burger 1995, 2008b; Matsumoto 2012). While permanent forms of art such as geoglyphs and architectural friezes occur late in Paracas history, ceramics, textiles, and pyro-engraved gourds continue to provide the richest sources for the study of visual culture (Figure 10.9).

Consideration of portable objects and the contexts in which they occur pose challenges. In the past, stirrup-spout bottles and painted textiles bearing the closest resemblance to Chavín iconography were recovered indiscriminately from tombs at Karwa, Ocucaje, Callango, and other south coast locations (e.g., Burger 1995:fig. 201, 209; Rowe 1962:figs. 48–55; Soldi 1956). Although the problem of insecure context continues to plague our analysis, today it is possible to compare earlier finds with

finds from more secure contexts with a wider range of features. Underrepresentation of systematically excavated materials from sites other than tombs and ceremonial contexts is a shortcoming. Urban overburden of subsequent cultures (Nasca and Wari) obscures or has destroyed earlier Paracas vestiges. Cultural remains may be deeply buried and without surface indicators, as Tello (1929; Tello and Mejía Xesspe 1979) experienced and as two recent case studies demonstrate (Balbuena 2013; Kaulicke et al. 2009). Differential preservation of material culture between the south coast and Ancash also affects comparison between the two.

Perhaps the thorniest issue remains the distinction between Chavín and other foreign influences in artifact assemblages, primarily for early Paracas history when the northern influence is most evident.[5] This problem is particularly acute with fineware ceramics and painted textiles, and it is compounded by the Chavín style, which is itself an emulation of northern Cupisnique and Tembladera styles (Burger 1996:82). This makes the search for a "pure" Chavín style on the south coast problematic.[6] With these challenges in mind, it is critical to consider Paracas agency in the selection of foreign iconographies, as well as the shared cultural practices in which the Paracas and Chavín engaged.

My analysis situates Chavín-influenced Paracas iconography in a range of contexts and media over time. By context, I am referring to tomb assemblages and stratigraphic artifact assemblages from domestic and ceremonial features, broadly defined. I am equally concerned with the ideas and practices that these material referents embody. I am as much concerned with those that are reinforced in public performances as those that are valued in funerary rituals. Critical to my analyses are the daily and thereby recurring messages conveyed through quotidian object iconographies. In these respects, the objects perform as well as inform.

I am interested in which icons persist and, by extension, continue to stimulate cultural memory after Chavín influence wanes and Paracas methods of interpreting and picturing are materialized (Weiner 1992:8). Of equal interest is the Chavín iconography that is destroyed, buried, or otherwise

figure 10.9

Feline images were seared into the perishable bottle gourd (*Lagenaria siceria*) of south coastal Peru. Pyro-engraved gourds were one of the principal portable objects that conveyed Cupisnique and Chavín ideology. Pre-Columbian Collection, PC.B. 563, Dumbarton Oaks Research Library and Collection, Washington, D.C. Drawing by Elizabeth Wahle.

removed from public view, as well as the significance of these practices (DeLeonardis 2013).

Ceramic Iconography and Ideology: Interpretation and Translation

Chavín and Paracas artists shared a number of approaches to ceramic iconography, design, and finishing. In some cases, the similarities are so striking that it is difficult to distinguish the two. Both employed post-fired paint, resist or negative paint, appliqué, and incision. The use of graphite in slip painting was common to Chavín, Chakinani, and Janabarriu ceramics (Burger 1984:104, 150–153), while the Paracas turned to the material long after Chavín influence had waned. One of the most ubiquitous design motifs—the circle-and-dot motif—was shared by both traditions but arranged and executed singularly by the Paracas.[7]

On the south coast, ceramics that show the strongest Chavín influence are finely polished stirrup-spout bottles and well-finished bowls with thick walls and beveled rims. They are distinguished for their dark color, flat bases, voluminous form, and iconography bearing a supernatural pantheon, of which the fanged feline is most common

(Figure 10.10). Textured surfaces, a hallmark of Chavín ceramic design, have been well-documented by Richard L. Burger at Chavín de Huántar (1984:figs. 104, 155, 233, 335, 338, 343). Texturing surfaces by stamping, brushing, or combing is less common on the south coast. Small fragments of rocker-stamped finewares are found in stratigraphic contexts, but they are rare (DeLeonardis 1999:3; Splitstoser et al. 2009:fig. 4a–c). The Paracas favored glossy surfaces on bottles and bowls, especially between post-fired painted and incised designs.

Chavín artists preferred a volumetric sculptural design in which the subject emerged carved from the block. This is apparent in early feline iconography, where the head is rendered in three-dimensional relief on bottles. Paracas sculptors initially emulated this approach in effigy bottles (Figures 10.10–10.11), then favored a planar design in which only the ears or nose was modeled. Felines and other prominent subjects are masked, flattened, and segmented into modular width or planiform arrangements. Design motifs that appear on a grand scale in architectural reliefs at Chavín de Huántar are narrowed to the smaller design field of the ceramic form. In addition to their reduced size, they are extracted from their

figure 10.10
The "Olsen" bottle is among a rare group of stirrup-spout
bottles that bear several finishing techniques that are foreign to
the south coast. It is considered one of the earliest renderings
of the cross-fanged feline. Photograph courtesy of Krannert Art
Museum, University of Illinois, Urbana-Champaign, 1967–29–2.

figure 10.11
The "Lucas" or "Tishman" bottle exemplifies an
early Paracas stirrup-spout bottle that employs
vibrant post-fired paint. Fowler Museum,
University of California, Los Angeles, FMCH
X90–481. Photograph by Don Cole.

original narrative, recombined with other design
motifs, and repeated. These approaches are uniquely
Paracas and represent a critical break from northern
design methods.

Chavín-influenced ceramics may be found
in tombs along with early Paracas forms, making it difficult to judge whether they are northern
imports or locally produced. A recent case from
Mollake Chico highlights this quandry, in which
northern and southern ceramic forms are combined together (Reindel 2009:fig. 25.4). In a second
case, Peter Kaulicke and his colleagues (2009:303,
fig. 16e) recovered *floreros* from an early Paracas
tomb in Coyungo. The *florero*, like the stirrup-spout
bottle, is attributed to northern Peru and is rare in
the Paracas ceramic sequence (see Alva 1986:fig.

424; Elera 1997:figs. 6, 8).[8] Both cases highlight the
mixing that occurs in early Paracas funerary contexts and provide the contextual evidence lacking in
other studies.[9]

There are idiosyncrasies in the Paracas
approach to northern iconography and design,
and these idiosyncrasies stand out as much as the
florero and stirrup-spout bottle do as foreign forms.
Double spout-and-bridge bottles are the southern
convention. The earliest forms are small and thick
walled (Figure 10.12). One spout is usually blind and
modeled with a bird or human head (Bird 1962:fig.
14, right).

Post-fired paint, often described as "resin
paint," is widely used.[10] The Paracas employed a
more varied color palette than Chavín painters

figure 10.12

Early Paracas double spout-and-bridge bottle with a blind spout modeled as a bird, Chiquerillo, Ica Valley. Note the snake hair on the fanged supernatural. Brooklyn Museum, Frank L. Babbott Fund, 59.197.1.

(Burger 1984:151). Post-fired paint is often combined with incision or other painting techniques on the same ceramic, creating a colorful, raised surface. In this manner, the application of thick, post-fired color distinguishes the Paracas approach to layering the surface from the Chavín method of texturing the clay body before firing. In the Paracas technique, paint encompasses the incised lines of designs (Figure 10.11), especially circles and other geometric shapes. Painting also occurs without incision. Paracas painted and incised ceramics are not restricted to tombs or ceremonial contexts; they are an integral part of domestic assemblages and were likely a key to the dissemination of the ideology encoded in them.

Along with the ubiquitous feline, human or composite human-supernatural faces constitute an early design theme, especially on bowls (Figure

10.13). Design motifs derived from bas-reliefs at Chavín de Huántar are common: squared eyes of the Staff God and other supernaturals, mouth bars with crossed fangs attributable to various supernaturals, the guilloche (twisted strand motif) as exemplified by the Lanzón, incised circle-and-dot motifs, or feline pelage are most frequent (Beresford-Jones et al. 2009:fig. 3e; DeLeonardis 1991:fig. 3.2–3.3, pl. 3.1, 1997:fig. 5.12, 6.13, 2005:fig. 5; Rowe 1962:figs. 50–51; Wallace 1962:fig. 4a). Birds (also modeled), caymans, profile faces, step motifs, and geometrical designs (crosses, herringbone patterns, lozenges, and triangles) are common (DeLeonardis 1997:fig. 7.11–b; Kaulicke et al. 2009:fig. 16c-1–3; Splitstoser et al. 2009:figs. 3, 5–6). San Pedro, a cactus with psychoactive properties, is also the rarer subject of iconography (DeLeonardis 1991:fig. 3.3b, 1997:fig. 7.22c; see also Torres 2008) (Figure 10.14).

figure 10.13
Early Paracas post-fired
painted and incised bowl
showing a human face,
Chiquerillo, Ica Valley.
As a design convention,
faces are rendered with
a human nose or shown
animated with bared teeth or
pronounced crossed fangs.
The Metropolitan Museum
of Art, Nathan Cummings
Collection, 62.266.62.

Modeled figures are shown seated as authorities with vacant, open eyes, as if in the initial stages of transformation (see Isla and Reindel 2006:fig. 20c; Lapiner 1976:cat. 140; Reindel and Isla 2004:fig. 6; Tello 1929:fig. 80) (Figure 10.15).[11] These figures form a sharp contrast with solid hand-modeled forms found in domestic assemblages (DeLeonardis 1997:fig. 5.13).

After ca. 650 BC, Chavín ceramic iconography becomes Paracas-translated, or post-mimetic. Paracas iconography follows new design canons. Regional and familiar flora and fauna are incorporated into the visual repertoire. Old Chavín icons are reconfigured into innovative arrangements of colors and patterns (e.g., Rowe 1962:figs. 52–52a) (Figure 10.16). Arguably, in their transfigured forms, some of the designs are as crowded and difficult to read as the polished granite stone monuments at Chavín de Huántar. This horror vacui speaks as much to changes in design methods as to a newly translated visual narrative that encodes esoteric knowledge.

Late in the ceramic sequence (ca. 500 BC), pronounced shifts occur in Paracas design methods. These changes parallel urbanization, the creation of geoglyphs, and the expansion of settlements across the south coast, including the Paracas Peninsula (Cavernas). Corresponding to Ocucaje Phase 8, some forms, such as the grater bowl and collared olla, proliferate. Design motifs are smaller, especially circles, which are mostly cane stamped rather than incised. Once restricted to the hair and belts of earlier figures, serpents (without fangs) become a common design motif as well as the subject of modeled effigy bottles.

Innovative icons such as the Occulate Being and the disembodied head are apparent in Paracas iconography after Ocucaje Phase 8. The fanged feline of the early period persists in the south, but the pampas cat, also a choice for embroidered textiles, is common in the north (see Peters 1991). The Topará style, characterized by thin, monochromatic vessels in the form of gourds and pumpkin squash (*calabaza*), becomes prevalent in the north (Paracas Peninsula "Necrópolis," Pisco, Chincha, and Cañete) and is interspersed with painted and incised traditions in the south. Miniature vessels contrast with large drums, panpipes (*antara*), and other musical instruments that are produced (see Tantalcán, Stanish, and Rodríguez 2020:figs. 3.45, 3.48). Turbaned chiefs occupy the blind spouts on

figure 10.14
Early Paracas cup incised with a San Pedro cactus motif, PV62D19, Callango west bank, Ica Valley. Photograph by Lisa DeLeonardis.

figure 10.15
Seated figures with supernatural attributes constitute a group of early Paracas bottles shown gesturing and possibly in trance. This bottle is said to be from Coyungo, Nazca drainage. Photograph by Lisa DeLeonardis.

bottles (DeLeonardis 2016:fig. 5.6). Ocucaje Phase 9 also marks the apogee of Animas Altas, where the greatest number of sculpted friezes have been recorded (Bachir 2017; Massey 1983).

The Paracas painted and incised tradition gradually diminishes in Ocucaje Phase 10, at around 200 BC. The design practice of modular width ends. Negative paint and black reduce fired ceramics are more common. The latter are marked with graphite designs. Well-attired masked figures holding weapons are a common motif on painted and incised ceramics. Life-sized painted and incised ceramic masks are also produced (see DeLeonardis 2016:fig. 5.9).

figure 10.16
Small bottles such as this one from Ocucaje show an approach to design in which the fanged feline appears as the attire of a human figure. Drawing by Lisa DeLeonardis (after Tello 1959:fig. 9).

Iconography and Ideology: Materialization of the Past

After an initial period of great iconographic similarity, certain icons persisted in the Paracas visual repertoire. These visual references may have served subsequent generations of viewers to trigger and reinforce cultural memory. Some are immortalized in landscape features, thereby leaving a permanent record that endured beyond the first millennium BC.

FANGED SUPERNATURALS

Fifty years ago, the tenacity of feline imagery (and other fanged creatures grouped with them) led scholars to conceptualize Paracas as a branch "cult of the feline" (Patterson 1971; Sawyer 1972). The Paracas-translated fanged feline of Cupisnique and Chavín persists long after its initial appearance. It is one of the most common motifs on ceramics and is found in all contexts. The motif, or its parts, is repeated as design motifs and modeled as effigy

bottles (e.g., DeLeonardis 2016:fig. 5.7). It also appears in various iterations on painted textiles (e.g., Lumbreras 1998:41).

AGNATHIC FACE

The agnathic face, a character with deep roots in Cupisnique visual culture, is limited in scope on early ceramics, appearing as the subject of design and as a subtle icon in combined representations or reconfigured as a repeating element in later compositions. It is pictured on textiles (Balbuena 2013:fig. 7), in crowded arrangements with south coast birds (Cordy-Collins 1999:pl. 8) or attached to other painted narratives (Cordy-Collins 1999:pl. 11a). Its persistence is exemplified in at least one petroglyph, where it gained permanence in the public eye (Fux 2011).

STEP MOTIF

Also of early Andean origin (e.g., Elera 1997:fig. 3), the step or terrace continued to persist in portable and permanent form. Largely recognized as a place of sacredness and of religious authority, the motif is used conservatively by the Paracas on early painted and incised ceramics (DeLeonardis 2013:fig. 7b, 2016:figs. 5.6, 5.9). In late Paracas Callango, it is materialized in the form of a patterned wall frieze (Bachir 2017:fig. 9) and itself forms an independent, three-dimensional construction (DeLeonardis 2022) (Figure 10.17).

EYE

A pre-Chavín icon, the squared-eye motif is prominent on the tenon head of a composite creature at Chavín de Huántar (Fux 2013:cat. 119, see also cat. 95) and is an important motif in the visual vocabulary of the Paracas. It appears as the subject of painted and incised designs (DeLeonardis 1997:fig. 7.16a) or is paired with birds in modular width bands (Balbuena 2013:fig. 9). On painted textiles, the eye is an outstanding feature of the Staff God (Burger 1996:pl. 6). The eye also gains permanence in geoglyph form (García 2013:fig. 5a–b).

GUILLOCHE

The twisted strand, or guilloche, and its angular forms endure throughout Paracas visual history.

a   b

figure 10.17

a) Excavations at the west bank cluster site of Casa Blanca (PV62D12) revealed a miniature stepped pyramid created from plastered adobe brick. Photograph by Lisa DeLeonardis. b) Post-fired painted and incised bowl with a pyramidal step motif. The Metropolitan Museum of Art, Nathan Cummings Collection, 1976.287.33.

It is recognized as an "Old Temple" icon, derived from the intertwined thread or axis mundi carved on the Lanzón at Chavín de Huántar. It first appears as the subject of ceramic design. Later, it is combined with other textile motifs, but rarely in modular width arrangements (DeLeonardis 2016:figs. 5.3, 5.5). Instead, it acts as a border element in complex designs where it is thought to protect sacred space (DeLeonardis 2016:fig. 5.3a; Paul 2000). The motif is found on many ceramic forms, including grater bowls and jars (DeLeonardis 2005:figs. 3, 13) (Figure 10.18). It also comprises a central motif on baskets (Fernández and Rodríguez 2017:fig. 7.22) and pyro-engraved gourds (Ministerio de Cultura 2013:fig. 60; Zorogastúa, Ávila, and Jones 2017:fig. 10.13). Anne Paul (2000) links the motif and its relatives to Paracas and Chavín-produced objects.

Ceramic Techné: Linking Materials and Practices

Techné situates the production of objects as an activity deeply embedded in social life. Through a number of sub-approaches (e.g., skill of artists, meaning, and raw materials), it considers the role that material culture plays in society (Costin 2016:5). Techné informs

the Chavín–Paracas relationship for its approach to identifying material choices in production and, indirectly, to locating and defining exchange networks on the basis of those materials. Its inquiry may also identify the presence of imported objects or confirm regional manufacture of those whose cultural affiliation is difficult to discern.

A developing body of research on Paracas ceramics seeks to identify the composition and sources of the binder and colorants that constitute post-fired paint (Dulanto, Gonzáles, and Guadalupe 2019; Kaplan 1999; Kriss et al. 2018). My interest in pigments stems from an earlier study in which I examined the value of color and the question of long-distance exchange for colorants and binders used in ceramic production (DeLeonardis 2016). A recent technical study undertaken by Dawn Kriss and her colleagues has identified two trends especially relevant to the present discussion.

On one stirrup-spout bottle bearing feline iconography, *Myroxylon balsumum*, or Balsam of Peru, was identified (Kriss et al. 2018:fig. 3-right; Lapiner 1976:fig. 145-left). *Myroxylon balsamum* is found in wet, lowland forests below 500 m (Pennington, Reynel, and Daza 2004:304). The bark from which the binder is derived is characterized by a resinous consistency and fragrance.[12] Its use by Paracas

a   b

figure 10.18

The twisted strand or guilloche motif is one of the most persistent design motifs in Paracas iconography: a) guilloche formed by post-fired painted, angular S-designs surrounding dots, Cerro La Capilla, Ocucaje, Ica Valley (The Metropolitan Museum of Art, Nathan Cummings Collection, 64.228.99); and b) the guilloche and related twisted strand are rendered on this ceramic jar by two methods—post-fired paint, and post-fired paint and incision in a modular width panel at the neck (Princeton University Art Museum, 2012.132).

painters would require long-distance exchange with the tropical lowlands of Amazonia. Among the larger sample, which included the full range of the Paracas ceramic sequence, the binder source was not identified. These trends indicate that, over time and independent of other changes (such as iconography and vessel shape), Paracas artists consistently used the same (but still unknown) binder material. Since there have been no comparable tests conducted on northern-sphere colorant binders, it is not clear if the results indicate early experimentation with binder substances, or if the binder or bottle on which it is found are imported. Early Paracas iconographic and design methods suggest a south coast manufacture.

A colorant palette for Paracas post-fired paints was also identified by Kriss et al. (2018), primarily for the Ica Valley. Cinnabar was employed for some of the earliest Chavín-influenced Paracas ceramics (see DeLeonardis 2016:fig. 5.2; Lapiner 1976:cat. 145), but not for all of the early Paracas ceramics in the sample. This finding points to the conservative use of the material early in the sequence, after which an iron-rich colorant, likely ochre, is preferred. This trend may be indicative of the use of cinnabar for specific icons, such as the cayman (DeLeonardis 2016:fig. 5.2), or a preference for its use as body

paint, among other uses (Burger and Leikin 2018). The results of the study compare to independent tests conducted on Puerto Nuevo–level ceramics at Puerto Nuevo by Jalh Dulanto (2013:120, fig. 18). More recently, a wider study by Dulanto and his colleagues shows an overall greater use of cinnabar for Chavín-influenced Paracas ceramics, perhaps reflecting stronger ties to the Huancavelica exchange route (Dulanto, Gonzáles, and Guadalupe 2019:73, 79–80, fig. 7).

In my study (DeLeonardis 2016:table 5.2), I identify a hiatus in the use of green pigments after Chavín influence wanes until late in the Paracas sequence. Test results from Kriss and colleagues (2018) confirm the decline in the use of copper-rich green colorants and a transition to iron-rich green colorants until late in the sequence, when copper-rich (atacamite, malachite) green colorants reoccur.[13] These results contrast with recent studies conducted on Ecuadorian post-fired pigments (Romero et al. 2018; Sánchez-Polo 2018). The Ecuador study identifies mostly iron oxides in paint composition for ceramics contemporaneous with Chavín and Paracas, perhaps distinguishing a narrower sphere in which Chavín and Paracas interacted, or indicating cultural preferences for certain colorants.

Fragmentation and the Question of Divine Substances

Textiles are the most celebrated art form in the Andes, encompassing a millennia-long history that continues to the present. Among Andean weavers, the Paracas are best known for their embroidered mantles and attire, first brought to the public's attention by Julio C. Tello at Wari Kayan. Equally distinguished are a group of textiles that appeared in the 1960s on the south coast. These are referred to as the "Chavín" or "Karwa" painted textiles.[14] The group consists of over two hundred painted cloths, primarily woven from cotton. This corpus includes some of the most orthodox Chavín images and has been the subject of several outstanding studies (Brugnoli and Hoces de la Guardia 1991; Conklin 2008; Cordy-Collins 1976, 1979, 1999; Wallace 1991).

Most scholarship has addressed iconography, since the cloths display compelling narratives of the gods and supernaturals of Chavín and their rituals. In particular, the Staff God, agnathic creatures (reminiscent of the Lanzón), and processional figures have received the greatest attention for their resemblance to the bas-reliefs at Chavín de Huántar (Figure 10.19). One well-studied cloth portrays activity associated with the consumption of San Pedro cactus (Cordy-Collins 1977; Torres 2008). Another, maritime life. One intersperses a dazzling repetition of Cupisnique-style agnathic faces with gliding birds, a south coast staple (Cordy-Collins 1999:pl. 8). There are no other caches of painted textiles of this thematic coherency known elsewhere in the Chavín–Paracas Interaction Sphere.

There is little doubt about the didactic value of the corpus in conveying ideology from the north. Some cloths stray from convention in their portrayal of maritime themes or female personae, unrecognized in the northern canon. These modifications suggest the hand of south coastal weavers or painters in reinterpreting or recreating the narrative(s).

William Conklin (2008:268) hypothesizes that some of the cloths—particularly those of circular composition—would have been lain horizontally to be read (see Conklin 2008:fig. 10.4). The design and horizontal orientation thereby enacted a cosmological chart, evoking memory of the sunken circular courtyard at Chavín de Huántar, and the meaning attendant to the architecture and the rituals held there. The final disposition of some cloths, directly into the ground, is consistent with the Andean practice of interring bundled textiles as offerings.

One of the noteworthy features of the cloths is their fragmentary state (Cordy-Collins 1999:128). There are no indications that the fabrics were cut in ancient times.[15] On the contrary, many are pastiches of cloths united together like a quilt. But unlike a quilt, the pieces do not align with each other or the themes portrayed. Joining the cloths together may have been a means of keeping the parts together to preserve them.[16] It is also possible that the cloths were manipulated to change the narrative.

Although the fragmentary nature of the cloths is lamented, I believe that fragmentation was intentional in many cases, likely from repeated action such as touch. This tactile practice would not be unusual if the cloths or the images represented on them were regarded as divine. A recent study by Kaulicke et al. (2009) supports this inquiry. His team recovered a small cloth bag, in which fragments of a painted textile were found, from a large Coyungo tomb. The fragments represent the fangs of a supernatural. He has since been able to match the fang fragments directly with a textile said to be from Callango (Burger 1996:pls. 7, 79) (Figure 10.20). Although Kaulicke is troubled by the fragmentation between tombs, I believe that the match is not coincidental.

In my research on Paracas ceramic fragmentation, I acknowledge that the practice is difficult to assess without controlled context (DeLeonardis 2013:211). When it is possible, pottery sherds distributed between graves as offerings can be crossmended. This act of distribution is an intervention by the living to unite and identify the deceased. The substance of the material that is distributed is important. The practice of interring sherds with the dead has been recorded by Walter Alva (1986) in his excavations of Cupisnique tombs in Jequetepeque and by Alfred Kroeber (Kroeber and Collier 1998) in Nasca tombs in Nazca. Packets of human hair distributed

figure 10.19

Painted textile with supernatural. The anatropic design of this image allows a 180-degree rotation: upright, the head of the fanged figure faces the viewer, while inverted, a newly defined creature spews stylized feathers. Pre-Columbian Collection, PC.B.545, Dumbarton Oaks Research Library and Collection, Washington, D.C.

among graves served a similar purpose (DeLeonardis 2012:209). We cannot say that this was a universal Andean practice, or that the meaning embodied in the practice was the same in all situations, but I assert that the intentional fragmentation of materials is more widespread than we acknowledge, and it often followed "killing" the object for distribution.[17]

When considered in a broader light, these acts of fragmentation and redistribution suggest that gaining a piece of cloth—and, in the Coyungo case, the fangs associated with a divine creature—was more than acquiring a piece of a place, but gaining possession of a sacred power. Powerful objects are subject to destruction by non-believers, which may explain the corpus's eventual interment, to preserve or hide them.

The ritual manipulation of images on cloth is not limited to the painted corpus. Some cloth fragments bearing Chavín iconography were united as pastiches in burials or intentionally destroyed. At Cerrillos, cloths portraying staff figures were indeed cut and deposited in architectural fill during temple reconstruction (Splitstoser 2009:449–450, 476; Splitstoser, Wallace, and Delgado 2009:figs. 9–10). At Pariahuana 5 (Pisco), two fragments were united in the burial shroud of an infant, each bearing different weaving techniques and icons: an agnathic face, and a profile staff figure (Balbuena 2013:figs. 6–8).

figure 10.20
Painted textile with cayman, Callango, lower Ica Valley. The fangs missing from the lower portion of this cotton fabric fragment were recovered from a tomb in Coyungo, Nazca drainage. Pre-Columbian Collection, PC.B.544, Dumbarton Oaks Research Library and Collection, Washington, D.C.

These cases underscore the power of images and locate their afterlife somewhere between iconoclastic destruction and careful preservation.[18]

From the Inside Looking Out

It is clear that Chavín ideology did not provide the sole impetus for Chavín–Paracas interaction as once thought. Our understanding of the south coast and adjacent areas indicates interaction spheres to have begun before the advent of Paracas, and to have become even more widespread between 1200 and 800 BC (Reindel and Isla 2009). Unrelated to the question of religious ideology, MacNeish, Patterson, and Browman (1975:43) have observed a similar pattern in their study, recognizing two different but simultaneous interaction spheres for central Peru. More recent investigations have defined a northern and south-central sphere for the circulation of obsidian (Matsumoto and Cavero Palomino, this volume; Matsumoto et al. 2018:59). The latter sphere, with its obsidian distribution center at Campanayuq Rumi, corresponds to the Quispisisa–south coast obsidian route. Undoubtedly, obsidian exchange was one stimulus for the exchange of ideas between Ancash, Ayacucho, Huancavelica, and the Paracas, as DeLeonardis and Glascock (2013:184), and Matsumoto et al. (2018:57–58) have proposed. Rather than a single force in one moment, we might envision spheres of interaction that multiplied and morphed, changing directions, tapping into others, and cementing relationships over time.

Chavín appears to have exerted their ideology into already active spheres by virtue of the power of their message and stimulated ideas that would have been attractive to the Paracas. For example, both the Paracas and Chavín claimed mythological origins and emphasized cultural practices such as ancestor veneration and ritual performance (Burger 2008a; DeLeonardis 2012; DeLeonardis and Lau 2004). The process of transformation is abundantly evident in Chavín and Paracas cosmology and art (DeLeonardis 2016; Roe 2008). The use of psychoactive substances in ritual may have been encouraged, since it is celebrated on textiles and quotidian materials alike. Those icons that persist are of an "old religion," an ideology with deep roots in Andean culture. The success of Chavín ideology may stem in part from an ability to ally with the old and familiar (and profoundly sacred) in their translation of ideology to others. As an ancient *waka*, Chavín and the material referents of its ideology were already deeply embedded in Andean thought. Paracas engagement with this old-new dogma and with Chavín as the meta-distant outsider would undoubtedly enhance the profile of its power-conscious leaders. We cannot rule out the possibility, however, of an ideological coercion linked to exchange culture.

Analysis of ceramic techné raises questions about the procurement of minerals and organic materials used in the production of post-fired painted ceramics relative to the circulation of materials. Recent studies indicate that the Paracas exchanged at great distances to procure pigments and materials to practice their craft (DeLeonardis 2016; Dulanto, Gonzáles, and Guadalupe 2019; Kaplan 1999; Kriss et al. 2018). Although there appears to be a brisk exchange of cinnabar between Huancavelica and Chavín de Huántar, and close resemblances in artifact assemblages between Chavín and Atalla, the relationship between Atalla and the greater south coast is less robust than expected. In Ica, the use of cinnabar is conservative and limited to early Chavín-influenced Paracas ceramics, but not all that bear Chavín iconography. On the other hand, stronger ties or better travel routes may have existed between Puerto Nuevo and Atalla, where exchange in cinnabar is more apparent. Further research is necessary to clarify the routes and exchange mechanisms for the circulation of materials used in ceramic production within the South Coast Interaction Sphere. Examination of a wider range of Chavín and Chavín-influenced Paracas post-fired painted icons may yield clues to the ideas inherent in the uses of one substance or another and their relevance to sacred objects, including painted textiles.

Technical analysis of colorants reveals disruption patterns in color use and materials, and it is worthwhile to pursue inquiry related to those disruptions relative to the spheres of Chavín influence.

Changes may correspond to the preferences of artists or to some sort of interference in the northern or central Andean exchange network after Chavín influence had waned. In this vein, questions are prompted about Chavín's role in the exchange network for materials such as Balsam tree bark. Determination of the direction of exchange would greatly aid in assessing whether the object(s) on which this substance was painted was imported and, ideally, identify the artists who were using or exchanging it. That the Paracas chose not to continue its use lends support to their agency in decision-making about how their ceramics were made.

The cultural act of fragmentation, in my view, provides the most convincing evidence for practices associated with Chavín ideological influence on the south coast and the value that such substances continued to hold. John Chapman (2000:23) has theorized about the interpretation of fragmentation in the archaeological record, understanding ritual redistribution as a form of enchainment between groups with commonalities, whether they be familial, religious, or political (or some combination).

Whether Chavín religion inspired all the painted textiles, it is clear that at least some of the icons painted on them rendered them as profoundly powerful. The social practices associated with textiles, from displaying them to destroying them, caching cloths and fragments, and burying those fragments in different places, provide convincing evidence for the divinity residing with them. In this light, we might envision Paracas tombs as the first Andean reliquaries.

Acknowledgments

I would like to express my sincerest appreciation to Richard Burger and Jason Nesbitt for the invitation to contribute to this volume. My work benefited from discussions with Jalh Dulanto, Michelle Young, Regina Harrison, Rubén García, Lucía Balbuena, Yuichi Matsumoto, Ann Rowe, Catherine Allen, Jeffrey Quilter, and Dawn Kriss and from the suggestions of two anonymous reviewers.

NOTES

1 See also Alana Cordy-Collins (1976:figs. 25–27) for a discussion of Chavín petroglyphs.

2 According to geochemical tests, obsidian exchange occurred in some iteration as early as 10,000 BC between San Nicolás in the Nazca drainage with Quispisisa in Ayacucho (Burger and Asaro 1979; DeLeonardis and Glascock 2013:169).

3 See Axel Nielsen's (2013:400) comprehensive study of southern Andean exchange routes and the role of llama caravans.

4 See also Edison Mendoza's (2017) discussion of the Paracas–Ayacucho relationship.

5 These concerns have been voiced by Elera (1997:178–179) and Kaulicke (2013) about the relationship between Cupisnique and Chavín material culture and the differentiation of each in the archaeological record.

6 The issue of composite style is not exclusive to the Early Horizon Andes (see, for example, Dean and Leibsohn 2003).

7 The circle-and-dot motif is widespread in the Central Andes, including the Ayacucho region, for the time period under question (Burger 1984; Matsumoto 2010; Ochatoma 1992, 1998).

8 Elera (1997:191) refers to this ceramic form as *florero* or *sombrero*. On the south coast, the Paracas iteration of this form appears later in the ceramic sequence and is described as a spittoon (Menzel, Rowe, and Dawson 1964:111, 115). Aside from its earliest appearance in the Coyungo tomb, it has been identified only at the Juan Pablo cemetery at Teojate (see Kriss et al. 2018:fig. 4, left).

9 When Dorothy Menzel, John Rowe, and Lawrence Dawson (1964:2) established their ten-phase relative chronology for Paracas ceramics, they

wrestled with the problem of how to sequence foreign influence. For this reason, they left open the possibility—Ocucaje Phases 1 and 2—of someday filling the gap. Alan Sawyer (1972:91) has chosen to fill the gap with a phase that he calls the "Chavinoid-Paracas Period."

10 In the early literature (e.g., Kroeber 1944:36–41; Soldi 1956), the term Cavernas is cited as a catch-all phrase for the whole of Paracas post-fired painted ceramics because the Cavernas tombs were thought to be the origin point for the painting technique.

11 The author has observed similar modeled figural bottles with winking or missing eyes.

12 The bark is recognized for its medicinal qualities. In the colonial era, it aided in the cleansing and healing of wounds (Newson 2017). Elsewhere, I have suggested that plants or minerals used in ceramic production may have served as health treatments or for related purposes (DeLeonardis 2016:144).

13 These changes may correspond to observations made by Richard MacNeish, Thomas Patterson, and David Browman (1975:45), who note a decline in the copper trade around 650 BC that is revived on the south coast in ca. 450 BC.

14 Karwa (also spelled Carhua) is a coastal site located south of the Paracas Peninsula. To date, none of the painted textiles for which the site is known have been encountered in scientific excavations. Painted textiles from the wider corpus are said to be from unregistered graves in Callango and Chincha. See Wallace 1991:62–64 for the history of their discovery.

15 At the Karwa site, extreme measures by vandals are said to have been used to expedite extraction of the cloths, resulting in the fragmentary state of some of the corpus.

16 In contemporary practice, textile fragments are randomly sewn together to increase their size and thereby market value.

17 Breaking objects, including the personal possessions of the deceased, was practiced by various Native Americans as part of their funerary rituals. Objects could also be broken and offered along with the ends of hair for entombment. In some cases, the practice followed the custom of forgetting or erasing the memory of the person after their death (Opler 1983:377).

18 The fragmentation of Chavín stone monuments at the time of collapse is beyond the scope of this paper. See Burger (1995:228–229) for an overview, and Burger (2008c) for discussion of the Yauya stela.

REFERENCES CITED

Alva, Walter

1986   *Cerámica temprana en el valle de Jequetepeque, norte del Perú*. Verag C. H. Beck, Munich.

Bachir B., Aïcha

2017   El edificio de los frisos de Ánimas Altas: Ser Paracas en el valle bajo de Ica. *Boletín de Arqueología PUCP* 22:191–225.

Balbuena, Lucía

2013   Evidencias Paracas en los valles de Pisco y Mala. *Boletín de Arqueología PUCP* 17:57–76.

Beresford-Jones, David, Carmela Alarcón, Susana Arce, Alex Chepstow-Lusty, Oliver Whaley, Fraser Sturt, Manuel Gorriti, Oscar Portocarrero, and Lauren Cadwallader

2009   Ocupación y subsistencia del horizonte temprano en el contexto de cambios ecológicos de largo plaza en las cuencas de Samaca y Ullujaya, valle bajo de Ica. *Boletín de Arqueología PUCP* 13:237–257.

Bird, Junius B.

1962   *Art and Life in Old Peru: An Exhibition.* American Museum of Natural History, New York.

Brugnoli B., Paulina, and Soledad Hoces de la Guardia

1991 Analisís de un textil pintado Chavín. *Boletín del Museo Chileno de Arte Precolombino* 5:67–80.

Burger, Richard L.

1984 *The Prehistoric Occupation of Chavín de Huántar, Peru.* University of California Press, Berkeley.

1995 *Chavín and the Origins of Andean Civilization.* Thames and Hudson, New York.

1996 Chavín. In *Andean Art at Dumbarton Oaks*, vol. 1, edited by Elizabeth H. Boone, pp. 45–86. Dumbarton Oaks Research Library and Collection, Washington, D.C.

2008a Chavín de Huántar and Its Spheres of Influence. In *Handbook of South American Archaeology*, edited by Helaine Silverman and William Isbell, pp. 681–704. Springer, New York.

2008b Los señores de los templos. In *Señores de los reinos de la luna*, edited by Krzysztof Makowski, pp. 12–37. Colección Arte y Tesoros del Perú, Banco de Crédito, Lima.

2008c The Original Context of the Yauya Stela. In *Chavín Art, Architecture, and Culture*, edited by William J. Conklin and Jeffrey Quilter, pp. 163–179. Cotsen Insitute of Archaeology, University of California, Los Angeles.

Burger, Richard L. (editor)

2009 *The Life and Writings of Julio C. Tello: America's First Indigenous Archaeologist.* University of Iowa Press, Iowa City.

Burger, Richard L., and Frank Asaro

1979 Análisis de rasgos significativos en la obsidiana de los Andes centrales. *Revista del Museo Nacional* 43:281–326.

Burger, Richard L., and Jerrold B. Leikin

2018 Cinnabar Use in Prehispanic Peru and Its Possible Health Consequences. *Journal of Archaeological Sciences* 17:730–734.

Burger, Richard L., and Ramiro Matos Mendieta

2002 Atalla: A Center on the Periphery of the Chavín Horizon. *Latin American Antiquity* 13(2):153–177.

Canziani A., José

1992 Arquitectura y urbanismo del período Paracas en el valle de Chincha. *Gaceta arqueológica andina* 6:87–117.

2013 Arquitectura, urbanismo y transformaciones territoriales del período Paracas en el valle de Chincha. *Boletín de Arqueología PUCP* 17:9–30.

Chapman, John

2000 *Fragmentation in Archaeology: People, Places and Broken Objects in Prehistory of Southeastern Europe.* Routledge, London.

Conklin, William J.

2008 The Culture of Chavín Textiles. In *Chavín Art, Architecture, and Culture*, edited by William J. Conklin and Jeffrey Quilter, pp. 261–278. Cotsen Insitute of Archaeology, University of California, Los Angeles.

Cook, Anita G.

1992 The Lower Ica Valley Ground Drawings on the South Coast of Peru. Paper presented at the 11th Annual Northeast Conference on Andean and Amazonian Archaeology and Ethnohistory, Hamilton.

1999 Asentamientos Paracas en el valle bajo de Ica, Perú. *Gaceta arqueológica andina* 9(25):61–90.

Cordy-Collins, Alana

1976 An Iconographic Study of Chavín Textiles from the South Coast of Peru: The Discovery of a Pre-Columbian Catechism. PhD dissertation, University of California, Los Angeles.

1977 Chavín Art: Its Shamanic/Hallucinogenic Origins. In *Pre-Columbian Art History: Selected Readings*, edited by Alana Cordy-Collins and Jean Stern, pp. 353–362. Peek, Palo Alto, Calif.

1979 Cotton and the Staff God: Analysis of an Ancient Chavín Textile. In *The Junius B. Bird Pre-Columbian Textile Conference*, edited by Ann P. Rowe, Elizabeth P. Benson, and Anne-Louise Schaffer, pp. 51–60. Textile Museum and Dumbarton Oaks, Washington, D.C.

1999 Telas pintadas Chavín del valle de Ica, costa sur. In *Tejidos milenarios del Perú / Ancient Peruvian Textiles*, edited by

José Antonio de Lavalle and Rosario de Lavalle de Cardenas, pp. 107–141. Integra AFP, Lima.

Costin, Cathy L.

2016   Introduction: Making Value, Making Meaning: Techné in the Pre-Columbian World. In *Making Value, Making Meaning: Techné in the Pre-Columbian World*, edited by Cathy L. Costin, pp. 19–30. Dumbarton Oaks Research Library and Collection, Washington, D.C.

Daggett, Richard E.

1991   Paracas: Discovery and Controversy. In *Paracas Art and Architecture: Object and Context in South Coastal Peru*, edited by Anne Paul, pp. 35–60. University of Iowa Press, Iowa City.

2009   Julio C. Tello: An Account of His Rise to Prominence in Peruvian Archaeology. In *The Life and Writings of Julio C. Tello: America's First Indigenous Archaeologist*, edited by Richard L. Burger, pp. 7–54. University of Iowa Press, Iowa City.

Dean, Carolyn, and Dana Leibsohn

2003   Hybridity and Its Discontents: Considering Visual Culture in Colonial Spanish America. *Colonial Latin American Review* 12(1):5–35.

DeLeonardis, Lisa

1991   Settlement History of the Lower Ica Valley, Peru, Vth–Ist Centuries, B.C. MA thesis, Catholic University, Washington, D.C.

1997   Paracas Settlement in Callango, Lower Ica Valley, Ist Millennium B.C., Peru. PhD dissertation, Catholic University, Washington, D.C.

1999   Preliminary Analysis of the Cerrillos Site PV6263: 1999 Excavations. Report submitted to Dwight Wallace, California Institute of Peruvian Studies.

2005   Paracas Cultural Contexts: New Evidence from the West Bank of Callango. *Andean Past* 7:27–55.

2012   Interpreting the Paracas Body and Its Value in Ancient Peru. In *The Construction of Value in the Ancient World*, edited by Gary Urton and John Papadopoulos, pp. 197–217. Cotsen Institute of Archaeology, University of California, Los Angeles.

2013   La sustancia y el contexto de las ofrendas rituales de la cerámica Paracas. *Boletín de Arqueología PUCP* 17:205–231.

2016   Encoded Process, Embodied Meaning in Paracas Post-Fired Ceramics. In *Making Value, Making Meaning: Techné in the Pre-Columbian World*, edited by Cathy L. Costin, pp. 129–166. Dumbarton Oaks Research Library and Collection, Washington, D.C.

2022   Modeling the Sacred: The Pyramidal Form and Its Resonance in Paracas Sculptural Ceramics. *Latin American and Latinx Visual Culture* 4(2):10–28.

DeLeonardis, Lisa, and Michael Glascock

2013   From Qhesqa to Callango: A Paracas Obsidian Assemblage from the Lower Ica Valley, Peru. *Ñawpa Pacha: Journal of Andean Archaeology* 33(2):163–191.

DeLeonardis, Lisa, and George Lau

2004   Life, Death, and Ancestors. In *Andean Archaeology*, edited by Helaine Silverman, pp. 77–115. Blackwell Press, Malden, Mass.

Dulanto, Jalh

2013   Puerto Nuevo: Redes de intercambio a larga distancia durante la primer mitad del primer milenio antes de nuestra era. *Boletín de Arqueología PUCP* 17:103–132.

Dulanto, Jalh, Patricia Gonzáles, and Enrique Guadalupe

2019   Los pigmentos utilizados en la pintura poscocción de vasijas de cerámica Paracas temprano de Puerto Nuevo y las redes de intercambio de la costa y sierra surcentral del Perú durante los siglos IX–VI a.c. *Boletín de Arqueología PUCP* 26:65–83.

Elera, Carlos G.

1997   Cupisnique y Salinar: Algunas reflexiones preliminares. In *Arquitectura y civilización en los Andes prehispánico*, edited by Elizabeth Bonnier and Henning Bischof, pp. 176–201. Reiss Museum, Mannheim.

Fernández, Abel, and Alexis Rodríguez

2017   Ofrendas depositadas durante el entierro del patio hundido de Cerro del Gentil. In *Cerro del Gentil: Un sitio Paracas en el valle de Chincha, costa sur del Perú*, edited by Henry Tantaleán and Charles Stanish, pp. 117–144. Publicaciones del Programa Arqueológico Chincha–PACH/PACH Press, Lima.

Fux, Peter

2011   The Petroglyphs of Chichictara, Palpa, Peru: Documentation and Interpretation Using Terrestrial Laser Scanning and Image-Based 3D Modeling. *Zeitschrift für Archäologie Außereuropäischer Kulturen* 4:127–205.

Fux, Peter (editor)

2013   Catalogue: Handcrafted Objects from the Early, Middle, and Late Formative Periods. In *Chavín: Peru's Enigmatic Temple in the Andes*, pp. 217–271. Museum Rietburg, Zurich.

García, Rubén

2009   Puerto Nuevo y los orígenes de la tradición estilístico-religiosa paracas. *Boletín de Arqueología PUCP* 13:187–207.

2013   Geoglifos parcas de la costa sur: Cerro Lechuza y Cerro Pico. *Boletín de Arqueología PUCP* 13:151–168.

Goldstein, Paul S.

2000   Exotic Goods and Everyday Chiefs: Long-Distance Exchange and Indigenous Sociopolitical Development in the South-Central Andes. *Latin American Antiquity* 11(4):335–361.

Gundrum, Darrell S.

1996   Ritual Landscape and Defensive Function at a Late Paracas Period Settlement, Peru. Paper presented at the 61st Annual Meeting of the Society for American Archaeology, New Orleans.

Isla, Johny, and Markus Reindel

2006   Una tumba Paracas Temprano en Mollake Chico, valle de Palpa, costa sur del Perú. *Zeitschrift für Archäologie Außereuropäischer Kulturen* 1:153–182.

Kaplan, Emily

1999   Technical Studies of Post-Fired Paint on Paracas Ceramics. Paper presented at the 64th Annual Meeting of the Society for American Archaeology, Chicago.

Kaulicke, Peter

2013   Paracas y Chavín: Variaciones sobre un tema longevo. *Boletín de Arqueología PUCP* 13:263–290.

Kaulicke, Peter, Lars Fehren-Schmitz, María Kolp-Godoy, Patricia Landa, Óscar Loyola, Martha Palma, Elsa Tomasto, Cindy Vergelh, and Burkhard Vogti

2009   Implicancias de un área funeraria del período formativo tardío en el Departamento de Ica. *Boletín de Arqueología PUCP* 13:289–322.

Kriss, Dawn, Ellen Howe, Judith Levinson, Federico Carò, Adriana Rizzo, and Lisa DeLeonardis

2018   A Material and Technical Study of Paracas Painted Ceramics. *Antiquity* 92(366):1492–1510.

Kroeber, Alfred L.

1944   *Peruvian Archeology in 1942.* Wenner Gren Foundation for Anthropological Research, New York.

Kroeber, Alfred L., and Donald Collier

1998   *The Archaeology and Pottery of Nazca, Peru: Alfred L. Kroeber's 1926 Expedition,* edited by Patrick H. Carmichael. Altamira Press, Walnut Creek, Calif.

Lapiner, Alan

1976   *Pre-Columbian Art of South America.* Harry H. Abrams, New York.

Lumbreras, Luis G.

1998   The Social Context of Art in Pre-Columbian America. In *Art in Pre-Columbian America,* pp. 10–63. Museo Chileno de Arte Precolombino, Santiago.

MacNeish, Richard S., Thomas C. Patterson, and David L. Browman

1975   *The Central Peruvian Prehistoric Interaction Sphere.* Papers of the Robert S. Peabody Foundation for Archaeology, Phillips Academy, Andover, Mass.

Massey, Sarah

1983   Antiguo centro Paracas, Animas Altas. In *Culturas precolombinas: Paracas,* edited by José Antonio de Lavalle and Werner Lang, pp. 134–160. Banco de Crédito del Perú en la Cultura, Lima.

Matsumoto, Yuichi

2010   Prehistoric Ceremonial Center of Campanayuq Rumi: Interregional Interactions in the South-Central Highlands of Peru. PhD dissertation, Yale University, New Haven.

2012   Recognizing Ritual: The Case of Campanayuq Rumi. *Antiquity* 86(333):746–759.

Matsumoto, Yuichi, Jason Nesbitt, Michael D. Glascock, Yuri I. Cavero Palomino, and Richard L. Burger

2018   Interregional Obsidian Exchange during the Late Initial Period and Early Horizon: New Perspectives from Campanayuq Rumi, Peru. *Latin American Antiquity* 29(1):44–63.

Mendoza Martínez, Edison

2017   Secuencia de cerámica Paracas en Pallaucha, Vilcashuamán, Ayacucho. *Boletín de Arqueología PUCP* 22:91–116.

Menzel, Dorothy, John H. Rowe, and Lawrence Dawson

1964   *The Paracas Pottery of Ica: A Study in Style and Time.* University of California Press, Berkeley.

Ministerio de Cultura

2013   *Paracas.* Museo Nacional de Arqueología, Antropología e Historia del Perú, Lima.

More More, Gabriel (editor)

2018   *Proyecto de rescate arqueológico de los geoglifos Pampa de Ocas, Paracas, Pisco-Ica.* Futura Consorcio Inmobiliario, S.A., Lima.

Newson, Linda A.

2017   *Making Medicines in Early Colonial Peru: Apothecaries, Science and Society.* Brill, Leiden.

Nielsen, Axel E.

2013   Circulating Objects and the Constitution of South Andean Society. In *Merchants, Markets, and Exchange in the Pre-Columbian World*, edited by Kenneth Hirth and Joanne Pillsbury, pp. 389–418. Dumbarton Oaks Research Library and Collection, Washington, D.C.

Ochatoma P., José

1992   Acerca del formativo en Ayacucho. In *Estudios de arqueología peruana*, edited by Duccio Bonavía, pp. 193–213. Fomciencias, Lima.

1998   El período formativo en Ayacucho: Balance y perspectivas. *Boletín de Arqueología PUCP* 2:289–302.

Opler, Morris E.

1983   The Apachean Culture Pattern and Its Origins. In *Handbook of North American Indians*, vol. 10, *Southwest*, edited by Alfonso Ortiz, pp. 368–392. Smithsonian Institution, Washington, D.C.

Patterson, Thomas C.

1971   Chavín: An Interpretation of Its Spread and Influence. In *Dumbarton Oaks Conference on Chavín*, edited by Elizabeth P. Benson, pp. 29–48. Dumbarton Oaks Research Library and Collection, Washington, D.C.

Paul, Anne

1990   *Paracas Ritual Attire.* University of Oklahoma Press, Norman.

2000   Protective Perimeters: The of Symbolism of Borders on Paracas Textiles. *Res: Anthropology and Aesthetics* 38:144–167.

Pennington, Terence D., Carlos Reynel, and Aniceto Daza

2004   *Trees of Peru.* David Hunt, Milborne Port Sherborne, England.

Peters, Ann H.

1991   Ecology and Society in Embroidered Images from the Paracas Necropolis. In *Paracas Art and Architecture: Object and Context in South Coastal Peru*, edited by Anne Paul, pp. 240–314. University of Iowa Press, Iowa City.

2013   Topará en Pisco: Patrón de asentamiento y paisaje. *Boletín de Arqueología PUCP* 17:77–102.

Reindel, Markus

2009   Life at the Edge of the Desert: Archaeological Reconstruction of the Settlement History in the Valleys of Palpa, Peru. In *New Technologies for Archaeology, Natural Science in Archaeology*, edited by Markus Reindel and Günther A. Wagner, pp. 439–461. Springer-Verlag, Berlin.

Reindel, Markus, and Johny Isla

2004   Archäeologie und Naturwissenschaften in Palpa. In *Neue naturwissenschaftliche Methoden und Technologien für die archäologische Forschung in Palpa, Peru*, edited by Markus Reindel and Günther A. Wagner, pp. 11–14. Goethe-Institut, Lima.

2009   El período inicial en Pernil Alto, Palpa, costa sur del Perú. *Boletín de Arqueología PUCP* 13:259–288.

2013   Early Cultural Developments in the Southern Andes. In *Chavín: Peru's Enigmatic Temple in the Andes*, edited by Peter Fux, pp. 40–49. Museum Rietburg, Zurich.

2017 Nuevo patrón arquitectónico paracas en Lucanas, sierra sur del Perú. *Boletín de Arqueología PUCP* 22:227–254.

Roe, Peter G.

2008 How to Build a Raptor: Why the Dumbarton Oaks "Scaled Cayman" Callango Textile Is Really a Jaguaroid Harpy Eagle. In *Chavín Art, Architecture, and Culture*, edited by William J. Conklin and Jeffrey Quilter, pp. 181–216. Cotsen Institute of Archaeology, University of California, Los Angeles.

Romero B., Martha, Alejandra Sánchez-Polo, Michelle Mármol V., and Fernanda Espinoza G.

2018 Los pigmentos del desarrollo regional en la costa ecuatoriana: Hallazgos de los análisis de laboratorio. In *Pigmentos y brillos en la costa del Ecuador precolombino*, edited by María Fernanda Cartagena and Alejandra Sánchez-Polo, pp. 76–83. Museo de Arte Precolombino Casa del Alabado, Quito.

Rowe, John H.

1962 *Chavín Art: An Inquiry into Its Form and Meaning*. Museum of Primitive Art, New York.

Sánchez-Polo, Alejandra

2018 Pigmentos y brillos en la costa del Ecuador precolombino. In *Pigmentos y brillos en la costa del Ecuador precolombino*, edited by María Fernanda Cartagena and Alejandra Sánchez-Polo, pp. 20–53. Museo de Arte Precolombino Casa del Alabado, Quito.

Sawyer, Alan R.

1972 The Feline in Paracas Art. In *The Cult of the Feline*, edited by Elizabeth P. Benson, pp. 91–112. Dumbarton Oaks Research Library and Collection, Washington, D.C.

Soldi, Pablo L.

1956 *Chavín en Ica*. Voz de Ica, Ica.

Splitstoser, Jeffrey C.

2009 Weaving the Structure of the Cosmos: Cloth, Agency, and Worldview at Cerrillos, An Early Paracas Site in Ica, Peru. PhD dissertation, Catholic University, Washington, D.C.

Splitstoser, Jeffrey, Dwight D. Wallace, and Mercedes Delgado

2009 Nuevas evidencias de textiles y cerámica de la época Paracas Temprano en Cerrillos, valle de Ica, Perú. *Boletín de Arqueología PUCP* 13:209–235.

Stanish, Charles, and Henry Tantaleán

2018 The Chincha Lines. *Ñawpa Pacha: Journal of Andean Archaeology* 38(1):1–31.

2020 *The Chincha Geoglyph Complex / El complejo de geoglifos de Chincha*. Instituto Peruano de Estudios Arqueológicos, Lima.

Tantaleán, Henry, Charles Stanish, and Alexis Rodríguez

2020 *La cerámica Paracas del valle de Chincha, costa sur del Perú*. Programa Arqueológico Chincha, Lima.

Tello, Julio C.

1929 *Antiguo Perú: Primera época*. Estado por la Comisión Organizadora del Segundo Congreso Sudamericano de Turismo, Lima.

1959 *Paracas, primera parte*. Publicación del Proyecto 8b del Programa 1941–1942 del Instituto Recursos Andinos de Nueva York. Empresa Gráfica, Lima.

Tello, Julio C., and Toribio Mejía Xesspe

1979 *Paracas segunda parte: Cavernas y Necrópolis*. Universidad Nacional Mayor de San Marcos, Lima; and Instituto Andino de Nueva York, New York.

Tomasto Cagiga, Elsa

2009 Talking Bones: Bioarchaeological Analysis of Individuals from Palpa. In *New Technologies for Archaeology, Natural Science in Archaeology*, edited by Markus Reindel and Günther A. Wagner, pp. 141–158. Springer-Verlag, Berlin.

Torres, Constantino M.

2008 Chavín's Psychoactive Pharmacopoeia: The Iconographic Evidence Art. In *Chavín Art, Architecture, and Culture*, edited by William J. Conklin and Jeffrey Quilter, pp. 239–259. Cotsen Institute of Archaeology, University of California, Los Angeles.

Verano, John W.

2016   *Holes in the Head: The Art and
        Archaeology of Trepanation in Ancient
        Peru.* Dumbarton Oaks Research Library
        and Collection, Washington, D.C.

Wallace, Dwight T

1962   Cerrillos: An Early Paracas Site in Ica,
        Peru. *American Antiquity* 27(3):303–314.

1991   A Technical and Iconographic Analysis
        of Carhua Painted Textiles. In *Paracas
        Art and Architecture: Object and Context
        in South Coastal Peru*, edited by Anne
        Paul, pp. 61–109. University of Iowa Press,
        Iowa City.

Weiner, Annette B.

1992   *Inalienable Possessions: The Paradox of
        Keeping-While-Giving.* University of
        California Press, Berkeley.

Young, Michele

2017   De la montaña al mar: Intercambio
        entre la sierra centro-sur y la costa sur
        durante el horizonte temprano. *Boletín de
        Arqueología PUCP* 22:9–34.

Zorogastúa, Paolo, Mary Ávila, and Terrah Jones

2017   Consumo aliméntico y ritual en Cerro del
        Gentil. In *Cerro del Gentil: Un sitio Paracas
        en el valle de Chincha, costa sur del Perú*,
        edited by Henry Tantaleán and Charles
        Stanish, pp. 183–206. Publicaciones del
        Programa Arqueológico Chincha–PACH/
        PACH Press, Lima.

The Chavín Interaction Sphere and Peru's South Coast

Maritime Communities, Long-Distance Exchange Networks, and Prestige Economies during the Early Horizon in the Central Andes

JALH DULANTO

The period between the tenth and sixth centuries BC is critical for our understanding of the prehispanic history of the Central Andes. As several researchers have noted, Central Andean populations experienced important political and economic changes during this time (e.g., Burger 1992; Kaulicke 1994). Notable among these shifts are two that are closely linked to each other. The first is the emergence of elites who emphasize their own status (see Seki, this volume), and the second is the consolidation of a prestige economy.

Several lines of evidence indicate that this new type of elite appears for the first time in the eighth century BC. For instance, during this period (but not before), certain individuals began to be buried in ways that highlighted their status in life and that elevated them above the rest of the population. Cases like those of Loma Macanche (Kaulicke 1998), Pacopampa (Seki, this volume; Seki et al. 2010), Chongoyape (Lothrop 1941), Cerro Corbacho (Alva 1992), and Kuntur Wasi (Onuki and Inokuchi 2011), on the north coast and in the

north highlands, are examples of this change. The burials of these individuals stand out because they are more elaborate, with an unusually high number and variety of associated offerings. But above all, they stand out because of the high proportion of offerings considered exotic and prestigious—either because they are imported or produced with raw materials from distant and foreign places, or because they are manufactured with strange and fascinating special technologies.

The fact that many of these offerings are objects of adornment and personal use reinforces that their main purpose was to aggrandize individuals who in life had been distinguished above others. The fact that some of these offerings are also pieces of ritual paraphernalia, are linked to the consumption of hallucinogens, or serve as support for complex iconographic representations suggests that one of the main means to achieve such aggrandizement and distinction was the possession of esoteric and mysterious knowledge (Burger 1992; Helms 1988, 1993, 2014).

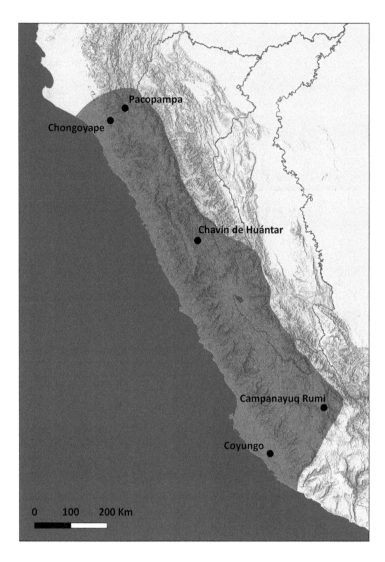

figure 11.1
Map of the Central
Andes, showing the
approximate area
covered by the Chavín
Interaction Sphere.
Map by Jalh Dulanto.

Other lines of evidence indicate that, around the eighth century BC, the exchange networks—through which these exotic and prestigious goods and information were transported—expanded and intensified rapidly until they integrated populations from regions as far apart as Lambayeque and Cajamarca (e.g., Pacopampa and Kuntur Wasi) in the north and Nasca and Ayacucho in the south (e.g., Coyungo and Campanayuq Rumi) (Burger 2008, 2013) (Figure 11.1). One node in these networks is a compelling case in point: Chavín de Huántar.

As Richard L. Burger (2013) has noted, at this ceremonial center, we find evidence of various imported goods from distant places, such as strombus and spondylus shells from the coast of Ecuador, pottery from different regions of the coast and highlands, stone vessels from the north coast, fish and marine mollusks from the Pacific coast, hallucinogens from the Eastern Andes and *ceja de selva*, cinnabar from Huancavelica, and obsidian from different sources of the southern highlands, among others. And this surge of exotic materials is not unusual. We find similar examples, not just in other ceremonial centers, but also in other types of settlements, scattered throughout the Central Andes.

Our research in Puerto Nuevo and other sites in the Paracas area (e.g., Dulanto 2013; Dulanto and Accinelli 2013) offers a unique opportunity to increase our knowledge of these exchange networks and their relationships with the political and economic changes I have just outlined. The evidence recovered so far from Puerto Nuevo leaves no doubt about the existence of interregional connections between the south coast and other distant coastal areas of the Central Andes, particularly contacts with the central coast (Burger and Salazar, this volume), the north-central coast and the north coast, and the adjacent south-central highlands of Huancavelica (Young, this volume) and Ayacucho (Matsumoto and Cavero Palomino, this volume).

The South Coast during the Tenth–Sixth Centuries BC

For several decades, we have known that the south coast—that is, the area made up of the lower and middle sections of the Chincha, Pisco, Ica, and Nasca Valleys—was not foreign to the political and economic changes of the tenth to sixth centuries BC. Although we know few sites from this period (Figure 11.2), there is clear evidence on the south coast of the two changes I mentioned before: the emergence of elites who emphasize their own status and the consolidation of a prestige economy.

Like the north coast and northern highlands, the south coast sees the emergence of elite burials beginning in the eighth century BC. Three cases worth mentioning in some detail are the elite burials found at Coyungo in the Rio Grande Valley, Mollake Chico in the Palpa Valley, and Karwa on the shore between the mouths of the Pisco and Ica Rivers. These burials show important similarities as well as significant differences with those of the northern regions.

In terms of the most recent and best constructed chronology of the south coast, that of the Nasca–Palpa Archaeological Project (Unkel et al. 2007; Unkel et al. 2012), these three burials clearly belong to the Early Paracas period (840–500 BC; all dates are calibrated) (Figure 11.3). However, it is worth noting that they predate most known cases of monumental architecture in this area, the vast majority of which date from the Middle Paracas period (500–380 BC) and Late Paracas period (380–260 BC).

The first of these tombs, that of Coyungo (Kaulicke 2013; Kaulicke et al. 2010; Loyola 2016), was looted in the late 1950s or early 1960s. At least part of its contents was sold on the antiquities black

market. Later, in 2006, Peter Kaulicke and his team excavated the remains of this tomb, and, thanks to his work, we know something about it today. The tomb has an unusually large quadrangular chamber with rounded corners constructed of conical adobes and *huarango* trunks. It is 3.4 m long, 3.3 m wide, and at least 1.2 m deep, and it is oriented northeast–southeast, with an access of three steps on its northeast side. Its walls were originally plastered and painted with various colors.

Within this chamber, archaeologists found the remains of at least nine individuals (two adult men, two adult women, four indeterminate adults, and an indeterminate adolescent), mixed with the remains of at least fifty-two textiles, thirty-eight ceramic vessels, and several gourds (at least one of them decorated). However, the most impressive finding was a fragment of a painted textile, which turned out to be one of the missing scraps of the so-called Callango textile at Dumbarton Oaks, which actually comes from Coyungo (Figure 11.4). This artifact, along with another less complex cloth, a ceramic vessel, and a decorated gourd—apparently all from the same tomb—have iconographic representations evoking the lithic sculpture of Chavín de Huántar. The latest of two radiocarbon dates for this tomb dates its use as sometime between 756 and 407 BC (Kaulicke et al. 2010).

The second of the tombs, Mollake Chico, was looted in 1969. Markus Reindel and Johny Isla excavated its remains in 2003 (Isla and Reindel 2006; Reindel and Isla 2006; Tomasto, Reindel, and Isla 2015). Like Coyungo, this tomb also had an unusually large quadrangular chamber with rounded corners, in this case built using stones and mud mortar. It was 2.5 m long, 1.8 m wide, and at least 1.1 m deep. Within this chamber, archaeologists found the remains of at least seventeen individuals: twelve adults and five infants, male and female in a similar proportion. Some of these human bones were burned. They also found at least nine pottery vessels, carved bones (one with the figure of a monkey), 369 shell beads, sixty-two stone and clay beads, a gold ring, and an obsidian point. The latest of two radiocarbon measurements from this tomb dates its use to between 792 and 431 BC.

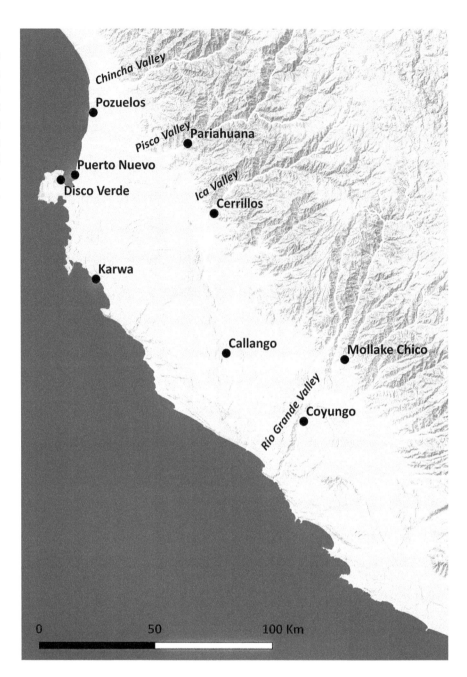

figure 11.2
Map of the south coast, showing the most important archaeological sites with Early Horizon occupations excavated by archaeologists. Map by Jalh Dulanto.

The third tomb, Karwa, was looted in the 1970s, but despite our efforts using ground penetrating radar (GPR) and digging several test pits, we have not yet been able to locate it. However, based on descriptions by apparent witnesses to the looting (Burger 1992), we suspect that it would have had a quadrangular chamber containing the remains of several individuals and a high number of offerings—among them, several fragments of Chavín-style textiles are believed to come from this tomb (Burger 1988).

Like the elite tombs of the north coast and northern highlands, these three tombs stand out for being unusually large and elaborate, as well as for containing more offerings and prestige goods than "common" tombs. However, unlike the burials from the northern regions, they contain not one but several individuals of both sexes and of different ages. Because of this, they could be interpreted as mausoleums of high-status family groups (Kaulicke 2013; Kaulicke et al. 2010).

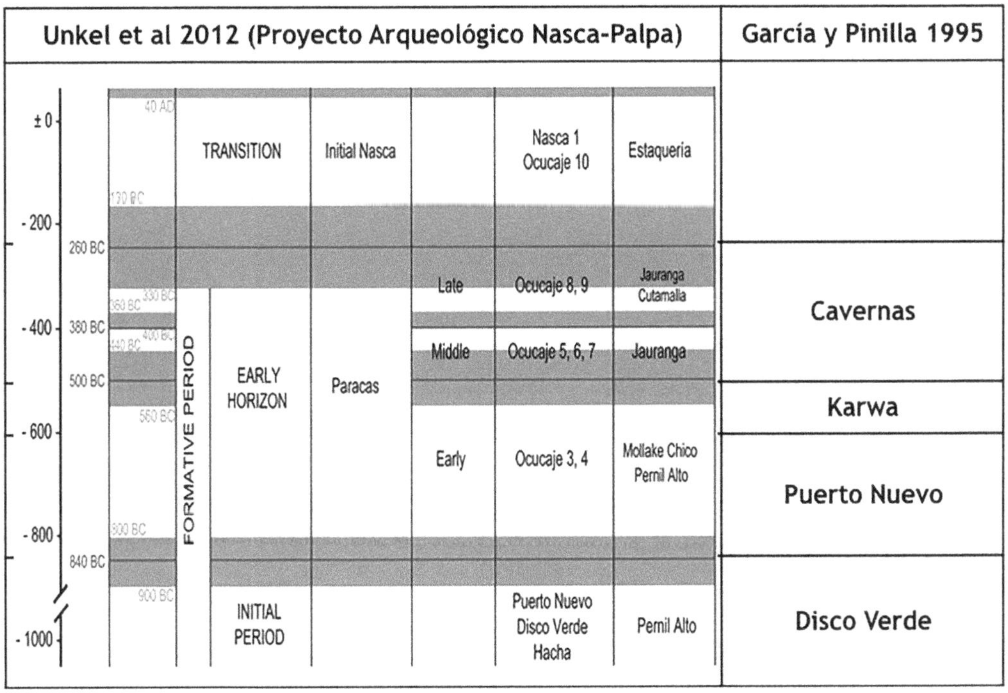

Unkel et al 2012 (Proyecto Arqueológico Nasca-Palpa)						García y Pinilla 1995
TRANSITION	Initial Nasca		Nasca 1 Ocucaje 10	Estaqueria		
		Late	Ocucaje 8, 9	Jauranga Cutamalla		Cavernas
FORMATIVE PERIOD	EARLY HORIZON	Middle	Ocucaje 5, 6, 7	Jauranga		
	Paracas					Karwa
		Early	Ocucaje 3, 4	Mollake Chico Pernil Alto		Puerto Nuevo
	INITIAL PERIOD		Puerto Nuevo Disco Verde Hacha	Pernil Alto		Disco Verde

Time axis (left): ±0 (40 AD), 130 BC, -200 (260 BC), 330 BC, 360 BC, 400 BC, -400 (380 BC, 440 BC), 500 BC, 560 BC, -600, 800 BC, 840 BC, -800, 900 BC, -1000

figure 11.3
The main periods and phases proposed for the first century BC in the south coast of Peru. The Puerto Nuevo and Karwa phases are dated to 850–500 BC (García and Pinilla 1995; Unkel et al. 2012).

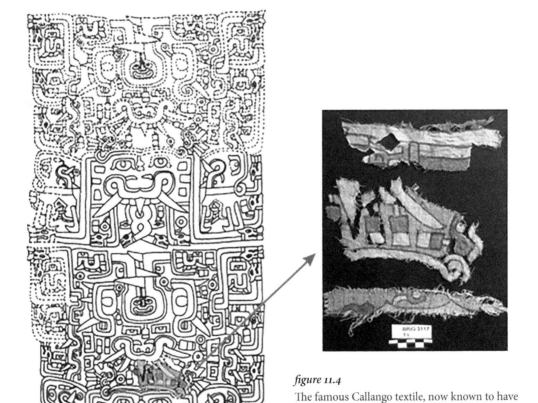

figure 11.4
The famous Callango textile, now known to have been looted from one of the tombs excavated by Peter Kaulicke and Oscar Loyola in Coyungo. Pre-Columbian Collection, PC.B.544, Dumbarton Oaks Research Library and Collection, Washington, D.C.

The textiles found in these tombs contain complex iconographic representations incorporating foreign and local elements. This suggests that the adoption and reformulation of beliefs and practices of other religious traditions would have been an important means through which these elites legitimized their power and maintained their status, distinguishing themselves from the rest of the population over several generations. On the south coast, no burials similar to the ones I have just described have been discovered for the period prior to the eighth century BC.

Puerto Nuevo

Puerto Nuevo (Dulanto 2013; Engel 1966, 1991; García 2009) is at least partially contemporary with these three tombs. As I will show, the site has several occupations in the Early Paracas period, even though its first occupations date from the pre-Paracas period. Located in the Bahía de Paracas, about 15 km from the mouth of the Pisco River and about 400 m from its current shoreline, Puerto Nuevo is about 150 km north of Coyungo and Mollake Chico and about 45 km from Karwa. Despite being located in a desert area typical of the Peruvian coast, even today it is possible to find fresh water by excavating only a few meters deep. Until a few years ago, you could still see *totora* reed fields in the vicinity of the site (Figure 11.5). The presence of subterranean water and sunken agricultural fields, next to a bay protected from currents and waves, helps explain why the Bahía de Paracas was occupied repeatedly by fishing communities over several millennia—or at least since the eighth

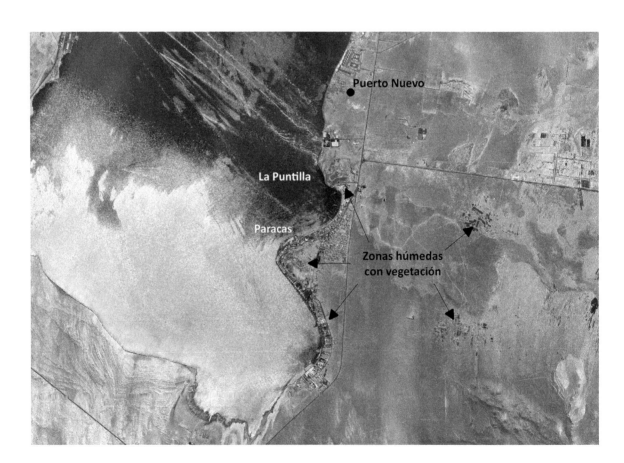

figure 11.5
The Puerto Nuevo archaeological site and the *totora* reed fields and sunken agricultural fields located on the Bahía de Paracas area. Illustration by Jalh Dulanto.

millenium BC, if we trust Frédéric Engel's (1991) dates for the Pampa de Santo Domingo Archaic site.

Today, Puerto Nuevo's concentration of archaeological remains is approximately 300 m in diameter. Within this area of about 6.5 ha, there are several mounds of less than 1.5 m in height. Most of these mounds are natural, and archaeological remains are deposited directly on them.

At the beginning of the 1960s, Engel excavated at least ten units of around 18 × 18 meters. Unfortunately, as far as we know, Engel never wrote a report on his excavations at the site, and his field notes have not yet been published. The only available information about his excavations comes from brief and extremely general observations scattered among several of his publications (e.g., Engel 1963a, 1963b, 1963c, 1966, 1976, 1987, 1991). From these general observations, we know that Engel found remains of several houses at the site. Some of them were circular pit-houses, while others were quadrangular aboveground houses. Both were usually built with a combination of perishable materials. Sometimes they had walls with foundations made of one or two rows of stones. Associated with these houses, Engel found sherds of at least two distinct local pottery styles, which he labeled Disco Verde and Chavín. He reports finding sherds of a third pottery style, Cupisnique, mixed with them. For Engel, these three styles overlapped considerably in time and were contemporary, at least in Puerto Nuevo.

In terms of the local pottery chronology proposed by Rubén García and José Pinilla (1995) for the Paracas area, Engel's Disco Verde style corresponds to the Disco Verde phase, while the Chavín style corresponds to the Puerto Nuevo phase. A third phase, called Karwa, corresponds to the Ocucaje 3 style of the neighboring Ica Valley and was later than the Puerto Nuevo phase, in García and Pinilla's opinion. They consider Karwa a Late Chavín phase (see Figure 11.3). The Karwa style is the one found in the Coyungo, Mollake Chico, and Karwa tombs. While the Disco Verde style can be clearly located in the pre-Paracas period of the Nasca–Palpa Archaeological Project chronology due to its clear similarities with the Pernil Alto style (Reindel and Isla 2009), the Puerto Nuevo and Karwa styles must

be dated to the Early Paracas period due to its clear similarities with the Ocucaje 3 style (Menzel, Rowe, and Dawson 1964).

Be that as it may, the important point here is that although the beginning of the Disco Verde style predates the beginning of the Puerto Nuevo style, which, in turn, predates the beginning of the Karwa style, the three styles overlap in time. If we add to this the well-known problems with the radiocarbon calibration curve for the period between 800 and 400 BC, the least we can say is that the end of the Puerto Nuevo style, the beginning of the Karwa style, and the overlap between the two cannot yet be dated with confidence.

The Paracas Archaeological Project Excavations at Puerto Nuevo

Our own investigations in Puerto Nuevo between 2013 and 2015 have confirmed several of Engel's observations—and have corrected others (Figure 11.6). During the first season, in 2013, our excavations were concentrated in the center of the site. That year, we excavated several units: three excavation units south of Engel's area, where we found an occupation dating from the tenth to ninth centuries BC and recovered mainly Disco Verde–style sherds (Figure 11.7a); a unit within Engel's area, where we found an occupation of the eighth to sixth centuries BC that included the remains of a quadrangular aboveground house with a central hearth and sherds of the Puerto Nuevo and Karwa styles as well as a few sherds of foreign northern styles (Figure 11.7b); and a unit north of Engel's area, where we documented occupations of the eighth to sixth centuries BC that were primarily associated with Puerto Nuevo and foreign-style sherds, laying directly above another occupation of the tenth to ninth centuries BC that included the remains of a circular pit-house primarily associated with Disco Verde sherds (Figure 11.7c).

During the second season, our excavations focused on a segmented trench north of Engel's area, where we found several occupations from the tenth to sixth centuries BC. We also excavated several test pits around the site and located a few small

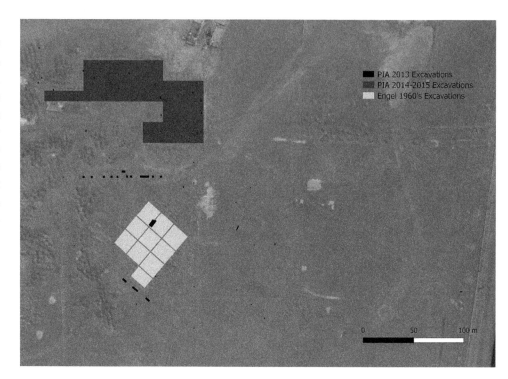

figure 11.6
Map of the Puerto
Nuevo archaeological
site, showing the
location of excavation
units excavated by
Engel in the early 1960s
and by the Paracas
Archaeological Project
between 2013 and 2015.
Map by Jalh Dulanto.

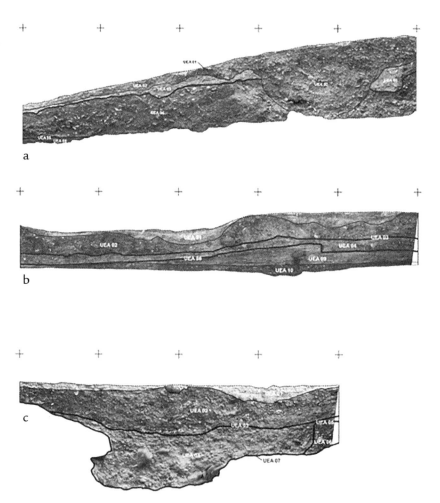

figure 11.7
Stratigraphic sections
exposed during the first
season of the Paracas
Archaeological Project
at the Puerto Nuevo site.
Photograph by Jalh Dulanto.

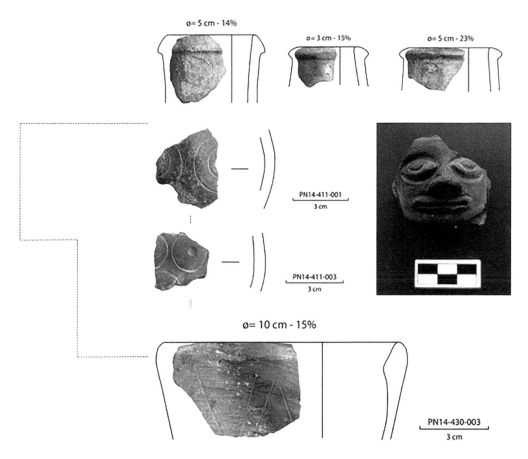

ø= 5 cm - 14%

ø= 3 cm - 15%

ø= 5 cm - 23%

PN14-411-001
3 cm

PN14-411-003
3 cm

ø= 10 cm - 15%

PN14-430-003
3 cm

figure 11.8

Karwa-style ceramics recovered from an isolated superficial concentration of materials found to the east of the Puerto Nuevo site during the second season of the Paracas Archaeological Project. Photograph by Jalh Dulanto.

and mainly superficial concentrations of archaeological materials (see Figure 11.6). One of these concentrations located to the east of the site was particularly interesting because we found mainly sherds of the Karwa style—some very similar to those of the tombs of Coyungo and Mollake Chico (Figure 11.8). Two dates from their associated features are consistent with the dates of the strata containing Puerto Nuevo materials and with the dates of the two "elite" tombs we have already described (817–551 BC and 799–509 BC). However, as I previously mentioned, problems with the calibration curve prevent us from ordering these events correctly in time.

During the third season, in 2014–2015, we excavated a large area at the north end of the site that had been severely affected by urban development activities. Here, we also found the remains of several occupations from the tenth to sixth centuries BC. Quadrangular aboveground houses were apparently superimposed over circular pit-houses. At least twenty-nine stone-lined hearths excavated within this area illustrate house density during the Puerto Nuevo occupation (Figure 11.9).

Our excavations during these three field seasons permit us to conclude that Puerto Nuevo was occupied for more than five centuries by fishing communities, probably linked to the Pisco and Ica Valleys. Beginning in the eighth century BC, these communities expanded their relationships with other communities on the south coast, as well as with other coastal communities to the south and especially to the north, and with groups living in the adjacent south-central highlands to the east (see Matsumoto and Cavero Palomino, this volume; Young, this volume).

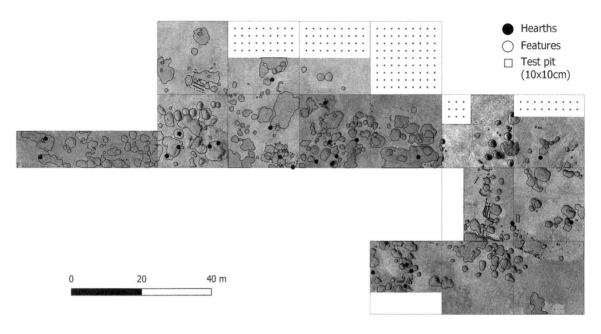

figure 11.9

Map of the large area excavated at the north end of the site during the third season of the Paracas Archaeological Project at the Puerto Nuevo site. Although the area was largely disturbed by modern roads and constructions, the concentration of different kinds of features and hearths gives a clear idea of the occupation density at the site between the eighth to sixth centuries BC. Map by Jalh Dulanto.

Complex Long-Distance Exchange Networks

Ongoing pottery analysis is shedding light on the interregional relations of the Puerto Nuevo communities (Druc et al. 2017; Dulanto 2013; Rey de Castro 2019). In our study, we combine stylistic and compositional analyses to differentiate between pottery produced locally in the Pisco and Ica Valleys, and pottery that could have been imported from other valleys of the south coast, or other regions from the coast and highlands. This is a multistep process involving, among other things, comparing pottery from different sites and clays from different sources. Hence, these results are preliminary. So far, we have been able to analyze the Puerto Nuevo pottery in detail and compare it with clay sources in the Pisco and Ica Valleys.

Stylistic analysis of 403 sherds accounted for technological, morphological, and decorative variables. We defined seven stylistic groups and one set of stylistically atypical vessels. Group I is a variant of the Disco Verde style; it predominantly includes

bowls decorated with one or two rows of stamped circles on the exterior rim (Figure 11.10). Group II, another variant of the Disco Verde style, includes mainly bowls and bottles decorated with negative painted geometric designs, usually lines, dots, crosses, and zigzags. (Figure 11.11). Group III, a variant of the Puerto Nuevo style, includes mostly large bowls whose rims are decorated with modeled step-fret designs (Figure 11.12). Group IV, also a variant of the Puerto Nuevo style, largely includes bowls and bottles decorated with complex geometric and figurative designs made with postfire paint applied on areas delimited by wide and deep incisions. Some of these designs clearly evoke those of Cupisnique pottery and murals from the north coast (see Alva 2010). Others appear to be antecedents of Middle and Late Paracas iconography from the fifth to third century BC (and this is one of the reasons to consider Puerto Nuevo to be an Early Paracas style) (Figure 11.13). Group V is yet another variant of the Puerto Nuevo style; it mainly includes bowls decorated with postfire painted geometric designs, usually diagonal parallel lines below

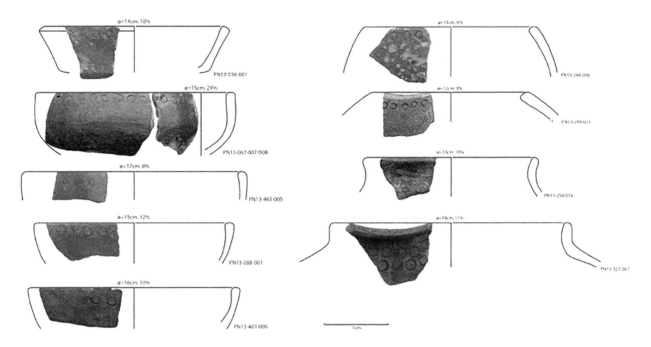

figure 11.10
Typical Group I Disco Verde–style ceramics from Puerto Nuevo. Illustration by Jalh Dulanto.

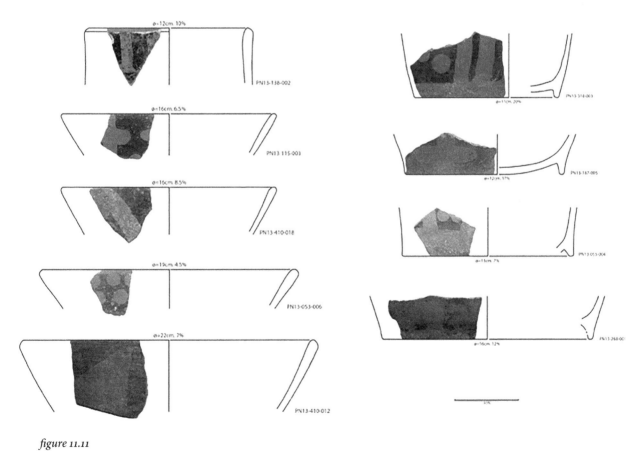

figure 11.11
Typical Group II Disco Verde–style ceramics from Puerto Nuevo. Illustration by Jalh Dulanto.

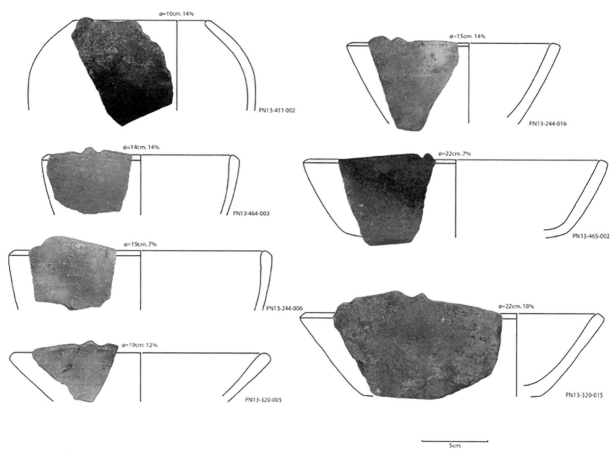

figure 11.12

Typical Group III Puerto Nuevo–style ceramics from Puerto Nuevo. Illustration by Jalh Dulanto.

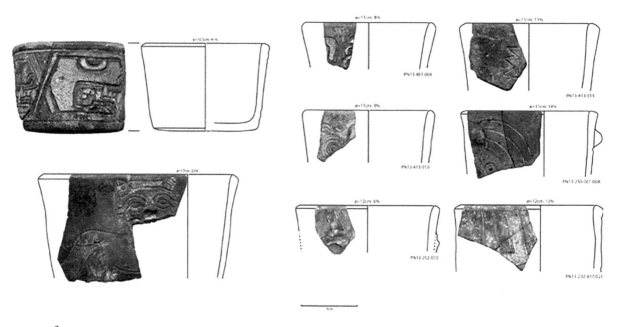

figure 11.13

Typical Group IV Puerto Nuevo–style ceramics from Puerto Nuevo. Illustration by Jalh Dulanto.

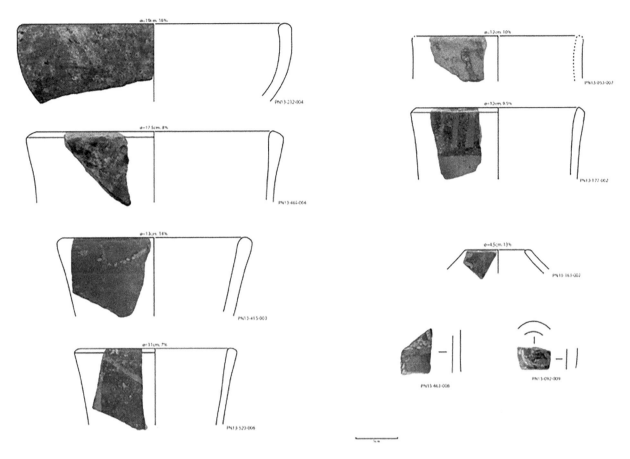

figure 11.14

Typical Group V Puerto Nuevo–style ceramics from Puerto Nuevo. Illustration by Jalh Dulanto.

the lip (Figure 11.14). Group VI, which is one more variant of the Puerto Nuevo style, includes bottles decorated with bands made of three or more rows of stamped circles (Figure 11.15). Group VII includes several foreign styles of pottery primarily from the central coast, the north-central coast, and the north coast. It includes bowls and bottles decorated with geometric and figurative designs made with a combination of incisions, stamped textures, and modeled reliefs. Stirrup-spout bottles are common in this group (Figure 11.16), as are some bowls that are practically identical to those recovered in the coastal site of Ancón, located about 300 km north of Puerto Nuevo (Figure 11.17). Group VIII is a set of stylistically atypical vessels that do not fit in any of the previous groups. It is worth highlighting one vessel: a bowl that is almost identical to those reported for the area between the Piura and Zaña Valleys, more than 1,000 km north of Puerto Nuevo.

Petrographic analysis of the same 403 sherds accounted for variables related to the mineral composition and size of the inclusions as well as to the texture of the paste. We defined six petrographic groups, designated here as A–F, and a set of petrographically atypical vessels designated AT (Druc et al. 2017; Rey de Castro 2019). Below, I provide a brief outline of the results of this analysis.

Groups A–F all seem to come from the lower and middle sections of the Pisco and Ica Valleys, and all the specimens of the AT group seem to be from coastal areas. Not one of the sherds we analyzed appears to be from the highlands. However, as I will discuss below, the compositional analysis of these sherds reveals a more complex reality.

How do these petrographic groups correlate with the stylistic groups I described (Table 11.1)? The petrographic groups A and B show a strong correlation with the stylistic groups I and II of the Disco

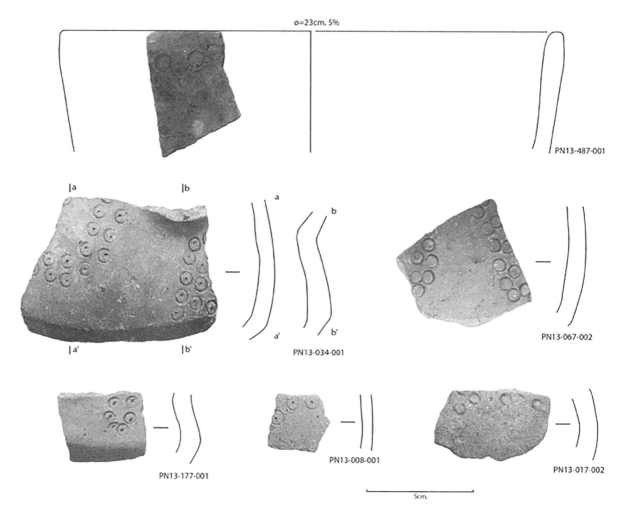

o=23cm. 5%

PN13-487-001

PN13-034-001

PN13-067-002

PN13-177-001

PN13-008-001

PN13-017-002

5cm.

figure 11.15

Typical Group VI Puerto Nuevo–style ceramics from Puerto Nuevo. Illustration by Jalh Dulanto.

Verde style. The petrographic groups C–F exhibit parallels with the stylistic groups III–VI of the Puerto Nuevo style. The petrographic groups C–E also show a strong connection with the stylistic group VII, which includes pottery from a wide variety of styles of the central coast and other coastal regions to the north. It is worth mentioning that seven out of nine sherds of the Karwa style are made with recipes typical of petrographic group E. Interestingly, the vast majority of atypical petrographic cases identified also belong to stylistic group VII. These are the vessels that could have been imported from other areas. They could have been used, at least in some cases, as models for making local copies. Finally, some of the vessels that we have not been able to assign to any of the

known stylistic groups are clearly correlated with petrographic groups A–B and could, therefore, be local variants linked to the Disco Verde style of the pre-Paracas period. Similarly, those correlated with the other petrographic groups could be local variants linked to the Puerto Nuevo style of the Early Paracas period.

Analysis by LA–ICP–MS (laser ablation inductively couple mass spectrometry) of the chemical composition of 220 of these 403 sherds and a few clay samples from the Pisco and Ica Valleys, conducted by Laure Dussubieux, Jalh Dulanto, and Alejandro Rey de Castro at the Field Museum of Natural History, reinforces several of these observations (Dulanto et al. 2019). The Principal Components Analysis of the concentration in ppm of fifty different

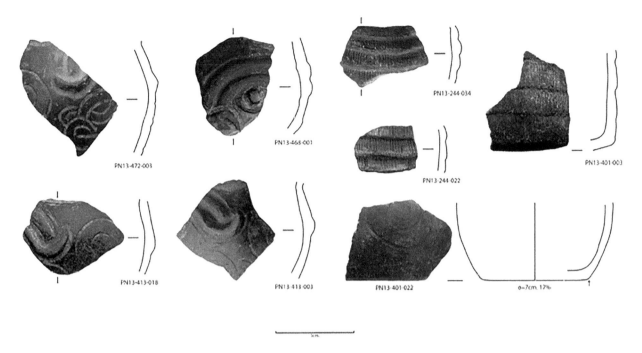

figure 11.16
Typical Group VII foreign-style ceramics from the central, north-central, and north coast recovered at Puerto Nuevo.
Illustration by Jalh Dulanto.

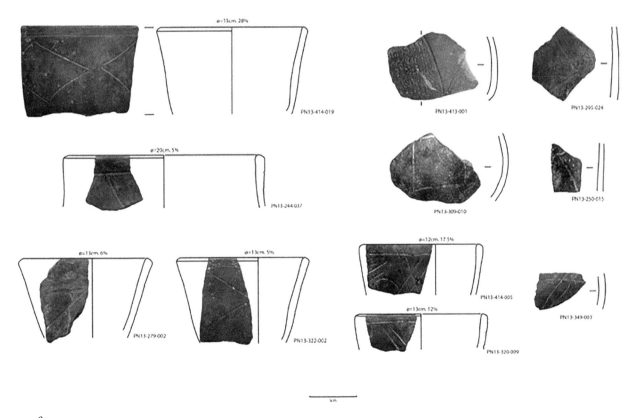

figure 11.17
Typical Group VII Ancón ceramics from the central coast recovered at Puerto Nuevo. Illustration by Jalh Dulanto.

PETROGRAPHIC GROUP

Stylistic Group	A	B	F	D	C	E	AT	Total
I	11	19	1					31
II	26	34						60
III	1	1	21	16	2		1	42
VI			3	9				12
V	1		11	13	4	7	1	37
IV				11	14	16	2	43
VII	1	1	6	11	55	73	19	166
AT	5	2	5					12
Total	45	57	47	60	75	96	23	403

PETROGRAPHIC GROUP

Stylistic Group	A	B	F	D	C	E	AT	Total
I	35%	61%	3%					100%
II	43%	57%						100%
III	2%	2%	50%	38%	5%		2%	100%
VI			25%	75%				100%
V	3%		30%	35%	11%	19%	3%	100%
IV				26%	33%	37%	5%	100%
VII	1%	1%	4%	7%	33%	44%	11%	100%
AT	42%	17%	42%					100%
Total	11%	14%	12%	15%	19%	24%	6%	100%

PETROGRAPHIC GROUP

Stylistic Group	A	B	F	D	C	E	AT	Total
I	24%	33%	2%					8%
II	58%	60%						15%
III	2%	2%	45%	27%	3%		4%	10%
VI			6%	15%				3%
V	2%		23%	22%	5%	7%	4%	9%
IV				18%	19%	17%	9%	11%
VII	2%	2%	13%	18%	73%	76%	83%	41%
AT	11%	4%	11%					3%
Total	100%	100%	100%	100%	100%	100%	100%	100%

table 11.1

Correlation between petrographic groups and stylistic groups of pottery vessels from Puerto Nuevo.

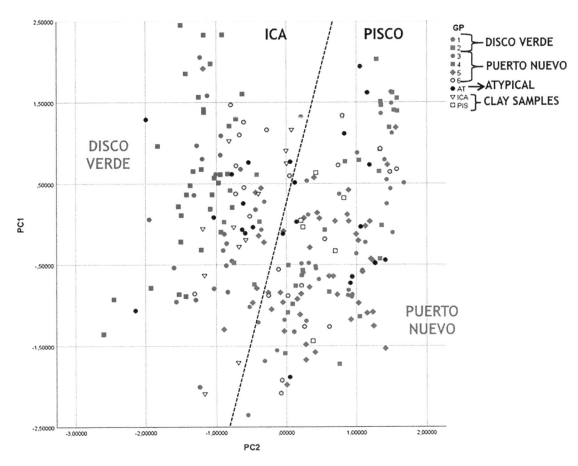

figure 11.18

Results of Principal Components Analysis of the concentration in ppm of fifty different chemical elements for 220 sherds, showing the separation of Disco Verde–style ceramics, on one side, and Puerto Nuevo– and foreign-style ceramics, on the other, and their association with different clay sources of the lower Pisco and Ica Valleys. These results strongly suggest that the vast majority of foreign-style sherds found in Puerto Nuevo were produced locally in the lower Pisco Valley. Illustration by Jalh Dulanto.

chemical elements in these 220 sherds reveals a clear separation between the petrographic groups A and B (linked to the Disco Verde style) and the petrographic groups C–F (linked to the Puerto Nuevo style and to foreign coastal styles). Furthermore, it suggests an association between the Disco Verde style and Ica sources of clay and the Puerto Nuevo style and Pisco sources of clay (Figure 11.18).

On the other hand, a simple bivariate analysis of specific chemical elements allows us to recognize chemically atypical cases precisely among the sherds which are also stylistically atypical. Notable is the case of the vessel mentioned above, stylistically identical to those reported for the area between the Piura and Zaña Valleys and compositionally probably

imported. Of course, to confirm that we need to continue with our research, including materials from other sites and regions in our comparisons.

Additional evidence of interregional contacts is found by studying the pigments used in the postfire painting of stylistic groups IV and V of the Puerto Nuevo style. PXRF (portable x-ray florescence) and Raman spectroscopy analyses that we started in 2013, together with Patricia Gonzales from the Department of Chemistry at Catholic University, show that these pigments include: an intense red made from cinnabar; an intense yellow made from pararcalgar, orpiment, or even a combination of both; a white, usually made from anatase; a dark red made from hematite; a green made from paratacamite; and a

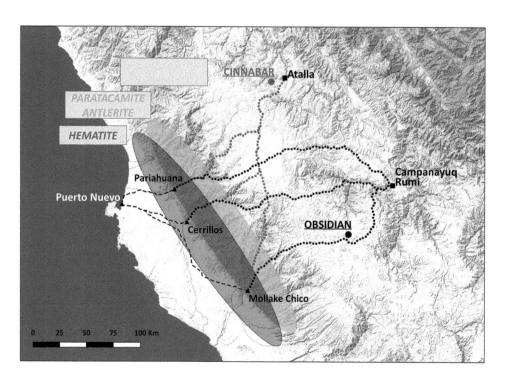

figure 11.19

Map of the south coast and highlands, showing the approximate distribution of sources of mineral pigments used in Early Paracas ceramics recovered at the Puerto Nuevo site. Note the location of the main source of cinnabar close to Atalla and the main source of obsidian close to Campanayuq Rumi. Map by Jalh Dulanto.

black made from antlerite (Dulanto, González, and Guadalupe 2019).

Minerals such as cinnabar, pararealgar, and orpiment are sourced mainly from the highlands; they are currently reported at Huancavelica mines (Cooke et al. 2013; Dulanto, González, and Guadalupe 2019; Young, this volume). Minerals such as hematite, paratacamite, and antlerite are reported from several sources in the middle and lower valleys of the Pisco, Ica, and Nasca Rivers (Dulanto, González, and Guadalupe 2019) (Figure 11.19). Although anatase is today reported for mines in the far south coast of Peru and the far north coast of Chile, it could be present in the south coast of Peru (Dulanto, González, and Guadalupe 2019). These results are consistent with those obtained independently by Dawn Kriss and Lisa DeLeonardis (DeLeonardis 2016, this volume; Kriss et al. 2018) for Early Paracas materials.

These pigments, imported and local, were used to paint vessels such as the one illustrated in the upper-left corner of Figure 11.13, which was produced in a local technical style to imitate a clearly foreign and intricate iconographic representation. This fact is an excellent example of the complex interregional interactions that south coast peoples were involved in between the eighth and sixth

centuries BC. Interestingly, the evidence we have about connections between Puerto Nuevo and other regions of the coast and the highlands is, apparently, at odds with the evidence we have for subsistence at Puerto Nuevo.

Analysis of the fauna and flora consumed at the site, and recovered during our first fieldwork season in 2013, shows that people in Puerto Nuevo exploited at least twenty-seven species of plants (four aquatic and twenty-three terrestrial) and seventy species of animals (forty-one vertebrates and twenty-nine invertebrates). We have not found remains of a single species of plant or animal that could not be obtained locally in Paracas. Notably, in the analyzed sample, we did not find camelid bones, skins, fiber, or excrement. Preliminary analyses of fauna and flora remains recovered in the other two fieldwork seasons suggest that the frequency of these camelid remains is very low in Puerto Nuevo. However, they are commonly found in contemporary inland sites. They are comparatively abundant in sites located on the foothills of the Andes, such as Pariahuana (Balbuena 2013), Cerrillos (Splitstoser 2009; Splitstoser, Wallace, and Delgado 2010; Wallace 1962), and Mollake Chico (Isla and Reindel 2006; Reindel and Isla 2006).

Conclusions

In conclusion, our research suggests that Puerto Nuevo was occupied between the tenth and sixth centuries BC by successive fishing communities. These communities were generally self-sufficient and very likely autonomous. However, they participated from the beginning in local and regional exchange networks, and from the eighth century BC onward, they became increasingly embedded in interregional exchange networks.

Pottery was imported from the central coast, and to a lesser extent from coastal regions to the north. Ceramics were also produced locally, imitating these imported styles, as well as in a distinctively local style that nonetheless incorporated the iconography of these imported styles. Together, this indicates that, beginning in the eighth century BC, Puerto Nuevo's inhabitants maintained close connections with the populations of other coastal regions. These connections could have been direct with peoples of the central coast, and through them, indirect, down-the-line, with more northern coastal regions (Figure 11.20).

Raw materials from the adjacent highlands, such as cinnabar, pararealgar, and orpiment, indicate contact with the highlands, but the relative absence of camelid remains, highland pottery, and highland textiles suggests that the inhabitants of Puerto Nuevo did not maintain close connections with highland groups during this period. These connections could have been indirect, most likely mediated by the inland populations of the coastal valleys, especially by those in the Andean foothills. Centers, such as Atalla in Huancavelica (Young 2017, this volume), and Campanayuq Rumi in Ayacucho (Matsumoto 2010; Matsumoto and Cavero Palomino 2010, this volume; Matsumoto et al. 2018), could have controlled llama caravans moving between the highlands and these inland coastal valleys populations (Figure 11.21).

The marginal location of a site like Puerto Nuevo in a desert area far from the agricultural areas of the surrounding valleys may surprise us. But it is consistent with our knowledge of fishing communities of later periods and with our understanding of

fishing communities in different parts of the world. These are often intermediaries in interregional exchange. Thanks in large part to the work of Maria Rostworowski (1989), we know that, in the early colonial period, the fishing communities of the coast stood out for their political, social, and linguistic separation from the farming communities of the coastal valleys. Although these communities exchanged maritime products for agricultural products, they did not usually marry each other, nor were they subject to the same lords. Rostworowski's reference to fishing communities such as Quilcay in the Lurín Valley, which was subject to its own lord and exchanged wives only with other fishing communities (some as far away as Magdalena de Cao in the Chicama Valley), is well-known. Although the existence of a "lengua pescadora" along the coast (Rabinowitz 1983) has been rightly criticized by Rodolfo Cerrón-Palomino (1995), the existence of linguistic differences between fishing and farming communities is mentioned in several early colonial documents and cannot be ruled out for earlier periods.

There are many ethnographic examples of geographically and socially marginal groups that, precisely because they are separated from others, occupy a convenient position in long-distance exchange networks. Sociologically, their marginality—and their autonomy—made it easier to assume the role of intermediaries in the movement of goods, beyond the reciprocal and redistributive obligations of those who are subject to a lord (Sahlins 2004:185–314). In fact, in the Central Andes, the sea-level coastal communities of fishermen, like the highland communities of herders, are in many ways marginal populations. They were not effectively controlled by lords until later periods. Both seem to have often been involved in interregional exchange: the former along the coast by land or sea, and the latter along the highlands, and between highlands and the coast, using llama caravans.

It is probably not a coincidence that fishing settlements with occupations contemporary to those of Puerto Nuevo, such as Curayacu (Lanning 1960), in the desert area south of the Lurín Valley, or Ancón (Burger and Salazar, this volume; Rosas 2007), in the desert area north of the Chillón Valley, share with

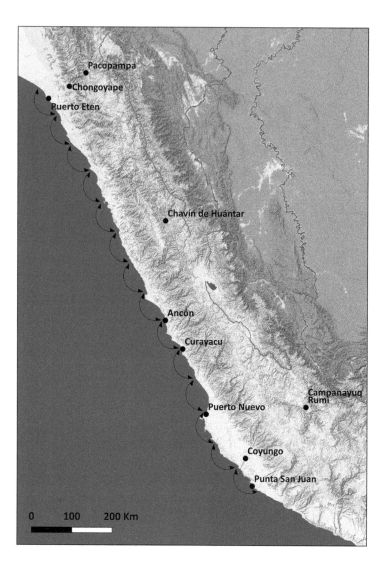

figure 11.20
Map of the Central Andes, showing a down-the-line model for the movement of prestige goods between fishing communities along the coast. In the case of Puerto Nuevo, the connections with fishing villages of the central coast, such as Curayacu and Ancón, are particularly clear. Map by Jalh Dulanto.

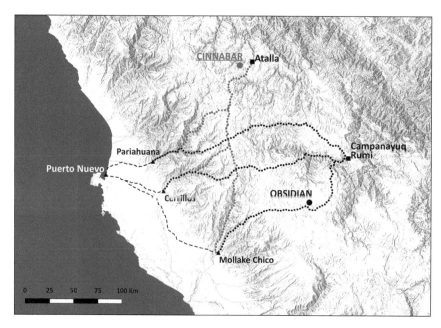

figure 11.21
Map of the south coast and highlands, showing the results of a least-cost-path analysis between the ceremonial centers of Atalla and Campanayuq Rumi; coastal inland sites such as Pariahuana, Cerrillos, and Mollake Chico; and the Puerto Nuevo site. According to the model proposed here, coastal inland sites could have served as intermediaries in the movement of goods between the ceremonial centers on the highlands and marginal fishing villages on the coast. Illustration by Jalh Dulanto.

Puerto Nuevo a marginal location. Their small harbors allow easy anchor of boats, far from the agricultural areas of the neighboring valleys. Prestigious ceramics imported from other coastal regions have been reported for all these sites. Researching these marginal settlements offers a unique opportunity to study the historical trajectories and complexities of long-distance exchange networks in the Central Andes in which the Chavín Interaction Sphere played an important role.

REFERENCES CITED

Alva, Ignacio

2010   Los complejos de Cerro Ventarrón y Collud-Zarpán: Del precerámico al formativo en el valle de Lambayeque. *Boletín de Arqueología PUCP* 12:97–117.

Alva, Walter

1992   Orfebrería del formativo. In *Oro del antiguo Perú*, edited by José A. Lavalle, pp. 17–116. Banco de Crédito del Perú, Lima.

Balbuena, Lucia

2013   Evidencias Paracas en los valles de Pisco y Mala. *Boletín de Arqueología PUCP* 17:57–75.

Burger, Richard L.

1988   Unity and Heterogeneity within the Chavín Horizon. In *Peruvian Prehistory*, edited by Richard W. Keatinge, pp. 99–144. Cambridge University Press, Cambridge.

1992   *Chavín and the Origins of Andean Civilization.* Thames and Hudson, New York.

2008   Chavín de Huántar and Its Sphere of Influence. In *Handbook of South American Archaeology*, edited by Helaine Silverman and William H. Isbell, pp. 681–703. Springer, New York.

2013   In the Realm of the Incas: An Archaeological Reconsideration of Household Exchange, Long-Distance Trade, and Marketplaces in the Pre-Hispanic Andes. In *Merchants, Markets, and Exchange in the Pre-Columbian World*, edited by Kenneth G. Hirth and Joanne Pillsbury pp. 321–336. Dumbarton Oaks Research Library and Collection, Washington, D.C.

Cerrón-Palomino, Rodolfo

1995   *La lengua de Naimlap: Reconstrucción y obsolescencia del Mochica.* Fondo Editorial de la Pontificia Universidad Católica del Perú, Lima.

Cooke, Colin, Holger Hintelmann, Jay J. Ague, Richard Burger, Harald Biester, Julian P. Sachs, and Daniel R. Engstrom

2013   Use and Legacy of Mercury in the Andes. *Environmental Science and Technology* 47:4181–4188.

DeLeonardis, Lisa

2016   Encoded Process, Embodied Meaning in Paracas Post-Fired Painted Ceramics. In *Making Value, Making Meaning: Techné in the Pre-Columbian World*, edited by Cathy L. Costin, pp. 129–166. Dumbarton Oaks Research Library and Collection, Washington, D.C.

Druc, Isabelle, Jalh Dulanto, Alejandro Rey de Castro, and Enrique Guadalupe

2017   Análisis de la composición mineral de las vasijas de cerámica de Puerto Nuevo: Algunas consideraciones preliminares sobre su producción y procedencia. *Boletín de Arqueología PUCP* 22:133–157.

Dulanto, Jalh

2013   Puerto Nuevo: Redes de intercambio a larga distancia durante la primera mitad del primer milenio antes de nuestra era. *Boletín de Arqueología PUCP* 17:103–132.

Dulanto, Jalh, and Aldo Accinelli

2013   Disco Verde 50 años después de Frédéric Engel: La primera temporada de excavaciones del proyecto de investigaciones arqueológicas Paracas en el sitio. *Boletín de Arqueología PUCP* 17:133–150.

Dulanto, Jalh, Isabelle Druc, Laure Dussubieux, Enrique Guadalupe, and Alejandro Rey de Castro

2019   Avances en la identificación de las fuentes de arcilla explotadas por los alfareros del valle de Pisco del primer milenio A.C. a partir del análisis por LA-ICP-MS de vasijas cerámica de Puerto Nuevo y muestras de arcillas de los valles de Pisco e Ica, costa sur del Perú. *Boletín de Arqueología PUCP* 27:27–47.

Dulanto, Jalh, Patricia Gonzáles, and Enrique Guadalupe

2019   Los pigmentos utilizados en la pintura postcocción de vasijas de cerámica Paracas temprano de Puerto Nuevo y las redes de intercambio de la costa y sierra surcentral del Perú durante los siglos IX–VI A.C. *Boletín de Arqueología PUCP* 26:65–83.

Engel, Frédéric

1963a   Datations à l'aide du radio-carbone et problèmes de la préhistoire du Pérou. *Journal de la Société des Américanistes* 52:101–132.

1963b   Notes relatives à des explorations archéologiques à Paracas et sur la cote sud du Pérou. *Travaux de l'Institute Français d'Études Andines* 9:10–72.

1963c   A Preceramic Settlement on the Central Coast of Peru: Asia, Unit 1. *Transactions of the American Philosophical Society* 53(3):1–139.

1966   *Paracas: Cien siglos de cultura peruana.* Juan Mejía Baca, Lima.

1976   *Le monde précolombien des Andes.* Hachette, Paris.

1987   *De las begonias al maíz: Vida y producción en el Perú antiguo.* Universidad Nacional Agraria—La Molina, Lima.

1991   *Un desierto en tiempos prehispánicos: Río Pisco, Paracas, Río Ica.* Universidad Nacional Agraria—La Molina, Lima.

García, Rubén

2009   Puerto Nuevo y los origenes de la tradición estilístico–religiosa Paracas. *Boletín de Arqueología PUCP* 13:187–207.

García, Rubén, and José Pinilla

1995   Aproximación a una secuencia de fases con cerámica temprana de la región

de Paracas. *Journal of the Steward Anthropological Society* 23:43–81.

Helms, Mary W.

1988   *Ulysses' Sail: An Ethnographic Odyssey of Power, Knowledge, and Geographical Distance.* Princeton University Press, Princeton.

1993   *Craft and the Kingly Ideal: Art, Trade, and Power.* University of Texas Press, Austin.

2014   *Access to Origins: Affines, Ancestors, and Aristocrats.* University of Texas Press, Austin.

Isla, Johny, and Markus Reindel

2006   Una tumba Paracas temprano en Mollake Chico, valle de Palpa, costa sur del Perú. *Zeitschrift für Archäologie Aussereuropäischer Kulturen* 1:153–182.

Kaulicke, Peter

1994   *Los orígenes de la civilización andina.* Brasa, Lima.

1998   El formativo de Piura. *Boletín de Arqueología PUCP* 2:19–36.

2013   Paracas y Chavín: Variaciones sobre un tema longevo. *Boletín de Arqueología PUCP* 17:289–263.

Kaulicke, Peter, Lars Fehren-Schmitz, Maria Kolp-Godoy, Patricia Landa, Oscar Loyola, Martha Palma, Elsa Tomasto, Cindy Vergel, and Burkhard Vogt

2010   Implicancias de un área funeraria del período formativo tardío en el Departamento de Ica. *Boletín de Arqueología PUCP* 13:289–322.

Kriss, Dawn, Ellen Howe, Judith Levinson, Adriana Rizzo, Federico Carò, and Lisa DeLeonardis

2018   A Material and Technical Study of Paracas Painted Ceramics. *Antiquity* 92:1492–1510.

Lanning, Edward P.

1960   Chronological and Cultural Relationships of Early Pottery Styles in Ancient Peru. PhD dissertation, University of California, Berkeley.

Lothrop, Samuel K.

1941   Gold Ornaments of Chavín Style from Chongoyape, Peru. *American Antiquity* 6:250–262.

Loyola, Oscar

    2016   Contextos funerarios del formativo tardío en Coyungo: Arquitectura y ajar funerario en el valle bajo de Río Grande, Ica. Tesis de licenciado, Pontificia Universidad Católica del Perú, Lima.

Matsumoto, Yuichi

    2010   The Prehistoric Ceremonial Center of Campanayuq Rumi: Interregional Interactions in the Peruvian South-Central Highlands. PhD dissertation, Yale University, New Haven.

Matsumoto, Yuichi, and Yuri Cavero

    2010   Una aproximación cronológica del centro ceremonial de Campanayuq Rumi, Ayacucho. *Boletín de Arqueología PUCP* 13:323–346.

Matsumoto, Yuichi, Jason Nesbitt, Michael Glascock, Yuri Cavero Palomino, and Richard Burger

    2018   Interregional Obsidian Exchange during the Late Initial Period and Early Horizon: New Perspectives from Campanayuq Rumi. *Latin American Antiquity* 29:44–43.

Menzel, Dorothy, John H. Rowe, and Lawrence E. Dawson

    1964   *The Paracas Pottery of Ica: A Study in Style and Time.* University of California Press, Berkeley.

Onuki, Yoshio, and Kinya Inokuchi

    2011   *Gemelos prístinos: El tesoro del Templo de Kuntur Wasi.* Fondo Editorial del Congreso / Mina Yanacocha, Lima.

Rabinowitz, Joel

    1983   La lengua pescadora: The Lost Dialect of Chimú Fishermen. In *Investigations of the Andean Past: Papers from the First Annual Northeast Conference on Andean Archaeology and Ethnohistory*, edited by Daniel H. Sandweiss, pp. 243–267. Cornell University, Ithaca, N.Y.

Reindel, Markus, and Johny Isla

    2006   Evidencias de culturas tempranas en los valles de Palpa, costa sur del Perú. *Boletín de Arqueología PUCP* 10:237–283.

    2009   El período inicial en Pernil Alto, Palpa, costa sur del Perú. *Boletín de Arqueología PUCP* 13:259–288.

Rey de Castro, Alejandro

    2019   Análisis estilístico y petrográfico de la cerámica de Puerto Nuevo, costa sur del Perú. Tesis de licenciatura, Pontificia Universidad Católica del Perú, Lima.

Rosas, Hermilio

    2007   *La secuencia cultural del período formativo en Ancón.* Avqi Eds., Lima.

Rostworowski, Maria

    1989   *Costa peruana prehispánica.* Instituto de Estudios Peruanos, Lima.

Sahlins, Marshall

    2004   *Stone Age Economics.* Routledge, London.

Seki, Yuji, Juan Pablo Villanueva, Masato Sakai, Diana Alemán, Mauro Ordóñez, Walter Tosso, Araceli Espinoza, Kinya Inokuchi, and Daniel Morales

    2010   Nuevas evidencias del sitio arqueológico de Pacopampa, en la Sierra Norte del Perú. *Boletín de Arqueología PUCP* 12:69–95.

Splitstoser, Jeffrey C.

    2009   Weaving the Structure of the Cosmos: Cloth, Agency, and Worldview at Cerrillos, and Early Paracas Site in the Ica Valley, Peru. PhD dissertation, Catholic University of America, Washington, D.C.

Splitstoser, Jeffrey C., Dwight D. Wallace, and Mercedes Delgado

    2010   Nuevas evidencias de textiles y cerámica de la época Paracas temprano en Cerrillos, valle de Ica, Perú. *Boletín de Arqueología PUCP* 13:209–235.

Tomasto, Elsa, Markus Reindel, and Johny Isla

    2015   Paracas Funerary Practices in Palpa, South Coast of Peru. In *Funerary Practices and Models in the Ancient Andes: The Return of the Living Dead*, edited by Peter Eeckhout and Lawrence S. Owens, pp. 69–86. Cambridge University Press, Cambridge.

Unkel, Ingmar, Bernd Kromer, Markus Reindel, Lukas Wacker, and Gunther Wagner

    2007   A Chronology of the Pre-Columbian Paracas and Nasca Cultures in South Peru Based on AMS 14C Dating. *Radiocarbon* 49:551–564.

Unkel, Ingmar, Markus Reindel, Hermann Gorbahn, Johny Isla, Bernd Kromer, and Volker Sossna

2012   A Comprehensive Numerical Chronology for the Pre-Columbian Cultures of the Palpa Valleys, South Coast of Peru. *Journal of Archaeological Science* 39:2294–2303.

Wallace, Dwight

1962   Cerrillos: An Early Paracas Site in Ica, Peru. *American Antiquity* 27:303–314.

Young, Michelle

2017   De la montaña al mar: Intercambio entre la sierra centro-sur y la costa sur durante el horizonte temprano. *Boletín de Arqueología PUCP* 22:9–34.

Horizon, Interaction Sphere, Cult?

A View of the Chavín Phenomenon from Huancavelica

MICHELLE YOUNG

This chapter explores the expression of the "Chavín horizon" in Huancavelica, contextualizing the region's participation in ritual practice, long-distance exchange, and sociopolitical transformations within the wider Central Andean region (see Figure 12.1 for locations of sites mentioned in this chapter). New findings from the late Initial Period and Early Horizon occupations of Atalla and other coeval sites in Huancavelica suggest the introduction of new exchange relationships, religious practices, craft technologies, and social identities, the spread of which was facilitated by an unprecedented increase in interaction between discrete communities; this is sometimes referred to as the Chavín Interaction Sphere (Brown 2017; Burger 2012; Matsumoto et al. 2018; Nesbitt, Matsumoto, and Cavero Palomino 2019; Young 2017). Examining the Chavín Phenomenon from a local, bottom-up perspective highlights how Huancavelica residents navigated a complex social landscape, producing layers of communal and individual identity through the selective creation, adoption, modification, and rejection of

certain styles and practices. This chapter investigates how the Indigenous tradition at Atalla articulates within a system of overlapping and nested exchange networks that incorporated both long-distance and regional spheres. I also introduce the concept of the Chavín International Style as a term that more accurately describes what have previously been referred to as "Chavín Horizon," "Chavín," "Chavínoid," or "Janabarroide" ceramics. I argue that the Chavín International Style is a kind of visual vocabulary used in the production of specialized ceramic vessel forms used in Chavín ritual practices. This research provides a valuable perspective on how large-scale material patterns that have traditionally been understood as archaeological "horizons" are mediated through local and regional social processes.

Early Village Life in the Huancavelica Region

The first evidence for the establishment of permanent settlements in the Huancavelica region date to

figure 12.1
Map of Peru,
showing the
locations of Initial
Period sites and
resource extraction
areas mentioned in
the chapter. Map
by Bebel Ibarra
Ascencios.

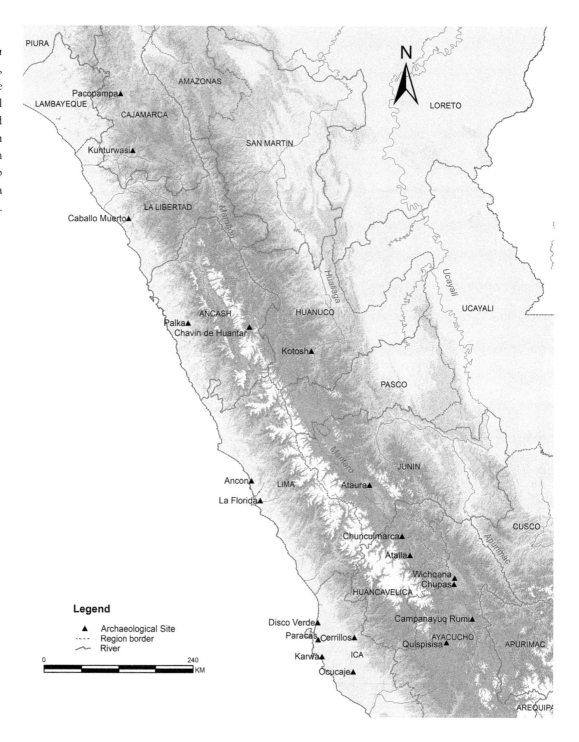

the Initial Period (1800–800 BC), when occupation sites associated with small sedentary communities formed on the banks of the Ichu River (Matos Mendieta 1959). A handful of early small-scale settlements have been identified within the current city limits of Huancavelica, including the sites of Chuncuimarca, Paturpampa, Seqsachaka, and

Arkosikimpampa (Ruiz Estrada 1977:37–38). Little is known about most of these sites, as they have been obscured by the modern development of the city of Huancavelica.

Of these sites, Chuncuimarca has received the most attention, and excavations there have provided some critical insights into the Initial Period

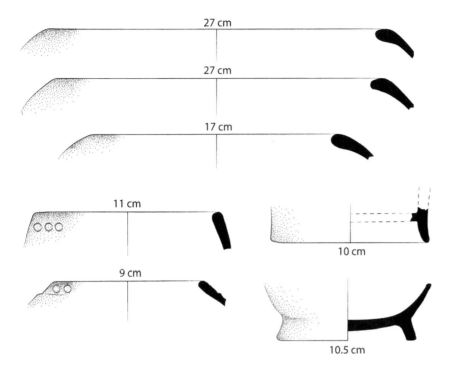

figure 12.2
Ceramics recorded from Chuncuimarca by Rogger Ravines. Images digitized by the author from Ravines 1969–1970:láminas 4, 6, and 7.

occupation of the area. Chuncuimarca is a small mound located in the lower part of Cerro Potocchi, where excavations uncovered quadrangular stone enclosures, burials, hearths, and deposits of ceramics, lithics, and bone (Espinoza 2006; Ravines 1969–1970). In his excavations of Chuncuimarca, Ravines noted that almost all of the ground stone tools presented traces of red colorant, which may have been cinnabar pigment (Ravines 1969–1970:250). Building upon this observation, Richard L. Burger and Ramiro Matos Mendieta (2002) have suggested that Chuncuimarca served as a locus of cinnabar pigment processing during the Early Horizon. This hypothesis is salient in light of more recent sourcing studies that have chemically confirmed that the Huancavelica region was a primary source for cinnabar pigment for the Central Andes between 1500 BC and the colonial period (Burger, Lane, and Cooke 2016; Cooke et al. 2013; Prieto et al. 2016).

The ceramics from Chuncuimarca are dominated by neckless ollas with thickened, coma-shaped rims and open bowls, but also include some plates, short-necked jars and bottles, and vessels with annular bases (Espinoza 2006; Ravines 1969–1970, 2009). The predominant form of decoration on

Chuncuimarca ceramics is a single row of small circles impressed beneath the rim of neckless ollas and open bowls (Figure 12.2). These ceramics form part of the same tradition with assemblages found at sites in the province of Castrovirreyna, including Ticrapo, San Francisco, Tambomachay, Yanamachay, and other rock shelters located between the Pucapampa and Pultoc lagoons along the Pisco-Huancavelica highway (García 2009; Ravines 1998, 2009). This ceramic group is also closely related to contemporaneous assemblages from Disco Verde in the Paracas Peninsula (Burger and Matos Mendieta 2002:164; Ravines 1998), which feature similar neckless olla and bowl forms, annular bases, and incised circles beneath the rim (e.g., Dulanto and Accinelli 2013; Engel 1991). Chuncuimarca ceramics also share traits with ceramics identified from the site of Pernil Alto in Palpa, including neckless ollas and bowls decorated with incised circles beneath the rim, as well as annular bases (e.g., Reindel and Isla 2009). One major difference between the Chuncuimarca style and that of the south coast styles of Disco Verde and Pernil Alto is the absence of negative painting in the highland assemblage (e.g., Dulanto and Accinelli 2013:143, fig. 11; Reindel and Isla 2009:fig. 15).

figure 12.3
View of the archaeological site of Atalla. Photograph by Michelle Young.

Connections with the south coast are further suggested by evidence from Paturpampa, another early settlement within the city of Huancavelica. At Paturpampa, ceramics recorded in surface scatters are decorated with impressed circles, punctation, and wide incision similar to the ceramics from Chuncuimarca; however, a few are decorated with geometric incision and postfire pigment, sharing similarities with Paracas ceramics (Ravines 1969–1970:257). Ceramic similarities with Paracas pottery observed in surface scatters from Paturpampa and Seqsachaka led Ruiz Estrada (1977:38) to suggest that these sites were settled by coastal peoples who had penetrated the highlands to exploit camelid meat, wool, and obsidian. Recent finds of Paracas ceramics found at the site of Pallaucha in Ayacucho (Mendoza Martínez 2017) are also comparable with published examples from Paturpampa (Matos Mendieta 1972a:fig. 7; Ravines 2009:62) and suggest connections to the south coast. It is within the context of these early networks, connecting settlements in the south-central highlands and the south coast, that we can contextualize the foundation and development of Atalla.

Atalla

The archaeological site of Atalla is located in the region and province of Huancavelica, district of Yauli, approximately 15 km east of the city of Huancavelica at an altitude 3535 masl (see Figure 12.1). The site is situated in a small plain on a natural terrace above the left bank of the Ichu River between the modern settlements of Yauli and the village center of the agrarian community of Atalla, which is located approximately 1.5 km to the northwest. Atalla covers an area of approximately 8 ha and consists of a natural hill, which was modified through the construction of artificial terraces (Figure 12.3).

The public architecture, concentrated in the most elevated part of the site, consists of a stepped platform mound that shares many similarities with other late Initial Period temples from the Peruvian highlands. The platformed mound measures approximately 115 × 85 m at the base and 12 m in height. The mound is formed by a series of quadrangular platforms with stone retaining walls that are drained by subterranean stone-lined canals and gallery-like features. A staircase constructed from cut and shaped

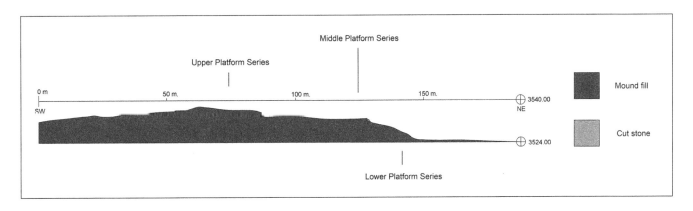

figure 12.4
Atalla temple profile. Image digitized by Luis Flores de la Oliva; courtesy of the Proyecto de Investigación Arqueológica Atalla.

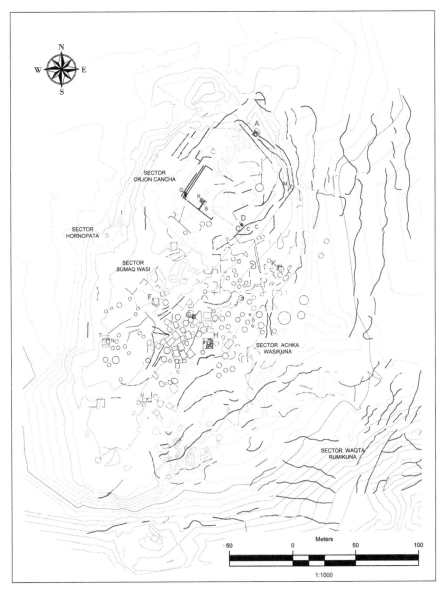

figure 12.5
Topographic and architectural plan of the archaeological site of Atalla, showing the locations of excavation units. Digitized by Luis Flores de la Oliva; courtesy of the Proyecto de Investigación Arqueológica Atalla.

LEGEND	
EARLY PLATFORM WALL	
POSSIBLE EARLY PLATFORM WALL	
LATE WALL	
POSSIBLE LATE WALL	
CIRCULAR STRUCTURE	○
POSSIBLE CIRCULAR STRUCTURE	○
COLONIAL STRUCTURES	
EXCAVATION UNITS	

stone blocks defines the northeast–southwest axis of the complex, leading up through a series of ascending platforms; the uppermost of these platforms measures approximately 30 × 25 m (Figure 12.4).

To the south of the temple is a sprawling domestic area littered with fragmented ceramic and lithic artifacts, collapsed stone architecture, and the remnants of several landscape modifications, including terracing and at least one drainage canal (Figure 12.5). Note that most of the architecture visible on the surface postdates the Early Horizon occupation. Today, the site is used as agricultural land by the neighboring community of the same name.

History of Investigations at Atalla

Atalla was first discovered in 1955 by Julio Espejo Núñez (1958). Ramiro Matos Mendieta followed up on the site's discovery in his bachelor's thesis, drawing attention to the site as a "Chavínoid" center (1959). From his observation of the architecture and materials at Atalla, he identified three phases: the Early/Formative phase, characterized by "Chavínoid" ceramics; the Early Intermediate Period phase, characterized by orange ceramics comparable to the "Caja" style; and the Late Intermediate Period occupation, characterized by light-colored ceramic paste, similar to the "Coras" style. Ruiz Estrada (1977) also visited Atalla, positing that it was an exceptionally large "Chavín" site that served as an administrative or ceremonial center for the smaller settlements identified in Huancavelica. Matos returned to Atalla with Burger in 1997 to record additional surface observations, publishing the results of the survey and posing several important hypotheses about the site's development and function (Burger and Matos Mendieta 2002). Based on relative dating of the ceramics and architecture observed on the surface, they hypothesized that the site was founded in the middle of the Early Horizon and concluded that Atalla represented an extraordinarily large sedentary community for the period (Burger and Matos Mendieta 2002).

Public architecture at Atalla consists of a large natural mound that has been significantly modified through the creation of a series of ascending platforms faced with large stone blocks. The platforms are accessed from the northeast through a central staircase of cut stone (Figure 12.6a) and are drained with stone-lined subterranean canals (Figure 12.6b–e) (Young 2017). The use of monumental stone blocks in the construction of public architecture is unique in the region at this time; foreign architectural canons used in the construction of platforms, walls, the staircase, and subterranean canals provide evidence of emulation of the great ceremonial centers of the north such as Chavín de Huántar and Kuntur Wasi (Burger and Matos Mendieta 2002).

Observations of similarities in style between the Atalla assemblage and ceramics from Chavín de Huántar provide an additional source of evidence for a connection between the sites. Burger and Matos Mendieta (2002) recorded detailed descriptions of the ceramic decoration of Atalla, which they describe as consisting essentially of a modification of the surface in the form of incision and texturing, which they note had strong parallels with Janabarriu-phase pottery from Chavín de Huántar. They also note stylistic similarities between ceramics observed from the surface of Atalla and those of the upper levels of the Tank site at Ancón near Lima, the site of San Blas in Junín, and the site of Kotosh in Huánuco (Burger and Matos Mendieta 2002:158).

The presence of architecture and ceramic styles at Atalla that have no antecedents in the region prompted Burger and Matos Mendieta (2002) to hypothesize that a foreign influence provided the impetus for Atalla's foundation. They suggest that the emergence of Atalla as a major center was related to its proximity to a source of cinnabar. The Santa Barbara mine, located 15 km to the west of Atalla, is the largest source of cinnabar in the Americas and was known to have been exploited in antiquity (Burger and Matos Mendieta 2002; Petersen [1970] 2010). Cinnabar, or mercuric sulfide (HgS), is a vermillion mineral pigment found decorating ritual objects and burial contexts from the Initial Period (e.g., Prieto et al. 2016) into the Early Horizon at ceremonial centers such as Chavín de Huántar, Kuntur Wasi, and Pacopampa (Cooke et al. 2013; Onuki 1997; Onuki and Inokuchi 2011; Seki, this volume; Seki et al. 2010:90) and at many occupational and burial sites on the north and south coasts of Peru,

figure 12.6
Stone architectural features at
Atalla: a) stone staircase providing
access to the Middle Platform
series and defining the primary
axis of the temple (Unit A);
b–c) two views of the large
subterranean stone-lined canal
with lintel construction built into
the temple architecture (Unit D);
d–e) one of the smaller stone-lined
canals held together with mortar
(Unit D); and f) wall foundation
from the residential sector (Unit T)
dating to 978–815 BC. Photographs
by the Proyecto de Investigación
Arqueológica Atalla.

among others (DeLeonardis, this volume). Using a core–periphery perspective, Burger and Matos Mendieta (2002) hypothesize that the emergence of a large settlement at Atalla was the outcome of an unequal relationship with Chavín de Huántar, in which Atalla was a periphery exploited for its raw-mineral resource (cinnabar) by the more powerful core (Chavín de Huántar). Recent studies have successfully verified that the cinnabar samples from Initial Period and Early Horizon archaeological sites originated in the Huancavelica region (Cooke et al. 2013; Prieto et al. 2016), supporting the notion that this deposit served as the primary source of cinnabar pigment during the Initial Period and Early Horizon.

Excavation Results

The remainder of this chapter will present the results from the first scientific excavations at Atalla, conducted between 2014 and 2016, which have clarified Atalla's role in the distribution of cinnabar and its relationship with Chavín de Huántar and other distant communities. The first section will characterize the site in terms of chronology, local traditions, and ritual practice, contextualizing the site within the Huancavelica region and the Central Andes. Next, the chapter will compare stylistic and chemical analyses of three types of materials—ceramics, cinnabar, and obsidian—to interpret shifting patterns of interaction and social identity.

Domestic Life

Atalla's domestic sectors, an area that spreads out to the south of the temple, provide evidence of intermittent occupation from the late Initial Period through the colonial era. According to the radiocarbon chronology established by the author, Atalla was first occupied in the Ichu phase (1150–925 BC) by a relatively small population. This settlement grew to form the largest village in Huancavelica during the Villa Hermosa phase (925–800 BC). It continued to be occupied during the subsequent Wilka phase (beginning in 800 BC) until its abandonment sometime between 500 and 400 BC (Young 2020). The site

was later heavily reoccupied after AD 150 by people using Caja- and Uchupas-style ceramics and may have been continuously occupied until the Late Intermediate Period. Later reoccupations of the site have obscured much of the late Initial Period settlement, but the few architectural remains associated with this occupation are represented by wall foundations constructed of single rows of lightly worked stones with flat exterior faces. These fragmentary foundations included part of a quadrangular structure held together with a fine clay mortar, an isolated straight segment of wall (Figure 12.6f), and a small circular structure measuring approximately 3 m in diameter. The fragmented remains of animal bones, cooking vessels, bone and stone tools, and hearth features point to residential activities associated with both quadrangular and circular structures. The texture, color, and composition of the mortar used in the rectangular plan foundations were highly comparable to the mortar used in the construction of the lower platform walls and small canals that form the temple architecture in Orjon Cancha. These shared architectural practices across the domestic and public architecture suggest contemporaneity in their occupations. A radiocarbon AMS date from one such feature located inside a rectangular structure produced a calibrated 2-sigma date range of 978–815 BC, a time frame that aligns with radiocarbon AMS dates from the temple platforms which place the temple construction between 900 and 800 BC (Young 2020).

Atalla's domestic architecture suggests that the residents originated within the south-central highlands, based on similarities with known traditions recorded from coeval sites in some neighboring regions of the central highlands. At Jargam Pata in Ayacucho, José Alberto Ochatoma Paravicino discovered rectangular structures whose walls consisted of a single row of field stones set in mud mortar with packed earthen floors and a double-walled circular structure constructed from irregular field stones, also set in mud mortar (1985:108–109, 1998:fig. 2). In the Jauja-Huancayo sector of the Mantaro River Basin, David Browman (1970) reports seasonally occupied villages with subterranean or semi-subterranean pit-houses that are both circular (2–3 m in diameter) or rectangular (4.5 m or more on a side). Houses at

Pirwapukio were associated with hearths outside of the dwellings, interpreted as suggestive of flammable superstructures, and small pits that measured approximately 1 m in diameter, perhaps for storage (Browman 1970). These examples demonstrate that the presence of both circular and rectangular domestic structures at Atalla is not uncommon for early villages in the neighboring Junín and Ayacucho highlands. In contrast, alternate house forms can be found in communities both near and far from Huancavelica. At other coeval sites in Ayacucho, houses are circular in plan, measuring between 1.5 and 7 m in diameter at sites like Campanayuq Rumi (Matsumoto et al. 2013, 2016:102) and Pallaucha (Mendoza Martínez 2017). Conversely, domestic areas from neighboring Chuncuimarca (Espinoza 2006) and the distant center of Chavín de Huántar are characterized by quadrangular stone architecture (Burger 1998; Sayre 2010; Sayre and Rosenfeld, this volume), as are houses from the Paracas culture area (Engel 1991; Kaulicke 2013:288; Reindel 2009). The observed residential structures from Atalla appear typical of select small late Initial Period villages in the south-central highlands but do not share obvious similarities with Chavín de Huántar, Campanayuq Rumi, or coastal Paracas sites despite some shared ceramic traits observed in the assemblage. The housing patterns at Atalla are also notably differentiated from their neighbors at Chuncuimarca. These observations suggest that Atalla residents maintained a unique and independent ethnic identity that distinguished them from both nearby and distant groups with whom they interacted.

Both domestic architecture and burial practices have been interpreted as material indicators of ethnic identity in the archaeological record (e.g., Aldenderfer and Stanish 1993; Reycraft 2005). The presence of multiple building shapes from the same late Initial Period occupation phase at Atalla may represent either different building functions or that the settlement was composed of multiple groups of people. Furthermore, differences in burial practices between Atalla and Chuncuimarca suggest at least the coexistence of different social groups living in proximity within the Huancavelica region. Burial practices at the site of Atalla are characterized by the placement of a single deceased individual in a flexed position into a simple, oval-shaped pit located in and/or adjacent to domestic structures. Graves are accompanied by meager grave goods that typically included one or more ground stone tools. Flexed burials are typical for this period in the highlands (Browman 1970; Grossman 1972; Matsumoto 2010; Onuki 1995), although the relative paucity of grave goods is somewhat anomalous compared to other coeval centers. Atalla's burial patterns contrast notably with those recorded from nearby Chuncuimarca, where Ruben Espinoza (2006) recorded multiple individuals (typically three) placed in formalized tombs lined with stones. The presence of both sub-adults and adults in these tombs suggests the interred individuals may have belonged to the same family unit. The divergent patterns of both residential architecture and burial practices between Atalla and Chuncuimarca further reinforce Atalla's status as a distinct community, separate even from other neighboring settlements in the Huancavelica region.

Evidence of Interaction: Personal Adornments, Metalworking, Flora, and Fauna

In the late Initial Period, bone pendants and simple conical ceramic objects, interpreted as possible earplugs, appear as personal adornments that may have served as early status markers (Figure 12.7). A string of small black, green, and turquoise-colored beads was also found in a ritual deposit at the site that likely dates to the Early Horizon occupation. A small number of ceramic and green stone ear spools appears in the Wilka phase (Figure 12.8), suggesting that material symbols of authority took on a new form in this period. The presence of simple ritual paraphernalia at Atalla suggests the possibility of emerging religious leaders who may have wielded a higher degree of influence or decision-making power over the rest of the community (e.g., Burger 1992:203), but there is little indication of elite class formation as has been demonstrated at other Early Horizon sites such as Pacopampa, Kuntur Wasi, Chongoyape, or Chavín de Huántar through the presence of rich burials or other archaeological indicators (Burger 1984:235–241, 1993; Lothrop 1941; Miller and Burger 1995; Nagaoka et al. 2012;

1 cm

figure 12.7
Bone pendant and ceramic earplug excavated from
Atalla. Photographs by the Proyecto de Investigación
Arqueológica Atalla.

Onuki and Inokuchi 2011; Seki 2014, this volume).
The humble burials and lack of signs of accumulated wealth or restricted access to certain materials
or goods suggest that Atalla maintained a relatively
egalitarian society compared with the increasingly
stratified societies in the northern highlands and the
south coast (Burger 1992; Kembel and Rick 2004;
Paul 1990; Seki 2014, this volume).

Finds at Atalla—including a lithic graver with
a remnant of a silver-colored metal where molten
metal had dribbled across the tool (Stone 2017), a
fragment of a stone crucible, and a simple hammered
gold ornament (Figure 12.9)—indicate that a form
of metal-working technology was present at Atalla,
likely informed by metallurgical knowledge shared
between craftspeople in the south-central highlands and the south coast (Young 2017). A fragment
of a stone crucible found at Atalla is comparable

figure 12.8
"Napkin ring" ear spools excavated
from Atalla, made of: a) ceramic;
b) ceramic and decorated on the
front with incised circles; and
c) greenstone. Photographs by
the Proyecto de Investigación
Arqueológica Atalla.

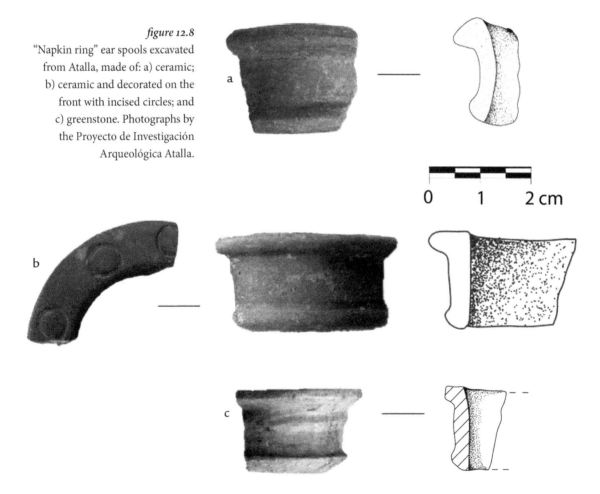

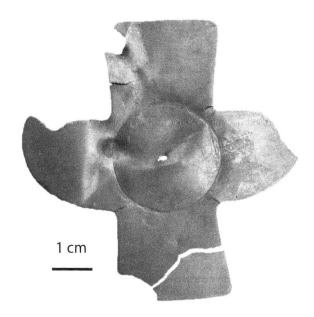

figure 12.9
Hammered gold ornament
found in Unit T at Atalla.
Photograph by the
Proyecto de Investigación
Arqueológica Atalla.

1 cm

a  b  c

CM

8 cm

figure 12.10
Examples of Early Horizon crucibles for metalworking found in south-central Peru: a) ceramic example from
Cerrillos (Splitstoser, Wallace, and Delgado 2012:fig. 15a); b) ceramic example from Campanayuq Rumi (Matsumoto
and Cavero Palomino 2012:fig. 9); and c) stone example from Atalla (photograph by the Proyecto de Investigación
Arqueológica Atalla).

to ceramic artifacts found at Campanayuq Rumi
(Matsumoto and Cavero Palomino 2010) in Ayacucho and Cerrillos (Splitstoser, Wallace, and
Delgado 2012) in the Ica Valley (Figure 12.10). It is
likely that this technology was transferred through
the movement of people within social networks that
connected communities within these regions, perhaps the same networks that were responsible for
the trade of obsidian, cinnabar, and other goods.

Microbotanical remains and isotopic evidence
from camelid teeth provide additional lines of evidence for Atalla's connections to communities

located in other ecological zones. Organic residues
analyzed by Sadie Weber contained non-local cultigens from both the coast and the eastern lowlands.
Algarroba (*Prosopis* sp.), chili pepper (*Capsicum* sp.),
and manioc (*Manihot esculenta*) appear at Atalla in
the late Initial Period alongside more traditional
highland cultigens like corn (*Zea mays*) and potato
(*Solanum tuberosum*), suggesting contact with societies in both the tropical forest and on the south
coast. Additional lowland crops, including achira
(*Canna edulis*), sweet potato (*Ipomoea batatas*), and
yam (*Dioscorea* sp.), appear at the site by the Early

Horizon, along with typical highland species like olluco (*Ullucus tuberosus*), quinoa (*Chenopodium quinoa*), and amaranth (*Amaranthus* sp.) (Weber 2019; Weber and Young 2023). Zooarchaeological analyses conducted by Weber in conjunction with isotopic evidence suggest that domesticated camelids were used for long-distance transport of goods from the late Initial Period onward (Weber 2019). Isotopic signatures of carbon and oxygen indicate that some camelids moved back and forth between the Huancavelica highlands and the coast and/or eastern lowlands, presumably as part of caravans bringing goods to and from these areas, while others lived exclusively in highland environs and were used for wool or meat (Weber 2019; Weber and Young 2023).

Ritual Architecture at Atalla

The temple at Atalla was built in at least two phases. Initial Period constructions established a series of ascending platforms and the central staircase defining the axis of the site in the Villa Hermosa phase, sometime between 900 and 800 BC. At least one later Early Horizon construction phase expanded upon the Villa Hermosa–phase design sometime between 750 and 425 BC during the subsequent Wilka phase. This construction phase increased the height and width of the original platforms, embedding small stone-lined canals within the construction fill for drainage (Young 2020).

The temple at Atalla uses construction conventions also observed from northern centers such as Chavín de Huántar (Burger and Matos Mendieta 2002); however, the plan of Atalla does not directly replicate that of Chavín de Huántar. The general layout of the temple complex at Atalla is most reminiscent of sites like Kuntur Wasi (Kato 1994; Onuki 1995) and Pacopampa (Morales 1998a, 2008; Seki, this volume; Seki et al. 2010) in Cajamarca or of Chupas in Ayacucho (Cruzatt Añaños 1966), each of which consists essentially of a series of ascending platforms, often built over a natural promontory. No sunken courts have been identified at Atalla, although most of the platforms have been destroyed by modern agricultural activity, so it is difficult to determine whether such a feature existed in antiquity.

The temple at Campanayuq Rumi, a coeval settlement in the neighboring region of Ayacucho, employed comparable construction techniques to those employed at Atalla but produced an alternative architectural layout. At Campanayuq Rumi, Yuichi Matsumoto (2010) has identified four mounds arranged around a central quadrangular plaza, which he compares to the U-shaped architecture of Chavín de Huántar (Matsumoto and Cavero Palomino, this volume). The platforms are faced with cut stone ashlars and feature monumental stairways and subterranean gallery features roofed with stone lintels, all of which are construction techniques observed from both Chavín de Huántar and Atalla (Burger and Matos Mendieta 2002; Matsumoto 2010; Matsumoto and Cavero Palomino, this volume). In the domestic sector of Campanayuq Rumi, recent finds of architectural models made of unbaked clay seem to emulate a cosmological ideal of a single stepped platform mound (Matsumoto et al. 2016). It is notable that the temple layout expressed in miniature differs significantly from the actual architectural plan of the temple complex at Campanayuq Rumi. The appearance of these clay models at Campanayuq Rumi suggests a relationship between the conceptual model of the single stepped platform mound and the construction of a full-scale U-shaped layout, as expressed in the building plans of Chavín de Huántar, Campanayuq Rumi, and other Initial Period coastal temples (Williams 1985).

Architectural models of ritual structures have been identified from later Andean cultures, suggesting that the making of *maquetas* in the form of existing temples was an important Andean practice that provided a material link between worshippers and specific temples. Scholars have convincingly argued that the elaborate *maquetas* made of clay or fired ceramic found in Moche elite tombs (Castillo and Donnan 1994; Castillo, Nelson, and Nelson 1997) manifest representations of particular Moche temples rather than idealized templates (McClelland 2010; Wiersema 2010). Stone architectural models of Tiwanaku temples were also intended to recreate specific structures in miniature. A *maqueta* discovered in a looted tomb at the site of Omo, a Tiwanaku-style temple in the Moquegua Valley, features a mound platform, pair of central staircases, and central sunken court that present an almost perfect replica of the Omo M10 ceremonial precinct (Goldstein 1993). It is reasonable to presume that these earlier manifestations of architectural models found in places like Campanayuq Rumi could have served a similar function, representing other temples that formed part of the Chavín religious network. Given coeval known temple layouts, the clay models found at Campanayuq Rumi likely represent distant temples that conform to the model of a single stepped mound such as those at Atalla, Kuntur Wasi, or Pacopampa. The presence of these models suggests that both stepped platform mound and U-shaped ceremonial configurations formed part of a larger system of interconnected Chavín ritual centers.

The coexistence of distinct but related ceremonial centers brings up questions about the nature and function of religious architecture in the late Initial Period. Do the different site layouts reflected in the U-shaped layout and single stepped platform mound represent different sects of a shared religious tradition, or different functions within the same religious system? One could venture a dualistic reading of Chavín temple architecture as comprising complementary male and female forms: stepped platform mounds, shaped like sacred apu mountain-tops (a holy protuberance) may embody masculine forces, while U-shaped mound configurations surrounding sunken plazas (a sacred recess) may manifest the feminine complement, the union of which can reproduce the universe both in full-scale temple complexes and reduced-scale models. Another possibility, originally suggested by Burger (1988), is that each site is dedicated to and may even house an oracle for separate deities within the Chavín pantheon, perhaps related to the main "Smiling God" or "Staff God" (Rowe 1967) represented on stone sculpture found in the temple of Chavín de Huántar. Thus, the differences in the overall form of each temple may be related to the representation of the particular deity within the Chavín religious system to which the temple is dedicated.

There are clear precedents in the Initial Period from the coast of temple layouts representing the bodies of supernatural creatures and/or deities. For example, Donald Lathrap (1985) has suggested that U-shaped ceremonial complexes from the central coast may represent the shape of the universe, conceptualized as the open jaws of a cayman. This interpretation is reinforced by the discovery of a clay frieze depicting a fanged mouth band across the entrance to the atrium of the Middle Temple at Cardal in the Lurín Valley (Burger and Salazar 1991). A tradition of temple entrances understood as the maw of a supernatural being emerges when we compare this example to another recorded in the Cupisnique area. Excavations at the temple of Limoncarro demonstrated that the temple itself embodies the Cupisnique "Spider Decapitator" (Salazar and Burger 1982), interpreted from architectural features in the shape of arachnid mouth pincers that were placed at the base of the staircase along the central axis of the temple (Sakai and Martínez 2010:198). The reason for formal variability in the layouts in highland temple architecture among apparently related late Initial Period centers is an issue that has yet to be sufficiently addressed. I highlight the possibility that observed variations may, in fact, correspond to different supernatural bodies within the Chavín pantheon as a potential path for future research.

Hallucinogenic Snuff

At Atalla, the consumption of hallucinogenic snuff is suggested by the discovery of a limited set of bone implements recovered in excavations. These include fragments of polished bone spatulas, three hollow bone tubes, and an elaborately carved bone spatula-tablet bearing distinctive iconography related to the Chavín religious complex (Figures 12.11 and 12.12a). One of the fragments of a polished bone spatula was found in excavations on the upper temple platform, suggesting that the inhalation of snuff powder was a part of the Early Horizon rituals that took place on the summit (e.g., Torres 2008). Bone tubes, found in a late Initial Period (1000–925 BC) domestic context, may also have served as ritual paraphernalia for snuff inhalation (e.g., Burger 2011; Mesía Montenegro 2014). The spatula-tablet was found alongside an

Bone tube and spatula fragment, examples of snuffing paraphernalia from Atalla. Photographs by the Proyecto de Investigación Arqueológica Atalla.

figure 12.12
Carved and perforated bone snuff spatulas depicting supernatural fanged beings, from: a) Atalla (note the faint traces of cinnabar powder rubbed into the incisions) (photograph by the Proyecto de Investigación Arqueológica Atalla); and b) from Kuntur Wasi (Burger 2011:fig. 9).

a   b

figure 12.13
Rollout drawing of the Lanzón monolith (Burger 1992:fig. 140).

unusually large, polished bone bead, forming an offering deposit of valuable items. The ritual deposit appears to have coincided with the abandonment of the Early Horizon occupation, as both artifacts were found intact, buried together in a cultural layer underneath the foundations of a reoccupation-period wall. Comparable bone implements to those found at Atalla have been excavated from Chavín de Huántar (Rick 2006:figs. 6, 8), Kuntur Wasi (Figure 12.12b), and Campanayuq Rumi (Matsumoto and Cavero Palomino 2010:fig. 8).

The snuff spatula-tablet measures approximately 6.4 cm long, 2.2 cm wide, and 0.35 cm thick, tapering both in width and thickness at the bottom edge. It is engraved with a mythological image separated into an upper and lower register. The lower register depicts part of an anthropomorphic face in profile with a single large round eye and circular central pupil, curved eyebrow feature, and mouth bearing a set of two crossed fangs that project beyond the mouth. In the upper register, the heads of three snakes in profile emanate upward

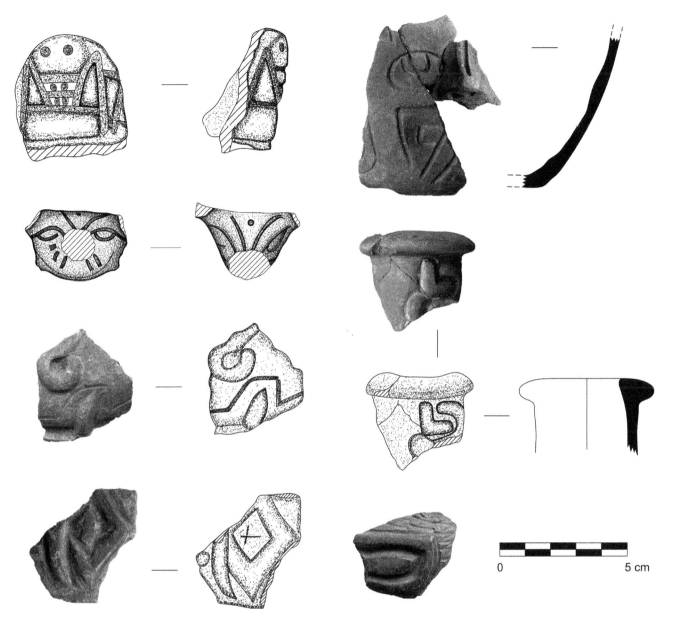

figure 12.14
Examples of ceramics from Atalla with Chavín religious iconography, including fanged anthropomorphic and avian figures. Photographs by the Proyecto de Investigación Arqueológica Atalla.

away from the face, representing the figure's hair or the feathers of a headdress. The overall composition and style of this image are strikingly similar to images of the deity depicted on the Lanzón and other stone sculpture from Chavín de Huántar (Figure 12.13). At some point in the object's history, the spatula-tablet was converted into a pendant with three biconically drilled holes, one of which pierces the eye of the central snake. This pendant could have been attached to clothing or worn hanging around the neck. At the site of Hualcayán in Ancash, a bone snuffing spoon was discovered around the neck of a sub-adult interred in one of the ceremonial mounds (Bria, this volume), providing a contemporary example of snuffing paraphernalia meant to be worn around the neck. At Atalla, the pendant's contextual association with the bone bead further reinforces its later use as an object of personal adornment, presumably one that imbued its owner with an elevated status or indicated spiritual acumen or authority.

Chavín cult iconography at Atalla is not limited to bone artifacts; several ceramic bottle fragments, found in association with both the temple platforms and the domestic sector, also depict mythological imagery such as fanged beings, felines, and raptorial birds (Figure 12.14). These finds indicate that not only does the Chavín International Style become popularized at Atalla, but the images of the mythical beings associated with the Chavín religion also propagated during this period—further proof of the adoption of the Chavín religion at the site.

Maize Chicha

The use of maize chicha as a ritual beverage has also been suggested as a potential component of the Chavín religious system (Burger 1992:138). At Chavín de Huántar, isotopic evidence supports the notion that maize was consumed in low amounts for ritual but did not constitute a significant part of the Early Horizon diet (Burger and Van der Merwe 1990). The ritual use of maize chicha has been widely identified in contexts from late Initial Period and Early Horizon ceremonial sites such as Campanayuq Rumi in Ayacucho (Matsumoto and Cavero Palomino 2010), Cerro Blanco in the Nepeña Valley (Ikehara, Paipay, and Shibata 2013), and as far south as the Taraco peninsula in the Titicaca Basin (Logan, Hastorf, and Pearsall 2012). A similar pattern of maize consumption appears at Atalla, where maize starch grains were identified in ceremonial contexts, but isotopic evidence from human bone samples taken from both the domestic and public sectors indicates a diet reliant on C3 plants, presumably potato, chenopods, and sweet potato, among other crops (Weber and Young 2016).

These finds from Atalla, which include evidence for the ritual consumption of hallucinogenic snuff and maize chicha in association with religious architecture and iconography associated with the Chavín religion, strongly suggest that Atalla residents participated in the Chavín religion beginning in the late Initial Period.

Ceramic Evidence

Three principal ceramic traditions appear in the late Initial Period and Early Horizon occupations at Atalla. These styles are relevant for understanding ethnic affiliation, as well as boundary maintenance and permeability between different communities in the Huancavelica region.

Atalla-Style Ceramics

Most pottery is of the Atalla style, identified from the earliest late Initial Period occupation layers at the site and continuing with some modifications into the Early Horizon. The Atalla style is characterized by burnished hemispherical bowls, short-necked jars, and ollas that are typically oxidized but can also be reduced (Figure 12.15). One common decorative technique is red paint, which appears on the rim and in horizontal and/or vertical bands on the vessel exterior. Rim modifications, including excision, punctation, incision, and modeled protuberances, are common, as are round appliqué nubbins and vertical appliqué fillets modeled on vessel bodies and decorated with a line of punctation (Young 2017, 2020).

The Atalla style is decidedly local in character; however, the forms, decorative techniques, and rim modifications present in the late Initial Period are most comparable to ceramics from Andahuaylas. For example, large neckless ollas and scalloped rim modifications are present in all phases of the Muyu Moqo style at Waywaka (Grossman 1972), and the braided appliqué decoration recorded in Chacamarca ceramics (Bauer, Kellett, and Aráoz Silva 2010) are very closely related to the Atalla style. Undulating appliqué bands with punctation, attributed at phase C–D at Waywaka (Grossman 1972), are also observed in the Early Horizon assemblages at Atalla.

At Campanayuq Rumi in Ayacucho, notched horizontal appliqué bands, bichrome painting, and negative painting are common decorative techniques but are virtually absent at Atalla. Nonetheless, the Atalla style does share some general commonalities with ceramics from Campanayuq Rumi. Forms such as Campanayuq I phase Neckless Jar 7A (Matsumoto

figure 12.15
Atalla-style ceramics. Photographs by the Proyecto de Investigación Arqueológica Atalla.

2010:fig 5.12) and Campanayuq II phase Oversized Bowl (Matsumoto 2010:fig. 6.23) resemble vessels from contemporary ceramic phases at Atalla. Decorations such as Campanayuq I phase plain ball-shaped appliqué (Matsumoto 2010:fig. 5.20) and Campanayuq II phase incised appliqués (Matsumoto 2010:fig. 6.10, neckless jar 11B) as well as rim modifications such as labial punctation (Matsumoto 2010:fig 5.13h), crenellation, and incision (Matsumoto 2010:fig 6.6, bowl 1E) also all appear commonly within the Atalla assemblage.

It is notable that the late Initial Period assemblage is most comparable to Waywaka and Chacamarca ceramics, since coeval centers within the same region, such as Chejo Orjuna (Matos Mendieta 1959), as well as those in the intervening region of Ayacucho are in closer proximity but maintained stylistically distinct ceramic traditions. The similarities between the Atalla style and assemblages from Andahuaylas may suggest migration or marriage ties between late Initial Period Atalla residents and settlements in Apurimac. Further investigation is required to clarify the nature of this connection.

Chuncuimarca-Style Ceramics

Another ceramic style present at Atalla from the late Initial Period is related to those found at Chuncuimarca in the province of Huancavelica (Figure 12.16). This style is also reported from sites in the province of Castrovirreyna, including Ticrapo (Ravines 1998), San Francisco (Engel 1991; Matos Mendieta 1959), Tambomachay, Yanamachay, and other rock shelters located between the Pucapampa and Pultoc lagoons along the Pisco-Huancavelica highway (Ravines 1971). These ceramics, whose similarities in form and decoration clearly place them within the same ceramic tradition, include neckless ollas with thickened rims, bowls with a single row of circles or ovals incised below the rim, and vessels with annular bases (Ravines 2009:53, 57). As past scholars have highlighted (Ravines 1971, 2009; Ruiz Estrada 1977), this ceramic group is also closely related to contemporaneous assemblages from Disco Verde in the Paracas Peninsula (e.g., Dulanto 2013, this volume; Engel 1991). These observed similarities in ceramic assemblages from the south coast to the Huancavelica highlands suggest a level of social cohesion in the late Initial Period that followed a route connecting the south coast to the Santa Barbara mine area. The presence of these ceramic styles in rock shelters suggests that these sites were used ephemerally by ceramic-using pastoralists, forming a route of mobility and exchange between the highlands and the coast. Zooarchaeological and isotopic evidence from camelid remains at Atalla demonstrate that camelids were used for transportation of goods to the coast beginning in the Initial Period, supporting the notion of late Initial Period

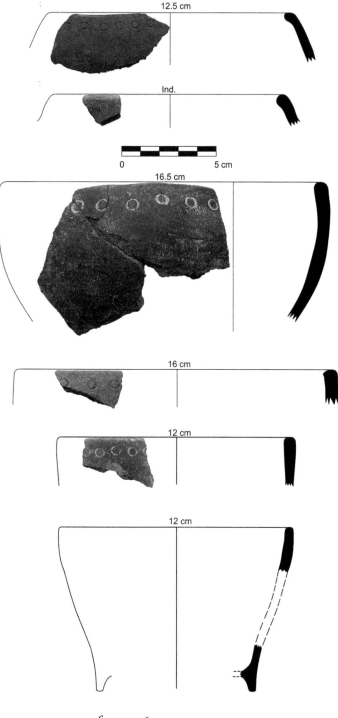

figure 12.16
Chuncuimarca style ceramics from Atalla.
Photographs by the Proyecto de Investigación
Arqueológica Atalla.

interaction networks between the south-central
highlands and the south coast.

Chavín International Style Ceramics

Claims about the relationship between Early Horizon centers and Chavín de Huántar have often been made based on the presence of what are referred to as Chavín or "Chavínoid" ceramics (Burger and Nesbitt, this volume). One of the challenges with evaluating these claims is the nebulous and subjective nature of these typological definitions. When applied to ceramics, the terms "Chavín" or "Chavínoid" generally refer to black polished and incised wares and/or ceramics bearing feline, avian, or serpentine motifs. Sometimes neckless ollas with comma-shaped rims are deemed sufficient evidence of Chavín "influence," although this vessel form is so ubiquitous during the late Initial Period as to render it meaningless as an indicator of interaction. As reported, the specific decorative techniques, motifs, and vessel forms are typically secondary to their typology as "Chavínoid," and thus they often do not receive enough illustration or careful description. Similar critiques were put forward decades ago by David Grove for the indiscriminate and uncritical use of the term "Olmec" (1989, 1993). Grove (1989) argues that the appearance of widespread motifs, previously described as "Olmec," may actually serve socio-religious functions for a local audience rather than indicate markers of contact with a specific site or region. Andeanists might do well to consider this possibility in the case of the Chavín "Horizon."

Additional obstacles facing investigators are the similarities between ceramic traditions labeled as Cupisnique, a general cultural category applied to ceramics found in burials from the north coast dating to 1200–800 BC (Burtenshaw-Zumstein 2014; Elera 1993; Larco Hoyle 1941), and ceramics described as "Chavín," representing the potting traditions from the site of Chavín de Huántar itself. The similarities between the styles are so striking that investigators in the mid-twentieth century sometimes used the terms "Cupisnique" and "coastal Chavín" interchangeably (e.g., Strong 1948; Willey 1945). Adding to the confusion is the fact that many ceramics that have been published as examples of classic Chavín (i.e., "Raku" from Lumbreras 1993) have more recently been shown to originate from the north or central coast (Nesbitt and Matsumoto 2014). Petrographic analyses have demonstrated that many of the vessels found in the Ofrendas Gallery at Chavín de Huántar were brought to the site from the coast or mid-valley and deposited at the site as offerings and thus are not representative of local ceramics from Chavín de Huántar (Burger 1993; Druc 1998). These issues have presented analytical challenges to evaluating relationships based on ceramic styles within the Cupisnique area and with the site of Chavín de Huántar.

Burger (1993) has attempted to address this problem by defining Chavín horizon ceramics in relation to those recorded in the Janabarriu phase (700–400 BC), which he defined based on stratigraphic excavations carried out in a domestic area of Chavín de Huántar (Burger 1984, 2019). He describes three vessel types and four decorative programs from the Janabarriu phase that appear unevenly in Early Horizon ceramic assemblages from the Central Andes region as far north as Pacopampa and as far south as Paracas (Burger 1988). By the same token, he acknowledges that these ceramic traits often appear in novel combinations, interpreted through the lens of local tastes. Later, John W. Rick and colleagues introduced the term "Janabarroide," defined as ceramics stamped with classic Chavín designs or icons, like those associated with the Janabarriu phase (Rick et al. 2009:113). Their illustrated examples include elaborate stamped motifs of fanged mouths, eyes, S's, circles, and circles with central dots (Rick et al. 2009:fig. 15).

The specific differences between assemblages that have traditionally been referred to as "Chavín horizon" ceramics deserve some attention, as these variations in style reflect the intentions of the people who created and consumed them. If we intend to use ceramic style as at least a partial indicator of contact between societies, then the virtual absence of certain forms and motifs must also be considered significant. An examination of some of the differences between the various manifestations of these Chavín International Styles can reveal more about the contexts of ceramic production and the meanings each society attributed to visual traits than the practice of lumping these styles together into a single category will permit. For example, stamped S's are a common decorative motif on Early Horizon ceramics at sites across central Peru, such as San Blas (Matos Mendieta 1999; Morales 1998b), Chawin Punta (Nick Brown, personal communication 2019), Kotosh (Izumi and Sono 1963; Izumi and Terada 1972), Sajara-Patac (Matsumoto and Tsurumi 2011), and Chavín de Huántar (Burger 1984; Rick and Bazán Pérez 2014). However, this motif was absent in excavations carried out at Atalla. This observation would seem to suggest that stamped S's were only relevant or intelligible within a more limited interaction sphere centered on the central highlands, which included the eastern slopes and the north-central highlands of Conchucos. The variation apparent in "Chavín horizon" ceramics makes it increasingly more difficult to pin down a discrete and bounded set of ceramic traits with which to define the style.

As our datasets from the central highlands continue to improve, the correlation between distant ceramic assemblages and Janabarriu traits becomes less tenable. For this reason, I build upon Burger's previous Janabarriu-based definition (1988) of Chavín horizon ceramics to propose a broader stylistic category that I refer to as the Chavín International Style. Rather than treating it as a monolithic and uniform stylistic category, I define the Chavín International Style as a stylistic vocabulary that includes a set of technological and decorative techniques accompanied by loosely bound sets of traits that are shared by a number of sites participating in the Chavín Interaction Sphere during the Early Horizon. With the introduction of this new ceramic terminology, I hope to acknowledge the flexibility and geographical particularity of ceramic production and encourage the comparison of specific ceramic attributes across sites and regions. This term serves as a blunt instrument to describe one material aspect of a complex and multifaceted phenomenon, but it is useful in allowing us to shed some of the explanatory assumptions embedded within alternate terminologies.

The term "international style" has been used in archaeology and art history to describe subsets of material culture, artistic expression, and even ideas that cross sociocultural boundaries whose symbolic content and stylistic conventions are determined through interaction rather than being set by any single group (Blanton et al. 1996; Feldman 2002, 2006; Robertson 1970; Smith and Berdan 2003). When applied to visual culture, the word "international" refers to the fluidity of a style across cultural boundaries rather than a narrow reference to modern nation states. In the Andes, this connection between distinctive sets of iconography and material culture and the formation of new international identities has been underscored for Wari and Tiwanaku in the Middle Horizon (Isbell 2008). I introduce the term "Chavín International" for this ceramic style to acknowledge the legacy of this terminology, as it encompasses a subset of what has previously been referred to as "Chavín," "Chavínoid," or even "Janabarroide" ceramics, while also emphasizing

that it arose through long-term cross-cultural interactions through which no single society dictated the visual agenda.

At Atalla, the Chavín International Style is easily recognized because it uses a suite of non-local forms, production, and decorative techniques that contrast markedly with the local ceramic tradition. The appropriation of foreign aesthetics and/or imagery—discussed in a variety of terms that include but are not limited to international style, visual hybridity, and transculturalism—presumably confers prestige on the owner or user of an object by suggesting their social connections with, and perhaps esoteric knowledge of, distant communities (Feldman 2006; Hitchcock and Maeir 2013:60–61). The Chavín International Style appears at Atalla in the Wilka phase (after 800 BC). Sherds belonging to the Chavín International Style constitute approximately 5 percent of diagnostic sherds in the Wilka-phase sample and 37 percent of decorated sherds from this phase (Young 2020:457; Young and Druc 2018). At Atalla, the Chavín International Style is characterized by unusually fine vessels with highly polished surfaces and a preference for black wares. Flat-bottomed bowls with beveled rims, sometimes with pouring lips, and bottles with flanged rims are typical forms (Burger and Matos Mendieta 2002:158 161; Young 2020). Characteristic decorative techniques include incised decoration, particularly circumferential incision beneath the rim, often accompanied by one or more rows of concentric circles or circles with central dots (Figure 12.17), and surface texturization such as rocker stamping or dentate rocker stamping, which often appears in zones defined by broad-line incision (Burger and Matos Mendieta 2002:161–163, Young 2017).

While the Chavín International Style that appears at Atalla shares much in common with Burger's list of Janabarriu-related ceramic traits (1988), it also differs in several meaningful ways. First, while fine polished bottles with thickened flanged rims have been identified from Atalla, stirrup spouts are extremely rare. Concentric circles and circles with central dot motifs are quite common at Atalla, but S-shapes, eccentric eyes, and the use of graphite paint on red-slipped vessels are virtually nonexistent. Additionally, while rows of repetitive designs do appear at Atalla, they are often incised rather than stamped, although several examples of stamped decoration do exist. These observations converge to demonstrate that direct and exclusive emulation of the Janabarriu-phase ceramics from Chavín de Huántar does not fully explain the variability apparent in Chavín International Style ceramics at Atalla, nor in other ceramic assemblages across the Central Andes. Instead, the prevalence of certain ceramic forms, motifs, and techniques in different regions suggests that what has formerly been referred to as a "horizon" style are regionally specific negotiations of a form of visual expression related to a supra-regional identity (Burger 1993). The Chavín International Style at Atalla, therefore, indicates the emergence of a social group in Huancavelica who negotiated their prestige and identity within their communities, strategically employing material symbols that linked them to other groups participating within the Chavín Interaction Sphere.

The expression of the Chavín International Style at any given site is dependent upon the technical knowledge of the potters, the community's relationship with other societies, and the social values projected onto a set of symbols. Within this framework, the repeated rows of concentric circles, circles with central dots, S-shapes, and/or horseshoe shapes are analogous to what Karl Taube refers to as "diagnostic symbol groups" for the international style of the Mesoamerican Late Postclassic (Taube 2010). These diagnostic symbol groups are significant for archaeologists, as they provide readily recognizable decorative elements used to assign ceramics—and by association, archaeological sites—chronological and cultural affiliation. Although these motifs are certainly laden with symbolic meaning related to the Chavín religious system (cf. Burger 1992), little attention has been paid to the presence of regional idiosyncrasies across these symbol groups and the significance of these iconographical variations. Future research on the distribution and significance of these diagnostic symbol groups and of the different ceramic recipes and manufacture techniques should help to clarify the social and economic mechanisms that connected communities of the south-central Andes during the first millennium BC.

Other Foreign Ceramic Styles

The fluorescence of a diverse range of stylistic imitations at Atalla during the Early Horizon suggests that the site's residents participated in wide and varied interaction networks, both regionally and with distant coastal societies. Other types of foreign ceramics, including Cupisnique- and Paracas-style vessels, have been identified at Atalla in small quantities (Young 2017). Examples of incised ceramics reminiscent of other south-central highland assemblages from places like Chejo Orjuna in Huancavelica (Matos Mendieta 1959), Ataura and Pirwapukio in Junín (Browman 1970; Matos Mendieta 1971, 1972b), and Wichqana, Chupas, Campanayuq Rumi, and Jargam Pata in Ayacucho (Flores Espinoza 1960; Lumbreras 1959, 1974; Matsumoto 2010; Ochatoma Paravicino 1985, 1998) also appear in small numbers alongside Chavín International Style ceramics in the Early Horizon. Atalla ceramics share less in common with highland assemblages from Rancha and San Blas (see Lumbreras 1959, 1974; Morales 1998b for comparative materials). These data taken together support the view of the Early Horizon as a period of increasing interaction between disparate parts of the Andes, which led to the exchange of exotic resources, shared sets of ritual practices, technological innovations, and ceramic production (Burger 1992; Contreras 2011).

Cinnabar

Cinnabar, also known as vermillion, is a highly valued mineral pigment that has been used by prehistoric peoples since at least the second millennium BC. It can appear red to pink to orange in color; these different shades may reflect particle morphology achieved through different types of pigment processing and/or through mixing with other minerals, such as hematite (Prieto et al. 2016). Cinnabar has been chemically identified from Initial Period contexts on the north coast (Prieto et al. 2016) and Early Horizon occupations from the northern highlands (Cooke et al. 2013) and the south coast (DeLeonardis, this volume; Dulanto 2013; Kriss et al. 2018), demonstrating that this resource moved considerable distances during these periods. Sourcing studies suggest that the Santa Barbara mine, located 15 km to the west of Atalla, was the primary source of cinnabar exploited throughout the Central Andes during the Initial Period and Early Horizon (Burger, Lane, and Cooke 2016; Cooke et al. 2013; Prieto et al. 2016).

Finds from Atalla support Burger and Matos Mendieta's (2002) hypothesis that Atalla's incorporation into the Chavín Interaction Sphere was related to its access to the major source of cinnabar for the Central Andes. At Atalla, cinnabar appears occasionally in the form of postfire pigment applied to incised ceramics, either inside of incisions or filling areas defined by incision, or adhering to human remains found in the upper temple platform (Young 2017). It appears most frequently as pigment applied to the surface of ceramic fragments, particularly the interior surface, indicating the intensive use of ceramic vessels as cinnabar containers at the site

(Figure 12.18). In some layers of the domestic sector, up to 9 percent of diagnostic sherds had evidence of cinnabar pigment, while over 20 percent of the diagnostic ceramics uncovered from Unit M, a segment of the lower platform series in the public sector, contained cinnabar residue. These data support the hypothesis that residents at Atalla played a role in administering the exportation of cinnabar pigment (e.g., Burger and Matos Mendieta 2002).

To chemically confirm the composition of the abundant pigment present at Atalla, fifty-three residue samples were taken from ceramic and lithic artifacts, forty-five of which were sampled from artifacts bearing visible pigment, to be analyzed with a Bruker Tracer III-SD pXRF device at Yale University. The eight artifacts sampled that did not exhibit visible pigment produced negative readings for cinnabar or other pigments. Visible pigments were also completely absent from the earliest identified occupation layer of the site, Layer 6 from Unit T, which dates to 1264–1131 cal BC (Young 2020:661). While cinnabar pigment was found across the public and domestic sectors of the site, analyses suggest a diachronic pattern in pigment exploitation: cinnabar was not present in red pigments sampled from Ichu-phase layers (prior to 925 BC) but constituted 40 percent of visible pigments sampled from Villa Hermosa layers (925–800 BC) and over 92 percent of visible pigments sampled from Wilka layers (800–500 BC) (Young 2020:658–661). Cinnabar pigment was not observed on ceramics from the Early Intermediate Period and Late Intermediate Period, indicating that after the abandonment of the site at the end of the Early Horizon, cinnabar distribution did not reclaim an important role in the local economy during these subsequent reoccupations.

An increasing engagement with cinnabar pigment seems to begin in Villa Hermosa, a phase of population growth and monumental construction at the site, leading to a peak in the importance of cinnabar in the Wilka phase. These results indicate that exploitation of cinnabar pigment became important to Atalla's economy only after the Ichu phase. Notable among the vessel fragments bearing cinnabar pigment residues are abundant fragments from an unusual class of ceramic vessels.

figure 12.18
Examples of ceramic
fragments with cinnabar
pigment adhered on
the interior surface.
Photographs by the
Proyecto de Investigación
Arqueológica Atalla.

0   5 cm

These fragmentary vessels are difficult to reconstruct because of their irregularity; they appear to
be unrestricted in form with flat sides that meet at
angular corners. These vessels appear within the
Atalla assemblage in the Wilka phase and are frequently observed with cinnabar residue adhered
to multiple surfaces (Figure 12.18), suggesting that
this unusual form may have been related to the processing, storage, and/or exportation of cinnabar
pigment. Lithic tools with pigment residue, on the
other hand, which one might expect to provide evidence for grinding and processing of cinnabar into
a powder form, were extremely rare at Atalla but are
reported from the nearby site of Chuncuimarca.

Chuncuimarca and Atalla are coeval sites whose
residents were likely deeply connected through a
collaborative endeavor to mine, process, and export
cinnabar pigment. Ravines (1969–1970) has noted a
lack of vertical variation in the material culture of
Chuncuimarca, leading him to suggest that the site
was inhabited over a relatively short period of time.
Nonetheless, an analysis that I conducted in 2019 of
ceramics collected by the Huancavelica Ministry of
Culture Office from the surface of Chuncuimarca

revealed ceramics diagnostic of both the Villa
Hermosa phase (925–800 BC) and the Wilka phase
(800–500 BC) at Atalla, demonstrating that the sites
were inhabited contemporaneously. The prevalence
of ceramic containers used to store cinnabar and
the dearth of pigment processing tools at Atalla
align with the suggestion by Burger and Matos
Mendieta (2002) that cinnabar would have been
extracted and processed closer to the ore source at
smaller sites such as Chuncuimarca, where Ravines
(1970) reports abundant ground stone tools covered in red pigment. The relationship between
Chuncuimarca and Atalla remains a topic for further exploration, but the differential material patterns of pigment at these sites—on ground stone
tools at Chuncuimarca and on ceramic vessels at
Atalla—would seem to indicate differing engage-
ments with cinnabar pigment.

Collections analyses of Paracas objects coincide
with the timeline for cinnabar exploitation from
Atalla and reinforce the relationship between the
Chavín cult iconography and this vibrant pigment.
A recent collections-based study carried out by
Kriss and colleagues (2018) found that cinnabar use

on Paracas ceramics was restricted to vessels depicting Chavín religious iconography and dating to the Early Paracas period, after which time cinnabar was replaced as a red colorant by iron-based ores. Based on a study of one hundred and fifty calibrated radiocarbon dates from archaeological sites in Palpa, Ingmar Unkel and colleagues (2012) have redefined the end of the Early Paracas period as falling between approximately 560 and 440 BC. Thus, the end of the Early Paracas phase and the use of cinnabar pigment on ceramics coincide with the date range for the abandonment of Atalla (500–400 BC). Additional studies carried out by the author as part of the Pre-Columbian Pigment Project have also identified cinnabar pigment used as a colorant on Karwa textiles in the Yale University Art Gallery (Brown et al. 2022). These findings underscore the observation that cinnabar, provisioned from Huancavelica, became intimately entwined with the production of Chavín religious iconography on the south coast during the Early Horizon.

What does the coincidental abandonment of Chavín cult iconography, cinnabar pigment use, and ritual centers like Atalla tell us about the reasons for the disintegration of the Chavín Interaction Sphere? Does this shift in Paracas painted ceramic technology reflect changing political alliances and/or the collapse of the supplier community at Atalla? Perhaps the surging popularity of a new religion among the Paracas archaeological culture, one that emphasized the Oculate Being and trophy-head taking, presented insuperable cultural differences that produced tensions and soured the relationship between societies of the south coast and the highland community of Atalla. Alternatively, the collapse of the Chavín religious system might have prompted the abandonment of ceremonial centers like Atalla between 500 and 400 BC, disrupting trade networks that relied on a shared religious code, and leaving the south coast and other areas of the Andes without a reliable source of cinnabar. Could the seismic event that apparently destroyed the temple of Chavín de Huántar around 500 BC (Rick 2008:18) have precipitated a "crisis of confidence" that encouraged people like the Paracas to abandon the Chavín religion and trade networks in favor of

new deities? While there are several possible explanations that remain to be tested, the disappearance of cinnabar on Paracas ceramics coincided with the introduction of new religious symbolism, suggesting that the disintegration of networks between the Huancavelica highlands and south coast was related to both the transformation of Paracas religious views and the abandonment of the settlement at Atalla.

Obsidian

Obsidian was a rare, valued material at Atalla, imported from Ayacucho beginning in the late Initial Period. Although less than 4 percent of the flaked stone assemblage at Atalla was made with obsidian, this non-local volcanic glass was present at Atalla from the late Initial Period onward. Obsidian appears at Atalla primarily in the form of broken tools and flakes from reduction and retouch. A small number of cores was also identified in lithic analyses carried out by Jane Stone (2016). Flaking practices geared toward conservation of the material suggest that obsidian was considered valuable (Stone 2016), but its presence in all areas of the site suggests that access to this resource was not restricted to certain segments of the population. A sample of fifty-two obsidian artifacts, which included eighteen tools and thirty-four flakes, was selected from a range of contexts to identify diachronic patterns in obsidian access at Atalla. Non-destructive energy dispersive x-ray fluorescence analyses of trace elements performed by Michael Glascock (2017) at MURR demonstrated that the vast majority of obsidian at Atalla came from the Quispisisa source in Ayacucho. Of the artifacts tested, fifty-one of fifty-two artifacts were confirmed to originate from the Quispisisa source, while a single flake from a mixed Early Horizon/Early Intermediate period context was identified as originating from the Alca-1 source.

These results provide an interesting point of comparison with the obsidian sourcing results from other Andean regions. The pattern of preferential exploitation of Quispisisa obsidian at Atalla is consistent with the consumption trends witnessed at other sites participating in the Chavín Interaction

Sphere, including Paracas sites on the south coast (Burger and Asaro 1977; DeLeonardis and Glascock 2013; Eerkens et al. 2010), Cerro Blanco on the north-central coast, Pacopampa and Kuntur Wasi in the northern highlands (Burger and Glascock 2009), and Chavín de Huántar in the north-central highlands (Burger 1984:264, 2006; Burger and Glascock 2009:22). At Campanayuq Rumi, in the neighboring region of Ayacucho, Matsumoto and colleagues (2018) also demonstrated multiple interaction spheres that changed through time; however, during the Campanayuq I phase (coeval with the Villa Hermosa phase and the beginning of the Wilka phase), Quispisisa was the predominant obsidian source, with occasional contributions from the Alca source in Arequipa. In other parts of the south-central highlands that do not appear to have participated in the Chavín Interaction Sphere, the pattern of obsidian exploitation deviates notably. For example, in Andahuaylas in the Apurimac region, communities relied on local sources, demonstrating more "insular" participation in regional interaction spheres oriented toward the southern highlands (Burger, Fajardo Rios, and Glascock 2006; Kellett, Golitko, and Bauer 2013). These observations support the notion that the exchange of Quispisisa obsidian was a hallmark of the Chavín Interaction Sphere (Burger and Glascock 2000:267, 2009) and that Atalla was connected within this pan-regional exchange network.

Discussion

Excavations at Atalla have allowed for the chronological disentanglement of the introduction of long-distance exchange, ritual syncretism, and stylistic emulation associated with the Chavín Interaction Sphere in Huancavelica. The ceramic, cinnabar, and obsidian data taken together support the view of Atalla as an important regional center participating in multiple nested and overlapping interaction networks through which residents took up new religious practices, exchanged resources, and adopted technological innovations in ceramics and metallurgy. Evidence from Huancavelica

and Ayacucho suggests that the significant movement of groups of people within the south-central highlands and between the highlands and the coast began in the late Initial Period, prior to the development of Chavín International Style ceramics. Decorative techniques in ceramics, including rim crenellation and incised circles that appear both in the Chuncuimarca highland assemblages and in those from the Muyu Moqo occupation at Waywaka in Andahuaylas (Grossman 1972) and coastal sites such as Puerto Nuevo (Dulanto 2013), underscore the preexistence of cross-regional interaction between the south coast and south-central highlands during the Initial Period. Ceramic evidence from other parts of the Andes also suggests the existence of overlapping spheres that connected Chavín de Huántar, northern ceremonial centers from Jequetepeque and Cajamarca, the Cupisnique area of the north coast, and the Manchay area of the central coast, as well as pan-regional interaction spheres connecting places like San Blas, Chawin Punta, Kotosh, and Sajara-Patac across the central highlands and the eastern slopes (Figure 12.19) (also see Matsumoto and Cavero Palomino, this volume). As these regional interaction spheres coalesced in the Early Horizon, people, ideas, resources, and the Chavín International Style traveled over great distances, producing supra-regional identities that emerged from this increasingly interconnected world (e.g., Burger 1988, 2008). Chavín de Huántar may have played an important role in unifying these disparate spheres as a central place of pilgrimage and exchange, but the processes that led to their creation had deep roots in the interregional social relations that formed between the small-scale villages of the Initial Period.

At Atalla, overlapping regional spheres may have carried cinnabar as far as the north coast (Prieto et al. 2016) and west to the Paracas Peninsula (Dulanto 2013), and Atalla residents acquired obsidian from the Quispisisa source in Ayacucho (Young 2020). Obsidian at Atalla was obtained almost exclusively from the Quispisisa source beginning in the late Initial Period and continuing through the Early Horizon, perhaps facilitated through relationships with sites located closer to the source such as

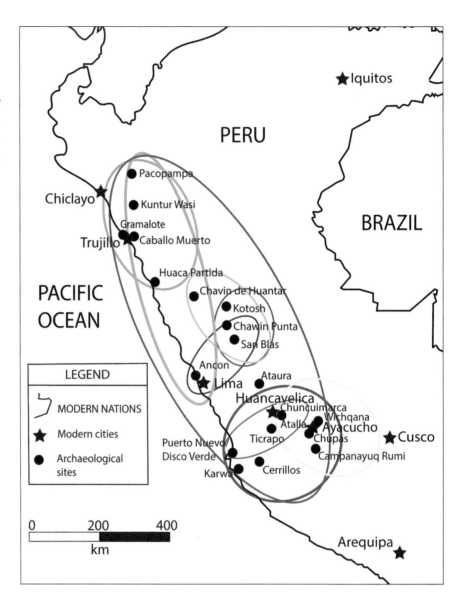

figure 12.19
Visualization of some of the
nested and overlapping regional
and pan-regional spheres of
interaction attested through
ceramic styles and other
material evidence. Illustration
by Michelle Young.

Arpiri and Campanayuq Rumi (Matsumoto et al. 2018; Nesbitt, Matsumoto, and Cavero Palomino 2019). Reliance on Quispisisa as the preferred source found at sites participating in the Chavín Interaction Sphere cannot be a mere coincidence. Preference for this source of obsidian among Chavín cult centers likely reflects trade relationships established in the late Initial Period that laid the foundation for those that were later responsible for funneling Quispisisa obsidian northward during the Early Horizon. Atalla residents had access to cinnabar from the Santa Barbara mine in the late Initial Period, but the dearth of cinnabar during the Ichu phase (1150–925 BC) suggests that local use of

the site was not motivated by its proximity to the Santa Barbara cinnabar mine. In the Villa Hermosa phase, cinnabar became more prevalent at the site, appearing on the interior of ceramic containers. A greater engagement with cinnabar pigment at Atalla coincides with the expansion of the original modest settlement into the largest village in the region of Huancavelica and precipitates the construction of the temple between 900–800 BC. By the Wilka phase, Atalla residents were participating in various scales of interaction with adjacent regions in the highlands and with distant trading partners on the north and south coasts and northern highlands. Novel vessel forms were produced in this phase, perhaps related to the processing, storage, and/or transportation of cinnabar pigment to accommodate an increased demand for this product. The lack of spondylus or other marine shell at Atalla indicates that the regional networks that brought this prized shell from the warm coastal waters of Ecuador to highland sites such as Chavín de Huántar were not linked to the more regionalized networks in which Atalla participated. The presence of non-local cultigens at Atalla suggests not only the exchange of perishable goods but also the movement of people who knew how to prepare these novel cultigens (Weber and Young 2023).

In spite of Atalla's incorporation into an increasingly connected world, Atalla residents continued to maintain their local cultural identities. This is attested archaeologically in the significant differences in ceramics, domestic structures, burial practices, and sociopolitical organization evidenced between Atalla and other sites connected in the Chavín Interaction Sphere, despite exhibiting other similarities, such as the adoption of Chavín religious practices and Chavín International Style ceramics.

The adoption of the Chavín religious system in the southern highlands becomes visible archaeologically at the end of the Initial Period, expressed at Atalla in the erection of monumental temple architecture following non-local canons, accompanied by rituals involving entheogens and maize chicha. A shared religious system would have facilitated contact between ethnically distinct groups and encouraged the expansion and intensification of the regional and long-distance trade relationships established in the late Initial Period (e.g., Burger 1992, 1988). Chavín de Huántar would likely have been considered a sacred place that loomed large in the minds of Atalla residents but may have been visited by only a select few of them.

Only in the Early Horizon, after generations of interaction, did Atalla residents develop and popularize the Chavín International Style. Stylistic and iconographic similarities in material culture across the Central Andes can be interpreted as the formation of a supra-regional identity, perhaps rooted in a kind of "sacred community" (e.g., Anderson [1983] 1991). This visual vocabulary employed novel sets of

decorative techniques and motifs to express a new corporate identity that was informed by the relationships each community forged with other groups. Ceramic evidence from Atalla and other coeval sites demonstrates that the Chavín International Style varies both regionally and between individual sites, defying its definition as a "horizon style." Beyond a mere reflection of local tradition and preference, the production of these discrete but related "international" styles can be best understood as part of a visual discourse between and within communities in which producers expressed locally embedded meanings through a self-consciously cosmopolitan and sacred visual system.

Conclusion

The Chavín Phenomenon is a complex series of interrelated processes that have traditionally been bundled together under a singular "horizon" concept. Recent excavations at Atalla have demonstrated that long-distance interaction, the adoption of Chavín religious ideology, and the production of Chavín International Style ceramics are related but not coterminous. In the case of Atalla, local and regional interaction spheres developed both prior to, and in tandem with, the rise to prominence of Chavín de Huántar to the north. The material expression of these networks includes the circulation of exotic goods such as obsidian and cinnabar and the creation and propagation of a shared "international" style of ceramics that reflect a supra-regional identity, rooted in commonly held religious ideologies.

My research at Atalla has highlighted regional interaction spheres that linked Huancavelica to other societies within the south-central highlands and the south coast to reconstruct how multi-scalar and historically particular relationships unfolded through time and ultimately were expressed through the material record. This research provides a valuable perspective on how the large-scale material patterns understood as archaeological "horizons" are mediated through local and regional processes. New data have led to a reconsideration of the horizon concept in favor of conceptualizing the Chavín Phenomenon as series of loosely bound and overlapping exchange networks facilitated by a common religious system that fostered cooperation and exchange between culturally distinct groups. These findings shift the emphasis from the leadership or elite at the site of Chavín de Huántar as the drivers of social and cultural change during the Early Horizon to consider the agency of various individuals and communities who participated in these networks. Future research will illuminate the means through which late Initial Period and Early Horizon social and economic relationships were forged, maintained, and transformed through time.

Acknowledgments

I would like to thank Richard Burger and Jason Nesbitt for their encouragement and invitation to participate in this conference and volume, and for their helpful feedback on previous drafts of this paper. I am grateful for the valuable perspectives and contributions of my research collaborators, Sadie Weber, Jane Stone, Daniela Wolin, Amy Krull, Isabelle Druc, Natali Lopez Aldave, José Luis Fuentes Sadowski, and Michael Glascock, many of whom worked alongside me in the field and/or lab and without whom the interpretations presented in this paper would not have been possible. I am appreciative of the comments and reflections from my colleagues Yuichi Matsumoto, Jalh Dulanto, Lisa DeLeonardis, and John Rick, and from two anonymous reviewers whose input improved the quality of the final version of this paper. Many thanks are also due to Lucy Salazar, Nick Brown, and Corey Hermann for their helpful feedback on early drafts of this paper. Funding for this research was provided by the NSF–DDRI, Fulbright, Rust Family Foundation, and Yale University.

REFERENCES CITED

Aldenderfer, Mark S., and Charles Stanish

1993   Domestic Architecture, Household Archaeology, and the Past in the South-Central Andes. In *Domestic Architecture, Ethnicity, and Complementarity in the South-Central Andes*, edited by Mark S. Aldenderfer, pp. 1–12. University of Iowa Press, Iowa City.

Anderson, Benedict

(1983) 1991   *Imagined Communities: Reflections on the Origin and Spread of Nationalism*. 2nd ed. Verso, New York.

Bauer, Brian S., Lucas C. Kellett, and Miriam Aráoz Silva

2010   *The Chankas: Archaeological Research in Andahuaylas (Apurimac), Peru*. Cotsen Institute of Archaeology Press, University of California, Los Angeles.

Blanton, Richard E., Gary M. Feinman, Stephen A. Kowalewski, and Peter N. Peregrine

1996   A Dual-Processual Theory for the Evolution of Mesoamerican Civilization. *Current Anthropology* 37(1):1–14.

Browman, David L.

1970   Early Peruvian Peasants: The Culture History of a Central Higlands Valley. PhD dissertation, Harvard University, Cambridge, Mass.

Brown, Nicholas E.

2017   Chawin and Chavín: Evidence of Interregional Interaction Involving the Peruvian Central Highlands during the Late Initial Period. *Ñawpa Pacha: Journal of Andean Archaeology* 37(2):87–109.

Brown, Nicholas E., Andrew D. Turner, Richard L. Burger, Lucy Salazar, and Michelle E. Young

2022   Towards a Holistic Approach to the Painted Textiles of Karwa, Peru. Paper presented as part of the IX

Jornadas Internacionales de Textiles Precolombinos y Amerindianos, Milan.

Burger, Richard L.

1984   *The Prehistoric Occupation of Chavín de Huántar, Peru*. University of California Press, Berkeley.

1988   Unity and Heterogeneity within the Chavín Horizon. In *Peruvian Prehistory*, edited by Richard W. Keatinge, pp. 99–144. Cambridge University Press, Cambridge.

1992   *Chavín and the Origins of Andean Civilization*. Thames and Hudson, London.

1993   The Chavín Horizon: Stylistic Chimera or Socioeconomic Metamorphosis? In *Latin American Horizons*, edited by Don S. Rice, pp. 41–82. Dumbarton Oaks Research Library and Collection, Washington, D.C.

1998   *Excavaciones en Chavín de Huántar*. Pontificia Universidad Católica del Perú, Fondo Editorial, Lima.

2006   Interacción interregional entre los Andes centrales y los Andes centro sur: El caso de la circulación de obsidiana. In *Esferas de interacción prehistóricas y fronteras nacionales modernas: Los Andes sur centrales*, edited by Heather Lechtman, pp. 423–447. Instituto de Estudios Peruanos, Lima.

2008   Chavín de Huántar and Its Sphere of Influence. In *The Handbook of South American Archaeology*, edited by Helaine Silverman and William Isbell, pp. 681–703. Springer, New York.

2011   What Kind of Hallucinogenic Snuff Was Used at Chavín de Huántar? An Iconographic Identification. *Ñawpa Pacha: Journal of Andean Archaeology* 31(2):123–140.

2012   Central Andean Language Expansion and the Chavin Sphere of Interaction. *Proceedings of the British Academy* 173:135–159.

2019   Understanding the Socioeconomic Trajectory of Chavín de Huántar: A New Radiocarbon Sequence and Its Wider Implications. *Latin American Antiquity* 30(2):373–392.

Burger, Richard L., and Frank Asaro

1977   Trace Element Analysis of Obsidian Artifacts from the Andes: New Perspectives on Pre-Hispanic Economic Interaction in Peru and Bolivia. Energy and Environment Division, Lawrence Berkeley Laboratory, University of California, Berkeley.

Burger, Richard L., Fidel A. Fajardo Rios, and Michael D. Glascock

2006   Potreropampa and Lisahuacho Obsidian Sources: Geological Origins of Andahuaylas A and B Type Obsidians in the Province of Aymaraes, Department of Apurimac, Peru. *Ñawpa Pacha: Journal of Andean Archaeology* 28(1):9–127.

Burger, Richard L., and Michael D. Glascock

2000   Locating the Quispisisa Obsidian Source in the Department of Ayacucho. *Latin American Antiquity* 11(3):258–268.

2009   Intercambio prehistórico de obsidiana a larga distancia en el norte Peruano. *Revista del Museo de Arqueología, Antropología e Historia* 11:17–50.

Burger, Richard L., Kris E. Lane, and Colin A. Cooke

2016   Ecuadorian Cinnabar and the Prehispanic Trade in Vermilion Pigment: Viable Hypothesis or Red Herring? *Latin American Antiquity* 27(1):22–35.

Burger, Richard L., and Ramiro Matos Mendieta

2002   Atalla: A Center on the Periphery of the Chavín Horizon. *Latin American Antiquity* 13(2):153–177.

Burger, Richard L., and Lucy C. Salazar

1980   Ritual and Religion at Huaricoto. *Archaeology* 33(6):26–32.

1991   The Second Season of Investigations at the Initial Period Center of Cardal, Peru. *Journal of Field Archaeology* 18(3):275–296.

Burger, Richard L., and Nikolaas J. Van der Merwe

1990   Maize and the Origin of Highland Chavin Civilization: An Isotopic Perspective. *American Anthropologist* 92(1):85–95.

Burtenshaw-Zumstein, Julia

2014   Cupisnique, Tembladera, Chongoyape, Chavín? A Typology of Ceramic Styles from Formative Period Northern Peru, 1800–200 BC. PhD dissertation, University of East Anglia, Norwich.

Castillo, Luis Jaime, and Christopher B. Donnan

1994   La ocupación Moche de San José de Moro, Jequetepeque. In *Moche: Propuestas y perspectivas; Actas del primer coloquio sobre la cultura Moche*, edited by Santiago Uceda and Elías Mujica, pp. 93–146. Universidad Nacional de la Libertad and Instituto Francés de Estudios Andinos, Trujillo.

Castillo, Luis Jaime, Andrew J. Nelson, and Chris S. Nelson

1997   Maquetas mochicas, San Jose de Moro. *Arkinka* 22:121–128.

Contreras, Daniel A.

2011   How Far to Conchucos? A GIS Approach to Assessing the Implications of Exotic Materials at Chavín de Huántar. *World Archaeology* 43(3):380–397.

Cooke, Colin A., Holger Hintelmann, Jay J. Ague, Richard L. Burger, Harald Biester, Julian P. Sachs, and Daniel R. Engstrom

2013   Use and Legacy of Mercury in the Andes. *Environmental Science and Technology* 47(9):4181–4188.

Cordy-Collins, Alana

1977   Chavin Art: Its Shamanic/Hallucinogenic Origins. In *Pre-Columbian Art History: Selected Readings*, edited by Alana Cordy-Collins, vol. 1, pp. 353–362. Peek Publications, Palo Alto, Calif.

1980   An Artistic Record of the Chavín Hallucinatory Experience. *The Masterkey* 54(3):84–93.

Cruzatt Añaños, Augusto

1966   Investigación arqueológica en Chupas. BA thesis, Facultad de Ciencias Sociales, Instituto de Antropología, Universidad Nacional de San Cristóbal de Huamanga, Consejo General de Investigaciones, Ayacucho.

DeLeonardis, Lisa, and Michael D. Glascock

2013   From Queshqa to Callango: A Paracas Obsidian Assemblage from the Lower Ica Valley, Peru. *Ñawpa Pacha: Journal of Andean Archaeology* 33(2):163–192.

Druc, Isabel C.

1998   *Ceramic Production and Distribution in the Chavín Sphere of Influence (North-Central Andes)*. Hadrian Books, Oxford.

Druc, Isabel C., Richard L. Burger, R. Zamojska, and P. Magny

2001   Ancon and Garagay Ceramic Production at the Time of Chavin de Huántar. *Journal of Archaeological Science* 28(1):29–43.

Dulanto, Jalh

2013   Puerto Nuevo: Redes de intercambio a larga distancia durante la primera mitad del primer mileno antes de nuestra era. *Boletín de Arqueología PUCP* 17:103–132.

Dulanto, Jalh, and Aldo Accinelli

2013   Disco Verde cincuenta años después de Frédéric Engel: La primera temporada de excavaciones del Proyecto de Investigaciones Arqueológicas Paracas en el sitio. *Boletín de Arqueología PUCP* 17:133–150.

Eerkens, Jelmer W., Kevin J. Vaughn, Moises Linares-Grados, Christina A. Conlee, Katharina Schreiber, Michael D. Glascock, and Nicholas Tripcevich

2010   Spatio-Temporal Patterns in Obsidian Consumption in the Southern Nasca Region, Peru. *Journal of Archaeological Science* 37(4):825–832.

Elera, Carlos

1993   El complejo cultural Cupisnique: Antecedent y desarollo de su ideologia religiosa. *Senri Ethnological Studies* 37:229–257.

Engel, Frédéric

1991   *Un desierto en tiempos prehispánicos: Río Pisco, Paracas, río Ica*. CIZA, Lima.

Espejo Núñez, Julio

1958   Vestigios arqueológicos "tipo Chavín" en la cuenca del Mantaro. *La voz de Huancayo* (January 10).

Espinoza, Ruben

2006   Excavaciones arqueológicas en Chuncuimarca, Huancavelica. Tesis de licenciado, Universidad Nacional de San Cristóbal de Huamanga, Ayacucho.

Feldman, Marian H.

2002   Luxurious Forms: Redefining a Mediterranean "International Style," 1400–1200 BCE. *The Art Bulletin* 84(1):6–29.

2006   *Luxury Arts and an "International Style" in the Ancient Near East, 1400–1200 BCE.* University of Chicago Press, Chicago.

Flores Espinoza, Isabel

1960   Wichqana, sitio temprano en Ayacucho. In *Antiguo Perú, espacio y tiempo: Trabajos presentados a la semana de arqueología peruana*, pp. 335–344. Librería Editorial Juan Mejía Baca, Lima.

García, Rubén

2009   Puerto Nuevo y los orígenes de la tradición estilístico-religiosa Paracas. *Boletín de Arqueología PUCP* 13:187–207.

Glascock, Michael

2017   Analysis of Obsidian Artifacts from Sites in Peru by X-Ray Fluorescence. Unpublished laboratory report, Archaeometry Laboratory, Research Reactor Center University of Missouri, Columbia.

Goldstein, Paul

1993   Tiwanaku Temples and State Expansion: A Tiwanaku Sunken-Court Temple in Moquegua, Peru. *Latin American Antiquity* 4(1):22–47.

Grossman, Joel W.

1972   Early Ceramic Cultures of Andahuaylas, Apurimac, Peru. PhD dissertation, University of California, Berkeley.

Grove, David C.

1989   Olmec: What's in a Name. In *Regional Perspectives on the Olmec*, edited by Robert J. Sharer, David C. Grove, and Jonathan Haas, pp. 8–14. Cambridge University Press, Cambridge.

1993   "Olmec" Horizons in Formative Period Mesoamerica: Diffusion or Social Evolution? In *Latin American Horizons*, edited by Don S. Rice, pp. 83–111. Dumbarton Oaks Research Library and Collection, Washington, DC.

Hitchcock, Louise A., and Aren M. Maeir

2013   Beyond Creolization and Hybridity: Entangled and Transcultural Identities in Philistia. *Archaeological Review from Cambridge* 28(1):51–74.

Hocquenghem, Anne-Marie

1993   Rutas de entrada del mullu en el extremo norte del Perú. *Bulletin de l'Institut Français d'Études Andines* 22(3):701–719.

Ikehara, Hugo C., J. Fiorella Paipay, and Koichiro Shibata

2013   Feasting with Zea Mays in the Middle and Late Formative North Coast of Peru. *Latin American Antiquity* 24(2):217–231.

Isbell, William

2008   Wari and Tiwanaku: International Identities in the Central Andean Middle Horizon. In *Handbook of South American Archaeology*, edited by Helaine Silverman and William H. Isbell, pp. 731–759. Springer, New York.

Izumi, Seiichi, and Toshihiko Sono

1963   *Andes 2: Excavations at Kotosh, Peru, 1960.* Kadokawa, Tokyo.

Izumi, Seiichi, and Kazuo Terada

1972   *Andes 4: Excavations at Kotosh, Peru, 1963 and 1966.* University of Tokyo Press, Tokyo.

Kato, Y.

1994   Resultados de las excavaciones en Kuntur Wasi, Cajamarca. In *El mundo ceremonial andino*, edited by L. Millones and Yoshio Onuki, pp. 199–224. Editorial Horizonte, Lima.

Kaulicke, Peter

2013   Paracas y Chavín: Variaciones sobre un tema longevo. *Boletín de Arqueología PUCP* 17:269–296.

Kellett, Lucas C., Mark Golitko, and Brian S. Bauer

2013   A Provenance Study of Archaeological Obsidian from the Andahuaylas Region of Southern Peru. *Journal of Archaeological Science* 40(4):1890–1902.

Kembel, Silvia R., and John W. Rick

2004   Building Authority at Chavin de Huantar: Models of Social Organization and Development in the Initial Period and Early Horizon. In *Andean Archaeology*, edited by Helaine Silverman, pp. 51–76. Blackwell, Malden, Mass.

Kriss, Dawn, Ellen Howe, Judith Levinson, Adriana Rizzo, Federico Caro, and Lisa DeLeonardis

2018   Examining Post-Fire Painted Paracas Ceramics: A Material and Technical Study. *Antiquity* 92(366):1492–1510.

Larco Hoyle, Rafael

1941   *Los Cupisniques*. Casa Editoria "La Cronica" y "Variedades" S.A., Lima.

Lathrap, Donald W.

1971   The Tropical Forest and the Cultural Context of Chavín. In *Dumbarton Oaks Conference on Chavín*, edited by Elizabeth P. Benson, pp. 73–100. Dumbarton Oaks Research Library and Collection, Washington, D.C.

1985   Jaws: The Control of Power in the Early Nuclear American Ceremonial Center. In *Early Ceremonial Architecture in the Andes*, edited by Christopher B. Donnan, pp. 241–267. Dumbarton Oaks Research Library and Collection, Washington, D.C.

Logan, Amanda L., Christine A. Hastorf, and Deborah M. Pearsall

2012   "Let's Drink Together": Early Ceremonial Use of Maize in the Titicaca Basin. *Latin American Antiquity* 23(3):235–258.

Lothrop, Samuel K.

1941   Gold Ornaments of Chavín Style from Chongoyape, Peru. *American Antiquity* 6(3):250–262.

Lumbreras, Luis Guillermo

1959   Esquema arqueológico de la sierra central del Perú. *Revista del Museo Nacional* 28:64–117.

1974   *Las fundaciones de Huamanga: Hacia una prehistoria de Ayacucho*. Nueva Educación, Lima.

1993   *Chavín de Huántar: Excavaciones en la Galería de las Ofrendas*. P. von Zabern, Mainz.

Matos Mendieta, Ramiro

1959   Exploraciones arqueológicas en Huancavelica. Undergraduate thesis, Facultad de Letras y Ciencias Humanas, Universidad Nacional Mayor de San Marcos, Lima.

1971   El período formativo en el valle del Mantaro. *Revista del Museo Nacional* 37:41–51.

1972a   Alfareros y agricultores. In *Pueblos y culturas de la sierra central del Perú*, edited by Duccio Bonavia and Rogger Ravines, pp. 35–43. Cerro de Pasco, Lima.

1972b   Ataura: Un centro Chavín en el valle del Mantaro. *Revista del Museo Nacional* 38(1):93–108.

1999   El período formativo en el altiplano de Junin, Peru. *Formativo sudamericano, una revaluación*, edited by Paulina Ledergerber-Crespo, pp. 189–200. Ediciones Abya-Yala, Quito.

Matsumoto, Yuichi

2010   The Prehistoric Ceremonial Center of Campanayuq Rumi: Interregional Interactions in the South-Central Highlands of Peru. PhD dissertation, Yale University, New Haven.

Matsumoto, Yuichi, and Yuri Cavero Palomino

2010   Una aproximación cronológica del centro ceremonial de Campanayuq Rumi, Ayacucho. *Boletín de Arqueología PUCP* 13:323–346.

Matsumoto, Yuichi, Yuri Cavero Palomino, and Roy Gutierrez Silva

2013   The Domestic Occupation of Campanayuq Rumi: Implications for Understanding the Initial Period and Early Horizon of the South-Central Andes of Peru. *Andean Past* 11(1):169–213.

Matsumoto, Yuichi, Jason Nesbitt, Yuri Cavero Palomino, and Edison Mendoza

2016   Actividades rituales en áreas circundantes al centro ceremonial de Campanayuq Rumi, Vilcashuamán, Ayacucho. *Actas del I Congreso Nacional de Arqueología* (2):99–104.

Matsumoto, Yuichi, Jason Nesbitt, Michael D. Glascock, Yuri Cavero Palomino, and Richard L. Burger

2018   Interregional Obsidian Exchange during the Late Initial Period and Early Horizon: New Perspectives from Campanayuq Rumi, Peru. *Latin American Antiquity* 29(1):44–63.

Matsumoto, Yuichi, and Eisei Tsurumi

2011   Archaeological Investigations at Sajara-Patac in the Upper Huallaga Basin, Peru. *Ñawpa Pacha: Journal of Andean Archaeology* 31(1):55–100.

McClelland, Donald

2010   Architectural Models in Late Moche Tombs. *Ñawpa Pacha: Journal of Andean Archaeology* 30(2):209–230.

Mendoza Martínez, Edison

2017   Secuencia de cerámica Paracas en Pallaucha, Vilcashuamán–Ayacucho. *Boletín de Arqueología PUCP* 22:91–116.

Menzel, Dorothy, John H. Rowe, and Lawrence E. Dawson

1964   *The Paracas Pottery of Ica: A Study in Style and Time.* University of California Press, Berkeley.

Mesía Montenegro, Christian

2014   Festines y poder en Chavín de Huántar durante el período formativo tardío en los Andes centrales. *Chungará* 46(3):313–343.

Miller, George R., and Richard L. Burger

1995   Our Father the Cayman, Our Dinner the Llama: Animal Utilization at Chavín de Huántar, Peru. *American Antiquity* 60(3):421–458.

Morales, Daniel

1998a   Investigaciones arqueológicas en Pacopampa, Departamento de Cajamarca. *Boletín de Arqueología PUCP* 2:113–126.

1998b   Importancia de las Salinas de San Blas durante el período formativo en la Sierra Central del Perú. *Boletín de Arqueología PUCP* 2:273–287.

2008   The Importance of Pacopampa Architecture and Iconography in the Central Andean Formative. In *Chavín: Art, Architecture, and Culture,* edited by William J. Conklin and Jeffrey Quilter, pp. 143–160. Cotsen Institute of Archaeology, University of California, Los Angeles.

Nagaoka, Tomohito, Yuji Seki, Wataru Morita, Kazuhiro Uzawa, Diana Alemán Paredes, and Daniel Morales Chocano

2012   A Case Study of a High-Status Human Skeleton from Pacopampa in Formative Period Peru. *Anatomical Science International* 87(4):234–237.

Nesbitt, Jason, and Yuichi Matsumoto

2014   Cupisnique Pottery from Campanayuq Rumi, South-Central Highlands of Peru: Implications for Late Initial Period Interaction. *Peruvian Archaeology* 1:47–61.

Nesbitt, Jason, Yuichi Matsumoto, and Yuri Cavero Palomino

2019   Campanayuq Rumi and Arpiri: Two Ceremonial Centers on the Periphery of the Chavín Interaction Sphere. *Ñawpa Pacha: Journal of Andean Archaeology* 39(1):57–75.

Ochatoma Paravicino, José Alberto

1985   Acerca del formativo en la sierra centro-sur. Tesis de licenciado, Universidad Nacional San Cristóbal de Huamanga, Ayacucho.

1998   El período formativo en Ayacucho: Balances y perspectivas. *Boletín de Arqueología PUCP* 2:289–302.

Onuki, Yoshio

1995   *Kuntur Wasi y Cerro Blanco: Dos sitios del formativo en el norte del Perú.* Hokusensha, Tokyo.

1997   Ocho tumbas especiales de Kuntur Wasi. *Boletín de Arqueología PUCP* 1:79–114.

Onuki, Yoshio, and Kinya Inokuchi

2011   *Gemelos pristinos: El tesoro del templo de Kuntur Wasi.* Fondo Editorial del Congreso del Perú, Minera Yanacocha, Lima.

Parsons, Jeffrey R., Charles M. Hastings, and Ramiro Matos Mendieta

2000   *Prehispanic Settlement Patterns in the Upper Mantaro and Tarma Drainages, Junín, Peru.* Memoirs of the Museum of Anthropology, University of Michigan, no. 34, pt. 2. Museum of Anthropology, Ann Arbor.

Paul, Anne

1990   *Paracas Ritual Attire: Symbols of Authority in Ancient Peru.* University of Oklahoma Press, Norman.

Petersen, Georg

(1970) 2010   *Mining and Metallurgy in Ancient Perú.* Translation by W. E. Brooks. Geological Society of America, Boulder, Colo.

Prieto, Gabriel, Véronique Wright, Richard L. Burger, Colin A. Cooke, Elvira L. Zeballos-Velasquez, Aldo Watanave, Matthew R. Suchomel, and Leopoldo Suescun

2016   The Source, Processing and Use of Red Pigment based on Hematite and Cinnabar at Gramalote, an Early Initial Period (1500–1200 cal. BC) Maritime

Community, North Coast of Peru. *Journal of Archaeological Science: Reports* 5:45–60.

Pulgar Vidal, Javier

1981   *Geografía del Perú: Las ocho regiones naturales del Perú*. Editorial Universo, Lima.

Ravines, Roger

1969–1970   El sitio arqueológico de Chuncuimarca, Huancavelica. *Revista del Museo Nacional* 36:235–257.

1971   Grupos de tradición cazadora en las tierras altas de Huancavelica, Perú. *Revista del Museo Nacional* 37:17–27.

1998   Ticrapo: Nuevo sitio del horizonte temprano. *Boletín de Lima* 111:25–30.

2009   Tradiciones alfareras prehispánicas de Huancavelica. *Boletín de Lima* 156:51–126.

Reindel, Markus

2009   Life at the Edge of the Desert— Archaeological Reconstruction of the Settlement History in the Valleys of Palpa, Peru. In *New Technologies for Archaeology: Multidisciplinary Investigations in Palpa and Nasca, Peru*, edited by Markus Reindel and Günther Wagner, pp. 439–461. Springer-Verlag Berlin, Heidelberg.

Reindel, Markus, and Johny Isla

2006   Evidencias de culturas tempranas en los valles de Palpa, costa sur del Perú. *Boletín de Arqueología PUCP* 10:237–283.

2009   El período inicial en Pernil Alto, Palpa, costa sur del Perú. *Boletín de Arqueología PUCP* 13:259–288.

Reycraft, Richard M. (editor)

2005   *Us and Them: Archaeology and Ethnicity in the Andes*. Cotsen Institute of Archaeology, University of California, Los Angeles.

Rick, John W.

2006   Chavín de Huántar: Evidence for an Evolved Shamanism. In *Mesas and Cosmologies in the Central Andes*, pp. 101–112. San Diego Museum of Man, San Diego.

2008   Context, Construction, and Ritual in the Development of Authority at Chavín de Huántar. In *Chavín: Art, Architecture, and Culture*, edited by William J. Conklin and Jeffrey Quilter, pp. 3–34. Cotsen Institute of Archaeology, University of California, Los Angeles.

Rick, John W., and Augusto E. Bazán Pérez

2014   *Proyecto de investigacion arqueologica y conservacion en Chavín de Huántar: Boletín de fin de temporada de excavaciones 2014*. Asociación Ancash and Compañía Minera Antamina, Huaraz, Ancash.

Rick, John W., Christian Mesia, Daniel Contreras, Silvia R. Kembel, Rosa M. Rick, Matthew Sayre, and John Wolf

2009   La cronología de Chavín de Huántar y sus implicancias para el período formativo. *Boletín de Arqueología PUCP* 13 (2009):87–132.

Robertson, Donald

1970   The Tulum Murals: The International Style of the Late Post-Classic. *Verhandlungen des XXXVIII internationalen Amerikanisten Kongresses* 2:77–88.

Rowe, John H.

1967   Form and Meaning in Chavín Art. In *Peruvian Archaeology: Selected Readings*, edited by John Rowe and Dorothy Menzel, pp. 72–103. Peek Publications, Palo Alto, Calif.

Ruiz Estrada, Arturo

1977   *Arqueología de la ciudad de Huancavelica*. Servicios de Artes Gráficos, Lima.

Sakai, Masato, and Juan José Martínez

2010   Excavaciones en el Templete de Limoncarro, valle bajo de Jequetepeque. *Boletín de Arqueología PUCP* 12:171–201.

Salazar, Lucy C., and Richard L. Burger

1982   La araña en la iconografía del horizonte temprano en la costa norte del Perú. *Beiträge zur allgemeinen und vergleichenden Archäologie* 4:213–253.

Sayre, Matthew P.

2010   Life across the River: Agricultural, Ritual, and Production Practices at Chavín de Huántar, Peru. PhD dissertation, University of California, Berkeley.

Seki, Yuji

2014   La diversidad del poder en la sociedad
        del período formativo: Una perspectiva
        desde la Sierra Norte. In *El centro cere-
        monial andino: Nuevas perspectivas para
        los períodos arcaico y formativo*, edited by
        Yuji Seki, pp. 175–200. Museo Nacional
        de Etnología, Osaka.

Seki, Yuji, Juan Pablo Villanueva, Masato Sakai, Diana
Alemán, Mauro Ordóñez, Walter Tosso, Araceli
Espinoza, Kinya Inokuchi, and Daniel Morales

2010   Nuevas evidencias del sitio arqueoló-
        gico de Pacopampa, en la Sierra Norte
        del Perú. *Boletín de Arqueología PUCP*
        12:69–98.

Smith, Michael Ernest, and Frances Berdan

2003   *The Postclassic Mesoamerican World*.
        University of Utah Press, Provo.

Splitstoser, Jeffrey, Dwight D. Wallace, and Mercedes
Delgado

2012   Nuevas evidencias de textiles y cerá-
        mica de la época Paracas Temprano en
        Cerrillos, valle de Ica, Perú. *Boletín de
        Arqueología PUCP* 13:209–235.

Stone, Jane

2016   Resultados preliminares del anali-
        sis de liticos tallados del Proyecto de
        Investigación Arqueológica Atalla,
        temporada 2015. Unpublished laboratory
        report, in possession of author.

2017   Resultados del analisis de liticos tallados
        del Proyecto de Investigación Arqueoló-
        gica Atalla, temporada 2016. Unpublished
        laboratory report, in possession of author.

Strong, William D.

1948   Cultural Epochs and Refuse Stratigraphy
        in Peruvian Archaeology. *Memoirs of
        the Society for American Archaeology*
        4:93–102.

Taube, Karl

2010   At Dawn's Edge: Tulum, Santa Rita, and
        Floral Symbolism in the International
        Style of Late Postclassic Mesoamerica.
        In *Astronomers, Scribes, and Priests:
        Intellectual Interchange between the
        Northern Maya Lowlands and Highland
        Mexico in the Late Postclassic Period*,
        edited by Gabrielle Vail and Christine
        Hernández, pp. 145–191. Dumbarton
        Oaks Research Library and Collection,
        Washington, D.C.

Torres, Constantino M.

2008   Chavín's Psychoactive Pharmacopoeia:
        The Iconographic Evidence. In *Chavín:
        Art, Architecture, and Culture*, edited
        by William Conklin and Jeffrey Quilter,
        pp. 239–260. Cotsen Institute of
        Archaeology, University of California,
        Los Angeles.

Unkel, Ingmar, Markus Reindel, Hermann Gorbahn,
Johny Isla Cuadrado, Bernd Kromer, and Volker Sossna

2012   A Comprehensive Numerical Chronol-
        ogy for the Pre-Columbian Cultures
        of the Palpa Valleys, South Coast of
        Peru. *Journal of Archaeological Science*
        39(7):2294–2303.

Weber, Sadie L.

2019   Pulling Abundance Out of Thin Air: The
        Role of Camelid Pastoralism at 3000 BP.
        PhD dissertation, Harvard University,
        Cambridge, Mass.

Weber, Sadie L., and Michelle E. Young

2016   Maize'd and Corn-fused: Microbotanical
        Confirmation of Early Horizon Maize
        Consumption at Atalla. Poster presen-
        tation at the Northeast Conference on
        Andean Archaeology and Ethnohistory.
        Harvard University, Boston, Mass.

2023   Eating Local, Drinking Imported: Chicha
        Recipes, Emulative Desire, and Identity
        Formation at Atalla, Huancavelica,
        Peru. In *Foodways of the Ancient Andes:
        Transforming Diet, Cuisine, and Society*,
        edited by Marta P. Alfonso-Durruty and
        Deborah E. Blom, pp. 68–88. University
        of Arizona Press, Tucson.

Wiersema, Juliet

2010   The Architectural Vessels of the Moche of
        Peru: Architecture for the Afterlife. PhD
        dissertation, University of Maryland,
        College Park.

Willey, Gordon R.

1945   Horizon Styles and Pottery Traditions
        in Peruvian Archaeology. *American
        Antiquity* 11(1):49–56.

Williams, Carlos

1985   A Scheme for the Early Monumental
        Architecture of the Central Coast of Peru.
        In *Early Ceremonial Architecture in the
        Andes*, edited by Christopher B. Donnan,
        pp. 227–240. Dumbarton Oaks Research
        Library and Collection, Washington, D.C.

Young, Michelle E.

2017   De la montaña al mar: Intercambio entre
         la sierra centro-sur y la costa sur en el
         período horizonte temprano. *Boletín de
         Arqueología PUCP* 22:9–34.

2020   The Chavín Phenomenon in Huancavel-
         ica, Peru: Interregional Interaction, Ritual
         Practice, and Social Transformations at
         Atalla. PhD dissertation, Yale University,
         New Haven.

Young, Michelle E., and Isabel C. Druc

2018   From Near and Far: Application
         of Archaeometric Techniques to
         Characterize Regional and Long-
         Distance Interaction at Atalla, Peru.
         Paper presented at the 83rd annual
         Society for American Archaeology
         conference, Washington, D.C.

Campanayuq Rumi and the Southern Periphery of the Chavín Phenomenon

YUICHI MATSUMOTO AND YURI CAVERO PALOMINO

The importance of the Peruvian south-central highlands is well recognized in the context of the Chavín Phenomenon, as it was a provider of important resources, such as cinnabar (Young, this volume) and obsidian, that were widely circulated in the Central Andes during the Early Horizon. However, the nature of the region's role in interregional interaction has not been well understood due to the scarcity of appropriate data sets. Our ongoing excavations at Campanayuq Rumi and survey in the Ayacucho region provide new information to examine this theme from a diachronic perspective. The main objective of this chapter is to describe the historical processes of interregional interaction between the "cores" of the Chavín Interaction Sphere and the sites located along its southern periphery. New data from recent excavations at Campanayuq Rumi and our survey around Vilcashuamán enable a synthesis that describes the formation of a regional interaction sphere that makes up an important part of the much larger pan-regional Chavín Interaction Sphere (Figure 13.1).

The South-Central Highlands as a Periphery of the Chavín Phenomenon

Interregional interaction is generally considered an important factor in the emergence of early complex societies in the Central Andes (Burger 1992, 2008; Burger and Matos Mendieta 2002; Goldstein 2000; Matsumoto 2010). In the study of the Chavín Phenomenon, exotic valuables such as obsidian, cinnabar, elaborated pottery, and spondylus and strombus shells are considered to be indicators of an interregional interaction sphere since they were exchanged over a wide geographic area during the late Initial Period (1100–800 BC) and the early half of the Early Horizon (ca. 800–400 BC) (Burger 1988, 1992, 2008, 2013; Druc 2004; Lumbreras 2007; Matsumoto 2010; Matsumoto et al. 2018; Nesbitt and Matsumoto 2014; Onuki 1997; Rick 2008; Seki et al. 2010). In this context, the Peruvian south-central highlands figure prominently, since this region includes all the available sources of cinnabar and obsidian (Burger and Glascock 2000, 2002,

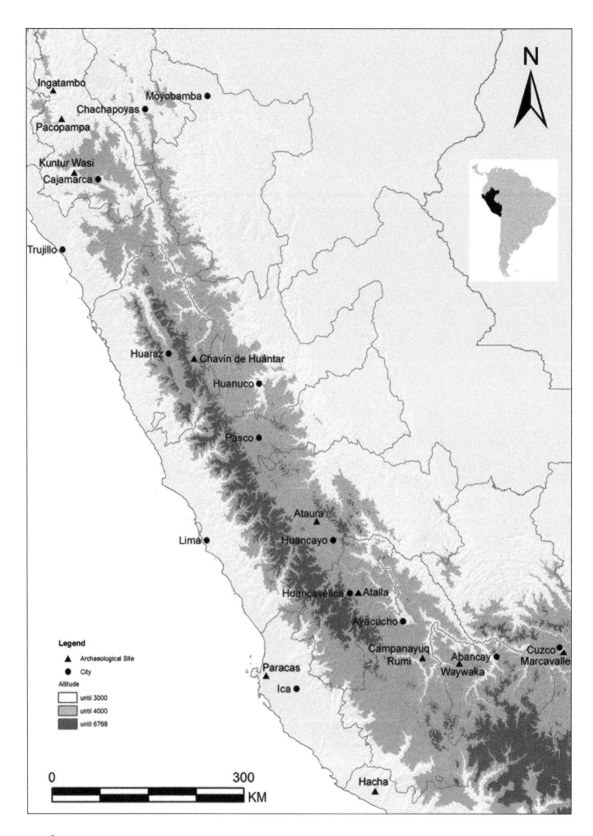

figure 13.1

The location of Campanayuq Rumi and other Chavín-related centers and areas mentioned in the text. Map by Bebel Ibarra Asencios.

2009; Burger and Matos Mendieta 2002; Cooke et al. 2013; Tripcevich and Contreras 2011, 2013; Young, this volume). We argue that the distribution pattern of these resources, in accordance with other archaeological data, can be explained through World Systems and core–periphery perspectives (Burger and Matos Mendieta 2002; Hornborg 2014; Matsumoto et al. 2018). Although these views have been critiqued because of their assumptions of asymmetric and/or unidirectional relationships between core and periphery (Dietler 1998, 2005; Schreiber 2005; Stein 1998, 1999, 2002), recent modifications of these theoretical frameworks and the nature of new data from the south-central highlands show that these models, when carefully applied, remain a useful heuristic tool for interpreting the Early Horizon (Algaze 2005; Chase-Dunn and Hall 1997; Hall, Kardulias, and Chase-Dunn 2011; Kardulias and Hall 2008; Smith and Berdan 2003).

It should be emphasized that we do not consider the Chavín Phenomenon to be the result of a single sociopolitical and economic system that unified the Central Andes (Burger and Nesbitt, this volume). Instead, we propose that the Chavín Phenomenon was a dynamic process of complex historical entanglements, in which multiple interaction spheres of different scale and character co-existed (Matsumoto 2019a; Young, this volume), and thus various local and regional agencies of the periphery need to be evaluated from a bottom-up perspective. This perspective does not require presumptions such as the core's exploitation of an underdeveloped periphery but is instead open to the possibility that mutually beneficial situations were generated that promoted socioeconomic developments in both the periphery and the core (Burger and Matos Mendieta 2002; Chase-Dunn and Hall 1997; Parkinson and Galaty 2007). Despite these caveats, Gil Stein's (2002) general critique of modified World Systems models is important. In his view, what remained from the original formulation of World Systems theory is little more than general characteristics of interregional interaction and thus its analytical value is limited. We value World Systems and core–periphery perspectives for the purpose of investigating the centers in the south-central highlands and think it helps us interpret the varieties of intra- and interregional interactions that occurred in the Central Andes during the Chavín Phenomenon. This approach enables one to understand the nested nature of the Chavín Interaction Sphere as a complex entity of multiple overlapping spheres of different scales and to compare them and consider their relationships (Burger 1988, 2008; Matsumoto et al. 2018).

Archaeological evidence suggests that the Early Horizon centers and societies tied to them experienced socioeconomic transformations that include the emergence of an elite social class that had differential access to wealth objects (Burger 1984, 1988, 1992; Dulanto, this volume; Matsumoto 2010; Matsumoto, Cavero Palomino, and Gutiérrez Silva 2013; Matsumoto et al. 2016; Seki, this volume). These changes are best recognized in the centers distributed along the north and north-central highlands, such as Chavín de Huántar, Kuntur Wasi, and Pacopampa, where large-scale and long-term excavations have been undertaken (Burger 1984, 1988, 1992; Inokuchi 2010; Lothrop 1941; Mesía 2007; Onuki 1995, 1997; Rick 2008; Sayre 2010; Seki 2014; Seki et al. 2010).

The political economies of these Early Horizon public centers are characterized by elite demand for non-local resources that come from distant sources that are sometimes hundreds of kilometers away (Burger and Nesbitt, this volume). Therefore, to better understand this phenomenon, it is necessary to adopt bottom-up perspectives that shed light on the provider of these resources. In other words, to understand the consumption and long-distance movement of exotic materials requires a far more nuanced understanding of the "peripheral" locations from which these varied items originate.

In this chapter, we will reconsider the southern periphery of the Chavín Phenomenon through archaeological data from Campanayuq Rumi and other sites situated in the south-central highlands (see Figure 13.1). For the purpose of considering the roles of these "peripheral" centers in the Chavín Interaction Sphere, the procurement and long-distance exchange of obsidian from this region are a matter of fundamental importance.

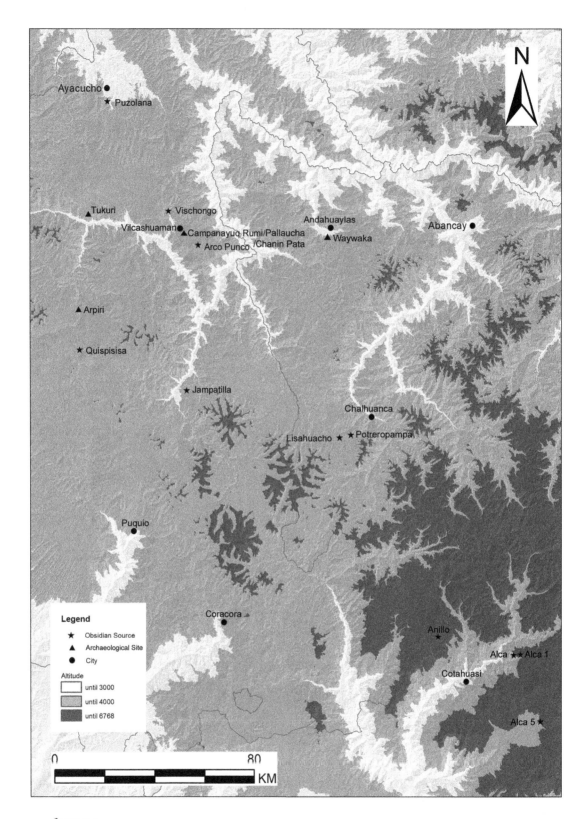

figure 13.2

Key obsidian sources and archaeological sites in the south-central highlands of Peru. Map by Bebel Ibarra Asencios.

Geochemical sourcing studies make it clear that all of the obsidian found at northern and north-central highland centers, including Chavín de Huántar, Kuntur Wasi, and Pacopampa, came from quarries located over a broad swath of the south-central highlands (Figure 13.2) (Burger and Glascock 2000, 2002, 2009; Glascock, Speakman, and Burger 2007). However, despite the recent advance in sourcing studies of obsidian outcrops, the south-central highlands, with few notable exceptions, are poorly explored with respect to its occupation during the Initial Period and Early Horizon (Bauer, Kellett, and Aráoz Silva 2010; Grossman 1972; Lumbreras 1974, 1981; Matsumoto 2010; Matsumoto, Cavero Palomino, and Nesbitt 2021; Mendoza 2010, 2018, 2020; Nesbitt, Matsumoto, and Cavero Palomino 2019). Past archaeological evidence clearly indicates that the most desired and preferred obsidian came from the Quispisisa source, situated roughly 16 km to the south of the modern town of Huancasancos in the Department of Ayacucho (Burger and Glascock 2000, 2002; see also Contreras 2011; Tripcevich and Contreras 2011, 2013). Richard L. Burger and Michael Glascock (2009) estimate that more than 90 percent of obsidian circulated in highland and coastal Peru during the Early Horizon came from this source.

Excavations at Campanayuq Rumi

Our excavations at the site of Campanayuq Rumi (Matsumoto 2010, 2012; Matsumoto and Cavero Palomino 2010a, 2010b, 2012; Matsumoto, Cavero Palomino, and Gutiérrez Silva 2013; Matsumoto et al. 2016), 52 km to the northeast of the Quispisisa source, provide a new corpus of archaeological data to reconsider the distribution of Quispisisa obsidian from its source region in the south, rather than from the perspective of recipients in the north (Matsumoto et al. 2018). Furthermore, research at Campanayuq Rumi enables us to better understand the development of sociopolitical complexity in a region long thought to be marginal to developments in the north.

In this section, we present a diachronic overview of the site of Campanayuq Rumi for the purpose of providing a chronological baseline to integrate fragmented archeological data from the Ayacucho region.

Site Description

The site of Campanayuq Rumi is located at an altitude of 3,500 masl, just 600 m east of the town and Inca administrative center of Vilcashuamán (Cavero Palomino 2014; González Carré and Pozzi-Escot 2002), in the Department of Ayacucho. Campanayuq Rumi is a large-scale civic-ceremonial center that flourished from the late Initial Period to the Early Horizon (950–450 cal. BC). Despite the recent discovery of contemporary sites with public architecture (Mendoza 2018; Nesbitt, Matsumoto, and Cavero Palomino 2019; Young 2017), it seems that Campanayuq Rumi was one of the largest ceremonial centers in the south-central highlands during this time.

Our excavations have demonstrated that Campanayuq Rumi is composed of a monumental core with stone masonry platforms arranged in a U-shaped layout covering an area of 3.5 ha (Figure 13.3); it is surrounded to the north and south by two residential areas that increase the site's overall size by at least an additional 12 ha (Figure 13.4) (Matsumoto 2010; Matsumoto and Cavero Palomino 2010a; Matsumoto, Cavero Palomino, and Gutiérrez Silva 2013; Matsumoto et al. 2016). In addition, based on the contextual correlations between the fifty-two AMS dates and relative chronology based on pottery styles and architectural sequences, the site history of Campanayuq Rumi can be divided into three phases: the Pre-Platform phase, Campanayuq I phase, and Campanayuq II phase (Matsumoto 2010; Matsumoto and Cavero Palomino 2010a).

The Pre-Platform Phase (1300–950 BC)

The first phase of occupation at Campanayuq Rumi is referred to as the Pre-Platform phase (1300–950 BC); it is defined as the time before the appearance of monumental architecture at the site. Excavations in both the monumental core and occupational contexts show evidence for domestic activity that extended in most of the excavated areas at Campanayuq Rumi, indicating that there

figure 13.3
The platform complex at Campanayuq Rumi. Map by Gentaro Miyano.

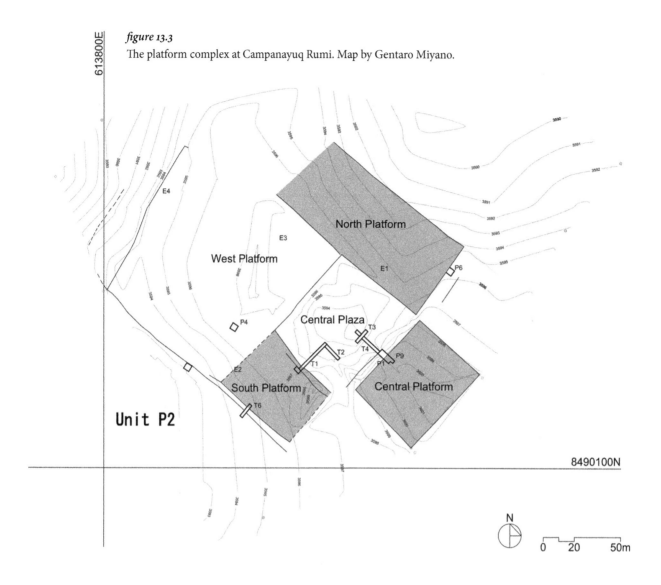

North Platform

West Platform

E4

E3

E1

P6

Central Plaza

T3

P4

T2

T4

P9

T1

P1

E2

South Platform

Central Platform

T6

Unit P2

8490100N

N

0   20   50m

was a relatively small village settlement before the beginning of the first monumental construction project. In other words, during the Pre-Platform phase, Campanayuq Rumi was probably one of many small-scale settlements that characterized the south-central highlands during the second millennium BC, as represented by sites in the Andahuaylas region to the east of Campanayuq Rumi (Bauer, Kellett, and Aráoz Silva 2010:53–55; Grossman 1972, 1983).

Portable x-ray florescence (pXRF) analysis of eleven obsidian artifacts from Campanayuq Rumi demonstrates that all of them came from Quispisisa, suggesting that the population of Campanayuq Rumi obtained high-quality obsidian even before its transformation into a major civic-ceremonial center

(Matsumoto et al. 2018:54). A handful of offering contexts, including a cache of red and black stones, suggests the inhabitants practiced local/domestic rituals. Moreover, it is highly probable that there was a specific place for head offerings (Matsumoto et al. 2016), indicating the presence of local religious beliefs and communal ritual activities before the installation of the monumental architecture.

The Campanayuq I Phase (950–700 BC)

In the Campanayuq I phase, the site transformed into a large-scale civic-ceremonial center, probably in accordance with the beginning of interaction with Chavín de Huántar, which is strongly indicated by architectural emulation. At this time, the monumental core of Campanayuq Rumi formed

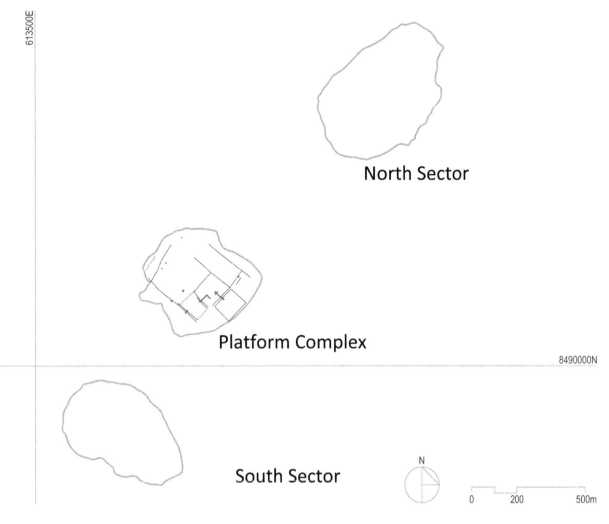

613500E

North Sector

Platform Complex

8490000N

South Sector

N

0   200   500m

figure 13.4
Map of Campanayuq Rumi, showing the locations of the south and north sectors. Map by Gentaro Miyano.

a U-shaped layout composed of stone masonry platforms surrounding a sunken rectangular plaza (Figure 13.5), which is similar to Chavín de Huántar. Other shared characteristics between the two centers include the presence of at least one gallery within Campanayuq Rumi's southern platform (Figure 13.6) that is similar to some of the gallery complexes at Chavín de Huántar (Matsumoto 2010:424–425; see Rick, this volume). In addition, excavations in 2016 and 2018 uncovered a sunken circular plaza measuring 14 m in diameter on the summit of the central platform with two stairs, which also shows certain similarities to the one found at Chavín de Huántar (Lumbreras 2014).

The combination of a U-shaped arrangement (see Figure 13.3), circular plaza, and interior gallery points to a close relationship with Chavín de Huántar, despite an approximate distance of 600 km separating the two centers (Matsumoto 2010; Matsumoto, Cavero Palomino, and Nesbitt 2021; Matsumoto et al. 2018; Nesbitt, Matsumoto, and Cavero Palomino 2019). Although the precise identification of its chronological position in the site history requires AMS dating, its stratigraphy indicates that the circular plaza was constructed by digging into bedrock and was closed sometime during the Campanayuq II phase, suggesting that its original construction occurred prior to this time. We,

figure 13.5
Southeastern corner of the sunken rectangular plaza at Campanayuq Rumi. Photograph by Yuichi Matsumoto.

figure 13.6
Gallery found at the southern platform of Campanayuq Rumi. Photograph by Yuichi Matsumoto.

therefore, hypothesize that this building was probably built in the Campanayuq I phase.

It remains difficult to precisely correlate these similarities with Chavín de Huántar, partially because of the ongoing debates over the relative and absolute chronology of its architectural sequence. In particular, the chronological position of the Circular Plaza of Chavín de Huántar is debated, with some scholars arguing that it is part of the temple's early phases and others placing it in its later phases (Burger 2021; Burger and Salazar 2008; Kembel 2008; Lumbreras 1977, 1993; Rick 2008; Rowe 1967; Watanabe 2013:50–64). Nevertheless, the greater scale and elaboration of the Chavín de Huántar public architecture, as well as the presence of earlier dates (Kembel and Haas 2015), strongly suggest that the ceremonial center of Campanayuq Rumi emulated Chavín architectural conventions. It should be emphasized that Campanayuq Rumi displays significantly greater monumentality than other Initial Period and Early Horizon centers known in the Ayacucho area (Cruzatt 1971; Lumbreras 1981). In the bottom lands of the Ayacucho Basin, the Wichqana site seems to be the earliest instance of public architecture in the region (Flores 1960; Lumbreras 1974, 1981:170–175). Luis Lumbreras excavated a possible rectangular plaza and platforms with a late Initial Period date (Lumbreras 1981:170, fig. 7-2). Though its precise size was unknown, the researchers believe that this site had a U-shape layout (Lumbreras 1981:171). If this was the case, Wichqana could have been an interesting comparative example to Campanayuq Rumi, but its destruction made their comparison impossible. However, in general, the stone masonry walls of Campanayuq Rumi were composed of large quarried stones and small flat stones. The spaces between the quarried stones were filled with flat stones and mud mortar. These stones were carefully selected and quarried to show a flat face on the wall surface, and thus they may have been used to create an aesthetic presentation of monumental architecture. It shows strong similarities to that of Chavín de Huántar, and this kind of architectural elaboration is lacking at Wichqana.

Chupas can be cited as another well-known early site in the Ayacucho region (Casafranca 1960;

Cruzatt 1966, 1971, 1977; Lumbreras 1981:177–181). Chupas is an early ceremonial center in the high grasslands at 3600 masl, about 20 km south of Wichqana, and the presence of an Early Horizon component was recognized from the pottery style and platform construction. Unlike Campanayuq Rumi, the monumental core of Chupas was composed of a single platform with multiple terraces. Several architectural phases were recognized, and during its final phase, the main platform was roughly 65 × 60 m and 5 m in height (Lumbreras 1981:178). The earliest phase of Chupas is not well-known, but its history might go back to the Initial Period. In any case, even in the final stage of its construction, the monumental core of Chupas extends less than 1 ha (Lumbreras 1981:176, fig. 7-10), making it much smaller than Campanayuq Rumi. Moreover, as was the case with Wichqana and Campanayuq Rumi, there seems to be obvious differences in the architectural sophistication and scale between Campanayuq Rumi and Chupas.

Despite the strong similarities observed in monumental architecture, the ceramic styles that characterize the Campanayuq I phase do not show clear affiliation to those of the contemporary Urabarriu phase at Chavín de Huántar (Burger 1984, 2019) or other contemporary assemblages in the Chavín heartland (Nesbitt, this volume). Instead, the ceramic assemblage of the Campanayuq I phase (Figure 13.7) was composed of styles that exhibit affinities with pottery documented in the south-central highlands and parts of the south coast (Matsumoto 2010, 2019b). For instance, stylistic linkages exist between Campanayuq Rumi and Pirwapukio in the Mantaro Valley (Browman 1970), Muyo Moqo in Andahuaylas (Bauer, Kellett, and Aráoz Silva 2010:51–52; Grossman 1972), Hacha in the Acari Valley (Neira Avendaño and Cardona Rosas 2000–2001; Riddell and Valdéz 1987–1988; Robinson 1994), and Marcavalle in Cuzco (Mohr Chávez 1977). A regional interaction sphere is indicated by the pottery styles mentioned above and it is to some extent concordant with the changes of the sources of obsidian artifacts at Campanayuq Rumi.

While Quispisisa obsidian continued to dominate, making up close to 90 percent of the sample,

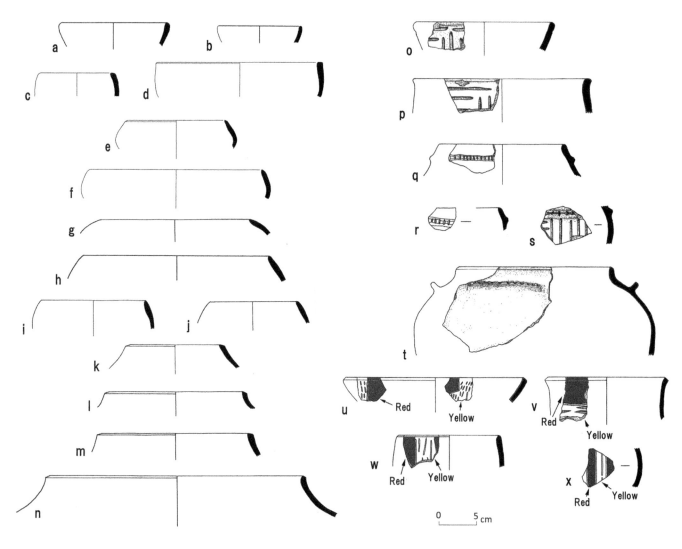

figure 13.7
Pottery assemblage of the Campanayuq I phase. Note that images u–x have bichrome painting. Drawing by Yuichi Matsumoto.

obsidian from other quarries appears in small quantities. Among them, it is important to note the presence of obsidian from the Alca source, which is located more than 200 km to the south of Campanayuq Rumi (Matsumoto et al. 2018). Despite the sporadic, though important, contact with Chavín de Huántar, Campanayuq Rumi also could have functioned as a regional node of interactions encompassing much of the south-central highlands. Although we believe that the changes in the Campanayuq I phase were partially linked to connections with Chavín de Huántar around 1000 BC, it is worth exploring and evaluating two alternative scenarios.

The first scenario assumes that the emergence of a U-shaped layout at Campanayuq Rumi was caused mainly by the interactions between Campanayuq Rumi and the U-shaped centers of the Manchay culture on the central coast (e.g., Burger and Salazar 1991, 2008, this volume; Ravines and Isbell 1976; Silva 1996, Williams 1985). The coexistence of a U-shaped platform layout and circular plazas at Cardal (Burger and Salazar 1991, 2008) might give the impression that Campanayuq Rumi possesses certain principal architectural elements in common with them. However, closer examination of these architectural features at the Manchay culture centers reveal stylistic differences that are more pronounced than some of the superficial formal similarities. Firstly, the U-shaped architecture at Manchay centers is much larger in size and more complex in its organization than the cases of Campanayuq Rumi. This difference was probably caused by construction processes at Manchay culture centers. The monumental constructions were achieved through repetitive and continuous building events over several centuries (Burger and Salazar 2012), which apparently resulted in the large size and irregular shape of each platform making up the U-shaped layout. In contrast, in the case of Campanayuq Rumi, the U-shaped layout was basically achieved through the first planned monumental construction project and was composed of rectangular stone-masonry platforms (Matsumoto 2010:87–90). As for the circular courts, Burger and Lucy C. Salazar (2008:103) have observed the difference between Chavín de Huántar and Manchay culture, stating that "[t]he sunken circular courts on the central coast differed from the Circular Plaza at Chavín de Huántar and those on the north-central coast in fundamental ways, most notably their location in relation to the central mound and the absence of fan-shaped stairway entrances." This observation is perfectly applicable to the circular plaza at Campanayuq Rumi and those of the Manchay culture, since the one at Campanayuq Rumi has two fan-shaped stairs (as at Chavín de Huántar) and is placed on the top of the central platform for public ceremonies. The core location of the circular plaza at Campanayuq Rumi contrasts well with that of Cardal, where circular courts/plazas are placed "on the periphery of the public architecture" (Burger and Salazar 2008:103). These data suggest that the circular plazas of the central coast are, as Burger and Salazar (2008) have observed, not the source of inspiration for those at Chavín de Huántar and Campanayuq Rumi. In addition, recent radiocarbon data imply that there is a chronological gap between them of more than a century (Burger and Salazar, this volume).

Other similarities in architectural techniques shared between Chavín de Huántar and Campanayuq Rumi, such as internal galleries and stone masonry composed of quarried and flat stones, are also missing among the Manchay centers. These data negate the hypothesis that the central coast centers of the Initial Period interacted intensively with Campanayuq Rumi and caused its emergence as a civic-ceremonial center of regional importance.

The other possible scenario is to relate the architectural layout of Campanayuq Rumi to the monumental architecture of the Lake Titicaca region—that is, to platforms surrounding a rectangular plaza, as seen in Early Horizon contemporary sites such as Chiripa (Janusek 2004; Mohr Chávez 1989). This may sound convincing because the U-shaped layout of Campanayuq Rumi was composed of four, not three, platforms. The east platform closed the open part of the "U," though the lack of excavation makes chronological estimation difficult. However, based on the stone masonry style observable on the surface and its base levels, we think it is reasonable to assume that the east platform was constructed during the Campanayuq I phase. In this case, there seems to be a chronological gap between the early monumental centers near Lake Titicaca and the Campanayuq I phase. At the Chiripa site, the radiocarbon dates indicate that the combination of a rectangular plaza and houses/platforms (lower house level) around it appeared somewhere between 800 and 400 BC (Bandy 1999:45), which is at least two centuries later than the beginning of Campanayuq Rumi as a large-scale civic-ceremonial center. In addition, interactions between Campanayuq Rumi and the south highlands of the Andes were not evident in the ceramic styles (Burger and Nesbitt, this volume; Matsumoto 2010; Steadman 1995, 1999). Most of the important data to demonstrate the lack of interaction between Campanayuq Rumi and the early centers around Lake Titicaca came from our recent study on obsidian provenience at Campanayuq Rumi. Campanayuq Rumi does not have any obsidian from the Chivay source located in the Colca Valley in the Department of Arequipa (Burger et al. 1998:210; Tripcevich and MacKay 2011). Available data indicate that Chivay obsidian was intensively exploited at Lake Titicaca sites such as Qaluyu and Chiripa (Burger et al. 1998:210; Burger, Mohr Chávez, and Chávez 2000) and thus the absence of

Chivay obsidian at Campanayuq Rumi delineates a clear boundary of interaction between these two regions (Matsumoto et al. 2018:57).

It is worth mentioning that despite the emulation of Chavín architectural conventions, local-style stone architecture was constructed in the residential sectors, and ritual activities represented by head offerings were carried out in specific ceremonial spaces. These features show some contrast to the situation at Chavín de Huántar and seem to reflect the local tradition. In other words, local domestic and religious traditions seem to have continued in residential sectors.

The Campanayuq II Phase (700–450 BC)

Several changes in architecture, ceramic styles, and social organization occur during the Campanayuq II phase (Matsumoto 2010). Around 700 BC, new pottery styles appeared in an intrusive manner, replacing some of the previous Campanayuq I–phase pottery styles (Matsumoto 2010, 2019b). Much of this pottery exhibits strong similarities to the ceramic styles of the contemporary Janabarriu phase at Chavín de Huántar (Burger 1984; see also Rick et al. 2010), as well as the Early Paracas style of the south coast (Figure 13.8) (Dulanto 2013, this volume; García and Pinilla 1995; Isla and Reindel

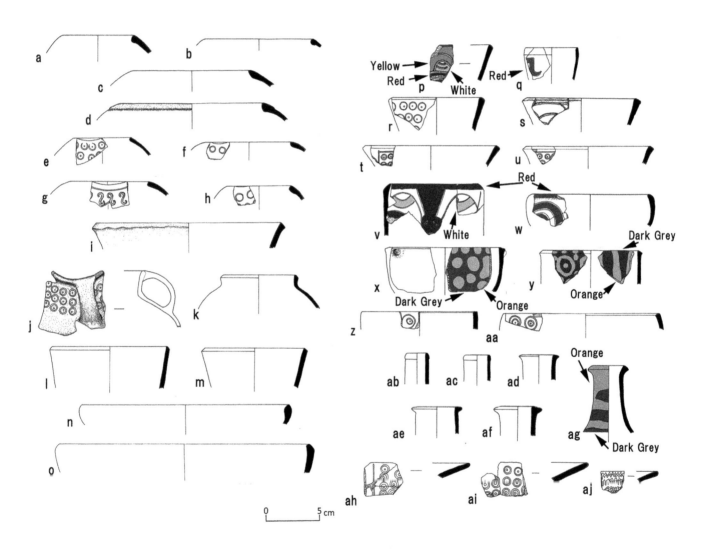

figure 13.8
Pottery assemblage of the Campanayuq II phase. Note that parts p, q, v, and w have postfired painting, and parts x, y, and ag have negative painting. Drawing by Yuichi Matsumoto.

figure 13.9
Local-style pottery of
the Campanayuq II
phase. Photograph by
Yuichi Matsumoto.

2006). It should be noted that the local pottery styles were not completely replaced (Matsumoto 2010:277, 2019b). Recent excavations in the residential sectors and the central platform demonstrate that certain aspects of the pottery assemblages, including utilitarian vessels, still maintain local styles (Figure 13.9) similar to the ones distributed in the south-central highlands such as Andahuaylas (Grossman 1972; Matsumoto 2019b).

This marked change in pottery style was associated with modifications in the monumental architecture. For instance, Campanayuq Rumi incorporated a new masonry technology of cut and polished stone referred to as ashlars. This new technique is important because it was popularized among the stone constructions of Chavín de Huántar (Kembel 2008) and applied only in important parts of the monumental core at Campanayuq Rumi, such as the staircase of the central platform (Figure 13.10). It is also during this time that the residential settlement of Campanayuq Rumi was occupied more intensively and possibly expanded (Matsumoto, Cavero Palomino, and Gutiérrez Silva 2013; Matsumoto et al. 2016).

The changes in material culture observed during the Campanayuq II phase serve as a proxy for significant socioeconomic transformations occurring at the site. Personal ornaments such as stone beads, bone ornaments with incised iconography, ear spools, gold jewelry (Figure 13.11), and elaborated pottery were used as funeral offerings (Figure 13.12) and suggest that social organization became more hierarchical during this phase (Matsumoto 2010, 2012; Matsumoto, Cavero Palomino, and Gutiérrez Silva 2013; Matsumoto et al. 2016). These artifacts also show clear stylistic affiliations to those found at Chavín de Huántar and other larger centers to the north such as Kuntur Wasi and Pacopampa (Onuki 1995; Seki et al. 2010).

Based on a comparison of ritual paraphernalia shown in the stone sculptures of Chavín de Huántar with material correlates from a ceremonial trash context at Campanayuq Rumi, Yuichi Matsumoto (2012) has hypothesized that the ritual activities carried out in the monumental core during this phase were an emulation of those performed at Chavín de Huántar (Burger 1992:200, 2013; Rick 2006). Based on this, Matsumoto concludes that "emulation of ceremonial

figure 13.10
Stone masonry platform
with a cut-stone staircase
at the central platform
of Campanayuq Rumi.
Photograph by Yuri
Cavero Palomino.

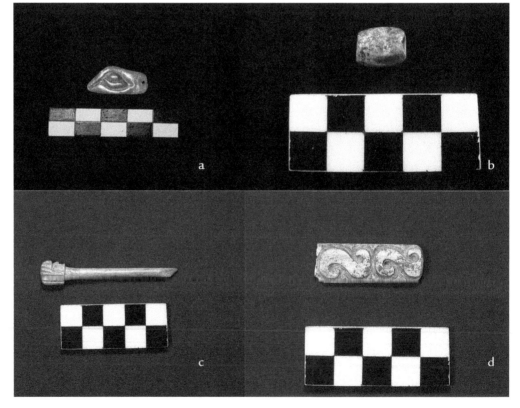

figure 13.11
Personal ornaments
unearthed from the
ceremonial trash of
the Campanayuq II
phase. Photograph by
Yuichi Matsumoto.

figure 13.12
Campanayuq II–phase burial and associated finely made vessels with religious iconography. Photograph by Yuichi Matsumoto.

activities suggests that people at Chavín de Huántar and Campanayuq Rumi shared specific religious experiences generated by similar ceremonies, which reflects the embracing of the religious ideology of Chavín de Huántar referred to as the 'Chavín cult' (Burger 1988, 1992)" (Matsumoto 2012:757).

This view is also supported by the changes in ritual activities in the residential sectors. Although head offerings continued to be carried out in the ritual spaces in the residential sector (Figure 13.13), several elements related to the religious activities carried out exclusively in the monumental core were associated with them. These includes small stone objects with possible feline iconography (Figure 13.14), clay architectural models depicting the temple platform (Figure 13.15), and a gold ear spool (Figure 13.16). In addition, there are several

examples in which high-quality Janabarriu-style vessels were used as offerings in residential areas. An offering placed at the time of architectural renovation in the north residential sector included both a local-style figurine and a typical Janabarriu bowl with a black-polished surface, pouring lip, and decorations of circles and dots (Figure 13.17).

It is reasonable to interpret this change as an intrusion of a foreign cult, even in the realm of local/domestic rituals. This is different from the Campanayuq I phase, where these rituals were clearly separated and coexisted independently. On the other hand, this might not have been a unidirectional change or an intrusion from the foreign tradition of the Chavín cult to the local ones. Local-style figurines popular in the residential sectors (Matsumoto, Cavero Palomino, and Gutiérrez Silva

figure 13.13
Circular structure found in the south sector of Campanayuq Rumi. Photograph by Yuri Cavero Palomino.

figure 13.14
Lithic artifact with Chavín-related feline iconography. Photograph by Yuichi Matsumoto.

2013:fig. 29) are found in the ceremonial trash contexts of the Campanayuq II phase mentioned earlier (Matsumoto 2010:fig.6.41), indicating that local-style ritual paraphernalia was partially utilized in the ceremonies of the monumental core of the site. It seems possible to assume that during this phase, the rituals conducted at the monumental architecture and residential sectors became interpenetrated in each other, suggesting the changing relationship between a local cult of the south-central highlands and a foreign "regional cult" (Werbner 1977), which might be referred to as the "Chavín Cult" (Burger 1988:113–114, 1992).

While these data indicate that in the Campanayuq II phase, Campanayuq Rumi was integrated into a much broader network of interregional interactions, both economic and religious, centered on

figure 13.15
Possible model of monumental architecture (41 cm in diameter) found in the circular structure in the south sector of Campanayuq Rumi (see Figure 13.13). Photograph by Jason Nesbitt.

figure 13.16
Gold ear spool (3.5 cm in diameter) found in the circular structure in the south sector of Campanayuq Rumi (see Figure 13.13). Photograph by Jason Nesbitt.

Chavín de Huántar, the obsidian proveniences of this phase enable us to take a more nuanced approach to the nature of interactions activated in this phase (Matsumoto et al. 2018). The obsidian sources of this phase are much more diverse than in previous phases. Though obsidian from the Quispisisa source still makes up the vast majority of the assemblage, it comprises a lower proportion of the assemblage than in the Campanayuq I phase and resulted in a much greater diversity of obsidian proveniences, as represented by a slight increase in obsidian coming from the Alca source. In addition, obsidian from three or possibly four new sources appear during this phase (see Figure 13.2). Among the most important sources is Potreropampa, which accounts for 5 percent of the obsidian at Campanayuq Rumi. Potreropampa is located in the southwest part of the Department of Apurimac, 104 km to the southeast of

figure 13.17
Local-style figurine and typical Janabarriu-related vessels found in an offering cache in the north sector at Campanayuq Rumi. Photograph by Yuichi Matsumoto.

Campanayuq Rumi (Burger, Fajardo, and Glascock 2006). An additional 4 percent of the obsidian comes from either Jampatilla or Lisahuacho, which are 62 km and 102 km to the south of Campanayuq Rumi, respectively (Burger, Schreiber, Glascock, and Ccencho 1998). Other sources present are distributed in the Andahuaylas and Arequipa regions with distances ranging from 60 to 200 km from Campanayuq Rumi. This obsidian data suggest that Campanayuq Rumi continued to be an important node of regional interactions in the south-central highlands despite its integration in the broader Chavín Interaction Sphere. The continuity of local pottery styles in coarse and utilitarian wares at Campanayuq Rumi also supports this view. Despite the decrease of bichrome decoration, several vessel forms and decorative techniques represented by appliqué and fine-line incisions survived during the Campanayuq II phase and these attributes are

popular in the contemporary sites in Vilcashuamán (Mendoza 2018) and Andahuaylas (Grossman 1972).

Summary: Campanayuq Rumi and the Chavín Phenomenon

The character of interaction at Campanayuq Rumi changed twice in its history. The first change occurred in the shift from the Pre-Platform phase to the Campanayuq I phase, corresponding to the transition from a small village to a major civic-ceremonial center that interacted with the south-central highlands and upper valleys of the south coast. During this time, Campanayuq Rumi first started emulating Chavín architectural conventions. The relationship between these two centers seems to have been religious rather than economic and might have caused certain interactions between them. The relative scarcity of obsidian in Chavín de Huántar's early phases (Burger 1984:188–195; Burger,

Asaro, and Michel 1984:264) probably suggests that the interactions between them were significant but sporadic. Therefore, it is reasonable to assume that pilgrimage and exchange activities were not carried out on a regular basis. Though Campanayuq Rumi likely benefited from its links to Chavín de Huántar, as represented by the knowledge tied to ritual and religion as well as by associated techniques for monumental construction projects, it also maintained much of its political-economic independence. This view is supported by the selective introduction of iconographic elements and material styles, and the separation of local/domestic ritual activities from the monumental core that reflects foreign religious ideology.

The other major transformation occurs during the transition from the Campanayuq I phase to the Campanayuq II phase. This change can be characterized by much stronger influence from Chavín de Huántar in terms of material culture and associated socioeconomic transformations. Based on Burger's model of a pilgrimage network centered at Chavín de Huántar (Burger 1988, 1993), Matsumoto has hypothesized that Campanayuq Rumi was incorporated into this religious network and functioned as a branch shrine during the Campanayuq II phase (Matsumoto 2010). We further hypothesize that, in accordance with the demands for Quispisisa obsidian from the emerging elite class of the north and north-central highlands, Campanayuq Rumi became embedded within this pan-regional interaction sphere as a gateway community (Hirth 1978; Matsumoto et al. 2018). On the other hand, it is worth noting that the demands for obsidian did not appear solely in relation to a prestige goods economy; the demand for obsidian was also guided by more practical reasons, including its potential value in a crafting economy (Matsumoto et al. 2018:57; Nesbitt, Johnson, and Horowitz 2019). The data from contemporary Chavín de Huántar demonstrate that obsidian tools were utilized in both high- and low-status areas of its occupation and suggest that during the Janabarriu phase obsidian tools were utilized for craft production, including hide processing (Burger 1984:238). These data also support the character of Campanayuq Rumi as a gateway community.

It should be stressed that Campanayuq Rumi continued to play an important role in the regional interaction sphere that had been established during the previous phase and that covered the south-central highlands and parts of the south coast, including the regions where clear affiliations to the Chavín cult cannot be recognized thus far (Matsumoto 2019b). In other words, the Campanayuq II phase can be characterized as the node to connect two overlapping, but different, kinds of interaction spheres.

Local Architectural Traditions in the South-Central Highlands

As discussed earlier, the architectural techniques of Campanayuq Rumi, especially that of stone masonry as well as galleries, and architectural layout, can be interpreted as an emulation of architectural conventions at Chavín de Huántar. Yet despite these similarities, the processes of platform construction at Campanayuq Rumi were quite different from those at Chavín de Huántar.

In general, Chavín de Huántar's monumental architecture is situated on a flat space that enabled a long-term construction sequence of expansion. From the late Initial Period to the early part of the Early Horizon, platforms with complex internal galleries and sunken plazas continued to be added as part of the vertical and horizontal expansion (Kembel 2001, 2008; Rick, this volume). However, in the case of Campanayuq Rumi, our excavations demonstrated that the location of the monumental core was selected to take advantage of a small natural hill and depression. The central platform of Campanayuq Rumi took the form we see today during the Campanayuq II phase, but it is the final product of five architectural phases of at least a few hundred years. Therefore, during its earliest phases of construction, its appearance was quite different from what we see in its final phase. The stratigraphic evidence of the central platform indicates that Campanayuq Rumi's central platform was built over a natural hill (Matsumoto 2010:78). Excavations on the top of the platform reached bedrock well above

figure 13.18
Sunken circular plaza found on top of the central platform at Campanayuq Rumi. Photograph by Yuri Cavero Palomino.

the level of the base of the platform, showing how a natural outcrop was incorporated into the first stages of monumental architecture. As for the most recent findings, in the 2016–2018 field seasons, we exposed about half of a circular plaza measuring 14 m in diameter (Figure 13.18). This plaza is placed on top of the central platform; it was constructed by digging into the bedrock and was sealed at some point in the Campanayuq II phase. In the early construction phases, the natural topography was not completely covered by the platform construction, exposing a hilltop and the low stone masonry walls surrounding it. This practice is somewhat reminiscent of the "framing" and "contouring" of sacred rock present in some instances of Inca architecture (Dean 2010:27–28; Nesbitt, Matsumoto, and Cavero Palomino 2019; see also Nesbitt 2012 for an example from the early Initial Period).

The Arpiri Site

We now believe that this architectural technique was common at other contemporary centers near Campanayuq Rumi. The one representative example

is the Arpiri site, which was identified by our survey in 2015 near the Quispisisa obsidian quarry (Matsumoto, Cavero Palomino, and Nesbitt 2021; Nesbitt, Matsumoto, and Cavero Palomino 2019). This site is situated 2 km to the southeast of the modern town of Huancasancos, above the eastern bank of the Caracha River at 3440 masl. Here, we recorded an artificial mound called Pasupata, where Initial Period/Early Horizon pottery sherds were recognized on the surface. Survey around the site located a stone wall and an Early Horizon ceramic sherd with a concentric circle motif that is typical of the Janabarriu-related pottery at Chavín de Huántar and the Campanayuq II phase at Campanayuq Rumi. Below Pasupata, several hills are located nearby and are artificially terraced by stone walls. Based on the survey there, we concluded that these hills, including Pasupata, made up a large site with monumental architecture, which is referred to as Arpiri by the local residents.

The site of Arpiri is composed of at least eight modified hills as well as the previously mentioned mound of Pasupata (Figure 13.19). On the surface

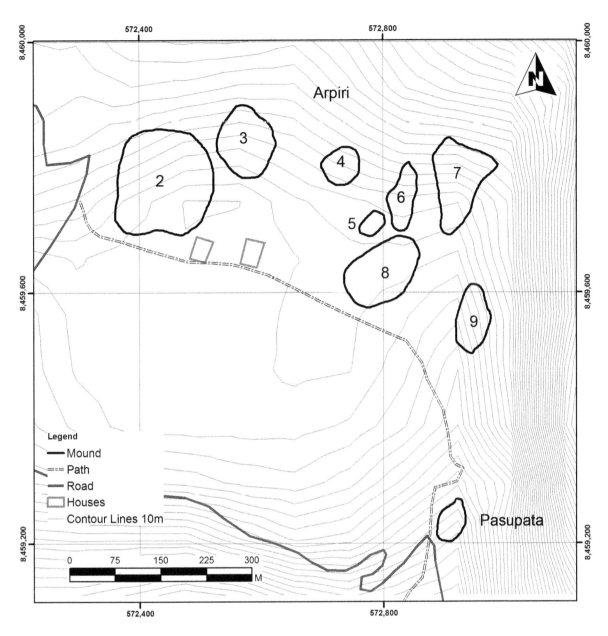

figure 13.19
Arpiri site. Map by Bebel Ibarra Asencios.

of these hills, we found artifacts including abundant obsidian flakes and points, as well as ceramic sherds that are stylistically similar to pottery found at Campanayuq Rumi. Among the hills, at least five of them exhibit evidence for artificial alteration. In particular, Arpiri 6, 7, and 8 (Figure 13.20) were intensively terraced using large stone retaining walls surrounding their base. In addition, at least two probable sunken rectangular plazas are located

in the spaces at the base of these hills. These architectural elements show clear monumentality, suggesting that Arpiri functioned as a local ceremonial center contemporary with Campanayuq Rumi.

If all of the areas associated with traces of ancient human activities are included, the total extension of Arpiri reaches 20 ha (see Figure 13.19). Thus, in terms of total area, Arpiri rivals Campanayuq Rumi in size. However, in the case

figure 13.20
Possible U-shaped layout at Arpiri, as seen from Arpiri 8. Photograph by Yuichi Matsumoto.

of Arpiri, labor investment for individual building projects, such as the terracing of natural hills and their associated retaining walls, is relatively modest when compared to the large volume invested in the construction of the largely artificial platforms of Campanayuq Rumi.

Many large quarried stones were used to construct walls of 10–50 m in length and 1–2 m in height. The largest walls at Arpiri were constructed from quarried stones that were probably brought from nearby rock outcrops, which would require low labor inputs by relatively small groups of people. Importantly, these walls only partially cover the hills; therefore, most of the natural landscape remained exposed. In other words, Arpiri exhibits an irregular architectural layout that integrates the local topography to create a type of natural monumentality. This does not fit the typical image of contemporary ceremonial centers such as Chavín de Huántar, Kuntur Wasi, and Pacopampa (Burger 1992, 2008; Inokuchi 2014; Rick 2005, 2008; Seki 2014), where

artificial monumentality was displayed by impressive stone masonry platform complexes. However, the architectural technique of Arpiri is identical to that of the central platform at Campanayuq Rumi, at least its early construction stage, and we believe they share important similarities in layout.

Based on surface observations, it is probable that there are at least two sunken plazas of rectangular shape in the space surrounded by Arpiri 6, 7, and 8. As a result, Arpiri 6, 7, and 8 seem to form a layout in which rectangular plazas are surrounded by adjacent monuments/platforms; this layout appears to form a U-shape, though the shape of the "U" is somewhat irregular and distorted compared to Campanayuq Rumi. In the case of Arpiri, it is reasonable to hypothesize that the U-shaped layout was achieved not through the planning and construction of artificial platforms to create this kind of ground plan, but rather through the selection and modification of natural topographic features that already had a preexisting configuration resembling a U-shape

(Matsumoto, Cavero Palomino, and Nesbitt 2021; Nesbitt, Matsumoto, and Cavero Palomino 2019).

Other Sites near Campanayuq Rumi

It is conceivable that the architectural technique of utilizing the natural landscape to achieve platforms or even U-shaped constructions characterizes early architecture at Campanayuq Rumi and Arpiri. Similar architectural practices are also evident at the site of Chanin Pata and Pallaucha. Chanin Pata is located approximately 3 km to the north of Campanayuq Rumi (Mendoza 2010:149) and consists of a series of low stone walls forming artificial terraces surrounding natural outcrops. Some of the revetment walls exhibit stone masonry styles similar to Campanayuq Rumi, as well as spaces that are roughly rectangular in shape. During our survey of this site in 2015, we observed pottery similar to the Campanayuq II phase and obsidian on the surface.

Pallaucha is a site with a long-term occupation from the Early Horizon to the Late Intermediate Period. This site was excavated by Edison Mendoza; he successfully demonstrated that the site clearly shows the "framing" technique for constructing monumental architecture, which is contemporary with the Campanayuq II phase (Mendoza 2017, 2018).

Recently, an important new discovery in the south-central highlands was made at the site of Tukri-Apu Urqu by Edison Mendoza and Cirilo Vivanco. This site is located on the western bank of the Caracha River near the town of Pampa Cangallo, about 40 km to the west of Campanayuq Rumi. At Tukri-Apu Urqu, Mendoza and Vivanco found an Early Horizon ceremonial center that shows clear architectural similarities to Campanayuq Rumi and Chavín de Huántar, including stone masonry platforms and a well-preserved gallery (Edison Mendoza and Cirilo Vivanco, personal communication 2018).

Monumental Architecture in the Ayacucho Area

These new data from the Ayacucho region clearly indicate that the combination of natural hills surrounded by stone walls and sunken plazas represents a local type of monumental architecture common in the Ayacucho region during the late

Initial Period and Early Horizon. Architectural variation is clearly observable among the Early Horizon ceremonial centers in the broader region. For example, at the site of Atalla in Huancavelica (Burger and Matos Mendieta 2002; Young 2017, this volume) and Chupas near the modern city of Ayacucho (Cruzatt 1966; Lumbreras 1981), monumental architecture is basically composed of a single platform and does not form a U-shaped layout. On the other hand, it is still possible that these centers were constructed by adopting this local technique first and later creating platforms covering the exposed parts of natural hills. This suggests that locally meaningful topography in relation to adjacent landscape was emphasized through the principles of "framing" and "contouring" sacred rock (Dean 2010:27–28) that might be framed more generally as a process of transforming natural places into a monument (Bradley 2000:103–110). The central platform of the Campanayuq I phase, which exposed the natural hill, implies that this architectural technique could have existed before 1000 BC as a local tradition. Only excavations of these ceremonial centers in the south-central highlands will allow us to evaluate the distribution of this architectural technique of incorporating natural topography as an important part of a site's monumentality and its chronological depth.

The presence of a possible Early Horizon U-shaped center with Janabarriu-related pottery that is positioned in a strategic location with respect to the Quispisisa quarry suggests that Arpiri, like Campanayuq Rumi, was closely connected to the interregional networks that characterize the Early Horizon. Yet, it is important to note that the U-shaped layout was achieved through local techniques, suggesting that foreign ideas were not passively accepted but rather actively modified and, in some instances, reinterpreted by local societies.

The Ayacucho Region and the Chavín Phenomenon

With these new findings, the picture of the late Initial Period and Early Horizon of the Ayacucho region in the south-central highlands is quite different from the common perspectives that prevailed until the 1990s that asserted that small centers and villages such as Chupas, Wichqana, and Jargam-pata characterized the degree of regional sociopolitical organization (Cruzatt 1971; Lumbreras 1974, 1981; Ochatoma 1998). Instead, it is now apparent that this area is crucial for understanding regional socioeconomic development in relation to the Chavín Phenomenon.

It is worth emphasizing that the Chavín Phenomenon in this region needs to be considered through two events. One occurred around 1000–950 BC and corresponds to the beginning of the Campanayuq I phase, when Campanayuq Rumi appeared as a civic-ceremonial center of regional importance and was centered on a regional interaction sphere covering the south-central highlands and upper valleys of the south coast (Matsumoto 2019b; Matsumoto et al. 2018). During this period, Campanayuq Rumi emulated architectural conventions at Chavín de Huántar. It is important to note that no other Initial Period sites that show evidence of direct contact with Chavín de Huántar have been identified thus far in this region. The obsidian data from Campanayuq Rumi and Chavín de Huántar suggest that their relationships were not economically driven, and evidence of socioeconomic transformation at the side of Campanayuq Rumi is still scarce. Though contact between the two sites could have stimulated the formation of a regional interaction sphere in the late Initial Period, it did not cause radical socioeconomic transformations in this region. Even at Campanayuq Rumi, presumable influence of Chavín de Huántar is rather limited; the local pottery styles and ritual activities in the domestic areas continued. In addition, iconographic elements of Chavín de Huántar have not yet been recognized in its monumental architecture and artifact styles. For example, the circular plaza at Campanayuq Rumi was not decorated at all by religious iconographies, which is quite different from the Circular Plaza at Chavín de Huántar (Lumbreras 1977, 2014).

The second major transition corresponds to the Chavín Phenomenon in a narrow sense. As described earlier, artifact styles, architectural techniques, and ritual activities in both the monumental core and residential areas significantly changed, suggesting much stronger affiliations to Chavín de Huántar. These changes occurred in accordance with the emergence of marked hierarchical organizations around 800–700 BC. As the data of obsidian proveniences suggest, the relationships between Chavín de Huántar and Campanayuq Rumi were both economic and religious (Burger 2013; Nesbitt, Matsumoto, and Cavero Palomino 2019; Matsumoto et al 2018:58). It is important to note that several civic-ceremonial centers appeared in the Ayacucho region in accordance with these changes. Despite the lack of AMS data outside of Campanayuq Rumi, pottery styles with stratigraphic evidence at Pallaucha (Mendoza 2017) and surface observations at other sites suggest that civic-ceremonial centers such as Pallaucha and Chanin-pata were probably constructed during this time. Arpiri and Tukri-Apu Urqu can also be included in this group (Nesbitt, Matsumoto, and Cavero Palomino 2019). These data probably indicate that a fundamental socioeconomic transformation occurred at a regional level. As represented by the recent discovery at Tukri-Apu Urqu, some sites show architectural configurations that are similar to Campanayuq Rumi. We argue that these regional changes were caused by their involvement in the larger Chavín Interaction Sphere. It should be noted that while this region was integrated into this pan-regional interaction network, it also maintained its more localized regional interaction sphere that was established in the late Initial Period. In other words, the sporadic but important contact between Chavín de Huántar and this region during the late Initial Period stimulated the formation of a regional interaction sphere where Campanayuq Rumi played an essential role. It is probable that the formation of this regional network during the late Initial Period prepared a feasible condition for this radical socioeconomic transformation in the Ayacucho region and south-central highlands in general during the Early Horizon. Even before the Early Horizon, the societies in the region had been aware of the ritual and religion of Chavín de Huántar through contact with Campanayuq Rumi, and information about the societies in the Ayacucho region and their available resources, such as the presence of multiple obsidian sources, had reached Chavín de Huántar. These preconditions could have enabled the local societies in the Ayacucho region to accept the foreign religion and get involved in this larger network of interregional interaction, which we call the Chavín Interaction Sphere. It is, therefore, of fundamental importance to recognize that Campanayuq Rumi continued to center on a regional interaction sphere of the south-central highlands, which includes the regions where the foreign cult of Chavín de Huántar was never accepted, such as Andahuaylas and the upper Colca Valley. Despite the presence of important obsidian sources of Potreropampa and Alca, clear evidence of interactions with Chavín de Huántar and other northern centers are not recognized in these regions. Two different spheres, one interregional and the other regional, overlapped independently, though they were interconnected by the sites that accepted the Chavín cult, such as Campanayuq Rumi, Arpiri, and Tukri-Apu Urqu.

Concluding Remarks

In conclusion, the Chavín Phenomenon triggered important socioeconomic changes at Campanayuq Rumi and more broadly in the south-central highlands during the Initial Period and Early Horizon (see also Young, this volume). While several material correlates suggest that the relationship between Campanayuq Rumi and Chavín de Huántar was significant, obsidian analysis likewise confirms the continued and broadened importance of Campanayuq Rumi as an important node of a regional interaction sphere within the south-central highlands, one that included portions of Arequipa, Apurimac, and the Peruvian south coast (Matsumoto et al. 2018).

The existence of a regional interaction sphere in south-central Peru during the Early Horizon is paralleled by other regional interaction spheres represented in northern Peru that incorporated highland Cajamarca. The pan-regional interaction sphere that emerged during the Early Horizon around 800–700 BC and covered the wide geographic area of the Central Andes should be considered as a complex entity of multiple regional spheres. These

regional interaction spheres articulated what is known as the Chavín Interaction Sphere (Matsumoto et al. 2018:59). These two are for now our best-documented and contrastive components, and we think comparing them is useful to capture the heterogeneity of the Chavín Phenomenon in a pan regional perspective as suggested by Burger (1988). For this purpose, we tentatively name the southern part (that includes Campanayuq Rumi) as the "Ayacucho Sphere" and the northern as the "Cajamarca Sphere" (Inokuchi 2010; Seki et al. 2010).

The Cajamarca Sphere includes two representative sites: Pacopampa and Kuntur Wasi, which show monumentality comparable to Chavín de Huántar and experienced major socioeconomic transformations after 800 BC, as represented by the emergence of marked hierarchical organization, technological innovations in metallurgy, and the expansion of monumental architecture (Seki, this volume). Despite the synchronicity of socioeconomic change, the relationships between these sites and Chavín de Huántar are quite different from that of Campanayuq Rumi and Chavín de Huántar. Many cultural elements at Campanayuq Rumi can be better interpreted as emulations or acceptance of conventions at Chavín de Huántar, and they appeared as intrusions within a local cultural matrix. Monumental architecture and religious iconographies are two representative examples that appeared at Campanayuq Rumi without any local antecedents (Matsumoto 2010, 2019b). In contrast, Chavín de Huántar, Kuntur Wasi, and Pacopampa had already been established as independent large-scale civic-ceremonial centers from the late Initial Period. Although these two northern centers and Chavín de Huántar share similar religious iconographies rooted in the north and central coasts and northern highlands (Elera 1998; Larco 1941; Lumbreras 1993; Ravines and Isbell 1976; Terada and Onuki 1985) as "sources of inspiration" (Burger and Salazar 2008), they interpret them in different ways, as exemplified by the different ceramic sequences and artifact styles between Kuntur Wasi and Pacopampa and by the lack of cultural elements from the central coast, despite the abundant presence at Chavín de Huántar as shown by the Tello Obelisk and fine pottery vessels found at the Ofrendas Gallery (Lumbreras 1993). Pottery styles, architectural styles, and religious iconography at Kuntur Wasi and Pacopampa maintain local characteristics despite the radical socioeconomic changes that occurred simultaneously with Chavín de Huántar. We, therefore, argue that the Chavín Phenomenon in the Cajamarca Sphere should be understood as a process of "peer polity interactions" (Renfrew 1982; Renfrew and Cherry 1986) rather than the core–periphery relations that we believe are applicable to the sites in the Ayacucho Sphere. We have argued that by around 800–700 BC, Campanayuq Rumi developed into an important "gateway community" (Hirth 1978) that served as a central redistributive point to provide a reliable flow of obsidian to Chavín de Huántar and other centers during the Early Horizon (Matsumoto 2010; Matsumoto et al. 2018). Campanayuq Rumi was situated on an advantageous trade route that connected the site to the Quispisisa obsidian quarries (Contreras 2011; Matsumoto 2010). In this perspective, demand for Quispisisa obsidian created intensified connections between Chavín de Huántar and the south-central highlands. Considering it with the fact that the influence from Chavín de Huántar appeared at Campanayuq Rumi as a radical intrusion, the Chavín Phenomenon in the Ayacucho Sphere needs to be considered as a relationship between core and periphery (Matsumoto et al. 2018).

Although these two spheres are currently the best understood, there could have existed others that might be similar. For example, in the Huánuco region in the central highlands, archaeological data demonstrate that around 800–700 BC all the centers in the region experienced important changes in artifacts, architecture, and settlement patterns. These changes include the destruction and/or relocation of local centers and the discontinuities of local material styles (Matsumoto 2010, 2019b; Matsumoto and Tsurumi 2011). Although they can be interpreted as acceptance of new religious beliefs from Chavín de Huántar, the changes in Huánuco, as was the case of the Ayacucho Sphere, are different in that local religious traditions were rejected in an exhaustive manner. Moreover, it is difficult to know if the centers in the Huánuco region functioned as gateway communities.

The data from Campanayuq Rumi and the Peruvian south-central highlands allow us to tentatively describe a regional process of the Chavín Phenomenon from the formation of a regional sphere to its integration to the pan-regional Chavín Interaction Sphere. Ongoing research in this and adjacent regions will provide archaeologists opportunities to evaluate how these different regional spheres are integrated to form a larger Chavín Interaction Sphere, in order to better understand the "unity and heterogeneity" (Burger 1988) of the Chavín Phenomenon from a macro perspective beyond a region.

Acknowledgments

We would like to express our deepest gratitude to the organizers of the symposium, Richard Burger, Jason Nesbitt, and Colin McEwan, for inviting us to contribute to this volume and for their helpful editorial comments. All of the comments from the symposium participants were quite inspiring and helped in shaping this paper. The excavations at Campanayuq Rumi were financed by the Coe Fund, Albers Fund, and Williams Fund of Yale University, The Roger Thayer Stone Center for Latin American Studies, Tulane University, JSPS KAKENHI Grant-in-Aid for Young Scientists (B) 25770282 (2013), and JSPS KAKENHI Grant-in-Aid for Young Scientists (A) 15H05383 (2014–). The AMS dating of Campanayuq Rumi was funded by NSF Doctoral Dissertation Improvement Grant (BCS-0950796) and the Matsushita International Foundation. The pXRF analysis of obsidian artifacts from Campanayuq Rumi was carried out as part of the archaeometry workshop in the Casa Concha with the financial support of Yale University, as part of the ongoing educational exchange program between the archaeology programs of Yale and UNSAAC. Costs for analysis of the artifacts were also covered by a National Science Foundation grant (1415403) to the Archaeometry Lab at the University of Missouri Research Reactor.

Special thanks to Cirilo Vivanco Pomacanchari and Edison Mendoza Martínez for inviting me to visit their excavations at the Tukri-Apu Urqu site. Ruben Cisneros Cardenas, Jhon Rene Huamani Diaz, Hilda Mirtha Bellido Huaña, Jorge Ronald Sulca Flores, Maribel Gutierrez Solier, and Roy Gutiérrez Silva participated in the excavations at Campanayuq Rumi and helped us with material analysis. Our deepest appreciation goes to Daniel Contreras, Lucy Salazar, Yuji Seki, and Michelle Young for providing us with valuable suggestions for shaping the ideas presented in this chapter. Bebel Ibarra Asencios created the maps shown in Figures 13.1, 13.2, and 13.19.

REFERENCES CITED

Algaze, Guillermo

2005 *The Uruk World System: The Dynamics of Expansion of Early Mesopotamian Civilization.* University of Chicago Press, Chicago.

Bandy, Matthew S.

1999 The Montículo Excavations. In *Early Settlement at Chiripa, Bolivia: Research of the Taraco Archaeological Project*, edited by Christine Hastorf, pp. 43–50. University of California Archaeological Research Facility, Berkeley.

Bauer, Brian S., Lucas C. Kellett, and Miriam Aráoz Silva

2010 *The Chanka: Archaeological Research in Andahuaylas (Apurimac), Peru.* Cotsen Institute of Archaeology, University of California, Los Angeles.

Bradley, Richard

2000 *An Archaeology of Natural Places.* Routledge, New York.

Browman, David L.

1970 Early Peruvian Peasants: The Culture of Central Highland Valley. PhD dissertation, Harvard University, Cambridge, Mass.

Burger, Richard L.

1984 *The Prehistoric Occupation of Chavín de Huántar, Peru.* University of California Press, Berkeley.

1988 Unity and Heterogeneity within the Chavín Horizon. In *Peruvian Prehistory*, edited by Richard W. Keatinge, pp. 99–144. Cambridge University Press, Cambridge.

1992 *Chavín and the Origins of Andean Civilization.* Thames and Hudson, New York.

1993 The Chavín Horizon: Stylistic Chimera or Socioeconomic Metamorphosis? In *Latin American Horizons*, edited by Donald Rice, pp. 41–82. Dumbarton Oaks Research Library and Collection, Washington, D.C.

2008 Chavín de Huántar and Its Sphere of Influence. In *Handbook of South American Archaeology*, edited by Helaine Silverman and William Isbell, pp. 681–703. Springer, New York.

2013 In the Realm of the Incas: An Archaeological Exploration of Household Exchange, Long-Distance Trade, and Marketplaces in the Pre-Hispanic Central Andes. In *Merchants, Markets, and Exchange in the Pre-Columbian World*, edited by Kenneth Hirth and Joanne Pillsbury, pp. 319–334. Dumbarton Oaks Research Library and Collection, Washington, D.C.

2019 Understanding the Socioeconomic Trajectory of Chavín de Huántar: A New Radiocarbon Sequence and Its Wider Implications. *Latin American Antiquity* 30(2):373–392.

2021 Evaluating the Architectural Sequence and Chronology of Chavín de Huántar: The Case of the Circular Plaza. *Peruvian Archaeology* 5:25–49.

Burger, Richard L., Frank Asaro, and Helen V. Michel

1984 Appendix E: The Source of Obsidian Artifacts at Chavín de Huántar, Peru. In *The Prehistoric Occupation of Chavín de Huántar, Peru*, edited by Richard L. Burger, pp. 263–270. University of California Press, Berkeley.

Burger, Richard L., Frank Asaro, Fred Stross, and Guido Salas

1998   The Chivay Obsidian Source and the Geological Origin of Titicaca Basin Type Obsidian Artifacts. *Andean Past* 5:203–224.

Burger, Richard L., Fidel A. Fajardo, and Michael D. Glascock

2006   Potreropampa and Lisahuacho Obsidian Sources: Geological Origins of Andahuaylas A and B Type Obsidians in the Province of Aymaraes, Department of Apurimac, Peru. *Ñawpa Pacha: Journal of Andean Archaeology* 28:109–127.

Burger, Richard L., and Michael D. Glascock

2000   Locating the Quispisisa Obsidian Source in the Department of Ayacucho, Peru. *Latin American Antiquity* 11(3):258–268.

2002   Tracking the Source of Quispisisa Type Obsidian from Huancavelica to Ayacucho. In *Andean Archaeology 1: Variations in Sociopolitical Organization*, edited by William Isbell and Helaine Silverman, pp. 341–368. Kluwer Academic/Plenum Publishers, New York.

2009   Intercambio prehistórico de obsidiana a larga distancia en el norte peruano. *Revista del Museo Arqueología, Antropología e Historia* 11:17–50.

Burger, Richard L., George F. Lau, Víctor M. Ponte, and Michael D. Glascock

2006   The History of Prehispanic Obsidian Procurement in Highland Ancash. In *La complejidad social en la sierra de Ancash*, edited by Alexander Herrera, Carolina Orsini, and Kevin Lane, pp. 103–120. Civiche Raccolte d'Arte Applicata del Castello Fozesco, Milan.

Burger, Richard L., and Ramiro Matos Mendieta

2002   Atalla: A Center on the Periphery of the Chavín Horizon. *Latin American Antiquity* 13(2):153–177.

Burger, Richard L., Karen L. Mohr Chávez, and Sergio J. Chávez

2000   Through the Glass Darkly: Prehispanic Obsidian Procurement and Exchange in Southern Peru and Northern Bolivia. *Journal of World Prehistory* 14:267–362.

Burger, Richard L., and Lucy C. Salazar

1991   The Second Season of Investigations at the Initial Period Center of Cardal, Peru. *Journal of Field Archaeology* 18(3):275–279.

2008   The Manchay Culture and the Coastal Inspiration for Highland Chavín Civilization. In *Chavín: Art, Architecture, and Culture*, edited by William Conklin and Jeffrey Quilter, pp. 85–106. Cotsen Institute of Archaeology, University of California, Los Angeles.

2012   Monumental Public Complexes and Agricultural Expansion on Peru's Central Coast during the Second Millennium BC. In *Early New World Monumentality*, edited by Richard L. Burger and Robert M. Rosenswig, pp. 399–430. University Press of Florida, Gainesville.

Burger, Richard L, Katharina Schreiber, Michael D. Glascock, and José Ccencho

1998   The Jampatilla Obsidian Source: Identifying the Geological Source of Pampas Type Obsidian Artifacts from Southern Peru. *Andean Past* 5: 225–239.

Casafranca, José

1960   Los nuevos sitios arqueológicos chavinoides en el Departamento de Ayacucho. In *Antiguo Perú: Espacio y tiempo*, edited by Ramiro Matos Mendieta, pp. 325–334. Librería Editorial Juan Mejía Baca, Lima.

Cavero Palomino, Yuri

2014   Evidencias arqueológicas en la Avenida Calle Real, Vilcashuamán-Ayacucho. *Arqueología y sociedad* 28:43–59.

Chase-Dunn, Christopher, and Thomas D. Hall

1997   *Rise and Demise: Comparing World-Systems*. Westview Press, Boulder.

Contreras, Daniel A.

2011   How Far to Conchucos? A GIS Approach to Assessing the Implications of Exotic Materials at Chavín de Huántar. *World Archaeology* 43(3):380–397.

Cooke, Colin A., Holger Hintelmann, Jay J. Ague, Richard L. Burger, Harold Biester, Julian P. Sachs, and Daniel R. Engstrom

2013   Use and Legacy of Mercury in the Andes. *Environmental Science & Technology* 47:4181–4188.

Cruzatt, Augusto V.

1966   *Investigación arqueológica en Chupas.* Consejo General de Investigaciones, Facultad de Ciencias Sociales, Universidad Nacional de San Cristóbal de Huamanga, Ayacucho.

1971   Horizonte temprano en el valle de Ayacucho. *Anales científicos* 1:603–631. Universidad Nacional del Centro, Huancayo.

1977   Ocupación aldeana en la altiplanicie de Chupas. BA thesis, Universidad Nacional de San Cristóbal de Huamanga, Ayacucho.

Dean, Carolyn

2010   *A Culture of Stone: Inka Perspectives on Rock.* Duke University Press, Durham, N.C.

Dietler, Michael

1998   Consumption, Agency, and Cultural Entanglement: Theoretical Implications of a Mediterranean Colonial Encounter. In *Studies in Culture Contact: Interaction, Culture Change, and Archaeology,* edited by James G. Cusick, pp. 288–315. Southern Illinois University Press, Carbondale.

2005   The Archaeology of Colonization and the Colonization of Archaeology: Theoretical Challenges from an Ancient Mediterranean Colonial Encounter. In *Archaeology of Colonial Encounters,* edited by Gil J. Stein, pp. 33–68. School of American Research Press, Santa Fe.

Druc, Isabel C.

2004   Ceramic Diversity in Chavín de Huántar, Peru. *Latin American Antiquity* 15:344–363.

Dulanto, Jalh

2013   Puerto Nuevo: Redes de intercambio a larga distancia durante la primera mitad del primer milenio antes de nuestra era. *Boletín de Arqueología PUCP* 17:103–132.

Elera, Carlos G.

1998   The Puémape Site and the Cupisnique Culture: A Case Study in the Origin and Development of Complex Society in the Central Andes. PhD dissertation, University of Calgary, Calgary.

Flores, Isabel

1960   Wichqana, sitio temprano en Ayacucho. In *Antiguo Perú: Espacio y tiempo,* edited by Ramiro Matos Mendieta, pp. 335–344. Librería Editorial Juan Mejia Baca, Lima.

García, Rubén, and José Pinilla

1995   Aproximación a una secuencia de fases con cerámica temprana de la región de Paracas. *Journal of the Steward Anthropological Society* 23:43–81.

Glascock, Michael D., Robert J. Speakman, and Richard L. Burger

2007   Sources of Archaeological Obsidian in Peru: Descriptions and Geochemistry. In *Archaeological Chemistry: Analytical Techniques and Archaeological Interpretation,* edited by Michael D. Glascock, Robert J. Speakman, and Rachel S. Popelka-Filcoff, pp. 522–552. American Chemical Society, Washington, D.C.

Goldstein, Paul S.

2000   Exotic Goods and Everyday Chiefs: Long-Distance Exchange and Indigenous Sociopolitical Development in the South-Central Andes. *Latin American Antiquity* 11:335–361.

González Carré, Enrique, and Denise Pozzi-Escot

2002   Arqueología y etnohistoria en Vilcas-huamán. *Boletín de Arqueología PUCP* 6:79–105.

Grossman, Joel W.

1972   Early Ceramic Cultures of Andahuaylas, Apurimac, Peru. PhD dissertation, University of California, Berkeley.

1983   Demographic Change and Economic Transformation in the South-Central Highlands of Pre-Huari Peru. *Ñawpa Pacha: Journal of Andean Archaeology* 21:45–126.

Hall, Thomas D., Nicholas P. Kardulias, and Christopher Chase-Dunn

2011   World-Systems Analysis and Archaeology: Continuing the Dialogue. *Journal of Archaeological Research* 3:233–279.

Hirth, Kenneth G.

  1978   Interregional Trade and the Formation
          of Prehistoric Gateway Communities.
          American Antiquity 43:35–45.

Hornborg, Alf

  2014   Political Economy, Ethnogenesis, and
          Language Dispersals in the Prehispanic
          Andes: A World-System Perspective.
          American Anthropologist 116:810–823.

Inokuchi, Kinya

  2010   La arquitectura de Kuntur Wasi: Secuencia
          constructiva y cronología de un centro
          ceremonial del período formativo. *Boletín
          de Arqueología PUCP* 12:219–247.

  2014   Cronología del período formativo de la
          Sierra Norte del Perú: Una consideración
          desde el punto de vista de la cronología
          local de Kuntur Wasi. *Senri Ethnological
          Studies* 89:123–158.

Isla, Johny, and Markus Reindel

  2006   Una tumba Paracas temprano en
          Mollake Chico, valle de Palpa, costa
          sur del Perú. *Zeitschrift für Archäologie
          Außereuropäischer Kulturen* 1:153–181.

Janusek, John W.

  2004   Tiwanaku and Its Precursors: Recent
          Research and Emerging Perspectives.
          Journal of Archaeological Research
          12(2):121–183.

Kardulias, Nicholas P., and Thomas D. Hall

  2008   Archaeology and World-Systems
          Analysis. *World Archaeology*
          40(4):572–583.

Kembel, Silvia R.

  2001   Architectural Sequence and Chronology
          at Chavín de Huántar, Peru. PhD disser-
          tation, Stanford University, Stanford.

  2008   The Architecture at the Monumental
          Center of Chavín de Huántar: Sequence,
          Transformations, and Chronology. In
          Chavín: Art, Architecture, and Culture,
          edited by William Conklin and Jeffrey
          Quilter, pp. 35–81. Cotsen Institute of
          Archaeology, University of California,
          Los Angeles.

Kembel, Silvia, and Herbert Haas

  2015   Radiocarbon Dates from the Monumen-
          tal Architecture at Chavín de Huántar,
          Perú. *Journal of Archaeological Method
          and Theory* 22:345–427.

Larco, Rafael

  1941   *Los Cupisniques.* Casa editora "La
          Crónica" y "Variedades" S.A., Lima.

Lothrop, Samuel K.

  1941   Gold Ornaments of Chavín Style from
          Chongoyape, Peru. *American Antiquity*
          6:250–266.

Lumbreras, Luis G.

  1974   *Las fundaciones de Huamanga: Hacia una
          prehistoria de Ayacucho.* Editorial Nueva
          Educación, Lima.

  1977   Excavaciones en el Templo Antiguo de
          Chavín (Sector R): Informe de la sexta
          campaña. *Ñawpa Pacha: Journal of
          Andean Archaeology* 15:1–38.

  1981   The Stratigraphy of the Open Sites. In
          Prehistory of the Ayacucho Basin, Peru,
          vol. 2, *Excavations and Chronology*, edited
          by Richard S. MacNeish, Angel G. Cook,
          Luis G. Lumbreras, Robert K. Vierra,
          and Antoinette N. Terner, pp. 167–198.
          University of Michigan Press, Ann Arbor.

  1993   *Chavín de Huántar: Excavaciones en la
          Galería de las Ofrendas.* P. von Zabern,
          Mainz.

  2007   *Chavín: Excavaciones arqueológicas.* 2 vols.
          Universidad Alas Peruanas Press, Lima.

  2014   *Excavaciones en la Plaza Circular y el
          Atrio del Lanzón en Chavín de Huántar.*
          Antamina, Lima.

Matsumoto, Yuichi

  2010   The Prehistoric Ceremonial Center
          of Campanayuq Rumi: Interregional
          Interactions in the Peruvian South-
          Central Highlands. PhD dissertation,
          Yale University, New Haven.

  2012   Recognizing Ritual: The Case of Campa-
          nayuq Rumi. *Antiquity* 86:746–759.

  2019a   South of Chavín: Interregional Inter-
          actions between the Central Highlands
          and South Coast during the Initial
          Period and Early Horizon. In *Perspectives
          on Early Andean Civilization in Peru
          Interaction, Authority, and Socioeconomic
          Organization during the First and Second
          Millennia BC*, edited by Richard L.
          Burger, Lucy C. Salazar, and Yuji Seki,
          pp. 173–188. Yale University Publications
          in Anthropology Number 94. Yale
          University Press, New Haven.

2019b   Paracas en la sierra: Interacción temprana entre la sierra centro-sur y costa sur. *Peruvian Archaeology* 3:33–64.

Matsumoto, Yuichi, and Yuri Cavero Palomino

2010a   Investigaciones arqueológicas en Campanayuq Rumi, Vilcashuamán, Ayacucho. *Revista Pacha Runa* 1:25–46.

2010b   Una aproximación cronológica del centro ceremonial de Campanayuq Rumi, Ayacucho. *Boletín de Arqueología PUCP* 13:323–346.

2012   Early Horizon Gold Metallurgy from Campanayuq Rumi in the Peruvian South-Central Highlands. *Ñawpa Pacha: A Journal of Andean Archaeology* 32(1):115–129.

Matsumoto, Yuichi, Yuri Cavero Palomino, and Roy Gutiérrez Silva

2013   The Domestic Occupation of Campanayuq Rumi: Implications for Understanding the Initial Period and Early Horizon of the South-Central Andes of Peru. *Andean Past* 11:169–213.

Matsumoto, Yuichi, Yuri Cavero Palomino, and Jason Nesbitt

2021   Utilización y adecuación del paisaje natural en construcciones monumentales durante el período inicial y el horizonte temprano en la sierra sur-centro. In *Paisaje y territorio en los Andes Centrales: Prácticas sociales y dinámicas regionales*, edited by Atsushi Yamamoto and Oscar Arias Espinoza, pp. 17–36. Fondo Editorial de la Universidad Nacional Mayor de San Marcos, Lima.

Matsumoto, Yuichi, Yuri Cavero Palomino, Jason Nesbitt, and Edison Mendoza

2016   Actividades rituales en áreas circundantes al centro ceremonial de Campanayuq Rumi, Vilcashuamán, Ayacucho. *Actas del I Congreso Nacional de Arqueología* 2:99–104.

Matsumoto, Yuichi, Jason Nesbitt, Michael D. Glascock, Yuri Cavero Palomino, and Richard L. Burger

2018   Interregional Obsidian Exchange during the Late Initial Period and Early Horizon: New Perspectives from Campanayuq Rumi. *Latin American Antiquity* 29:44–63.

Matsumoto, Yuichi, and Eisei Tsurumi

2011   Archaeological investigations at Sajara-patac in the Upper Huallaga Basin, Peru. *Ñawpa Pacha: Journal of Andean Archaeology* 31:55–100.

Mendoza Martínez, Edison M.

2010   Investigaciones arqueológicas en la margen izquierda de los Ríos Yanamayu y Pampas, Vilcashuaman-Ayacucho 2008. *Revista Pacha Runa* 1:123–162.

2017   Secuencia de cerámica Paracas en Pallaucha, Vilcashuamán-Ayacucho. *Boletín de Arqueología PUCP* 22:91–116.

2018   El período formativo tardío y final en Ayacucho, con una perspectiva desde Pallaucha–Vilcashuamán. MA thesis, Pontificia Universidad Católica del Perú, Lima.

Mendoza Martínez, Edison, Jason Nesbitt, Yuichi Matsumoto, Yuri Cavero Palomino, and Michael D. Glascock

2020   pXRF Sourcing of Obsidian from Pallaucha, Vilcashuamán: Insights into Exchange Patterns in South-Central Peru during the Early Horizon. *Bulletin de l'Institut Français d'Études Andines* 49:255–276.

Mesía, Christian M.

2007   Intrasite Spatial Organization at Chavín de Huántar during the Andean Formative: Three-Dimensional Modeling, Stratigraphy and Ceramics. PhD dissertation, Stanford University, Stanford.

Mohr Chávez, Karen L.

1977   Marcavalle: The Ceramics from an Early Horizon Site in the Valley of Cusco, Peru, and Implications for South Highland Socio-economic Interaction. PhD dissertation, University of Pennsylvania, Philadelphia.

1989   The Significance of Chiripa in Lake Titicaca Developments. *Expedition* 30 (3):17–26.

Neira Avendaño, Máximo, and Augusto Cardona Rosas

2000–2001   El período formativo en el área de Arequipa. In *Andes 3: Boletín de la Misión Arqueológica Andina*, edited by Mariusz Ziółkowski and Luis Augusto Belan Franco, pp. 27–60. Universidad de Varsovia, Varsovia.

Nesbitt, Jason

2012   Excavations at Caballo Muerto: An Investigation into the Origins of the Cupisnique Culture. PhD dissertation, Yale University, New Haven.

Nesbitt, Jason, and Yuichi Matsumoto

2014   Cupisnique Pottery at the South Highland Site of Campanayuq Rumi: Implications for Late Initial Period Interaction. *Peruvian Archaeology* 1:47–61.

Nesbitt, Jason, Rachel Johnson, and Rachel A. Horowitz

2019   Was Obsidian Used for Camelid Shearing in Ancient Peru? An Experimental and Use-Wear Study. *Ethnoarchaeology: Journal of Archaeological, Ethnographic and Experimental Studies* 11:80–94.

Nesbitt, Jason, Yuichi Matsumoto, and Yuri Cavero Palomino

2019   Campanayuq Rumi and Arpiri: Two Ceremonial Centers on the Periphery of the Chavín Interaction Sphere. *Ñawpa Pacha: Journal of Andean Archaeology* 39: 57–75.

Ochatoma, José

1998   El período formativo en Ayacucho: Balances y perspectivas. *Boletín de Arqueología PUCP* 1:79–114.

Onuki, Yoshio

1995   *Kuntur Wasi y Cerro Blanco: Dos sitios del formativo en el norte del Perú.* Hakusen-sha, Tokyo.

1997   Ocho tumbas especiales de Kuntur Wasi. *Boletín de Arqueología PUCP* 1:79–114.

Parkinson, W. A., and M. Galaty

2007   Secondary States in Perspective: An Integrated Approach to State Formation in the Prehistoric Aegean. *American Anthropologist* 109:113–129.

Ravines, Rogger, and William H. Isbell

1976   Garagay: Sitio temprano en el valle de Lima. *Revista del Museo Nacional* 41:253–272.

Renfrew, Colin

1982   Polity and Power: Interaction, Intensification and Exploitation. In *An Island Polity: The Archaeology of Exploitation in Melos*, edited by Colin Renfrew and Malcolm Wagstaff, pp. 264–290. Cambridge University Press, Cambridge.

Renfrew, Colin, and John F. Cherry (editors)

1986   *Peer Polity Interaction and Socio-Political Change.* Cambridge University Press, Cambridge.

Rick, John W.

2005   The Evolution of Authority and Power at Chavín de Huántar, Peru. In *Foundations of Power in the Prehispanic Andes*, edited by Kevin J. Vaughn, Dennis Ogburn, and Christine Conlee, pp. 71–89. Archaeological Papers of the American Anthropological Association 14. Arlington, Va.

2006   Chavín de Huántar: Evidence for an Evolved Shamanism. In *Mesas and Cosmologies in the Central Andes*, edited by Douglas Sharon, pp. 101–112. San Diego Museum, San Diego.

2008   Context, Construction, and Ritual in the Development of Authority at Chavín de Huántar. In *Chavín: Art, Architecture, and Culture*, edited by William Conklin and Jeffrey Quilter, pp. 3–34. Cotsen Institute of Archaeology, University of California, Los Angeles.

Rick, John W., Christian Mesía, Daniel A. Contreras, Silvia Rodríguez Kembel, Rosa M. Rick, Matthew Paul Sayre, and John Wolf

2010   La cronología de Chavín de Huántar y sus implicancias para el período formativo. *Boletín de Arqueología PUCP* 13:87–132.

Riddell, Francis A., and Lidio Valdéz

1987–1988   Hacha y la ocupación temprana del Valle de Acarí. *Gaceta arqueológica andina* 16:6–10.

Robinson, Roger W.

1994   Recent Excavations at Hacha in the Acarí Valley, Peru. *Andean Past* 4: 9–37.

Rowe, John H.

1967   Form and Meaning in Chavín Art. In *Peruvian Archaeology: Selected Readings*, edited by John Rowe and Dorothy Menzel, pp. 72–103. Peek Publications, Palo Alto.

Sayre, Matthew

2010   Life across the River: Agricultural, Ritual, and Production Practices at Chavín de Huántar, Peru. PhD dissertation, University of California, Berkeley.

Schreiber, Katharina

2005   Imperial Agendas and Local Agency: Wari Colonial Strategies. In *Archaeology of Colonial Encounters*, edited by Gil J. Stein, pp. 237–261. School of American Research Press, Santa Fe.

Seki, Yuji

2014   La diversidad del poder en la sociedad del período formativo: Una perspectiva desde la Sierra Norte. In El *centro ceremonial andino: Nuevas perspectivas para los períodos arcaico y formativo*, edited by Yuji Seki, pp. 175–200. National Museum of Ethnology, Osaka.

Seki, Yuji, Juan Pablo Villanueva, Masato Sakai, Diana Alemán, Mauro Ordóñez, Walter Tosso, Araceli Espinoza, Kinya Inokuchi, and Daniel Morales

2010   Nuevas evidencias del sitio arqueológico de Pacopampa, en la Sierra Norte del Perú. *Boletín de Arqueología PUCP* 12:69–95.

Silva, Jorge

1996   Prehistoric Settlement Patterns in the Chillón River Valley, Peru. PhD dissertation, University of Michigan, Ann Arbor.

Smith, Michael E., and Frances F. Berdan

2003   *The Postclassic Mesoamerican World*. University of Utah Press, Salt Lake City.

Steadman, Lee

1995   Excavations at Camata: An Early Ceramic Chronology for the Western Titicaca Basin, Peru. PhD dissertation, University of California, Berkeley.

1999   The Ceramics. In *Early Settlement at Chiripa, Bolivia: Research of the Taraco Archaeological Project*, edited by Christine Hastorf, pp. 61–72. University of California Archaeological Research Facility, Berkeley.

Stein, Gil J.

1998   World System Theory and Alternative Modes of Interaction in the Archaeology of Culture Contact. In *Studies in Culture Contact: Interaction, Culture Change, and Archaeology*, edited by James G. Cusick, pp. 220–255. Southern Illinois University Press, Carbondale.

1999   Rethinking World-Systems: Power, Distance, and Diasporas in the Dynamics of Interregional Interaction. In *World-Systems Theory in Practice: Leadership, Production, and Exchange*, edited by Nicholas P. Kardulias, pp. 153–177. Rowman and Littlefield, New York.

2002   From Passive Periphery to Active Agents: Emerging Perspectives in the Archaeology of Interregional Interaction. *American Anthropologist* 104(3):903–916.

Terada, Kazuo, and Yoshio Onuki (editors)

1985   *The Formative Period in the Cajamarca Basin, Peru: Excavations at Huacaloma and Layzón, 1982.* University of Tokyo Press, Tokyo.

Tripcevich, Nicholas, and Daniel A. Contreras

2011   Quarrying Evidence at the Quispisisa Obsidian Source, Ayacucho, Peru. *Latin American Antiquity* 22:121–136.

2013   Archaeological Approaches to Obsidian Quarries: Investigations at the Quispisisa Source. In *Mining and Quarrying in the Ancient Andes*, edited by Nicholas Tripcevich and K. Vaughn, pp. 23–44. Springer, New York.

Tripcevich, Nicholas, and Alex MacKay

2011   Procurement at the Chivay Obsidian Source, Arequipa, Peru. *World Archaeology* 43:271–297.

Watanabe, Shinya

2013   *Estructura en los Andes antiguos*. Editorial Shumpusha, Yokohama.

Werbner, Richard P.

1977   Introduction. In *Regional Cults*, edited by Richard P. Werbner, pp. ix–xxxvi. Academic Press, London.

Williams, Carlos L.

1985   A Scheme for the Early Monumental Architecture of the Central Coast of Perú. In *Early Ceremonial Architecture in the Andes*, edited by Christopher Donnan, pp. 227–240. Dumbarton Oaks Research Library and Collection, Washington, D.C.

An *Olmequista's* Thoughts on Chavín

CHRISTOPHER A. POOL

The Dumbarton Oaks Pre-Columbian sym-posium has been critical in shaping what we understand and how we think about ancient societ-ies and cultures in the Americas—none more so than the foundational "Formative" cultures, particularly Chavín and Olmec. The first Pre-Columbian confer-ences dealt specifically with these two cultural phe-nomena (Benson 1968, 1971), and both Michael Coe and Kent Flannery participated in the 1968 Chavín conference after serving on the panel of the 1967 Olmec conference. Inspirations for the interpretation of the Chavín and Olmec Phenomena intertwine in Dumbarton Oaks publications, often in their com-mon use of ethnographic analogies drawn from the tropical forests of South America to understand ico-nography and its sociopolitical context. Examples include Peter Furst's (1968) evaluation of Olmec "were-jaguar" imagery in light of shamanic practice in South America, David Grove's (1981) analysis of Olmec political practice and iconography drawing on Donald Lathrap's (1974) and Norman Whitten's (1976) research among forest-dwelling groups

in Ecuador and Peru, and in this volume, Ryan Clasby's reevaluation of Chavín's interaction with tropical forest regions, also citing Lathrap's (1971) Dumbarton Oaks chapter. Likewise, *Olmequistas* will hear echoes of Flannery's (1968) seminal chap-ter on the highland Olmec Phenomenon in chapters herein that discuss exchange and marriage bonds as part of the social glue of interregional interaction.

Some Chavín and Olmec Parallels

Both Chavín and Olmec have, at one point or another, been considered "Mother Cultures" of their respective regions, constituting the *fons et origo* of Andean and Mesoamerican civilization (Caso 1942; Coe 1968; Tello 1960). With their refined chronolo-gies and expanded research into the Initial Period (Burger 1992), scholars have liberated Chavín from the burden of giving birth to all later civilizations, allowing the contributors to this volume to focus on what are ultimately more interesting questions about the nature and diversity of interactions in the Early Horizon—or as David Chicoine and colleagues (this volume) put it, to "move beyond chronology and Chavín."

The same has not proved true for Olmec studies, in which a model that argues for more balanced interaction among societies in an evolving Formative co-tradition continues to compete with a narrative of Olmec cultural and political dominance (Flannery and Marcus 2000; Grove 1989; Hammond 1989; cf. Diehl and Coe 1995). Though the last two decades have seen calls to move beyond this "Mother Culture–Sister Culture" debate, it seems that most researchers find themselves drawn with magnetic force toward these poles, each of which, in pushing a single vision of interaction, is conceptually homogenizing. Archaeology in both our regions has seen its share of chronological confusion as well, both substantively and terminologically. For example, an outside reader can easily become lost in differential usages of Luis Lumbreras's Formative periods and John Rowe's Initial Period and Early Horizon, as well as variant temporal divisions thereof (see Burger and Nesbitt, this volume, for a clear discussion). With Richard Burger's recent (2019) reassessment of dates for his Urabarriu, Chakinani, and Janabarriu phases, developments elsewhere seem to align better with the waxing and waning of Chavín de Huántar (Burger and Nesbitt, this volume).

Religion and Ritual

In contrast to interpretations of Formative "Olmec" horizons, there appears to be a remarkable degree of consensus that the Chavín Phenomenon represented a religious cult and Chavín de Huántar was a pilgrimage center. In Mesoamerica, Gordon Willey (1962) first characterized Olmec as a transregional cult, and soon thereafter Michael Coe (1972) described Olmec religion as a royal cult. Coe's and Burger's former student, Jeffrey P. Blomster (1998), has productively applied the Chavín cult model to understand Olmec interregional interaction as well. In this light, Burger's (1988) suggestion that Chavín specifically represents a crisis cult is intriguing and may find resonance with

changes in representations of Olmec interaction during the Middle Formative period (1000–400 BC) in the wake of San Lorenzo's collapse.

By and large, though, recent models of Olmec interregional interaction and site function have tended to focus more on the political and economic realms, while recognizing that symbols reflect cosmological belief and ritual. Perhaps this is due to the more explicitly political message of ruler imagery in colossal heads, thrones, and stelae.

Olmec and Chavín archaeology share a common interest in the spaces of ritual (e.g., Cyphers 1999; Cyphers and Di Castro 2009; González Lauck 2010; Grove 1999; Pool 2010; Tate 1999), but the complexity and consistent layouts of Chavín architecture have attracted more attention than earthen Olmec mounds and have inspired more sophisticated research on proxemics, as reflected in the contributions by John Rick and Yuji Seki to this volume. In Olmec research, site extent and population are used as much or more than architectural form and volume as measures of importance, with the notable exceptions of Ann Cyphers's (1999; Arieta Baizabal and Cyphers 2017) work on the artificial modification of the San Lorenzo Plateau and Rebecca González Lauck's (2010) and David Grove's (1999) discussion of La Venta's ceremonial core.

Iconography, Meaning, and Ritual Practice

There are many iconographic parallels between Olmec and Chavín—so many that they sparked early speculation about a historical connection between the two cultures (Lathrap 1985). Those parallels extend to a focus on tropical forest animals such as jaguars, harpy eagles, caimans, and fish (Clasby, this volume), as well as complex and fanciful composite supernaturals, such as that on the Yauya stela (Burger 2008). We can ponder how closely meaning and material style are tied to one another in various settings. For example, Rebecca Bria sees material style, especially ceramics, as evidence that people also adopted a system of beliefs involving Chavín's supreme deity and hallucinogenic transformation, while Michelle Young asks whether simpler motifs are not merely stylistically or aesthetically popular, apart from whatever associations they might have had with the Chavín cult "package." Though others might disagree, I think there is ample evidence that meanings of Olmec iconography shifted with their specific social contexts of use outside the Gulf Coast heartland.

It is interesting that the use of hallucinogens seems so closely tied to, even innovative with, Chavín (Burger 1992, 2011; Cordy-Collins 1980; Torres 2008). This contrasts with the general assumption that the Olmec use of hallucinogens and "techniques of ecstasy" (Eliade 1964) is simply part of a deeply shared shamanic substrate (Furst 1968, 1995; Tate 1995).

Memory and Forgetting

The chapters in this volume have provided very interesting examples of the preservation, manipulation, and erasure of social memory. This theme is well represented by Rick's detailed analysis of the galleries at Chavín de Huántar, particularly regarding the maintenance of access to the Lanzón monument and the filling of Gallery 4. Yuji Seki provides another example in his description of the reuse of stones at Pacopampa, in which he argues that leaders always take advantage of social memory to establish power. Likewise, Lisa DeLeonardis thoughtfully addresses the use of iconography in ceramics as stimulating social memory.

Rebecca Bria provides a fascinating discussion of the initial conversion and later reconstruction of the temple at Hualcayán, as well as its destruction and decommissioning. I find compelling the argument, expressed in the abstract to her symposium presentation, "that the process of reconstruction not only generated new sets of locally oriented meanings and values, but also transformed the temple's physical substance from the inside out," as well as her contention that "the subsequent return to repetitive building practices reveals potential tensions between long-standing local ritual traditions, such as the cyclical practices of temple building in the north-central highlands, and the emplaced rituals of

Chavín, which emphasized permanence and absolute authority." In contrast to Seki's inference of top-down manipulation of social memory, Bria views the materialization and erasure of social memories from the bottom up as an act of community formation. These uses of social memory—building community and exercising power—are not mutually exclusive, though, as contemporary political practice reveals (Pool and Loughlin 2017).

The Political Economy and the Emergence of Elite Authority

From the perspective of Olmec studies, it is striking that there was not more discussion in this volume about the emergence of elites and their manipulation of sources of power. Jalh Dulanto and Seki are the most explicit in identifying the Early Horizon as a time of the emergence of an exclusionary elite in many parts of the Andes (see also Burger and Nesbitt, this volume). Dulanto situates the power of these elites in their control over a prestige economy and their importation and use of exotic goods for personal adornment and ritual use, expressed in larger and more sumptuous tombs. Dulanto's perspective from the south coast contrasts most sharply with Young's characterization of Atalla as lacking an elite class. It remains an open question whether this and other contrasts in these chapters are more reflective of regional differences or of theoretical orientations.

Sources of Elite Power

Seki, Yuichi Matsumoto and Yuri Cavero Palomino, and others in this volume also discuss control over exotic goods as a source of elite power. Certainly, control over a prestige economy would have provided elites with one source of power, but in the Early Horizon that economy seems inextricably bound up with ritual (as Matthew Sayre and Silvana Rosenfeld interpret production at La Banda). It may be more useful to conceive of the use of exotic and highly crafted goods as elements of a ritual economy, as Patricia McAnany and E. Christian Wells (2008), among others, have discussed in the Maya context.

Ideological power (*sensu* Earle 1987) seems broadly acknowledged to have been a critical component of the Chavín Phenomenon, and it seems generally accepted that a formal priesthood wielded ideological power at Chavín de Huántar (Burger 1992) through the control of esoteric knowledge, partially grounded in the use of hallucinogens and the ritual manipulation of space, light (or perhaps sound), and iconography. With respect to the expansion or emergence of a Chavín horizon, it is striking the degree to which authors have tended to emphasize voluntary participation over the coercive imposition of a Chavín cult (e.g., Burger and Salazar, this volume); there is a lesson there for how we think of Olmec interaction, which harkens back to Flannery's (1968) original model of the "highland Olmec" problem.

Economic and ideological power articulate a kind of social power, particularly in the context of feasting, as discussed by Matthew Sayre and Silvana Rosenfeld, Jason Nesbitt, Michelle Young, and other authors in this volume. Such feasts and rituals in general seem to have been broadly inclusive, but Sayre and Rosenfeld make the excellent point that feasts can be simultaneously inclusive and exclusive, and Bria echoes that notion with her discussion of proxemics at Hualcayán.

Interregional Interaction

Of course, interregional interaction is intrinsic to any discussion of archaeological horizons, and this volume offers a great deal to think about in that regard. It is hard not to compare this book with the landmark volume *Regional Perspectives on the Olmec*, which was based on an advanced seminar at the School of American Research (Sharer and Grove 1989). Whereas that volume exposed a rift that keeps getting reopened in Olmec archaeology, the current volume and the symposium that produced it point toward a more nuanced understanding.

What especially stands out in these papers is the great variability in the adoption, expression, and local importance of Chavín interaction. It appears that Chavín specialists have not only set aside the mother culture narrative but have truly *embraced*

variability and local agency in their understandings of the Chavín Phenomenon, as Burger (1988) has long urged them to do. This variability extends not only to interregional interaction, but within Chavín de Huántar itself, as John Rick demonstrates in his discussion of the diverse forms, content, and functions of the galleries in the monumental core.

At the interregional scale, variability in interaction seems to be variously a result of the directness of interaction (Clasby, this volume); the intersection of multiple nested networks of interaction (Burger and Salazar, this volume; Matsumoto and Cavero Palomino, this volume; Young, this volume); and the critical influence of local politics, which, as Bria (this volume) illustrates, lies at the core of how communities became and ceased to be Chavín. The willingness of the authors to entertain the idea that different modes of interaction operated in different regions is impressive, particularly in the case of Matsumoto and Cavero Palomino, who argue for a core–periphery model in the south-central "Ayacucho Sphere," simultaneous with more peer-polity interactions in the northern "Cajamarca Sphere." This parallels the Olmec case, where David Cheetham (2010a, 2010b) has argued for an Olmec colonial enclave on the Pacific coast, while researchers in Oaxaca argue for more even relations. Given Matsumoto and Cavero Palomino's speculation that stonemasons from Chavín may have been working at Campanayuq Rumi, it would be interesting to learn how similar residential architecture and domestic assemblages may have been at the two sites. On the other hand, it is worth asking to what extent variation was also shaped by the application of different strategies by Chavín leaders.

In aggregate, the pattern of variation in the Andean and Mesoamerican cases seems more complex than indicated by either the World Systems model or Gil Stein's (1999) distance-parity model—that is, one single model does not seem to fit all cases. Furthermore, it seems that we are not just seeing regional difference in interaction, but also what Wes Stoner (2011; Stoner and Pool 2015) has theorized as *disjuncture in different realms* of interaction that do not map cleanly one on the other. This emerges, for example, in Young's (this volume) speculation that a multiethnic community may have existed at Atalla. One can also detect evidence of disjuncture in the maintenance of local traditions with partial adoption of Chavín practices described in the chapters by Matsumoto and Cavero Palomino, Young, and Bria, as well as in the differential articulation of interregional and regional interaction spheres described by Matsumoto and Cavero Palomino for their Ayacucho and Cajamarca Spheres and echoed by Burger and Lucy Salazar for the central coast. Disjuncture seems especially evident in the noncontinuous patterns of demographic, stylistic, and local change in the Nepeña Valley (Chicoine, Ikehara-Tsukayama, and Shibata, this volume). In comparison, Olmec studies have been preoccupied with relationships with the Gulf Olmec to the detriment of other interregional interactions—which clearly occurred, even during Mesoamerica's Early Horizon, based on movement of obsidian, greenstone, iron ore, and shell. Far from a unidirectional model still popular in some circles of Olmec studies, the Andean case closely parallels the lattice model that Arthur Demarest (1989) has proposed for Middle Formative Mesoamerican interactions. For the Andes, there seems to be a clearer lattice/complex network of interaction than many models of Olmec contemplate.

Methodologically, as well as conceptually, Young's approach to the analysis of "Chavínoid" ceramics and DeLeonardis's emphasis on techné offer very productive venues for evaluating models of interregional interaction. Young's complaint about the "nebulous, subjective nature" of Chavín or Chavínoid ceramics mirrors in general and specific ways David Grove's complaints vis-à-vis "Olmec"— but without a concern for refuting a mother culture narrative for Chavín. Her approach resonates with Jeffrey Blomster and Cheetham's (2017) efforts in an earlier Dumbarton Oaks workshop, which were similar to Young's attribute-level consideration of similarities and differences among assemblages to get beyond mere typological or iconographic analysis. In the furtherance of such efforts, Young (and others) might consider a "communities of practice" perspective, grounded in research on situated learning (Blomster and Cheetham 2017; Joyce 2013; Lave and Wenger 1991). The communities of practice

approach is commensurate with Young's "stylistic vocabulary that includes a set of technological and decorative techniques accompanied by loosely bound sets of traits that are shared by a number of sites participating in the Chavín Interaction Sphere during the Early Horizon," and her observation that, "[t]he prevalence of certain ceramic forms, motifs, and techniques in different regions" suggests that what has formerly been referred to as a "horizon" style are regionally specific negotiations of a form of visual expression related to a supra-regional identity (Burger 1993). Young's assessment that the Chavín International Style's expression at individual sites was "dependent upon the technical knowledge of the potters, the community's relationship with other societies, and the social values projected onto a set of symbols" echoes a "constellation of practice" model (Joyce 2013:151) that can be applied as well in Olmec studies to the Mesoamerican Early Horizon. The "communities of practice" perspective is not incommensurate with a concern for agency, as some critics have charged, because it is focused on practice and choice, as well as the transmission of knowledge. Neither is it mutually exclusive with the social, political, economic, or religious contexts within which communities of practice operate. Therefore, we can also go beyond identifying communities of practice to ask what *kind* of community of practice exists.

Conclusion

The chapters of this volume move beyond the conceptualization of Chavín as a horizon (Burger and Nesbitt, this volume) to more nuanced interpretations and more complicated narratives like those of Bria; Burger and Salazar; Chicoine, Ikehara-Tsukayama, and Shibata; Matsumoto and Cavero Palomino; and Young. As these chapters imply, our view of the Chavín Phenomenon in the twenty-first century is less of a horizon and more of an intricate web of social relationships unfolding through time. Working out such complex interactions will benefit from close attention to ceramics and other crafting. At the same time, work needs to continue on precisely how Chavín's leaders and local leaders converted their social relationships into political and social prestige. Finally, with such a variety of models for interaction, future research should focus on whether different models accurately reflect actual patterns of interaction in the past or the theoretical perspectives of researchers in the present.

REFERENCES CITED

Arieta Baizabal, Virginia, and Ann Cyphers
2017   Densidad poblacional en la capital olmeca de San Lorenzo, Veracruz. *Ancient Mesoamerica* 28:61–73.

Benson, Elizabeth P. (editor)
1968   *Dumbarton Oaks Conference on the Olmec.* Dumbarton Oaks Research Library and Collection, Washington, D.C.
1971   *Dumbarton Oaks Conference on Chavín.* Dumbarton Oaks Research Library and Collection, Washington, D.C.

Blomster, Jeffrey P.
1998   Context, Cult, and Early Formative Public Ritual in the Mixteca Alta: Analysis of a Hollow Baby Figurine from Etlatongo, Oaxaca. *Ancient Mesoamerica* 9:309–326.

Blomster, Jeffrey P., and David Cheetham (editors)
2017   *The Early Olmec and Mesoamerica: The Material Record.* Cambridge University Press, Cambridge.

Burger, Richard L.
1988   Unity and Heterogeneity within the Chavín Horizon. In *Peruvian Prehistory*, edited by Richard Keatinge, pp. 99–144. Cambridge University Press, Cambridge.
1992   *Chavín and the Origins of Andean Civilization.* Thames and Hudson, London.
1993   The Chavín Horizon: Stylistic Chimera or Socioeconomic Metamorphosis? In *Latin America Horizons*, edited by Donald Rice, pp. 41–82. Dumbarton Oaks Research Library and Collection, Washington, D.C.
2008   The Original Context of the Yauya Stela. In *Chavín Art, Architecture, and Culture*, edited by William J. Conklin and Jeffrey Quilter, pp. 163–179. Cotsen Institute of Archaeology, University of California, Los Angeles.

2011   What Kind of Hallucinogenic Snuff Was Used at Chavín de Huántar. *Ñawpa Pacha: Journal of Andean Archaeology* 31(2):123–140.
2019   Understanding the Socioeconomic Trajectory of Chavín de Huántar: A New Radiocarbon Sequence and Its Wider Implications. *Latin American Antiquity* 30(2):373–392.

Caso, Alfonso
1942   Definición y extensión del complejo "olmeca." In *Mayas y Olmecas, segunda reunión de mesa redonda*, pp. 43–46. Sociedad Mexicana de Antropología, Mexico City.

Cheetham, David
2010a   America's First Colony: Olmec Materiality and Ethnicity at Cantón Corralito Chiapas, Mexico. PhD dissertation, Arizona State University, Tempe.
2010b   Cultural Imperatives in Clay: Early Olmec Carved Pottery from San Lorenzo and Cantón Corralito. *Ancient Mesoamerica* 21(1):165–185.

Clark, John E., Julia Guernsey, and Barbara Arroyo (editors)
2010   *The Place of Stone Monuments: Context, Use, and Meaning in Mesoamerica's Preclassic Transition.* Dumbarton Oaks Research Library and Collection, Washington, D.C.

Coe, Michael D.
1968   *America's First Civilization: Discovering the Olmec.* American Heritage, New York.
1972   Olmec Jaguars and Olmec Kings. In *The Cult of the Feline*, edited by Elizabeth P. Benson, pp. 1–18. Dumbarton Oaks Research Library and Collection, Washington, D.C.

Cordy-Collins, Alana K.

1980 An Artistic Record of the Chavín Hallucinatory Experience. *The Masterkey for Indian Lore and History* 54(3):84–93.

Cyphers, Ann

1999 From Stone to Symbols: Olmec Art in Social Context at San Lorenzo Tenochtitlán. In *Social Patterns in Pre-Classic Mesoamerica*, edited by David C. Grove and Rosemary A. Joyce, pp. 155–181. Dumbarton Oaks Research Library and Collection, Washington, DC.

Cyphers, Ann, and Anna Di Castro

2009 Early Olmec Architecture and Imagery. In *The Art of Urbanism: How Mesoamerican Kingdoms Represented Themselves in Architecture and Imagery*, edited by William Fash and Leonardo López Luján, pp. 21–52. Dumbarton Oaks Research Library and Collection, Washington, D.C.

Demarest, Arthur A.

1989 The Olmec and the Rise of Civilization in Eastern Mesoamerica. In *Regional Perspectives on the Olmec*, edited by Robert J. Sharer and David C. Grove, pp. 303–344. Cambridge University Press, Cambridge.

Diehl, Richard A., and Michael D. Coe

1995 Olmec Archaeology. In *The Olmec World: Ritual and Rulership*, edited by Jill Guthrie and Elizabeth P. Benson, pp. 11–25. The Art Museum, Princeton University, Princeton, N.J.

Earle, Timothy K.

1987 *How Chiefs Come to Power: The Political Economy in Prehistory*. Stanford University Press, Stanford.

Eliade, Mircea

1964 *Shamanism: Archaic Techniques of Ecstasy*. Bollingen Foundation/Pantheon, New York.

Flannery, Kent V.

1968 The Olmec and the Valley of Oaxaca: A Model for Interregional Interaction in Formative Times. In *Dumbarton Oaks Conference on the Olmec*, edited by Elizabeth P. Benson, pp. 79–110. Dumbarton Oaks Research Library and Collection, Washington, D.C.

Flannery, Kent V., and Joyce Marcus

2000 Formative Mexican Chiefdoms and the Myth of the "Mother Culture." *Journal of Anthropological Archaeology* 19:1–37.

Furst, Peter T.

1968 The Olmec Were-Jaguar Motif in the Light of Ethnographic Reality. In *Dumbarton Oaks Conference on the Olmec*, edited by Elizabeth P. Benson, pp. 143–178. Dumbarton Oaks Research Library and Collection, Washington, D.C.

1995 Shamanism, Transformation, and Olmec Art. In *The Olmec World: Ritual and Rulership*, edited by Jill Guthrie and Elizabeth P. Benson, pp. 69–81. The Art Museum, Princeton University, Princeton.

González Lauck, Rebecca

2010 The Architectural Setting of Olmec Sculpture Clusters at La Venta, Mexico. In *The Place of Stone Monuments: Context, Use, and Meaning in Meso-america's Preclassic Transition*, edited by Julia Guernsey, John E. Clark, and Barbara Arroyo, pp. 129–148. Dumbarton Oaks Research Library and Collection, Washington, D.C.

Grove, David C.

1981 Olmec Monuments: Mutilation as a Clue to Meaning. In *The Olmec and Their Neighbors: Essays in Memory of Matthew W. Stirling*, edited by Elizabeth P. Benson, pp. 48–68. Dumbarton Oaks Research Library and Collection, Washington, D.C.

1989 Olmec: What's in a Name? In *Regional Perspectives on the Olmec*, edited by Robert J. Sharer and David C. Grove, pp. 8–14. Cambridge University Press, Cambridge.

1999 Public Monuments and Sacred Mountains: Observations on Three Formative Period Sacred Landscapes. In *Social Patterns in Pre-Classic Mesoamerica*, edited by David C. Grove and Rosemary A. Joyce, pp. 255–295. Dumbarton Oaks Research Library and Collections, Washington, D.C.

Hammond, Norman

1989 Cultura Hermana: Reappraising the Olmec. *Quarterly Review of Archaeology* 9(4):1–4.

Joyce, Rosemary

2013   Thinking about Pottery Production as Community of Practice. In *Potters and Communities of Practice: Glaze Paint and Polychrome Pottery in the American Southwest, A.D. 1250 to 1700*, edited by Linda S. Cordell and Judith A. Habicht-Mauche, pp. 149–154. University of Arizona Press, Tucson.

Lathrap, Donald W.

1971   The Tropical Forest and the Cultural Context of Chavín. In *Dumbarton Oaks Conference on Chavín*, edited by Elizabeth P. Benson, pp. 73–100. Dumbarton Oaks Research Library and Collection, Washington D.C.

1974   The Moist Tropics, the Arid Lands, and the Appearance of Great Art Styles in the New World. In *Art and Environment in Native America*, edited by Mary Elizabeth King and Idris R. Traylor Jr., pp. 115–158. Special Publication no. 7. The Museum, Texas Tech University, Lubbock.

1985   Jaws: The Control of Power in the Early Nuclear American Ceremonial Center. In *Early Ceremonial Architecture in the Andes*, edited by Christopher Donnan, pp. 241–267. Dumbarton Oaks Research Library and Collection, Washington, D.C.

Lave, Jean, and Étienne Wenger

1991   *Situated Learning: Legitimate Peripheral Participation*. Cambridge University Press, Cambridge.

McAnany, Patricia, and E. Christian Wells

2008   Toward a Theory of Ritual Economy. *Research in Economic Anthropology* 27:1–16.

Pool, Christopher A.

2010   Stone Monuments and Earthen Mounds: Polity and Placemaking at Tres Zapotes, Veracruz, Mexico. In *The Place of Stone Monuments: Context, Use, and Meaning in Mesoamerica's Preclassic Transition*, edited by John E. Clark, Julia Guernsey, and Barbara Arroyo, pp. 97–126. Dumbarton Oaks Research Library and Collection, Washington, D.C.

Pool, Christopher A., and Michael L. Loughlin

2017   Creating Memory and Negotiating Power in the Olmec Heartland. *Journal of Archaeological Method and Theory* 24(1):229–260.

Sharer, Robert J., and David C. Grove (editors)

1989   *Regional Perspectives on the Olmec*. University of Cambridge Press, Cambridge.

Stein, Gil J.

1999   *Rethinking World-Systems: Diasporas, Colonies, and Interaction in Uruk Mesopotamia*. University of Arizona Press, Tucson.

Stoner, Wesley D.

2011   Disjuncture among Classic Period Cultural Landscapes in the Tuxtla Mountains, Southern Veracruz, Mexico. PhD dissertation, University of Kentucky, Lexington.

Stoner, Wesley D., and Christopher A. Pool

2015   Toward an Archaeology of Disjuncture: Scale and Variability in Long-Distance Interaction Networks. *Current Anthropology* 56:385–420.

Tate, Carolyn E.

1995   Art in Olmec Culture. In *The Olmec World: Ritual and Rulership*, edited by Jill Guthrie and Elizabeth P. Benson, pp. 47–67. The Art Museum, Princeton University, Princeton.

1999   Patrons of Shamanic Power: La Venta's Supernatural Entities in Light of Mixe Beliefs. *Ancient Mesoamerica* 10:169–188.

Tello, Julio C.

1960   *Chavín: Cultura matriz de la civilización andina*. Publicación Antropológica del Archivo "Julio C Tello" de la Universidad Nacional Mayor de San Marcos, Lima.

Torres, Constantino Manuel

2008   Chavín's Psychoactive Pharmacopoeia: The Iconographic Evidence. In *Chavin Art, Architecture, and Culture*, edited by William J. Conklin and Jeffrey Quilter, pp. 239–259. Cotsen Institute of Archaeology, University of California, Los Angeles.

Whitten, Norman E., Jr.

1976   *Sacha Runa: Ethnicity and Adaptation of Ecuadorian Jungle Quichua*. University of Illinois Press, Urbana.

Willey, Gordon R.

1962   The Early Great Styles and the Rise of the Pre-Columbian Civilizations. *American Anthropologist* 64(1):1–14.

CONTRIBUTORS

Rebecca E. Bria received her PhD from Vanderbilt University in 2017 and is assistant professor in the Department of Anthropology at the University of Texas at San Antonio. She is the founding director and principal investigator of the Proyecto de Investigación Arqueológico Regional Ancash (PIARA; piaraperu.org), a research and community outreach project that has focused on the province of Huaylas, Ancash, Peru, since 2009. Her research is primarily centered on understanding processes of long-term community transformation, which she has investigated at the site of Hualcayán. While concerned with long-term change, much of her work has concentrated on understanding the evolving social landscape of highland Ancash between the Chavín (900–500 BC), Huarás (400 BC–AD 100), and Recuay (AD 100–700) cultural phases, which shaped a pivotal transition in the Pre-Columbian Andes.

Richard L. Burger received his BA in Archaeology from Yale College and his PhD in Anthropology from the University of California, Berkeley. After several years excavating in highland Peru, he returned to Yale, where he is currently the Charles J. MacCurdy Professor of Anthropology and Curator of South American Archaeology at the Peabody Museum of Natural History. Burger has directed excavations at Chavín de Huántar and Huaricoto in the highlands, and at Initial Period sites along the central coast of Peru. He also has pioneered the study of obsidian and cinnabar sourcing and exchange in the Central Andes. Along with Lucy Salazar, he organized *Machu Picchu: Unveiling the Mystery of the Incas*, a major traveling exhibit that was shown in seven venues in 2003 and 2004. Burger served as the director of Yale's Peabody Museum of Natural History from 1995 to 2002 and is currently president of the Institute of Andean Research. He has written and edited numerous books and articles on Andean archaeology, including *Chavín and the Origins of Andean Civilization* (1992), *Emergencia de la civilización en los Andes: Ensayos de interpretación* (1993), *Excavaciones en Chavín de Huántar* (1998), and *Arqueología del período formativo en la cuenca baja de Lurín* (with Krzysztof Makowski, 2009).

Yuri Cavero Palomino obtained his BA from the Universidad Nacional de San Cristóbal de Huamanga, Ayacucho, and MA from Yamagata University, Japan. He participated in various archaeological research projects in Peru, Italy, and France. He is currently an associate professor at the Faculty of Letters and Human Sciences of the Universidad Nacional Mayor de San Marcos; prior to that appointment, he taught at the School of Archeology and History of the Universidad Nacional de San Cristóbal de Huamanga, Ayacucho. Since 2007 he has been the national director of the Campanayuq Rumi Archaeological Project. His research focuses on the study of ritual practices, the emergence of complex societies, and the presence of the Chavín Phenomenon in the south-central highlands of Peru. He has published various books and articles related to the Formative period and the Late Horizon in the Andes, including *Inkapamisan: Ushnus y santuario inka en Ayacucho* (2010).

David Chicoine is an anthropological archaeologist who specializes in the development of complex societies in the Americas. He holds a PhD from the Sainsbury Research Unit for the Arts of Africa, Oceania, and the Americas at the University of East Anglia. After a postdoctoral fellowship in the Department of Archaeology at Simon Fraser University, he joined the faculty at Louisiana State University, where he is currently professor in the Department of Geography and Anthropology. His research intersects various fields and lines of evidence in order to document the complex and relational aspects of ancient Andean societies. Since 2003, he has directed interdisciplinary archaeological fieldwork in Nepeña, a small valley of the Department of Ancash on the north-central coast of Peru. His collaborations and publications have explored various interrelated dimensions of Early Horizon societies in Nepeña, including architecture (*Journal of Field Archaeology*, 2006), chronology (*Boletín de Arqueología PUCP*, 2010), feasting (*Journal of Anthropological Archaeology*, 2011), ritual performance (*Ñawpa Pacha: Journal of Andean Archaeology*, 2012; and *Antiquity*, 2013), maritime economies (*Andean Past*, 2012; and *Journal of Island and Coastal Archaeology*, 2013), urbanism (*Journal of Field Archaeology*, 2014), camelid management (*Environmental Archaeology: The Journal of Human Paleoecology*, 2016), and plaza settings (*Americae: European Journal of Americanist Archaeology*, 2018).

Ryan Clasby is a postdoctoral research associate in the NAGPRA Office at the University of Illinois at Urbana-Champaign. He has recently taught at Skidmore College and Central Washington University and was a fellow in Pre-Columbian Studies at Dumbarton Oaks. He received his PhD in Anthropology from Yale University in 2014, specializing in

Andean and Amazonian archaeology. Since 2007, he has conducted archaeological research in the Jaén region of the northeastern Peruvian Andes and the lower Marañon, focusing on the sociopolitical developments of the *ceja de selva* and their relationship to the rise of Andean civilization. His work has been published in journals such as *Latin American Antiquity*; he is the coeditor, with Jason Nesbitt, of *The Archaeology of the Upper Amazon: Complexity and Interaction in the Andean Tropical Forest* (2021).

Lisa DeLeonardis is the Austen-Stokes Professor in Art of the Ancient Americas at Johns Hopkins University. Her research on the Paracas has addressed questions about visual culture, ancestor veneration, and mortuary practices. Her work has appeared in a number of articles and edited volumes, including *Andean Archaeology* (edited by Helaine Silverman, 2004), *The Construction of Value in the Ancient World* (edited by John K. Papadopoulos and Gary Urton, 2012), and *Making Value, Making Meaning: Techné in the Pre-Columbian World* (edited by Cathy Costin, 2016). She is concurrently completing manuscripts on Paracas sculptural design and the architectural and social history of Santa Cruz de Lancha. She is the recent recipient of the Charles K. Williams II Rome Prize Fellowship in Historic Preservation and Conservation at the American Academy in Rome.

Jalh Dulanto is a professor of Archaeology and chair of the Archaeology Program at the Pontificia Universidad Católica del Perú. His most recent research focuses on the maritime communities and long-distance exchange networks of the first millennium BC in the Central Andes. He is the author of several articles and the editor of several volumes on Andean archaeology and ethnohistory. He has been a visiting professor at Colgate University (2008), Rollins College (2008–2010), and DePauw University (2010–2011) in the United States, as well as at the University of Lund in Sweden (2015) and L'École des Hautes Études en Sciences Sociales and the University of Paris IV—La Sorbonne in France (2015–2017). He has served as the director of the Paracas Archaeological Program on the south coast of Peru since 2010, and he has been a member of the Grupo de Investigaciones de Materiales de Patrimonio Cultural de la Pontificia Universidad Católica del Perú since 2014.

Hugo Ikehara-Tsukayama is an anthropological archaeologist who specializes in the development and dynamics of early complex societies in the Americas. He holds an MA and a PhD from the Department of Anthropology at the University of Pittsburgh; he is currently a senior research associate in the Michael C. Rockefeller Wing at the Metropolitan Museum of Art. His research focuses on several topics related to the formation of complex organizations such as cooperation and warfare (*World Archaeology*, 2016; and *Journal of Anthropological Archaeology*, 2019), foodways and feasting (*Boletín de Arqueología PUCP*, 2008; and *Latin American Antiquity*, 2013), and architecture (*Boletín de Arqueología PUCP*, 2010; *Ñawpa Pacha: Journal of Andean Archaeology*, 2018; and *Journal of Andean Archaeology*, 2021). He coedited *Global Perspectives on Landscapes of Warfare* (2022), and his new research in the coastal valley of Nepeña (Ancash, Peru) is a multidisciplinary effort to study the transformation of landscapes from earlier to contemporary times.

Yuichi Matsumoto obtained his BA and MA at the University of Tokyo and his PhD from Yale University in 2010; he is currently an associate professor at the National Museum of Ethnology and Graduate University of Advanced Studies, Japan. His doctoral research explored the periphery of the Chavín Interaction Sphere during the Initial Period and Early Horizon by focusing on the ceremonial center of Campanayuq Rumi. His research interests include the development of complex societies, the emergence of monuments, and interregional interactions in the ancient Andes. Currently, he is conducting an archaeological project in the Peruvian south-central highlands for the purpose of understanding the emergence, growth, and collapse of the Chavín Phenomenon from its periphery. His most recent work is *Prehistoric Settlement Patterns in the Upper Huallaga Basin, Peru* (2020). He has served as the director of the Campanayuq Rumi Archaeological Project since 2007.

Jason Nesbitt is an anthropological archaeologist specializing in the emergence of complex societies in the Central Andes. He is currently an associate professor of Anthropology in the Department of Anthropology at Tulane University. Before receiving his PhD from Yale University, he completed his BA in Archaeology from Simon Fraser University and his MA in Anthropology from Trent University. His master's thesis was focused on Cerro Icchal, a late prehistoric oracular center in Huamachuco. For his doctoral research, he shifted his focus to the famous Initial Period/Early Horizon center of Caballo Muerto in the Moche Valley, where he carried out extensive excavations at Huaca Cortada and other Cupisnique mounds. More recently, he has concentrated on research in the Callejón de Conchucos in the northern highlands and the south-central highlands near Vilcashuamán. He has broad interests spanning from archaeometry to the archaeology of religion. He has published numerous articles, including "El Niño and Second Millennium B.C. Monumental Building at Huaca Cortada (Moche Valley, Peru)" (2016).

Christopher A. Pool is an archaeologist whose research focuses primarily on the evolution of complex societies in the tropical lowlands of southern Veracruz, Mexico, including the Olmecs and their Epi-Olmec and Classic-period successors. He studies the interactions among environment, economy, ideology, and political practice at scales ranging from the individual household to supra-regional political economies. In pursuing his research, he draws on an interdisciplinary training in anthropology, geology, and geochemical characterization to understand patterns of resource exploitation and exchange within their social and cultural contexts. His research attempts to move the archaeological investigation of culture change toward approaches that address variability within and between ancient cultures and away from typological approaches that obscure variability within cultural types and present culture change as a sequence of steady states. The analysis of variability provides a more accurate characterization of cultural systems and allows more sophisticated analysis of dynamic change. Beginning in 1983, he has investigated ceramic production and exchange at the Classic-period site of Matacapan as well as household organization at the Late and Terminal Formative site of Bezuapan; he has also directed survey and excavations at Tres Zapotes. He is currently professor of Anthropology at the University of Kentucky.

John W. Rick is an associate professor (emeritus) of Anthropology, former chair of the Department of Anthropological Sciences at Stanford University, and past director of Stanford's Archaeology Center. He earned his BA from the University of California, Santa Cruz, and his MA and PhD from the University of Michigan. His teaching concentrates on South American archaeology, the beginnings of sociopolitical complexity, hunter-gatherers, stone tools, and digital methodologies in archaeology. For the last twenty-six years, he has directed a large fieldwork program at Chavín de Huántar. His interests there concentrate on understanding how early religious cults strategized the beginnings of political authority in the Andes.

Silvana A. Rosenfeld received her BA from the Universidad de Buenos Aires and her MA and PhD from Stanford University. She is currently an assistant professor of Anthropology at High Point University in North Carolina. She has conducted archaeological field and lab work in Ancash, Ayacucho, and Cuzco in Peru, as well as in Patagonia and northwest Argentina. Her research centers on the dynamics of sociopolitical inequality and ritual through the analysis of foodways and exchange in ancient Andean societies, specifically at Chavín de Huántar and in the Wari empire. Her work has been published in several edited volumes and journals, including *Antiquity* (2021), *Latin American Antiquity* (2016), *Ñawpa Pacha* (2013), and *Quaternary International* (2008). Her book *Rituals of the Past: Prehispanic and Colonial Case Studies in Andean Archaeology*, coedited with

Stefanie L. Bautista, was published in 2017 by the University Press of Colorado.

Lucy C. Salazar received her bachelor's degree in Archaeology from the Universidad Nacional Mayor de San Marcos in Lima, Peru, and carried out graduate studies at Yale University, writing her master's thesis on the ceramics from the Machu Picchu burial caves. She has extensive field experience in Peru, including excavations at Initial Period and Early Horizon sites such as Curayacu and Bandurria on the coast as well as Pacopampa, Huaricoto, and Chavín de Huántar in the highlands. More recently, she has acted as codirector in the excavation of Initial Period sites in the Lurín Valley, including Cardal, Mina Perdida, and Manchay Bajo. She has a strong interest in museums and has been on the staff of the Museo de Arqueología y Antropología of the Universidad Nacional Mayor de San Marcos and the Peabody Museum of Natural History at Yale University. In 2003, she was the cocurator of the blockbuster traveling exhibit *Machu Picchu: Unveiling the Mystery of the Incas*; in 2011, she played a central role in the design and installation of the Museo Machu Picchu in Cuzco. She has numerous edited books and articles on early Andean civilization, prehispanic Peruvian textiles, cultural heritage, and Inca culture. Her most recent book is *Finding Solutions for Protecting and Sharing Archaeological Heritage Resources* (with Anne Underhill, 2016). Salazar was awarded the Tumi USA Award in 2015 for Outstanding Contributions by Peruvians in the United States.

Matthew P. Sayre is an archaeologist who has conducted his primary fieldwork work at the site of Chavín de Huántar. He completed his MA and PhD in Anthropology at the University of California, Berkeley, and his BA in Latin American Studies and Anthropology at the University of Chicago. He is currently associate professor of Anthropology, and chair of the Department of Sociology and Anthropology, at High Point University in North Carolina. He was previously an associate professor and chair of the Department of Anthropology and Sociology at the University of South Dakota;

prior to that appointment, he was a postdoctoral fellow at Stanford University with a teaching focus on heritage issues. His work has been published in *Anthropological and Archaeological Sciences*; *Andean Past*; *Ñawpa Pacha: Journal of Andean Archaeology*; *Culture, Agriculture, Food and the Environment*; and *Latin American Antiquity*. His book, *Social Perspectives on Ancient Lives from Paleoethnobotanical Data*, with Maria Bruno, was published in 2017.

Yuji Seki is an archaeologist and anthropologist who is currently professor emeritus of the National Museum of Ethnology, Japan. He is vice president of the Japan Consortium for International Cooperation in Cultural Heritage. He has carried out excavations at several monumental sites, including Huacaloma, Layzón, Kuntur Wasi, and Pacopampa in the north highlands of Peru since 1979 as a member of the Japanese Archaeological Team and as director of a Japanese–Peruvian archaeological project to study the formation of Andean civilization. At the same time, he has been working on the issues of conservation and social use of cultural heritage. He has authored or edited several books about the Formative period, including *El centro ceremonial andino* (2014) and *New Perspectives on the Early Formation of the Andean Civilization* (2023). He has been awarded the Meritorious Person of Peruvian Culture by the Ministry of Culture of Peru (2015) and the Commendation of the Foreign Minister of Japan (2016).

Koichiro Shibata is an archaeologist specializing in the Andean Formative period. He holds an MA and a PhD from the Department of Interdisciplinary Cultural Studies at the University of Tokyo. After a postdoctoral fellowship at the Yamagata University and an affiliated research position at the Pontificia Universidad Católica del Perú, he joined the faculty at the Kobe City University of Foreign Studies and then at the Hosei University, where he is currently a professor in the Department of Economics. He has directed archaeological projects in the lower Nepeña Valley since 2002, focusing on topics around interregional interaction and the Chavín Phenomenon (*Boletín de Arqueología PUCP*, 2010), chronology (*Andes*, 2011), factional competition (*Senri Ethnological Studies*, 2014), and architecture and cosmology (*Indiana*, 2017).

Michelle Young received her BA from the University of Virginia in both the History of Art and Anthropology, and her M.Phil. and PhD in Anthropology from Yale University in the Department of Anthropology. She has conducted archaeological field and lab work in the United States, Belize, Ecuador, Peru, Bolivia, and Madagascar, and has held an internship at the Museo Larco in Lima, a junior fellowship at Dumbarton Oaks in Washington, D.C, and a postdoctoral fellowship at the National Museum of the American Indian in Suitland, Maryland. Between 2014 and 2017, she directed the Proyecto de Investigación Arqueológica Atalla, carrying out mapping, survey, excavation, sample collection, and laboratory analyses of archaeological materials from the site of Atalla alongside a robust community outreach program. Her dissertation project investigates the archaeological site of Atalla, located in the highlands of Huancavelica, Peru, and its relationship to the Chavín Interaction Sphere during the first half of the first millennium BC. She currently holds the position of assistant professor of Anthropology at Vanderbilt University, where she continues her field and collections-based research.

INDEX

Page numbers in *italics* indicate illustrations.

bird wing bone tubes for inhaling hallucinogens, *48*, 49, 57
Bischof, Henning, 210
Black and White phase, 38, 43, 47, 53, 54, 55, 64
Blomster, Jeffrey P., 394
Bolivian altiplano and Chavín, 19–20
Bonavia, Duccio, 210, 238
bone. *See* animal bone; burials and remains; marine shell
 and bone
Bonnier, Elizabeth, 114
Bria, Rebecca E., *vii*, 13–14, 17, 111, 394, 395, 396, 397, 401
Browman, David L., 289, 291n13, 330
Bueno Mendoza, Alberto, 121
Building A, Chavín de Huántar, 46, 64
Building B, Chavín de Huántar, 46, 64
Building C, Chavín de Huántar, 36, 46
Burger, Richard L.: on Atalla, 325, 328, 330, 335, 341, 343,
 345; biographical information, 401; on Campanayuq
 Rumi, 363, 383; on central coast, 237; on Chavín
 Phenomenon, *vii*, ix, 1, 6, 8, 12, 16–17; La Banda sector
 and, 63, 64, 71, 72, 74; on Nepeña Valley, 226, 228;
 Olmec and Chavín compared, 394, 397; on Paracas, 278;
 on south coast, 300; on tropical forest, 175, 186, 189
burials and remains: at Atalla, 331, 332; auditory exostosis,
 evidence of, 160; at Campanayuq Rumi, *373*; at Canchas
 Uckro, 93; on central coast, 250, 256–257; Chavín,
 absence of cemeteries at, 61; cranial deformations, 50,
 55, 57, 152, 156, 159–160, 272, 274; elite burials, 15, 17, 20;
 fragmentation and redistribution of objects between
 tombs, 286–287; in Galería de las Visitantes (Gallery
 4), 50, 57; in Galería de los Inhaladores (Gallery 3), 46,
 47, 57; at Hualcayán, *121*, 121–122, 124, *125–127*, 125–129;
 at Huayurco, 189–191, *190*; Huayurco burial cache, Jaén
 region, 179, *180*; Kareycoto, child burials at, 127; at
 Kuntur Wasi, 15, 17, 20, 159–160, 163; at La Capilla, 167;
 Manchay culture's lack of elite burials, 248; in Ofrendas
 Gallery, 50, 52; at Pacopampa, 15, 17, 20, 148, *149*, 150–155,
 152–154, 156, 160, 163, 165; in Paracas, 272, 274–275, 277,
 279, 286; on south coast, 301–304; trepanning, 272, 274.
 See also child burials
Bushnell, Geoffrey, 179, 198nn1–2

C

Caballo Muerto, 10, 16
Cajamarca Interaction Sphere, 20, 347, 383–384, 396–397
Cajamarca pottery style, 51, 253
Cajamarca/Cajamarca Valley, 14, 20, 101, 143, 155, 177, 196,
 253, 300, 334, 347, 383
Caja-style ceramics, 328, 330
Caldwell, Joseph, 7
Callango, *275*, *276*, *282*, 286, *288*
Callango textile, *301*, *303*
Callejón de Huaylas, 13, 17, 97, 116, 124, 228. *See also*
 Hualcayán
camelids: at Atalla, 18, 339; at Canchas Uckro, 99; *ch'arki*
 (dried camelid meat), 71, 72, 74; at Chavín de Huántar, 7,
 12; at Huayurco, 192; La Banda, bone beads and camelid
 meat consumption at, 70, *71*, 71–72; long-distance
 llama caravans, use of, 14, 18; in Nepeña Valley, 225; at

Pacopampa and Kuntur Wasi, 161, 162; Puerto Nuevo,
 absence at, 316
Campamento Gallery, 38, 53
Campanayuq Rumi, 18–19, 359–385; architectural models
 from, 334–335, 373, *375*; Arpiri and other nearby
 sites compared, 378–381; burials and remains, *373*;
 Campanayuq I Phase, 364–370, *365*, *366*, *368*, 376–377,
 382; Campanayuq II Phase, 370–376, *370–376*, 377,
 382–383; Canchas Uckro compared, 99, 100; ceramics
 from, 333, 338–339, 343, 367, *368*, *370*, 370–371, *371*, *373*,
 376; Chavín–Ayachuco Sphere at, 20, 276; chicha/
 maize beer, use of, 338; chronology of, 9, 18–19, 363;
 circular plaza, 365–367, 369, *378*, 382; engagement
 with Chavín Phenomenon in, 381–384; excavations
 and site description, 363, *364*; exchange relationships
 with, 14, 317, *318*; hallucinogenic paraphernalia from,
 99, 336; localized traditions at, 370, 377–378, *378*;
 map of area, *360*; map of platform complex, *364*;
 obsidian distribution from, 19, 316, 347, 348, *362*,
 363, 367–368, 369–370, 375–377, 382, 384; Paracas
 and, 276, 289; personal ornamentation from, 371, *372*,
 375; Pre-Platform phase, 363–364, *376*; residential
 settlement and domestic architecture, 331, 370, 371,
 373, *374*; ritual paraphernalia and iconography from,
 371–373, *373*, *374*; site description, 363; south-central
 highlands, importance of, 18; temple at, 334; U-shaped
 architectural tradition at, 18, 334, 365, 368–369, 381
canal systems, Chavín de Huántar, 34, 45, 54, 69
Canchas Uckro, 13, 81–102; abandonment of, 94, 95,
 101–102; agriculture and diet at, 86; ceramics at, 86,
 92, 94, 95–98, *96*, *97*, 101; in Chavín heartland, 82–85,
 83, *84*; chronology of, 13, 88, 94–95, 98, *101*; domestic
 occupation at, *91*, 91–92; early development at
 Chavín de Huántar and, 98, 99–101, *100*; excavations
 at, 86–94, *87–94*; exchange and interaction at, 95–98,
 96–98, 101; exotic goods at, 95, 99; feasting/communal
 consumption events at, 94, 99; first architectural phase,
 88–92, *89–92*, 95; hallucinogens and paraphernalia, 99;
 huancas, 93, 93–94; landscape setting, 85, 85–86, *86*;
 map of main platform, *87*; monumentality and labor
 organization at, 99–100; as peer center with Chavín
 de Huántar, 85, 100–101; retaining walls, *94*; second
 architectural phase, 92–94, *93*, 95; stone figurine, 91–92,
 92; Structure 4, *93*, 93–94
Cápac Ñan, 184
Capilla Gallery, 36
Caracolas Gallery: ceramics from, 41–43, 53; ducts into
 other galleries from, *39*; excavation of, 34–35, 38, 40–43,
 41; exotic goods recovered from, 11; ritual function of,
 57; strombus shell from, 40, *41*, *42*, 51, 57, 70, 74
Caracolas Gallery series, *39*, 39–40, 53, 54; ceramics in,
 55–57, *56*, *57*; Galería de las Visitantes (Gallery 4), 40,
 49–51, 49–52, 54, 55, *56*, 57; Galería de los Inhaladores
 (Gallery 3), 40, *45*, 45–49, *47*, *48*, 51, 52, 54, 55, *56*, 57;
 Galería del Fuego (Gallery X), 38–40, *39*, 43–45, *44*, 46,
 49, 52, 54, *56*, 57; Ofrendas and Campamento Galleries
 compared, 52, 53–54; symmetry of, 54–55, *55*

Cardal, 239–243, *240, 242–244*, 245–251, *246, 248*, 255, 335, 368

Carrión Cachot, Rebeca, 3, 6, 7, 209, 237, 238

Casa Blanca (PV62D12), Paracas, *284*

Casafranca, Jose, 238

Casma/Casma Valley, 21, 177, 211, 221, 228, 246, 252

Castrovirreyna, 325, 339

Cavern ("Cavernas") tomb, Paracas, 272, 291n10

Cavero Palomino, Yuri, 18–19, 20, 359, 396, 397, 403

Caylán: camelids at, 225; ceramics from, *222, 223, 223*; chronology of, 211, *212*; excavation of, 210; fortress, *215*; resistance to Chavín Interaction Sphere at, 16; ritual settings and practices, 218–219, *220*, 221; settlement patterns at, 214, *215*

ceja de selva. See tropical forest

central coast, 16–17, 22, 237–264; appearance of Chavín Phenomenon on, 249–252, *250, 251*; archaeological investigations into Chavín's impact on, 237; burials and remains, 250; ceramics from, and appearance of Chavín Phenomenon, 249, *251*, 251–252; ceramics from, Early Horizon, 255, *257, 258, 259–263, 260–262*; ceramics from, Initial Period, 228, 243, 245, 249; ceramics from, left by Chavín de Huántar pilgrims, 252–254; defined, 237–238; food and agriculture on, 259; Manchay culture of Initial Period, 238–250, *239–246, 248*; maps, *239, 243*; pilgrimages to Chavín de Huántar from, 252–255, 260; public spaces during Early Horizon, 255–257, *256, 257*, 264; relationship to Chavín Phenomenon, 263–264; transformation of, during Early Horizon, 255–263, *256–258, 260–262*; U-shaped architectural tradition on, 237, 238–240, *239, 243*, 245–247, 250–251, 255–257, *261*. *See also specific locations*

Central Coast Interaction Sphere, 20

ceramics: cultural break, change from Janabarriu to Huarás at Chavín de Huántar indicating, 228; itinerant or "swallow" potters, 249; petrographic analysis of, 247, 253, 311–315, *314*, 341; spondylus shell depicted in ceramic, Santa Ana–La Florida, 183; tombs, pottery sherds distributed between, 286; tropical forest fauna, representations of, 177–178. *See also specific types, styles, techniques, and locations*

ceramics at Chavín de Huántar: at canal intersections, 69; Caracolas Gallery, 41–43, 53; in Caracolas Gallery series generally, 55–57, *56, 57*; Galería de las Visitantes (Gallery 4), 50, *51*, 55, *56, 57*; Galería de los Inhaladores (Gallery 3), 45–46, *47*, 49, 55, *56*; Galería del Fuego (Gallery X), 43, *56, 57*; Ofrendas Gallery, 52, *53*, 166, 211, 252–254

ceremonial life. *See* religion, ritual, and ceremony

Cerrillos, 257, 259, 261, 272, *274*, 287, 316, *318*, 333

Cerro Blanco: ceramics from, 211–213, 221–224, *222, 225*; Chavín-Cupisnique Religious Complex, 16, 228, 229; chicha/maize beer, use of, 338; cultural history and chronology, 211–213, *212, 213*; discovery and excavation of site, 207, 208–210; exchange networks and exotic goods, 224, *225*; map of site, *213*; obsidian from, 347; ritual settings and practices, 217–219, *219*, 221, 226–227; settlement patterns at, 214, 215

Cerro Corbacho, 299

Cerro Lampay, 99

Cerro Ñañañique, 186

Cerro San Isidro, 214, 215

Cerro San Juan, fortress at, *215*

Cerro Sapo, sodalite from, 20

Cerro Sechín, 246

Chacamarca ceramics, 338, 339

Chachapoyas, 177, 196, 197

Chakinani ceramics, 278

Chaullabamba, 186

Chanapata pottery style, 19

Chancay, 16, 20, 238, 251

Chanin Pata, 381, 382

Chapdelaine, Claude, 214

Chapman, John, 290

ch'arki (dried camelid meat), 71, 72, 74

Chávez Ballón, Manuel, 8

Chavín: Cultura matriz de la civilización andina (Tello, 1960), 82

Chavín de Huántar, 10–13, 61; architectural damage at/ abandonment of, 22, 46, 57, 346; authority and power at, evolution of, 63; canal systems at, 34; Canchas Uckro as peer center with, 85, 100–101; central coast, pilgrimages from, 252–255; chronology of, 12, 394; compared to Kuntur Wasi and Pacopampa, 14–15, 143–156, 166–167; early development at, 98, 99–101, *100*; exotic goods at, 11, 12, 13, 14, 15, 20, 82, 101, 300, 347; Huarás groups at, 115; landscape setting of, 85–86; location and elevation, 11; map of, *62*; peer polity model applied to, 166–167; public architecture at, 7, *10–11*, 11–12; religious, ritual, and ceremonial significance of, 11, 13, 62, 69, 72–74, 167, 336, 347, 394; residential population at, 12, 64, 81–82, 92, 95, 101, 331; socioeconomic organization of, 61; stone sculpture at, 7, *10–11*, 11–12, 253, 254, 281, 335; as urban or proto-urban center, 13, 82, 85. *See also* ceramics at Chavín de Huántar; Circular Plaza, Chavín de Huántar; La Banda sector; Ofrendas Gallery; underground galleries at Chavín de Huántar; Urabarriu residences, exotic goods from; *specific features and buildings*

Chavín heartland, 13–14, 82–85, *83, 84*, 102. *See also* Canchas Uckro; Hualcayán

Chavín horizon style, 6, 21

Chavín Interaction Sphere, concept of, 7–8, 21

Chavín International Style, 21, *251*, 260, 340–343, *342*, 347, 397

Chavín Phenomenon, 1–23; archaeological/excavation history, 8; bottom-up perspective on, 21; Chavín de Huántar and its heartland, 10–14 (*See also* Chavín de Huántar; Chavín heartland); chronologies and dating, 2–3, *4–5*, 8–10, 20; community, viewed through lens of, 115–116; comparative perspectives on, 22–23; as "crisis cult," 252; decline and "collapse" of, 10, 20, 21–22, 346; Dumbarton Oaks Pre-Columbian conferences on, ix–x, 1–3; local chronologies, importance of establishing, 9, 20; map of key sites, *2, 300*; multiple overlapping interaction networks, recognition of, 20–21, 347, *348*, 361, 383–384, 396–397; Olmec and Chavín, 23, 340, 393–398; pan-regional perspective on, 14–20, 396–397

of, in eighth century BC, 300; fishing communities
involved with, 317–319, *318*; at Huaca Partida, 224, *225*;
in Nepeña Valley, 224–226, *225*; at Paracas, 275–277, *276*,
284–285, 289; at Puerto Nuevo, 289, 300–301, 308–317,
316; socially marginal groups and, 317; tropical forest
and, 177–178, 197, 285. *See also* exotic goods

exoετοειϛ, 160

exotic goods: at Ancón, *260–262*, 260–263; at Canchas
Uckro, 95, 99; ceremonial centers, facilitating contact
between, 141; at Chavín de Huántar, 11, 12, 13, 14, 15,
20, 82, 101, 300, 347; emergence of prestige economy,
between tenth and sixth centuries BC, 299, 395–396;
galleries at Chavín de Huántar, recovered from, 11, 12,
13, 14, 15, 20, 70, 74, 82, 101; at Hualcayán, 111, 114, 124,
131; Huancavelica, exotic minerals from, 14, 300, 316,
325; interregional interaction spheres, as indicators of,
359; from Jaén region, 186–187; at Kuntur Wasi, 14, 160–
161, 347; La Banda sector of Chavín de Huántar, exotic
materials and craft manufacture at, *67, 68, 69–70, 73,*
74; at La Capilla, 167; at Nepeña, 16; at Nepeña Valley,
16, 218, 224–226, *225*; at Pacopampa, 14, 160–161, 347;
in Paracas, 275–277, *276*, 284–285, 289, 347; at Puerto
Nuevo, 289, 300–301, 308–317, *316*; social inequality
and status differentiation, emergence of, 299, 395–396;
Urabarriu residences at Chavín de Huántar, found in
refuse associated with, 14. *See also* exchange networks;
specific goods, e.g., marine shell and bone

F

farming. *See* food and agriculture

feasting/communal consumption events: at Canchas
Uckro, 94, 99; at Cerro Blanco, 226–227; at Hualcayán,
133, 134; in Manchay culture, 248; at Pacopampa, 153,
154–155, 156; social power and, 396

feline iconography: at Atalla, 338, 340; at Campanayuq
Rumi, 373, *374*; on central coast, 245, 254; Chavín
Phenomenon and, 7, 16; in Nepeña Valley, 217, *218*, 224,
226; in north highlands, 148, *150, 154*; Olmec were-
jaguar imagery, 394; in Paracas, *278, 279*, 280, 281, *283*,
284; in tropical forest, 191, *195*

fishing communities and exchange networks, 317–319, *318*

Flannery, Kent V., 393, 396

florero ceramic form, 279, 290n8

food and agriculture: access to food and social inequality
at La Banda sector, 70–72; at Atalla, 333–334, 338; on
central coast, 259; chicha/maize beer, 134, 197, 224,
254, 338; cotton as industrial crop in Paracas, 275, *276*;
at Huayurco, 192; in Manchay culture, 247; manioc
replaced by maize at Pacopampa, 161; in Paracas, 275;
at Puerto Nuevo, 316; at Santa Ana–La Florida, 183;
tropical rainforest, domestication of plants in, 177. *See
also* feasting/communal consumption events

formative cultures, concept of, 393–394

Fortaleza, 238

fragmentation, practice of, 272, 286–289, *287, 288*, 290,
291nn16–18

Fung, Rosa, 8

Furst, Peter, 393

G

galleries: at Canchas Uckro, 89, *90*, 92, 98; defined, 34. *See
also* underground galleries at Chavín de Huántar

Gamboa, Jorge, 12

Garagay, 238, 243, *245, 246, 247*, 249, 251, 253, 255

gendered temple architecture, 335

geoglyphs, Paracas, 272, 277

Glascock, Michael, 346, 363

gold jewelry and objects: at Atalla, 332, *333*; at Campanayuq
Rumi, 371, *372, 375*; at Kuntur Wasi, 159–160; at
Pacopampa, 151–153, *153, 154*, 160–161

Gonzales, Marino, 8

Gonzales, Patricia, 315

González Lauck, Rebecca, 394

Gotush, 82

gourds, pyro-engraved, from Paracas, 277, *278*

Grieder, Terence, 121

Grove, David, 340, 393, 394, 397

guilloche (twisted strand) motif, 283 284, *285*

H

Hacha, 367

hair bundles, 286–287

Haley, Kevin J., 155

hallucinogens and paraphernalia, 7, 395; at Atalla, 335–338,
336; bird wing bone tubes for inhaling hallucinogens,
8, 49, 57; at Campanayuq Rumi, 99, 336; at Canchas
Uckro, 99; at Hualcayán, *128*, 337; at Kuntur Wasi, 336;
from La Banda sector, 61; from Paracas, 289; San Pedro
cactus, 280, *282*, 286; on south coast, 300; from tropical
forest, 175; from underground galleries at Chavín de
Huántar, *48*, 49

Harrison, John B., 208

Hastorf, Christine A., 62, 165

Hayden, Brian, 155

hematite, 154, 315, 316, 344

Herrera, Alexander, 210

Huaca Cortada, 224

Huaca de los Reyes, 224

Huaca La Florida, 238, 239, 247, 255

Huaca Partida: ceramics at, 223, *225*; Chavín–Cupisnique
Religious Complex and, 16, 228, 229; chronology
and cultural history of, 211, *212, 213*; excavation of,
210; exchange networks and exotic goods, 224, *225*;
polychrome frieze at, 217, *218*, 227; ritual settings and
practices, 217, 217–219, *218, 221*, 226, 227; settlement
patterns at, 214, *215*

Huaca Prieta, *182, 183*

Huacaloma, 14, 155, 177

Huacoy, 253

Hualcayán, 13–14, 111–135; ceramics found at, *123*, 123–124,
125, 126, 130, 132, 133, 134; Chavín culture, embracing
and replacing, 111–114, 116, 134–135; Chavín-era temple,
124–131, *125–130*; chronology of, 13; community, viewed
through lens of, 115–116; exotic goods at, 111, 114, 124,
131; hallucinogenic paraphernalia from, *128*, 337;
highland Ancash, in context of, 111–114, *112*, 134–135;
Huarás culture following Chavín at, 114–115, 116,

131–133, 131–134; between Kotosh and Chavín, 121–123, 121–124; Kotosh Religious Tradition preceding Chavín at, 114, 117–120, 117–121, 124, 134; La Galgada compared, 117, 118, 119, 120, 121; Lurín Valley on central coast compared, 17; Mito tradition at, 117, 118, 119, 120; PC-A ritual enclosure, 117–24, 118–23; PC-C platform, 121–23, 121–24; PC-E complex, 124–26, 125, 130; PC-H complex, child burials at, 124, 125–27, 125–28, 130, 131, 134; PC-J platform complex, 128–132, 129–133; Perolcoto temple mound and plaza complex at, 113, 114, 116–117, 117, 395; rejection of Chavín cultural patterns at, 22; social inequality and status differentiation at, 121; Sunken Plaza area, 116–117, 117

Huambacho: camelids at, 225; ceramics from, 222, 223, 224; chronology of, 211; excavation of, 210; resistance to Chavín interaction sphere at, 16; ritual settings and practices, 218–219, 221; settlement patterns at, 214

huancas: at Canchas Uckro, 93, 93–94; in Chavín's CPA galleries, 47, 51, 55, 57

Huancavelica, 323–326, 347–350; early village life in, 323–326; exotic minerals from, 14, 300, 316, 325; map, 324; Paracas and, 285; south-central highlands, importance of, 18. *See also* Atalla

Huánuco Basin and Ucayali, stylistic relationships between, 174

Huarás: Chavín, relationship to, 115; Hualcayán, Huarás culture at, 114–115, 116, 131–133, 131–134; *huancas* at, 47; as pottery style, 22, 50, 132, 228; rise of culture of, 22, 57

Huaricoto, 95–97, 114

Huaura, 238

Huayurco, 15, 179, 180, 187–192, 187–193, 196–197

human remains. *See* burials and remains

human sacrifice, 154

I

Ibarra Ascensios, Bebel, 83

Ikehara-Tsukayama, Hugo, *vii*, 15–16, 207, 210, 214, 397, 402–403

inequality, socioeconomic. *See* social inequality and status differentiation

Ingatambo, 15, 184–187, 185, 186, 188, 196–197

inscribed memory practices, 165, 166

interregional interaction spheres, concept of, 14–20, 396–397

Isla, Johnny, 301

Izumi, Seiichi, 121

J

Jaén region, 15, 176–177, 178–197; archaeological exploration of, 178–184, 180–183; Bagua, 177–178, 180, 193, ceramics from, 51, 179, 180, 181–186, 186, 192, 192–193, 196; dry forest in, 178, 179; exotic goods found at, 186–187; Huaca Prieta, 182, 183; Huayurco burial cache, 179, 180; Huayurco site, 15, 179, 180, 187–192, 187–193, 196–197; Ingatambo site, 15, 184–187, 185, 186, 188, 196–197; map, 176; Montegrande, 183, 183–184, 185, 188; Santa Ana–La Florida site, 181–184, 182, 185, 188, 194;

serpent and avian imagery, 179, 180, 182, 183; shaman figurine, 195; spiral architecture of, 181, 182, 183, 183–184, 185; stone bowl tradition, 179, 180, 193, 193–195, 194, 197

Jampatilla, 376

Janabarriu pottery, 18–19, 341; at Aalla, 18, 328, 343; at Arpiri, 378; at Campanayuq Rumi, 19, 370, 373, 376; Canchas Uckro lacking, 101; on central coast, 252, 259; Chavín de Huántar, change from Janabarriu to Huarás at, 228; from CPA galleries, 40, 41, 43, 46, 47, 49, 51, 57; graphite, use of, 278; at Hualcayán, 13, 124, 125, 126, 130; at Huayurco, 193; at Ingatambo, 186; at La Banda sector, 64; from Moro Pocket, Nepeña Valley, 224; use of term, 21, 40

Jargampata, 330, 343, 382

Jequetepeque pottery style, 260, 347

Joyce, Rosemary, 166

Juan Pablo, Paracas, 274

K

Kareycoto, child burials at, 127

Karwa: burials and remains at, 17, 277, 291nn14–15, 301; cinnabar used on textiles from, 346; as pottery style, 305, 307, 312

Kauffmann Doig, Federico, 8

Kaulicke, Peter, 279, 286, 301

Kembel, Silvia Rodriguez, 35, 38, 64, 100–101

Kiske, fortress at, 215

Kosok, Paul, 210

Kotosh ceramics: Atalla and, 347; Kotosh-Wairajirca pottery style, 97, 177; tropical forest imagery, use of, 177

Kotosh Religious Tradition: at coastal sites, 136n1; at Hualcayán, 114, 117–120, 117–121, 124, 134

Kriss, Dawn, 284, 285, 345–346

Kroeber, Alfred, 3–6, 9, 237

Kuntur Wasi, 14–15, 156–160; architectural plan, 158; Atalla's public architecture resembling, 334, 335; burials and remains at, 15, 17, 20, 159–160, 163; Cajamarca Interaction Sphere and, 20; Campanayuq Rumi and, 371; Canchas Uckro compared, 100; ceramics from, 158, 160, 161, 186; "Chavín culture" not appearing at, 7; Chavín horizon style and, 6; chronology of, 9, 10, 156, 158; compared to Pacopampa and Chavín de Huántar, 14–15, 143–156, 166–167; destruction and rebuilding between phases at, 165, 166; exotic goods at, 14, 160–161, 347; hallucinogenic paraphernalia from, 336; Jaén region, interaction with, 187; local characteristics at, 384; Main Platform, 157; map of north highlands, 142; ritual activity at, 157–158, 383; social inequality and status differentiation, emergence of, 160–167, 299; Sunken Square and Circular Courts, 157, 163

Kushipampa: ceramics from, 222, 224; chronology of, 211, 212; exotic goods at, 225; ritual settings and practices, 219, 219–221; settlement patterns at, 215

L

La Banda sector, 12–13, 61–74; archaeological background and excavations, 64–67, 66–68; camelid bone beads from, 70, 71, 71–72; chronology of, 12–13, 64, 65;

evidence for asymmetrical relations at, 61, 63; exotic materials and craft manufacture at, 67, 68, 69–70, 73, 74; food access and inequality at, 70–72; hallucinogens and paraphernalia, 61; intersection between inequality, ritual, and daily life at, 61, 62, 63–64; lithic staff from, 70; map of, 66; residential population and domestic architecture at, 12, 63, 64, 65, 67, 68, 69; ritual practice and inequality at, 62–63, 65, 69, 72–74; social inequality and status differentiation at, 63–64, 69–72

La Capilla, 142, 148, 167

La Galgada: Hualcayán compared, 117, 118, 119, 120, 121; textiles from, 182, 183

La Laguna, 142, 148

Laberintos Gallery, 36, 54

labor organization at Canchas Uckro, 98–99

"Lady of Pacopampa," tomb of, 148, 149, 151–153, 152, 155, 156, 159, 165

Laguna Pomacochas, 177

Lambayeque, 246, 300

Lane, Kevin, 210

Lanning, Edward, 237, 238, 262

Lanzón Gallery, 35, 36, 37, 38, 54, 73

Lanzón monolith, 69, 73, 336, 337, 395

Larco Hoyle, Rafael, 14, 15, 150, 173, 210

Las Haldas pottery style, 211, 221

Lathrap, Donald, 15, 69, 174, 177, 179, 183, 195, 393

Layzón, 14

Limoncarro, temple of, 335

Lisahuacho, 376

llamas. See camelids

Lobatus shell. See strombus shell

Loco Gallery, 36

Loma Macanche, 299

Lucas or Tishman bottle, 279

Lumbreras, Luis, 8, 9, 34, 35, 40, 51, 52, 195, 252, 367, 394

Lurín/Lurín Valley, 16–17, 20, 238–239, 242, 247, 249–252, 255–257, 317, 335

M

MacNeish, Richard S., 289

maize. See chicha/maize beer; food and agriculture

Makowski, Krzysztof, 256, 257

malachite, 154, 163, 285

Malpaso, 238

Manachaqui Cave site, 177–178

Manchay Bajo, 238, 240, 250, 255, 256, 257

Manchay culture: on central coast during Initial Period, 238–249, 239–246, 248, 347; ceramics associated with, 228, 243, 245, 249, 253–254; Chavín, relationship to, 113; crises and demise of, 249–252; elite burials, lack of, 248; feasting/communal consumption events, 248; food and agriculture in, 247; Nepeña Valley and, 207, 227, 229, 230; religious iconography of, 243–245, 245, 246, 251; social inequality and status differentiation, lack of, 247–248; tropical forest fauna, representations of, 177; U-shaped architectural tradition in, 16, 238–240, 245–247, 368–369

Mantaro, 18, 92, 330, 367

maquetas, 334–335

Marcavalle, 19, 367

Mariash-Recuay period/structures/deposits, 43, 44, 45, 49–50, 51

marine shell and bone: Ancón shell middens, 237, 247; Atalla's lack of, 349; at Canchas Uckro, 92, 95, 99; at Cerro Blanco, 218; at Chavín de Huántar, 300; at Hualcayán, 123, 124, 127, 128, 130, 131, 133; at Huayurco, 191, 191–192; Huayurco burial cache, Jaén region, 179; from Ingatambo, 186; at Kuntur Wasi, 160; in Kushipampa and Moro Pocket, 225; at La Banda, 67, 69–70, 74; at La Capilla, 167; at Pacopampa, 152, 161; in Paracas, 275; pututus (shell trumpets), 40, 41, 42, 51, 57, 179; rocker-stamping techniques for decorating ceramics, 224. See also spondylus shell; strombus shell

Matibamba, 82, 83

Matos Mendieta, Ramiro, 325, 328, 330, 345

Matsumoto, Yuichi, vii, 18–19, 20, 334, 359, 371–373, 377, 396, 397, 403

Maya, 166, 210, 395

McAnany, Patricia A., 70, 395

McEwan, Colin, vii, ix

Mejía Xesspe, Toribio, 209

memory: inscribed memory practices, 165, 166; social memory, 163–166, 395

Mendoza, Edison, 381

Mendoza, Rosa, vii

metals and metalworking: at Atalla, 332–333, 333. See also copper, copper pigments, and copper ores; gold jewelry and objects

Miasta Gutiérrez, Jaime, 179

Middendorf, Ernst, 8

Miller, Alberto, 259

Miller, George, 71, 72

Mina Perdida, 238, 239, 240, 241, 247–250, 255

Mito tradition: Hualcayán's PC-A ritual enclosure and, 117, 118, 119, 120; West Field, Chavín, Mito-style architecture at, 69

Moche state, 156, 334–335

Mohr Chávez, Karen, 19

Mollake Chico, 17, 301, 307

Montegrande, 183, 183–184, 185, 188

Moore, Jerry D., 165

Morales Chocano, Daniel, 178

Moro Pocket, 214–216, 216, 222, 223, 224, 225

Moseley, Michael, 237

mother cultures, concept of, 393–394

Muelle, Jorge, 8, 237

mummies/mummy bundles, 250, 272, 274, 277

Munro, Kimberly, 210

mural art: on central coast, 243, 245, 246; of Nepeña Valley, 16, 207, 208, 217, 219, 221, 224, 226–229, 230; at Puerto Nuevo, 308; tropical forest plants and animals in, 177

Muyu Moqo, 338, 347, 367

Myers, Thomas, 178

Myroxylon balsamum (Balsam of Peru), 284–285, 291n12

DUMBARTON OAKS PRE-COLUMBIAN SYMPOSIA AND COLLOQUIA

PUBLISHED BY DUMBARTON OAKS,
TRUSTEES FOR HARVARD UNIVERSITY, WASHINGTON, D.C.

The Dumbarton Oaks Pre-Columbian Symposia and Colloquia Series volumes are based on papers presented at scholarly meetings sponsored by the Pre-Columbian Studies program at Dumbarton Oaks. Inaugurated in 1967, these meetings provide a forum for the presentation of advanced research and the exchange of ideas on the art and archaeology of the ancient Americas.

Further information on the Dumbarton Oaks Pre-Columbian series and publications can be found at www.doaks.org/publications.

Dumbarton Oaks Conference on the Olmec, edited by Elizabeth P. Benson, 1968

Dumbarton Oaks Conference on Chavín, edited by Elizabeth P. Benson, 1971

The Cult of the Feline, edited by Elizabeth P. Benson, 1972

Mesoamerican Writing Systems, edited by Elizabeth P. Benson, 1973

Death and the Afterlife in Pre-Columbian America, edited by Elizabeth P. Benson, 1975

The Sea in the Pre-Columbian World, edited by Elizabeth P. Benson, 1977

The Junius B. Bird Pre-Columbian Textile Conference, edited by Ann Pollard Rowe, Elizabeth P. Benson, and Anne-Louise Schaffer, 1979

Pre-Columbian Metallurgy of South America, edited by Elizabeth P. Benson, 1979

Mesoamerican Sites and World-Views, edited by Elizabeth P. Benson, 1981

The Art and Iconography of Late Post-Classic Central Mexico, edited by Elizabeth Hill Boone, 1982

Falsifications and Misreconstructions of Pre-Columbian Art, edited by Elizabeth Hill Boone, 1982

Highland-Lowland Interaction in Mesoamerica: Interdisciplinary Approaches, edited by Arthur G. Miller, 1983

Ritual Human Sacrifice in Mesoamerica, edited by Elizabeth Hill Boone, 1984

Painted Architecture and Polychrome Monumental Sculpture in Mesoamerica, edited by Elizabeth Hill Boone, 1985

Early Ceremonial Architecture in the Andes, edited by Christopher B. Donnan, 1985

The Aztec Templo Mayor, edited by Elizabeth Hill Boone, 1986

The Southeast Classic Maya Zone, edited by Elizabeth Hill Boone and Gordon R. Willey, 1988

The Northern Dynasties: Kingship and Statecraft in Chimor, edited by Michael E. Moseley and Alana Cordy-Collins, 1990

Wealth and Hierarchy in the Intermediate Area, edited by Frederick W. Lange, 1992

Art, Ideology, and the City of Teotihuacan, edited by Janet Catherine Berlo, 1992

Latin American Horizons, edited by Don Stephen Rice, 1993

Lowland Maya Civilization in the Eighth Century AD, edited by Jeremy A. Sabloff and John S. Henderson, 1993

Collecting the Pre-Columbian Past, edited by Elizabeth Hill Boone, 1993

Tombs for the Living: Andean Mortuary Practices, edited by Tom D. Dillehay, 1995

Native Traditions in the Postconquest World, edited by Elizabeth Hill Boone and Tom Cummins, 1998

Function and Meaning in Classic Maya Architecture, edited by Stephen D. Houston, 1998

Social Patterns in Pre-Classic Mesoamerica, edited by David C. Grove and Rosemary A. Joyce, 1999

Gender in Pre-Hispanic America, edited by Cecelia F. Klein, 2001

Archaeology of Formative Ecuador, edited by J. Scott Raymond and Richard L. Burger, 2003

Gold and Power in Ancient Costa Rica, Panama, and Colombia, edited by Jeffrey Quilter and John W. Hoopes, 2003

Palaces of the Ancient New World, edited by Susan Toby Evans and Joanne Pillsbury, 2004

A Pre-Columbian World, edited by Jeffrey Quilter and Mary Ellen Miller, 2006

Twin Tollans: Chichén Itzá, Tula, and the Epiclassic to Early Postclassic Mesoamerican World, edited by Jeff Karl Kowalski and Cynthia Kristan-Graham, 2007

Variations in the Expression of Inka Power, edited by Richard L. Burger, Craig Morris, and Ramiro Matos Mendieta, 2007

El Niño, Catastrophism, and Culture Change in Ancient America, edited by Daniel H. Sandweiss and Jeffrey Quilter, 2008

Classic Period Cultural Currents in Southern and Central Veracruz, edited by Philip J. Arnold III and Christopher A. Pool, 2008

The Art of Urbanism: How Mesoamerican Kingdoms Represented Themselves in Architecture and Imagery, edited by William L. Fash and Leonardo López Luján, 2009

New Perspectives on Moche Political Organization, edited by Jeffrey Quilter and Luis Jaime Castillo B., 2010

Astronomers, Scribes, and Priests: Intellectual Interchange between the Northern Maya Lowlands and Highland Mexico in the Late Postclassic

Period, edited by Gabrielle Vail and Christine Hernández, 2010

The Place of Stone Monuments: Context, Use, and Meaning in Mesoamerica's Preclassic Transition, edited by Julia Guernsey, John E. Clark, and Barbara Arroyo, 2010

Their Way of Writing: Scripts, Signs, and Pictographies in Pre-Columbian America, edited by Elizabeth Hill Boone and Gary Urton, 2011

Past Presented: Archaeological Illustration and the Ancient Americas, edited by Joanne Pillsbury, 2012

Merchants, Markets, and Exchange in the Pre-Columbian World, edited by Kenneth G. Hirth and Joanne Pillsbury, 2013

Embattled Bodies, Embattled Places: War in Pre-Columbian Mesoamerica and the Andes, edited by Andrew K. Scherer and John W. Verano, 2014

The Measure and Meaning of Time in Mesoamerica and the Andes, edited by Anthony F. Aveni, 2015

Making Value, Making Meaning: Techné in the Pre-Columbian World, edited by Cathy Lynne Costin, 2016

Smoke, Flames, and the Human Body in Mesoamerican Ritual Practice, edited by Vera Tiesler and Andrew K. Scherer, 2018

Sacred Matter: Animacy and Authority in the Americas, edited by Steve Kosiba, John Wayne Janusek, and Thomas B. F. Cummins, 2020

Teotihuacan: The World Beyond the City, edited by Kenneth G. Hirth, David M. Carballo, and Barbara Arroyo, 2020

Waves of Influence: Pacific Maritime Networks Connecting Mexico, Central America, and Northwestern South America, edited by Christopher S. Beekman and Colin McEwan, 2022

Reconsidering the Chavín Phenomenon in the Twenty-First Century, edited by Richard L. Burger and Jason Nesbitt, 2023